Survey of Accounting

The Robert N. Anthony / Willard J. Graham Series in Accounting

Survey of Accounting
Sixth Edition

Gary L. Schugart
Texas A&M University

James J. Benjamin
Texas A&M University

Arthur J. Francia
University of Houston

Robert H. Strawser
Texas A&M University

1988
IRWIN
Homewood, Illinois 60430

Previous editions published by Dame Publications, Inc.,
Houston, Texas

ISBN 0-256-06534-9

Library of Congress Catalog Card No. 87-83209

Printed in the United States of America

2 3 4 5 6 7 8 9 0 F 5 4 3 2 1 0 9 8

Preface

THIS UNIQUE TEXTBOOK has been prepared for use in an introductory or survey course in accounting. It is ideal for use in a one or a two term first course (depending on the material selected and the depth of coverage desired) at either the undergraduate or graduate level. The text has been written to provide a broad overview of all aspects of accounting from the basic concepts, through the accounting information system to financial statements and special reports, emphasizing the interpretation of these statements and reports. It stresses the analysis of financial and managerial accounting data. Twenty comprehensive chapters have been prepared to permit maximum flexibility in topic selection without any loss of continuity or instructional benefit. Choices of materials may range from a balanced financial-managerial orientation to an emphasis on either, depending upon material selection. The text presents a balanced perspective of practice and theory emphasizing decision-making using accounting information. A direct, straightforward approach achieves completeness of coverage using simple but accurate terms, examples and illustrations. *SURVEY OF ACCOUNTING* is a usable text geared to the understanding of basic concepts, principles and practices. This unique text emphasizes financial statement understanding and analysis, decision-making using financial information, managerial planning, control and performance evaluation. A wealth of end-of-chapter materials (Summary, Key Definitions, Questions and Problems) are available to reinforce understanding. A descriptive outline of the text and its contents follows:

1. Introduces the basic accounting concepts and discusses the basic financial statements, including the balance sheet, income statement, statement of changes in financial position.

2. Discusses the basic financial statements and introduces the accounting equation.

3. Traces and explains the process of recording transactions, end of period adjustments and the preparation of financial statements.

4. Illustrates the operational differences among companies with special emphasis on the differences between retailing and service organizations and considers the alternative methods for accounting for inventories.

5. Discusses the procedures used for recording, allocating and disposing of long-term assets and the accounting for intangibles and natural resources, including oil and gas accounting, ACRS procedures, as modified by the Tax Reform Act of 1986 are discussed.

6. Considers the issues related to the accounting for firms organized as sole proprietorships and partnerships.

7. Discusses the issues related to the formation of a corporation, the issuance of capital stock and considers matters related to the retained earnings and dividends of a corporation.

8. Discusses the accounting procedures which are used to record and control cash, accounts and notes payable and current liabilities.

9. Discusses the accounting for bonds payable and investments in corporate securities and explains and illustrates the preparation and use of consolidated financial statements.

10. Discusses and illustrates the basic techniques of analyzing and using the information presented in financial statements.

11. Explains and illustrates the procedures employed in preparing the statement of cash flows.

12. Presents a general discussion of the federal income tax as modified by the Tax Reform Act of 1986. Explanation and illustration of both interperiod and intraperiod tax allocation is included.

13. Discusses the basic differences between managerial and financial accounting, product costs and period costs and considers cost behavior and costs for planning.

14. Explains and illustrates the cost accounting for inventories by focusing on the elements of product cost—direct materials, direct labor and manufacturing overhead. Covers both job order and process cost accounting systems.

15. Discusses the concept of standard costs and illustrates the operation of a standard cost system.
16. Explains and illustrates the variable costing format as contrasted to absorption costing and discusses the various approaches to cost-profit-volume analysis.
17. Continues the discussion and illustration of short-range planning and provides a comprehensive example of the budgeting process.
18. Discusses the cost concepts and accounting approaches which are related to the planning and execution of special decisions. The appendices cover learning curve analysis and the role of quantitative techniques in short-range planning and decisions.
19. Explains and illustrates the basic steps of the capital budgeting process, with special emphasis on evaluating and choosing among alternative long-term investments. Sensitivity analysis and the cost of prediction errors is discussed.
20. Introduces the concept of responsibility accounting and the role that it plays in a management accounting system. Cost centers, profit centers and investment centers are discussed.

Acknowledgments

We are indebted to many students and colleagues for their assistance, comments, and constructive criticisms which assisted in making this text a reality. A necessary ingredient in the writing of any textbook is the environment in which the effort took place. Our special thanks go to James McFarland of the University of Houston, A. Benton Cocanougher, William H. Mobley, William V. Muse and the late John E. Pearson of Texas A&M University for providing us with encouragement in our efforts and with environments in which this book could be created.

We appreciate the permissions received from the American Institute of Certified Public Accountants and the Institute of Management Accounting of the National Association of Accountants allowing us to use selected problem materials from past Uniform CPA Examinations and CMA Examinations, respectively. Of course, the authors are responsible for any shortcomings of this text.

August, 1987

Gary L. Schugart
James J. Benjamin
Arthur J. Francia
Robert H. Strawser

Contents

11 The Statement of Cash Flows

INTRODUCTION. IMPORTANCE OF CASH FLOWS. A BRIEF HISTORY. ALL FINANCIAL RESOURCES CONCEPT. THE STATEMENT OF CASH FLOWS. Cash From Operations. Preparation of the Statement of Cash Flows. Change in Cash. Changes in Noncash Accounts. The Statement of Cash Flows. Worksheet Approach. Additional Problems in the Analysis of the Statement of Cash Flows. SUMMARY. KEY DEFINITIONS. QUESTIONS. EXERCISES. PROBLEMS.

12 Income Tax Considerations

INTRODUCTION. THE FEDERAL INCOME TAX. CLASSES OF TAXPAYERS. INDIVIDUAL FEDERAL INCOME TAX. CORPORATE INCOME TAX. DIFFERENCES BETWEEN ACCOUNTING INCOME AND TAXABLE INCOME. Interperiod Tax Allocation. Allocation of Income Tax Within a Period. INCOME TAXES AND MANAGEMENT DECISIONS. SUMMARY. KEY DEFINITIONS. QUESTIONS. EXERCISES. PROBLEMS.

13 Management Accounting: An Introduction

INTRODUCTION. BASIC DIFFERENCES BETWEEN FINANCIAL AND MANAGEMENT ACCOUNTING—FURTHER COMMENTS. The Objectives of Management Accounting. COST CLASSIFICATIONS. PRODUCT COSTS: FOR INCOME DETERMINATION. PRODUCT COST FLOWS IN MANUFACTURING. PERIOD COSTS: FOR INCOME DETERMINATION. IMPORTANCE OF THE DISTINCTION BETWEEN PRODUCT AND PERIOD COST. COSTS FOR PLANNING: COST BEHAVIOR. VARIABLE COSTS. FIXED COSTS. Per Unit Fixed Cost. Total Costs. COMMITTED AND MANAGED FIXED COSTS. Committed Fixed Costs. Managed Fixed Costs. SEMIVARIABLE COSTS. STEP COSTS. SUMMARY. KEY DEFINITIONS. QUESTIONS. EXERCISES. PROBLEMS.

Survey of Accounting
Sixth Edition

Chapter 1 introduces certain basic accounting concepts. Studying this chapter should enable you to:

1. Describe the basic accounting definition and discuss accounting as a process of communication.

2. Describe the role of the accountant and explain why this role has increased in significance.

3. Compare and contrast accounting and bookkeeping.

4. Contrast financial accounting with managerial accounting and identify the primary users of each.

5. Describe the objectives of financial reporting.

6. Discuss the qualitative characteristics of accounting information.

7. Explain "generally accepted accounting principles" and discuss the major concepts underlying these principles.

8. Define and discuss the elements of financial statements.

9. Explain recognition and measurement in financial statements.

10. Identify the basic financial statements and explain the purpose and use of each.

11. Trace the process of developing generally accepted accounting principles.

12. List and briefly describe certain of the more important influences on accounting principles.

13. Discuss the accounting standard setting process.

14. Discuss the extent and nature of opportunities in accounting.

1

Accounting: An Introduction

INTRODUCTION   Accounting has been described as ". . . the art of recording, classifying, and summarizing in a significant manner and in terms of money, transactions and events which are, in part at least, of a financial character, and interpreting the results thereof."[1] This definition emphasizes the ". . . creative skill and ability with which the accountant applies his knowledge to a given problem."[2] Another view of the function of accounting, very similar to that reported above, is that "the primary function of accounting is to accumulate and communicate information essential to an understanding of the activities of an enterprise, whether large or small, corporate or non-corporate, profit or non-profit, public or private."[3] The importance of this second definition is the direct relevance of accounting to many and varied types of undertakings, both private and public, and profit and not-for-profit.

Implicit in any definition of accounting is the importance of the accountant's role in the reporting function. In fact, the primary role of the accountant is reporting and communicating information which will aid various users in the financial community in making economic decisions. These users of accounting information include current and potential owners, managers, creditors, and others.

It should be noted however, that "financial reporting is not an end in itself but is intended to provide information that is useful in making business and economic decisions."[4]

In the past, when businesses were less complex than they are today, there were usually only a very limited number of users of accounting information. For example, at the turn of the century, most businesses in the United States were managed and operated by their owners. Since these owners were intimately involved in the day-to-day operations of their businesses, there was little or no need for accounting reports. The owner or decision-maker already had firsthand knowledge of the information he required in order to operate the business effectively. Today, however, the situation is quite different. Many organizations have increased in both size and complexity. In many instances, the ownership and the management of a business have been separated. Firms are frequently managed by professional managers for their absentee owners who exercise a minimal amount of formal control over the operations of the business except in the most general sense. These owners often have virtually no involvement in the day-to-day activities of the business. Even professional managers (at all but the most basic levels of authority in the firm) have little *firsthand* involvement in the most fund-

---

[1] American Institute of Certified Public Accountants, *Accounting Terminology Bulletin No. 1—Review and Resume* (New York: AICPA), p. 9.

[2] *Ibid.*

[3] *Accounting and Reporting Standards for Corporate Financial Statements* (Columbus, Ohio: American Accounting Association, 1957), p. 1.

[4] "Objectives of Financial Reporting by Business Enterprises," FASB Statement of Financial Accounting Concepts No. 1 (Stamford, Conn. FASB, 1978), para. 9.

damental of these activities. Their decisions are, more often than not, made on the basis of reports and summaries which are prepared by their subordinates. It should be noted here that these reports and summaries are prepared using accounting estimates. Too often, managers and other users of financial information may overlook this fact.

Although the above discussion might overstate the case just a bit (the corner pizza parlor may still be owner-operated, but it could well be a franchise operation), the basic point is that most decisions are made on the basis of summary-type reports rather than firsthand information.

What is the role of accounting and the accountant in this process? One observation that has been made is that the task of the accountant is to observe, interpret, summarize, and communicate information in a form which will enable the user of the data to evaluate, control, plan, and even predict performance. It is essential to note the importance of the term "user" in this context. A user could be a manager involved in the evaluation and direction of the continuing operations of the business; a present or a potential stockholder (owner) seeking information for an impending investment decision; a bank officer in the process of reviewing a loan application; a supplier making a decision with regard to a credit application; a federal, state, or local revenue officer evaluating the propriety of a tax return; or even a citizen attempting to assess the performance of some governmental unit. In each of the circumstances mentioned above, and in countless other situations as well, user needs are met, at least in part, by a report prepared by an accountant on the basis of accounting information.

Not to be overlooked is the impact of accounting on our society. The transfer and distribution of the economic resources of society are often related to the actions of the users described above, taken in response to accounting information. Thus, the failure of accounting information systems to report information on an accurate and timely basis could alter the decisions made by various users and thereby create undesirable economic consequences for society.

ACCOUNTING AS A PROCESS OF COMMUNICATION[5]

Accounting may be regarded as a process of communication in a very real sense. Events occur on a continuing basis which affect the operations of an organization. The accountant acts as an observer-reporter, observing events or transactions as they take place, evaluating the significance of these events, then recording, classifying, and summarizing the events in an accounting report. The user receives the report, analyzes its content, and utilizes the information in making economic decisions. Of course, these decisions made by the user cause new events to take place, again setting the chain in process through another cycle.

---

[5] This discussion is based on Norton M. Bedford and Vahe Baladouni, "A Communication Theory Approach to Accountancy," *The Accounting Review*, October 1962, pp. 650-59.

Two factors are of major importance in this communication. First, there should be mutual understanding and agreement between the accountant preparing the report and the persons using the report on the basis of its preparation and content. The accountant must know the user's needs and perceptions and prepare the report so that what the user understands the report to express will indeed correspond with what the accountant intended to express in the report. Bedford and Baladouni call this fidelity—the relationship between what is understood by the user of accounting statements and what the accountant intended to express in his report.

The second factor is that the accountant's report should show a reliable and relevant relationship to the events it attempts to summarize. The report should, to the degree possible and/or practicable, include and describe all the significant events which did, in fact, take place. In the ideal situation, a user would make the same decision based on the analysis of a report that would have been made if firsthand information obtained on a personal basis was used. Bedford and Baladouni refer to this factor as significance—the relationship between the events which take place and the accounting report which attempts to summarize these events.

ACCOUNTING VS. BOOKKEEPING

Often, the distinction between accounting and bookkeeping is not understood. Bookkeeping refers to the actual recording of business transactions. This clerical recordkeeping function may be done manually or electronically with the use of computers. Accounting goes far beyond bookkeeping. The accounting function encompasses the design of the recordkeeping system, the preparation of reports, and the analysis and interpretation of financial and quantitative data. The decision-making involved in the accounting function requires a much greater knowledge and comprehension than the clerical skills which are needed in bookkeeping.

FINANCIAL ACCOUNTING AND MANAGERIAL ACCOUNTING

Although there is considerable overlap between the two, accounting may be thought of as consisting of two basic segments, financial accounting and managerial accounting. The basic difference between these two segments or divisions of accounting lies in their orientation.

Financial accounting is primarily concerned with users who are *external* to the firm and managerial accounting is concerned with *internal* users. Financial accounting attempts to provide external user groups such as current or potential owners, creditors, government agencies, and other interested parties with information concerning the status of the firm and the results of its operations. The objective of financial accounting is to provide these users with the information they require for making decisions.

Managerial accounting attempts to provide the information which is necessary for internal decision-making to those who are charged with this responsibility within the firm. Managerial accounting, unlike financial accounting, is not constrained by the requirements of the standard setting bodies discussed later in this chapter.

This text is concerned with both financial accounting and managerial accounting. Again, it is important to note that the two overlap. For example, the determination of the cost of the products which are produced by a manufacturing firm may be regarded as a problem that lies within the domain of managerial accounting; however, it is also a concern of financial accounting, because determining the cost of inventory is an important consideration for financial reporting purposes.

OBJECTIVES OF FINANCIAL REPORTING

Financial reporting includes not only the financial statements but also such other forms of communicating financial information as annual reports filed with the SEC (Securities and Exchange Commission), news releases, and management forecasts.

The users of financial information may be divided into internal and external groups. Internal users such as managers and directors can specify the information that they want, can receive additional and more detailed information than is appropriate or necessary for external reports, and can receive information pertaining to planning and controlling operations. External users include owners, lenders, suppliers, potential investors, potential creditors, employees, customers, stockbrokers, financial analysts, taxing authorities, regulatory authorities, trade associations, and teachers. Certain of these external users (e.g., taxing authorities) can specify and obtain both the form and content of the information desired; others lack the authority to prescribe the financial information desired.

Investors and creditors are the most obvious external groups who use financial information and cannot obtain all the information that they may wish to have. Their decisions significantly affect the allocation of resources in the economy. In addition, information which meets the needs of investors and creditors is likely to meet the needs of those other external users who rely on external financial reporting.

A primary objective of financial reporting is to ". . . provide information that is useful to present and potential investors and creditors and other users in making rational investment, credit, and similar decisions."[6] In order to accomplish this goal, it is necessary that the information which is communicated must be understood; it ". . . should be comprehensible to those who have a reasonable understanding of business and economic activities and are willing to study the information with reasonable diligence."[7]

The users of financial information are concerned not only with past and current performance but also with the future expectations of a business. Recognizing these needs, *the primary focus of financial reporting is on the disclosure of information concerning the earnings of a business*, although

---

[6] FASB Statement of Financial Accounting Concepts No. 1, "Objectives of Financial Reporting By Business Enterprises," (Stamford: FASB, 1978), para. 34.

[7] *Ibid.*

information concerning the resources of an enterprise also is emphasized. Consequently, two other important objectives which are stated in FASB Statement of Financial Accounting Concepts No. 1, "Objectives of Financial Reporting by Business Enterprises," are as follows:

> Financial reporting should provide information to help present and potential investors and creditors and other users in assessing the amounts, timing, and uncertainty of prospective cash receipts from dividends or interest and the proceeds from the sale, redemption, or maturity of securities or loans. The prospects for those cash receipts are affected by an enterprise's ability to generate enough cash to meet its obligations when due and its other cash operating needs, to reinvest in operations, and to pay cash dividends and may also be affected by perceptions of investors and creditors generally about that ability, which affect market prices of the enterprise's securities. Thus, financial reporting should provide information to help investors, creditors, and others assess the amounts, timing, and uncertainty of prospective net cash inflows to the related enterprise.[8]
>
> Financial reporting should provide information about the economic resources of an enterprise, the claims to those resources (obligations of the enterprise to transfer resources to other entities and owners' equity), and the effects of transactions, events, and circumstances that change its resources and claims to those resources.[9]

The Board emphasized that accrual accounting is a superior indicator of an enterprise's performance than is accounting on a cash basis. *The measurement of income under the conventions of accrual accounting is intended to provide users with more useful information concerning an enterprise's present and future ability to generate desirable cash flows than is indicated by the income measured on a cash basis. Investors, creditors, and other users of financial information are interested in the current and future cash flows of an enterprise.* Therefore, these users of financial information prefer that information concerning an enterprise's performance to be measured on an accrual rather than a cash basis.

QUALITATIVE CHARACTERISTICS OF ACCOUNTING INFORMATION

Pervasive Constraint

In order to be useful, accounting information should possess certain qualitative characteristics.

Benefits and Costs. *In order to justify providing accounting information, the benefits which may be derived from the use of this information must exceed the costs of providing the data.* There are several costs of providing information, including: (1) costs of collecting, processing, and disseminating; (2) costs of auditing; (3) costs associated with dangers of litiga-

---

[8] *Ibid.*, para. 37.
[9] *Ibid.*, para. 38.

tion and loss of competitive advantage; and (4) costs to the user for analysis and interpretation. Also, there are benefits to the preparers of the information as well as to the users. These benefits include improved access to capital markets and favorable impact on public relations.

User-Specific Qualities

       Understandability. *The information which is provided by financial reporting should be understandable to those who have a reasonable understanding of business and economic activities* and who are willing to study the information with reasonable diligence. Useful information which is difficult to understand should not be excluded. In this context, understandability is the quality which enables users to perceive the significance of information.

       Decision Usefulness. The determination as to whether or not information is useful is dependent upon the particular decision to be made, the manner in which the decision is to be made, the other information which already is available, and the ability of the decision maker to process and use the information. *SFAC No. 2 identifies usefulness for decision-making as the most important quality of accounting information.* Usefulness provides the benefits from information to set against the costs of providing the information; without usefulness, there would be no benefits. Decision usefulness may be separated into the qualities of *relevance* and *reliability*, both of which are defined below.

       Relevance. *In order to be relevant, accounting information must be capable of making a difference in a particular decision* by helping users to form predictions concerning the outcomes of past, current, or future events or to confirm or correct prior expectations. In this context, an "event" is a happening of consequence to an enterprise (for example, receipt of a sales order or a change in the price of a good which is bought or sold), while an "outcome" is the effect or result of a series of events (for example, the amount of last year's profit or the expected profit for the current year). Relevant information does not necessarily mean that a new decision should be made; the information may support the decision which was made previously.

       Reliability. *Reliable information is information which is reasonably free from both error and bias and which faithfully represents what it is intended to represent.* To be reliable, accounting information must be verifiable, neutral and possess representational faithfulness.

       Reliability and relevance often conflict with one another in the standard setting process. The type of information which is most desired by users of financial accounting information (relevance) is often the most difficult information to obtain in a reliable fashion. Traditionally, standard setters have favored reliability over relevance in those situations in which the two are in conflict.

Ingredients of Primary Qualities

       Predictive and Feedback Value. *Accounting information has predictive value when it assists the decision maker in correctly forecasting the out-*

comes of past or present events. It possesses feedback value when it assists the decision maker in either confirming or correcting prior expectations.

Timeliness. *Timeliness means having information available to decision makers before the information loses its capacity to influence decisions.* Timeliness by itself does not make information relevant. However, information may lose relevance if it is not communicated on a timely basis. Often, a gain in relevance from increased timeliness may involve, for example, a sacrifice of reliability; therefore, trade-offs in the qualitative characteristics of accounting information must be considered by decision makers.

Verifiability. *Verifiability (sometimes referred to as objectivity) of accounting information means that several measurers are likely to obtain the same measure, so that measurement results may be duplicated independently.* The Certified Public Accountant (CPA) is an independent accountant who examines or audits financial statements and attests to or reports as to whether or not the financial statements "present fairly" financial position, results of operations and changes in financial position of an entity. In accounting, verification is a primary concern of auditing and the CPA.

Representational Faithfulness. *Representational faithfulness means that there is correspondence or agreement between the accounting numbers and the resources or events that those numbers are supposed to represent.* For example, if a firm reports that its cash account has a balance of $50,000 when the correct balance is actually $35,000, the concept of representational faithfulness is violated. Information that is biased (consistently too high or too low) is not representationally faithful. Bias may arise because the measurement method is not used properly or the measurement method does not represent what it is supposed to represent.

Secondary and Interactive Qualities

Neutrality. *Accounting information should be free from any bias toward or against a predetermined result.* The effect of an accounting rule on the interests of a particular user should not be a major consideration in its selection. The primary concern here is the relevance and reliability that results from the application (or the formulation) of accounting standards.

Comparability. *The significance of information is enhanced greatly when it can be contrasted with similar information concerning other enterprises and with similar information about the same enterprise for some other period or point in time.* Information, especially quantitative information, is most useful when it can be compared with such benchmarks. The purpose of these comparisons is, of course, to detect and explain similarities and differences.

Consistency. The concept of consistency is linked closely to comparability. *Consistency is conformity from one period to another in the use of accounting methods and procedures.*

Accounting principles do not comprise a detailed set of rules and procedures that apply to each and every situation. Rather, they are more in the nature of general guidelines. This is why the accountant may record a particular transaction in alternative ways. Also, different firms may use different accounting methods. Thus, the concept of consistency is essential.

Briefly stated, *the consistency concept requires that once an entity adopts a particular accounting method for its use in recording a certain type of transaction, the enterprise should continue to use that method for all future transactions of the same category.* Note that this concept applies only to the accounting methods used by a particular entity. It does not apply to the methods used by different companies, even though these firms may be engaged in the same line of business or industry.

Consistency, for example, would require that General Motors use the same accounting methods in its reports from one year to the next so that the users of its financial statements are able to make comparisons of the financial position of the company, the results of its operations, and the changes in its financial position between and among years. It would not require, however, that General Motors and Chrysler use the same accounting methods, even though these firms may be somewhat similar in many respects. The financial statements of General Motors and Chrysler may or may not be readily comparable, depending upon the accounting methods which are selected by each of these firms.

Threshold for Recognition

Materiality. *Materiality indicates that the amount involved is sufficiently large to affect or make a difference in a decision. The materiality concept indicates that the accountant should be concerned primarily with those transactions which are of real significance or concern to the users of financial information.* For example, assume that a company acquires a pencil sharpener at a cost of $10. It is expected that this sharpener will be used by the business over a five-year period before it will be replaced. In theory, a portion of the cost of the pencil sharpener should be considered as an expense of each year in which it will be used, because it will be of benefit to the company during each of these years. In practice, however, this would be neither realistic nor practical. The benefits which might be obtained by allocating the cost of the pencil sharpener over the five-year period simply would not be worth the cost that this procedure would involve. This example is, of course, a clear-cut case. A precise definition of what is or is not material is often elusive in particular circumstances.

A general understanding of the basic concept of materiality may be obtained from the following example. Assume that a transaction occurs. It is recorded in Accounting Report #1 in a manner that is theoretically correct. In alternative Accounting Report #2, it is recorded in a way that is expedient, but not necessarily correct in terms of accounting theory. If a user of an accounting report would make the same decision irrespective of whether it was based on Accounting Report #1 (theoretically correct) or Accounting Report #2 (expedient, but not necessarily theoretically correct), then the item obviously does not affect the decision at hand and is, therefore, clearly immaterial or insignificant in amount. On the other hand, if the user would make a different decision on the basis of Accounting Report #1 than might be made using Accounting Report #2, then the item would be considered to be material, because it affected the decision which was made by the user.

Clearly then, decisions as to whether a particular item is or is not material must be made by the accountant and depends on the exercise of professional judgment. Quantitative factors alone are not sufficient to judge the materiality of an item. The nature of the item and the circumstances under which the judgement is to be made must be considered.

OTHER BASIC ACCOUNTING PRINCIPLES, UNDERLYING ASSUMPTIONS AND CONCEPTS

Entity Assumption

The entity assumption is the basis for the distinction which is made by the accountant between a business and its ownership. In accounting, an organization, often referred to as an entity, is treated as a unit which is separate and distinct from its ownership and is accounted for as such. The affairs and transactions of the owners of a business are not combined or co-mingled with those of their firms. This is true irrespective of the legal form of organization which is used by the business.

There are three basic forms of business enterprises. A *proprietorship* is an enterprise which is owned by a single person who is personally liable for all of the debts of the business. A *partnership* is a business which is owned by two or more persons who share profits or losses according to an agreement, and who are personally liable for all of the debts of the business. A *corporation* is a business which has a legal identity separate from its owners, or stockholders. Therefore, the stockholders are not personally liable for the debts of the corporation.

The entity assumption is a distinction which always is made in accounting, even though the distinction may not be true in a legal sense for businesses which are organized as either single proprietorships or partnerships. In addition, the accounting entity could be a department or a division, or the accounting entity could be a group of companies even though each one is a legal entity.

Going-Concern Concept

The going-concern concept means that it is assumed that an entity will continue its operations for an indefinite future period of time, at least long enough to fulfill its plans and commitments. (This assumption is used in accounting unless there is conclusive evidence to the contrary—for example, if a firm is in the process of bankruptcy proceedings.)

Monetary Unit Assumption

The monetary unit assumption means that the transactions and events which occur in a business should be recorded in terms of money. As its definition indicates, accounting is ". . . the art of recording, classifying, and summarizing in a significant manner and *in terms of money* . . ."[10] The monetary unit is a useful means to communicate financial results.

---

[10] American Institute of Certified Public Accountants, Accounting Terminology Bulletin No. 1 "Review and Resume," *op. cit.*, para. 9 (emphasis added).

Stable Dollar Assumption

The stable dollar assumption is closely related to the monetary assumption. *The stable dollar assumption assumes that all dollars are of equal worth or value, that is, of the same purchasing power.* Thus, the relevant transactions of an entity are recorded and its accounting reports are prepared on the assumption that a dollar is a stable unit of measure. Under the stable dollar concept, a dollar spent in 1930 is assumed to be equal to a dollar spent in 1975, or a dollar spent today. In other words, any changes which may have occurred in the purchasing power of the dollar due to either inflation or deflation are ignored.

Time Period Assumption

The most accurate determination of an enterprise's performance would be made at the time in which the business ceases to function. However, investors, creditors, and other interested parties need financial information concerning an enterprise on a much more timely basis. *Therefore, financial statements are prepared for such time intervals as a year or a quarter.* Of course, because of estimates and other factors, the resulting information becomes less reliable as the time period is shortened, although the relevance of the information is increased.

Historical Cost Concept

The historical cost concept is the assumption that the original cost (acquisition price) of a resource, and not its current market value or replacement cost, is the basis which normally is used to account for the resources of an entity. This assumption has been justified by accountants on the grounds of its reliability. Its proponents argue that historical cost is a fact, whereas, in many instances, alternative measures such as market values or replacement costs may be somewhat subjective and must be determined each time that the financial statements are prepared. Historical cost also has been justified on the basis of the going-concern concept. An entity is assumed to have an indefinite life, and many (if not most) of its resources are acquired for use rather than for resale. Therefore, there is little need to consider the amount which might be realized if these resources were sold.

Of course, there have been serious objections to the use of historical cost, especially when prices have risen substantially. Under these circumstances, critics believe that the historical cost of an asset has no relation to its "value".

Matching Concept

(*The matching concept is related to the measurement of the earnings or income of an entity. It provides that expenses that can be associated with revenue should be matched with that revenue when the revenue is realized and recognized during a particular period.*) Thus, the matching concept emphasizes a cause and effect association in which efforts are matched with accomplishments.

Revenue is recorded in accordance with the realization principle (discussed below), not necessarily as cash is received. For example, assume that an accountant prepares a tax return for her client during the month of March, bills the client for this service in April, and is paid in May. The revenue which is earned by the accountant from the preparation of this tax return is included in income for the month of March, because that is the month in which the accountant performed the work which entitled her to the fee.

Likewise, expenses are recorded as they are incurred, not necessarily as they are paid. The expenses incurred by the accountant in performing her work in March should be recorded in March. When she pays for these expenses is not relevant. From the viewpoint of the client, the cost of having the tax return prepared by the accountant is an expense. This expense should be recorded by the client at the point in time in which it was incurred (in March) rather than when it was actually paid (in May).

Revenue Realization

Revenue from sales usually is recognized as a component of earnings when it is realized or realizable and earned. A revenue is earned when the ". . . entity has substantially accomplished what is must do to be entitled to the benefits represented by the revenue."[11] Recognition differs from realization. *Recognition is the process of formally recording an item in the financial statements; realization is the process of converting noncash resources and rights into cash or claims to cash.*[12]

Revenue from sales usually is recognized at the time that both an exchange transaction takes place and the earnings process is complete or virtually complete. Revenue from sales usually is recognized at the time of delivery of the product; revenue from services is recognized when the service has been performed. Recognizing revenue at these times is objective and verifiable, because the sales price provides a measure for the amount of revenue realized.

Revenue which is earned by allowing others to use the enterprise's resources is recognized as time passes (examples of such revenue include interest and rent). The amount of revenue which is recognized is determined by the amount which is received or is expected to be received.

Cash may be received prior to production and delivery. Revenue is recognized as the goods are produced and delivered. An example of recognizing revenue in this manner is magazine subscriptions. A publisher may receive payment from subscribers either before or after the subscription period but would recognize income as the magazine is produced and distributed to subscribers.

Conservatism

Conservatism traditionally has meant that accountants who are selecting an alternative from two equally possible ones choose the accounting alternative that is least likely to overstate assets and income. APB Statement No. 4 stated the following:

---

[11] FASB Statement of Financial Accounting Concepts No. 5, "Recognition and Measurement in Financial Statements of Business Enterprises," (Stamford: FASB , December, 1984). para. 83.

[12] FASB Statement of Financial Accounting Concepts No. 6, "Elements of Financial Statements," (Stamford: FASB, December, 1985), para. 143.

Frequently, assets and liabilities are measured in a context of significant uncertainties. Historically, managers, investors, and accountants have generally preferred that possible errors in measurement be in the direction of understatement rather than overstatement of net income and net assets. This has led to the convention of conservatism. . .[13]

The FASB believes that such a preference not only introduces a bias into financial reporting, but also conflicts with such qualitative characteristics as representational faithfulness, neutrality, and comparability. The Board discussed conservatism in its Statement of Financial Accounting Concepts No. 2 and stated that "[c]onservatism in financial reporting should no longer connote deliberate, consistent understatement of net assets and profits."[14] Continuing, the Board stated the following:

Conservatism is a prudent reaction to uncertainty to try to ensure that uncertainties and risks inherent in business situations are adequately considered. Thus, if two estimates of amounts to be received or paid in the future are about equally likely, conservatism dictates using the less optimistic estimate; however, when two amounts are not equally likely, conservatism does not necessarily dictate using the more pessimistic amount rather than the more likely one. Conservatism no longer requires deferring recognition of income beyond the time that adequate evidence of its existence becomes available or justifies recognizing losses before there is adequate evidence that they have been incurred.[15]

Full Disclosure Concept

Full disclosure means that information which is needed by the users of financial statements should be disclosed in an understandable form. The information may be presented in the main body of the financial statements or in the related notes. In addition to the required financial statements, information should be presented on such items as the following:

1. Details pertaining to elements within the financial statements.

2. Summary of accounting policies.

3. The effect of current value on earnings.

4. Management's discussion of the significance of the company's performance and of future prospects.

5. The effect of changes in accounting principles.

---

[13] APB Statement No. 4, "Basic Concepts and Accounting Principles Underlying Financial Statements of Business Enterprises," (New York: AICPA, 1970), para. 171.

[14] FASB Statement of Financial Accounting Concepts No. 2, "Qualitative Characteristics of Accounting Information," (Stamford: FASB, 1978), para. 93.

[15] *Ibid.*, para. 95.

Full disclosure is very important to the efficient operations of the securities market. Efficiency means that security prices react quickly to published financial information.

ELEMENTS OF FINANCIAL STATEMENTS OF BUSINESS ENTERPRISES

Elements[16]

Financial statements require certain elements to be reported or disclosed in order to measure the performance and status of an enterprise. Ten interrelated elements of financial statements have been identified and defined.

Assets. *Assets are probable future economic benefits obtained or controlled by a particular entity as a result of past transactions or events.* For example, an acre of land purchased by a company is considered to be an asset, because the company can obtain the future economic benefits, can control others' access to these benefits, and has completed the transaction for the purchase of the land. If access to the land cannot be controlled by the company because the city can use it as a right-of-way or if the transaction has not yet occurred, but will in the future, then the land is not considered to be an asset.

Liabilities. *Liabilities are probable future sacrifices of economic benefits arising from present obligations of a particular entity to transfer assets or provide services to other entities in the future as a result of past transactions or events.* An obligation to pay an account which arose on the credit purchase of inventory or the use of electricity in advance of payment are examples of liabilities. An obligation to pay an executive a bonus in cash is a liability; an obligation to pay an executive a bonus in the company's own stock is not a liability because it does not involve a commitment of assets. An agreement to purchase inventory in the future is not considered to be a liability because no transaction has taken place.

Equity. *Equity is the residual interest in the assets of an entity that remains after deducting its liabilities (i.e., Equity = Assets − Liabilities).* In a business enterprise, the equity is the ownership interest. Equity is the source of distributions to the owners of an enterprise. These distributions are made at the discretion of the owners after any restrictions imposed by law, regulation, or agreements with other entities have been satisfied. Equity is increased by owners' investments and by comprehensive income. The division between liabilities and equity is clear in concept but not always in practice. For example, securities such as convertible bonds and preferred stock have characteristics of both liabilities and equity.

The example on the next page distinguishes between the sources of changes in equity (Class B) and the other transactions, events, and circum-

---

[16] FASB Statement of Financial Accounting Concepts No. 6, "Elements of Financial Statements," (Stamford: FASB, December, 1985).

stances affecting an enterprise during a period (Class A and Class C). The changes in assets and liabilities under Class A do not produce changes in equity—examples include purchasing inventories for cash, issuing a note payable to settle an account payable, purchasing equipment on account, and repaying bonds payable. The changes in assets and liabilities under Class B produce changes in equity—examples include comprehensive income (revenues, expenses, gains and losses) and changes in equity due to investments by owners and distributions to owners. Changes which affect the composition of equity but not the amount are represented by Class C—examples include stock dividends and the conversion of preferred stock into common stock.

Investments By Owners.   Investments by owners are increases in equity of a particular business enterprise resulting from transfers to the enterprise from other entities of something of value to obtain or increase ownership interests (or equity) in it. Assets are most commonly received as investments by owners, but that which is received may also include services or satisfaction or conversion of liabilities of the enterprise.

Distributions to Owners.   Distributions to owners are decreases in equity of a particular business enterprise resulting from transferring assets, rendering services, or incurring liabilities by the enterprise to owners. Distributions to owners decrease ownership interest (or equity) in an enterprise.

Comprehensive Income.   *Comprehensive income is the change in equity (net assets) of a business enterprise during a period from transactions and other events and circumstances from non-owner sources.* It includes all changes in equity during a period except those resulting from investments by owners and distributions to owners.

Revenues.   *Revenues are inflows or other enhancements of assets of an entity or settlements of its liabilities (or a combination of both) from delivering or producing goods, rendering services, or other activities that constitute the entity's ongoing major or central operations.* For example, a sale of furniture by a furniture manufacturer is considered to be revenue, whereas the sale of one of its short-term investments at a price exceeding its cost is not considered to be revenue.

Expenses.   *Expenses are outflows or other consumption or using up of assets or incurrences of liabilities (or a combination of both) from delivering or producing goods, rendering services, or carrying out other activities that constitute the entity's ongoing major or central operations.* For example, the cost of the furniture sold by the furniture manufacturer above is considered to be an expense, whereas the sale of one of its short-term investments at a price less than its cost is not considered to be an expense.

Gains.   *Gains are increases in equity (net assets) from peripheral or incidental transactions of an entity and from all other transactions and other events and circumstances affecting the entity during a period except those that result from revenues or investments by owners.* The sale of the short-term investment by the furniture manufacturer at a price exceeding its cost is considered to be a gain.

Losses. *Losses are decreases in equity (net assets) from peripheral or incidental transactions of an entity and from all other transactions and other events and circumstances affecting the entity during a period except those that result from expenses or distributions to owners.* The sale of the short-term investment by the furniture manufacturer at a price less than its cost is considered to be a loss.

RECOGNITION AND MEASUREMENT IN FINANCIAL STATEMENTS OF BUSINESS ENTERPRISES

Since financial statements are the principal means by which financial accounting information is communicated, it is essential to know what information should be incorporated into the financial statements. *SFAC No. 5 identifies this formal incorporation of information as the process of recognition.* For items that meet the criteria for recognition, disclosure by such other means as notes to the financial statements and supplementary information is not a substitute for recognition in the financial statements.

The Role of Financial Statements

According to SFAC No. 5, financial statements should contribute to meeting the objectives of financial reporting both individually and collectively. A complete set of financial statements for a period should include:

1. Financial position at the end of the period;

2. Earnings for the period;

3. Comprehensive income for the period;

4. Cash flows during the period; and

5. Investments by and distributions to owners during the period.[17]

Statement of Financial Position. *A statement of financial position (balance sheet) is designed to provide information concerning an entity's assets, liabilities, and equity and their relationship among one another at a moment in time.* It is not designed to present the value of a business enterprise but should assist users in assessing this value.

Statements of Earnings and of Comprehensive Income *Together, these two statements show the degree to which and the ways in which the equity of an entity increased or decreased. The concept of earnings is defined as a measure of entity performance based on the extent to which asset inflows (revenues and gains) associated with cash-to-cash cycles substantially com-*

---

[17] *FASB Statement of Financial Accounting Concepts No. 5, "Recognition and Measurement in Financial Statements of Business Enterprises," (Stamford: FASB, December, 1984), p. vii.*

pleted during the period exceed asset outflows (expenses and losses). Earnings is similar to net income for a period but, unlike comprehensive income, excludes the effects of certain accounting adjustments of earlier periods that are recognized in the current period—primarily the cumulative effect of a change in accounting principle—as well as changes in net assets attributable to certain types of holding gains and losses.

Statement of Cash Flows.   An entity should report its sources of cash receipts and uses of cash payments in a statement of cash flows. Cash flow information should also be provided concerning an entity's operating, financing, and investing activities.

Statement of Investments By and Distributions to Owners.   This statement is designed to reflect an entity's capital transactions during a period, including the extent and ways to which the equity of the entity was changed from capital transactions with the owners.

Recognition and Measurement

A revenue, expense, gain, or loss item and information about it should meet four criteria subject to the cost-benefit constraint and materiality threshold to be recognized. These are:

1.   The item fits one of the definitions of elements in SFAC No. 6 (formerly SFAC No. 3);

2.   The item has a relevant attribute measurable with sufficient reliability;

3.   The information is relevant; and

4.   The information is reliable.

The item can be measured by different attributes (e.g., historical cost, current market value, replacement cost, net realizable value, and present value of future cash flows), depending on the nature of the item and the relevance and reliability of the attribute measured.

SFAC No. 5 provides guidance for the recognition of revenues and gains and of expenses and losses. As a reaction to uncertainty, more stringent requirements are imposed for recognizing revenues and gains than for recognizing expenses and losses.

Recognition of revenues and gains involves the consideration of two factors:

1.   Revenues and gains are generally not recognized until realized (assets or services exchanged for cash or claims to cash) or realizable (assets are readily convertible to known amounts of cash or claims to cash).

2.   Revenues are not recognized until earned (the entity has substantially accomplished what is needed to be entitled to the benefits); being earned is generally less significant for gains than being realized or realizable.

Recognition of expenses and losses also involves the consideration of two factors:

1. Consumption of economic benefits are recognized by matching the expense with revenues (e.g., cost of the goods sold), by recognizing the expense in the period in which cash is spent or liabilities are incurred (e.g., administrative salaries), and by systematically allocating expenses to the periods during which the related assets are expected to provide benefits (e.g., depreciation).

2. An expense or loss is recognized if an asset no longer has a future economic benefit or if a liability has been incurred without associated economic benefits.

DEVELOPING GENERALLY ACCEPTED ACCOUNTING PRINCIPLES

Generally accepted accounting principles (GAAP) are concerned with the measurement and disclosure of economic activity. GAAP determines the manner in which the accounting process is to be applied in specific situations. *Generally accepted accounting principles are defined by the APB in its Statement No. 4 as follows:*

> . . . Generally accepted accounting principles incorporate the consensus at a particular time as to which economic resources and obligations should be recorded as assets and liabilities by financial accounting, which changes in assets and liabilities should be recorded, when these changes should be recorded, how the assets and liabilities and changes in them should be measured, what information should be disclosed and how it should be disclosed and which financial statements should be prepared.
>
> Generally accepted accounting principles therefore, is a technical term in financial accounting. Generally accepted accounting principles encompass the conventions, rules, and procedures necessary to define accepted accounting practice at a particular time. The standard of "generally accepted accounting principles" includes not only broad guidelines of general application, but also detailed practices and procedures.
>
> Generally accepted accounting principles are conventional—that is, they become generally accepted by agreement (often tacit agreement) rather than by formal derivation from a set of postulates or basic concepts. The principles have developed on the basis of experience, reason, custom, usage, and, to a significant extent, practical necessity.[18]

INFLUENCES ON ACCOUNTING PRINCIPLES

Accounting principles derive their authority from their general acceptance and use by the accounting profession and the financial community. Some of the more important influences on accounting are described in the paragraphs which follow.

---

[18] *Ibid.*, para. 95.

American Institute of Certified Public Accountants

The American Institute of Certified Public Accountants (AICPA) is the primary professional association of certified public accountants (CPAs) in the United States today. For CPAs, it is the accounting profession's equivalent of the American Bar Association (for attorneys) and the American Medical Association (for physicians). The AICPA is responsible for the preparation of the Uniform CPA Examination that is used in all states and which must be completed successfully in order for an individual to become a certified public accountant. For a number of years this organization has been involved actively in research, which is intended to improve accounting practices and procedures, through its numerous committees and by the publication of *The Journal of Accountancy*, the most widely read professional publication of the practicing CPA.

Within the last decade, the role of the AICPA has changed. An example of this increased activity is the formation of the Auditing Standards Executive Committee (ACSEC). *ACSEC represents the AICPA in the area of financial accounting and reporting.* It issues Statements of Position (SOP) in response to the pronouncements of other accounting governing bodies. SOPs have the dual purpose of providing guidance where none previously existed and of influencing the standard-setting process. ACSEC also attempts to bridge the gap between the accounting standard setting bodies and practicing accountants with the use of issue papers which identify current financial reporting problems, present alternative treatments, and recommend solutions.

The Committee on Accounting Procedure

The Committee on Accounting Procedure (CAP) was formed by the AICPA in 1939 to establish, review, and evaluate accepted accounting procedures. During the period 1939-1959, the CAP issued 51 Accounting Research Bulletins dealing with a variety of accounting practices, problems, and issues. The success of this committee was limited somewhat, because it dealt with specific problems as they arose, rather than establishing an overall framework to deal with these issues, and because the authority of its pronouncements depended solely upon their general acceptance. As the need for additional research into accounting principles intensified, the reasons for the continued existence of the CAP were less evident.

The Accounting Principles Board

In 1959, the AICPA replaced the CAP with the Accounting Principles Board (APB). The APB attempted to establish the basic postulates of accounting as a basis for the formulation of a set of broad accounting principles that would be used to guide the accountant in the specific circumstances of his or her practice. An Accounting Research Division was established simultaneously to assist the Board with the research which was necessary to carry out its assigned tasks.

During its fourteen years of existence, the APB issued a total of thirty-one Opinions and four Statements. *APB Opinions are authoritative pronouncements which established generally accepted accounting principles; APB Statements are designed to increase the understanding of financial reporting.*

The APB's membership ranged from eighteen to twenty-one. Although all of the members belonged to the AICPA and were CPAs, not all were practicing public accountants; some members were selected from industry, government, and the academic community.

The Accounting Reseach Division issued fifteen research studies during its term of existence. However, the Division did not interact with the APB in selecting the topics to analyze, nor did the APB request the Division to examine specific accounting problems. This lack of coordination resulted in the Board's issuance of Opinions on topics for which little or no prior research had been conducted.

Prior to 1964, the enforcement of APB Opinions depended primarily on the prestige and influence of the AICPA and the support of the Securities and Exchange Commission, an independent regulatory agency of the Federal government responsible for administering the Federal laws governing the trading of securities. Then the AICPA issued *Rule 203 of the Rules of Conduct of the Code of Professional Ethics. This rule prohibits a member of the AICPA from expressing an opinion that financial statements have been prepared in accordance with generally accepted accounting principles if there is any material departure from the pronouncements of the APB (and now the FASB as well), unless the member can demonstrate that the financial statements otherwise would be misleading due to unusual circumstances.* In addition, all material departures from these pronouncements must be disclosed and the reasons for such departure must be explained in the financial statements.

The APB was criticized for its structure. In addition, the APB's positions on several controversial topics were perceived to be compromises. In 1971, the AICPA established the Study Group on Establishment of Accounting Principles to examine the organization and operation of the APB and to determine the improvements which were necessary. Its recommendations were accepted and led to the creation of the Financial Accounting Standards Board.

Financial Accounting Standards Board

The Financial Accounting Standards Board (FASB) came into existence in July of 1973 as the successor to the APB. Unlike its predecessor, the APB, *the FASB is an independent board whose membership consists of seven full-time, well-paid, distinguished accountants who are experienced in industry, government, education, and public accounting.* FASB members must sever all ties with former employers or private firms. Like its predecessor, the FASB conducts research in accounting matters using its own full-time technical staff members or commissions outside researchers from the academic and financial communities to work on specific projects of interest to the Board.

The research activities of the FASB serve as the basis for an invitation to comment or a discussion memorandum, which is prepared to outline the key issues involved in a particular accounting problem and to invite public comment. After further consideration, the discussion memorandum or invitation to comment is modified and an exposure draft is issued for additional public comment. Depending upon the reaction to the initial exposure draft, the Board may issue a new exposure draft for additional comment or, if it is satisfied at this point, may issue its final Statement, or may do neither. A majority vote of the seven members is required for a Statement to be issued.

The major types of pronouncements which are issued by the FASB are: (1) *statements of financial accounting standards,* which define GAAP; (2) *interpretations of financial accounting standards,* which modify or extend existing standards and which have the same authority as standards; (3) *statements of financial accounting concepts,* which set forth the fundamental objectives and concepts to be used by the FASB in developing financial accounting standards; and (4) *technical bulletins,* which provide guidance on financial accounting and reporting problems. To date, the FASB has issued over 150 statements, interpretations and technical bulletins.

Securities and Exchange Commission

The Securities and Exchange Commission (SEC) was established as an independent governmental regulatory agency with the authority to prescribe accounting practices and standards for the financial reporting of firms that offer securities for sale to the public through national (and interstate) securities exchanges, such as the New York Stock Exchange and the American Stock Exchange. The Securities Act of 1933 and the Securities Exchange Act of 1934 require that these companies file registration statements, periodic reports, and audited annual financial statements with the SEC.

The SEC has worked closely with the accounting profession in establishing and improving accounting practices, particularly in the area of financial reporting. The SEC has stated that the standards issued by the FASB are considered to have authoritative support, and that practices which are contrary to the positions taken by the FASB are considered to be lacking in such support.

Internal Revenue Service

Although in most cases the Internal Revenue Service (IRS) influences accounting in an indirect rather than a direct manner, the income tax code and regulations do affect accounting procedures and methods. The effects of income taxes on accounting information will be discussed throughout this text.

National Association of Accountants

The National Association of Accountants (NAA) is the professional association of accountants who are employed in industry, and as such, is concerned normally with matters which are primarily related to managerial accounting. Of course, many of these issues also have an effect on financial accounting matters as well. Like the AICPA, the NAA sponsors research in accounting and issues periodic reports to its membership.

Governmental Accounting Standards Board

The Governmental Accounting Standards Board (GASB), which was formed in 1984, is an independent organization in the private sector. *The GASB establishes standards for activities and transactions of state and local governmental entities.* The GASB's pronouncements are applicable to such entities and activities as utilities, authorities, hospitals, colleges and universities, and pension plans. If the GASB has not issued a pronouncement applicable to such entities or activities, the FASB's standards should be used.

Like the FASB, the GASB follows due process procedures to provide for broad public participation at all stages of the standard-setting process. The GASB, like the FASB, issues invitations to comment, discussion memorandums, exposure drafts, statements, interpretations, and technical bulletins.

Cost Accounting Standards Board

The Cost Accounting Standards Board (CASB) was the managerial accounting equivalent of the FASB. The CASB was charged with establishing uniform cost accounting standards for defense contractors awarded government contracts. The CASB was established in 1971, and the costs of research and investigation into defense contract problems were paid by the U.S. Government. Reports of the Board were presented to the Congress of the United States. Although its standards are still in effect, the CASB ceased to exist in 1980 when Congress failed to fund its operations.

American Accounting Association

The American Accounting Association (AAA) is concerned primarily with matters relating to accounting education. A sizable portion of its membership consists of accounting faculty of colleges and universities. Like the other professional organizations mentioned above, the AAA sponsors research in accounting and related matters and issues reports from time to time.

Congress

Congress also has involved itself directly in the rule-making process. In 1971, the APB adopted a rule concerning the accounting for the investment tax credit. At that time, the SEC stated its support for the APB's position. However, Congress then passed legislation that stated no particular method of accounting for the investment tax credit is required. The APB subsequently rescinded its earlier pronouncement.

The brief descriptions which were included above are intended to provide a general indication of the major thrust and composition of these organizations. In many cases, there is considerable overlap in the objectives and even the membership of these groups. All of these organizations (with the possible exception of Congress) share the common objective of seeking to improve accounting practice and financial reporting on both a national and multi-national basis.

THE ACCOUNTING STANDARD—SETTING PROCESS

A well-accepted view of the accounting standard-setting process asserts that it is essentially a political process involving various user groups each of which is attempting to advance its own self-interests.[19] User groups often react negatively to those proposed standards which are perceived to be damaging to them and positively to those proposed standards which they perceive to be favorable for them.

User groups are able to politicize the standard-setting process by means of their lobbying efforts with Congress, the SEC, and the President. Since the SEC has both the authority and power to enact accounting standards, the FASB must remain responsive to these user groups or assume the risk of having its standard setting power usurped. Therefore, accounting standards sometimes lack the theoretical background one might expect as greater emphasis is given to the economic consequences of a proposed standard on various user groups.

Some accountants believe that the FASB should not only take accounting theory and the usefulness of accounting information into consideration, but also should support the economic goals of our government. Others believe that if accounting standards are promulgated to achieve macroeconomic objectives, then the confidence in these standards would be destroyed.

Most accounting standards have a definite economic impact. For example, the requirement to expense rather than to capitalize research and development costs has been considered to be a threat to technological progress. The requirement to use the method initially required by the FASB for accounting for the exploration and development costs of oil and gas companies was believed to be injurious to these enterprises.

At the time that the FASB issues a Discussion Memorandum, Invitation to Comment, or Exposure Draft, those companies that would be most affected submit their comments. There are always companies that dislike and oppose a proposed standard, and these companies may appeal to the government to become involved. If a standard is adopted that a company does not feel is beneficial, that company may not follow the standard on the basis of immateriality, or the company may alter its behavior in order to circumvent the effect of the standard. In addition, the company may increase its lobbying efforts in an attempt to have the standard modified or repealed.

OPPORTUNITIES IN ACCOUNTING

The accounting profession in the United States has achieved a professional status that is comparable to that of both the legal and medical professions. Certified Public Accountants (CPAs) are accountants who have completed educational requirements specified by the state in which they are licensed and who have successfully completed the uniform CPA examination. Accountants are employed in a wide variety of positions; any organ-

---

[19] Charles Horngren, "The Marketing of Accounting Standards," *Journal of Accountancy*, (October, 1973), pp. 61-66.

nization, regardless of its purpose, that requires information to be recorded, processed, and communicated usually needs the services of an accountant.

CPAs, in large and small public accounting firms, render a wide variety of services to their clients on a professional basis, much as do attorneys. The services offered by CPA firms include: auditing—the conducting of examinations and rendering of professional opinions as to the fairness of the presentation of the financial statements of organizations; taxes—tax planning and preparation of local, state, and federal tax returns; SEC work—assisting organizations in filings with the Securities and Exchange Commission; and management services—assisting in the design and installation of accounting systems and, in general, services of an advisory nature that do not fall under any one of the other categories mentioned above.

Many accountants are employed by industry and other profit and not-for-profit organizations. These accountants work in maintaining and improving the information systems of their organizations and are engaged in a wide variety of other tasks and duties.

Accountants also find employment in local, state, and federal government, ranging from small local municipal agencies to large federal organizations such as the Internal Revenue Service, Securities and Exchange Commission, and the General Accounting Office. It may interest the reader that special agents of the Federal Bureau of Investigation are often either trained attorneys or accountants.

At the turn of the present century there were fewer than 250 certified public accountants in the United States. Today there are more than 150,000 CPAs, and the accounting profession continues to grow at an astonishing rate. An indication that this growth is likely to continue is the increasing demand for accounting graduates reflected in the starting salaries paid to accounting graduates. Along these same lines it is interesting to note that presidents of large U.S. corporations more often have a background in accounting than in any other single functional area. Clearly, there is a future in accounting.

SUMMARY

The accounting profession has grown rapidly in recent years both in terms of the number of accountants demanded and employed and in terms of professional stature. Accounting is basically a process of reporting and communicating financial information to a variety of internal and external users. As more and more decisions are based on information obtained from accounting reports, the communication aspect of accounting is of particular significance.

Financial accounting is concerned primarily with providing financial information to users who are external to the firm. Managerial accounting provides necessary information to those individuals responsible for internal decision-making. Information is typically provided to external users in the form of four basic financial statements: the balance sheet, the income statement, the statement of owners' equity, and the statement of changes in financial position.

Underlying all accounting practices are certain basic accounting concepts. Once accounting principles based on these concepts are accepted and used by the accounting profession, they become authoritative and are referred to as "generally accepted accounting principles." Many groups influence the acceptance of accounting principles.

Chapter 1 has discussed certain of the basic accounting concepts and definitions that will form a framework for the more detailed explanations included in subsequent chapters.

KEY DEFINITIONS

Accounting Principles Board   The Accounting Principles Board (APB) was formed in 1959 to replace the Committee on Accounting Procedures (CAP) as the primary agency responsible for establishing, reviewing, and evaluating accounting principles. The APB was replaced in 1973 when criticisms of its structure and positions created the Financial Accounting Standards Board (FASB).

American Accounting Association   The American Accounting Association (AAA) is an accounting organization which is primarily concerned with accounting education and research. Its membership consists of accounting faculty of colleges and universities as well as the practicing accountants.

American Institute of Certified Public Accountants   The American Institute of Certified Public Accountants (AICPA) is the primary professional association of Certified Public Accountants (CPAs) in the United States. It is involved in research intended to improve accounting practices and procedures.

Assets   Assets are probable future economic benefits obtained or controlled by a particular entity as a result of past transactions or events.

Balance sheet   The balance sheet or statement of financial position is a general purpose financial report which presents the financial position of the firm as of a particular point in time.

Benefits and costs   In order to justify providing accounting information, the benefits which may be derived from the use of this information must exceed the costs of providing the data.

Bias   Bias in measurement is the tendency of a measure to fall more often on one side than the other of what it represents instead of being equally likely to fall on either side. Bias in accounting measures means a tendency to be consistently too high or too low.

Bookkeeping   Bookkeeping is the actual recording of business transactions. It is a clerical function which may be done manually or electronically with the use of computers.

Committee on Accounting Procedure   The Committee on Accounting Procedure (CAP) was established in 1939 by the AICPA for the role of establishing, reviewing, and evaluating accepted accounting principles. The CAP's successor in this role was the Accounting Principles Board (APB).

Comparability   Comparability is the quality of information that enables users to identify similarities in and differences between two sets of economic phenomena.

Completeness   Completeness is the inclusion in reported information of everything material that is necessary for faithful representation of the relevant phenomena.

Comprehensive income   Comprehensive income is the change in equity (net assets) of a business enterprise during a period from transactions and other events and circumstances from non-owner sources.

Concept of earnings   The concept of earnings is defined as a measure of entity performance based on the extent to which asset inflows (revenues and gains) associated with cash-to-cash cycles substantially completed during the period exceed asset outflows (expenses and losses).

Conservatism   Conservatism is a prudent reaction to uncertainty to try to ensure that uncertainty and risks inherent in business situations are adequately considered.

Consistency concept   This concept requires that once a firm adopts a particular accounting method for its use in recording a certain type of transaction, it should continue to use that method for all future transactions of the same category.

Corporation   A corporation is an artificial being which has a legal identity that is separate and distinct from its owners or stockholders.

Cost Accounting Standards Board   The CASB, which went out of existence in 1980, was the managerial accounting equivalent of the FASB. It was charged with establishing uniform cost accounting standards for defense contractors awarded government contracts. Its standards are still in effect.

Elements of Financial Statements   The elements are the components of the financial statements (e.g., assets, liabilities, revenues, and expenses).

Entity assumption   This assumption is the basis for the distinction which is made between the entity and its owners. The entity is treated as a unit separate and distinct from its ownership and is accounted for as such.

Equity   Equity is the residual interest in the assets of an entity that remains after deducting its liabilities (i.e., Equity = Assets − Liabilities).

Expenses   Expenses are outflows or other consumption or using up of assets or incurrences of liabilities (or a combination of both) from delivering or producing goods, rendering services, or carrying out other activities that constitute the entity's ongoing major or central operations.

Feedback value   Feedback value is the quality of information that enables users to confirm or correct prior expectations.

Fidelity of accounting information   Fidelity of accounting information is the correspondence between the information the accountant wishes to convey and the user's perception of the meaning of the information the accountant reports. The accountant and the user must have a mutual understanding as to certain basic concepts in order for the communication to be valid.

Financial accounting   The segment of accounting primarily concerned with the needs of users who are external to the firm.

Financial reporting   Financial reporting includes not only the financial statements but also such other forms of communicating financial information as annual reports filed with the SEC, news releases, and management forecasts.

Financial Accounting Standards Board   The Financial Accounting Standards Board is an independent board which conducts research and issues opinions as to the correct treatment and presentation of financial information. Its membership includes accountants from industry, government, education, and public accounting. It is the successor to the Accounting Principles Board of the AICPA.

Full disclosure concept   The full disclosure concept requires that all information needed by the users of financial statements should be disclosed in an understandable form.

Gains   Gains are increases in equity (net assets) from peripheral or incidental transactions of an entity and from all other transactions and other events and circumstances affecting the entity during a period except those that result from revenues or investments by owners.

Going-concern concept   This concept is the assumption made by the accountant that the business will operate indefinitely unless there is evidence to the contrary.

Governmental Accounting Standards Board   The Governmental Accounting Standards Board (GASB) establishes standards for activities and transactions of state and local governmental entities.

Historical cost concept   The historical cost concept is the assumption that the original acquisition cost of a resource, not its current market value nor replacement cost, is the basis to be used in accounting for the resources of an entity.

Income statement   The income statement is a summary of the operations of a firm. It reports the income (or loss) of the company during a specified period of time.

Internal Revenue Service   The Internal Revenue Service (IRS) is a government agency which is charged with the collection of taxes. The income tax code and regulations often affect the procedures and methods of accounting.

Liabilities   Liabilities are probable future sacrifices of economic benefits arising from present obligations of a particular entity to transfer assets or provide services to other entities in the future as a result of past transactions or events.

Losses   Losses are decreases in equity (net assets) from peripheral or incidental transactions of an entity and from all other transactions and other events and circumstances affecting the entity during a period except those that result from expenses or distributions to owners.

Managerial accounting   The segment of accounting concerned with the needs of users who are internal to the firm.

Matching concept   The matching concept requires the accountant to match the revenues earned during the accounting period with the expenses which were incurred to generate these revenues during this period.

Materiality concept   This concept indicates that the accountant should be primarily concerned with those transactions which are of real significance to the users of his report. No specific value can be assigned to any transaction to determine materiality, but if the information would affect a financial statement user's decisions, then it is material. It is the magnitude of an omission or misstatement of accounting information that, in the light of surrounding circumstances, makes it probable that the judgment of a reasonable person relying on the information would have been changed or influenced by the omission or misstatement.

Monetary unit assumption   This is the assumption made by the accountant that all transactions of the business can be recorded in terms of dollars.

National Association of Accountants   The National Association of Accountants (NAA) is a professional association of industrial accountants which is concerned primarily with managerial accounting.

Neutrality   Neutrality is the absence in reported information of bias intended to attain a predetermined result or to induce a particular mode of behavior.

Objective of financial reporting   A primary objective of financial reporting is to ". . . provide information that is useful to present and potential investors and creditors and other users in making rational investment, credit, and similar decisions. In order to accomplish this goal, it is necessary that the information which is communicated must be understood; it . . . should be comprehensible to those who have a reasonable understanding of business and economic activities and are willing to study the information with reasonable diligence."

Objectives of Financial Statements   The objectives of financial statements which are derived from the needs of the users of the financial statements, are the most basic components of the conceptual framework.

Partnership   A partnership is a business owned by two or more persons who share profits or losses according to an agreement and who are personally liable for all of the debts of the business.

Predictive value   Predictive value is the quality of information that helps users to increase the likelihood of correctly forecasting the outcome of past or present events.

Primary focus of financial reporting   The primary focus of financial reporting is on the disclosure of information concerning the earnings of a business.

Proprietorship   A proprietorship is a business owned by one person who is individually liable for all of the debts of the business.

Qualitative characteristics of financial statements   The qualitative characteristics are the criteria to be used in the selection and evaluation of accounting and reporting policies.

Relevance   Relevance is the capacity of information to make a difference in a decision by helping users to form predictions about the outcomes of past, present, and future events or to confirm or correct prior expectations.

Reliability   Reliability is the quality of information that assures that information is reasonably free from error and bias and faithfully represents what it purports to represent.

Representational faithfulness   Representational faithfulness is the correspondence or agreement between a measure or description and the phenomenon that it purports to represent (sometimes called validity).

Revenues   Revenues are inflows or other enhancements of assets of an entity or settlements of its liabilities (or a combination of both) from delivering or producing goods, rendering services, or other activities that constitute the entity's ongoing major or central operations.

Securities and Exchange Commission   The Securities and Exchange Commission (SEC) is a government regulatory agency which reviews the financial reporting practices of companies that offer securities for public sale through any national or interstate stock exchange. It works closely with the accounting profession to improve financial accounting practices.

Significance of accounting information   Significance of accounting information is the relationship between the actual transactions of the company and the reports which summarize them. The accounting statements should disclose the events which occurred in a manner such that the user would reach the same decision based on the report that he would have made with firsthand information.

Stable dollar assumption   This concept assumes that any fluctuation in the purchasing power of the dollar is not significant. For this reason, changes in the purchasing power of the dollar are not recognized in the accounts.

Statement of cash flows   An entity should report its sources of cash receipts and uses of cash payments in a statement of cash flows.

Statement of changes in owners' equity   The statement of changes in owners' equity summarizes investments made by the owners, additions to equity from earnings, and withdrawals made by owners during the accounting period.

Statement of financial position   A statement of financial position (balance sheet) is designed to provide information concerning an entity's assets, liabilities, and equity and their relationship among one another at a moment in time.

Statement of investments by and distributions to owners   This statement is designed to reflect an entity's capital transactions during a period, including the exent and ways to which the equity of the entity was changed from capital transactions with the owners.

Statements of earnings and of comprehensive income   These two statements show the degree to which and the ways in which the equity of an entity increased or decreased.

Timeliness   Timeliness is having information available to a decision maker before it loses it capacity to influence decisions.

Time period assumption   The time period assumption requires the preparation of financial statements at such intervals as a year or a quarter to meet users' needs on a timely basis.

Understandability   Understandability is the quality of information that enables users to perceive its significance.

Users of accounting information   A user of accounting information is anyone who will read and analyze the financial statements in order to use the information contained therein to meet his own needs.

Verifiability   Verifiability is the ability through consensus among measures to ensure that information represents what it purports to represent or that the chosen method of measurement has been used without error or bias.

QUESTIONS

1. What is the purpose of accounting?

2. Is accounting useful for both profit and not-for-profit businesses? Explain.

3. Has the need for accounting (and accountants) increased in the United States since the turn of the century? Explain.

4. Who are some of the users of financial statements? Do their needs differ? Why?

5. Explain the similarities and differences between managerial accounting and financial accounting.

6. What are the objectives of financial reporting?

7. Define: (a) understandability; (b) decision usefulness; (c) relevance; and (d) reliability.

8. Why is it important that accounting information be timely and verifiable?

9. How does comparability enhance accounting information?

10. Why have accountants adopted the consistency concept?

11. How can the accountant determine whether a particular item is material in amount?

12. Why is the entity assumption necessary in accounting?

13. Discuss the relationship between the monetary unit assumption, the historical cost concept, and the stable dollar assumption. Are these assumptions realistic?

14. Distinguish between revenue recognition and revenue realization.

15. What is meant by full disclosure?

16. Identify and define the elements of financial statements.

17. What are the basic financial statements issued by the typical business? (Briefly describe each statement.)

18. Financial statements are prepared in accordance with "generally accepted accounting principles." What are "generally accepted accounting principles" and how are they determined?

19. What is the role of the Financial Accounting Standards Board in accounting?

20. If you were uncertain as to whether a particular procedure was in accordance with "generally accepted accounting principles," what would you do to find out?

21. What is meant by the term "certified public accountant (CPA)"? How does one become a CPA?

Chapter 2 discusses three of the major financial statements prepared by the accountant. The basic steps in the recording process are traced and explained. Studying this chapter should enable you to:

1. Present and explain the accounting equation.

2. Identify the two basic sources of a firm's assets.

3. Discuss the purpose, format, and major classifications of the balance sheet, income statement and statement of capital.

4. Analyze transactions as to the effect on the balance sheet and income statement accounts.

Transaction Analysis: The Accounting Process

2

INTRODUCTION

Financial statements are the end product of the financial accounting process. The basic objective of the financial statements of a business is to provide the information which is required by various users for making economic decisions. As was indicated earlier, the basic accounting statements which are included in the accounting reports normally issued to users are the balance sheet, the income statement, the statement of capital, and the statement of cash flows. We will discuss the balance sheet, income statement, and statement of capital in this chapter. The statement of cash flows will be considered in Chapter 10.

THE BALANCE SHEET

The balance sheet, or statement of financial position, is the accounting statement which provides information regarding the financial position of the firm at a particular point in time. It includes information as to the assets, liabilities, and equities of the business as of a given date.

Assets are probable future economic benefits obtained or controlled by a particular entity as a result of past transactions or events.[1] They are the economic resources of the business. An asset is an economic right or a resource that will be of either present or future benefit to the firm. In general, assets are things of value that are owned by the business. The assets of a business may take various forms. For example, assets include: cash, merchandise held for sale to customers, land, buildings, and equipment. In other words, assets are the resources which are used by the business in its continuing operations.

At any point in time, the total of the assets of a business are, by definition, equal to the total of the sources of these assets. A business obtains its assets from two basic sources: its owners and its creditors. Creditors lend resources to the firm. These debts, referred to as liabilities, must be repaid at some specified future date. Liabilities may be defined as probable future sacrifices of economic benefits arising from present obligations of a particular entity to transfer assets or provide services to other entities in the future as a result of the past transactions or events.[2] Owners invest their personal resources in the firm. Investments by owners are increases in net assets of a particular enterprise resulting from transfers to it from other entities of something of value to obtain or increase ownership interests (or equity) in it. Assets are most commonly received as investments by owners, but that which is received may also include services or satisfaction or conversion of liabilities of the enterprise.[3] In other words, the investments of owners in the firm and any profits retained in the business are its equity (or

---

[1] "Elements of Financial Statements of Business Enterprises," FASB Statement of Financial Accounting Concepts No. 3 (Stamford, Conn. FASB, 1980), p. xi.

[2] *Ibid.*

[3] *Ibid.*

capital). Equity is the residual interest in the assets of an entity that remains after deducting its liabilities. In a business enterprise, the equity is the ownership interest.[4] Thus, the sources of a firm's assets are its liabilities and owner's equity.

BALANCE SHEET CLASSIFICATIONS

The various classifications included in the balance sheet are intended to assist the user of the statement in acquiring as much information as possible concerning the business. The individual elements of the financial statements are the building blocks with which financial statements are constructed— the classes of items that financial statements comprise. The items included in financial statements represent in words and numbers certain enterprise resources, claims to those resources, and the effects of transactions and other events and circumstances that result in changes in those resources and claims.[5]

It might appear that if a firm desired to provide the user of its statements with the maximum information possible, it could supply him with a listing of all transactions which took place during the period so that the user could perform his own analysis. However, large firms routinely enter into hundreds of thousands or even millions of transactions during any given period. It is therefore highly unlikely that any user would have either sufficient time, the inclination, or the ability to analyze this type of listing. To simplify the analysis of financial statements, firms group similar items in order to reduce the number of classifications which appear on the balance sheet. For example, a chain store may own many buildings of different sizes, at various locations and serving different functions, but instead of listing these assets separately, all buildings will normally be grouped and presented as a single amount on the balance sheet.

Assets

When assets are acquired by a business they are initially recorded at the cost of acquisition or original purchase price. This is true even if the business has paid only a portion of the initial cost in cash at the time of acquisition and owes the remaining balance to the seller of the asset.

Assets will vary somewhat in their characteristics such as their useful life in relationship to the business' operating cycle, physical attributes, and frequency of use. Accountants attempt to describe certain of the relevant characteristics of assets on the balance sheet by the use of general classifications such as current assets, long-term (or fixed) assets, and other assets. Within these broad categories there are also several sub-classifications. The usual ordering of assets on the balance sheet is in terms of liquidity—the order in which the assets would normally be converted into cash or used up.

---

[4] *Ibid.*
[5] *Ibid.*, p. xii.

Current Assets. Generally, current assets include cash and other assets which are expected to be converted into cash, sold, or used in operations or production during the current accounting period. The accounting period is usually considered to be one year for most businesses. The general sub-classifications of current assets normally found in the balance sheet include cash, marketable securities, accounts receivable, inventories, and prepaid expenses. These individual asset categories are briefly described below.

Cash. Cash includes all cash which is immediately available for use in the business including cash on hand, in cash registers, and in checking accounts. Cash is discussed in detail in Chapter 7.

Marketable Securities. Marketable securities are temporary investments in stocks, bonds, and other securities which are readily salable and which management intends to hold only for a relatively short period of time. Marketable securities are discussed in Chapter 8.

Receivables. The accounts receivable balance represents the amount which is owed to the business by its customers. If a business has a significant amount of receivables from sources other than its normal trade customers, the receivables from customers are normally classified as trade accounts receivable and the amounts owed by others are classified as other accounts receivable.

A balance sheet may also include notes receivable. Notes receivable are the receivables (from customers or others) for which the business has received written documentation of the debtors' intent to pay. Both accounts receivable and notes receivable are discussed in Chapter 7.

Inventories. Inventories represent the cost of goods or materials which are held for sale to customers in the ordinary course of business, in the process of production for such sale, or to be used in the production of goods or services to be available for sale at some future date. Inventories are described in Chapter 3.

Prepaid Expenses. Prepaid expenses represent expenditures which were made in either the current or a prior period and which will provide benefits to the firm at some future time. For example, a fire insurance policy which protects the assets of a firm for a three-year period may be purchased during the current year. Although the policy was paid for and a portion of the protection was used during the current year, the firm benefits from the insurance protection in future years as well. Therefore, the portion of the cost of the policy which is applicable to future years would be considered a prepaid expense at the end of the current year.

Fixed Assets. Fixed or long-term assets are those assets which are acquired for use in the business rather than for resale to customers. They are assets from which the business expects to receive benefits over a number of future accounting periods. Since fixed assets are used in the operations of the firm and benefits are derived from this use or availability, the cost of these assets is considered an expense of those periods which benefit from their use.

The actual classifications which may be included in the balance sheet under the fixed asset caption will, of course, vary depending upon the type of business and the nature of its operations. The accounting for fixed assets is described in Chapter 4.

Other Assets. The classification, other assets, includes those assets which are not appropriately classified under either the current or the fixed asset categories described above. This classification may include both tangible and intangible assets. Tangible assets are those that have *physical* substance, such as land held for investment purposes. Intangibles are assets *without* physical substance, such as patents, copyrights, goodwill, etc. This distinction will be discussed in detail in Chapter 4.

Liabilities

Liabilities are debts. They represent claims of creditors against the assets of the business. Creditors have a prior legal claim over the owners of the business. In the event a business is liquidated, creditors will be paid the amounts owed them before any payments are made to owners. Creditors are, of course, concerned with the ability of the business to repay its debts. In certain instances, creditors may earn interest on the amount due them. Normally, a liability has a maturity or due date at which time it must be satisfied.

Liabilities, just as assets, fall into several descriptive categories. The two basic classifications which are usually employed in the balance sheet are current liabilities and long-term liabilities. Both of these general classes may also have sub-classifications.

Current Liabilities. Current liabilities include those obligations for which settlement is expected to require the use of current assets or the origination of other current liabilities. Examples of current liabilities include accounts payable, notes payable, taxes payable, and unearned revenues. These are described in the following paragraphs.

Accounts Payable. Accounts payable are claims of vendors who sell goods and services to the company on a credit basis. Accounts payable are usually not evidenced by a formal, written document such as is the case with a note.

Notes Payable. Notes payable normally arise from borrowing or, on occasion, from purchases, and are evidenced by a written document. Notes payable may or may not be interest bearing. Notes usually have a fixed or determinable due date.

Taxes Payable. This liability includes any local, state, and federal taxes which are owed by the business at the end of the accounting period but are payable in the next period.

Unearned Revenues. Unearned revenues are amounts collected from customers for goods which have not been shipped or services which have not yet been performed.

Long-Term Liabilities. Long-term liabilities generally represent claims which will be paid or satisfied in a future accounting period (or periods). Examples of long-term liabilities are bonds payable and mortgages payable.

Owner's Equity

Owner's equity, also referred to as capital, represents the claims of the owners against the net assets of the firm. Owners normally assume risks which are greater than those of creditors since the return on investment to the owners is usually undefined. In the event of bankruptcy, claims of creditors take priority over those of owners and must be satisfied first. After all creditors have been paid, any assets that remain will then be available to the owners of the firm.

Accounting for owner's equity is influenced by the legal status of the company—the form of its organization. The legal forms of business recognized and used most extensively in the United States are the sole proprietorship, the partnership, and the corporation. There are certain legal differences associated with these types of organizations which will be considered in Chapters 5 and 6. Basically, the owner's equity of a business is normally divided into two major classifications based on the source of the equity: direct investments made by the owner and profits retained in the business. Owner's equity accounts will be discussed in detail in later chapters.

THE INCOME STATEMENT

The income statement or operating statement provides data concerning the results of operations of the firm for a specific period of time, usually a year. The results of the operations of a business are determined by its revenues, expenses, and the resulting net income.

Revenues and expenses are defined as follows:

> *Revenues* are inflows or other enhancements of assets of an entity or settlements of its liabilities (or a combination of both) during a period from delivering or producing goods, rendering services, or other activities that constitute the entity's ongoing major or central operations.[6]
> *Expenses* are outflows or other using up of assets or incurrences of liabilities (or a combination of both) during a period from delivering or producing goods, rendering services, or carrying out other activities that constitute the entity's ongoing major or central operations.[7]

Put simply, revenues are the gross increases in assets or gross decreases in liabilities which are recognized and result from the sale of either goods or

---

[6] *Ibid.*
[7] *Ibid.*

services. Expenses are gross decreases in assets or gross increases in liabilities that occur as a result of the operations of a business. Net income is the excess of revenues over the related expenses for an accounting period. The revenues, expenses, and the resulting net income for a period are presented in the firm's income statement.

The usual accounting concept of income is based on determining, as objectively as possible, the income earned during a particular accounting period by deducting the expenses which were incurred from the revenues earned. Revenues are the proceeds received from the sale of goods and the rendering of services. Expenses are the costs which are incurred in the process of generating revenues. The accounting concept of income assumes that various rules and principles will be followed. These principles require the accountant to exercise his professional judgment in their application since the accounting concept of income measurement stresses the fair determination of income. The reader should note that fair presentation of income does not mean precise presentation. Accounting is an estimating process that requires the accountant to view transactions as objectively as possible in determining both the financial position of a firm and its income for the period.

Since the income statement presents the results of operations for an accounting period, information included in this statement is usually considered to be among the most important data provided by the accountant. This is because profitability is a major concern of those interested in the economic activities of an enterprise.

INCOME STATEMENT CLASSIFICATIONS

As was the case with the balance sheet, classifications which appear in the income statement are intended to be descriptive, functional categories of revenues and expenses. There are many different formats employed for income statements. Variations among industries are substantial and, to compound this problem, variations among firms in the same industry can also be significant. Consequently, the classifications which are used in the income statement will be discussed in detail in later chapters of this text.

THE STATEMENT OF CASH FLOWS

The statement of cash flows explains the causes of changes in cash plus highly liquid marketable securities and provides a summary of the investing and financing activities of an enterprise during a period of time. While the basic purpose of this statement is to provide information concerning the changes in cash plus highly liquid marketable securities, the statement also is useful in appraising other factors such as the firm's financing policies, dividend policies, ability to expand productive capacity, and the ability to satisfy future debt requirements.

Information concerning the amount, sources, and uses of the liquid resources of a business is considered to be of considerable interest and great value to a wide variety of users of financial statements in making economic decisions. While certain information concerning the sources and uses of resources can be derived from comparative balance sheets and income statements, neither of these statements provides complete disclosure of the financing and investing activities of an enterprise over a period of time. An income statement discloses the results of operations for a period of time but does not indicate the amount of resources provided by other activities. Further, reported revenues and expenses may not represent increases or decreases in liquid resources during the period. Comparative balance sheets show net changes in assets and equities but do not indicate the specific causes of these changes. Therefore, while partial information concerning the sources and uses of liquid funds may be obtained from comparative balance sheets and income statements, a complete analysis of the financial activities of a business can be derived only from a third financial statement, referred to as a statement of cash flows. This statement is discussed in Chapter 11.

THE FINANCIAL ACCOUNTING PROCESS

The relationship among the assets, liabilities, and owner's equity of a business may be summarized by the accounting equation: Assets = Liabilities + Owner's Equity (A = L + OE). The concept expressed in this simple equation underlies the recording process of accounting and also serves as the basis of one of the principal financial statements, the balance sheet. In other words, the balance sheet includes a listing of the assets owned by the firm (and the sources from which these assets were obtained), liabilities, and owner's equity.

$$\frac{\text{Assets}}{A} = \frac{\text{Sources}}{L + OE}$$

The balance sheet or statement of financial position is a statement which reports the financial position of the firm at a particular point in time. The balance sheet discloses the three major categories included in the above equation: assets, liabilities, and owner's equity.

The accounting equation also indicates that the owner's equity is equal to the interest of the owners in the net assets (assets − liabilities) of the business. That is, by transposition, the accounting equation may be restated as follows:

$$A - L = OE$$

Transaction Analysis

A transaction is an event which takes place during the life of a business. In order to illustrate the process of recording transactions and the effect this has on the financial position of a business, we will review the transactions of a small service organization, Kilmer Contractors, during May 19x1, the initial month of its operations.

May 1.   Bill Kilmer organized Kilmer Contractors and invested cash of $10,000 in the business.

This increase in the asset cash and the corresponding increase in the investment by the owner, referred to as capital, would be reflected in the balance sheet as follows:

	Assets	=	Liabilities	+	Owner's Equity
	Cash	=			*Capital*
May 1	$10,000	=			$10,000

This transaction is an investment of funds in a business by its owner. The asset, cash, was received by the firm and the owner's equity or capital was increased. Note that the basic accounting equation balances.

May 2.   The company purchased painting supplies, paying the $3,000 purchase price in cash.

The increase in supplies and the offsetting decrease in the cash of the business would be reflected in the balance sheet as follows:

	Assets		=	Liabilities	+	Owner's Equity
	Cash + *Supplies*		=			*Capital*
Balance	$10,000		=			$10,000
May 2	(3,000)	$3,000				
	$ 7,000 + $3,000		=			$10,000

This transaction represents an exchange of one asset for another. The asset supplies was increased while the asset cash was decreased. Capital was not affected. The equation is still in balance.

May 5.   Kilmer Contractors borrowed $2,000 from the Virginia National Bank.[8]

---

[8] For purposes of illustration, it will be assumed that this is a non-interest bearing note.

This increase in both assets (cash) and liabilities (notes payable) would affect the balance sheet as follows:

	Assets			=	Liabilities	+	Owner's Equity
					Note		
	Cash	+	*Supplies*	=	*Payable*	+	*Capital*
Balance	$7,000	+	$3,000	=			$10,000
May 5	2,000				$2,000		
	$9,000	+	$3,000	=	$2,000	+	$10,000

This transaction is the receipt of an asset, cash, in exchange for a liability, the promise to pay a creditor at some future time. It reflects the promise of the business to repay $2,000 at a future date in order to have cash on hand and available for use at this time. Again, capital is not affected; what has occurred is an exchange of a promise to pay the liability, notes payable, for the asset cash. The basic accounting equation remains in balance.

May 10. Kilmer signed a contract whereby he agreed to paint two houses sometime during the next few weeks. The customer paid the fee of $1,100 per house in advance.

This increase in cash and the corresponding increase in liabilities, unearned fees, would be reflected by the business as follows:

	Assets			=	Liabilities			+	Owner's Equity
					Note		*Unearned*		
	Cash	+	*Supplies*	=	*Payable*	+	*Fees*	+	*Capital*
Balance	$ 9,000	+	$3,000	=	$2,000			+	$10,000
May 10	2,200						$2,200		
	$11,200	+	$3,000	=	$2,000	+	$2,200	+	10,000

The company has agreed to paint two houses at a future date and has received its fee now, before it has done the work. The receipt of the $2,200 increases cash and the liability, unearned fees, by the same amount. Unearned fees is not a liability in the sense that the company will be required to repay the money. Rather, it represents an obligation on the part of Kilmer Contractors to perform a service at some future date. Capital is not affected by this transaction and the accounting equation, $A = L + OE$, remains in balance.

May 12.   Bill Kilmer, the owner, withdrew $1,000 from the business for his personal use.

This decrease in cash and the corresponding decrease in the owner's equity balance would be reflected in the balance sheet as follows:

	Assets			=	Liabilities			+	Owner's Equity
	Cash	+	Supplies	=	Note Payable	+	Unearned Fees	+	Capital
Balance	$11,200	+	$3,000	=	$2,000	+	$2,200	+	$10,000
May 12	(1,000)								(1,000)
	$10,200	+	$3,000	=	$2,000	+	$2,200	+	$ 9,000

This transaction represents a withdrawal of a portion of the owner's investment from the business. Cash and capital were both decreased by $1,000. The accounting equation is still in balance.

May 15.   Kilmer Contractors repaid $500 of the $2,000 it borrowed from the Virginia National Bank.

This decrease in both cash and liabilities would affect the balance sheet as follows:

	Assets			=	Liabilities			+	Owner's Equity
	Cash	+	Supplies	=	Note Payable	+	Unearned Fees	+	Capital
Balance	$10,200	+	$3,000	=	$2,000	+	$2,200	+	$9,000
May 15	(500)				(500)				
	$ 9,700	+	$3,000	=	$1,500	+	$2,200	+	$9,000

This transaction is a reduction of both liabilities and assets. The business repaid $500 of the $2,000 it owed to the bank. Both cash and the note payable decreased by this amount. Capital is not affected and the accounting equation remains in balance. (Recall that it was assumed this was a non-interest bearing note.)

The transactions of Kilmer Contractors for the first fifteen days of May are summarized below.

Kilmer Contractors
Total Transactions
May 1 to May 15, 19x1

	Assets			=	Liabilities			+	Owner's Equity
	Cash	+	Supplies	=	Note Payable	+	Unearned Fees	+	Capital
May 1	$10,000								$10,000
May 2	(3,000)		$3,000						
May 5	2,000				$2,000				
May 10	2,200						$2,200		
May 12	(1,000)								(1,000)
May 15	(500)				(500)				
	$ 9,700	+	$3,000	=	$1,500	+	$2,200	+	$ 9,000

At this point in time, we will prepare a balance sheet for Kilmer Contractors. This balance sheet appears below.

Kilmer Contractors
Balance Sheet
May 15, 19x1

Assets		Liabilities + Owner's Equity	
Cash....................	$ 9,700	Note Payable..............	$ 1,500
Supplies................	3,000	Unearned Fees.............	2,200
		Capital...................	9,000
	$12,700		$12,700

The balance sheet example for Kilmer Contractors was overly simplified for purposes of illustration. The actual balance sheet for General Motors is presented in the appendix to the text, and includes far more additional account titles and classifications. The reader should note that these classifications are not arbitrary distinctions made by the accountants who prepared the balance sheet. They represent generally followed classifications which are intended to assist the user of the balance sheet in analyzing and interpreting it for his use.

The operations of Kilmer Contractors for the first fifteen days of May, 19x1, were analyzed earlier. None of the transactions which occurred during this period were relevant to the income statement since they affected neither the revenues earned nor the expenses incurred. We will now follow the activities for the remainder of May to see how revenue and expense transactions affect *both* the income statement and the balance sheet.

The balance sheet is the starting point for the continuation of our example. Before proceeding, however, certain fundamental relationships should be reexamined. Recall that all assets are obtained from two basic sources, creditors and owners. At this point, we are concerned with the latter, the assets contributed by owners.

Owners may contribute assets either: (1) directly, that is, by investment; or (2) indirectly, by allowing the *income* earned by the firm to remain with the business and not withdrawing it for their personal use. In other words, just as a direct investment made by the owner increases his equity, the income earned by the firm also increases both the assets and the owner's equity of the firm. Since income is the excess of revenues over expenses (R − E), the basic accounting equation expressed earlier in the chapter may be expanded and restated for purposes of illustration as follows:

$$\text{Assets} = \text{Liabilities} + \text{Owner's Equity} + \text{Revenue} - \text{Expense}$$

$$A = L + OE + R - E$$

Keep in mind that this restatement is made for purposes of illustration only and does not really change either the substance or the meaning of the equation itself. It merely emphasizes the fact that one way in which the owner's equity of a business may be increased is by income—that is, revenues less expenses. Nothing else is changed. Now let us return to the Kilmer Contractors example.

May 17. Kilmer Contractors painted its first house and billed and collected cash of $700 from the customer.

This transaction was a sale of services for cash. It would affect Kilmer Contractors as follows:

	Assets			=	Liabilities			+	Owner's Equity		
	Cash	+	Supplies	=	Note Payable	+	Unearned Fees	+	Capital	+	Revenue (Expense)
Balance May 17	$ 9,700	+	$3,000	=	$1,500	+	$2,200	+	$9,000		
	700										$700
	$10,400	+	$3,000	=	$1,500	+	$2,200	+	$9,000	+	$700

This transaction reflects the fact that the firm has begun to earn revenue. Cash was received and the owner's equity of the business was increased by the amount of the revenue earned, $700. The basic accounting equation is still in balance.

May 19. Kilmer Contractors painted a second house and billed (but did not collect) its fee of $900.

This transaction was a sale of services to a customer on a credit basis. It would affect the business as indicated below:

	Assets					=	Liabilities			+	Owner's Equity		
	Cash	+	*Accounts Receivable*	+	*Supplies*	=	*Note Payable*	+	*Unearned Fees*	+	*Capital*	+	*Revenue (Expense)*
Balance May 19	$10,400			+	$3,000	=	$1,500	+	$2,200	+	$9,000	+	$ 700
			$900										900
	$10,400	+	$900	+	$3,000	=	$1,500	+	$2,200	+	$9,000	+	$1,600

Again, this transaction records the revenue earned by the firm in painting a customer's house. Unlike the previous transaction, however, cash was not received. The customer was billed for the service and will pay Kilmer Contractors at some future date. Accounts receivable have increased and owner's equity (revenue) has increased by $900, the fee which was charged for painting the house. This transaction illustrates the very important point that revenue is recorded as it is earned, not necessarily as cash is received. This concept reflects the *accrual* basis of accounting.

May 25.   Kilmer paid his employees salaries of $400.

This transaction was the payment of an expense in cash. It would affect Kilmer Contractors as follows:

	Assets					=	Liabilities			+	Owner's Equity		
	Cash	+	*Accounts Receivable*	+	*Supplies*	=	*Note Payable*	+	*Unearned Fees*	+	*Capital*	+	*Revenue (Expense)*
Balance May 25	$10,400	+	$900	+	$3,000	=	$1,500	+	$2,200	+	$9,000	+	$1,600
	(400)												(400)
	$10,000	+	$900	+	$3,000	=	$1,500	+	$2,200	+	$9,000	+	$1,200

Expenses of $400 were incurred and paid in cash. This transaction reduces both cash and owner's equity. The reduction in owner's equity is due to the fact that an expense has been incurred, thereby reducing income. (Remember that revenues less expenses equals income.) The accounting equation is still in balance.

May 31.   Kilmer Contractors painted one of the two houses contracted for on May 10.

By painting one of the two houses, Kilmer Contractors has partially satisfied a non-cash liability by the rendering of services and therefore earned income. This transaction would be reflected as follows:

			Assets			=		Liabilities		+		Owner's Equity	
			Accounts				*Note*		*Unearned*				*Revenue*
	Cash	+	*Receivable*	+	*Supplies*	=	*Payable*	+	*Fees*	+	*Capital*	+	*(Expense)*
Balance May 31	$10,000	+	$900	+	$3,000	=	$1,500	+	$2,200 (1,100)	+	$9,000	+	$1,200 1,100
	$10,000	+	$900	+	$3,000	=	$1,500	+	$1,100	+	$9,000	+	$2,300

On May 10, Kilmer signed a contract to paint two houses and received his fee of $1,100 per house in advance. No income was earned at the point the cash was received because no work had been done at that time. Kilmer Contractors had an obligation to paint the two houses at some future date. This was a liability to perform services, which was previously recorded as unearned fees. Now one of the two houses contracted for has been painted and that portion of the income has been earned. The liability, unearned fees, has been reduced by $1,100 and the income for the current period has been increased by the same amount. These facts require that the statements be adjusted in order to reflect the current status of the contract. Again, this transaction emphasizes the point that income is recorded as it is earned, *not* as cash is received. The accounting equation remains in balance.

May 31.   The unused painting supplies on hand at this date had an original cost of $2,000.

The facts of this transaction indicate that an expense has been incurred and should be recorded. It will affect Kilmer Contractors as indicated below:

	Assets					=	Liabilities			+	Owner's Equity		
	Cash	+	Accounts Receivable	+	Supplies	=	Note Payable	+	Unearned Fees	+	Capital	+	Revenue (Expense)
Balance May 31	$10,000	+	$900	+	$3,000 (1,000)	=	$1,500	+	$1,100	+	$9,000	+	$2,300 (1,000)
	$10,000	+	$900	+	$2,000	=	$1,500	+	$1,100	+	$9,000	+	$1,300

During the month of May, Kilmer Contractors used supplies that had an original cost of $1,000. This amount was determined by subtracting the $2,000 cost of the supplies which were on hand at May 31 from the $3,000 total cost of supplies available for use (that is, the supplies on hand at the beginning of the month plus the supplies purchased during the month). As in the previous May 31 transaction, an adjustment is required. The asset, supplies, was decreased by $1,000 (the cost of the supplies used) from $3,000 (the total supplies available for use during the month of May) to $2,000 (the cost of supplies on hand at May 31). This transaction reflects the fact that expenses, like revenues, are recorded as they are incurred or used rather than when cash is disbursed. The accounting equation remains in balance.

All of the transactions of Kilmer Contractors for the month of May are summarized as follows:

Kilmer Contractors
All Transactions
For the Month of May, 19x1

	Assets					=	Liabilities			+	Owner's Equity		
	Cash	+	*Accounts Receivable*	+	*Supplies*	=	*Note Payable*	+	*Unearned Fees*	+	*Capital*	+	*Revenue (Expense)*
May 1	$10,000										$10,000		
May 2	(3,000)				$3,000								
May 5	2,000						$2,000						
May 10	2,200								$2,200				
May 12	(1,000)										(1,000)		
May 15	(500)						(500)						
	$ 9,700	+	$ 0	+	$3,000	=	$1,500	+	$2,200	+	$ 9,000	+	$ 0
May 17	700												700
May 19			900										900
May 25	(400)												(400)
May 31									(1,100)				1,100
May 31					(1,000)								(1,000)
	$10,000	+	$900	+	$2,000	=	$1,500	+	$1,100	+	$ 9,000	+	$1,300

We are now in a position to prepare a balance sheet and an income statement for Kilmer Contractors. The balance sheet would be as follows:

Kilmer Contractors
Balance Sheet
May 31, 19x1

Assets		Liabilities and Owner's Equity	
Cash	$10,000	Note payable.........	$ 1,500
Accounts receivable...	900	Unearned fees........	1,100
Supplies	2,000	Capital	10,300
	$12,900		$12,900

The income statement for the month of May would appear as follows:

Kilmer Contractors
Income Statement
For the Month Ended May 31, 19x1

Revenue..............................		$2,700
Less: Expenses:		
Supplies used..................	$1,000	
Salaries......................	400	
Total Expenses..............		1,400
Income..............................		$1,300

The revenues reported in the income statement include $700 earned by painting the house on May 17, $900 earned on May 19 by painting a second house, and $1,100 earned by painting one of the two houses contracted for on May 10 ($700 + $900 + $1,100 = $2,700). The expenses of $1,400 include the salaries of $400 paid to Kilmer Contractors' employees on May 25 and the cost of the painting supplies used during the month of May. The cost of the supplies used was determined by subtracting the cost of the supplies on hand at May 31, $2,000, from the $3,000 cost of the supplies which were available for use during the month ($3,000 − $2,000 = $1,000). Again, note that revenues are recorded as they are earned and expenses are recorded as they are incurred, not necessarily as cash is either paid or received. As previously indicated, this practice is referred to as the accrual basis of accounting.

The income for the month is the difference between the total revenues earned ($2,700) and the total of the expenses ($1,400) which were incurred in order to generate these revenues ($2,700 − $1,400 = $1,300). At the end of the period, this income is added to the owner's equity account.

STATEMENT OF CAPITAL

At this point, it might be helpful to examine the changes between the balance sheet of May 15 and that of May 31 in order to fully understand the relationship between the income statement and the balance sheet. Balance sheets at May 15 and May 31 are reported in a comparative format as follows:

Kilmer Contractors
Comparative Balance Sheets

	May 15	*May 31*	*Change*
ASSETS			
Cash..............................	$ 9,700	$10,000	$ 300
Accounts receivable...................	0	900	900
Supplies...........................	3,000	2,000	(1,000)
	$12,700	$12,900	$ 200
LIABILITIES AND OWNER'S EQUITY			
Note payable.......................	$ 1,500	$ 1,500	$ 0
Unearned fees......................	2,200	1,100	(1,100)
Capital...........................	9,000	10,300	1,300
	$12,700	$12,900	$ 200

Each change in the comparative balance sheets can be explained by the transactions that affected the particular asset, liability, or the owner's equity (these were summarized previously).

The change in owner's equity is particularly important because it represents the net increase or decrease in the owner's investment in the firm. This change can be explained by the transactions which occurred on May 17, 19, 25, and the two adjustments which were made on May 31. These same transactions are the ones which appear in summarized form in the income statement. In other words, the change in capital or owner's equity which took place during the period May 15 to 31 is due to the earnings of the company. These changes in owner's equity are included in a statement of capital (referred to as a statement of retained earnings for a corporation). The statement of capital reports the details of the equity of the owners in the business. Capital is equal to the direct investments made by the owners plus the earnings of the business and less any withdrawals made by owners.

> Withdrawals or distributions to owners are decreases in net assets of a particular enterprise resulting from transferring assets, rendering services, or incurring liabilities by the enterprise to owners. Distributions to owners decrease ownership interests (or equity) in an enterprise.[9]

---

[9] "Elements of Financial Statements of Business Enterprises," *op.cit.*

Note that the statement of capital for Kilmer Contractors, which covers the entire month of May, includes the investment made by Kilmer on May 1 and the withdrawal made on May 12. In other words, it summarizes all of the transactions which affected owner's equity during the month of May.

A statement of capital for Kilmer Contractors is presented below:

Kilmer Contractors
Statement of Capital
For the Month Ending May 31, 19x1

Capital at May 1, 19x1..................		$ 0
Add:		
Investment......................	$10,000	
Income for May..................	1,300	11,300
Deduct:		
Withdrawal		(1,000)
Capital at May 31, 19x1.................		$10,300

As indicated above, this statement of capital indicates how and why the owner's equity of Kilmer Contractors changed during the month of May.

The balance sheet, income statement, and statement of capital presented above were deliberately kept brief and simple for purposes of illustration. They do, however, illustrate the basic principles and procedures which are followed in the preparation of financial statements. An income statement for General Motors is presented in the appendix to the text.

SUMMARY

The balance sheet, income statement, and statement of capital are three of the basic accounting statements that provide data to various external users to be used in making economic decisions. These and other financial statements are the end products of the accountant's work. Although companies may vary somewhat in the exact detail and format of the data provided, all companies will include essentially the same type of information in their financial statements.

The balance sheet reflects the financial position of a firm at a particular point in time by providing information regarding the economic resources (assets) of the firm and the sources of these resources (liabilities and owner's equity). The format of the balance sheet reflects the basic accounting equation: Assets = Liabilities + Owner's Equity. By convention, the assets of the firm are generally presented on the balance sheet in the order of their liquidity. The usual subcategories include current assets, fixed assets, and other assets. Similarly, the liabilities (or debts) of the firm are generally subdivided into current and long-term liabilities. The owner's equity section of the balance sheet contains information regarding the direct investment of the owners as well as the income earned by the firm and not withdrawn by the owners.

The income statement is of particular importance to many users of financial statements because it provides information regarding the results of operations of the firm for a specified period of time, usually a year. Only those transactions involving revenues (the proceeds received from the sale of goods and the rendering of services) and expenses (the costs incurred in the process of generating revenues) will be reflected on the income statement. Net income is the excess of revenues over related expenses for an accounting period.

The statement of capital presents a summary of the transactions that affected owner's equity in a given time period. Any change in owner's equity that occurred in that time period will be reflected and explained in the statement of capital.

KEY DEFINITIONS

Accounting equation or dual-aspect concept The accounting equation may be expressed as follows: *assets = sources of assets* or *assets = liabilities + owner's equity*.

Accounting cycle The length of the accounting or operating cycle of any company is the period of time required for the company to acquire the basic resources to produce, manufacture goods, receive purchase orders, ship goods, and collect cash from the sale. This cycle depends on many factors and could vary from a short period of time for a company in the grocery industry to a long period of time for a company in the liquor industry.

Accounting period The accounting period is the longer of one year or one accounting cycle.

Accounts payable Accounts payable represent amounts the company owes to its creditors for purchases of goods or services in the ordinary course of business.

Accounts receivable Accounts receivable represent the amounts owed by customers to the company for goods or services which were sold in the ordinary course of business.

Cash Cash is any medium of exchange which is readily accepted and used for transactions. Besides currency or demand deposits, cash usually includes certain negotiable instruments, such as customers' checks.

Current assets Current assets include cash and other assets which are expected to be converted into cash, sold, or used in operations or production during the current accounting period.

Current liabilities Current liabilities include those obligations for which settlement is expected to require the use of current assets or the creation of other current liabilities.

Fixed assets Fixed or long-term assets are those assets which are acquired for use in the continuing operations of a business over a number of accounting periods rather than for resale to customers.

Income statement   The income statement is a summary of the operations of a firm. It reports the income (or loss) of the company during a specified period of time.

Intangibles   Intangibles are assets without physical substance, such as patents.

Inventory   Inventories include materials which are used in production, goods which are in the process of production, and finished products held for sale to customers.

Investments by owners   Investments by owners are increases in net assets of a particular enterprise resulting from transfers to it from other entities of something of value to obtain or increase ownership interests (or equity) in it. Assets are most commonly received as investments by owners, but that which is received may also include services or satisfaction or conversion of liabilities of the enterprise.

Liquidity   Liquidity normally refers to the order in which assets would be converted into cash or used up.

Long-term liabilities   Long-term liabilities generally represent claims which will be paid or satisfied in a future accounting period.

Managerial accounting   The segment of accounting concerned with the needs of users who are internal to the firm.

Marketable securities   Marketable securities are temporary investments in stocks, bonds, and other securities which are readily salable and which management intends to sell within a relatively short period of time.

Net income   Net income is the excess of revenues earned over the related expenses incurred for an accounting period.

Notes payable   Notes payable normally arise from borrowing and are evidenced by a written document or formal promise to pay.

Owner's equity   Owner's equity, also referred to as net worth or capital, represents claims against the assets by the owners of the business. The total owner's equity represents the amount that the owners have invested in the business including any income which may have been retained in the business since its inception.

Owner's withdrawals   Distributions to owners are decreases in net assets of a particular enterprise resulting from transfering assets, rendering services, or incurring liabilities by the enterprise to owners. Distributions to owners decrease ownership interests (or equity) in an enterprise. Owner's withdrawals are the removal from the business of cash or other assets by the owners of that business.

Prepaid expenses   Prepaid expenses represent expenditures which were made in either the current or a prior period and which will provide benefits to the firm at some future time.

Statement of capital   The statement of capital summarizes investments made by the owners, additions to capital from earnings, and withdrawals made by owners during the accounting period.

Statement of cash flows.   This statement explains the causes of changes in cash plus highly liquid marketable securities and provides a summary of the investing and financing activities of a company during a period of time.

Tangible assets   Tangible assets are those assets that have physical substance.

Transactions   Transactions are events which occur during the life of a business.

Unearned revenues   Unearned revenues are amounts collected from customers for goods which have not been shipped or services which have not yet been performed.

QUESTIONS

1. What are the main sources of assets for a company? Why does each source provide assets?

2. A = L + OE expresses what accounting concept? Explain the concept.

3. What is a transaction?

4. What is an asset? Distinguish between current and long-term assets.

5. What is a liability? Distinguish between current and long-term liabilities.

6. Explain the difference between liabilities and owner's equity.

7. What does the balance in the capital account represent?

8. What are some advantages of preparing a balance sheet?

9. What periods of time are covered by the income statement, the statement of capital, and the balance sheet? How is this recorded in the headings of the statements?

10. What is the relationship between the balance sheet and the income statement at the end of the accounting period?

EXERCISES

11. Using these abbreviations, classify each of the following account titles as to what section of the balance sheet they would appear in.

$$
\begin{array}{ll}
\text{CA} & - \text{ Current assets} \\
\text{FA} & - \text{ Fixed assets} \\
\text{OA} & - \text{ Other assets} \\
\text{CL} & - \text{ Current liabilities} \\
\text{LTL} & - \text{ Long-term liabilities} \\
\text{OE} & - \text{ Owner's equity}
\end{array}
$$

_____ Cash	_____ Taxes payable
_____ Capital	_____ Inventory
_____ Note payable	_____ Wages payable
_____ Prepaid insurance	_____ Accounts payable
_____ Accounts receivable	_____ Marketable securities
_____ Plant and equipment	_____ Land
_____ Investments	_____ Goodwill
_____ Patents	_____ Interest payable

12. Fill in the missing amounts:

	Company	
	Allen	_Barr_
Assets — January 1, 19x1	$120	_(d)_
Liabilities — January 1, 19x1	80	$ 55
Owner's equity — January 1, 19x1	_(a)_	95
Assets — December 31, 19x1	130	_(e)_
Liabilities — December 31, 19x1	_(b)_	70
Owner's equity — December 31, 19x1	_(c)_	120
Revenues in 19x1	15	_(f)_
Expenses in 19x1	19	24

13. Give an example of a transaction which will:

    a. Increase an asset and increase owner's equity.
    b. Increase an asset and increase a liability.
    c. Increase one asset and decrease another asset.
    d. Decrease an asset and decrease owner's equity.
    e. Decrease an asset and decrease a liability.

14. Given the following information, answer the questions below:

Revenue, 19x1.................................	$24,000
Liabilities — December 31, 19x1...................	25,000
Investments by owner, 19x1.......................	4,000
Withdrawals, 19x1.............................	12,000
Owner's equity — January 1, 19x1.................	27,000
Owner's equity — December 31, 19x1...............	35,000

    a. What are the total assets on December 31, 19x1?
    b. What is net income for the year?
    c. What is total expense for 19x1?

15. Fill in the missing figures in the information below:

	19x1	19x2	19x3
Assets — January 1.................	$100,000	$120,000	(f)
Liabilities — January 1..............	60,000	(c)	$72,000
Owner's equity — January 1..........	(a)	(d)	75,000
Withdrawals......................	20,000	15,000	17,000
Investments by owners..............	18,000	16,000	0
Owner's equity — December 31.......	(b)	(e)	57,000
Income (Loss).....................	20,000	16,000	(g)

16. For each transaction listed below, indicate the effect on the total assets, total liabilities, and owner's equity of the business. Identify the effect of each transaction by using a (+) for an increase, a (−) for a decrease and a (0) for no effect.

		Assets	Liabilities	Owner's Equity
a.	The owner invested cash in the business.....	( )	( )	( )
b.	Purchased a building for cash.............	( )	( )	( )
c.	Borrowed cash from the bank.............	( )	( )	( )
d.	Purchased equipment on credit............	( )	( )	( )
e.	Provided a service and collected cash.......	( )	( )	( )
f.	Paid wages in cash to employees...........	( )	( )	( )
g.	Paid a bank loan........................	( )	( )	( )

17. Classify each of the following items as to whether they would be found on the balance sheet (B), income statement (I), or statement of capital (C).

_____ Cash	_____ Insurance expense
_____ Revenue	_____ Building
_____ Wages payable	_____ Supplies
_____ Withdrawal	_____ Rental expense
_____ Accounts payable	_____ Rental income
_____ Goodwill	_____ Accounts receivable
_____ Unearned fees	_____ Bonds payable
_____ Salary expense	_____ Prepaid insurance

18. Fill in the missing amounts:

Lee Company
Balance Sheet
June 30, 19x1

Assets		Liabilities and Owner's Equity		
Cash	$ 12,000	Accounts payable..	$33,000	
Marketable securities.....	31,000	Taxes payable.....	*(b)*	
Accounts receivable......	7,000	Bonds payable.....	76,000	
Inventory	44,000	Total liabilities...		$120,000
Buildings	193,000			
Land...................	75,000	Capital		*(c)*
	(a)			*(d)*

19. Longhorn Company had sales revenue of $5,700 for the month of October 19x1. Total expenses incurred during this period were $2,900; including rent for the store of $400; salaries amounting to $900; and the cost of the supplies used of $1,600. Prepare an income statement for October.

20. Fill in the missing amounts:

Nourallah Company
Comparative Balance Sheets

	April 30	May 31	Change
ASSETS			
Cash	$13,500	$20,000	*(a)*
Accounts receivable....................	7,000	*(b)*	$3,300
Inventory	*(c)*	2,700	(5,100)
	(d)	*(e)*	*(f)*
LIABILITIES AND OWNER'S EQUITY			
Accounts payable......................	$14,900	*(h)*	$ 100
Unearned revenue......................	*(g)*	$ 8,000	8,000
Capital	*(i)*	*(j)*	*(k)*
	(d)	*(e)*	*(f)*

PROBLEMS

21. Certain transactions of the Ricketts Company for September 19x1 are shown below in equation form. Give a short explanation of the probable nature of each transaction.

	Cash	+	Accounts Receivable	+	Supplies	+	Equipment	=	Accounts Payable	+	Capital
											Owner's Equity
			Assets					=	Liabilities	+	
Beginning Balance	$10,000	+	$5,000	+	$3,000	+	$12,000	=	$10,000	+	$20,000
(a)							+ 8,000		+ 8,000		
(b)	+ 1,000										+ 1,000
(c)	− 3,000								− 3,000		
(d)	+ 2,000		− 2,000								
(e)	− 4,000				+ 4,000						
(f)	− 3,000										− 3,000
Ending Balance	$ 3,000	+	$3,000	+	$7,000	+	$20,000	=	$15,000	+	$18,000

22. Certain transactions of the Kreuger Company for the month of October are shown below in equation form. Provide a description of the probable nature of each transaction.

	Cash	+ Accounts Receivable +	Supplies	+ Equipment =	Accounts Payable	+	Wages Payable	+	Capital	+	Revenue (Expense)
		Assets		=		Liabilities		+	Owner's Equity		
Beginning Balance	$ 8,000	+ $ 9,000 +	$3,000	+ $ 8,000 =	$7,000	+	$1,000	+	$20,000	+	$ 0
(a)		+ 6,000									+ 6,000
(b)	− 2,000								− 2,000		
(c)			+ 2,000		+ 2,000						
(d)	− 5,000			+ 5,000							
(e)	+ 10,000	− 10,000									
(f)	− 4,000				− 4,000						
(g)			− 3,000								− 3,000
(h)							+ 2,000				− 2,000
Ending Balance	$ 7,000	+ $ 5,000 +	$2,000	+ $13,000 =	$5,000	+	$3,000	+	$18,000	+	$1,000

23. Dave Karwin opened a roofing business on June 1 and during the month of June completed the following transactions.

June   1   Dave Karwin formed the Karwin Roofing Service with an initial investment of $15,000.

         3   The company purchased roofing shingles, paying the $4,000 purchase price in cash.

         7   Karwin received $3,500 as advance payment on a contract to roof two houses during the month of July.

      12   Karwin Roofing Service borrowed $3,000 from the Sharpstown State Bank.

June   15   Dave Karwin withdrew $2,500 from the business for personal use.

      30   Karwin Roofing Service made its first payment of $1,000 on the $3,000 loan from Sharpstown State Bank.

Indicate the effects of the transactions on the equation provided below.

Assets		=	Liabilities		+	Owner's Equity
Cash	Roofing Supplies	=	Notes Payable	Unearned Fees	+	Karwin, Capital

24. The following transactions occurred during the initial month of operations of Kingsbery Automotive Service.

Sept.   3   The owner contributed $15,000 cash.

       9   Auto parts purchased on account, $5,000.

     12   Paid rent for the first month, $2,500.

     18   Repaired cars for a $2,200 fee and billed the customers.

     20   Auto parts used, $1,150.

     26   Collected $850 on customers' accounts.

     29   Paid $1,000 to creditors.

a.   Indicate the effects of these transactions on the equation provided below.

Assets			=	Liabilities	+	Owner's Equity	
Cash	Auto Parts	Accounts Receivable	=	Accounts Payable	+	Kingsbery, Capital	Revenue (Expense)

b.   Prepare a balance sheet and an income statement at the end of the month.

25. Sam Jones opened an auto repair business on January 1, 19x1. At the end of 19x1, Jones Auto Repair had the following balances of assets, liabilities, and owner's equity:

Accounts payable.........................	$ 5,000
Accounts receivable.......................	20,000
Building	30,000
Capital	?
Cash	10,000
Land	12,000
Notes payable...........................	12,000
Prepaid insurance........................	5,000
Supplies	8,000
Unearned fees...........................	16,000
Wages payable...........................	2,000

Required:

Determine the amount in the capital account at year-end and prepare a balance sheet at December 31, 19x1.

26. Below is a balance sheet for Rich Exterminator Company at October 31, 19x1.

Rich Exterminator Company
Balance Sheet
October 31, 19x1

Assets		Liabilities and Owner's Equity	
Cash	$7,500	Note payable............	$2,200
Supplies	2,000	Unearned fees...........	300
		Capital	7,000
	$9,500		$9,500

The unearned fees are the result of receiving in advance a $100 fee for each of three jobs to be performed in the future.

During the month of November, the following transactions occurred.

Nov.	2	Rich Company exterminated a house and billed and collected $100 cash from the customer.
	7	Rich Company exterminated a house and billed but did not collect its fee of $150.
	11	Rich paid his employees salaries of $200.
	17	Rich Company exterminated two of the three houses contracted for in October.
	30	The unused supplies on hand at this date had an original cost of $1,500.

Required:

a. Prepare an income statement for Rich Exterminator Company for the month of November.
b. Prepare a balance sheet at November 30, 19x1.

27. Given the following information, prepare an income statement, a statement of capital and a balance sheet for Pate Company on December 31, 19x1.

Prepaid insurance	$ 500		Wages payable	$ 1,550
Cash	16,600		Goodwill	2,000
Accounts payable	8,800		Equipment	7,900
Unearned revenue	3,840		Salary expense	15,000
Utility expense	750		Rent expense	3,200
Withdrawals	3,000		Office furniture	4,000
Accounts receivable	8,160		Marketable securities	1,200
Revenues	25,000		Capital, January 1, 19x1	17,860
Building	20,000		Bonds payable	20,000
Supplies expense	2,600		Capital, December 31, 19x1	26,310
Supplies	140			

28. The following information was taken from the books of the Dawson Company on December 31, 19x1:

Withdrawal	$ 3,000		Revenue	$60,000
Insurance expense	2,400		Prepaid rent	18,000
Cash	28,000		Wages expense	13,400
Utilities expense	1,900		Supplies expense	1,500
Rent expense	10,200			

Required:

Prepare an income statement for 19x1.

29. Prepare a balance sheet for the Kang Company as of June 30, 19x1.

Kang Company
Balance Sheet
January 1, 19x1

Assets		Liabilities and Owner's Equity	
Cash	$13,000	Accounts payable	$20,000
Accounts receivable	49,000	Salaries payable	9,000
Inventory	1,000	Capital	34,000
	$63,000		$63,000

Transactions which occurred between January 1, 19x1 and June 30, 19x1 were:

a. Accounts receivable of $19,000 was collected in cash.
b. Accounts payable increased by $10,000 due to a purchase of inventory.
c. Salaries payable of $9,000 were paid in cash.

30. Prepare a statement of capital for the Hoffmans Company as of October 31, 19x1, given the following information:

    a.   On March 27, 19x1, Anne Hoffmans invested $20,000 in the business.
    b.   Anne Hoffmans invested an additional $57,000 on June 26, 19x1.
    c.   The capital balance as of January 1, 19x1 was $79,000.
    d.   The owner withdrew $13,000 on March 8, 19x1.
    e.   The net income for the period from January 1, 19x1 until October 31, 19x1 was $44,000.

31. The effects on the accounting equation of The Hartford Company are shown on the next page. Write a short explanation of the probable nature of each of the transactions.

32. John King began operating a tax return preparation service on January 1. During the month of January, the following transactions were completed.

Jan.   2   The owner invested $10,000 cash in the business.
         4   The business acquired $3,000 of supplies on account.
         5   Rent of $500 was paid for an office building.
      11   Prepared tax returns on credit for a $3,000 fee.
      15   Salaries of $1,000 were paid to employees.
      25   Collected $1,500 on customer accounts.
      30   Cash of $1,000 was paid to creditors.
      31   Supplies of $1,000 were used.

Required:

    a.   Show the effects of these transactions on the equation provided below.

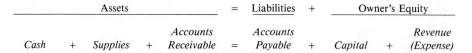

Assets			=	Liabilities	+	Owner's Equity		
Cash	+ Supplies	+ Accounts Receivable	=	Accounts Payable	+	Capital	+	Revenue (Expense)

    b.   Prepare an income statement for the month of January.
    c.   Prepare a balance sheet as of January 31.

	ASSETS					LIABILITIES			OWNER'S EQUITY	
	Cash	Accounts Receivable	Land	Supplies	Prepaid Insurance	Accounts Payable	Unearned Fees	Wages Payable	Capital	Revenue (Expense)
Beginning Balance	$4,320	$9,370	$19,780	$470	$1,400	$5,460	$1,500	$1,320	$27,060	0
(a)					− 400					− 400
(b)				− 290						− 290
(c)							− 300			+ 300
(d)								+ 1,200		− 1,200
(e)	+ 4,000	− 4,000								
(f)	− 3,000					− 3,000				
(g)	+ 2,000									+ 2,000
Ending Balance	$7,320	$5,370	$19,780	$180	$1,000	$2,460	$1,200	$2,520	$27,060	$ 410

33. The following information was taken from the records of J.S. Wylie and Company as of July 31, 19x1. Prepare the balance sheet at that date.

Wages payable	$ 5,000
Cash	2,345
Land	30,000
Prepaid rent	300
Accounts payable	1,470
Capital	?
Inventory	5,990
Equipment	15,200
Buildings	33,450
Accounts receivable	1,350
Patents (just purchased)	7,000
Mortgage payable (due January 31, 19x9)	40,000
Marketable securities	1,035
Estimated taxes payable	3,000
Unearned revenue	750

Refer to the Annual Report included in the Appendix at the end of the text:

34. What was the income for the most recent year?

35. Did the most recent year's income increase or decrease from the prior year?

36. Were the increases/decreases in income because of a change in revenue, a change in expenses, or both?

37. What was the largest expense in the most recent year?

38. Which expense increased the most during the most recent year? What expense decreased the most?

39. Which current asset is the largest at the end of the most recent year?

40. Comparing the two years presented, what was the change in long-term debt? What factors might have caused these changes?

41. What is the largest asset amount in the balance sheet at the end of the most recent year?

42. Comparing the two years presented, how much did total stockholders' equity increase/decrease?

43. Comparing the two years presented, did dividends increase or decrease for stockholders?

Chapter 3 traces and explains the basic steps in the recording process. Studying this chapter should enable you to:

1. Explain what an account is and how it is used in the recording process.

2. Discuss the use of debits and credits and how they affect asset, liability, and owners' equity accounts.

3. List the basic steps in the recording process.

4. Describe a trial balance and identify the types of errors it will (and will not) detect.

5. Explain the use of adjusting entries.

6. Discuss the purpose and illustrate the process of closing the temporary accounts.

7. Identify when revenues and expenses are recognized in an accrual system of accounting.

8. List the five common types of adjusting entries and give examples of each.

The Recording Process

INTRODUCTION   Because the number of transactions which occur in even a small business causing its assets, liabilities, equities, revenues, and expenses to increase and decrease occur much too frequently to prepare a new set of financial statements each time a transaction takes place, an alternative method of recording information must be employed. The description of this recording process, which is basic to every accounting system, is the subject matter of this chapter. The accounting system described, referred to as the "double-entry" system, is applicable to all situations in which financial information must be collected and processed. In small firms the system may be maintained manually, just as described in this chapter, while in larger organizations it will usually be implemented using mechanical or electronic data processing equipment. In any situation, however, the basic principles involved are the same.

THE ACCOUNT   For purposes of reporting and analysis, the transactions of an entity are summarized or grouped in individual accounts. An account is simply a place or means of summarizing all of the transactions that affect a particular asset, liability, equity, revenue, or expense item. The accounting system of a firm includes an individual account for each type or classification of individual asset, liability, owners' equity, revenue, and expense. The increase or decrease in each of these items will be recorded in its own account using "debits" and "credits." At this point we cannot overemphasize the fact that the words "debit" and "credit" are simply terms used to identify *left* and *right* sides of an account, respectively, and have absolutely no other meaning in their accounting usage. (The reader who accepts this statement as a fact and keeps it in mind will save himself untold grief and will greatly enhance his understanding of the recording process.) For purposes of discussion, a typical account may be illustrated as follows:

(Account Title)

(debit side)	(credit side)

This form of presentation is often referred to as a "T-account."

It was indicated earlier that the "double-entry" method is used in accounting in order to record transactions. To understand the double-entry method a simple rule must be kept in mind: for every transaction recorded, the total dollar amount of the debits must be equal to the total dollar amount of the credits. Since we already know that assets must be equal to liabilities plus owners' equity, the following rules of "debit" and "credit" may be established and used in recording the transactions of an entity:

Assets		Liabilities		Owners' Equity	
debit (+)	credit (−)	debit (−)	credit (+)	debit (−)	credit (+)

Because of the equation:

$$\text{Assets} = \text{Liabilities} + \text{Owners' Equity}$$

and the rule:

$$\text{Total Debits} = \text{Total Credits}$$

the procedures (or rules) for recording increases and decreases in the accounts logically follow:

> To increase an ASSET, debit the account.
> To decrease an ASSET, credit the account.
>
> To increase a LIABILITY or OWNERS' EQUITY, credit the account.
> To decrease a LIABILITY or OWNERS' EQUITY, debit the account.

Since revenues and expenses increase and decrease owners' equity respectively, the rules of debit and credit for owners' equity apply to revenue and expense accounts. Because revenues increase owners' equity, the rule for recording increases or decreases in this account is the same as that for owners' equity:

> To increase REVENUE, credit the account.
> To decrease REVENUE, debit the account.

On the other hand, since expenses decrease owners' equity, the rule for recording expenses is opposite of that for owners' equity:

> To increase an EXPENSE, debit the account.
> To decrease an EXPENSE, credit the account.

In order to illustrate the operation of these rules, assume that a firm obtains a $2,000 cash loan from its bank. This transaction would increase the firm's cash, an asset, by $2,000 and also increase its loans payable, a liability, by the same amount. In order to record this transaction, the firm would debit (increase) its cash account for $2,000 and, at the same time, credit (increase) its loans payable account for $2,000. This transaction would be summarized in the accounts of the firm as follows:

Cash	Loans Payable
2,000	2,000

Note that the total of the debits (in this instance a debit to the cash account of $2,000) is equal to the total of the credits (a credit to the liability account, loans payable for the same amount). In addition, the accounting equation, $A = L + OE$ remains in balance since the assets and liabilities were both increased by $2,000 (owners' equity was not affected).

When the firm repays its loan to the bank, the payment of $2,000 would decrease the firm's asset, cash, by $2,000 and decrease its liability, loans payable, by the same amount. This transaction would be recorded in the accounts by a debit (decrease) to loans payable of $2,000 and a credit (decrease) to cash of $2,000. The effects of the two transactions, the loan and its repayment, are recorded in the accounts as follows:

Cash		Loans Payable	
(1) 2,000	(2) 2,000	(2) 2,000	(1) 2,000

(1) Borrow $2,000 from bank.
(2) Repay $2,000 to bank.

Again the total debits are equal to the total credits and the accounting equation remains in balance.

It is often useful to consider, analyze, and record the transactions of a business as they occur. The simplest example of this process is the use of the general journal entry, which could be used to record the two transactions explained above as follows:

	Debit	Credit
Cash	2,000	
Loans Payable.		2,000
Loans Payable.	2,000	
Cash		2,000

A general journal entry, usually referred to as a journal entry, is a simple means of recording the transactions of a firm in terms of debits and credits. As illustrated above, the format for each journal entry is to write the title of the account to be debited and the amount of the debit on the first line, then indent and write the title of the account to be credited and the amount of the credit on the second line. This is simply a matter of convention.

For purposes of illustration, transactions will be recorded initially in general journal form and then transferred to the individual "T-accounts" (as illustrated in the foregoing). This latter process is referred to as "posting," transferring information from the general journal to the ledger (the book of entry which contains all the accounts of the firm). The same data which were used in Chapter 2 in order to illustrate the preparation of financial statements for Kilmer Contractors will be employed again in this example.

AN ILLUSTRATION

To illustrate the recording process described above, we will again follow the activities of Kilmer Contractors, the small painting contractor described in Chapter 2, through May, the initial month of its operations. In this process we will review the procedures which are involved in:

1. The preparation of general journal entries.
2. Posting these general journal entries to the ledger.
3. The preparation of a trial balance before adjustment.
4. The preparation of adjusting journal entries.
5. Posting these adjusting entries to the ledger.
6. The preparation of the adjusted trial balance.
7. The preparation of closing entries.
8. Posting these closing entries to the ledger.
9. The preparation of the after-closing trial balance.
10. The preparation of the financial statements.

General Journal Entries

The transactions of Kilmer Contractors which occurred during the month of May 19x1, would be recorded as follows:

May 1.   Bill Kilmer organized Kilmer Contractors and invested cash of $10,000 in the business.

This transaction is an investment of funds in a business by its owner. Cash held by the firm and the owner's equity account, capital, were both increased. It would be recorded as follows:

Cash 10,000
    Bill Kilmer, Capital.   10,000

Cash		Capital	
5/1 10,000			5/1 10,000

As indicated above, the increase in the asset cash would be recorded by a debit to the cash account and the corresponding increase in the investment by the owner would be recorded by a credit to the capital account. This entry illustrates the rule that increases in assets are recorded by debits and increases in equities are recorded by credits. Note that the basic accounting equation, $A = L + OE$, is in balance and the total debits are equal to the total credits. This will hold true for each of the transactions of the business as they are recorded.

May 2.   The Company purchased painting supplies, paying the $3,000 purchase price in cash.

This transaction represents an exchange of one asset for another. The asset supplies was increased while the asset cash was decreased. It would be recorded as follows:

Supplies 3,000
    Cash   3,000

Cash		Supplies	
5/1 10,000	5/2 3,000	5/2 3,000	

The increase in the asset supplies would be recorded by a debit to the supplies account while the cash outlay would be recorded by a credit to the cash account. This entry follows the rule that increases in assets are recorded by debits while decreases in assets are recorded by credits.

May 5. Kilmer Contractors borrowed $2,000 from the Virginia National Bank.[1]

This transaction is the receipt of an asset, cash, in exchange for a liability, the promise to pay a creditor at some future date. It reflects the promise of the business to repay $2,000 at a future date in order to have cash on hand and available for use at this time. It would be recorded by the following entry:

Cash 2,000
    Note Payable   2,000

Cash		Note Payable	
5/1 10,000	5/2 3,000		5/5 2,000
5/5 2,000			

---

[1] For purposes of illustration, it was assumed that this was a non-interest bearing note.

The increase in the asset cash is recorded by a debit to the cash account and the increase in the liability, note payable, is recorded by a credit to the note payable account. This transaction illustrates the rule that increases in assets are recorded by debits and increases in liabilities are recorded by credits.

May 10.   Kilmer signed a contract whereby he agreed to paint two houses sometime during the next few weeks. The customer paid Kilmer the fee of $1,100 per house in advance.

The company has agreed to paint two houses at a future date and has received its fee now, before it has done the work. The receipt of the $2,200 increases cash and the liability, unearned fees, by the same amount. Unearned fees are not a liability in the sense that the company will be required to repay the money. Rather, this account represents an obligation on the part of Kilmer Contractors to render a service at some future date. This transaction would be recorded by the following entry:

Cash 2,200
    Unearned Fees   2,200

	Cash				Unearned Fees	
5/1	10,000	5/2	3,000		5/10	2,200
5/5	2,000					
5/10	2,200					

The increase in the asset cash would be recorded by a debit to the cash account while the increase in the liability, unearned fees, would be recorded by a credit to the unearned fees account. Again, this entry illustrates the rule that increases in assets are recorded by debits and increases in liabilities are recorded by credits.

May 12.   Bill Kilmer, the owner, withdrew $1,000 from the business for his own personal use.

This transaction is a withdrawal of a portion of the owner's investment from the business. Cash and capital were both decreased by $1,000. It would be recorded as follows:

Withdrawals 1,000
    Cash   1,000

	Cash				Withdrawals	
5/1	10,000	5/2	3,000	5/12	1,000	
5/5	2,000	5/12	1,000			
5/10	2,200					

The withdrawal of $1,000 in cash from the business by the owner would be recorded by a debit to the withdrawals account and a credit to the cash account. This entry illustrates the rule that decreases in equity accounts are recorded by debits and decreases in asset accounts are recorded by credits.

May 15. Kilmer Contractors repaid $500 of the $2,000 it borrowed from the Virginia National Bank.

This transaction is a reduction of both liabilities and assets. The business repaid $500 of the $2,000 it owed to the bank. Both cash and the note payable decreased by this amount. (Recall that it was assumed that this note was not interest bearing.) The following entry would be made:

Note Payable 500
    Cash 500

	Cash				Note Payable		
5/1	10,000	5/2	3,000	5/15	500	5/5	2,000
5/5	2,000	5/12	1,000				
5/10	2,200	5/15	500				

The repayment of $500 to the bank would be recorded by a debit to the liability account, note payable, and a credit to the asset account, cash. This entry illustrates the rule that decreases in liabilities are recorded by debits while decreases in assets are recorded by credits.

May 17. Kilmer Contractors painted its first house and billed and collected a fee of $700 from the customer.

This transaction indicates that the firm has begun to earn revenue. It is a sale of services for cash. Cash was received and the owner's equity of the business was increased by the amount of the revenue earned. It would be recorded by the following entry:

Cash 700
    Painting Fees 700

	Cash				Painting Fees	
5/1	10,000	5/2	3,000	5/17	700	
5/5	2,000	5/12	1,000			
5/10	2,200	5/15	500			
5/17	700					

The sale of services for cash would be recorded by a debit to the cash account and a credit to the revenue account, painting fees. This entry illustrates the rule that increases in assets are recorded by debits and increases in revenues are recorded by credits.

May 19. Kilmer Contractors painted a second house and billed (but did not collect) its fee of $900.

Again, this transaction records the revenue earned by the firm in painting a customer's house. Unlike the previous transaction, however, cash was not received. The customer was billed for the service rendered and will pay Kilmer Contractors at some future date. Accounts receivable have increased and owner's equity (revenue) has increased by $900, the fee charged for painting the house. This transaction illustrates the very important point that revenue is recorded as it is earned, not necessarily as cash is received. This concept reflects the *accrual* basis of accounting. The transaction would be recorded by the following entry:

Accounts Receivable 900
    Painting Fees   900

Accounts Receivable		Painting Fees	
5/19 900		5/17 700	
		5/19 900	

This sale of services to a customer on a credit basis would be recorded by a debit to the asset, accounts receivable, and a credit to the revenue account, painting fees. Again, this transaction illustrates the rule that increases in assets are recorded by debits and increases in revenues are recorded by credits.

May 25. Kilmer paid salaries of $400 to his employees.

Expenses of $400 were incurred and paid in cash. This transaction reduces both the cash balance and owner's equity. The reduction in owner's equity is due to the fact that an expense has been incurred, thereby reducing income. (Remember that revenues less expenses equals income.) The transaction would be recorded by the following entry:

Salaries 400
    Cash   400

Cash				Salaries	
5/1	10,000	5/2	3,000	5/25 400	
5/5	2,000	5/12	1,000		
5/10	2,200	5/15	500		
5/17	700	5/25	400		

The payment of salaries to employees would be recorded by a debit to the expense account, salaries, and a credit to the asset account, cash. This entry illustrates the rule that increases in expenses are recorded by debits and decreases in assets are recorded by credits. An example of the recording of these journal entries in a general journal is shown in Illustration 1.

Posting

The second step in the recording process would be to post each of the journal entries to the appropriate ledger accounts. Posting is the process of transferring the individual debits and credits of each entry to the appropriate account or accounts in the ledger. This step enables the accountant to summarize and group the transactions which occurred according to the individual accounts which they affect. For each transaction, the debit amount in the journal entry is posted by entering it on the debit side of the appropriate ledger account and each credit amount in the entry is posted by entering it on the credit side of the appropriate ledger account. This process was illustrated in the previous section on general journal entries. Recall that the initial transaction of Kilmer Contractors was as follows:

May 1. Bill Kilmer organized Kilmer Contractors and invested cash of $10,000 in the business.

This transaction was recorded by the following general journal entry:

```
Cash  . . . . . . . . . . . . . . . . . . . . . . . . . . . . . . . . . . . 10,000
    Bill Kilmer, Capital. . . . . . . . . . . . . . . . . . . . . . . .        10,000
```

It would be posted to the ledger as follows:

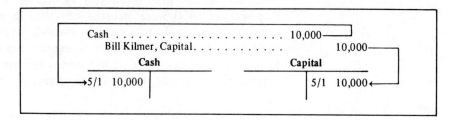

The debit to cash of $10,000 in the journal entry is posted to the debit side of the cash account in the general ledger and the credit to capital of $10,000 is posted to the credit side of the capital account in the general ledger. The date in the ledger accounts provides a reference back to the original source of the posting, the general journal. Usually, a page reference will also be provided by each entry in the journal and each account in the general ledger in order to facilitate the cross-referencing of transactions.

Illustration 1

GENERAL JOURNAL

DATE		ACCOUNT TITLES AND EXPLANATION	FO. LIO	DEBIT	CREDIT
May	1	Cash		1 000 00	
		Capital			1 000 00
	2	Supplies		300 00	
		Cash			300 00
	5	Cash		200 00	
		Note Payable			200 00
	10	Cash		220 00	
		Unearned Fees			220 00
	12	Withdrawals		100 00	
		Cash			100 00
	15	Note Payable		50 00	
		Cash			50 00
	17	Cash		70 00	
		Painting Fees			70 00
	19	Accounts Receivable		90 00	
		Painting Fees			90 00
	25	Salaries		400 00	
		Cash			400 00

Each of the transactions of Kilmer Contractors would be posted in this manner. In our example, the transactions journalized in the previous section are posted to the "T-accounts" included below. The dates of the transactions appear by each amount and are included for reference purposes.

	Cash		
5/1	10,000	5/2	3,000
5/5	2,000	5/12	1,000
5/10	2,200	5/15	500
5/17	700	5/25	400
	10,000		

	Accounts Receivable	
5/19	900	
	900	

	Supplies	
5/2	3,000	
	3,000	

	Note Payable		
5/15	500	5/5	2,000
			1,500

	Unearned Fees	
	5/10	2,200
		2,200

	Capital	
	5/1	10,000
		10,000

	Withdrawals	
5/12	1,000	
	1,000	

	Painting Fees	
	5/17	700
	5/19	900
		1,600

	Salaries	
5/25	400	
	400	

An alternative to the "T-account" format for posting is the three-column running balance format shown in Illustration 2. This format utilizes the debit and credit columns for the posting of journal entries, but also requires the new, or current, balance to be entered each time.

Trial Balance

After all of the transactions which were initially recorded in the general journal have been posted to the general ledger, the next step in the accounting process would be to prepare a trial balance. A trial balance is simply a listing of all of the accounts included in the general ledger along with the balance, debit or credit, of each account. The purpose of a trial balance is simply to prove the equality of the debits and credits and to "catch" or detect any obvious errors which may have occurred in either

Illustration 2

GENERAL LEDGER

ACCOUNT *Cash*   ACCT. No. *101*

DATE	DESCRIPTION	POST-ING REF.	DEBIT	CREDIT	BALANCE
May 1			10 000 00		10 000 00
2				3 000 00	7 000 00
5			2 000 00		9 000 00
10			2 200 00		11 200 00
12				1 000 00	10 200 00
15				500 00	9 700 00
17			700 00		10 400 00
25				400 00	10 000 00

ACCOUNT *Accounts Receivable*   ACCT. No. *111*

DATE	DESCRIPTION	POST-ING REF.	DEBIT	CREDIT	BALANCE
May 19			900 00		900 00

ACCOUNT *Supplies*   ACCT. No. *121*

DATE	DESCRIPTION	POST-ING REF.	DEBIT	CREDIT	BALANCE
May 2			300 00		300 00

ACCOUNT *Note Payable*   ACCT. No. *321*

DATE	DESCRIPTION	POST-ING REF.	DEBIT	CREDIT	BALANCE
May 5				2 000 00	2 000 00
15			500 00		1 500 00

ACCOUNT *Unearned Fees*   ACCT. No. *331*

DATE	DESCRIPTION	POST-ING REF.	DEBIT	CREDIT	BALANCE
May 10				2 200 00	2 200 00

ACCOUNT *Capital*   ACCT. No. *401*

DATE	DESCRIPTION	POST-ING REF.	DEBIT	CREDIT	BALANCE
May 1				10 000 00	10 000 00

ACCOUNT *Withdrawals*   ACCT. No. *402*

DATE	DESCRIPTION	POST-ING REF.	DEBIT	CREDIT	BALANCE
May 12			1 000 00		1 000 00

ACCOUNT *Painting Fees*   ACCT. No. *501*

DATE	DESCRIPTION	POST-ING REF.	DEBIT	CREDIT	BALANCE
May 17				700 00	700 00
19				900 00	1 600 00

ACCOUNT *Salaries*   ACCT. No. *701*

DATE	DESCRIPTION	POST-ING REF.	DEBIT	CREDIT	BALANCE
May 25			400 00		400 00

the recording or the posting process. The reader should note, however, that even if the total of the debits in the trial balance is equal to the total of the credits, this only proves that the accounts are "in balance"; it does not indicate that errors have not been made. (For example, a posting could have been made to the wrong account.)

The trial balance of Kilmer Contractors at May 31, 19x1, before adjustments would be as follows:

Kilmer Contractors
Trial Balance Before Adjustment
May 31, 19x1

	Debit	Credit
Cash	$10,000	
Accounts receivable	900	
Supplies	3,000	
Note payable		$ 1,500
Unearned fees		2,200
Capital		10,000
Withdrawals	1,000	
Painting fees		1,600
Salaries	400	
Total	$15,300	$15,300

Adjusting Entries

As previously indicated, the accrual basis of accounting requires that revenues be recorded as they are earned and expenses be recorded as they are incurred. This procedure is followed without regard to either the receipt or disbursement of cash. At the end of any period, then, there will usually be transactions which are still in the process of completion or which have occurred but have not yet been recorded. These transactions require adjusting entries. In the case of Kilmer Contractors, adjustments are required for: (1) the revenue which was earned by painting one of the two houses contracted for on May 10, and (2) the painting supplies which were used during the month of May. These adjustments, referred to as adjusting entries, would be recorded in the accounts by the general journal entries presented below.

May 31. Kilmer Contractors painted one of the two houses contracted for on May 10.

This adjustment records the partial satisfaction of a non-cash liability by the rendering of services (that is, painting one of the two houses) and the earning of income. It would be recorded by the following journal entry:

Unearned Fees	1,100	
Painting Fees		1,100

Unearned Fees		Painting Fees	
5/31 1,100	5/10 2,200	5/17	700
		5/19	900
		5/31	1,100

Recall that on May 10 Kilmer signed a contract whereby he agreed to paint two houses at a future date and received his fee of $1,100 per house in advance. No income was earned at the point the contract was signed and the cash received, because no work had been done at that time. Kilmer Contractors had an obligation to paint the two houses at a future date. This was a liability to perform services, which was reflected as unearned fees. Now, at the end of May, one of the two houses contracted for has been painted and that portion of the income has been earned. The liability, unearned fees, has been reduced by $1,100 and the income for May has been increased by the same amount. These facts require that the financial statements be adjusted in order to reflect the current status of the contract. Again, this transaction emphasizes the fact that income is recorded as it is earned, *not* as cash is received.

The decrease of $1,100 in the liability, unearned fees, would be recorded by a debit to the unearned fees account and the increase in the revenue, painting fees, would be recorded by a credit to the painting fees account. This adjusting entry illustrates the rule that decreases in liabilities are recorded by debits and increases in revenues are recorded by credits.

May 31.   The unused painting supplies on hand at this date had an original cost of $2,000.

The facts of this transaction indicate that an expense has been incurred during the month which has not yet been recorded in the accounts. The following adjusting entry would be required at May 31:

Supplies Used	1,000	
Supplies		1,000

Supplies Used		Supplies	
5/31 1,000		5/2 3,000	5/31 1,000

During May, Kilmer Contractors used supplies that had an original cost of $1,000. This amount was determined by subtracting the $2,000 cost of the supplies which were still on hand at May 31 from the $3,000 total cost of supplies that were available for use (that is, the supplies on hand at the beginning of the month plus the supplies purchased during the month). As in the previous May 31 transaction, an adjusting entry was required. The asset, supplies, was decreased by $1,000 (the cost of the supplies used), from $3,000 (the total supplies available for use during the month of May) to $2,000 (the cost of supplies still on hand at May 31). This transaction reflects the fact that expenses are recorded when incurred or used rather than when cash is disbursed.

The increase in the supplies used expense would be recorded by a debit to the supplies used account. The decrease in the asset, supplies, would be recorded by a credit to the supplies account. This adjusting entry illustrates the rule that increases in expenses are recorded by debits and decreases in assets are recorded by credits.

After these two journal entries have been made, all of the transactions of Kilmer Contractors which occurred during the month of May have been recorded in the accounts.

Posting the Adjusting Entries

The adjusting entries would then be posted to the ledger in the same manner as were the regular journal entries. This has been done below. Again, the dates of the transactions are included for the use of the reader for purposes of reference. (Note that the two adjusting entries are dated May 31.)

Cash			
5/1	10,000	5/2	3,000
5/5	2,000	5/12	1,000
5/10	2,200	5/15	500
5/17	700	5/25	400
	10,000		

Accounts Receivable		
5/19	900	
	900	

Supplies			
5/2	3,000	5/31	1,000
	2,000		

Note Payable			
5/15	500	5/5	2,000
			1,500

Unearned Fees			
5/31	1,100	5/10	2,200
			1,100

Capital			
		5/1	10,000
			10,000

Withdrawals	
5/12	1,000
	1,000

Painting Fees		
	5/17	700
	5/19	900
	5/31	1,100
		2,700

Salaries	
5/25	400
	400

Supplies Used	
5/31	1,000
	1,000

**Trial Balance
After Adjustment**

The next step in the recording process would be the preparation of a trial balance *after* adjustment. This trial balance is simply the trial balance which was prepared after the adjusting entries were made and posted to the general ledger. The trial balance after adjustment for Kilmer Contractors is presented below.

Kilmer Contractors
Trial Balance After Adjustment
May 31, 19x1

	Debit	Credit
Cash	$10,000	
Accounts receivable	900	
Supplies	2,000	
Note payable		$ 1,500
Unearned fees		1,100
Capital		10,000
Withdrawals	1,000	
Painting fees		2,700
Salaries	400	
Supplies used	1,000	
Totals	$15,300	$15,300

Again, the only difference between the trial balance after adjustment and the trial balance before adjustment presented previously is the inclusion of the effect of the adjusting entries which were made.

Closing Entries

The purpose of closing entries is to close out the temporary accounts (revenues, expenses, and withdrawals) into the owners' equity (capital) account. This process is facilitated by the introduction of a temporary account created solely for the closing process. This account is known as the *income summary account* and is used to collect or summarize all of the revenues and expenses of the firm in a single account which is then, in turn, closed to the capital account (or the retained earnings account for a corporation).

The purpose of the closing process is to systematically reduce all of the balances in the temporary accounts to a zero balance at the end of the accounting period. This means that at the beginning of the next period all revenues, expenses, and drawing accounts will have a zero balance so that these accounts can again be used in order to record the results of operations of that period.

The closing process is accomplished by the preparation of journal entries known as closing entries. These entries are recorded in the general journal and posted to the ledger in the same manner as all other transactions are processed.

We will now illustrate the closing process for Kilmer Contractors. The journal entries which are required to close out the revenue and expense accounts would be made at the end of the month of May, the accounting period used in this illustration. Referring back to the trial balance after adjustment for Kilmer Contractors, the temporary accounts were as follows:

	Balance	
	Debit	Credit
Withdrawals	$1,000	
Painting fees		$2,700
Salaries	400	
Supplies used	1,000	

The entry to close out the revenue account would be:

May 31. Painting Fees 2,700
           Income Summary. 2,700

Painting Fees				
		5/17	700
		5/19	900
		5/31	1,100
5/31	2,700		2,700
		0	

Income Summary	
5/31	2,700

Revenue accounts have credit balances. Therefore, the entry which is required in order to close out the balance in a revenue account consists of a debit to the revenue account for the total revenue for the period and a credit to the income summary account for the same amount. This entry closes out (i.e.—brings the account balance to zero) the revenue account and transfers the total for the period to the credit side of the income summary account.

In our illustration, the painting fees account is now closed and has a zero balance, and the $2,700 revenue from painting fees has been transferred to the credit side of the income summary account.

The two expense accounts would be closed out by the following entry:

May 31. Income Summary 1,400
           Salaries. 400
           Supplies Used 1,000

Salaries					Supplies Used					Income Summary			
5/25	400				5/31	1,000				5/31	1,400	5/31	2,700
	400	5/31	400			1,000	5/31	1,000					
	0					0							

Expense accounts have debit balances. Therefore, the entry which is required in order to close out the balance in an expense account credits the account for the total expense for the period and debits the income summary account for this amount. This closing entry reduces the expense account balance to zero and transfers the expense for the period to the debit side of the income summary account.

In our example, both the salaries and the supplies used expense accounts are now closed out and the total of these two accounts ($400 + $1,000) which is the total expense for the period has been transferred to the debit side of the income summary account.

The balance in the income summary account ($2,700 − $1,400 = $1,300) is then transferred to Kilmer's capital account by the following closing entry:

May 31.   Income Summary.   1,300
                  Capital.   1,300

Income Summary				Capital	
5/31	1,400	5/31	2,700	5/1	10,000
5/31	1,300		1,300	5/31	1,300
			0		

As indicated above, all revenue and expense accounts are closed to the income summary account. Therefore, the credit side of the income summary account will include the total revenue for the period while the debit side of the account will include the total expenses. The account balance will be the income or loss of the business for the period. If the total of the credits (revenues) in the income summary account exceeds the total of the debits (expenses), revenues are greater than expenses and the difference is the income for the period. On the other hand, if the total of the credits (revenues) is less than the total of the debits (expenses), expenses exceed revenues and the difference is the loss for the period. In either case the balance in the income summary account after all of the revenue and expense accounts have been closed is transferred to the capital account.

In the Kilmer Contractors example the balance in the income summary account, a credit of $1,300 (revenues of $2,700 less expenses of $1,400), was closed out and the income for the period was transferred to the capital account.

As a final step in the closing process the balance in any drawing or withdrawals account is closed out to owner's equity. In the Kilmer Contractors illustration this step would be to close the balance in the withdrawals account directly to capital.

May 31.   Capital   1,000
                  Withdrawals.   1,000

	Withdrawals		
5/12	1,000		
	1,000	5/31	1,000
	0		

	Capital		
5/31	1,000	5/1	10,000
		5/31	1,300

Withdrawals made by the owner do not pass through the income summary account since they are not an expense of the period and therefore do not enter into the determination of income. Withdrawal or drawing accounts have debit balances. Therefore, the closing entry which is required to close withdrawals credits the withdrawal account and debits the capital account for the drawings made by the owner during the period.

In the Kilmer Contractors example, the withdrawals of $1,000 are closed out and transferred to the capital account as a reduction of the end-of-period capital balance.

The closing process can be depicted graphically as follows:

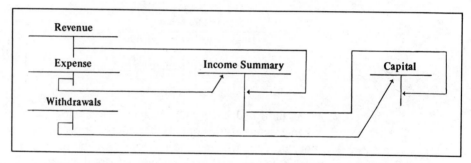

In terms of the specific accounts which were used in the Kilmer Contractors illustration, the closing process is shown below, after all of the closing entries are posted to the accounts.

After-Closing Trial Balance

After all of the temporary accounts have been closed out, a trial balance, referred to as an after-closing trial balance, may be prepared as a test of the equality of the total debits and credits. The after-closing trial balance of Kilmer Contractors is presented below. Since all of the temporary accounts have been closed out, the after-closing trial balance includes only the permanent or balance sheet accounts.

Financial Statements

After all of the adjusting and closing entries have been prepared and made and the posting process has been completed, the general ledger account balances will be up to date as of the end of the period. The information regarding the assets, liabilities, capital, revenues, and expenses included in the general ledger will be used as a basis for preparing the financial statements. Asset, liability, and capital balances as of the end of the period

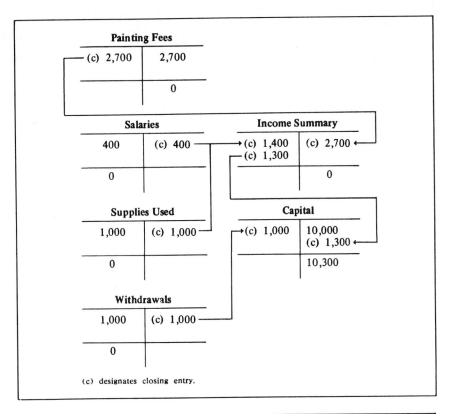

(c) designates closing entry.

Kilmer Contractors
After-Closing Trial Balance
May 31, 19x1

	Debits	Credits
Cash	$10,000	
Accounts receivable.	900	
Supplies	2,000	
Note payable		$ 1,500
Unearned fees		1,100
Capital		10,300
	$12,900	$12,900

will be taken from the general ledger accounts and used to prepare the balance sheet or statement of financial position. As previously indicated, the after-closing trial balance may be used to check the accuracy of the balance sheet since it includes all permanent accounts which appear in the balance sheet.

The revenues and expenses for the period will also be taken from the general ledger and used to prepare the income statement. The trial balance after adjustment and the detailed amounts which are included in the income summary account may be used as a check on the accuracy of the income statement since both of these sources include the details of the revenues and expenses for the period.

The statement of capital will also be prepared using the capital account from the general ledger as a source. The financial statements for Kilmer Contractors for the month of May are included below.

Kilmer Contractors
Balance Sheet
May 31, 19x1

ASSETS		LIABILITIES AND OWNER'S EQUITY	
Cash	$10,000	Note Payable	$ 1,500
Accounts Receivable	900	Unearned Fees.	1,100
Supplies	2,000	Capital	10,300
	$12,900		$12,900

Kilmer Contractors
Income Statement
For the Month Ending May 31, 19x1

Revenue from painting services		$2,700
Supplies Used	$1,000	
Salaries	400	
Total Expenses		1,400
Income		$1,300

Kilmer Contractors
Statement of Capital
For the Month Ending May 31, 19x1

Capital at May 1, 19x1		$ -0-
Add:		
Investment.	$10,000	
Income for May	1,300	11,300
Deduct:		
Withdrawal		(1,000)
Capital at May 31, 19x1		$10,300

At this time, several points should be noted by the reader in review. First, the general journal entries were prepared as the transactions occurred. These entries represent a chronological record of the transactions of the company which took place during the month of May. These journal entries were then posted to the ledger accounts. At the end of the month, a trial balance was prepared and the transactions and the status of the company at that point in time were reviewed. All adjustments which were necessary to bring the accounts up to date were made.

The next step in the process was the preparation of a trial balance after adjustment. Again, it is important to note that any trial balance only proves the equality of the totals of the debits and the credits; it gives no other assurance as to the absence of errors.

Entries were then prepared to "close-out" all temporary accounts, the revenues, expenses, and withdrawals for the period. These are the only accounts closed. The permanent accounts, assets, liabilities, and capital, which appear in the balance sheet, are not closed out. The closing entries summarize the balances of the revenue and expense accounts in an income summary account.[2] The balance in the withdrawals account is then closed out to the capital account. The closing entries were then posted to the ledger and the after-closing trial balance. Then the financial statements were prepared.

TRANSACTIONS REQUIRING ADJUSTING ENTRIES

As previously indicated, the accrual basis of accounting requires that all revenues be recorded as they are earned and that expenses be recorded as they are incurred. That is, there is a proper matching of revenues and expenses only if the income statement for the period includes all of the revenues and expenses which are applicable to the accounting period without regard to the timing of either the receipt or the disbursement of cash. At the end of any accounting period, then, there will usually be certain transactions which are still in the process of completion or which have occurred but which have not been recorded in the accounts. These transactions require adjusting entries to record revenues and expenses and to allocate them to the proper period or periods. In the case of Kilmer Contractors, adjustments were required to record for the revenue which was earned by painting one of the two houses for which payment had been received in advance and to record the cost of the painting supplies which were used during the month of May. In general, the types of transactions which require end-of-period adjusting entries fall into the following groups:

1. Allocation of prepaid expenses to the proper periods.
2. Recognition of unrecorded (accrued) expenses.

---

[2] The reader will note that the income summary is, in fact, a duplication of the income statement itself. That is, the credits to the summary are the revenues for the period and the debits are the expenses for the period. The difference, or balancing figure, is, of course, the income (or loss) for the period.

3. Allocation of a portion of the recorded cost of a fixed asset to the accounting periods which benefit from its use (depreciation).
4. Allocation of recorded revenue to the proper periods.
5. Recognition of unrecorded (accrued) revenues.

The remainder of this chapter will discuss these types of adjusting journal entries. In order to illustrate the different types of adjusting entries, the trial balance before adjustment of Brown Company as of December 31, 19x1, will be used. This trial balance appears below.

Brown Company
Trial Balance Before Adjustment
December 31, 19x1

	Debit	Credit
Cash	$ 2,760	
Accounts receivable	4,000	
Supplies	3,000	
Office furniture	3,600	
Accumulated depreciation— office furniture		$ 360
Accounts payable		2,000
Unearned rent		3,000
Capital		5,000
Withdrawals	1,000	
Service revenues		20,000
Rent expense	9,000	
Salaries	6,000	
Other expense	1,000	
	$30,360	$30,360

Prepaid Expenses

Certain goods and services, such as insurance, rent, and supplies, are purchased prior to their use by the business. If these goods have been used or the services have expired during the accounting period, these costs should be classified as expenses. However, the portion of the goods which is unused or the services which have not expired should be included in the balance sheet and classified as an asset. These assets are referred to as prepaid expenses. A prepaid expense will be reclassified as an expense in a subsequent accounting period (or periods) as it is used or as it expires. Adjusting entries are necessary in order to allocate the cost of each item between the asset account and the expense account.

To illustrate, assume that Brown Company purchased supplies at a cost of $3,000 on June 30. This transaction was recorded by the following journal entry:

Supplies	3,000	
Cash		3,000

This entry indicates that an asset has been acquired by the company. Supplies will be carried in the accounts as an asset until they are used, at which time they will become an expense and be reclassified as such. Note that the trial balance before adjustment reflects the $3,000 balance in the supplies account as an asset.

At the end of December the supplies which were still on hand had a cost of $2,000. Subtracting the cost of the supplies on hand at December 31 ($2,000, as indicated above) from the cost of the supplies which were available for use during the year ($3,000 of supplies purchased on June 30) indicates that it is necessary to record the difference of $1,000, the cost of the supplies used during the year, as an expense. This would be accomplished by means of the following entry:

```
Supplies Used . . . . . . . . . . . . . . . . . . . . . . . . . . . . . . . . . . 1,000
    Supplies . . . . . . . . . . . . . . . . . . . . . . . . . . . . . . . . . .            1,000
```

Alternatively, a prepaid expense may be initially recorded as an expense. For example, Brown Company could have recorded the purchase of the supplies on June 30 with the following journal entry:

```
Supplies Used . . . . . . . . . . . . . . . . . . . . . . . . . . . . . . . . . . 3,000
    Cash . . . . . . . . . . . . . . . . . . . . . . . . . . . . . . . . . . . . .            3,000
```

Since only $1,000 of the supplies were actually used and should be considered as an expense, the following entry would be necessary at the end of the accounting period in order to reclassify the $2,000 of supplies which were still on hand as an asset:

```
Supplies . . . . . . . . . . . . . . . . . . . . . . . . . . . . . . . . . . . . 2,000
    Supplies Used . . . . . . . . . . . . . . . . . . . . . . . . . . . . . . .            2,000
```

Note that this alternative method results in identical balances at the end of the period in both the Supplies account ($2,000) and the Supplies Used account ($1,000). Thus, either method is acceptable as long as the appropriate adjusting entries are made at the end of the period.

In some instances, companies will purchase supplies or prepay expenses which will be entirely used or consumed prior to the preparation of financial statements. In these instances, the amounts paid may be charged directly to expense when the outlay is made, simply as a matter of convenience. For example, assume that Brown Company pays the monthly rent on its office space in advance on the first day of each month. This outlay could be recorded on December 1 as follows:

```
Prepaid Rent. . . . . . . . . . . . . . . . . . . . . . . . . . . . . . . . . . 750
    Cash . . . . . . . . . . . . . . . . . . . . . . . . . . . . . . . . . . . .            750
```

If the transaction is recorded in this manner, the following adjusting entry would be required at the end of December in order to reclassify a part of the outlay which was made for two months' rent as an expense:

```
Rent Expense .....................................  750
    Prepaid Rent ..................................        750
```

Alternatively, it might be expedient to record the expenditure as follows, since the rent is paid and the benefit is received during the month:

```
Rent Expense .....................................  750
    Cash .........................................        750
```

Assuming that Brown Company recorded the transaction in this manner, an adjusting entry would not be required at the end of the month since the expense has been fully incurred and the "prepayment" has been fully used by December 31.

Accrued Expenses   At the end of an accounting period there are usually expenses which have been incurred but which have not been paid because payment is not due until a subsequent period. Many expenses, such as wages and salaries or interest on loans, may be incurred during a period but not recorded in the accounts because they have not been paid. These expenses are referred to as accrued expenses. Adjusting entries are necessary at the end of an accounting period in order to record all accrued expenses. For example, assume that Brown Company placed a newspaper advertisement which appeared during the month of December, but was not billed for the ad until some time in January. Since Brown Company did not pay for the advertisement during December, this amount does not appear on the trial balance before adjustment. Therefore, the following adjusting entry would be required at the end of December:

```
Advertising Expense ...............................  75
    Accounts Payable. .............................        75
```

This adjusting entry records the expense which was incurred but not paid during December and the corresponding liability which exists at the end of the month.

When the bill is received in January and is paid, the payment would be recorded by the following journal entry:

```
Accounts Payable..................................  75
    Cash .........................................        75
```

This entry records the fact that the liability has been satisfied (and assets reduced) by the cash payment. The timing of the recognition of the expense is not determined by the date of the payment; the expense was recorded during the previous month when it was incurred.

Depreciation

Businesses normally acquire assets which are used in their operations over a number of years. Buildings and equipment are examples of this type of asset. A business may purchase equipment and use it for a number of years. For example, assume that Brown Company acquired office furniture on January 1, 19x0, and expects to use this furniture for ten years before it will be replaced. Assuming that the cost of this furniture was $3,600, the purchase would have been recorded as follows:

```
Office Furniture. . . . . . . . . . . . . . . . . . . . . . . . . . . . . . . 3,600
    Cash . . . . . . . . . . . . . . . . . . . . . . . . . . . . . . . . . . .         3,600
```

The office furniture is an asset of the business and is recorded as such. Its cost should be charged to expense over the period that it is used, in this case ten years. The process of allocating the cost of an asset to expense over its useful life is referred to as depreciation. Depreciation is the systematic allocation of the cost of an asset to the periods which benefit from its use. The primary difference between allocating the cost of a fixed asset to expense (i.e., depreciation) and the allocation of the cost of a prepaid item, such as supplies or insurance, to expense is that it is normally much more difficult to measure the portion of the cost of a fixed asset which has been used during an accounting period. Therefore, the allocation of the cost of a fixed asset to expense during an accounting period is only an *estimate* of the part of the usefulness of the asset which has expired or been used during the year. Since the cost of the furniture was $3,600 and the expected useful life of this asset was 10 years or 120 months, depreciation in the amount of $360 ($3,600 divided by 10) should be recorded annually. Assuming that Brown Company did not make monthly entries to record the depreciation, the adjusting entry which should be made on December 31, 19x0 and 19x1 in order to record depreciation expense would be as follows:

```
Depreciation Expense . . . . . . . . . . . . . . . . . . . . . . . . . . . . 360
    Accumulated Depreciation . . . . . . . . . . . . . . . . . . . . . . .         360
```

The debit to depreciation expense records the portion of the cost of the asset which is recorded as an expense of the year. The credit is to accumulated depreciation, a contra account which would appear as an offset or deduction from the related asset account in the balance sheet. As the title accumulated depreciation implies, the depreciation taken over the useful life of the asset is accumulated in this account. Usually a reduction in an asset account is recorded with a credit made directly to the account. However, a contra account is used for fixed assets in order to provide additional information concerning the asset—that is, both the original cost and the depreciation expense which has been taken to date may be recorded and reported in the balance sheet. The asset and the related accumulated depreciation account would appear in the balance sheet as follows at the end of 19x1:

Office Furniture. $3,600
Less: Accumulated Depreciation 720 $2,880

A more complete discussion of the procedures which are involved in determining depreciation expense is presented in Chapter 4.

Unearned Revenues   Revenue which is collected before a business actually performs a service or delivers goods to a customer is referred to as unearned revenue. Since cash is received prior to the performance of the service or delivery of the goods, the amount received represents a liability to the firm. Unearned revenues are not a liability in the sense that the company will be required to repay the money. Rather, they represent an obligation of the company to perform a service or deliver goods at some future date (i.e., revenues that have been received but not earned). Examples of unearned revenues include rent collected in advance and subscription fees received prior to delivery of a magazine or newspaper.

To illustrate, assume that Brown Company subleased a portion of its office space to Smith for a rental of $3,000 per year. Terms of the lease agreement specify that Smith will pay the yearly rental in advance on July 1. The entry to record the receipt of the $3,000 advance payment on July 1, 19x1 would be as follows:

Cash 3,000
    Unearned Rent   3,000

Note that the trial balance before adjustment includes the $3,000 balance in the unearned rent account. Since no service had been performed at the time the cash was received, the entire amount was initially recorded in a liability account, unearned rent. Since rent is earned over the 12 month period that Brown Company provides office space to Smith, exactly one-half of the service will be rendered during the period July 1 to December 31, 19x1. Thus $1,500 ($\frac{1}{2} \times$ $3,000) of the rent has been earned and would be recorded by the following adjusting entry on December 31:

Unearned Rent 1,500
    Rental Income   1,500

The liability account, unearned rent, has been reduced by $1,500 and revenue for the period has been increased by this amount. The remaining balance in the unearned rent account represents an obligation to provide office space to Smith during the first six months of 19x2. This adjusting entry made on December 31 emphasizes the fact that income is recorded as it is earned, not as cash is received.

Accrued Revenues   Accrued revenues are revenues that have been earned but not recorded in the accounts during an accounting period because cash has not yet been received. As such, accrued revenues are the opposite, so to speak, of unearned revenues. Therefore, adjusting entries are necessary in order to record any revenue which has been earned but not recorded in the accounts as of the end of the accounting period. To illustrate, assume that Brown Company entered into an agreement with the Fooler Brush Company on December 1, 19x1. Brown Company agreed to display a line of brushes at their offices in return for a commission of 10 percent on any sales made by Fooler if the initial contact with the customer was made by Brown Company. The commissions are payable on a quarterly basis. Assume that Brown Company earned commissions of $100 during the month of December. The following adjusting journal entry would be made on December 31:

Commissions Receivable 100
    Commissions Earned   100

This entry increases the assets (commissions receivable) of Brown Company by the $100 due from Fooler Brush Company and records the revenue which has been earned to date by providing the agreed-upon service. When payment is received from the Fooler Brush Company, the following journal entry would be made:

Cash 100
    Commissions Receivable   100

It is important to note that this second entry simply records the fact that one asset, cash, was received in exchange for another, commissions receivable; revenues were not affected. The revenues were recorded at the time the service was performed, which was when they were earned by Brown Company.

**ACCRUAL BASIS
OF ACCOUNTING**

When a company records revenues as they are earned and records its expenses as they are incurred, the company is using the *accrual* basis of accounting. Under the accrual basis, revenues must be recorded as they are earned and expenses recorded as they are incurred without regard to the timing of either the receipt or disbursement of cash. Thus, the purpose of end-of-period adjusting entries is to update the accounting records of a business so that they are on the accrual basis.

SUMMARY

Transactions that affect the financial statements of a firm occur much too frequently to permit a revision of the statements after each transaction takes place. Therefore, firms use various "accounting systems" that record and accumulate the essence of these transactions. This allows the accountant to use the summarized data provided by the accounting system to prepare financial statements at designated points in time. The most commonly used accounting system, and the one discussed in this chapter, is the "double-entry" system.

The basic element of the double-entry system, as well as other systems, is the account. An account is simply a place or means of collecting and summarizing all of the transactions that affect a particular asset, liability, or owners' equity account. Each account is increased or decreased by use of debits (left-side entries) and credits (right-side entries). A debit entry increases assets and expenses, but decreases liabilities, owners' equity, and revenue accounts. Conversely, a credit entry increases liabilities, owners' equity, and revenues, but decreases assets and expenses.

The actual recording process involves a number of separate but related steps. The initial step is the preparation of general journal entries at the time the transactions take place. These general journal entries are then posted to the individual accounts in the ledger. After these two steps are completed, the accountant prepares a trial balance before adjustment. This trial balance is simply a listing of each account and the corresponding debit or credit balance in the account. This listing will only detect the most obvious errors and does not guarantee that other errors have not been made.

The next step in the recording process is the preparation of adjusting entries. These entries are necessary to adjust the accounts so that the final balances will reflect the proper updated balances as of the end of the accounting period. The adjusting entries are then posted to the appropriate ledger accounts and a trial balance after adjustment is prepared.

The next phase in the recording process is the preparation of closing entries. These entries are required to close the temporary accounts (revenues, expenses, and withdrawals) so that these accounts can be used to accumulate similar data for the next accounting period. To accomplish this, all revenues and expenses are closed to the income summary account. The income summary account and the withdrawal account are then closed to the capital account. Once the closing entries are prepared and entered into the general journal, they are then posted to the ledger accounts and an after-closing trial balance is prepared.

The final step is the actual preparation of the financial statements. The primary financial statements prepared by the accountant are the balance sheet, income statement, and statement of capital.

KEY DEFINITIONS

Account An account is a place or means of summarizing all of the transactions that affect a particular asset, liability, equity, revenue, or expense item.

Accrual basis of accounting The accrual basis of accounting is the process of recording revenues in the period in which they are earned and recording expenses in the period in which they are incurred.

Accrued expenses Accrued expenses are expenses, such as wages and salaries or interest on loans, which have been incurred during a period but not yet recorded in the accounts because they have not yet been paid.

Accrued revenues Accrued revenues are revenues which have been earned but not yet recorded in the accounts during the accounting period because cash has not yet been received.

Accumulated depreciation Accumulated depreciation is a contra account which appears as an offset or deduction from the related asset account in the balance sheet. The depreciation taken over the useful life of the asset is accumulated in this account.

Adjusted trial balance The adjusted trial balance is prepared by combining the trial balance before adjustments with the related adjusting entries.

Adjusting entries At the end of any accounting period there will usually be certain transactions which are still in the process of completion or which have occurred but which have not yet been recorded in the accounts. These transactions require adjusting entries in order to record revenues and expenses and to allocate them to the proper period.

Closing entries The purpose of closing entries is to close out or transfer the balances in the temporary accounts (revenues, expenses, and withdrawals) into the capital account.

Contra account A contra account is an account which is offset against or deducted from another account in the financial statements.

Credit "Credit" is the term used to identify the right-hand side of an account. A credit decreases an asset and increases a liability, equity, or revenue account.

Debit "Debit" is the term used to describe the left-hand side of an account. By debiting an asset or expense account, the account is increased and by debiting a liability or equity account, the account is decreased.

Depreciation Depreciation is the systematic allocation of the cost of an asset to the periods which benefit from its use.

Double-entry method This method requires that for every transaction recorded, the total dollar amount of debits must be equal to the total dollar amount of the credits.

General journal entry The general journal entry is a means of recording the transactions of a firm chronologically in terms of debits and credits.

General ledger The general ledger is a compilation of all the accounts of a firm and their balances.

Posting Posting to ledger accounts is the process of transferring the information from the general journal to the individual accounts of the general ledger. This enables the accountant to review and summarize all changes in the accounts.

Prepaid expenses   Certain goods and services, such as insurance, rent, and supplies, are often paid for prior to their use by the business. The portion of the goods which has not been used up or the services which have not expired should be included in the balance sheet and classified as an asset.

Trial balance   The trial balance is a listing of all the accounts in the general ledger. If the accounts are "in balance," the total of the accounts with debit balances will equal the total of those with credit balances. The trial balance only indicates that the accounts are in balance. It does not prove that errors have not been made in the recording process.

Unearned revenues   Unearned revenues are revenues which are collected before a business actually performs a service or delivers goods to a customer.

Appendix

INTRODUCTION

A primary function of accounting is to accumulate the information which is required by decision makers and to communicate this data to them. The accounting system used for communicating information consists of business documents (such as invoices, checks, and records) that are used in recording transactions and preparing reports. A financial accounting system must communicate data to users in such a way that the operating performance and current financial position of a company is reported in a manner that is both meaningful and useful. All pertinent information which is required for decision making, planning, and control purposes must be made available to the user on a timely basis. There are also certain other basic housekeeping functions that the system should accomplish. For example, detailed information must be made available in order to identify the specific accounts receivable balance of each customer, detailed information regarding payroll and deductions is required in order to pay employees and satisfy government regulations, and inventory balances must be available on a current basis for purposes of inventory planning and control. The accounting system of an organization should be designed to handle all of the many facets of accounting and this system must operate in a manner which is efficient, effective, accurate, and timely.

Model of a Financial Accounting System

A model of a basic financial accounting system is presented in tabular form and in the form of a diagram below. The financial accounting system shown in these illustrations indicates the procedures which are followed during the accounting cycle. Presentation of the system in these illustrations is intended to provide a comprehensive picture or overview of the information flows that are required in a typical organization. Note that this example is a summarization of the steps in the recording process discussed in Chapters 1 and 2. The next illustration diagrams the same general data flows in a financial accounting system. Certain features, which will be discussed in this chapter, have been added to the system which provide for more efficient means of processing the accounting data.

The basic components of the system are as follows:

1. A Chart of Accounts
2. A Coding System
3. A General Journal
4. A General Ledger
5. Subsidiary Ledgers
6. Special Journals
7. Internal Control
8. An Audit Trail

These components of the financial accounting system are discussed in the following paragraphs.

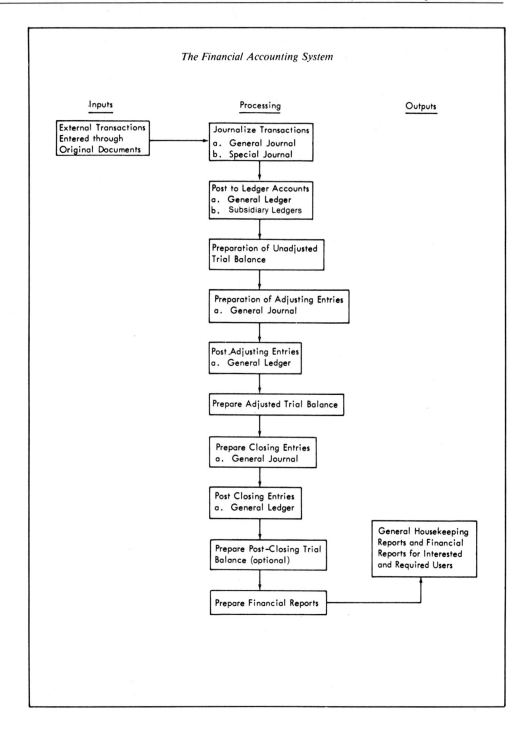

The Financial Accounting System

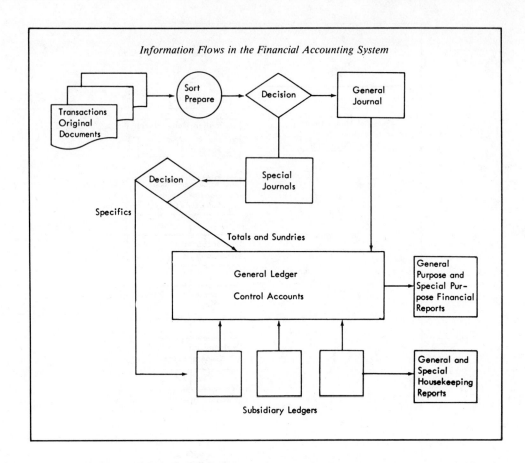

Information Flows in the Financial Accounting System

The Chart of Accounts

A chart of accounts is a listing of all of the accounts that an organization may use in its accounting system. The scope of the chart of accounts and the ability to adapt new account titles to the existing listing is a very important factor to be considered in the process of designing and installing an accounting system. The design of the chart of accounts will affect the manner in which accounting information will be accumulated, summarized, and used by the organization.

At a minimum, the chart of accounts should include all of the accounts that appear on the balance sheet, income statement, and statement of capital or retained earnings. In most cases, however, limiting the chart to only these accounts would be inadequate since management often requires information which is more detailed than that which is included in the basic financial statements. This detailed information is required in order to manage the day-to-day operations of the business. Also, external users such as governmental agencies frequently require information not included in the financial statements, often in detailed and specified formats. In addition to the basic functional classifications, management normally requires:

1. Accounting information which is based on cost behavior patterns for purposes of planning and control.
2. Accounting information which is based on areas of responsibility for purposes of performance measurement and control. For example, information regarding divisions or geographical regions may be used in order to measure the performance of these segments.

Many of the accounts used by the organization will be utilized for multiple purposes in the management and operations of the business. For example, production cost data is required in the process of inventory valuation, but it is also necessary for evaluating the performance of the specific departments which are involved in the production process.

Coding the Chart of Accounts

In order to facilitate the use of data and to provide a unique identity for each account, the chart of accounts is normally coded numerically. A normal pattern of arrangement and coding of the chart of accounts is in the format and the order of the financial statements and the accounts included in these statements. A simplified example of the broad categories of accounts which might be included in a typical chart of accounts is presented below.

1000–1999	Asset Accounts
2000–2999	Liability Accounts
3000–3999	Owners' Equity Accounts
4000–4999	Revenue Accounts
5000–5999	Manufacturing Cost Accounts
6000–6999	Distribution Expense Accounts
7000–7999	Administrative Expense Accounts
8000–8999	Other Income Accounts
9000–9999	Other Expense Accounts

To illustrate the usefulness of coding and the means of identifying specific items using numerical codes, a code for asset accounts will be expanded and explained. The first digit in the code may be used to identify the general account classification. Any search of the accounts is then limited to one thousand possible accounts in that category. The second digit could be used to identify an asset's location; that is, for example, whether the asset is located at the home office or at a division. The third digit could be used to identify the classification of the asset; that is, whether the asset is a current asset, a long-term asset, an intangible asset, etc. The fourth digit might be used to identify the specific asset itself.

Obviously, in a large organization, the coding structure may be very complex. In order to deal with the complexity of the coding structure, a code dictionary, identifying the specific account and its code, is often employed. In situations where automated equipment with sensing or scanning capability is used, numerical characters are usually considered necessary for reasons of both economy and efficiency.

The General Journal and General Ledger

Until this point, the mechanics of recording and handling transactions described in this text has been limited to the general journal and the general ledger. As previously indicated, each transaction is recorded in the general journal chronologically, and then the debits and credits from the general journal are posted individually to the appropriate accounts in the general ledger.

In the accounting procedures illustrated to this point, the general journal was used as the book of original entry while the general ledger served as the book of final entry. Financial statements were usually prepared from an adjusted trial balance or worksheet. The mechanics of this system would make it almost impossible for all but the smallest business to operate effectively or, at least, efficiently. This type of system is simply unable to process large volumes of transactions on a timely basis, primarily because no effective division of labor is possible since each and every journal entry must be written out on an individual basis.

In addition, this system might not provide the detailed information necessary to operate a business efficiently. For example, the system previously described did not always identify the specific individual who purchased goods on account. Likewise, it did not provide information as to the identity of individual creditors. Division of labor and necessary detail may be accomplished in this basic system by the addition and use of special journals and subsidiary ledgers in addition to the general journal and general ledger.

Subsidiary Ledgers

Subsidiary ledgers are supplemental detailed records which provide underlying support for the amounts recorded in control accounts included in the general ledger. An example of a subsidiary ledger is the accounts receivable subsidiary ledger. An individual record must be maintained on a current basis for every customer for purposes of control, billing, and handling of any inquiries.

The use of individual customer records eliminates the problem of including large numbers of detailed accounts receivable accounts in the general ledger. There are also many other obvious advantages to the use of subsidiary ledgers other than the accumulation of necessary detail. Subsidiary ledgers permit a division of duties among employees by allowing a number of different individuals to assist in the preparation of the records. In addition, personnel with less experience may be used to post to subsidiary ledgers. Also, an error in a trial balance may be localized in a subsidiary ledger, thus reducing the effort necessary to locate the error.

Subsidiary ledgers are necessary to permit the classification of a large group of accounts under a single control account in the general ledger. The subsidiary ledgers found in most systems include: accounts receivable, accounts payable, inventories, employee pay records, property records, and the stockholders' register.

When a company maintains a subsidiary ledger, the corresponding general ledger account is referred to as a control account. If no recording errors are made, the total of the balances in a subsidiary ledger should be equal to the total in the corresponding control account which is included in the general ledger.

Special Journals

The initial step in the flow of information through the financial accounting system is identifying the transactions that will be processed. One means of reducing the amount of individual recording and posting is to separate the transactions into groups that have common elements and to provide special journals for recording the transactions in each group. A decision is then made as to whether the transaction falls into a class that should be entered in a special journal or is an infrequently occurring transaction that should be entered directly in the general journal. A special journal is useful in those instances where there is a large volume of transactions which result in debits and credits to the same accounts. For such transactions, the recording process is facilitated by entering the amounts in the columns of a special journal and posting the totals periodically to the general ledger. The types of transactions which normally occur with sufficient frequency to justify the use of special journals include receipts of cash, disbursements of cash, sales of merchandise on credit, and the purchase of merchandise on account. Of course, transactions not recorded in any of the special journals are recorded in the general journal. That is, every transaction must be recorded in some type of journal, and the effects of all transactions are still posted, either individually or by cumulative totals, to the ledger.

The accounts receivable example which was employed to illustrate the use of subsidiary ledgers is also applicable to special journals. When goods are sold on account, the sale is made and should be recorded at that time. The relevant aspects of credit sales from a data gathering standpoint include: identity of the customer; amount of the sale; nature of any credit terms;[1] date of the sale; and, for any future inquiries, the invoice number. This is repetitive data which will be accumulated for each and every sale.

---

[1] Credit terms include the time allowed for payment and any discounts allowed. Payment required within 30 days would be shown by the notation N/30 indicating that the full amount is due in 30 days.

Special journals permit a division of labor, allow the use of less experienced personnel, employ preprinted account columns or summaries which reduce the incidence of error, and allow special transactions of like kind to be easily analyzed since the original data was accumulated by category rather than on an individual basis.

If a specific type of transaction occurs frequently in the business, a special journal should be designed and used for these transactions. As previously indicated, the types of special journals most frequently used by a business normally include: sales, cash receipts, cash disbursements, and purchases.

INTERNAL ACCOUNTING CONTROL

Certain accounting controls are necessary within a business to safeguard the assets from waste, fraud, and inefficiency and to ensure the accuracy and reliability of the accounting data. Ideally, the system of internal control should provide assurance regarding the dependability of the accounting data relied upon in making business decisions. Generally, these accounting controls include a specified system of authorization and approval of transactions, separation of the recordkeeping and reporting functions from the duties concerned with asset custody and operations, physical control over assets, and internal auditing.

A subdivision of responsibility in a financial accounting system is necessary to provide adequate checks on the work of company personnel. When one transaction is handled from beginning to end by a single individual and that person makes an error, the mistake will probably be carried through in the mechanics of recording the transaction and will be very difficult to locate. On the other hand, if different aspects of a transaction are processed by different people, each acting on an independent basis, an error will be much more readily identifiable. Many of the errors that would have affected the accounts will never occur because the mistake may be identified and corrected on a timely basis.

A division of responsibility among employees is also necessary for control purposes. In a properly designed accounting system that has adequate division of duties, fraud and embezzlement should be very difficult and require the collusion of two or more people. However, even in a properly designed system, the possibility of errors and embezzlement cannot be completely eliminated.

The division of duties should, of course, be logically based on the desired purposes of the system. For example, the person who maintains the subsidiary ledger of accounts receivable should not have access to cash. This will prevent him from being able to manipulate the accounts receivable and retain the cash. Likewise, a single individual should not be given the responsibility of both approving purchases and then signing the checks that are used to pay for them. Payments made to nonexistent companies for fictitious purchases would be difficult to prevent if one person is able to approve both the purchase and the payment.

A system of internal control is frequently justified because it assists the business in the detection of errors and the prevention of embezzlement. Another major benefit of a system of internal control is that it provides an atmosphere and system which are deterrents to inefficient utilization of the company's resources, fraudulent conversion of assets, and inefficient and inaccurate handling of the company's accounts.

The Audit Trail

An audit trail is the traceability factor that is built into an accounting system. It permits a person, normally an independent certified public accountant (referred to as an auditor), to follow the processing of a specific transaction from the beginning of the system described to the final output of the system. This procedure should also be reversible, that is, the final output of the system should be traceable back to the original source documentation that represents the transactions which caused the final output. An audit trail provides a path that can be followed in order to verify the accuracy with which transactions were handled as well as their legitimacy. The audit trail relies on a good system of internal control and documentation of transactions.

A flowchart of the purchase, receipt, payment, and use of office supplies for the Brown Grass Seed Company is presented below. This flowchart describes both the internal control and audit trail for these types of transactions. Note that only three sets of forms are used: a purchase requisition, the invoice prepared by purchasing (which is the first of a series of invoices in this case), and the bill of lading and the invoice received from the vendor. Multiple copies of these documents are used by the business for internal control purposes. The entire transaction may be traced from the financial statements to any point in the accounting system.

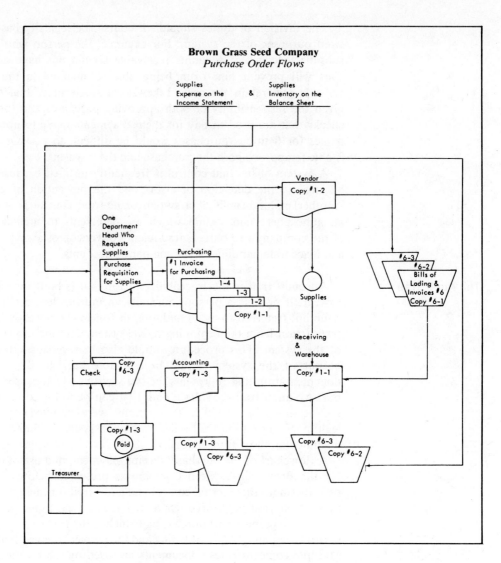

Brown Grass Seed Company
Purchase Order Flows

AUTOMATED ACCOUNTING SYSTEMS

The introduction of a computer system into the accounting function does not alter the data flow but instead parallels the manual processing system. The computer system simply performs many functions that would be performed by people in a manual system. Any automated system will, however, affect the form of transaction documentation and other factors such as:

1. Methods of establishing source documents
2. Methods of transmitting data
3. Techniques of data preparation

4. Amount of data handled
5. Speed and accuracy
6. Processing of the data
7. Methods of data storage
8. Methods of information retrieval
9. Number of accounting reports used
10. Types of controls necessary for adequate internal control

The objective of any accounting information system (whether manual or automated) is to produce the financial information required by internal and external users. The basic components of any computer system are the "hardware" and appropriate "software."

Computer Hardware

Computer hardware is the equipment used to process the accounting information. Hardware can change from the very sophisticated and expensive system which possesses tremendous computing capability to the relatively simple and inexpensive system such as a personal computer which costs less than two thousand dollars. In general, the equipment can be classified into three categories; mainframe computers, minicomputers, and microcomputers.

Mainframe computers are large-scale systems that would be used when a large volume of data needs to be processed rapidly. Minicomputers are much cheaper and, obviously, much less powerful. Minicomputers provide the computing capacity needed by many small to medium size companies which need the capability to process many transactions but do not necessarily need the power and efficiency of a mainframe computer.

A microcomputer is a system which is smaller than a minicomputer and could be used by a small business that does not have a large number of transactions to process. The "home computer" is a microcomputer as are word processors. The microcomputer has been referred to as the "computer on a chip." Any transaction processing is not as fast nor can the system be as sophisticated as the mainframe or minicomputers.

Computer Software

Computer software are the instructions that are developed to make the hardware perform the functions that are necessary to process transactions. The software controls the computer activities by instructing the hardware, in a step-by-step program, to perform a specific function. For example, in a payroll program (software) all the deductions from each person's paycheck (such as taxes and other payroll deductions) would have.to be programmed and "read" into or made available to the computer. When each employee's hours and pay rate are entered, the program could calculate payroll deductions and, with the proper hardware, print the employees' checks. When a program is written to handle a specific application such as payroll or order handling or inventory, the programs for that application are usually called a software package. Software packages are available from most computer vendors to perform the usual accounting functions. In addition, a company can have a program "tailored" or written to their specifications when they have unique processing and/or control requirements.

SUMMARY

A financial accounting system must communicate economic information efficiently, effectively, accurately, and on a timely basis. Basic components of the system include: (1) a chart of accounts, (2) a coding system, (3) a general journal, (4) a general ledger, (5) special journals, (6) subsidiary ledgers, (7) a system of internal control, and (8) an audit trail.

A chart of accounts is a listing of all the accounts that may be used by a company. The basic design of the chart of accounts determines how accounting information will be accumulated, summarized, and used. A coding system is necessary for the chart of accounts to provide a unique identity for each account included in the chart of accounts. A general journal is used to record those transactions which occur on an infrequent basis. A general ledger contains the control accounts for the system. Special journals will be used for recording transactions which occur frequently. Subsidiary ledgers are supplemental detailed records which provide underlying support for the control accounts included in the general ledger. An effective system of internal control serves as a deterrent to the inefficient utilization of a company's resources; it discourages the fraudulent conversion of assets and the inefficient and inaccurate handling of a company's accounts. An audit trail is necessary to allow traceability of transactions after the fact.

The use of automated equipment in the financial accounting system does not alter the data flows in the system per se; but the equipment may cause significant changes in: (1) the source documents, (2) methods of transmitting data, (3) techniques of data preparation, (4) amount of data handled, (5) speed and accuracy, (6) processing of data, (7) methods of data storage, (8) methods of information retrieval, (9) the number of accounting reports used, and (10) the controls necessary for adequate internal control.

KEY DEFINITIONS

Audit trail The audit trail is the traceable sequence of steps through which a transaction is processed from the beginning of the accounting system to the final output. The procedures and documentation should be clear so as to provide traceability from the output back to the original documents.

Cash disbursements journal A cash disbursements journal is a special journal which may be used to record all expenditures of cash made by the business.

Cash receipts journal A cash receipts journal is a special journal which may be used to record all transactions involving the receipt of cash.

Chart of accounts The chart of accounts is the list of all accounts that a company will use in conducting its business. It includes all accounts used in the preparation of the balance sheet, income statement, and statement of capital, and in addition, all accounts that management needs for planning and control purposes. The design of the chart of accounts will determine how the information will be gathered, summarized, and used in its accounting system.

Coding Coding is the process of assigning a system of numbers to the various accounts included in the chart of accounts.

Coding dictionary The coding dictionary identifies an account with its coding number to simplify use of the coding system and the accounts.

Control account A control account is a general ledger account which is supported by detailed information included in subsidiary accounts.

Internal control Internal control comprises the plan of organization and all of the coordinate methods and measures adopted within a business to safeguard its assets, check the accuracy and reliability of its accounting data, promote operational efficiency, and encourage adherence to prescribed managerial policies.

Payroll journal A payroll journal is a specialized form of a cash disbursements journal used exclusively to record the payment of salaries and wages to employees.

Purchases journal A purchases journal is a special journal which may be used to record credit purchases.

Special journals Special journals are designed to record the type of transactions where there is a large volume of transactions that occur on a frequent basis. Special journals are often used for accounts receivable, accounts payable, and cash receipts and disbursements.

Subsidiary ledgers A subsidiary ledger is a supplementary record which provides underlying support for control accounts which are included in the general ledger. A subsidiary ledger will include more detail than the related general ledger account, and the total of all subsidiary accounts will equal the balance of the applicable control account.

QUESTIONS

1. What is the purpose of the double-entry system of recording business transactions?

2. Explain the terms "debit" and "credit." What effect does each of these have on asset and liability accounts?

3. What is the general rule of the double-entry system?

4. Describe a general journal entry.

5. What is a T-account?

6. What is "posting"?

7. What is the purpose of a trial balance?

8. What concept of accounting requires adjusting entries? Explain.

9. What type of accounts do closing entries affect? Why are these accounts closed?

10. How is the adjusted trial balance prepared?

11. Which accounts are closed at the end of the period?

12. Are prepaid expenses reclassified as expenses in future periods? Why?

13. How is revenue which is collected before a business actually performs a service classified in the financial statements?

14. Explain the accrual basis of accounting.

EXERCISES

15. The first nine transactions of a newly formed business, Smart Company, appear in the T-accounts below. For each set of debits and credits, explain the nature of the transaction. Each entry is designated by the small letters to the left of the amount.

Cash		Accounts Receivable		Equipment	
(a) 10,000	(c) 2,000	(d) 6,000	(g) 2,000	(b) 3,000	
(g) 2,000	(e) 4,000				
(i) 2,500	(f) 1,000				
	(h) 1,500				

Accounts Payable		Unearned Fees	
(f) 1,000	(b) 3,000		(i) 2,500

Capital		Land		Fees Earned	
	(a) 10,000	(c) 2,000			(d) 6,000

Wage Expense		Rent Expense	
(e) 4,000		(h) 1,500	

16. Assume that the ledger accounts given in Exercise 15 are for the Smart Company as of December 31, 19x1. Prepare a trial balance for Smart Company as of that date.

17. Prepare the closing entries, the income statement for 19x1 and the balance sheet as of December 31, 19x1, for the Smart Company assuming the data given in Exercise 15.

18. Bob Feller opened a driving range and the following transactions took place in July, 19x1:

July 1 The owner invested $10,000 cash in the business.
      5 Purchased fixed assets for $5,000; made a cash down payment of $2,000 and signed a 60 day note for the balance.
     10 The total revenue for the month was $1,500; $1,200 in cash was collected and the balance was owed on account by customers.
     15 The total expenses for the month were $1,100; $900 was paid in cash and the balance was owed on account.
     25 The owner withdrew $100 in cash.

Required:

Prepare the journal entries to record these transactions and enter the debits and credits in T-accounts.

19. After recording and posting the transactions from Exercise 18, prepare a trial balance for Feller Company as of July 31, 19x1.

20. Given the following T-accounts, prepare the closing entries for the White Company for the month of August, 19x0.

Cash			Accounts Receivable			Supplies		
B.B. 20,000	1,100	(2)	B.B. 4,000	2,000	(1)	B.B. 800	1,000	(8)
(1) 2,000	5,000	(4)	(6) 7,000			(2) 1,100		
(3) 35,000	2,800	(5)						
	14,000	(9)						
	900	(10)						
	500	(11)						
32,700			9,000			900		

Note Payable		Unearned Fees		Capital	
(5) 2,800	2,800 B.B.	(7) 30,000	7,000 B.B.		15,000 B.B.
			35,000 (3)		
			12,000		15,000

Withdrawals		Fees Earned		Supplies Used	
(4) 5,000			7,000 (6)	(8) 1,000	
			30,000 (7)		
5,000			37,000	1,000	

Salaries		Utilities		Property Taxes	
(9) 14,000		(10) 900		(11) 500	
14,000		900		500	

21. Using the information in Exercise 20, prepare an After-Closing Trial Balance for White Company.

22. From the information given in Exercise 20, prepare a balance sheet, income statement, and statement of capital for White Company.

23. Prepare the journal entries for the Wicks Company for the month of December.

Dec. 1   Office supplies were purchased on credit for $5,000.
       3   A new machine was purchased for $15,000 cash.
       4   Revenues of $7,500 were received in advance of services being rendered.
       7   Services were performed on credit for $400.
       9   The bank loaned Wicks Company $10,000.
     12   Ivan Ingot invested $25,000 in the company.
     16   The $400 credit extended for services performed was collected.
     18   A remittance was sent for the office supplies.
     19   Services were performed for one-half of the revenues received in advance.
     21   Ivan Ingot withdrew $3,000 from the company.
     24   Performed services and collected amount due of $600 in cash.
     27   Repaid one-fourth of the bank loan.
     30   Salaries of $2,500 were paid to employees.

24. Post each journal entry in Exercise 23 to the appropriate ledger account and prepare closing entries.

25. Boyd Company purchased a two-year insurance policy on June 30 for $900 and recorded the transaction with a debit to the Prepaid Insurance account. Give the adjusting journal entry necessary to record the insurance that has expired as of December 31.

26. Below are the 19x1 adjusting entries for Branson Shoe Repairs.

a.	Supplies expense	275	
	Supplies		275
b.	Rent expense	500	
	Prepaid rent		500
c.	Interest receivable	150	
	Interest income		150
d.	Wage expense	75	
	Wages payable		75
e.	Repair fees	25	
	Unearned fees		25
f.	Fees receivable	33	
	Repair fees		33

Give a possible explanation for each of the above adjusting entries.

27. Gardner Company leases a building to a client at a rental of $2,400 per year on June 1, 19x1. Give the required December 31, 19x1, adjusting entry on the books of Gardner Company under each of the following assumptions.

   a. The rent is paid in advance on June 1, 19x1, and is recorded by crediting Unearned Rent.
   b. The rent is paid in advance on June 1, 19x1, and is recorded by crediting Rental Income.
   c. The rent for the period of June 1, 19x1, to May 31, 19x2, is to be paid on May 30, 19x2.

28. Prepare the adjusting entries required at December 31, 19x1, in each of the following cases:

   a. Herman Company was assessed property taxes of $350 for 19x1. The taxes were due April 15, 19x2.
   b. Norton Company's payroll was $6,000 per month and wages were paid on the 15th of the following month. The company closes its books on December 31.
   c. Frazier Company has $3,000 of savings bonds. Interest receivable on these bonds was $180 at December 31.
   d. Foreman Company owns a building costing $30,000. $1,000 of the cost is to be allocated to expense in 19x1.

29. The income statement for 19x2 for the Lang Company reflected wage expense of $80,000. The year-end balances in the wages payable account were $10,000 at December 31, 19x1, and $12,000 at December 31, 19x2. Determine the amount of cash paid for salaries during 19x2.

30. Yestramski, Inc. signed a contract on June 30, 19x1 to rent a building for three years. The total contract price of $9,000 was paid on June 30, 19x1. Give the journal entry to record payment and the adjusting entries made on December 31, 19x1 and 19x2.

31. On March 30, 19x1 the Dandridge Company purchased a truck for $8,000 cash. The company planned an annual depreciation of $2,000. Give the journal entries to record the purchase of the truck and depreciation on December 31, 19x1 and December 31, 19x2.

32. Henderson Incorporated purchased $7,800 of office supplies on August 1. On December 31, it was determined that 35 percent of these supplies had been used. Prepare the journal entries for the initial purchase and the later adjustment. Prepare one set of entries assuming supplies are initially recorded as an asset and another assuming they are recorded as an expense.

33. The Kupchak Company is adjusting its accounts as of December 31. Make the adjusting entries for the following accounts:

a. Depreciation on equipment is $2,000 for the year.
b. Two years' rent was paid on January 1. The amount paid ($36,000) was debited to prepaid rent.
c. Unpaid salaries as of December 31 were $9,000.
d. Interest not yet received on an investment was $1,700.
e. Unearned revenues were reduced by $4,500.

34. Below are two partial trial balances for the Bing Company, one before and the other after closing entries have been posted to the accounts as of December 31, 19x1. You are required to reconstruct the closing entries for December 31, 19x1.

	Before Closing	After Closing
Rent expense....................	$ 500	$ 0
Accounts receivable..............	2,200	2,200
Capital	350	2,600
Withdrawals.....................	425	0
Fees for services..................	4,543	0
Income summary.................	0	0
Accounts payable................	1,350	1,350
Insurance expense................	110	0
Salaries expense..................	1,200	0
Prepaid insurance................	25	25
Supplies used....................	58	0

PROBLEMS

35. Presented below are the transactions of the Home Finder Realty Company for the month of May, 19x1.

May 1   The owner invested $20,000 cash in the business.
3   Purchased office equipment for $1,800 on account.
5   Purchased a car for $3,000, giving $1,000 in cash and a note payable of $2,000.
10   Purchased $500 of office supplies on account.
15   Paid $300 office rent for the month of May.
16   Paid for office supplies purchased on May 10.
18   Received a bill for $200 for radio advertising.
20   Earned and collected $1,500 commission for the sale of a house.
21   Paid bill for advertising that was received on May 18.
23   Earned but did not collect an $800 commission.
25   Paid salaries of $400.
27   Received payment in full from customer of May 23.
29   Paid the telephone bill, $50.

Required:

Prepare the general journal entries that would be required to record the above transactions.

36. On September 1, 19x1 Mark Walls, a bookkeeper, organized a bookkeeping service business. The following events occurred during September.

Sept. 1 · Walls withdrew $10,000 from his personal savings and invested this amount in the business.
2 Paid September rent of $250.
4 Purchased office furniture for $2,000 on account.
6 Received and paid a bill for $200 for advertising in the local newspaper.
9 Received cash of $1,400 as payment for services to customers.
15 Paid the $300 salary of a part-time secretary.
17 Paid for office furniture purchased on account.
18 Purchased $150 of office supplies on account.
20 Received a utilities bill for $75.
21 Completed $600 of services on credit for customers.
23 Collected $200 of receivables for credit services provided.
27 Walls withdrew $600 from the business.

Required:

1. Prepare the general journal entries to record the above transactions.
2. Post the above journal entries to T-accounts.
3. Prepare a trial balance as of the end of September.
4. Prepare closing entries.

37. The following transactions involving the Mantle Company occurred during the month of July, 19x1:

July 1 Mantle organized the company, contributing $1,000 as an initial investment.
3 Purchased office supplies paying $100 in cash.
6 Performed services for his first customer and collected $500 in cash.
9 Performed services for another customer and agreed to accept his payment of $700 later in the month.
13 Contracted to perform certain services for a third customer and received the full payment of $1,000 in advance.
18 Received the payment from the customer for whom services were performed on July 9.
24 Paid the following operating items:

Salaries for July......................... $250
Office rent for July and August............. 300
Other July expense....................... 75

(Mantle will prepare financial statements at the end of July.)
31 Noted that exactly one-fourth of the services contracted for on the thirteenth by a customer had been performed. Counted the office supplies on hand and ascertained that supplies with an original cost of $65 were still on hand.

Required:

1. Record the above transactions with general journal entries.
2. Post the journal entries by entering debits and credits in T-accounts.
3. Prepare a trial balance as of July 31, 19x1.
4. Prepare closing entries.

38. Below is the trial balance of the Nittany Lion Company as of October 31, 19x1.

Cash	$10,000	
Accounts receivable	4,000	
Notes receivable	2,500	
Supplies	1,000	
Accounts payable		$ 4,500
Note payable		3,000
Unearned revenue		1,500
Capital		7,500
Withdrawals	500	
Revenues		3,000
Expenses	1,500	
	$19,500	$19,500

Required:

1. Prepare the entries which are necessary to close the accounts as of October 31, 19x1.
2. Prepare the following statements:

   a. Balance sheet
   b. Income statement
   c. Statement of capital

39. Certain data relating to River Corporation are presented below:

Trial balance data as of June 30, 19x1.

Advertising expense...........................	$ 75
Capital.......................................	3,195
Cash...	895
Commissions earned...........................	1,900
Commissions receivable........................	950
Interest earned................................	5
Land	2,000
Mercantile Company bonds......................	1,000
Notes payable................................	700
Office rent....................................	80
Salaries expense...............................	800

Adjusted trial balance data as of June 30, 19x1.

Accrued interest receivable......................	5
Accrued interest payable........................	7
Accrued rent receivable.........................	55
Accrued salaries payable........................	100
Advertising expense............................	75
Capital.......................................	3,195
Cash...	895
Commissions earned...........................	1,960
Commissions receivable........................	1,010
Interest earned................................	10
Interest expense...............................	7
Land	2,000
Mercantile Company bonds......................	1,000
Notes payable................................	700
Office rent....................................	80
Rent earned...................................	55
Salaries expense...............................	900

Required:

Compare the unadjusted and adjusted account balances and prepare the adjusting journal entries made by River Corporation as of June 30, 19x1. Also prepare the closing entries as of June 30, 19x1. (No withdrawals were made during the period ending June 30, 19x1.)

40. The following information has been developed by the bookkeeper of the Sneed Company. It relates to the company's operations for 19x1.

Cash receipts
    From customers............................... $46,100
Cash disbursements
    For expenses................................. 10,600

Account balances as of December 31	*19x0*	*19x1*
Accounts receivable from customers, (all collectible).	$10,400	$9,600
Accrued expenses payable......................	1,900	1,600

Required:

Prepare the company's income statement for the year ended December 31, 19x1.

41. On June 30, 19x1, the Repertory Theater Co. was organized. On that date the owners invested $25,000 in cash and the company manager signed a 10-year lease on a building. The lease called for a monthly rental of $4,000. The first payment under the lease was made immediately; all future rentals were to be paid on the last day of each month. The theater capacity was 800 seats which were to be sold for $3 at each performance. A 3-year comprehensive insurance policy was paid for on July 1, 19x1, at a cost of $600.

The theater opened on August 1, 19x1. There were 8 performances each week (each evening Monday through Saturday and matinees on Wednesday and Saturday). Through December 31, 19x1, there had been exactly 22 full weeks of performances. The player companies who were engaged to perform received 40 percent of the gate with settlement to be made after each Saturday evening performance for the 8 performances of the week then ending. At the beginning of the 19th week of business a smash hit opened. This show played to capacity crowds and was sold out through the first 7 weeks of 19x2.

A refreshment counter in the lobby dispensed soft drinks, candy, etc., and proved to be most lucrative. This was the only source of revenue other than ticket sales. Refreshments with an invoice cost of $19,000 had been purchased during 19x1. The inventory of refreshments on hand at December 31, 19x1, had an invoice price of $2,200. All purchases had been paid for except one made on December 27, 19x1, at a cost of $1,200.

Prior to the opening of the smash hit, the theater enjoyed good success, averaging exactly 75 percent of capacity of all performances. All receipts during the year had been deposited intact and deposit slips showed a total of $517,400 deposited through December 31, 19x1.

Salaries for ushers, ticket-takers, the manager, and other employees were paid after each Friday evening performance for work done through that performance. These salaries averaged $900 per week. Advertising had been run in local newspapers and $2,900 had been paid for as of December 31, 19x1. The bill for ads run during the last week of 19x1 had not been received by

December 31, but based upon knowledge of the rates it was estimated that it would be $150. Utilities bills through December 31 totaled $2,700 and had been paid.

There were no liabilities at December 31, 19x1, other than those which have been specifically mentioned or alluded to above. No additional investments by the owners had been made and no withdrawals were made.

Required:

1. A statement of financial position as of December 31, 19x1.
2. An income statement for the six months ended December 31, 19x1.

42. Following are given the *total debits* and *total credits* for the year (which include beginning-of-the-year balances) in certain accounts of the Ace Company, *after the closing entries have been posted to the accounts* as of December 31, 19x1.

	Debits	Credits
Advertisting expense................	$ 210	$ 210
Salaries expense....................	700	700
Telephone expense..................	48	48
Prepaid insurance...................	90	15
Insurance expense..................	15	15
Fees earned.......................	1,880	1,880
Drawings..........................	600	600
Income summary...................	1,880	1,880
Accounts receivable................	2,330	2,330
Capital...........................	600	19,257

Required:

Reconstruct the December 31, 19x1, *closing entries* (in general journal form).

43. Given the following T-accounts, prepare the following items for the Cowens Company for the month of January, 19x1:

a. Closing entries
b. After-closing trial balance
c. Balance sheet
d. Income statement
e. Statement of capital

Cash

25,000	(1) 3,500
(2) 4,700	(3) 2,300
(4) 12,000	(5) 9,000
	(6) 1,000
25,900	

Accounts Receivable

11,710	(2) 4,700
(7) 1,000	
8,010	

Note Payable

(1) 3,500	3,800
	300

Supplies

1,090	
(3) 2,300	(8) 1,900
1,490	

Unearned Fees

(9) 7,000	4,000
	(4) 12,000
	9,000

Fees Earned

	(7) 1,000
	(9) 7,000
	8,000

Capital

	30,000
	30,000

Withdrawals

(6) 1,000	
1,000	

Salaries

(5) 9,000	
9,000	

Supplies Used

(8) 1,900	
1,900	

44. Given the following data for the Havlicek Company for March, 19x1, prepare the following items:

a.   Adjusting entries
b.   Closing entries
c.   Income statements
d.   Statement of capital
e.   Balance sheet

Havlicek Company
Trial Balance Before Adjustment
March 31, 19x1

	Debit	Credit
Cash	$57,000	
Accounts receivable....................	4,500	
Supplies.............................	2,000	
Note payable........................		$ 7,000
Unearned fees........................		20,000
Capital		33,000
Withdrawals.........................	2,000	
Earned fees..........................		12,000
Salaries	6,500	
	$72,000	$72,000

Additional data:

1.   Supplies on hand at the end of March were $1,500.
2.   Unearned fees decreased by $10,000 in March.

45.   Presented below are the transactions of the Goodson Realty Company for the month of June, 19x1.

June   2   The owner invested $15,000 cash in the business.
        5   Purchased office furniture for $1,500 cash.
        7   Paid $300 in cash for June rent.
        9   Office supplies of $200 were purchased on account.
     10   Received and paid a bill for $300 for advertising in a local newspaper during June.
     13   Paid wages of $200 in cash for the month of June.
     15   Received a cash advance of $500 from a customer for services to be rendered during July.
     16   Sold a house and collected $800 commission.
     17   Sold a house and will collect the $600 commission in July.
     21   The owner withdrew $500 from the business.
     23   Received and paid the June telephone bill for $100.
     25   Paid for office supplies purchased on June 9.
     27   Paid the utilities bill for the month, $35.

Required:

Prepare the general journal entries necessary to record the above transactions.

46.   On August 1, 19x1, Bill King began operating a bicycle repair shop. The transactions of the business during the month of August were as follows:

Aug.   2   King began the business by investing $15,000 in cash and repair equipment with a fair value of $2,000.
        4   Purchased land for $4,000 cash.
        7   Purchased a building for $20,000. The terms of the purchase required a cash payment of $5,000 and the issuance of a note payable for $15,000.
     11   Purchased supplies on account in the amount of $700.
     13   Completed repair work for customers and collected $700 cash.
     15   Paid the $400 salary of an employee.
     17   Completed repair work of $500 on credit.
     19   Paid for supplies purchased on account.
     21   Withdrew $300 from the business to be used for personal expenses.
     25   Received $500 cash for repair work previously completed.
     27   Paid a $50 utility bill.
     30   Made first payment of $1,000 on the note payable.

Required:

1.   Prepare the general journal entries to record each of the above transactions.
2.   Post the above journal entries to T-accounts.
3.   Prepare a trial balance as of the end of August.
4.   Prepare closing entries.

47. Below is given certain data relating to the operations of Maxwell Company for the year ended December 31, 19x1.

Trial balance data as of December 31, 19x1:

	Before Adjustment	After Adjustment
Advertising expense..................	$ 210	$ 210
Salaries expense......................	700	750
Accrued salaries payable.............	0	50
Telephone expense...................	48	58
Accrued telephone expenses payable.....	54	64
Capital	19,350	19,350
Land................................	5,600	5,600
Cash	365	365
Prepaid insurance....................	90	55
Fees earned..........................	1,880	1,960
Insurance expense....................	30	65
Unearned fees.......................	175	95
Withdrawals.........................	600	600
Accounts receivable..................	2,330	2,330

Required:

Prepare adjusting entries as of December 31, 19x1 by comparing the above data. Also, prepare the closing entries as of December 31, 19x1.

48. The Maryland Wholesale Company has kept no formal books of accounts. The owner has, however, made up a statement of assets and liabilities at the end of each year. For 19x1 and 19x2, a portion of this statement appears as follows, as of December 31:

	19x1	19x2
Cash	$3,000	$ 5,000
Accounts receivable..............	7,000	5,000
Accounts payable for expenses......	8,000	10,000

An analysis of the checkbook for 19x2 shows (1) deposits of all amounts received from customers totaling $50,000 and (2) cash payments to creditors for expenses amounting to $33,000.

Required:

Prepare the company's income statement for the year ended December 31, 19x2.

49. On January 1, 19x1, the Rowe Realty Company began operations. On that date, Rowe executed a contract for the purchase of five apartment buildings costing $30,000 each. Rowe paid $40,000 of the total purchase price and gave a mortgage note payable for the balance. This note was to be paid in equal installments of $10,000 due each December 31. In addition to the $10,000 principal payment, Rowe must also pay interest of $1,000 each year on December 31.

Additional information:

1. Each apartment building consisted of 24 apartments, each apartment renting for $150 a month including all utilities. During the year, every apartment was rented for the full 12 months, and all rent had been collected to date. Cash receipts were immediately deposited in a checking account when collected, and all cash disbursements were made by check.

2. Salaries for the year consisted of $200 per week for maintenance and $10,000 per year for the apartment manager. Utilities expense paid by Rowe Realty amounted to an average of $500 per month for six months out of the year and $700 for the other six months. Property taxes paid were $6,000. Other expenses paid were $3,500.

3. All expenses have been paid to date and there have been no additional investments or withdrawals made by Rowe.

Required:

1. An income statement for the year ended December 31, 19x1.
2. A balance sheet as of December 31, 19x1.

50. The following information for adjustments was available at December 31, the end of the accounting period. Prepare the necessary adjusting entry for each item of information.

a. Annual office rent of $1,200 was paid on July 1, when the lease was signed. This amount was recorded as prepaid rent.

b. The office supplies account had a $100 balance at the beginning of the year and $600 of office supplies were purchased during the year. An inventory of unused supplies at the end of the year indicated that $150 of supplies were still on hand.

c. Wages earned by employees during December but not yet paid amounted to $700 on December 31.

d. The company subleased part of its office space at a rental of $50 per month. The tenant occupied the space on September 1 and paid six months rent in advance. This amount paid was credited to the unearned rent account.

e. Equipment was purchased on January 1 for $5,000. The useful life was estimated to be ten years with no salvage value.

f. Services provided for clients which were not chargeable until January amounted to $800. No entries had yet been made to record these earned revenues.

51. From the information given below concerning the College Inn Ski Resort, prepare the adjusting entries required at December 31, 19x1.

    a.   Accrued property taxes at December 31, 19x1, were $500.

    b.   Accrued wages payable at December 31, 19x1, were $2,400.

    c.   Interest receivable on United States government bonds owned at December 31, 19x1, was $75.

    d.   A tractor had been obtained on October 31 from Equipment Rentals, Inc., at a daily rate of $4. No rental payment had yet been made. Continued use of the tractor was expected through the month of January.

    e.   A portion of the land owned by the resort had been leased to a riding stable at a yearly rental of $3,600. One year's rent was collected in advance at the date of the lease (November 1) and credited to Unearned Rental Revenue.

    f.   Another portion of the land owned had also been rented on October 1 to a service station operator at an annual rate of $1,200. No rent had as yet been collected from this tenant.

    g.   On December 31, the College Inn Ski Resort signed an agreement to lease a truck from Gray Drive Ur-Self Company for the next calendar year at a rate of 10 cents for each mile of use. The Resort estimates that they will drive this truck for about 1,000 miles per month.

    h.   On September 1, the Company purchased a three-year fire insurance policy for $360. At the time the policy was acquired, the Company debited insurance expense and credited cash.

52. Below is given the September 30, 19x1, trial balance *before* adjustment of the Cavilier Company.

Cavilier Company
Trial Balance
September 30, 19x1

Cash	$ 2,700	
Supplies	1,250	
Prepaid rent	1,800	
Land	10,000	
Accounts payable		$ 3,500
Fees received in advance		2,500
Capital		7,250
Drawings	500	
Commissions earned		5,800
Fees earned		2,200
Wages and salaries expense	4,000	
Utilities expense	550	
Miscellaneous expense	450	
	$21,250	$21,250

Other data:

1. Supplies on hand at the end of September totaled $750.
2. In accordance with the terms of the lease, the annual rental of $1,800 was paid in advance on April 1, 19x1.
3. Wages and salaries earned by employees but unpaid at September 30, 19x1, amounted to $450.
4. Of the balance in the Fees Received in Advance account, $1,500 had not been earned as of September 30, 19x1.
5. On September 1, 19x1, Cavilier Company rented certain equipment to the Alpha Fraternity under the following terms: $50 per month payable on the first day of each month following the start of the rental arrangement.

Required:

Prepare all journal entries necessary to: (1) adjust the accounts and (2) close the books as of September 30, 19x1.

53. Given below is the trial balance before adjustment and the adjusted trial balance for Doak Company at December 31, 19x1.

Doak Company
Trial Balance and Adjusted Trial Balance
December 31, 19x1

	Trial Balance		Adjusted Trial Balance	
Cash............................	$ 3,000		$ 3,000	
Accounts receivable..............	2,500		2,500	
Rent receivable..................	0		200	
Prepaid insurance................	1,000		600	
Supplies........................	1,200		400	
Office furniture.................	3,000		3,000	
Accumulated depreciation—				
office furniture................		$ 900		$ 1,200
Land	7,000		7,000	
Accounts payable................		1,500		1,500
Notes payable...................		2,000		2,000
Interest payable.................		0		100
Unearned fees...................		800		300
Wages payable...................		0		600
Withdrawals.....................	500		500	
Capital.........................		9,000		9,000
Service fees.....................		10,000		10,500
Rental income...................		600		800
Wage expense...................	6,000		6,600	
Insurance expense...............	0		400	
Depreciation expense.............	0		300	
Interest expense.................	100		200	
Supplies expense.................	0		800	
Other expenses..................	500		500	
	$24,800	$24,800	$26,000	$26,000

Prepare the adjusting journal entries made by Doak Company on December 31, 19x1. Prepare the closing entries as of December 31, 19x1.

54.   Below is the trial balance for the Martin Company:

Martin Company
Trial Balance
December 31, 19x1

Cash	$ 800	
Notes receivable.	2,500	
Prepaid insurance.	750	
Land	21,000	
Service revenue received in advance. .		$ 3,500
Mortgage payable.		5,000
Capital		14,700
Commissions earned.		9,000
Salaries expense.	6,500	
Miscellaneous expense.	650	
	$32,200	$32,200

Data for adjustments:

a.   Accrued salaries at December 31, 19x1, were $220.
b.   Accrued interest on the mortgage at December 31, 19x1, was $250.
c.   At year-end, one-half of the service revenue received in advance had been earned.
d.   Insurance expense for 19x1 was $375.
e.   Accrued interest on the notes receivable at December 31, 19x1, was $20.

Required:

1.   Prepare the adjusting and closing journal entries for Martin Company at December 31, 19x1.
2.   Prepare an income statement for the year and the balance sheet as of December 31, 19x1.

55. As chief accountant for Ford Company, it is your job to prepare end-of-period financial statements for the firm. You had an assistant prepare the following unadjusted trial balance from the books of the company.

Ford Company
Trial Balance
December 31, 19x1

Cash	$ 1,100	
Accounts receivable..............................	800	
Prepaid insurance...............................	900	
Office furniture.................................	4,000	
Accumulated depreciation—		
office furniture.................................		$ 400
Land	8,000	
Accounts payable................................		900
Unearned revenues..............................		1,500
Note payable...................................		2,500
Capital		9,600
Withdrawals....................................	400	
Service revenues................................		4,100
Rent expense...................................	600	
Salaries expense................................	1,000	
Supplies expense................................	2,000	
Other expenses.................................	200	
	$19,000	$19,000

The following information was also gathered from the books of the Ford Company:

a.   The company paid $900 for a three-year insurance policy on June 30, 19x1.

b.   The office furniture was purchased January 1, 19x0, and is expected to have a 10-year life and no salvage value. Depreciation for 19x1 has not been recorded.

c.   The unearned revenues account was created when Ford Company was paid $1,500 for services to be rendered. One-third of these services were rendered on December 1, 19x1.

d.   Interest of $20 has accrued on the note payable at December 31.

e.   Ford Company paid $600 on August 1 as annual rent for its warehouse. This amount was debited to rent expense.

f. $100 of salaries have been earned by employees but not yet paid or recorded on the books.

g.   Supplies on hand at December 31 had a cost of $500.

Required:

1.   Prepare the adjusting and closing entries for Ford Company at December 31, 19x1.

2.   Prepare the company's balance sheet, income statement, and statement of capital.

56.   Given below is a trial balance before adjustment for Unseld Company.

Unseld Company
Trial Balance Before Adjustment
December 31, 19x3

Cash....................................	$ 2,500	
Accounts receivable......................	1,600	
Notes receivable.........................	2,100	
Office furniture.........................	3,000	
Accumulated depreciation—		
office furniture.........................		$ 300
Accounts payable.........................		1,800
Unearned fees............................		425
Capital..................................		5,900
Withdrawals..............................	360	
Service fees.............................		2,050
Rent income.............................		350
Supplies expense........................	800	
Insurance expense.......................	115	
Wage expense............................	350	
	$10,825	$10,825

On December 31, the accountant for Unseld Company found several items which he thought needed adjustment in the preparation of the worksheet. Below are listed these items which may or may not need adjustment.

a.   The office furniture which was purchased on January 1, 19x1 is being depreciated over a 20-year life with no salvage value.

b.   Wages for the last week of the year amounted to $50 which would not be paid until January 6, 19x4.

c.   Unearned fees worth $200 will be earned as of December 31, and the rest will be earned in January.

d.   Insurance of $100 was unexpired as of December 31.

e.   Supplies worth $500 were on hand at the end of the year.

f.   Accrued interest on notes receivable amounts to 6 percent of the ending notes receivable balance.

g.   Rental income earned but not yet received included $200 for the month of November and $100 for December.

Required:

Prepare the adjusting and closing journal entries as of December 31, 19x3 for Unseld Company.

57. Given below is a trial balance before adjustment for Holmes Company.

Holmes Company
Trial Balance Before Adjustment
December 31, 19x1

Cash	$1,100	
Accounts receivable...........................	800	
Notes receivable.............................	1,500	
Office furniture.............................	2,000	
Accumulated depreciation—		
office furniture.............................		$ 400
Accounts payable.............................		1,250
Unearned fees................................		500
Capital		4,350
Withdrawals.................................	400	
Service fees..................................		2,000
Rent income.................................		300
Supplies expense............................	1,500	
Insurance expense...........................	900	
Wage expense...............................	600	
	$8,800	$8,800

After preparing the adjusting and closing journal entries, the accountant for Holmes Company produces the following balance sheet for the year.

Holmes Company
Balance Sheet
As of December 31, 19x1

ASSETS

Cash		$1,100
Accounts receivable...........................		800
Interest receivable...........................		20
Supplies....................................		250
Prepaid insurance............................		600
Notes receivable.............................		1,500
Office furniture.............................	$2,000	
Less: Accumulated depreciation................	600	1,400
Total Assets............................		$5,670

LIABILITIES AND OWNERS' EQUITY

Accounts payable............................	$1,250
Unearned fees................................	300
Unearned rent...............................	100
Total Liabilities...........................	$1,650
Capital	4,020
Total Liabilities and Owners' Equity..........	$5,670

Required:

Reproduce the adjusting and closing journal entries prepared by the accountant for Holmes Company.

58. The trial balance of the Aggie Company as of September 30, 19x1, was as follows:

Aggie Company
Trial Balance
September 30, 19x1

Cash..	$ 6,000	
Supplies......................................	500	
Prepaid rent.................................	900	
Land	8,500	
Accounts payable.............................		$ 4,000
Unearned revenues............................		1,050
Capital......................................		10,000
Withdrawals	1,000	
Commissions earned...........................		10,100
Salaries expense.............................	7,500	
Miscellaneous expense........................	750	
	$25,150	$25,150

Other financial data:

a.   The cost of supplies on hand at the end of September was $100.

b.   In accordance with the terms of its lease, the company paid its annual rent of $900 on September 1.

c.   Salaries earned by employees but not paid as of September 30, 19x1 totaled $500.

d.   Of the balance in the unearned revenues account, $450 had not been earned as of September 30, 19x1.

e.   Included in the miscellaneous expense account was the cost of a fire insurance policy purchased on August 31, 19x1, at a cost of $180. The policy expires on August 31, 19x3.

Required:

Prepare adjusting journal entries for the above data. Prepare closing entries.

59. Below is given a trial balance before and after adjustment for Bonham Company at December 31, 19x1.

Bonham Company
Trial Balance Before Adjustment
December 31, 19x1

Cash	$ 800	
Accounts receivable	1,100	
Prepaid insurance	600	
Supplies	2,250	
Office furniture	2,500	
Accumulated depreciation—		
office furniture		$ 500
Land	4,000	
Accounts payable		700
Unearned fees		750
Note payable		2,000
Capital		5,450
Withdrawals	150	
Service fees		3,750
Rent income		200
Salaries expense	1,200	
Other expenses	750	
	$13,350	$13,350

Bonham Company
Trial Balance After Adjustment
December 31, 19x1

Cash	$ 800	
Accounts receivable	1,100	
Rent receivable	200	
Prepaid insurance	300	
Supplies	750	
Office furniture	2,500	
Accumulated depreciation—		
office furniture		$ 1,000
Land	4,000	
Accounts payable		775
Interest payable		20
Unearned fees		500
Unearned rent		50
Note payable		2,000
Capital		5,450
Withdrawals	150	
Service fees		4,000
Rent income		350
Salaries expense	1,200	
Advertising expense	75	
Insurance expense	300	
Depreciation expense	500	
Interest expense	20	
Supplies expense	1,500	
Other expenses	750	
	$14,145	$14,145

Required:

Prepare the adjusting entries for Bonham Company for 19x1. Also, prepare closing entries.

Refer to the Annual Report included in the Appendix at the end of the text:

60.   Which account *does not* appear in the financial statements, but *is* used in the closing process?

61.   Were more debits or credits made to the cash account during the most recent year?

62.   Referring to the previous question, why is this the case?

63.   Were more debits or credits made to the accounts payable account during the most recent year?

64.   Referring to the previous question, why is this the case?

65.   At the end of the most recent year, how much of that year's net income was not in the equity accounts?

66.   Where did the net income mentioned in the previous question go?

Chapter 4 discusses the accounting for a company that sells a product and the alternative methods of accounting for inventory. Studying this chapter should enable you to:

1. Illustrate the accounting for a retailing firm.

2. Discuss the components of inventory cost, including purchase discounts, freight-in, returns and allowances.

3. Distinguish between periodic and perpetual inventory methods.

4. Explain the concept of cost allocation.

5. Distinguish between product and period costs.

6. Describe basic inventory control procedures.

7. Discuss the objective of inventory accounting.

8. Identify the primary cost basis used in accounting for inventories and describe the elements of this cost.

9. Discuss inventory cost flow methods and the basic assumption each makes.

10. Explain the concept of lower of cost or market as it relates to inventories.

11. Apply the retail and gross profit methods of estimating inventory costs.

Merchandising Transactions and Inventories

4

INTRODUCTION

The preceding chapters have illustrated the basic steps of the complete accounting cycle for Kilmer Contractors, a firm rendering personal services. The income of a service business is equal to the excess of its revenues (i.e., its fees, commissions, etc.) earned for the services it provides over the expenses which were incurred by the company in rendering these services. Service companies, such as travel agencies, hotels and airlines, are responsible for a significant dollar volume of business in our economy. However, the majority of businesses in the United States are engaged in selling products. Businesses which earn revenues by selling products may be either merchandising firms or manufacturing companies. Merchandising companies, both wholesalers and retailers, acquire merchandise in ready-to-sell condition, whereas manufacturing companies acquire input materials and produce a product for sale. In contrast to a service type business, the net income of a merchandising or manufacturing company results when the revenues earned from selling products exceed the total of the cost of goods sold and the operating expenses.

While many of the accounting concepts discussed previously are also applicable to product oriented companies, there are certain additional techniques required to account for the purchase and sale of products.

ACCOUNTING FOR MERCHANDISING OPERATIONS

Accounting for Cost of Goods Sold

The cost of merchandise sold during the period is included in the income statement as an expense referred to as the cost of goods sold. The merchandise which was available for sale but which was not sold during the period is referred to as inventory on hand at the end of the year. The cost of this inventory is included in the balance sheet as an asset.

There are two general methods of recordkeeping which are used in accounting for inventories: the periodic and the perpetual inventory methods. The basic difference between these two methods is in the timing of the recording of the cost of goods sold for the period.

Under the periodic method the cost of goods sold is determined at the end of the period by making a physical count of the goods on hand and subtracting the cost of the goods which are still on hand from the total cost of goods which were available for sale. Using the perpetual method, an entry recording the cost of goods sold is usually made at the time a sale is made. A physical inventory is still taken, either at the end of the year or periodically during the year, and the inventory amounts on the books are then adjusted, if necessary, in order to reflect the cost of the actual goods which are on hand. The perpetual inventory method is most appropriate for a business which has only a limited number of sales each day. In such a case, it would not be difficult to determine the cost of each item sold and to record the specific cost of goods sold expense at the time of the sales transaction. However, in a business with a high volume of sales and/or a variety of merchandise items, it may not be practical to record the cost of each item sold at the time the sale is made. Instead, the periodic method could be used by taking a physical count of goods on hand at the end of the period to determine the cost of goods sold. To illustrate the application of accounting for merchandising operations, assume that Kilmer Contractors decided to expand its decorating operations by selling carpet to its customers in addition to its painting activities. Recall that its balance sheet at May 31, 19x1, was as follows:

Kilmer Contractors
Balance Sheet
May 31, 19x1

ASSETS		_LIABILITIES AND OWNER'S EQUITY_	
Cash	$10,000	Note payable	$ 1,500
Accounts receivable	900	Unearned fees	1,100
Supplies	2,000	Capital	10,300
	$12,900		$12,900

Cost of Merchandise Purchased

The cost of items purchased for resale is debited to a Purchases account. This Purchases account is used to accumulate the cost of all merchandise acquired for resale during an accounting period. To illustrate, assume that on June 1, the company purchased 1,000 square yards of carpet, paying $5 per yard in cash. The journal entry to record the purchase of this carpet would be as follows:

Purchases	5,000	
Cash		5,000

This transaction represents an exchange of one asset for another, i.e., cash for inventory. The debit to the Purchases account records the acquisition of the carpet, and the credit to cash indicates the Cash expenditure. Because the carpet has not been sold, its cost is considered an asset and not reclassified as an expense until the period the carpet is sold. Under the periodic inventory system, the Purchases account accumulates the total cost of merchandise purchased during the period. Therefore, the balance in the Purchases account during the period does not normally indicate whether the goods purchased during the period are still on hand or were sold.

Sales of Merchandise

When a business sells merchandise to its customers, it either receives immediate payment in cash or acquires a receivable from its customer which will be collected in cash at a future date. In this illustration, assume that during the month of June, Kilmer sold 800 square yards of this carpet at a selling price of $9 per yard. These sales would be recorded as follows, assuming that they were made for cash:

```
Cash ................................... 7,200
     Sales ..............................              7,200
```

This transaction was a sale of a product for cash. The debit to the cash account records the increase in cash, and the credit to sales records the total amount of revenue generated from the sale of the carpet. If this sale had been made on a credit basis, the entry would have been a debit to accounts receivable and a credit to sales.

Determination of Cost of Goods Sold and Net Income

To continue our illustration, we will assume that the only expense (other than the cost of the carpet itself) incurred by Kilmer Contractors during the month of June was the payment of salaries to the crew which was hired to install carpet. This outlay of $1,500 would be recorded as follows:

```
Salaries expense........................ 1,500
     Cash ..............................              1,500
```

This journal entry reflects the fact that period expenses of $1,500 were incurred and paid in cash. This cost is a period cost since it cannot be associated with the purchase or manufacture of a product and since the benefits were obtained by the firm from this outlay (that is, installation of the carpet sold) during the current accounting period.

The next step in the recording process would be to post the journal entries to appropriate ledger accounts in order to summarize the transactions which have occurred. This process would be identical to that described in Chapter 2 and will not be repeated here.

After the posting process is completed, the trial balance would appear as follows:

Kilmer Contractors
Trial Balance Before Adjustment
June 30, 19x1

Cash............................	$10,700	
Accounts receivable.................	900	
Supplies.........................	2,000	
Note payable......................		$ 1,500
Unearned fees.....................		1,100
Capital...........................		10,300
Sales.............................		7,200
Purchases	5,000	
Salaries expense...................	1,500	
	$20,100	$20,100

At the end of the accounting period, the balance accumulated in the Purchases account represents the total cost of the merchandise purchased during the period. An adjusting journal entry would now be required to determine the product cost for the month. Note that the balance in the Purchases account is $5,000, representing the cost of the 1,000 square yards of carpet which were purchased during the month of June. It is necessary to allocate this balance to record the cost of carpet which was still on hand as of June 30 and the cost of the carpet which was sold during the month of June. The cost of the items still on hand at the end of the period represents an asset referred to as *inventory*. The cost of the items sold during the period is an expense called *cost of goods sold*. The adjusting entry necessary to record the cost of the 800 square yards of carpet sold during June and the cost of the 200 square yards of carpet still on hand at June 30, 19x1, would be as follows:

```
Inventory  . . . . . . . . . . . . . . . . . . . . . . . . . . . . . . . .   1,000
Cost of Goods Sold . . . . . . . . . . . . . . . . . . . . . . . . . . .   4,000
    Purchases  . . . . . . . . . . . . . . . . . . . . . . . . . . . . .            5,000
```

The debit to Cost of Goods Sold records the cost of the carpet which was sold during June (800 yards × $5) and the debit to Inventory records the cost of the carpet still on hand at June 30 (200 yards × $5). Since the Purchases account is closed out, it has a zero balance at the beginning of the next accounting period, July 1. The balance in the Inventory account at June 30 is also the inventory at the beginning of the next period. Thus, the cost of goods available for sale during the next accounting period will include the beginning inventory plus any purchases made during July. Note that cost of goods available for sale is divided into two components at the end of the period—the cost of goods sold and the inventory on hand. This is done by means of an adjusting entry which would then be posted to the ledger accounts. The next step in the recording process would be the preparation of a trial balance *after* adjustment. This trial balance is presented below:

Kilmer Contractors
Trial Balance After Adjustment
June 30, 19x1

Cash	$10,700	
Accounts receivable.	900	
Supplies	2,000	
Inventory	1,000	
Note payable		$ 1,500
Unearned fees		1,100
Capital		10,300
Sales		7,200
Salaries expense	1,500	
Cost of goods sold	4,000	
	$20,100	$20,100

Again, the only difference between the trial balance above and the one presented previously is the inclusion of the effect of the adjusting entry which was made to record the cost of goods sold for June.

The next step in the recording process would be to prepare closing entries. The journal entries required to close out the revenue and expense accounts of Kilmer Contractors are as follows:

Sales	7,200	
Income Summary.		7,200
Income Summary	5,500	
Salaries Expense		1,500
Cost of Goods Sold.		4,000

The balance in the income summary account is then transferred to Kilmer's capital account by the following entry:

Income Summary	1,700	
Capital.		1,700

The closing entries would then be posted to the general ledger. The reader should note that the closing entries for a retailing concern are almost identical to those for a service organization.

After the closing entries have been made and posted to the ledger, the financial statements would then be prepared as follows:

Kilmer Contractors
Balance Sheet
June 30, 19x1

ASSETS		LIABILITIES AND OWNER'S EQUITY	
Cash	$10,700	Note payable	$ 1,500
Accounts receivable.	900	Unearned fees	1,100
Supplies	2,000		
Inventory.	1,000	Capital	12,000
	$14,600		$14,600

Kilmer Contractors
Income Statement
For the Month Ending June 30. 19x1

Sales		$7,200
Less: Cost of goods sold:		
Beginning inventory.	$ –0–	
Purchases.	5,000	
Goods available for sale	$5,000	
Ending inventory	1,000	4,000
Gross profit		$3,200
Salaries		1,500
Income		$1,700

Kilmer Contractors
Statement of Capital
For the Month Ending June 30, 19x1

Capital at June 1, 19x1.......................... $10,300
Add: Income for the month of June...............   1,700
Capital at June 30, 19x1.......................... $12,000

Note that the difference between the balance sheet for a service business and that of a retailing firm is that the latter includes inventory as an asset. The primary difference between the financial statements of the two types of organizations is in the income statement. The income statement for a service business (see Chapter 2) usually includes a revenue account for each major source of revenue followed by a grouping of expenses which are deducted, in total, from the total revenues for the period in order to determine income. The income statement for a retailing firm includes three major segments or sections. The revenue from the sale of goods is shown first. The determination of the cost of the goods sold (product cost) is then made and is deducted from sales in order to disclose the gross profit from sales for the period (sales less cost of goods sold). The other expenses (period costs) are then subtracted from the gross profit figure in order to determine the net income for the period.

OBJECTIVE OF INVENTORY ACCOUNTING

The objective of inventory accounting is two-fold. First, it is concerned with valuation of the asset inventory. Valuation of the asset account is important because the funds invested by a firm in its inventories are usually quite significant; the inventory of a business is often the largest of its current assets. Second, and at least of equal importance, is the proper determination of net income of the business for the period by matching the appropriate costs (the cost of the inventory sold) against the related revenue (the revenue received from the sale of the inventory). In other words, the matching process requires that costs be assigned: (1) to those goods which were sold during the period and (2) to those goods which are still on hand and available for sale at the end of a period. It should be noted that this is really a single process; the procedures which are employed in the valuation of inventories also simultaneously determine the cost of goods sold. In order to illustrate this general process, consider the following activities of Art's Wholesalers for the month of June:

1.   Purchased 100 cases of coca-cola at a cost of $3 per case.
2.   Sold 80 cases of coca-cola at a price of $5 per case.
3.   Selling expenses for June totaled $25.
4.   On June 1, Art had 10 cases of coke which had also cost him $3 per

case on hand. At June 30, Art's inventory consisted of 30 cases of coke.

If Art were to prepare an income statement for the month of June, it would appear as follows:

Art's Wholesalers
Income Statement
For the Month of June

Sales (80 cases @ $5)		$400
Less: Cost of goods sold		
Beginning inventory, June 1 (10 cases @ $3)	$ 30	
Add: Purchases (100 cases @ $3)	300	
Goods available for sale	$330	
Deduct: Ending inventory, June 30 (30 cases @ $3)	90	
Cost of goods sold		240
Gross profit from sales		$160
Selling expenses		25
Income		$135

Several points should be noted from the analysis of the above income statement. The total inventory of coke which was available for sale, identified in the income statement as the *goods available for sale*, was accumulated by combining the cost of goods which were on hand at the start of the period (*beginning inventory*) with the cost of coke purchased during the period (*purchases*).

Goods available for sales was then divided into its two components: (1) the cost of coke which was still on hand and available for sale at the close of the period (*ending inventory*) and (2) the cost of coke which was sold during the period (*cost of goods sold*). *Cost of goods sold* was subtracted from the sales revenue for the period (*sales*) in order to determine *gross profit from sales*. Note that the gross profit from sales is determined and presented before the other costs and expenses incurred during the period are considered. The next step in the preparation of the income statement is the deduction of these expenses, in this example *selling expenses*, in order to arrive at the income for the period.

Of course, the example used above was very simple for purposes of illustration. All coke was assumed to be acquired at a single price and no discounts, returns, or losses were encountered. Our purpose was to illustrate the general concepts of inventory accounting; we will now consider some of the detailed procedures which are normally involved in this process.

INVENTORY COSTS Inventory values should reflect all costs that are required in order to obtain merchandise (retailer or wholesaler) in the desired condition and location. If any costs of obtaining inventory (in addition to the purchase price) are not included as product costs and instead are considered to be costs of the period, inventory values on the balance sheet would be understated and expenses on the income statement would be overstated. When these goods are sold in a later period, expenses on the income statement of that period would be understated.

All indirect costs that were incurred by the business in obtaining and placing the goods in a marketable condition should be included as a part of inventory cost if it is possible and practical to identify these costs with inventory purchases. Examples of these costs would include such items as sales taxes, duties, freight-in, and insurance. The cost of merchandise is also reduced by any discounts, returns and allowances.

PERIODIC AND PERPETUAL INVENTORIES

There are two general methods of recordkeeping which are used in accounting for inventories: the periodic and the perpetual inventory methods. The basic difference between these two methods is in the timing of the recording of the cost of sales.

Under the periodic method the cost of goods sold is determined at the end of the period by making a physical count of the goods on hand and subtracting the cost of the goods which are still on hand from the total cost of goods which were available for sale. Using the perpetual method, an entry recording the cost of goods sold is usually made at the time a sale is made. A physical inventory is still taken, either at the end of the year or periodically during the year, and the inventory amounts on the books are then adjusted, if necessary, in order to reflect the cost of the actual goods which are on hand.

The above procedures describe periodic and perpetual systems in terms of dollar amounts. Either of these inventory systems can also be maintained on a quantity basis. For example, with a perpetual system on a quantity basis, a "running count" of each class or category of inventory item may be maintained, either manually or by the use of electronic data processing equipment, in order to provide information with regard to the quantity of a particular inventory item on hand at any particular point in time.

The basic difference between the two methods is illustrated by the following example:

1. Purchased 10 cases of beer @ $3 per case (assume that the firm had no inventory at the beginning of the period).

Perpetual			*Periodic*		
Inventory	30		Purchases	30	
Cash		30	Cash		30

2. Sold 7 cases of beer for $5 per case.

	Perpetual				Periodic	
Cash		35		Cash		35
Sales			35	Sales			35
Cost of Goods Sold		21				
Inventory			21			

3. Ending inventory is 2 cases of beer.

	Perpetual				Periodic	
Loss		3		Cost of Goods Sold		24
Inventory			3	Inventory		6
				Purchases			30

An analysis of the entries presented above indicates that using the perpetual system the cost of goods sold is $21 and a loss of $3 is shown for the missing case of beer (10 cases purchased minus 7 cases sold minus 2 cases in the ending inventory indicates that 1 case was "missing"). Using the periodic method, the $3 cost of the missing case would be included in the cost of goods sold since the cost of goods sold under this method was determined by subtracting the $6 cost of ending inventory from goods available for sale of $30 and assuming that the difference represented inventory that was sold. This is a disadvantage of the periodic method, because the cost of sales under this method will include not only the cost of the goods actually sold, but also the cost of any merchandise lost or stolen as well. More effective control over inventories may be established by using the perpetual method, either on a dollar or a quantity basis.

INVENTORY LOSSES Under a periodic inventory system, it is assumed that all Cost of Goods Available for sale during the period are either sold or are on hand at the end of the period. Based upon this assumption, the cost of any merchandise lost through shrinkage, spoilage, or theft by shoplifting, etc. is automatically included in Cost of Goods Sold for the period. To illustrate, assume that a firm purchased ten cases of coke at $3 per case during a period, and the firm had no inventory at the beginning of the period. Further assume that the business sold seven cases of coke during the period, and that one case of coke was stolen by shoplifters. Thus, the ending inventory as determined by a physical count would be two cases of coke. Under the periodic method, the following entry would be made at the end of the period:

Cost of goods sold	24	
Inventory	6	
Purchases		30

In this circumstance, the $3 cost of the stolen merchandise is included in Cost of Goods Sold because the Cost of Goods Sold was determined by subtracting the ending inventory ($6) from the Cost of Goods Available ($30). If the theft had not occurred, the ending inventory would have been $3 greater. In reality, the Cost of Goods Sold was $21 and the Cost of Goods Stolen was $3.

More effective control over inventories and inventory losses may be established by using the perpetual inventory method which was discussed earlier. However, because the perpetual method is impractical for many types of businesses, a means of estimating inventory losses have been developed. This estimation technique is discussed later in this chapter.

The above procedures describe periodic and perpetual systems in terms of dollar amounts. Either of these inventory systems can also be maintained on a quantity basis. For example, with a perpetual system on a quantity basis, a "running count" of each class or category of inventory item may be maintained, either manually or by the use of electronic data processing equipment, in order to provide information with regard to the quantity of a particular inventory item on hand at any particular point in time.

BASIS OF ACCOUNTING

Historical cost is the primary basis used in accounting for inventories. This cost includes not only the price of the asset itself, but also any direct or indirect outlays which were made or incurred in order to bring the inventory to the firm's location in the desired form and condition. For example, shipping costs would be considered a part of the cost of the inventory if they were paid by the purchaser.

PURCHASE DISCOUNTS

Sellers of goods frequently offer discounts to their customers to recognize quantity purchases and to encourage prompt payment for goods sold on account. Quantity discounts, often referred to as trade discounts, usually represent an adjustment of a catalog or list price which is made to arrive at the selling price of merchandise to a particular customer. For this reason, trade discounts are not usually reflected in the accounts. For example, assume that the distributor offered coke at a list price of $4 per case and allowed Art's Wholesalers a trade discount of 25 percent. From an accounting viewpoint, Art would determine the cost to be employed in his accounts as follows:

List price per case.	$4
Less: Trade discount	
(25% of $4)	1
Cost per case ·	$3

Art would use the $3 figure as his cost; the $4 list price and the $1 discount would not appear anywhere in the accounts.

Discounts which are offered to encourage the prompt payment of purchases made on a credit basis are another matter. These discounts usually are reflected in the accounts. Such discounts, often referred to as purchase discounts, are usually stated in terms such as 2/10; n/30. This notation means that a 2 percent discount is offered to the customer if his account is settled within 10 days of the date of sale, the full amount is due at the end of the 30 day period. Two methods may be used in accounting for these discounts, the *net* method and the *gross* method. In order to illustrate these two methods, we will return to the transactions of Art's Wholesalers for the month of June and record the purchase of the 100 cases of coke at $3 per case in Art's books and in the distributor's accounts using both the net and gross methods. We will assume that the terms offered were 2/10; n/30.

Note that the seller of merchandise normally records the sale at the gross amount. One reason for this procedure lies in the fact that the seller has no control over whether or not the purchaser will make payment during or after the discount period. If payment is made by the purchaser during the discount period, the difference between the cash payment and the amount of the receivable (which was set up for the gross amount of the sale) is recorded by the seller as a *sales discount*. Of course, if payment is made after the expiration of the discount period there is no problem since the purchaser will be required to pay the gross amount in full. If this is the case, the seller will simply debit cash and credit accounts receivable for the amount of cash received.

In the purchaser's accounts, the sales price *less* the purchase discount will be recorded at the time of the purchase if the net method is used. If payment for the goods is made during the discount period, there is no problem. The purchaser will simply debit accounts payable and credit cash for the amount paid. On the other hand, if payment is made after the discount period has passed, the purchaser will be required to pay the full or gross price. Since the payable was originally recorded at the net amount, the entry for payment will require a debit to accounts payable for the net amount and a credit to cash for the amount paid (gross price); the difference between the gross and the net price will be debited to a *Discounts Lost* account. Discounts Lost is considered to be an expense of the period and is included as such in the income statement.

Under the gross method of recording purchases, the initial entry will be for the buyer to debit purchases and credit accounts payable for the full (gross) price. If payment is made during the discount period, the entry will consist of a debit to accounts payable for the original amount recorded as a liability (gross price), a credit to cash for the amount actually paid (net price), and the difference will be credited to a Purchase Discounts

Transaction	Coca-Cola Distributor	Art Net Method	Art Gross Method
Sale of 100 cases of Coca-Cola; terms: 2/10; n/30	Accounts receivable...... 300 Sales............... 300	Purchases............. 294 Accounts payable....... 294	Purchases............ 300 Accounts payable...... 300
Payment made *during* the discount period.	Cash.............. 294 Sales discounts......... 6 Accounts receivable... 300	Accounts payable....... 294 Cash............... 294	Accounts payable....... 300 Cash............... 294 Purchase discount..... 6
Payment made *after* the discount period.	Cash.............. 300 Accounts receivable.... 300	Accounts payable....... 294 Discount lost............ 6 Cash.................. 300	Accounts payable....... 300 Cash................. 300

account. Purchase Discounts is reported as a deduction from the purchases made during the period. If the payment is made after the discount period has passed or expired, the entry will simply consist of a debit to accounts payable and a credit to cash for the full or gross price.

Note that the difference between the two methods lies in the information which is provided by each. The net method provides information as to the discounts which were lost but gives no data as to those which were taken. The gross method indicates the amount of discounts taken but gives no information as to the discounts which were lost. Because of the significance[1] of discounts lost to the business, the authors feel that information regarding the discounts not taken is critical and for this reason believe that the net method should be used by purchasers. We feel that any discounts lost are, in fact, interest costs and should be disclosed as such and not included as a part of the cost of inventories.

FREIGHT-IN, RETURNS, AND ALLOWANCES

The purchase of merchandise often involves payment of shipping costs necessary to bring the goods to the purchaser's place of business. The cost of the merchandise logically includes these transportation costs.

Frequently purchasers of goods will also find it necessary to return goods to their suppliers because the goods are damaged or unacceptable. In other instances, such goods will be retained by the purchaser and the supplier will allow him an adjustment of the purchase price, known as an allowance. To illustrate these occurrences, we will assume the following facts:

1. Art ordered 100 cases of Coke, 50 cases of Pepsi, and 50 cases of Dr. Pepper, all at a price of $3 per case. The terms were F.O.B. shipping point,[2] 2/10; n/30, and Art uses the net method for recording purchases. Art pays the freight of $10.
2. Art's distributor ships him 100 cases of Coke, 50 cases of Pepsi, and, by mistake, 50 cases of Orange Crush instead of the Dr. Pepper.
3. Art returns 50 cases of the Coke, agrees to keep the Orange Crush in lieu of the Dr. Pepper since the distributor gave him a $5 allowance, and pays the balance in full within the discount period.

---

[1] Failure to take a discount when the terms are 2/10; n/30 represents an interest cost in excess of 36 percent per annum. ($294 \times R \times {}^{20}\!/_{360} = 6; solving for R, the interest rate is 36.7 percent.)

[2] The initials F.O.B. stand for free on board. F.O.B. shipping point means that the seller pays the costs *to* the shipping point only; the buyer pays the cost of transit from the shipping point to the destination. Alternatively, F.O.B. destination terms would require the seller to pay all shipping costs.

The entries to record these transactions would be as follows:

Art			*Distributor*		
Purchases	588		Accounts Receivable	600	
Freight-in	10		Sales		600
Accounts Payable		588			
Cash		10			
			Cash	436	
Accounts Payable	588		Sales Returns	150	
Purchase Returns		147	Sales Allowance	5	
Purchase Allowance		5	Sales Discount	9	
Cash		436	Accounts Receivable		600

Art debits Purchases and credits Accounts Payable for the net amount of the purchase ($600 less 2 percent of $600 or a net amount of $588). He debits Freight-in and credits Cash for the $10 freight charge that he paid in cash, since according to the terms of the purchase (F.O.B. shipping point) this is his responsibility. The seller, using the gross method, simply debits Accounts Receivable and credits Sales for the full price of the sale (200 cases @ $3).

At the time payment is made, Art would debit Accounts Payable for the amount of the liability originally recorded (net price). He would credit Purchase Returns for the net cost of the 50 cases of Coke that he returned to the seller (50 cases @ $3 or $150, less 2 percent of $150, or a net of $147) and credit Purchase Allowances for the $5 adjustment made to Art for keeping the Orange Crush, rather than the Dr. Pepper that he ordered. The credit to Cash would be for the net cash paid ($588 less the $147 return, less the $5 allowance, or a net amount of $436).

When the seller receives Art's payment, he would debit Cash for the $436 received, debit Sales Returns for $150 (the 50 cases of Coke returned @ $3), debit Sales Allowance for the $5 adjustment, and debit Sales Discounts for $9 (150 cases @ $3 or $450 multiplied by 2%). The distributor would credit Accounts Receivable for the amount he originally recorded, the gross amount of $600.

The partial income statement presented on the following page indicates how these items would be disclosed in the statements.

The reader should note that the account Purchase Discounts does not appear in the statements since we assumed that Art is using the net method of recording purchases. If the gross method were used, purchases would be included at their gross rather than net amount and purchase discounts would appear along with purchase returns and purchase allowances as a deduction in arriving at the net purchases for the period. Discounts lost would not appear in the statements when using the gross method.

Art's Wholesalers
(Partial) Income Statement
For the Year Ending December 31, 19x1

Sales			$102,800
Less: Sales returns.		$ 500	
Sales allowances.		300	
Sales discounts		2,000	2,800
Net sales			$100,000
Less: Cost of goods sold			
Beginning inventory		$10,000	
Purchases	$70,000		
Less: Purchase returns	$1,000		
Purchase allowances	100	1,100	
Net purchases		$68,900	
Add: Freight-in		600	$69,500
Goods available for sale		$79,500	
Ending inventory		15,500	
Cost of goods sold			64,000
Gross profit on sales			$ 36,000
Discounts lost		$ 100	
All other expenses		20,000	20,100
Income			$ 15,900

INVENTORY COST FLOW METHODS

Once the quantities of goods on hand at the end of the period and the quantity of goods sold during the period are determined, the next step is to decide how costs should be allocated between cost of goods sold and ending inventory. If all purchases of inventory were made at the same unit price, this allocation does not create any problems. However, if the inventory items were acquired at different unit costs, it is necessary to determine which costs should be assigned to each inventory item. One method of determining the cost of the inventory on hand would be to maintain records of the exact cost of each item sold during the period and each item on hand at the end of the period. In many cases, this specific identification procedure would require excessive recordkeeping costs, while in other instances it would be impossible to do so. Consequently, some arbitrary method for assigning costs to inventory must be used. The three most common methods used in pricing inventories (and therefore determining cost of goods sold for the period) are the average method; the first-in, first-out (Fifo) method; and the last-in, first-out (Lifo) method. The application of these methods result in a different amount of ending inventory and cost of goods sold for each period because they are based upon different arbitrary assumptions as to the flow of costs of merchandise through the business.

These methods are assumptions regarding the flow of inventory *costs* and not about the actual *physical* flow of goods. The following data relating to a special brand of foreign beer, again taken from the inventory records of Art's Wholesalers, will be used to illustrate these methods:

January 1—Beginning inventory (100 cases @ $2).	$200
February 7—Purchase (150 cases @ $3)	450
March 25—Purchase (200 cases @ $4)	800
October 6—Purchase (150 cases @ $5)	750
November 10—Purchase (100 cases @ $6)	600

Thus, the goods available for sale during the year were 700 cases at a total cost of $2,800. Art's records indicate that 500 cases were sold during the year. The accounting problem is in assigning or allocating the $2,800 cost of goods available for sale between the ending inventory and the cost of goods sold. The valuation of the ending inventory (and therefore the determination of the cost of goods sold) under each of the alternative methods of inventory valuation is illustrated in the paragraphs which follow.

Average Method

The average cost method assumes that no definite relationship exists between the receipt and the usage of quantities of inventory. This method averages costs on the assumption that one unit cannot be distinguished from another. One feature of the average method is the assignment of cost on an equal unit basis to both the ending inventory and cost of goods sold. The average cost is computed by dividing the total cost of the beginning inventory plus purchases by the total number of units included in the inventory.

In the example stated above, the average cost would be calculated as follows:

January 1—Inventory (100 cases @ $2).	$ 200
February 7—Purchase (150 cases @ $3)	450
March 25—Purchase (200 cases @ $4)	800
October 6—Purchase (150 cases @ $5)	750
November 10—Purchase (100 cases @ $6)	600
Total 700 cases	$2,800

The total cost of the goods available for sale ($2,800) would be divided by the number of cases (700) and the result of $4 would be the average cost of the inventory. This average cost figure would be used both in valuing the ending inventory (200 × $4 = $800) and in determining the cost of goods sold for the period (500 × $4 = $2,000).

First-in, First-out (Fifo) Method

The Fifo method assumes that the cost of the first item acquired or produced is the cost of the first item used or sold. Its use is advantageous because it assigns a current cost to inventories on the balance sheet and is relatively easy to apply. In many cases, the assumption is also consistent with the actual flow of goods. (Fifo inventories are priced by using the actual invoice costs or production costs for the latest quantities purchased or produced which are still on hand.) It is a good method to use in those instances where the inventory turnover is rapid or where changes in the composition of the inventory are frequent since the costs associated with the oldest inventory are always transferred to cost of goods sold first.

Its disadvantage is that it does not match the most recent costs with current revenues. On the other hand, it does give a fairly current valuation of the ending inventory balance. The Fifo inventory and the related cost of goods sold for Art's Wholesalers would be calculated as follows:

Fifo Cost of Goods Sold—the First 500 Units

January 1—Inventory (100 cases @ $2)	$ 200
February 7—Purchase (150 cases @ $3)	450
March 25—Purchase (200 cases @ $4)	800
October 6—Purchase (50 cases @ $5)	250
Fifo Cost of Goods Sold	$1,700

Fifo Ending Inventory—the Last 200 Units

October 6—Purchase (100 cases @ $5)	$ 500
November 10—Purchase (100 cases @ $6)	600
Fifo Cost of Ending Inventory	$1,100

Last-in, First-out (Lifo) Method

This method assumes that the cost of the last item received or produced is the cost of the first item used or sold. A principal advantage of the Lifo method is that it matches current costs more nearly with current revenues. Another advantage of Lifo is the fact that in periods of price increases, net income computed using Lifo is less than the amount that would result from using Fifo or the average cost method. Therefore, it reduces federal income taxes. Providing that prices do not decline below the prices of the year in which Lifo was adopted, the method results in a postponement of income taxes. Unlike many other instances where alternative accounting procedures exist, Federal income tax laws require the use of the Lifo inventory method for financial reporting purposes whenever it is used for income tax purposes.

Its disadvantages are that it gives a "noncurrent" value to inventories in the balance sheet and it reduces reported income in periods of rising prices.

When there is an increase in the quantity of inventory, the year-end Lifo inventory consists of the prior year-end inventory plus the earliest additions at cost in the current year. The cost of the Lifo inventory and the related cost of goods sold would be calculated as follows:

Lifo Ending Inventory–the First 200 Units

January 1–Inventory (100 cases @ $2)	$200
February 7–Purchase (100 cases @ $3)	300
Lifo Cost of Ending Inventory	$500

Lifo Cost of Goods Sold–the Last 500 Units

February 7–Purchase (50 cases @ $3)	$ 150
March 25–Purchase (200 cases @ $4)	800
October 6–Purchase (150 cases @ $5)	750
November 10–Purchase (100 cases @ $6)	600
Lifo Cost of Goods Sold	$2,300

Differences in Methods

The effect of the differences in the three methods which we described above are illustrated by the following summary.

	Average	*Fifo*	*Lifo*
Sales (500 cases @ $10)	$5,000	$5,000	$5,000
Less: Cost of goods sold			
Beginning inventory (100 cases)	$ 200	$ 200	$ 200
Purchases (600 cases)	2,600	2,600	2,600
Goods available for sale (700 cases)	$2,800	$2,800	$2,800
Ending inventory (200 cases)	800	1,100	500
Cost of goods sold (500 cases)	$2,000	$1,700	$2,300
Gross profit on sales	$3,000	$3,300	$2,700

The total cost of goods available for sale ($2,800) was allocated either to cost of goods sold or ending inventory in every case. The sales, beginning inventory, and purchases included in the example are identical irrespective of the inventory method chosen. An inventory method is only used to cost the ending inventory and determine the cost of goods sold. It does not necessarily reflect the actual physical flow of goods. That is, a bakery could use the Lifo method for accounting purposes although obviously the physical flow would be Fifo—who wants a ten-year-old cake!

Although a firm may select any one of several acceptable methods, the consistency principle requires that a firm use the same method over time. The selection of the method to be used should depend upon such factors as the potential effect upon the balance sheet and the income statement, and the effect on taxable income.

LOWER OF COST OR MARKET

As previously indicated, the primary basis for accounting for inventories is cost. Therefore, if the value of the item increases or decreases prior to its sale, no record of this fact is normally entered in the books. However, an exception to this rule may occur when the market price, which is defined as the current replacement cost of the goods, is less than their historical cost. In this case, the inventory may be carried at its replacement cost. In other words, inventories may be carried at the lower of their cost or their market value. If the market price for a firm's inventory falls below its original cost, an entry is made recognizing the difference between cost and market as a loss and reducing the carrying value of the inventory to market. The reduced figure becomes the new "cost" of the inventory for accounting purposes. However, if the market price exceeds the original cost, no entry is made in the accounts. The recognition of losses but not gains prior to sale is based on the principle of conservatism. To illustrate the lower of cost or market method, assume the same facts as presented above—that a firm had 700 cases of beer available for sale and that this beer had been purchased at an average price of $4 per case. Sales for the period were 500 cases at a selling price of $10 per case. If the business used the "average" inventory method, the gross profit on sales would be calculated as follows:

Sales (500 cases @ $10)	$5,000
Less: Cost of goods sold	
Beginning inventory (100 cases)	$ 200
Purchases (600 cases)	2,600
Goods available for sale (700 cases)	$2,800
Ending inventory (200 cases)	800
Cost of goods sold	$2,000
Gross profit on sales	$3,000

If the replacement cost of the ending inventory had declined to $750 as of the end of the period, the ending inventory might be written down from its original cost of $800 to its current replacement cost of $750 by the following entry:

Loss on Inventory Decline	50	
Inventory		50

The effect of the write-down of inventory would be to reduce income for the period by $50 by recognizing the reduction in the replacement cost of the inventory below its original cost. In subsequent periods, inventory would be carried at a "cost" of $750 in the balance sheet and this amount would be used in determining the cost of goods sold when the inventory was sold. The lower of cost or market method may be applied: (1) to each individual type of inventory item; (2) to major classes of inventory; or (3) to the inventory as a whole. Although the application of lower of cost or market valuation is optional, once the method is adopted it should be followed consistently from year to year.

GROSS PROFIT METHOD

In many instances, such as in the case of the preparation of interim financial statements, it may be desirable simply to estimate the amount of the ending inventory rather than go to the time and trouble of taking a physical inventory. One method which is often used in estimating inventories is the gross profit method.

This method assumes that the relationship between sales, the cost of goods sold, and gross profit will remain relatively constant from one accounting period to the next. This relationship is normally based upon actual amounts from the preceding year, adjusted for any changes which occurred in the current year. To illustrate, consider the following example for Art's Wholesalers for the month of January, 19x1.

Sales	$10,500
Sales returns	500
Purchases	5,500
Purchase returns	100
Purchase allowances	50
Freight	150
Inventory, January 1, 19x1	15,500

In addition to the data summarized above, information concerning the gross profit percentage (gross profit of $36,000 divided by net sales of $100,000 or 36%)[3] and the inventory at the beginning of the year ($15,500) was obtained from the 19x0 income statement. This information would be used to estimate the cost of the ending inventory on hand at January 31, 19x1 as follows:

1. Determine the cost of goods available for sale to date, using the ledger accounts.
2. Estimate the cost of goods sold by multiplying the net sales by the estimated gross profit rate.

---

[3] Information from the 19x0 income statement was as follows:

Sales	$100,000	(100%)
Cost of goods sold	64,000	(64%)
Gross profit on sales	$ 36,000	(36%)

3. Subtract the estimated cost of goods sold from the cost of goods available for sale to determine the estimated inventory on hand.

The calculation of the estimated inventory at January 31, 19x1 for Art's Wholesalers is as follows:

Beginning inventory			$15,500
Purchases		$ 5,500	
Less: Purchase returns.	$100		
Purchase allowances	50	150	
Net purchases		$ 5,350	
Freight-in		150	5,500
Goods available for sale			$21,000
Less: Estimated cost of goods sold			
Sales		$10,500	
Less: Sales returns.		500	
Net sales		$10,000	
Multiply by the cost of goods sold percentage (100% – 36%).		X 64%	
Estimated cost of goods sold			6,400
Estimated cost of January 31, 19x1 inventory.			$14,600

The reader should keep in mind that the gross profit method is a method of *estimating* inventories, not *costing* inventories. The gross profit method can be used in order to estimate inventories for interim statement purposes; to test the accuracy of inventories determined by physical count; and to estimate inventory destroyed by fire, lost by theft, etc.

RETAIL INVENTORY METHOD

The retail inventory method is commonly used by retail businesses to simplify their accounting for inventories. An advantage of the use of this method is that the physical inventory is computed on the basis of selling prices, which are readily available. The physical inventory at selling prices is then converted to its estimated cost by applying the average ratio of costs to selling prices of goods that were on hand during the period. Thus, it is an averaging method which assumes that the cost of merchandise on hand at any time bears the same relationship to total retail prices as the total cost of all goods handled during the period bears to original selling prices. In using this method, when sales are subtracted from goods available for sale at retail selling prices, the result is the estimated ending inventory at retail prices. Then, this amount is multiplied by the average ratio of cost to selling prices to give an estimate of ending inventory at cost. Its principal advantages are: it provides a clerically feasible means of determining inventories on hand; it provides a measure of control over inventories and a means of computing the cost of merchandise sold at any time, even though the store handles a large number of items and has a very high volume of sales transactions; it simplifies the taking and pricing of physical inventories; it provides information for a monthly determination of gross profit for each department and store; and it helps control inventory by disclosing shortages which may indicate either thefts or sales made at unauthorized prices.

As goods are purchased, information regarding the goods is accumulated on both a cost and a selling price basis. The determination of the estimated cost of inventory using the retail method is illustrated with the following example:

	Cost	Selling Price
Beginning inventory	$ 1,500	$ 2,000
Add: Purchases	10,000	18,000
Freight	500	
	$12,000	$20,000
Deduct: Sales		16,000
Ending inventory, at retail		$ 4,000

Cost percentage: $\dfrac{\$12,000}{\$20,000} = 60\%$

Ending inventory, at cost: $4,000 \times 60\% = \$2,400$

SUMMARY

This chapter has discussed certain of the operational differences in companies, with special emphasis placed on the differences in retailing and service organizations.

For accounting purposes, inventories include all goods which are held for sale to customers, those in the process of being produced for sale, and those to be used in the production of goods for sale. The objective of inventory accounting is to provide a proper valuation of inventory, both for balance sheet reporting purposes and for the proper determination of income.

Inventories are normally accounted for at historical cost, with any savings due to trade and purchase discounts and expenses due to freight charges considered in the determination of historical cost. In addition, inventory costs must be adjusted for any returns or allowances on inventory items. When the market price falls below cost, inventories may be written down to their current replacement cost using the lower of cost or market concept.

The periodic and perpetual inventory methods are the two general methods of determining inventory amounts. The perpetual method requires recording the cost of goods sold as inventory items are sold. The periodic method involves making a physical count of goods on hand and subtracting this amount from the total goods available for sale to determine the cost of goods sold. Each inventory system can be maintained on either a dollar or unit basis or both.

Two basic general classifications of cost used for purposes of income determination are product costs and period costs. A product cost is a cost which can be directly identified with the purchase or manufacture of goods that are available for sale. A period cost, which is usually associated with the passage of time, is recognized on the income statement as an expense of the period in which it is incurred.

Where inventory items are purchased at different prices, certain assumptions regarding cost flows must be made to allocate costs between cost of goods sold and ending inventory. The average cost method assumes that all units should carry the same cost. The first-in, first-out (Fifo) method assumes that the cost of the first item acquired or produced is the cost of the first item used or sold. The last-in, first-out (Lifo) method assumes that the cost of the last item received or produced is the cost of the first item used or sold. Currently, the Fifo method results in balance sheet valuations that reflect current cost more appropriately than Lifo, but the Lifo method results in a better matching of current costs with current revenues.

For a variety of reasons, firms may wish to estimate ending inventory amounts instead of taking an actual physical count. Two methods for such estimation are the retail method and the gross profit method. Neither of these should be considered costing methods; they are basically methods of estimating cost.

KEY DEFINITIONS

Average inventory method The average inventory method is a method based on the theory that one unit cannot be distinguished from another. The average cost is computed by dividing the total cost of the beginning inventory plus purchases by the total number of units.

Beginning inventory Beginning inventory includes the goods which are on hand and available for sale at the beginning of the period.

Cost of goods sold Cost of goods sold is the cost of the inventory sold during the period. Beginning inventory plus purchases minus the ending inventory equals the cost of goods sold.

Cost of inventory Cost of inventory is the price of the inventory itself plus all direct and indirect outlays incurred in order to bring it to the firm's location in the desired form.

Cost percentage Cost percentage is the percentage obtained from the ratio of the goods available for sale at cost to the goods available for sale at selling price. This percentage is used in the retail method in order to calculate the estimated cost of the ending inventory.

Discounts lost Discounts lost is an account used under the net method of recording purchases to record the amount of the discounts which were not taken.

Ending inventory Ending inventory is goods which are still on hand and available for sale at the end of the period.

Expenses Expenses are outflows or other using up of assets or incurrences of liabilities (or a combination of both) during a period from delivering or producing goods, rendering services, or carrying out other activities that constitute the entity's ongoing major or central operations.

F.O.B. F.O.B. means "free on board."

F.O.B. destination F.O.B. destination terms would require the seller to pay all shipping costs.

F.O.B. shipping point F.O.B. shipping point means that the seller pays the costs to the shipping point only. The buyer pays the cost of transit from the shipping point to the destination.

Finished goods inventory Finished goods inventory includes completed goods which are held for resale.

First-in, first-out (Fifo) Fifo is an inventory method which assumes that the cost of the first item acquired or produced is the cost of the first item used or sold.

Freight-in Freight-in is the shipping costs incurred for goods purchased.

Goods available for sale Goods available for sale includes the beginning inventory plus the net purchases for the period.

Gross method Gross method is a method of recording purchases (sales) whereby purchases (sales) are recorded at the gross price.

Gross profit from sales Gross profit from sales is the difference between the revenue from sales and the cost of the goods sold.

Gross profit method This is a method which estimates the cost of the ending inventory by assuming that the relationship between sales, cost of goods sold, and gross profit remains constant.

Gross profit percentage Gross profit percentage is the gross profit or gross margin (sales minus cost of goods sold) divided by sales.

Inventories Inventories include those assets which are acquired and/or produced for sale in the continuing operations of a business.

Last-in, first-out (Lifo) Lifo is an inventory method which assumes that the cost of the last item received or produced is the cost of the first item used or sold.

Lower of cost or market Lower of cost or market is a method of pricing inventory whereby the original cost or the market value, whichever is lower, is used to value inventory for financial statement purposes.

Net method The net method is a method of recording purchases whereby purchases are recorded at the net price—that is, the gross price less the purchase discount.

Period cost A period cost is a cost which cannot be directly identified with the production of a specific product or products. It is usually more closely associated with the passage of time.

Periodic inventories Under the periodic method, the cost of goods sold is determined at the end of the period by making a physical count of the goods on hand and subtracting the cost of the goods which are still on hand from the total cost of goods available for sale. This inventory system may also be maintained on a quantity basis.

Perpetual inventories Under the perpetual method, an entry recording the cost of goods sold is usually made at the time a sale is made. This inventory system may also be maintained on a quantity basis.

Product cost A product cost is a cost which is directly associated with the production or purchase of goods that are available for sale.

Purchases Purchases include all inventory acquired by purchase during the period.

Purchase allowances Purchase allowances is an adjustment of the purchase price allowed the buyer by the seller. See sales allowances.

Purchase discounts Purchase discounts are discounts which are offered to encourage the prompt payment of purchases made on account. Purchase discounts are reflected in the accounts. It is also an account used under the gross method to record purchase discounts taken. See sales discounts.

Purchase returns Purchase returns is the account used by the buyer to record the cost of goods returned to the seller. See sales returns.

Retail method This is a method of estimating inventories which assumes that the cost of merchandise on hand at any time bears the same relationship to total retail prices as the total cost of all goods handled during the period bears to the original selling prices.

Revenues Revenues are inflows or other enhancements of assets of an entity or settlements of its liabilities (or a combination of both) during a period from delivering or producing goods, rendering services, or other activities that constitute the entity's ongoing major or central operations.

Sales allowances Sales allowances are adjustments of the purchase price allowed the buyer by the seller. See purchase allowances.

Sales discount This is a discount offered by the seller to the purchaser. See purchase discounts.

Sales returns Sales returns is the account used by the seller to record the goods returned by the buyer. See purchase returns.

Trade discount A trade discount is a quantity discount that represents an adjustment of a catalog or list price which is made in order to arrive at the selling price to a particular customer. Trade discounts are not reflected in the accounts.

QUESTIONS

1. What are the major differences between the income statements of a service organization and that of a retailer?

2. Why do businesses offer discounts and how are they recorded in the accounts?

3. Explain how the gross price method and the net price method each provide an evaluation of management. Which method is preferred?

4. Explain F.O.B. shipping point and F.O.B. destination. What effect do these have on the valuation of inventory?

5. What are two methods of inventory recordkeeping? Describe these methods.

6. How is the cost of goods sold figure arrived at under the periodic inventory method?

7. How does the perpetual inventory method act as a control?

8. Why should a company have accounting control over its inventory?

9. What are "goods available for sale"?

10. Explain the term "cost" with respect to accounting for inventories.

11. Briefly discuss three inventory cost flow methods.

12. Give examples of some kinds of inventories in which average cost, Fifo, and Lifo would actually match the flow of goods.

13. What problems of valuation occur with Fifo? With Lifo?

14. What is the main advantage of Lifo?

15. Explain the exception to the general cost rule for inventories.

16. What are some reasons why a company would want to estimate its inventory?

17. What is the basic assumption of the retail method of estimating inventory? What are some advantages of this method?

18. What is the gross profit method? When is it especially useful?

EXERCISES

19. Using the following information, calculate the total sales for the period.

Inventory purchases...................... $ 50,200
Beginning inventory...................... 10,350
Wage expense............................ 9,300
Rent expense............................ 1,500
Interest expense........................ 700
Ending inventory........................ 9,350
Net income............................. 12,000

20. The following balances were taken from the accounts of Norris Company. Using this information, calculate the amount of the beginning inventory.

Sales $510,000
Ending inventory........................ 84,000
Purchases............................... 300,000
Net income.............................. 162,000
Other expenses.......................... 108,000

21. Fill in the blanks:

Beginning inventory...................... $ 20,000
Purchases............................... *(a)*
Ending inventory........................ 22,000
Cost of goods sold...................... 54,000
Expenses................................ *(d)*
Net income............................. *(c)*
Beginning owners' equity................. 200,000
Owners' additional investments........... 12,000
Owners' withdrawals..................... 8,000
Ending owners' equity................... 230,000
Gross margin............................ *(b)*
Net sales............................... 108,000

22. Determine and fill in the missing amounts in the following situations. Each column of figures is a separate situation.

	A	B	C	D
Sales	$100,000	$100,000	$200,000	?
Beginning inventory.........	10,000	?	30,000	$15,000
Purchases...................	?	70,000	100,000	75,000
Ending inventory............	20,000	10,000	?	10,000
Cost of goods sold...........	50,000	?	110,000	?
Gross profit................	?	25,000	?	40,000
Expenses...................	?	?	60,000	25,000
Net income.................	20,000	10,000	?	?

23. Prepare journal entries to record the following transactions under both a perpetual and a periodic inventory system.

    a.   Purchased 15 dozen apples @ $2 per dozen (assume that the firm had a beginning inventory of 3 dozen apples which were purchased at $2 per dozen).

    b.   Sold 14 dozen apples @ $3 per dozen.

    c.   Counted the remaining apples and discovered that 3 dozen were on hand.

24. Scott ordered 50 cases of Swan soap, 90 cases of Sweet Breath mouthwash, 70 cases of Brush-It toothpaste, and 40 cases of Talc deodorant. Each case cost $15 regardless of the item. Carbo Distributor, the seller, extended credit terms of 2/10; n/30; however, Scott must pay the freight of $50. Carbo made an error in shipping the merchandise. Instead of the Swan soap, they shipped Rose soap. Scott agreed to keep this soap in return for a $20 allowance. Scott also returned 30 cases of Sweet Breath. Scott uses the net method for recording the purchases, and pays the balance within the discount period.

Required:

    1.   Make the journal entries for Scott.

    2.   Make the journal entries for Carbo.

25. Given below are the pertinent data for Griswold's Bookkeeping Services for August.

    a.   Purchased 100 cartons of ledger tablets @ $5 per carton during August.

    b.   Sold 90 cartons of tablets at $7.50 per carton during the month.

    c.   Incurred selling expenses of $35 during August.

    d.   On August 1, Griswold had 15 cartons of tablets on hand which had cost $5 per carton.

From the above information, prepare an income statment for Griswold's Services for the month of August.

26. Determine the missing figures in each of the following independent cases.

	Sales	Beginning Inventory	Ending Inventory	Gross Profit	Expenses	Net Income	Purchases	Cost of Goods Sold
1.	$1,000	$300	a	b	$100	c	$500	$600
2.	a	100	$200	$400	b	$200	700	c
3.	800	a	150	100	100	b	400	c

27. Grasso, Inc. began its operations on January 1, 19x1. It purchased goods for resale during the month as follows:

        January 3............................ 3 units @ $3
        January 11........................... 2 units @ $4
        January 20.......................... 3 units @ $5
        January 30.......................... 2 units @ $6

Sales for the month totaled 6 units. The selling price per unit was $10. A count of the units as of January 31, 19x1, shows four (4) units on hand.

Required:

The inventory at January 31, 19x1 would be carried at the following amounts (for each method listed below):

Fifo..................................... _____
Lifo..................................... _____
Weighted Average....................... _____

All computations should be shown.

28. On December 31, 19x1, the end of its first year of operations, the management of the Busby Company is trying to decide whether to use the Fifo or Lifo method of measuring inventory. It determines that the Lifo method would produce the lower asset amount.

Required:

1. Which method would produce the higher cost of goods sold?
2. Which method would produce the higher net income for 19x1?
3. Which method would produce the higher cost of goods available for sale for 19x1?
4. In what direction do you think prices have been moving during the year?

29. The following information was available from the records of a merchandising company at the end of an accounting period.

	At Cost	At Retail
Beginning inventory...............	$10,000	$ 20,000
Net purchases....................	69,000	100,000
Freight-in	1,000	(n/a)
Sales	(n/a)	90,000

Required:

Estimate the cost of the ending merchandise inventory using the retail inventory method.

30. Bando Company determines its ending inventory by taking a physical inventory at the end of each accounting period. On June 15, the merchandise inventory was completely destroyed by a fire. In the past, the normal gross profit rate was 20 percent. The following data were salvaged from the accounting records:

```
Inventory, January 1....................... $ 20,000
Purchases, January 1 to June 15.............  90,000
Sales, January 1 to June 15.................  100,000
```

Required:

Estimate the cost of the merchandise destroyed by the fire.

31. For the month of March, Lynn Distributors had the following transactions:

```
Sales ................................... $ 50,000
Sales returns............................   6,000
Purchases...............................  24,000
Purchase returns.........................     900
Purchase allowances......................     200
Freight .................................     575
```

Inventory at the beginning of March was $32,700. This amount, as well as the gross profit percentage of 34 percent, was obtained from the February financial statements.

Required:

Use the gross profit method to estimate the ending inventory for March.

32. For each of the following five inventory cases, give the necessary journal entry to reflect the lower of cost or market rule.

	1	*2*	*3*	*4*	*5*
Cost......................	900	750	400	1,000	620
Market (replacement cost)....	950	600	300	1,200	590

PROBLEMS   **33.** The following transactions took place during October, 19x1. Prepare the journal entries to record these transactions.

Oct. 1   Purchased merchandise from supplier A on account, $5,000.
2   Merchandise was sold on account to R.P. Jones for $1,000.
3   A $1,500 credit sale was made to J.R. Lowry.
6   Purchased merchandise from supplier B on account, $3,000.
9   Received payment from R.P. Jones.
15   Sales on account of $2,000 and $2,500 were made to K.L. Putnam and A.R. Hardy, respectively.
17   Paid supplier A in full.
18   Received payment from J.R. Lowry.
23   Sold merchandise on account to M.S. Fletcher for $2,500.
24   Received payment of half of K.L. Putnam's account.
25   Paid supplier B half of the amount owed to him.
26   Received full payment from A.R. Hardy.
30   Received balance of payment from K.L. Putnam.
31   Paid supplier B the balance of the account.

34. A trial balance of the Sport Shop at the end of the first year of its operations is:

Sport Shop
Trial Balance
December 31, 19x1

Cash..................................	$ 7,000	
Accounts receivable......................	9,000	
Supplies..............................	3,000	
Inventory, January 1.....................	0	
Accounts payable........................		$ 1,000
Notes payable..........................		4,000
Capital................................		15,000
Sales.................................		20,000
Purchases	15,000	
Wage expense..........................	4,000	
Other expense..........................	2,000	
	$40,000	$40,000

The inventory on hand at December 31, 19x1 was determined to be $3,000.

Required:

Prepare the income statement for the year ended December 31, 19x1.

35. Paul Peach opened a small office supply store on January 1, 19x1. The following trial balance was taken from the ledger at the end of the first year of operation.

Peach Office Supply
Trial Balance
December 31, 19x1

Cash.................................	$ 3,500	
Accounts receivable....................	13,500	
Inventory.............................	0	
Prepaid insurance......................	1,000	
Equipment............................	20,000	
Accounts payable......................		$ 5,000
Unearned revenue......................		15,000
Peach, capital.........................		13,000
Sales.................................		75,000
Purchases............................	40,000	
Wage expense..........................	10,000	
Rent expense..........................	12,000	
Other expense.........................	8,000	
	$108,000	$108,000

A physical count taken on December 31, 19x1, showed merchandise on hand in the amount of $7,000. Other information available on December 31 included the following:

a.   The equipment was purchased on January 1, 19x1, and had an estimated useful life of 10 years and no salvage value.

b.   The amount of insurance that expired during the year was $400.

c.   Certain customers paid in advance for regular deliveries of supplies. The amounts collected were credited to Unearned Revenue. As of December 31, $5,000 of the supplies purchased had been delivered.

d.   Accrued wages payable amounted to $500.

Required:

1.   Prepare the necessary adjusting journal entries at December 31, 19x1.

2.   Prepare the entries required to close the books.

3.   Prepare an income statement for the year ended December 31, 19x1.

36.   The following transactions took place between Flintstone's Friendly Fish Market and Barney's Beanery during June of 19x1.

June   1   Barney buys the following items from Flintstone:

> 10 cases of Charlie the Tuna Fish @ $10 per case
> 1 Fishing submarine @ $2,000,000

Terms of the sale are 2/10; n/30. The purchase was made on account.

9   Barney notifies Flintstone that the shipment included eight cases as ordered, one case of horse meat, and one case of caviar. The submarine was O.K. Barney proposes that he keep the caviar and deduct 50¢ from the net amount which would otherwise be due. He plans to return the horse meat. Flintstone agrees and Barney mails him a check for the net amount after making the agreed-on deductions.

15   Barney pays for the submarine.

Required:

1.   Record the above transactions on Flintstone's books assuming that he records sales using the gross method.

2.   Record the above transactions on Barney's books assuming he uses:

a.   The net method of recording purchases.

b.   The gross method of recording purchases.

37. Prepare the necessary journal entries for the Doyle Company for the following transactions. Make one set of entries assuming a perpetual inventory system, then make another assuming a periodic inventory system. In each case, assume inventory is determined on a Fifo basis.

Jan. 1   Purchased 7 stoves at $300 each (assume no beginning inventory).
      3   Sold 2 stoves for $380 each.
      7   Sold 3 stoves for $370 each.
     11   Purchased 11 stoves at $260 each.
     19   Sold 1 stove for $370.
     23   Sold 3 stoves for $350.
     28   Purchased 5 stoves at $310 each.
     31   Ending inventory was 14 stoves.

38. Peterson Company sells a single product. The company began 19x1 with 20 units of the product on hand with a cost of $4 each. During 19x1 Peterson made the following purchases:

February 3, 19x1......................10 units @ $5
April 16, 19x1........................25 units @ $6
October 6, 19x1.......................10 units @ $7
December 7, 19x1......................10 units @ $8

During the year, 50 units of the product were sold. The periodic inventory method is used.

Required:

Compute the ending inventory balance and the cost of goods sold under each of the following methods:

1.   Fifo.
2.   Lifo.
3.   Weighted Average.

39. Dente Company began business on January 1, 19x1. Purchases of merchandise for resale during 19x1 were as follows:

January 1.....................	300 units @ $3.00	$ 900.00
February 7....................	600 units @ $3.50	2,100.00
March 25.....................	400 units @ $3.00	1,200.00
October 6....................	800 units @ $2.50	2,000.00
November 10.................	300 units @ $2.50	750.00
November 16.................	300 units @ $2.25	675.00
	2,700 units	$7,625.00

A total of 2,200 units were sold during 19x1.

Required:

1. Compute the ending inventory at December 31, 19x1, under each of the following methods: (1) Fifo; (2) Lifo; (3) Average.
2. Considering the information given above and your computations for Dente Company, answer the following:

    a. Would the net income for 19x1 have been greater if the company had used (a) Fifo or (b) Lifo in computing its inventory?
    b. Assume that the market cost of the merchandise sold by Dente Company was $2.15 per unit at December 31, 19x1. Assuming the Fifo method of inventory valuation, what would the *total* carrying value of the inventory be if the lower of cost or market method is used?
    c. Give the journal entry necessary to reduce the inventory to market in (b) above.

40. On February 1, 19x1, the Sporting Goods Department of the Most Store had an inventory of $11,000 at retail selling price; the cost of this merchandise was $8,000.

    During the three months ended April 30, purchases of $18,000 were made for that department and were marked to sell for $25,000. Freight-in on this merchandise was $1,000. Sales for the period amounted to $25,000. Sales returns and allowances were $900.

    The physical inventory at retail amounted to $2,500.

Required:

Estimate the cost of theft or shrinkage.

41. The McDermott Company had a fire on June 30, 19x2, which completely destroyed its inventory. No physical inventory count had been taken since December 31, 19x1. The company's books showed the following balances at the date of the fire:

Sales		$180,000
Sales returns and allowances..............	$ 1,400	
Inventory, December 31, 19x1.............	40,000	
Purchases.............................	130,000	
Purchases returns and allowances..........		2,000
Transportation-in	1,600	
Selling expenses........................	50,000	
Administrative expenses..................	30,000	

Assume that the company's records show that in prior years it made a gross profit of approximately 25 percent of net sales, and there is no indication that this percentage cannot be considered to have continued during the first six months of this year.

Required:

Determine the cost of inventory destroyed by fire on June 30, 19x2.

42. A condensed income statement for the year ended December 31, 19x1 for Murcer Products shows the following:

Sales	$80,000
Cost of goods sold	50,000
Gross profit on sales	$30,000
Expenses	20,000
Net income	$10,000

An investigation of the records discloses the following errors in summarizing transactions for 19x1.

a. Ending inventory was overstated by $3,100.
b. Accrued expenses of $400 and prepaid expenses of $900 were not given accounting recognition at the end of 19x1.
c. Sales of $250 were not recorded although the goods were shipped and excluded from the inventory.
d. Purchases of $3,000 were made at the end of 19x1 but were not recorded although the goods were received and included in the ending inventory.

Required:

1. Prepare a corrected income statement for 19x1.
2. Prepare the entries necessary to correct the accounts in 19x1, assuming the books have not been closed.

43. The Yost Company began business on January 1, 19x1. Its reported net losses for the calendar years 19x1 and 19x2 were as follows:

19x1	$95,000 loss
19x2	$40,000 loss

Selected information from its accounting records is presented below:

Purchases of Goods for Resale

Date	Units		Price
February 1, 19x1.................	10,000	@	$10
May 1, 19x1......................	10,000	@	12
September 1, 19x1................	10,000	@	15
December 1, 19x1................	10,000	@	18
January 1, 19x2..................	10,000	@	20
March 1, 19x2....................	10,000	@	24
June 1, 19x2.....................	10,000	@	25
November 1, 19x2................	10,000	@	26

Sales

19x1	25,000 units
19x2	40,000 units

Other data:

The company uses the last-in, first-out (Lifo) method of inventory valuation.

Required:

1. Using the company's present inventory method (Lifo) compute:

    a. Ending inventory for the calendar years 19x1 and 19x2.
    b. Cost of goods sold for the calendar years 19x1 and 19x2.

2. Determine what the net income or net loss for each year would have been if the company had used the first-in, first-out (Fifo) method of inventory valuation.

44. Selected data for the Vernon Co., is as follows:

	Sales	Purchases
October	$10,000	$ 8,000
November	12,000	8,000
December	13,000	10,000

The inventory on hand at October 1st had a cost of $4,000. Goods are sold at a gross profit of 20 percent on sales.

Required:

Estimate the cost of the inventory on hand at October 31, November 30, and December 31.

45. Purchases and sales for the Yastrzemski Company are as follows:

Date		Event	Units	Unit Cost	Total Value
June	1	Balance	300	$1.00	$300.00
	8	Sale	150		
			150		
	15	Purchase	330	2.00	660.00
			480		
	23	Sale	300		
			180		
	29	Purchase	400	2.10	840.00
	30	Balance	580		

Required: (Assume a periodic inventory.)

1. What is ending inventory under Fifo?
2. Determine ending inventory under Lifo.
3. Under Fifo, what is the cost of goods that were sold on June 23?
4. Using the average price, what is ending inventory?
5. Determine gross profit on sales of $4,000 for June, assuming the average, Fifo, and Lifo methods of inventory accounting.

46. Tiant Company began business on January 1, 19x1. During 19x1, it reported a loss of $104,000; during 19x2, it had a loss of $60,000.

Selected information from its accounting records is presented below.

Purchases of Goods for Resale

Date	Units		Price
January 1, 19x1....................	10,000	@	$11
April 1, 19x1.....................	10,000	@	13
August 1, 19x1....................	10,000	@	14
November 1, 19x1.................	10,000	@	16
February 1, 19x2.................	10,000	@	17
May 1, 19x2......................	10,000	@	20
August 1, 19x2...................	10,000	@	22
October 1, 19x2..................	10,000	@	23

Sales

19x1	27,000 units
19x2	42,000 units

Other data:

The company uses Lifo in valuing its inventory.

Required:

1.   Using the company's present inventory method (Lifo) compute:

    a.   Ending inventory for 19x1 and 19x2.
    b.   Cost of goods sold for 19x1 and 19x2.

2.   Determine what the net income or net loss for each year would have been if the company had used first-in, first-out (Fifo) method of inventory valuation.

Refer to the Annual Report included in the Appendix at the end of the text:

47.   Comparing the two years presented, was there an increase or decrease in inventories?

48.   What was the average inventory maintained during the most recent year?

49.   During the most recent year, what percentage profit was earned in relation to sales?

50.   During the most recent year, what were net sales?

51.   What inventory method is used?

Chapter 5 discusses the accounting procedures used for recording and allocating the cost of plant and equipment, the disposition of plant and equipment, and the accounting for intangible assets and natural resources. Studying this chapter should enable you to:

1. Identify the purpose of and information included on a fixed asset ledger card.

2. Recognize the three basic factors that must be considered in recording periodic depreciation.

3. Discuss and apply the depreciation methods discussed in the chapter.

4. Differentiate between capital expenditures and revenue expenditures.

5. Record the disposition of plant and equipment.

6. Discuss the nature of intangible assets and the computation of amortization.

7. Explain the concept of depletion of natural resources.

5

Long-Term
Assets

INTRODUCTION

The term plant and equipment refers to long-lived tangible assets which are used in the continuing operations of a business over a number of years. They are assets which are acquired for *use* in the firm's operations as contrasted to those assets which are purchased for *resale* to the customers of a business. Examples of plant and equipment include land, buildings, equipment, furniture, and fixtures. Plant and equipment may be regarded as a "bundle" of services that are used over the life of the asset in the process of generating revenue. In accordance with the matching principle, as these services expire through use in generating revenue, a portion of the cost of the asset should be allocated to expense. The costs which are to be allocated to expense in future periods may be considered deferred costs and are shown as assets on the balance sheet. This process of periodically allocating the cost of tangible plant and equipment to expense is referred to as *depreciation*.

In this chapter we will discuss the accounting procedures used to record the acquisition of long-lived assets and to determine the depreciation expense for the period.

CONTROL OVER TANGIBLE LONG-TERM ASSETS

A fixed asset ledger card should be prepared and maintained for each individual asset purchased. This card should include all of the pertinent information relating to the asset and its use. This data will enable the management of the firm to establish and maintain control over each individual asset (for example, by providing the basis for taking a physical inventory of all fixed assets owned by the firm). It will also assist in accounting for all transactions relating to plant assets. For example, the fixed asset ledger card will provide the information which is required in order to calculate the periodic depreciation expense for the asset and the data required to adjust the accounts as assets are sold or retired.

Using a ledger card for an automobile as an illustration, the following information should ordinarily be provided:

Asset Ledger Account

Description	*Cost*	*Depreciation*	*Other Information*
Name of asset	Date acquired	Estimated life	Repairs
Account number	Invoice cost	Estimated salvage	Date
Asset number	Other costs	value	Amount
Manufacturer's		Depreciation to	Actual life
serial number		date	Data on disposal:
Horsepower			Date
Insurance carried			Sales price
Property tax			(if any)
valuation			Gain or loss
			To whom sold

TYPES OF PLANT AND EQUIPMENT

Plant and equipment may be classified into two categories for accounting purposes: land and depreciable assets. Since the assumption is made that land is not used up over time, the cost of land is not subject to depreciation. All other items of plant and equipment are assumed to have a limited useful life and, therefore, the cost of these items is allocated to expense through periodic depreciation charges.

ACCOUNTING FOR TANGIBLE FIXED ASSETS

All costs incurred in acquiring an asset and preparing the asset for productive use are capitalized as the cost of the asset by debiting them to the asset account. The costs include the net invoice price, transportation costs and installation costs. All costs that are incurred before the asset becomes productive, such as demolition of old buildings on a building site or repairs of or to used equipment acquired for production, is considered to be a cost of the acquired asset. A proper determination of the total cost of a plant asset is important because the cost of an asset (less any salvage value, i.e., the amount the firm can recover when the firm has finished using it) becomes an expense which should be charged against the income of the business during the periods the asset is used by the firm. . This process of allocating the cost of an asset to expense is known as depreciation.

Plant assets are normally acquired either by cash purchase or by incurring a liability (or by a combination of a cash down payment and incurring a liability for future payments). If a liability is incurred, the interest cost associated with the liability should be recorded as interest expense and not as a cost of the asset acquired. Plant assets may also be acquired in exchange for other assets owned by the firm. The procedures used in accounting for assets acquired by exchange are discussed later in this chapter.

In certain cases, more than a single asset may be acquired for a lump sum purchase price. Because the assets acquired may have different useful lives (or, in the case of land, an unlimited life), it is necessary to allocate the total purchase price among the assets acquired. Normally, this allocation is based upon the relative appraisal values of the assets involved. For example, assume that a company acquired land, building, and equipment for a total cost of $200,000. Assume that the company making the acquisition determined the following appraisal values for the individual items:

Land	$ 75,000
Building	150,000
Equipment	25,000
Total appraised value	$250,000

The apportionment of the $200,000 purchase price is made on the basis of the relative values of the assets and would be as follows:

Asset	Appraisal Value	Fraction of Total Appraisal Value	Allocation of Cost
Land	$ 75,000	$ 75,000/$250,000 = .3	$ 60,000
Building	150,000	$150,000/$250,000 = .6	120,000
Equipment	25,000	$ 25,000/$250,000 = .1	20,000
	$250,000		$200,000

The cost of an asset includes all expenditures which are necessary to acquire the asset and place it in use. For example, a company buys a delivery truck with a list price of $10,000. The company received a 10% reduction in price from the dealer and also a 2% cash discount. The company pays a 5% sales tax and in addition, purchases a stereo for the truck paying $300 including installation. The cost of the new truck is computed as follows:

List price......................	$10,000
Less 10% reduction.............	1,000
	$ 9,000
Less 2% cash discount..........	180
	$ 8,820
Sales taxes....................	441
Stereo........................	300
Cost of the truck..............	$ 9,561

The $9,561 cost is the balance in the asset account and is the basis for computing depreciation. To charge the sales tax and the stereo to the expenses in the year the truck is acquired would overstate expenses for that period and understate expenses for the following periods.

Land. The cost of land includes the purchase price, commissions, any taxes due, and other similar costs. Any cost incurred to grade, level and demolish old buildings are added to the cost of the land but any proceeds from the sale of scrap reduces the cost. Land is not subject to depreciation and its cost is retained in the land account until it is sold.

Buildings. The cost of constructing a building includes excavation, building materials, labor, and all other costs necessary to place the building in use. Costs such as interest on borrowed construction funds and real estate taxes incurred during the construction are also part of the total building cost.

Machinery and equipment. In addition to the normal costs of acquiring machinery and equipment, such costs as supports, wiring, inspection and testing are charged to the machinery and equipment account.

DEPRECIATION   Depreciation is the process of allocating the cost of an asset to the periods in which services are received from the asset. The basic nature of and the problems involved in depreciation accounting may be illustrated by the use of a simple example. Assume that you decide to purchase a Chevrolet Impala for use as a taxi cab. The cost of the auto is $9,000. You feel that you will be able to earn approximately $12,000 each year in fares, and the estimated operating costs (gas, oil, repairs, insurance, etc.) will be approximately $4,000 per year. You further estimate that the auto will last for four years at which time it will probably have to be replaced. At the end of the four-year period you estimate that your used Chevrolet may be sold for about $1,000. What would your earnings be over the four years if your estimates prove to be accurate? Total income for the four-year period might be calculated as follows:

Your Taxi Company
Income Statement
For Four Years

Revenues ($12,000 per year for 4 years)................		$48,000
Operating costs ($4,000 per year for 4 years)............	$16,000	
Cost of the taxi ($9,000 cost less $1,000 received from its sale at the end of the four-year period)................................	8,000	
Total costs......................................		24,000
Net income.......................................		$24,000

Assume now that you wished to prepare separate income statements for each of the four years. You could do the following:

Your Taxi Company
Income Statements

			For the Year		
	1	*2*	*3*	*4*	*Total*
Revenues............	$12,000	$12,000	$12,000	$12,000	$48,000
Operating costs......	$ 4,000	$ 4,000	$ 4,000	$ 4,000	$16,000
Cost of the taxi.......	9,000	0	0	(1,000)[1]	8,000
	$13,000	$ 4,000	$ 4,000	$ 3,000	$24,000
Net income (loss).....	($1,000)	$ 8,000	$ 8,000	$ 9,000	$24,000

---

[1] The negative thousand dollars shown as "cost of the taxi" represents the proceeds received from its sale at the end of the fourth year—i.e., its salvage value.

But do these statements really reflect the actual facts of the situation? Is it reasonable to report that your income increased significantly during year 2, remained constant during the third year and then increased slightly in year 4? Of course not. The total for the four years seems to be reasonable, but the problem lies in attempting to measure the income for *each* individual year. This difficulty arises because you purchased the car and paid for it at the beginning of year 1, used it for four years and sold it at the end of the fourth year. In order to measure the income for each year properly, it is necessary to allocate, in a rational and systematic manner, the net cost of owning the auto (i.e., the purchase price of the car less its estimated salvage value) over the periods which benefit from its use.

As previously indicated, the process of amortizing or charging the cost of a fixed asset to expense over the period of its useful life is referred to as depreciation. A more formal definition of depreciation is ". . . the systematic allocation of the cost of an asset, less salvage value (if any) over its estimated useful life."

From a theoretical viewpoint, depreciation expense for a particular period represents an estimate of the portion of the cost of an asset which is used up or which otherwise expires during that period. A precise determination of the depreciation expense related to an individual asset for any given year is difficult because it is almost impossible to accurately predict the exact useful life of an asset. The life of an asset, and therefore its depreciation, is affected by a combination of factors such as the passage of time, normal wear and tear, physical deterioration, and obsolescence. Even though the various techniques which can be employed in determining the depreciation may appear to be precise, and from a mathematical viewpoint they are, it should be noted that because of the estimating of useful life, salvage value, etc., depreciation is always an estimate or approximation. However, periodic measurement of that portion of the cost of an asset which has been used up or has expired during a period is a necessary element in determining the income of the firm for that period. Depreciation accounting is a method of allocation by which an attempt is made to "match" the cost of an asset against the revenue which has been generated or produced from using the asset.

ELEMENTS AFFECTING THE DETERMINATION OF PERIODIC DEPRECIATION

The depreciation process represents the allocation of the costs (less any estimated residual or salvage value) of property, plant and equipment over the expected useful life of the asset. As discussed previously, the cost of a long-lived asset includes all of the expenditures associated with its acquisition and preparation for use. The additional factors which must be considered in the estimate of periodic depreciation for an asset include:

1.　Estimated Useful Life
2.　Estimated Salvage (Residual) Value
3.　Methods of Allocation

USEFUL LIFE

The useful life of an asset is that period of time during which it is of economic use to the business. The estimation of the useful life of an asset should consider such factors as economic analysis, engineering studies, previous experience with similar assets, and any other available information concerning the characteristics of the asset. However, regardless of the quantity of information available, the determination of the useful life of an asset is a judgment process which requires the prediction of future events.

The period of economic usefulness of an asset to a business is a function of both physical and functional factors. Physical factors include normal wear, deterioration and decay, and damage or destruction. These physical factors limit the economic useful life of an asset by rendering the asset incapable of effectively performing its intended function. Thus, the physical factors limit the maximum potential economic life of the asset.

Functional factors may also cause the useful life of an asset to be less than its physical life. The primary functional factors which may limit the service life of an asset are obsolescence and inadequacy. Obsolescence is caused by changes in technology or changes in demand for the output product or services which cause the asset to be inefficient or uneconomical before the end of its physical life. Inadequacy may result from changes in the size or volume of activity which cause an asset to be economically incapable of handling or processing the required output. In a high technology, growth-oriented economy such as that of the United States, functional factors generally impact significantly upon the determination of the useful life of an asset.

SALVAGE VALUE

Salvage value is the estimated realizable value of an asset at the end of its expected life. Depending upon the expectations regarding the disposition of an asset, this amount may be based on such factors as scrap value, second-hand market value or anticipated trade-in value. The depreciation base used for an asset normally is equal to the difference between the acquisition cost of the asset and its salvage value.

This depreciation base is the amount of the cost of an asset which is allocated to expense over the expected useful life of the asset.

The relationship between salvage value and the cost of an asset varies considerably. In some cases, particularly when the estimated useful life of an asset is significantly less than its physical life, salvage value may be substantial. On the other hand, in certain instances, the estimated residual value of an asset may be so small that the salvage value is assumed to be zero in computing the depreciation base. Of course, the validity of the periodic depreciation expense is dependent upon a reasonably accurate estimate of both the salvage value of an asset and its useful life.

DEPRECIATION METHODS

Theoretically, the selection of a depreciation method should be based on the expectations regarding the pattern of decline in the service potential of the asset under consideration. Because both the nature and the characteristics of various assets may vary significantly, alternative depreciation patterns may be justified. Accordingly, there are a number of acceptable depreciation methods which mathematically approximate the possible pattern of use expected from an asset. However, in practice, the criteria for selecting a particular depreciation method are often not determinable. It has been suggested by some that depreciation accounting is used by management as a factor in implementing its financial policy. That is, management may select the method(s) which contribute to the desired financial results that it hopes to achieve over time. The consistency principle does require that once a method has been adopted for a particular type of asset, the firm must continue to use that method over time. Because of the number of alternative methods which are available, the depreciation expense for each period may vary significantly depending upon the method selected. Each of the methods, however, results in the identical total depreciation expense over the useful life of the asset(s).

In recording the periodic depreciation for fixed costs, three basic factors must be considered:

1.   The cost of the asset—the invoice cost plus all costs which are necessary to place it in use.
2.   The estimated useful life of the asset.
3.   The estimated salvage or scrap value of the asset—the amount which will be recovered when the asset is retired.

This section of the chapter will discuss four of the methods which are used in accounting for the use of long-term tangible assets in the operations of businesses: the straight-line method, the declining-balance method, the sum-of-the-years'-digits method and the accelerated cost recovery system. Each of these methods results in identical total depreciation over the life of a fixed asset—an amount equal to the original cost of the asset or, when appropriate, the original cost less its estimated salvage value. The methods differ, however, in the amount of cost which is allocated to expense during each year of the life of the asset. To illustrate these techniques, the following data will be used:

```
Type of asset................................ Chevrolet Impala
Date acquired............................... January 1, 19x1
Cost (including delivery, sales tax, etc.)............ $9,000
Estimated useful life.......................... 4 years
Estimated salvage value....................... $1,000
```

Straight-Line Depreciation. One of the simplest and most commonly used methods of computing depreciation is the straight-line method. This method considers the passage of time to be the most important single factor or limitation on the useful life of an asset. It assumes that other factors such as wear and tear and obsolescence are somewhat proportional to the elapsed time; this may or may not be the case in fact. The straight-line method allocates the cost of an asset, less its salvage value, to expense equally over its useful life. A formula which may be employed in calculating depreciation using the straight-line method is as follows:

$$\frac{\left(\begin{array}{c}\text{Cost of} \\ \text{the Asset}\end{array} - \begin{array}{c}\text{Estimated} \\ \text{Salvage} \\ \text{Value}\end{array}\right)}{\text{Estimated Useful Life}} = \text{Depreciation for the Period}$$

Substituting the illustrative data presented above in the formula, we obtain the following calculation of depreciation for 19x1:

$$\frac{(\$9,000 - \$1,000)}{4 \text{ years}} = \$2,000 \text{ Per Year}$$

Since the straight-line method of depreciation allocates an identical dollar amount of depreciation expense to each period, depreciation for the years 19x2, 19x3 and 19x4 (the remaining useful life of the automobile) would also be $2,000 each year.

Accelerated Methods of Depreciation. Businessmen recognize that the benefits obtained from the use of a fixed asset frequently may not be uniform over its useful life. Both the revenue-producing ability of an asset and its value may decline at a faster rate during the early years of its life. Also, the costs of repairing and maintaining the asset may increase during the later years of its life. Furthermore, one accelerated depreciation method, Accelerated Cost Recovery System (ACRS) is permitted for income tax purposes and may benefit the taxpayer by postponing or deferring the payment of taxes to a later year. Although a business may use different methods of computing depreciation for accounting and tax purposes, firms often wish to simplify their recordkeeping by using the same method for both purposes. For these reasons, many businesses will adopt ACRS. In general, accelerated methods of calculating depreciation allow the recording of larger amounts of depreciation in the early periods of an asset's life than in later years. As indicated above, a business may choose to employ the ACRS method for computing the expense relating to the use of its fixed assets for tax purposes because the increased depreciation charges (which do not require the outlay of cash, since the cash expenditure was made at the time the asset was acquired) reduce taxable income and therefore reduce the amount of income tax currently payable. By postponing or deferring the payment of income taxes from an earlier to a later year of an asset's life, the business has obtained, in effect, an interest-free loan from the taxing authority.[2]

Three commonly-used methods of accelerated depreciation will be illustrated: the double-declining balance method, the sum-of-the-years'-digits method and ACRS.

The Double-Declining Balance Method. The procedures used in applying the double-declining balance method arbitrarily double the depreciation rate which would be used in calculating depreciation under the straight-line method.[3] This increased rate is then applied to the book value (i.e., the cost of the asset less the total depreciation taken to date) of the assets. The formula used in calculating double-declining balance depreciation is as follows:

$$(2 \times \text{Straight-Line Rate}) \times (\text{Cost} - \text{Depreciation Taken in Prior Periods})$$
$$= \text{Depreciation for the Period}$$

Salvage value is ignored in the computation of depreciation under the double-declining balance method with the exception of the final year. In the final year of the asset's life, the formula is ignored and the depreciation taken is simply whatever amount is necessary to reduce the book value of the asset to its salvage value.

Using the same data as in the previous example, the calculation of double-declining balance depreciation may be illustrated as follows:

$$(2 \times 25\%) \times (\$9,000 - \$0) = \$4,500 \text{ Depreciation for 19x1}$$

The straight-line rate is 25 percent; since the asset has a useful life of four years, one-fourth (or 25 percent) of the cost is expensed each year using the straight-line method. The doubled rate (2×25 percent) is applied to the full cost of $9,000 since the salvage value is ignored in the initial years of the asset's life and there is, of course, no depreciation from prior years.

The depreciation charge for 19x2 would be calculated as follows:

---

[2] See Chapter 12 for a detailed discussion of income tax allocation.

[3] The straight-line rate may be calculated by dividing the useful life of the asset (in years) into 100%. For the example used, the straight-line rate would be 100% divided by 4 or 25%.

$$(2 \times 25\%) \times (\$9,000 - \$4,500) = \$2,250 \text{ Depreciation for 19x2}$$

The only change from the previous year is that $4,500, the depreciation taken in 19x1, is substituted for $0 in the first calculation.

Depreciation for 19x3 would be:

$$(2 \times 25\%) \times (\$9,000 - \$6,750) = \$1,125 \text{ Depreciation for 19x3}$$

Again, the only change in the formula is in the depreciation taken in prior years. The $6,750 amount used in the computation of depreciation for 19x3 is the 19x1 depreciation of $4,500 plus the 19x2 depreciation of $2,250.

The formula would not be used to calculate the depreciation expense for 19x4, since this is the final year of the asset's useful life. Depreciation for 19x4 would be computed as follows:

Cost of the asset..............................		$9,000
Less: Depreciation taken in prior years:		
19x1....................................	$4,500	
19x2....................................	2,250	
19x3....................................	1,125	7,875
Net book value of the asset at January 1, 19x4.....		$1,125
Less: Estimated salvage value...............		1,000
Depreciation for 19x4........................		$ 125

The Sum-of-the-Years'-Digits Method. The use of the sum-of-the-years'-digits method also produces greater charges for depreciation in the early years of an asset's useful life. The life-years of an asset are totaled[4] and utilized as the denominator of a fraction that uses the number of years of life remaining from the beginning of the year (i.e., the years in reverse order) as the numerator. This fraction is then applied to the cost of the asset less its estimated salvage value in order to compute the depreciation for the period.

Again, using the same data as in the previous illustrations, the depreciation expense for each of the four years, 19x1 through 19x4, using the sum-of-the-years'-digits method, would be calculated as follows:

Sum-of-the-years'-digits:

$$1 + 2 + 3 + 4 = 10$$

---

[4] The sum of the numbers from one to the estimated life of an asset in years. For example, the life-years of an asset with a 3-year estimated life would be $1 + 2 + 3 = 6$. [Sum of arithmetic progression of n consecutive numbers $= n \dfrac{(n + 1)}{2}$.]

Depreciation for each period:

$$19x1: \quad \frac{4}{10} \times (\$9,000 - \$1,000) = \$3,200$$
$$19x2: \quad \frac{3}{10} \times (\$9,000 - \$1,000) = \$2,400$$
$$19x3: \quad \frac{2}{10} \times (\$9,000 - \$1,000) = \$1,600$$
$$19x4: \quad \frac{1}{10} \times (\$9,000 - \$1,000) = \$\ 800$$

Effective January 1, 1981, the Accelerated Cost Recovery System (ACRS) was implemented, introducing significant changes in the manner in which depreciation expense is computed for federal income tax purposes. ACRS procedures were modified by the Tax Reform Act of 1986. While the straight-line, sum-of-the-years'-digits and double-declining balance methods may still be used for financial accounting and reporting purposes, ACRS methods are the only accelerated methods which may be used for federal income tax purposes.[5] Essentially, ACRS places all depreciable assets into six classes of depreciable personal property or to one of two classes of real property using pre-1981 asset depreciation range (ADR) guidelines as a basis for classification, as summarized below:

Recovery Property

ACRS Class and Method	ADR Midpoint	Special Rules
3- year, 200% declining balance	4 years or less	Includes some race horses. Excludes cars and light trucks.
5-year, 200% declining balance	More than 4 years to less than 10	Includes cars and light trucks, semiconductor manufacturing equipment, qualified technological equipment, computer-based central-office switching equipment, some renewable and biomass power facilities, and research and development property.
7-year, 200% declining balance	10 years to less than 16	Includes single-purpose agricultural and horticultural structures and railroad track. Includes property with no ADR midpoint.
10-year, 200% declining balance	16 years to less than 20	None
15-year, 150% declining balance	20 years to less than 25	Includes sewage treatment plants, telephone distribution plant and comparable equipment for two-way voice and data communication.
20-year, 150% declining balance	25 years or more	Excludes real property with ADR midpoint of 27.5 years or more. Includes municipal sewers.
27.5-year, straight-line	N/A	Residential rental property
31.5-year, straight-line	N/A	Nonresidential real property

---

[5] As a general statement for plant and equipment acquired prior to 1981, the depreciation methods that are permissable for tax purposes are: straight-line, double-declining balance, and sum-of-the-years'-digits. For years after 1980, the Economic Recovery Tax Act of 1981 provides an Accelerated Cost Recovery System (ACRS) that was modified by the Tax Reform Act of 1986.

Although the property classes described above are identified by years, the concept of useful life for the calculation of depreciation expense has been discontinued under the ACRS rules. Rather, depreciation expense for the 3-, 5-, 7- and 10-year classes is calculated using double-declining balance depreciation. Depreciation on assets in the 15- and 20-year classes is computed using the 150 percent declining balance method. A switch to a straight-line approach is permitted in the year that the depreciation expense using the straight-line method exceeds ACRS depreciation. The straight-line method must be used for all real estate and under ACRS rules, a taxpayer may elect to use the straight-line method of depreciation rather than ACRS. Also, the taxpayer electing ACRS must use the half-year convention which requires that the taxpayer take one-half year's depreciation expense in the year an asset is acquired and disposed of, regardless of the actual dates. Salvage value may be ignored in calculating depreciation under ACRS.

Using the same data as in the previous examples, the depreciation expense using ACRS would be calculated as follows:

					Annual	Cumulative
19x1:	$(2 \times 20\%)$	$\times$	$(\$9,000 - 0) \times \frac{1}{2}$	$=$	$1,800	$1,800
19x2:	$(2 \times 20\%)$	$\times$	$(\$9,000 - \$1,800)$	$=$	2,880	4,680
19x3:	$(2 \times 20\%)$	$\times$	$(\$9,000 - \$4,680)$	$=$	1,728	6,408
19x4:	$(2 \times 20\%)$	$\times$	$(\$9,000 - \$6,408)$	$=$	1,037	7,445
19x5:	$(2 \times 20\%)$	$\times$	$(\$9,000 - \$7,445)$	$=$	622	8,067
19x6:	$\$9,000 - \$8,067$			$=$	833	9,000

Note that only one-half year's depreciation is taken in 19x1, the year of acquisition, because of the half-year convention. The remaining undepreciated cost is charged to depreciation in 19x6, also because of the half-year convention.

As is now apparent, except for ACRS (which ignores salvage value), the *total* amount of depreciation taken for a fixed asset over its useful life will be identical regardless of the method used, although the timing and pattern of the depreciation charges vary widely according to the particular method chosen. The effects of the various methods on the example data are illustrated below.

Year	Straight-line	Double-Declining Balance	Sum-of-the Years'-Digits	ACRS
19x1	$2,000	$4,500	$3,200	$1,800
19x2	2,000	2,250	2,400	2,880
19x3	2,000	1,125	1,600	1,728
19x4	2,000	125	800	1,037
19x5	0	0	0	622
19x6	0	0	0	833
Total............	$8,000	$8,000	$8,000	$9,000

The differences in the depreciation expense depending on the method chosen are illustrated graphically below.

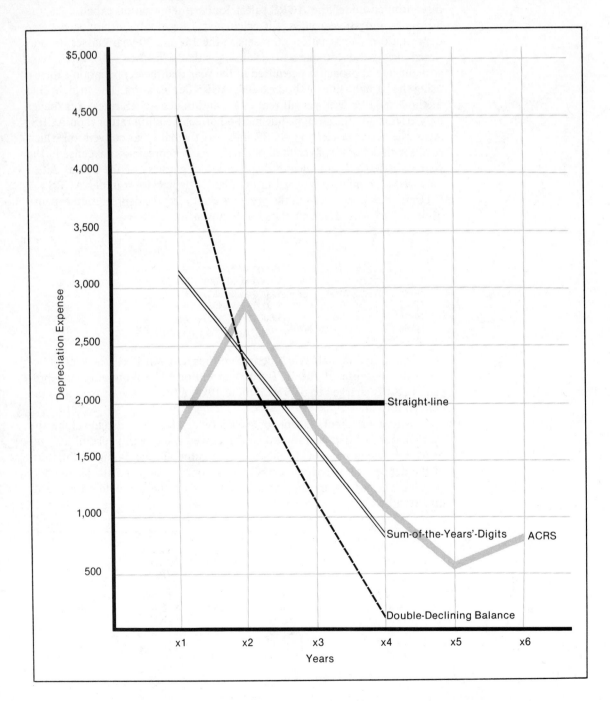

Because depreciation expense is an important factor which enters into the determination of the income of a firm for a period, the reported income will also vary according to the depreciation method selected. The effect of depreciation on the reported income of the firm (and therefore its income taxes) is an important factor in the selection of the depreciation method(s) a firm will use.

RECORDING LONG-TERM ASSETS

Using the Chevrolet Impala acquired by Your Taxi Company as an example, the accounting procedures for recording the acquisition and use of plant assets will be illustrated.

On January 1, 19x1, the acquisition of the automobile would be recorded as follows:

Automobile	9,000	
Cash		9,000

It should be noted that the debit to the asset account was for the total cost of the Chevrolet including delivery charges, sales tax, etc. In this instance the car was paid for in cash. Had a liability been incurred, it would have been recorded by a credit. The procedures required when an old asset is traded in on a new asset are discussed later in this chapter.

At the end of 19x1, it would be necessary to record depreciation on the asset in order to charge to expense the portion of the cost of the asset which had been "used up" during the period. For purposes of illustration, we will assume that the straight-line method of depreciation was used. On December 31, 19x1, depreciation would be recorded in the books of Your Taxi Company by the following entry:

Depreciation expense	2,000	
Accumulated depreciation		2,000

The debit to depreciation expense records the portion of the cost of the asset which is to be charged as an expense of the period. The credit to the accumulated depreciation account adds the current period's depreciation to that which was taken in prior years (in this case zero since this is the initial year of the asset's useful life); the total of this account indicates the total amount of depreciation taken to date at any given point in time. The depreciation expense of $2,000 would appear in the income statement along with the other expenses of the period and would be deducted from revenue in the determination of income. Accumulated depreciation would appear as an offset (called a contra account) against the related asset account in the balance sheet as follows:

Current assets............................			$10,000
Automobile............................		$9,000	
Less: Accumulated depreciation..........		2,000	7,000
Total assets...........................			$17,000

Since the straight-line method of depreciation was used, the entries which are required in order to record depreciation expense for the years 19x2, 19x3 and 19x4 will be the same as the one which was made on December 31, 19x1, shown above. The automobile and accumulated depreciation accounts would appear as follows:

Automobile		Accumulated Depreciation	
(a) 9,000		(b) 2,000	
		(c) 2,000	
		(d) 2,000	
		(e) 2,000	
		(f) 8,000	

Key:

(a) Cost of the automobile on January 1, 19x1.
(b) Depreciation for 19x1.
(c) Depreciation for 19x2.
(d) Depreciation for 19x3.
(e) Depreciation for 19x4.
(f) Balance in the account at December 31, 19x5.

Occasionally, plant assets are used for periods of time beyond their originally estimated lives. Since the purpose or objective of depreciation accounting is to allocate the cost of a plant asset to expense over its useful life, no additional depreciation should be recorded for an asset which has already been fully depreciated. The cost of the asset, along with the associated accumulated depreciation, should remain in the accounts until the asset is disposed of.

Assets Acquired During the Period

In the example used in the previous section, the automobile was acquired at the beginning of the period. In practice, assets will be acquired throughout the accounting period and this will require that depreciation be recorded for a part of a period in the year of acquisition. For example, the purchase of the automobile on June 1, 19x1, would be recorded as follows:

Automobile............................	9,000	
Cash		9,000

At the end of 19x1, it would be necessary to record depreciation on the asset for the seven-month period that it was used during the year (June 1, 19x1 to December 31, 19x1). Again, we will assume the same facts as before (4-year life, $1,000 salvage value) and that the straight-line method of depreciation was used, so the calculation would be as follows:

$$\frac{(\$9,000 - \$1,000)}{4 \text{ years}} = \$2,000 \text{ per year}$$

$$\frac{\$2,000}{12 \text{ months}} = \$166.67 \text{ per month}$$

Depreciation for the period June 1, 19x1 to December 31, 19x1 would be 7 months × \$166.67 per month or a total of \$1,167 (rounded). At December 31, 19x1, depreciation for the period would be recorded by the following entry:

Depreciation expense...................	1,167	
Accumulated depreciation.............		1,167

The entries to record depreciation expense for the years 19x2, 19x3, and 19x4 would each cover a full year and each would be as follows:

Depreciation expense...................	2,000	
Accumulated depreciation.............		2,000

In 19x5, depreciation would be recorded for the final five months of the life of the asset (5 months × \$166.67 per month or \$833) by the following entry:

Depreciation expense...................	833	
Accumulated depreciation.............		833

The automobile and accumulated depreciation accounts would appear as follows:

Automobile		Accumulated Depreciation	
(a) 9,000		(b)	1,167
		(c)	2,000
		(d)	2,000
		(e)	2,000
		(f)	833
		(g)	8,000

Key:
(a)	Cost of the automobile on June 1, 19x1.
(b)	Depreciation for 19x1 (7 months).
(c)	Depreciation for 19x2 (12 months).
(d)	Depreciation for 19x3 (12 months).
(e)	Depreciation for 19x4 (12 months).
(f)	Depreciation for 19x5 (5 months).
(g)	Balance in the account at May 31, 19x5.

In the above example, depreciation was calculated from the exact date of acquisition until the end of the useful life of the asset. In practice, as a matter of convenience, a business may establish a procedure whereby it will always take six months' depreciation in the year an asset is acquired and six months' depreciation in the year it is disposed of irrespective of the exact dates of acquisition or disposal. Alternatively, a firm might take a full year's depreciation in the year of acquisition and no depreciation in the year of disposal, or vice-versa. The use of procedures such as those described above do not change the entries illustrated and are generally acceptable as long as there is no significant distortion of depreciation expense or income.

Interest Costs

Frequently, firms borrow substantial sums for the purpose of constructing or acquiring property, plant, and equipment. A basic accounting issue which exists with regard to the interest costs relating to these borrowings is whether the interest should be considered an expense of the period or included (capitalized) as a part of the cost of the asset acquired or constructed. The charging of interest to expense has been defended on the grounds that interest represents the cost of financing and is not a cost which should be associated with a specific asset. Capitalizing interest costs, on the other hand, has been justified on the basis that an asset should be charged with all of the costs necessary to place it in its intended use. It may be argued that the interest incurred is as much a cost of acquiring an asset as is the cost of any other resources used or expended.

Until recently, the proper accounting for interest costs had been an unresolved issue. In 1979, however, the FASB issued its *Statement No. 34*, ''Capitalization of Interest Costs,'' which *requires* capitalizing interest as a part of the cost of acquiring *certain* assets. In this pronouncement, the FASB concluded:

> On the premise that the historical cost of acquiring an asset should include all costs necessarily incurred to bring it to the condition and location necessary for its intended use,... in principle, the cost incurred in financing expenditures for an asset during a required construction or development period is itself a part of the asset's historical acquisition cost.

The assets which qualify for interest capitalization generally are those assets that require a period of time to place them in their intended use. Examples of these qualifying assets include those constructed for an entity's own use (e.g., a manufacturing facility) or those intended for sale or lease that are constructed as discrete projects (e.g., ships or real estate projects). Interest should not be capitalized as a part of the cost of inventories that are routinely manufactured or otherwise produced in large quantities on a repetitive basis even if these inventories require lengthy maturation periods, such as is the case with whiskey or tobacco. Interest cost eligible for capitalization is limited to amounts incurred on borrowings and other obligations. The amount to be capitalized is determined by applying an interest rate to the average amount of accumulated expenditures for the asset during the construction or development period.

**Disclosure in the
Financial Statements**

Because the amount of periodic depreciation depends on the method or methods of depreciation in use, it is necessary that information on the depreciation method(s) be disclosed in the financial statements. Such information is necessary for a meaningful comparison of the depreciation charges of different companies or for prediction of future depreciation charges of a company. Consequently, the Accounting Principles Board in Opinion No. 12 indicated that the following disclosures should be made in the financial statements or accompanying notes:

1. Depreciation expense for the period.
2. Balances of major classes of depreciable assets, by nature or function, at the balance sheet date.
3. Accumulated depreciation, either by major classes of depreciable assets or in total, at the balance sheet date.
4. A general description of the method or methods used in computing depreciation with respect to major classes of depreciable assets.[6]

**COSTS INCURRED
AFTER ACQUISITION**

It is often necessary to make additional expenditures relating to plant assets subsequent to the date of acquisition. Such expenditures are classified into one of two groups:

1. *Capital Expenditures*—Expenditures which extend the useful life or the quality of services of plant assets.
2. *Revenue Expenditures*—Expenditures for ordinary maintenance, repairs, and other items necessary for the operation and use of plant and equipment.

Since capital expenditures increase the future economic benefits of an asset, the costs incurred are recorded in an asset account. On the other hand, revenue expenditures benefit only the current operations, and these costs are recorded by debits to expense accounts.

Capital expenditures for existing assets are often classified as additions or improvements. An addition represents an increase in the physical substance

---

[6] Opinions of the Accounting Principles Board No. 12, "Omnibus Opinion - 1967" (New York: AICPA, 1967), Par. 5.

of an asset, such as a new wing on a building. Improvements (or replacements) involve the substitution of new parts on an existing asset. Examples of improvements include the installation of elevators in a building or an air conditioner in a delivery truck. If the addition or improvement has the same economic life as the existing asset, the cost should be capitalized directly to the asset account. When the expenditure extends the economic life of the asset, the depreciable life of the asset should be extended accordingly. If the item has a different economic life than the existing asset, the cost should be capitalized in a separate asset account and expensed over the period of expected benefit.

Revenue expenditures are routine and recurring expenditures which are incurred to maintain an asset in operating condition and which do not increase the economic benefits associated with the asset. Examples of typical revenue expenditures are routine maintenance (i.e., oil change and lubrication) and ordinary repairs (i.e., replacing a worn out tire).

Theoretically, if an expenditure increases the economic benefits originally expected from an asset, then the cost should be capitalized. In practice, however, it is often difficult to make a distinction between a capital expenditure and a revenue expenditure. In many companies, arbitrary policies are established for defining capital and revenue expenditures. For example, an expenditure might be capitalized only if it (1) clearly increases the economic benefits associated with an existing asset and (2) exceeds a minimum cost (such as $50). The use of a minimum cost for capitalization eliminates the need to recompute depreciation schedules for minor improvements or additions.

To illustrate the accounting for a capital expenditure, assume that in January, 19x5 a company spent $3,000 to recondition an existing delivery truck. The truck had been acquired on January 1, 19x1 for $16,000, and at that time had an estimated useful life of 5 years and a salvage value of $1,000. The truck was depreciated using the straight-line method. Therefore, as of December 31, 19x4, the balance in accumulated depreciation was $12,000 [($15,000 ÷ 5) × 4]. The company estimated that the reconditioning process would both significantly improve the gas mileage of the truck and extend the useful life to a total of 7 years (with no change in salvage value). The journal entry to record the improvement is:

Delivery truck	3,000	
Cash		3,000

The new balance in the asset account is $19,000 (the original cost plus the improvement). The remaining book value of $7,000 ($19,000 − $12,000) less the estimated salvage value is divided equally over the three remaining years of the estimated life. Thus, the depreciation expense for 19x5, 19x6, and 19x7 would be recorded as follows:

```
Depreciation expense.................... 2,000
    Accumulated depreciation.............        2,000
```

DISPOSAL OF PLANT AND EQUIPMENT

At some point in time, the cost of continuing to use a particular asset will exceed the benefits derived from its use and it will be to the advantage of the firm to dispose of it. Upon disposal of an asset, the cost of the asset must be removed from the asset account and the accumulated depreciation at the date of disposal also must be removed from the accumulated depreciation account.

For example, assume that after using the Chevrolet as a taxi for four years, it was sold for $1,000, its book value at that time. (Recall that the auto had an original cost of $9,000, an estimated life of four years, and an anticipated salvage value of $1,000.) The entry to record the sale of the Chevrolet would be as follows:

```
Cash ................................... 1,000
Accumulated depreciation................. 8,000
    Automobile ...........................        9,000
```

The debit to cash records the amount of cash received while the debit to accumulated depreciation and the credit to automobile remove the automobile and its related accumulated depreciation account from the books of Your Taxi Company. In this example, the estimate of useful life and salvage value were precise. This would occur only infrequently in actual practice.

At the time of the disposal of an asset, if the book value of the asset (cost less accumulated depreciation) is not exactly equal to the amount received from the sale, the difference is a gain or loss on disposal. If the selling price exceeds the book value there is a gain, while if the sales price is less than book value there is a loss. Such gains or losses are included in the income statement in the determination of income from operations.

For example, if the same Chevrolet were sold at the end of the fourth year for $1,100, the entry to record this transaction would be as follows:

```
Cash ................................... 1,100
Accumulated depreciation................. 8,000
    Automobile ...........................        9,000
    Gain .................................        100
```

The only difference between this entry and the preceding entry is that the amount of cash received increased from $1,000 to $1,100. This amount exceeds the book value of the asset (original cost of $9,000 less accumulated depreciation of $8,000 or $1,000) and therefore a gain ($1,100 minus $1,000 or $100) is realized. On the other hand, if the car had been sold for $350, a loss would have been incurred. The calculation of the gain and/or loss on the disposal of the automobile in all three cases mentioned above may be summarized as follows:

		A	B	C
Selling price...........................		$1,000	$1,100	$350
Cost of automobile...................	$9,000			
Accumulated depreciation............	(8,000)			
Book value...........................		(1,000)	(1,000)	(1,000)
Gain (loss) on the sale of the automobile.....		$ 0	$ 100	($650)

The entries for the disposal of the asset under Cases A and B have been presented above. The entry for Case C, the loss situation, is as follows:

Cash..................................	350	
Accumulated depreciation..................	8,000	
Loss..................................	650	
Automobile...........................		9,000

Again, the only difference between this entry and the two preceding entries is the amount of cash received, $350. Since the cash received was less than the book value of the automobile ($9,000 less $8,000 or $1,000) a loss equal to the difference ($1,000 less $350 or $650) occurred and should be recorded in the accounts.

In some instances, an asset may be discarded prior to the end of its useful life. For example, assume that the automobile was involved in an accident at the end of its third year of use and was damaged to the extent that repairs were not considered to be feasible. The entry to record the loss from the accident would be as follows:

Loss..................................	3,000	
Accumulated depreciation..................	6,000 *	
Automobile...........................		9,000

* For purposes of the example, it was assumed that the straight-line method of depreciation was used.

Of course, the taxi would probably be insured. If this was the case and $1,000 was received from an insurance policy on the automobile, the entry would be as follows:

Cash..................................	1,000	
Accumulated depreciation..................	6,000 *	
Loss..................................	2,000	
Automobile...........................		9,000

* For purposes of the example, it was assumed that the straight-line method of depreciation had been used.

In any case, cash is debited for the amount received (if any), accumulated depreciation is debited for the depreciation taken to the date of disposal, and the asset is credited for its original cost in order to remove these accounts from the books. A loss (or gain) is recorded for the difference between the book value of the asset and the cash received (if any).

In each of the illustrations included above, it was assumed that the disposal of the asset took place at the end of the period. If the disposal is made during the period, the only difference would be that an entry would be required to record the depreciation for the period from the end of the preceding year up to the date of the disposal. The entry to record the disposal itself would be exactly the same as those illustrated above.

In the above examples it was assumed that cash was received in the disposition of the asset. In some cases, however, a plant asset may be simply retired from productive service. When this occurs, the asset's cost and accumulated depreciation are removed from the accounts, and any difference is recorded as a loss on retirement.

Trade-Ins

In acquiring assets, a firm will frequently trade in an old asset in purchasing the new asset. In these cases, a trade-in allowance is given on the old asset and the balance of the purchase price is paid in cash or by a combination of cash and debt. The accounting procedures used in recording a trade-in depend on whether the assets exchanged are *similar* (an automobile traded in on another automobile) or *dissimilar* (an automobile traded in on a printing press). When items of property, plant, and equipment are acquired by trading in a *dissimilar* asset, the transaction should be accounted for using the fair market values of the assets involved as the base. Thus, the cost of the acquired asset is the fair market value of the assets given up (old asset and cash) or the fair market value of the asset acquired, if its fair value is more clearly determinable. Any difference between the fair value of the asset surrendered and the book value of the old asset should be recognized as a gain or a loss on the disposition of the old asset. Caution must be used in determining and recording the fair values of the assets involved, as the quoted list prices of new assets and trade-in allowances are often not good or accurate indicators of actual or true market values. Dealers often establish list prices that are in excess of the actual cash price to allow them to offer inflated trade-in allowances to their customers.

When *similar* assets are exchanged, a loss may be recognized based upon the fair market value of the asset traded in but not a gain. If the terms of the exchange of similar assets indicates that there is a gain, this "gain" is not recognized. Rather, the new asset is recorded at an amount equal to the total of the book value of the old asset traded in and the cash paid. The logic supporting the nonrecognition of gains is that the income of a firm should not be increased by the act of substituting a new productive asset for an old one. The "gain" is recognized in future years because the recorded cost of the new asset will be less than if the gain was recognized in the current period. Thus, depreciation expense will be less in future years (and income greater) because of the reduced recorded cost of the new asset.

Assume that Your Taxi Company traded in its Chevrolet on a new asset on January 1, 19x5. The following data will be used in the example:

List-price of the new asset	$10,000
Cost of the Chevrolet (at January 1, 19x1)	9,000
Accumulated depreciation on the Chevrolet (at December 31, 19x4)	8,000
Trade-in allowance	500
Fair market value of the Chevrolet (at January 1, 19x5)	200
Cash difference paid	9,500

The entry to record the acquisition of the new asset would be as follows:

New asset	9,700	
Accumulated depreciation	8,000	
Loss	800	
Automobile		9,000
Cash		9,500

The debit to new asset records the $9,700 "cost" of the new asset as the $9,500 cash paid plus the $200 fair market value of the Chevrolet traded-in. The debit to accumulated depreciation of $8,000 and the credit to autombile of $9,000 remove the original cost of the Chevrolet and its related accumulated depreciation from the accounts. The debit to loss of $800 records the loss on the disposal of the Chevrolet and was calculated as follows:

Original cost of the Chevrolet	$9,000
Less: Accumulated depreciation as of the date of trade-in	8,000
Book value of the Chevrolet at the date of trade-in	$1,000
Less: Fair market value of the Chevrolet at the date of the trade-in	200
Loss	$ 800

The credit to cash of $9,500 records the cash outlay which was made in order to acquire the new asset.

If, in the above example, the fair market value of the old car was not available, but it was known that the new asset could have been acquired for a cash price of $9,800, this value would have been used in recording the acquisition of the new asset. In this situation, the apparent value of the old asset is $300 ($9,800 − $9,500) even though the trade-in allowance is stated at $500. Thus, the loss on this exchange is $700, the difference between the actual or apparent trade-in value ($300) and the book value ($1,000) of the old asset. The entry required to record this transaction would be as follows:

New asset	9,800	
Accumulated depreciation	8,000	
Loss	700	
Automobile		9,000
Cash		9,500

In the above example, there was a loss on the trade, so the entries would be the same whether the assets were similar or dissimilar.

We will now modify the example as follows:

Trade-in allowance....................................	$1,500
Fair market value of the Chevrolet (at January 1, 19x5).......	1,500
Cash difference paid...................................	8,300

These facts indicate a gain on the disposal of the Chevrolet, calculated as follows:

Fair market value of the Chevrolet at the date of the trade-in..................		$1,500
Original cost of the Chevrolet..............	$9,000	
Less: Accumulated depreciation as of the date of trade-in................	8,000	
Book value of the Chevrolet at the date of the trade-in.........................		1,000
Gain		$ 500

If the assets are dissimilar, the entry to record the acquisition of the new asset would be as follows:

New asset...............................	9,800	
Accumulated depreciation..................	8,000	
Automobile		9,000
Cash		8,300
Gain		500

If the assets are assumed to be similar, the entry required to record the trade would be as follows:

New asset...............................	9,300	
Accumulated depreciation..................	8,000	
Automobile		9,000
Cash		8,300

Note that the debit of **$9,300** to the new asset is the total of the cash paid and the book value of the asset traded in ($8,300 + $1,000).

In the preceding examples, the trade-in took place at the beginning of the period. If a trade-in is made during the period, depreciation should be recognized on the old asset for the period up to the time of the trade-in, and the entry to record the exchange should recognize the book value of the old asset as of the date of exchange.

In APB, *Opinion No. 29,* "Accounting for Nonmonetary Transactions" (1973), the Accounting Principles Board recognized several exceptions to the general requirement of using market values to determine the gain or loss on the exchange of nonmonetary assets. The circumstances which require exceptions to the general rule include:

1. If market values are not determinable within reasonable limits.
2 . If the general rule indicates a gain, and the exchange is:

   a. An exchange of inventory between dealers to facilitate sales to customers other than the parties involved in the exchange.
   b. An exchange of *similar* productive assets not held for sale.

3. If nonmonetary assets are transferred to owners in a spin-off, or other forms of reorganization.

The details of the accounting procedures required to record the other exceptions are beyond the scope of this text.

For federal income tax purposes, a gain or loss is never recognized on the exchange of similar productive assets. Rather, the cost of the new asset is considered to be the book value (cost less accumulated depreciation) of the old asset plus the additional cash paid (or cash and debt incurred) in the exchange.

Natural Resources

In addition to plant assets such as property, plant, and equipment described in the earlier sections of this chapter, a firm may also own assets in the form of natural resources. These resources include such items as oil deposits, tracts of timber, and coal deposits. Like the other long-term assets of the firm, the basis for accounting for these resources is primarily cost. As these resources are converted into salable inventory by drilling, cutting, and mining operations, the cost of these operations along with the original cost of the resources themselves are transferred to expense.

The process of writing off or amortizing the cost of these natual resources is generally referred to as depletion. Since the natural resource provides a salable product, the depletion charges are included in inventory costs as production occurs and cost of goods sold as the natural resource is sold. The primary difference between depreciation and depletion is that depreciation represents the allocation of the cost of a productive asset in relation to the decline in service potential, while depletion represents the allocation of cost of a natural resource in relation to the quantitative physical exhaustion of the resource.

Depletion Base and Amortization

The depletion base of any wasting asset is the total cost of acquiring and developing the property less the estimated residual value of the land after the natural resource has been economically exhausted. The total cost of the natural resource may be classified in three categories: (1) acquisition cost of the property, (2) exploration costs, and (3) development costs.

Generally, depletion for the period is determined on the basis of the relationship between actual production for the period and total estimated production during the economic life of the resource. To apply this approach, the quantity of economically recoverable units of the natural resource must be estimated. Then the total cost of the natural resource less any estimated residual value is divided by the estimated number of recoverable units to obtain a cost per unit of output. This cost per unit is multiplied by the number of units extracted during the period to determine the depletion charge.

To illustrate this process, consider the following example:

1. An oil field is acquired at a cost of $1,000,000. Geological surveys indicate that a total of approximately 400,000 barrels of oil will ultimately be taken from the field.
2. The estimated residual value of the field after the oil has been extracted is approximately $200,000 (net of restoration costs).
3. During the first year of operations, the drilling costs total $75,000. A total of 25,000 barrels of oil are extracted and sold at a price of $40 per barrel.

These transactions would be recorded as follows:

Acquisition of the Field

Oil field..............................	1,000,000	
Cash		1,000,000

Drilling during the First Year

Inventory of oil........................	75,000	
Cash		75,000
Inventory of oil........................	50,000	
Accumulated depletion—oil field........		50,000

The $75,000 cost of drilling was assumed to be entirely applicable to the oil taken during the year and was therefore assigned to the inventory of oil as a part of its costs. The depletion of $50,000 was calculated as follows:

Cost of the field.....................................	$1,000,000
Estimated residual value of the field....................	200,000
Cost of the 400,000 barrels of oil......................	$ 800,000
Divide by 400,000 in order to obtain the cost per·barrel..................................	$2

The total cost per barrel would be the cost of the oil, that is the depletion per barrel, of $2 plus the drilling cost of $3 per barrel[7] or $5.

Sale of the 25,000 Barrels of Oil

Cash	1,000,000	
Sales		1,000,000
Cost of goods sold	125,000	
Inventory of oil		125,000

Frequently, additional development costs may be incurred after the production begins or estimates of recoverable units are revised based on production data. In either case, a revision in the unit depletion charge is necessary. In the revision process, a new rate is determined by dividing the unamortized total cost less the estimated residual value by the estimate of the remaining recoverable units.

The procedures described above are known as cost depletion and are required for accounting and financial reporting purposes. For income tax purposes, firms use either depletion based on cost or percentage depletion. Further, if cost depletion is used for tax purposes, the amount of periodic tax depletion need not be equal to the cost depletion determined for financial reporting purposes. It is often advantageous from a tax standpoint to use the percentage depletion method, since depletion calculated by this method frequently exceeds depletion on a cost basis. Furthermore, in many cases it allows the taxpayer to deduct more than the cost of the property over its useful life. The percentage depletion method allows the firm to deduct from revenues a given percentage of gross income depletion without regard to the number of units produced or the cost of the property. In this method, the amount of depletion for tax purposes may exceed the total cost of the natural resource. Percentage depletion is not acceptable for financial accounting purposes.

Accounting for Oil and Gas Producers

Normally the exploration costs of oil and gas companies are substantial. There have been two methods which have long been used by oil and gas companies to account for costs incurred in the exploration, development and production of crude oil and natural gas—the successful efforts method and the full cost method. The larger oil and gas companies have tended to use the successful efforts method; the smaller companies have tended to use the full cost method.

Under the successful efforts method, only the costs of successful drilling

---

[7] Drilling costs of $75,000 divided by the 25,000 barrels extracted, or $3 per barrel.

efforts are capitalized and subsequently charged against the revenue of the producing wells. Costs in connection with nonproducing wells are written off as expenses in the period incurred. Under the full cost method, the costs of both successful and unsuccessful drilling efforts are capitalized and amortized against subsequent petroleum production in the same relatively large cost center (e.g., a country or a continent).

There has been considerable pressure on the accounting profession to eliminate the alternatives available for accounting for exploratory costs in the oil and gas industry. In December 1977, the FASB issued Statement No. 19, "Financial Accounting and Reporting by Oil and Gas Producers," which essentially required the adoption of a form of the successful efforts method by all oil and gas producers. However, in Accounting Series Release No. 253 issued in August 1978, the SEC rejected the FASB's attempt to eliminate use of the full cost method, asserting that both cost-based methods were so inadequate that it did not matter which method was employed.

In 1982, the FASB issued Statement No. 69, "Disclosures about Oil and Gas Producing Activities," which superceded the disclosure requirements of all previous FASB statements concerned with oil and gas producing activities. In applying Statement No. 69, companies are required to disclose information about quantities of reserves, capitalized costs, costs incurred, and a standardized measure of discounted cash flows related to proved reserves.

Intangible Assets

Intangible assets are resources such as organization costs, trademarks, patents, copyrights, and goodwill which have value but do not have physical substance. An intangible asset derives its value from certain special rights and privileges which accrue to the firm which owns it. For example, the ownership of a patent has value because it gives the owner of the patent exclusive right to the manufacture, sale, or other use of an invention or process for a period of 17 years.

A firm may obtain an intangible asset by purchase or by development within the firm. The objectives of accounting for intangible assets are similar to those for tangible assets which were described earlier in the chapter—the cost of the asset is recorded upon acquisition and this cost is allocated to expense over the useful life of the intangible. The cost of an intangible asset includes all expenditures which are incurred in the acquisition of the rights or privileges. The cost of an intangible asset acquired by purchase can usually be measured with little difficulty. The cost of internally developed intangibles is often more difficult to determine. For example, it may be quite difficult to estimate how much of the total research and development cost for a particular period should be allocated to the development of a single patent. For this reason the cost of internally developed patents includes only legal fees. Any other costs incurred in developing the patent are expenses as they are incurred. This treatment is consistent with the handling of research and development costs in general.

The costs of intangible assets are written off to expense over their estimated useful lives in a manner similar to the depreciation of tangible fixed assets. This is referred to as amortization. Amortization is recorded by a debit to amortization expense and a credit to the intangible asset account. Like tangible fixed assets, the cost of intangibles should be amortized over their estimated useful lives. However, according to Accounting Principles Board *Opinion No. 17,* the period of amortization should not exceed a maximum of 40 years. The Board also concluded that the straight-line method of amortization should be used unless the firm shows evidence that some other systematic method is more appropriate in the circumstances.

To illustrate the accounting for intangible assets, assume that Landry Company purchased a patent from Allen Company for $10,000 on January 1, 19x1. The purchase would be recorded as follows:

Patents	10,000	
Cash		10,000

If the remaining useful or economic life of the patent was ten years, the adjusting entry required to record the amortization of the patent at the end of each year of its useful life would be as follows:

Amortization expense	1,000	
Patents		1,000

Note that the amortization is credited directly to the asset account rather than to an accumulated amortization account as in the case of tangible fixed assets. There appears to be no logical reason for this procedure other than tradition.

Certain intangibles, such as patents, copyrights, and franchises, may be identified with a specific right or privilege. The costs of these intangibles when purchased can be measured and amortized or allocated to expense over their useful lives. Other intangibles, however, cannot be specifically identified. This type of intangible is usually referred to as goodwill. The intangible asset goodwill represents the sum of all the special advantages which are not identifiable and which relate to the business as a whole. It encompasses such items as a favorable location, good customer relations, and superior ability of management. The existence of such factors enables the firm to earn an above normal rate of return.

Unlike tangible assets or identifiable intangible assets, goodwill cannot be sold or acquired separately from the business as a whole. Because of the uncertainty involved in estimating the goodwill of a business enterprise, goodwill is normally recorded only when a business is acquired by purchase. In a purchase transaction, goodwill may be measured as the excess of the purchase price of an entity over the sum of the fair values of all its identifiable assets less its liabilities. The source of this excess is the potential of the firm to earn an above average rate of return.

To illustrate, assume that Richard Smith purchased the Campus Book Store on January 1, 19x1, for $100,000 cash. Further assume that the identifiable assets were determined to have a total fair value of $90,000 at the date of purchase (including inventory, $10,000; equipment, $20,000; building, $40,000; and land, $20,000). The liabilities assumed by the purchaser were accounts payable of $20,000. The $30,000 excess of the purchase price over the value of all the identifiable assets less the liabilities represents the value of the goodwill. The purchase would be recorded as follows:

Inventory	10,000	
Equipment	20,000	
Building	40,000	
Land	20,000	
Goodwill	30,000	
Accounts Payable		20,000
Cash		100,000

Once goodwill is recorded in a purchase transaction, it is amortized like all other intangible assets—the recorded cost is allocated to expense over its estimated life with a maximum of 40 years.

Many businesses engage in research and development (R&D) activities in order to develop new products or processes, or to improve present products. A problem in accounting for R&D expenditures lies in determining the amount and timing of the future benefits which are associated with such activities. Prior to 1974, there was considerable diversity in the procedures used in accounting for R&D costs. In 1974, however, the FASB issued its *Statement No. 2* which simplified the accounting for R&D expenditures by requiring that most research and development costs should be charged to expense as they are incurred. This treatment eliminated the need to assess the uncertain future benefits associated with R&D costs and to measure the cause and effect relationship of these costs for accounting purposes.

FASB *Statement No. 2* stated that R&D costs include the costs of materials, personnel, purchased intangibles, contract services, and a reasonable allocation of indirect costs which are specifically related to R&D activities and have no alternative future uses. Disclosure should be made in the financial statements of the total R&D costs charged to expense for each period for which an income statement is presented.

Plant and Equipment in the Financial Statements

Plant assets are carried in the balance sheet at their acquisition cost, less any accumulated depreciation. The depreciation on long-term assets is included in the income statement as an expense and is deducted in determining income from operations. Gains or losses on the disposal of long-term assets would appear on the income statement in a special section after income from operations, since they are normally not considered to be a part of the normal operations of the firm.

SUMMARY

The resources of a firm which are used in the continuing operations of a business over a number of years are referred to as plant and equipment or fixed assets. Such assets are generally classified as tangible fixed assets if they have physical substance and are depreciable or non-depreciable assets (land).

Control over tangible fixed assets is usually achieved by the use of a ledger card that includes all data related to the asset item. This card will reflect the cost of the item, which includes all expenditures necessary to place the asset in use as well as the actual invoice price.

Since long-term assets benefit a firm over an extended period of time, the cost of the asset must be allocated in some manner to the periods which benefit from its use. This is achieved through the process of depreciation. In the case of most tangible fixed assets, the depreciation process will result in either a uniform charge for each year (under the straight-line depreciation method) or larger charges in the early years of operation (under the accelerated depreciation methods). In either case, the consistency principle requires that the same method of depreciation be used in all periods. Fixed tangible assets are presented on the balance sheet at their acquisition cost along with an offset or deduction for accumulated depreciation.

Costs incurred for existing assets subsequent to acquisition are classified as either capital expenditures or revenue expenditures. Capital expenditures increase the economic benefits of the existing asset and the cost is debited to an asset account. Revenue expenditures are routine expenditures incurred to maintain an asset in operating condition and such costs are debited to expense.

Eventually, the economic usefulness of an item of plant and equipment expires and the asset must be sold, scrapped, retired or traded-in on a new asset. When an asset is disposed of, the cost of the asset is removed from the asset account and the accumulated depreciation balance is eliminated. When a plant asset is sold, there is a gain or loss equal to the difference between the asset's book value (cost less accumulated depreciation) and its sales price.

When an old asset is traded in on a new asset, the accounting treatment depends upon the nature of the assets involved. If the assets are dissimilar, the cost of the new asset is equal to the fair market value of the old asset plus the cash paid, and a gain or loss on the disposition of the old asset is recognized for the difference between the book value and the fair market value at the date of exchange. If the assets are similar, the accounting treatment is the same as for dissimilar assets if a loss is indicated. However, if the fair market value is greater than the book value of the old asset, no gain is recognized and the new asset is recorded at the book value of the old asset plus the cash paid.

Identifiable intangible assets, which generally involve property rights rather than physical property, are written off in a similar manner referred to as amortization. Goodwill differs from tangible assets and identifiable intangible assets in that it cannot be sold or acquired separate from the business. Therefore, due to the uncertainty of measuring goodwill, it is only recorded and amortized if purchased with a business already in existence. A similar uncertainty exists in matching expenses incurred by research and development efforts with possible future revenues resulting from these efforts. Therefore, R&D expenditures are considered expenses of the period in which they are incurred.

Allocation of the cost of natural resources is referred to as depletion. For financial accounting purposes, depletion must be calculated on a cost basis over the estimated units to be produced. However, for tax purposes, firms must take the higher of cost depletion or a specified percentage of gross income (referred to as percentage depletion).

KEY DEFINITIONS

Accelerated Cost Recovery System (ACRS)   ACRS is an accelerated method of depreciation permitted for federal income tax purposes and may also be used for financial accounting purposes.

Accelerated methods of depreciation   Accelerated methods of depreciation are techniques for computing depreciation that assume the rate of depreciation decreases with the passage of time.

Accumulated depreciation   Accumulated depreciation is a contra account which appears as an offset or deduction from the related asset account in the balance sheet. The depreciation taken over the useful life of the asset is accumulated in this account.

Book value of an asset   The book value of an asset is the cost of an asset less accumulated depreciation. The book value of an asset is the remaining undepreciated cost.

Capital Expenditures   Expenditures which extend the useful life or quality of services provided by plant assets.

Contra account   A contra account is an account which is offset against or deducted from another account in the financial statements.

Declining balance method   The declining balance method is an accelerated method of depreciation that assumes the rate of depreciation to be some multiple of the rate which would have been used in the case of the straight-line method.

Depletion Depletion is the process of writing-off or amortizing the cost of natural resources over the periods which benefit from their use.

Depreciation Depreciation is the systematic allocation of the cost of an asset, less the salvage value (if any), over its estimated useful life.

Fixed asset ledger card A fixed asset ledger card is prepared for each individual asset purchased. It includes all of the important information relating to the asset and its use.

Goodwill Goodwill may be measured as the excess of the purchase price of an entity over the sum of the fair values of all its identifiable assets less its liabilities.

Intangible fixed asset An intangible fixed asset is one that does not have physical substance, usually a property right.

Plant and equipment Long-term or fixed assets are those resources of a firm which are used in the continuing operations of a business over a number of years.

Revenue Expenditures Expenditures for ordinary maintenance, repairs, and other items necessary for the operation and use of plant and equipment.

Salvage value Salvage value is the residual amount of a long-term tangible asset that the firm expects to recover at the end of the useful life of the asset.

Straight-line depreciation This method of depreciation assumes that factors such as wear and tear and obsolescence are somewhat uniform over time. The method allocates the cost of an asset, less its salvage value, to expenses equally over its useful life.

Sum-of-the-years'-digits method This is an accelerated method of depreciation where the life-years of an asset are totaled and utilized as the denominator of a fraction that uses the number of years of life remaining from the beginning of the year as the numerator.

Tangible fixed asset A tangible fixed asset is a long-term asset that has physical substance.

QUESTIONS

1. Which expenditures are included in the total cost of a fixed asset?

2. What is the purpose of depreciation accounting?

3. What factors should be considered when determining periodic depreciation?

4. Explain the equations used in calculating straight-line, double-declining balance, and sum-of-the-years'-digits depreciation.

5. Four basic depreciation methods are straight-line, sum-of-the-years'-digits, double-declining balance and ACRS. In what ways are the four depreciation methods similar? In what ways are they different?

6. What is the purpose of the accumulated depreciation account?

7. What does the balance in the accumulated depreciation account indicate at any given point in time?

8. What is the difference between a capital expenditure and a revenue expenditure?

9. Why is periodic depreciation not recorded for land?

10. What factors must be known to compute depreciation on a plant asset?

11. How is accumulated depreciation reported in the balance sheet?

12. When a plant asset is disposed of for cash, how is the gain or loss on the sale determined?

13. If an old asset is traded in on a dissimilar new asset, how should the cost basis of the new asset be measured?

14. Explain the rules for recognizing gains or losses on the exchange of similar productive assets.

15. Over what period should the cost of an intangible asset be amortized?

16. When should goodwill be recorded in the accounts?

17. Discuss the appropriate accounting treatment of research and development costs.

18. List some possible causes of goodwill.

19. What is the basis for accounting for natural resources? Is this basis the same as that for other long-term assets?

20. What is depletion? Is it similar to depreciation, and if so, in what way?

21. What is the difference in the accounting for intangible assets and the accounting for tangible assets?

EXERCISES

22. A machine was purchased for an invoice price of $10,000, F.O.B. destination. The freight charges were $200. Costs of installation amounted to $500. At what cost should the machine be recorded?

23. Determine which of the following accounts is to be debited for each of the transactions below.

A.	Buildings	F.	Machinery
B.	Accumulated Depreciation	G.	Insurance Expense
C.	Land	H.	Freight Expense
D.	Patents	I.	General Repairs
E.	Depreciation Expense	J.	Legal Fees

_____ Purchased land and unusable building.
_____ Paid legal fees for above purchase.
_____ Constructed new building on site.
_____ Purchased machinery for building.
_____ Paid freight on machinery.
_____ Paid cost of installing machinery.
_____ Paid minor repairs on building.
_____ Recorded depreciation of equipment.
_____ Paid insurance for year on building.
_____ Obtained patent from U.S. Patent Office.

24. A machine was installed at a total cost of $8,000, assumed to have an estimated useful life of 5 years and a salvage value of $2,000. Calculate the initial year's depreciation assuming (a) the straight-line method is used, (b) the sum-of-the-years'-digits method is used, (c) the double-declining balance method is used, and (d) ACRS depreciation is used.

25. In each of the following cases, make the journal entry for the initial year of depreciation, assuming the straight-line method is used by Pat Kelly. (Round to the nearest dollar.)

a. Original cost, $9,000; salvage value, $500; useful life, 4 years; purchased on April 1.

b. Original cost, $25,000; salvage value, $5,000; useful life, 5 years; purchased on October 1.

c. Original cost, $16,000; salvage value, $0; useful life, 8 years; purchased on December 1.

d. Original cost $5,000; salvage value, $1,000; useful life, 2 years; purchased on July 31.

e. Original cost, $30,000; salvage value, $2,000; useful life, 7 years; purchased on May 31.

26. Smith Company paid $100,000 to acquire land, building, and equipment. At the time of acquisition, appraisal values for the individual assets were determined as: land, $30,000; building, $60,000; and equipment, $30,000. What cost should be allocated to the land, building, and equipment, respectively?

27. Putnam Company purchased a new machine on January 1, 19x1 for a $1,000 down payment and a liability for six monthly payments of $2,000 beginning on February 1, 19x1. The machine could have been purchased for a cash price of $8,600. The company paid delivery and installation costs of $400. Prepare the journal entry to record the acquisition of the machine.

28. Which of the following items are capital expenditures and which are revenue expenditures?

    a. Cost of a major overhaul of a machine.
    b. Routine maintenance of a delivery truck.
    c. Replacement of an oil furnace with a gas furnace.
    d. Replacement of stairs with an escalator.
    e. Annual repainting of the administrative offices.
    f. Lubricating, inspecting, and cleaning factory machinery.
    g. Addition to a new wing on the factory building.

29. A truck with an original cost of $10,000 and accumulated depreciation to date of $8,000 was traded in on a new truck with a list price of $20,000. The dealer allowed a trade-in allowance of $3,000 on the old truck (which was equal to the fair market value). Give the journal entry to record the exchange.

30. Assume the same facts as in Exercise 29, except that the trade-in allowance and the fair market value of the old truck were $1,000. Give the journal entry to record the exchange.

31. A company had a plant asset with an original cost of $15,000 and accumulated depreciation to date of $12,000. Give the journal entry to record the disposition of the asset under the following circumstances:

    a. Sold the asset for $5,000.
    b. Sold the asset for $2,000.
    c. The asset was destroyed by fire; insurance proceeds of $1,500 were received.
    d. Abandoned the asset.

32. The Get Rich Quick Mining Company obtained a uranium mine for $1,350,000 on February 1, 19x1. It is estimated that approximately 335,000 pounds of uranium can be extracted from the mine. The residual value of the property after uranium has been removed is approximately $10,000. In 19x1, 74,000 pounds of uranium were extracted from the mine and in 19x2, 90,000 pounds were extracted. Mining costs were $14,800 for 19x1 and $22,500 for 19x2. The uranium is sold for $10 per pound.

Required:

Record the above transactions on the books of the Mining Company.

33. The Bratton Company purchased a patent for $56,000 on January 1, 19x1. Additional legal costs of $4,000 were incurred in obtaining the patent. The patent was estimated to have a useful life of 10 years. (Its legal life is 17 years.) What will be the patent amortization expense for 19x1?

34. From the following information make the necessary journal entries for the trade-in of an asset by the Singleton Company. Assume that the old and new assets were dissimilar.

List-price of new machine	$20,795
Original cost of old machine	18,560
Accumulated depreciation on old machine at trade-in date	10,560
Trade-in allowance	2,000
Fair market value of old machine at trade-in date	1,000
Cash difference paid	18,795

35. Al Bumbry bought Billy's Grocery on March 27 for $250,000 cash. On the date of purchase, the following fair values were determined: inventory, $50,000; equipment, $18,000; building, $68,000; land, $45,000; and accounts payable, $7,000. Make the entry required on the date of purchase.

36. For each of the following items owned by Mark Belanger, determine what the gain or loss will be upon the disposition of the asset and make the necessary journal entries.

a. Original outlay, $7,900; sales price, $1,750; accumulated depreciation, $6,450.

b. Original outlay, $13,050; sales price, $5,110; accumulated depreciation, $10,250.

c. Original outlay, $21,400; sales price, $9,790; accumulated depreciation, $8,330.

d. Original outlay, $91,625; sales price, $40,000; accumulated depreciation, $40,580.

e. Original outlay, $47,985; sales price, $25,470; accumulated depreciation, $29,645.

PROBLEMS

37. The Carson Carton Company purchased a new cutting machine at an invoice price of $13,000. It paid the seller in time to take advantage of a 3 percent discount. Carson Carton then paid $400 shipping charges and $550 installation costs. However, after the machine was installed, it was discovered that the electrical wiring in the plant was not adequate to carry the additional current needed by the new asset. The company rewired that section of the building at a cost of $875. At what amount should Carson Carton Company value the new cutting machine on its books?

38. Cutler Cutlery Company purchased a large storage cabinet on January 1, 19x1, at a cost of $7,500. It was assigned an estimated useful life of 5 years and a salvage value of $500. Prepare a depreciation schedule for the cabinet under the straight-line, double-declining balance, sum-of-the-years'-digits, and ACRS methods.

39. For each of the depreciation methods listed, complete the following schedule of depreciation over the first two years of the life of a delivery truck costing $8,800 and having a salvage value of $800. The truck has an estimated life of 5 years.

Method	Year	Depreciation Expense	Accumulated Depreciation	Book Value
Straight-line	1	$ _____	$ _____	$ _____
Straight-line	2	_____	_____	_____
Sum-of-the-years'-digits	1	_____	_____	_____
Sum-of-the-years'-digits	2	_____	_____	_____
Double-declining balance	1	_____	_____	_____
Double-declining balance	2	_____	_____	_____
ACRS	1	_____	_____	_____
ACRS	2	_____	_____	_____

40. During the course of your audit of Confused, Inc. for the year ended December 31, 19x2, you find the following account:

Equipment

(a) 20,000	(c) 3,400
(b) 14,000	(d) 6,600

Key:
(a) Cost of machine A purchased on January 1, 19x1.
(b) Cost of machine B purchased on January 1, 19x1.
(c) Credit resulting from the recording of depreciation expense for 19x1. (Debit was to "depreciation expense.")
(d) Credit resulting from the recording of the sale of machine B on April 1, 19x2. (Debit was to cash.)

Each machine had an estimated life of ten years with no salvage value anticipated. The company uses the straight-line method of recording depreciation.

Required:

Give all the adjusting and correcting entries (or entry) required on April 1, 19x2.

41. Snowden Manufacturing Company decided to construct a new plant in 19x1 rather than continue to rent its present plant. On January 1, 19x1, the company purchased 10 acres of land with two old buildings standing on it. The old buildings were demolished and construction of the new plant was begun. The company set up a Land and Buildings account to which all expenditures relating to the new plant were charged.

The balance in the Land and Buildings account after completion of the plant was $740,450. Entries in the account during the construction period were:

a.	Cost of land and old buildings (old buildings appraised at $17,000)	$137,000
b.	Legal fees involved in securing title to property	250
c.	Cost of demolishing old buildings	9,500
d.	Surveying costs	1,200
e.	Price paid for construction of new building	425,000
f.	Salary paid to Jim Seales, engineer, supervisor of construction of new plant	12,500
g.	Fencing of plant property	3,000
h.	Machinery for new plant	113,000
i.	Installation costs of new machinery	9,500
j.	Landscaping of grounds	6,250
k.	Office equipment	12,000
l.	Payment to architect for designing plans and for services during construction	13,000
m.	Paneling and finishing work done on executive offices	2,250
	Total Debits	$744,450
n.	Proceeds from sale of scrap from old buildings	4,000
	Total Credit	$ 4,000
	Balance	$740,450

Required:

Reclassify the items presently in the Land and Buildings account to the proper general ledger accounts.

42.   Blintz, Inc. has followed the practice of depreciating its building on a straight-line basis. The building has an estimated useful life of 20 years and a salvage value of $20,000. The company's depreciation expense for 19x3 was $20,000 on the building. The building was purchased on January 1, 19x1.

Required:

1.   The original cost of the building.
2.   Depreciation expense for 19x2 assuming:

   a.   The company has used the double-declining balance method.
   b.   The company has used the sum-of-the-years'-digits method.

43.   The Silver Fox Company purchased a parcel of land on which was located a large home and a riding stable on January 7, 19x2, for $87,500. Additional expenditures made at the time of settlement were as follows:

Attorney's fees in connection with the purchase.........	$ 500
Cost of property transfer taxes......................	1,000
Real estate taxes for 19x1 (the seller was to	
repay Silver Fox for these taxes)....................	2,000
Title insurance....................................	500
Broker's commission...............................	500
Gardening equipment..............................	1,000
	$5,500

Silver Fox had the property appraised by a professional appraiser on the purchase date. His appraisal showed the following valuations:

Land	$ 55,000
Home...	45,000
Stable..	10,000
Total appraised value of property.................	$110,000

Extensive remodeling and redecorating was undertaken immediately to ready the property for rental. The following outlays were made during the month of January:

Cost of tearing down the stable......................	$ 10,000
Cost of removing fourth story of home................	35,000
Architect's fee.....................................	15,000
Replacement of plumbing...........................	11,000
New electrical wiring...............................	14,000
Landscaping......................................	25,000
Payment of hospital bill of passer-by injured	
by falling debris................................	5,000
	$115,000
Less: Sale of materials salvaged from stable..........	1
	$114,999

Required:

Indicate the accounts which would be charged with the cost of each of the items listed below. If an item is to be allocated to more than one account, simply list each account that would be charged.

In indicating your answers, use the following code:

Land......................	L	Any expense or loss account......	E
Home....................	H	Any revenue or gain account.....	R
Stable...................	S	Any other account.............	X
Any other asset account......	A		

Purchase price of $87,500................. ( )
Attorney's fees.......................... ( )
Property transfer taxes................... ( )
Real estate taxes for 19x1................. ( )
Title insurance.......................... ( )
Broker's commission..................... ( )
Gardening equipment.................... ( )
Cost of tearing down stable............... ( )
Cost of tearing down fourth
   floor of home........................ ( )
Architect's fee.......................... ( )
Plumbing.............................. ( )
Electrical wiring......................... ( )
Landscaping............................ ( )
Hospital bill........................... ( )
Sale of materials salvaged
   from stable.......................... ( )

44. On October 30, 19x1, Thomas Brothers, Inc. purchased a used machine for $7,800 from a company in a neighboring state. The machine could not be shipped until November 15 so Thomas Brothers were forced to pay $150 storage costs and $35 insurance fees. After the asset was received and $250 shipping costs had been paid, it was overhauled and installed at a cost of $320, including parts costing $130. On December 21, additional repair work was performed at a cost of $180 in order to put the asset in working condition. At what value should this machine be recorded on the balance sheet on December 31?

45. For each of the depreciation methods listed, complete the following schedule of depreciation over the first two years of the life of a building costing $57,500. The building is expected to have a salvage value of $7,500 at the end of 10 years.

Method	Year	Depreciation Expense	Accumulated Depreciation	Book Value
Straight-line	1	$ _____	$ _____	$ _____
Straight-line	2	_____	_____	_____
Sum-of-the-years'-digits	1	_____	_____	_____
Sum-of-the-years'-digits	2	_____	_____	_____
Double-declining balance	1	_____	_____	_____
Double-declining balance	2	_____	_____	_____
ACRS	1	_____	_____	_____
ACRS	2	_____	_____	_____

46. Crowley Company decided to construct a new plant in order to meet the rising demand for its product. On January 1, 19x1, the company purchased five acres which adjoin their present plant site. The land had an old barn on it and a number of trees which had to be cleared before construction could begin. A Land & Buildings account was charged with all expenditures relating to the new plant. Entries in the account included:

a.	Cost of land..............................	$ 50,000
b.	Survey costs...............................	750
c.	Legal fees involved in securing title to property.....	500
d.	Cost of clearing trees and removing barn.........	1,600
e.	Proceeds from sale of trees for lumber...........	(2,000)
f.	Construction costs for new plant................	375,000
g.	Cost of parking lot at new plant...............	87,000
h.	Machinery for new plant.....................	167,500
i.	Shipping costs for machinery...................	875
j.	Installation cost of machinery.................	980
k.	Office equipment...........................	7,800
l.	Office supplies.............................	690
m.	Raw materials to be used in production of product..	10,750
	Balance...................................	$701,445

Required:

Reclassify the items presently in the Land & Buildings account to the proper general ledger accounts.

47. Anderson Aerospace Company traded in its Boeing 707 for a new Boeing 747 on January 1, 19x5. The following is the pertinent data for the transaction:

Cost of the 707 (at January 1, 19x1)................ $785,000
Accumulated depreciation on the 707
   (at December 31, 19x4)........................ 300,000
Fair market value of the 707 (at January 1, 19x5)...... 325,000
List price of the 747............................. 925,000
Trade-in allowance............................. 350,000
Note payable given for difference.................. 575,000

Required:

Record the acquisition of the Boeing 747. Discuss the theoretical validity of this accounting treatment.

48. Marshall Furniture Manufacturers purchased a new lathe on January 1, 19x1, for $1,600. It has an estimated salvage value of $100 and an estimated useful life of 3 years. The company uses the sum-of-the-years'-digits depreciation method and maintains records on a calendar year basis. Prepare the journal entries to record the disposal of the lathe under each of the following independent conditions:

a. Sold for $725 cash on October 1, 19x2.
b. Destroyed by flood on July 1, 19x3. Insurance proceeds were $200.
c. Traded in on purchase of new lathe on January 1, 19x2. List price of new lathe was $2,000, market value of old lathe was $1,200, and $700 cash was paid on the transaction.

49. On January 1, 19x1, the Confused Company purchased a new truck for $5,600 paying cash. On May 1, 19x2, the Company purchased a new truck which had a list price of $6,200. They were given a trade-in allowance of $2,000 for the old truck, the balance being paid in cash. On December 1, 19x2, the second truck was completely destroyed by fire. Confused received $3,200 from their insurance company as full settlement for the loss. Truck operating expense for 19x2 totaled $2,200.

    You are called in by the company's accountant who states that in preparing the December 31, 19x2, trial balance he noted that the truck account had a balance of $8,800 although the company does not own any trucks. He also tells you that he failed to record depreciation on either truck during 19x2, although the company's accounting manual requires straight-line depreciation, two-year life, and $800 salvage value for all automotive equipment.

    You obtain a copy of the company's ledger account "Trucks," which shows the following:

Trucks	
5,600	2,000
6,200	3,200
2,200	
8,800	

Required:

1.   Prepare all journal entries regarding the trucks as they *should* have been made originally.
2.   Prepare an entry to correct the accounts as of December 31, 19x2. You may assume that the books have not yet been closed for 19x2.

50.   During an audit of Lee May Company for the year ended December 31, 19x2, you find the following account:

Machinery		
(a) 42,000	*(b)*	7,273
(c) 200	*(d)*	6,545
	(e)	5,600

Key:

(a)   Cost of machinery purchased on January 1, 19x0.
(b)   Credit to record the depreciation expense for 19x0. (Debit was to Depreciation Expense.)
(c)   Cost of minor repairs which will not lengthen the life of the machine.
(d)   Credit to record depreciation expense for 19x1. (Debit was to Depreciation Expense.)
(e)   Credit to record sale of machinery on March 31, 19x2.

The machinery had an estimated life of ten years with a salvage value of $2,000. The company uses the sum-of-the-years'-digits method of recording depreciation.

Required:

Give all of the adjusting and correcting entries (or entry) required.

51.   King Company purchased a truck on January 1, 19x1, at a cost of $4,200. The truck was depreciated using the straight-line method with an estimated useful life of four years and a salvage value of $200. On January 1, 19x3, the truck was traded in on a new truck with a list price of $6,000. The fair market value of the old truck was $1,500 and the truck dealer gave a trade-in allowance of $2,400 on the old truck. King Company gave a note payable for the balance of the purchase price.

Required:

Record the acquisition of the new truck.

52.   A truck was purchased on October 1, 19x1, at a cost of $29,400. The expected life of this truck was 4 years with an expected salvage value of $600. The company used the straight-line depreciation method and the accounting records are maintained on a calendar year basis.

Required:

Prepare journal entries to record the disposal of the truck on *May 1, 19x3* under *each* of the following *separate* conditions:

a. Sold for $18,000 cash.

b. Completely destroyed by fire, and the insurance company paid $6,000 as full settlement of the loss.

c. Traded in on the purchase of another truck which had a cash price of $34,000; trade-in allowance granted on the old truck was $20,000 and the balance was paid in cash.

53. Kelly Company acquired a mine for $2,500,000. It was estimated that the land would have a value of $400,000 after completion of the mining operations, and that 1,000,000 tons of ore could be extracted from the mine. During the first year of operations, 100,000 tons of ore were extracted and additional production costs of $200,000 were incurred.

Required:

Prepare the journal entries to record the acquisition of the property and the cost of production for the year.

Refer to the Annual Report included in the Appendix at the end of the text:

54. Comparing the two years, what is the change in gross investment in real estate and plant and equipment?

55. What causes the difference in the change in net investment and in the change in gross investment mentioned above?

56. Which account included in the asset sections always carries a credit balance?

57. What is the balance in the accumulated depreciation account at the end of the most recent year?

58. Why does an asset account carry a credit balance?

59. What is the amount of the intangible assets at the end of the most recent year?

60. Where else in the financial statements does the change in accumulated depreciation appear?

61. Referring to the above question, how is this shown?

62. What is the total of net fixed assets for GM at the end of the most recent year?

Chapter 6 discusses the issues related to the accounting for sole proprietorships and partnerships. Studying this chapter should enable you to:

1. Discuss the advantages and disadvantages of the sole proprietorship and partnership forms of business organization.

2. Explain how the owners' equity accounts are affected by investments, withdrawals, and earnings.

3. Identify the purpose of the partnership agreement and the information it normally includes.

4. Summarize the significant characteristics of a partnership.

5. Describe the procedures for recording the formation of a partnership, division of profits and losses, admission and withdrawal of partners, and liquidation of a partnership.

6

Unincorporated Business Organizations

INTRODUCTION   There are three basic types of business organizations: (1) the sole proprietorship; (2) the partnership; and (3) the corporation. This chapter considers the accounting for unincorporated business organizations—sole proprietorships and partnerships.

THE SOLE   The simplest form of business organization is the sole proprietorship, a
PROPRIETORSHIP   business owned by a single individual. In terms of the absolute number of business firms, the sole proprietorship greatly outnumbers all other forms of business organizations in the United States. Because of their size, however, corporations account for the greatest dollar amount of both assets and sales. Sole proprietorships are the dominant form of business organization among smaller firms, particularly among businesses engaged in retail trade and in the rendering of services.

One of the principal advantages of the sole proprietorship is the ease of establishing this type of business. Other than local and possibly state licensing requirements, an owner need only have the necessary capital and begin operations in order to establish his firm. Legal contracts are not necessary and the proprietor is not required to comply with provisions of certain regulations or laws which apply to corporations. A proprietor owns, controls, and usually manages the firm's assets and receives the profits (or losses) from its operations. All earnings of the business are taxable to the owner whether he withdraws them from the firm or not. A sole proprietorship is not considered to be a separate entity for income tax purposes.

Usually, the primary disadvantage of a sole proprietorship as a form of business organization is its unlimited liability feature. If the assets of the business are insufficient to meet its obligations, a sole proprietor will be required to satisfy business creditors from his own personal resources. Other principal disadvantages of the sole proprietorship form of business organization include limitations on the availability of funds to the business and difficulties involved in the transferability of ownership. Funds or resources available to a sole proprietorship are limited to the personal assets of the owner and what he is able to borrow. Ownership may be transferred only by selling the entire business or by changing to another form of business organization.

Accounting for   It is primarily in the accounting for owner's equity that the accounts
a Proprietorship   of an unincorporated business differ significantly from those of a corporation. The owner's equity accounts of a sole proprietorship normally include only a capital account and a drawing account.

The capital account reflects the proprietor's equity in the assets of the business as of a specific point in time. Capital is credited for the investments made by the owner in the business and for the earnings of the period, and it is debited for a net loss during the period.

A separate drawing or withdrawals account may be maintained which is debited for the withdrawals of cash or other business assets made by the owner, or for any payments which are made from business funds in order to satisfy personal debts of the owner. The balance in the drawing account is closed or transferred to the capital account during the preparation of closing entries which are made at the end of the period. As an alternative, the drawing account may be omitted with all changes in the owner's equity recorded directly in the capital account. Either procedure accomplishes the same end result.

THE PARTNERSHIP

A somewhat more complicated form of business organization is the partnership. A major difference between the sole proprietorship and the partnership is that the partnership has more than a single owner. The partnership form of business organization is often used as a means of combining the resources and special skills or talents of two or more persons. In addition, state laws sometimes prevent the incorporation of certain businesses which provide professional services such as certified public accounting firms or associations of physicians. Although only two persons are required to form a partnership, there is no limit as to the number of partners. For example, in some CPA firms there are more than 800 partners.

The Uniform Partnership Act defines a partnership as "an association of two or more persons to carry on, as co-owners, a business for profit." Even though two or more persons may, in fact, operate a business as a partnership without a formal agreement, it is important that a written contract, known as the articles of co-partnership, be drawn up in order to clearly delineate the rights and duties of all partners and thereby avoid possible misunderstandings and disagreements. The partnership agreement serves as the basis for the formation and operation of the partnership. At a minimum, the partnership contract should usually include the following points:

1. Names of all partners.
2. Rights and duties of each partner.
3. Name of the partnership.
4. Nature and location of the business.
5. Effective date and the duration of the agreement.
6. Capital contribution of each partner.
7. Procedures for dividing profits and losses.
8. Any rights or limitations of withdrawals by partners.
9. Accounting period to be used.

10. Provisions for dissolution.
11. Procedures for arbitrating disputes.

Characteristics of a Partnership

The significant characteristics of the partnership form of organization are summarized briefly in the following paragraphs.

Ease of Formation. Partnerships may be formed with little difficulty. As was the case with a sole proprietorship, there are few legal formalities or regulations (aside from local and possibly state licensing requirements) to be complied with.

Mutual Agency. Normally, all partners act as agents of the partnership and as such have the power to enter into contracts in the ordinary course of business. These contracts bind the remaining partners. The concept of mutual agency provides an important reason for the careful selection of partners.

Unlimited Liability. Usually each partner may be held personally liable to partnership creditors for all the debts of the partnership in the event that the partnership assets are insufficient to meet its obligations. If one partner is unable to meet his obligations under the partnership agreement, the remaining partners are liable for these debts.

If a new partner is admitted to a partnership, the partnership agreement should indicate whether he assumes a liability for debts which were incurred prior to his admission into the partnership. When a partner withdraws from a partnership, he is not liable for partnership debts incurred *after* his withdrawal if proper notice has been given to the public, for example, by a legal notice in a newspaper. He is, however, liable for all debts which were incurred prior to his withdrawal unless he is released from these obligations by the creditors of the partnership.

Since any partner may bind the entire partnership when making contracts in the normal scope of business, a lack of good judgment on the part of a single partner could jeopardize both partnership assets and the personal resources of the individual partners. The mutual agency and unlimited liability features may discourage certain individuals with substantial personal resources from entering into a partnership agreement.

Limited Life. Since a partnership is based on a contract, a partnership is legally ended by the withdrawal, death, incapacity, or bankruptcy of any of its partners. Addition of a new partner also terminates the old partnership. Although the entry of a new partner or the exit of an old partner legally dissolves the partnership, the business may be continued without interruption by the formation of a new partnership. This is done on a continual basis by firms of attorneys, doctors, and CPAs.

Co-ownership by Partners. Partners are the co-owners of both the assets and the earnings of a partnership. The assets invested by each partner in the partnership are owned by all of the partners collectively. The income or loss of a partnership is divided among the partners according to the terms which are specified in the partnership agreement. If the partnership agreement specifies a method of dividing profits among the partners but is silent as to the division of losses, losses will be shared in the same manner as profits. If the manner of dividing profits or losses is not specified in the partnership agreement, partners will share profits and losses equally.

Evaluation of the Partnership Form of Organization

The primary disadvantages of organizing a business as a partnership include the unlimited liability of the owners, the mutual agency of all partners, and the limited life of the partnership. However, a partnership has certain advantages over both the sole proprietorship and the incorporated forms of business organization. In comparison to a sole proprietorship, a partnership has the advantage of being able to combine the individual skills or talents of partners and of pooling the capital of several individuals, both of which may be required to carry on a successful business. A partnership is much easier to form than a corporation and is subject to much less governmental regulation. In addition, a partnership may provide certain tax advantages. Like the sole proprietorship, the partnership itself is not subject to taxes. Individual partners are, however, required to pay income taxes on their share of the income of the partnership, whether or not these earnings are withdrawn from the business.

Accounting for a Partnership

The accounting for a partnership is very similar to that of a proprietorship except with regard to specific transactions involving the accounting for owners' equity. Since a partnership is owned by two or more persons, a separate capital account must be maintained for each owner and a separate drawing account may also be used for each partner. Further, the net income or loss for a period must be divided among the partners as specified by the terms of the partnership agreement. Additional accounting problems which are unique to partnerships may occur with the formation of a partnership, admission of a partner, withdrawal or death of a partner, and liquidation of a partnership.

Formation of a Partnership

Upon the formation of a partnership, resources invested by the partners are recorded in the accounts. A capital account for each partner is credited for the amount of net assets invested (assets contributed less liabilities assumed by the partnership). Individual asset accounts are debited for the assets contributed and liability accounts are credited for any debts assumed by the partnership.

If the investments made by the partners are entirely in the form of cash, the entry required would be a debit to cash and a credit to the partner's capital account for the amount of cash invested. When noncash assets such as land, equipment, or merchandise are invested, these assets should be recorded at their fair market values as of the date of investment. The valuations assigned to these assets may differ from the cost or book value of the assets on the books of the contributing partner prior to the formation of the partnership. Of course, the amounts recorded by the partnership must be agreed upon by all partners. Amounts agreed upon represent the acquisition cost of the assets to the newly formed partnership. The recording of assets at their current market value as of the date they were contributed to the partnership is necessary in order to provide a fair presentation in the partnership financial statements, and to assure a fair distribution of the property among partners in the event a dissolution of the partnership occurs.

To illustrate the entries which are required at the formation of a partnership, assume that Mantle and Maris, who operate separate sporting goods stores as sole proprietorships, agree to form a partnership by combining their two businesses. It is agreed that each partner will contribute $10,000 in cash and all of his individual business assets, and that the partnership will assume the liabilities of each of their separate businesses. Assuming that the partners have agreed upon the amounts at which noncash assets are to be recorded, the following journal entries on the books of the partnership would be necessary in order to record the formation of the M & M partnership:

Cash	10,000	
Accounts receivable	15,000	
Merchandise inventory	30,000	
Accounts payable		5,000
Mantle, Capital		50,000
Cash	10,000	
Merchandise inventory	35,000	
Building	50,000	
Land	15,000	
Notes payable		10,000
Maris, Capital		100,000

Division of Profits and Losses

The net income or loss of a partnership is divided among the partners according to the terms or procedures specified in the partnership agreement. As previously indicated, if provisions are made only for dividing profits, any losses are divided in the same manner as profits. In the absence of any provisions for sharing profits and losses in the partnership agreement, the law provides that they must be shared equally among the partners.

The specific method of dividing profits and losses selected in a partnership situation may be designed to recognize and compensate the partners for differences in their investments in the partnership, for differences in their personal services rendered, for special abilities or reputations of individual partners, or for some combination of these and other factors. The following are examples of some of the methods which may be given consideration in the division of partnership profits or losses:

1.   A fixed ratio base.
2.   A capital ratio base.
3.   Interest on capital.
4.   Salaries to partners.

The specific method chosen by the partners may incorporate one or more of the methods of dividing partnership profits and losses which are mentioned above and illustrated in the following paragraphs. As a basis for these illustrations, assume that the M & M partnership had net income of $30,000 for the year ended December 31, 19x1. The following capital accounts reflect the investments made by Mantle and Maris during 19x1.

Mantle, Capital		Maris, Capital	
	1/1/x1 50,000		1/1/x1 100,000
	7/1/x1 20,000		5/1/x1 60,000

Fixed Fractional Basis.   Partners may agree on any fractional or percentage basis as a means of dividing partnership profits and losses. For example, assume that in order to reflect differences in their initial capital contributions, services provided, and abilities, Mantle and Maris agreed to allocate one-fourth of any profits or losses to Mantle and three-fourths to Maris. Consequently, at the end of 19x1 the $30,000 net income would be allocated $7,500 to Mantle ($\frac{1}{4} \times$ $30,000) and $22,500 to Maris ($\frac{3}{4} \times$ $30,000). The division of net income is recorded with a closing entry—the income summary account is closed to each partner's individual capital account according to the terms of the partnership agreement. The entry required in order to divide the net income among the two partners is as follows:

```
Income summary  . . . . . . . . . . . . . . . . . . . . . . . . . . .  30,000
    Mantle, Capital  . . . . . . . . . . . . . . . . . . . . . . . . . .         7,500
    Maris, Capital  . . . . . . . . . . . . . . . . . . . . . . . . . .        22,500
```

Additional closing entries are also necessary in order to transfer any balances in the partners' drawing accounts to their respective capital accounts.
   Capital Ratio.   When the invested capital of a partnership is a major factor in the generation of income, net income is often divided on the basis of the relative capital balances of the partners. If a capital ratio is used, the partners must agree whether the beginning capital balances or average capital balances should be used.

For example, the partners may agree to distribute net income on the basis of capital balances at the beginning of the period. Division of the $30,000 net income of the M & M partnership on the basis of the ratio of the partners' beginning capital balances would be as follows:

Partner	Capital Balance 1/1/x1	Fraction of Total Capital	Division of Income
Mantle	$ 50,000	$50/$150 or 1/3	$10,000
Maris	100,000	$100/$150 or 2/3	20,000
Total	$150,000		$30,000

Thus, the income summary account would be closed to the partners' capital accounts at the end of the year by the following journal entry.

Income summary	30,000	
Mantle, Capital		10,000
Maris, Capital		20,000

In order to reflect any significant changes in the capital accounts which may occur during a period in the division of income, the partners may agree to use the average capital balance ratio as a means of sharing partnership income. The average capital balance for each partner is equal to the weighted average of the different balances in their capital account during a period. In order to compute the weighted average, each balance in a partner's capital account is multiplied by the number of months until the next transaction affected the balance or to the end of the period. The sum of these amounts is divided by 12 in order to yield the partner's average capital balance during the period.

For purposes of illustration we will assume that Mantle's capital balance at the beginning of the year was $50,000 and that Maris's was $100,000. Maris invested an additional $60,000 on May 1 and Mantle invested an additional $20,000 on July 1. The computation of the average capital balance for Mantle and Maris is as follows:

Partner	Date	Balance × Time	Total	Weighted Average
Mantle	1/1/x1	$ 50,000 × 6	= $ 300,000	
	7/1/x1	70,000 × 6	= 420,000	
			$ 720,000 ÷ 12 =	$ 60,000

Partner	Date	Balance × Time	Total	Weighted Average
Maris	1/1/x1	$100,000 × 4	= $ 400,000	
	5/1/x1	160,000 × 8	= 1,280,000	
			$1,680,000 ÷ 12 =	$140,000

After the average capital balances have been computed, the division of net income is based on the ratios of average capital per partner to total average capital. In the case of the M & M partnership, the calculation would be as follows:

Partner	Average Capital	Fraction of Total Average Capital	Division of Income
Mantle	$ 60,000	$60/$200 or 3/10	$ 9,000
Maris	140,000	$140/$200 or 7/10	21,000
Total	$200,000		$30,000

Interest on Capital. In some instances, only partial recognition may be given to unequal investments made by the partners in determining the division of income. This may be accomplished by allowing some fixed rate of interest on the capital balances and dividing remaining profits on some other basis. As in the use of capital ratios, interest may be based on beginning or on average capital balances during the period.

To illustrate, assume that Mantle and Maris agreed to allow each partner interest at the rate of 8 percent on his beginning capital balance, with any remaining profit to be divided equally. Under this agreement, the $30,000 net income for 19x1 would be divided as follows:

	Mantle	Maris	
Income.			$30,000
Interest:			
8% × $50,000.	$ 4,000		$ 4,000
8% × $100,000		$ 8,000	8,000
			$12,000
Remainder:			$18,000
$18,000 × ½	$ 9,000		$ 9,000
$18,000 × ½		$ 9,000	9,000
Total	$13,000	$17,000	$30,000

Salaries to Partners. As a means of recognizing differences in the value of personal services contributed to the partnership by individual partners, the partnership agreement may provide for "salary" allowances in the division of income. For this purpose, the agreed-upon salaries are used in the allocation of income but need not actually be paid to the partners. The partnership agreement may also allow for withdrawals of cash by the partners described as salaries. These withdrawals are treated like all withdrawals made by partners and debited to the drawing accounts; they are *not* salary expenses similar to those paid to employees. Salary allowances may be used in the division of partnership income whether or not the partners make any cash withdrawals.

To illustrate, assume that Mantle and Maris are allowed annual salaries of $6,000 and $8,000 respectively, with any remaining profits divided equally. The following division of the $30,000 profit for 19x1 would be made:

	Mantle	Maris	Total
Salaries.	$ 6,000	$ 8,000	$14,000
Remainder	8,000	8,000	16,000
Total	$14,000	$16,000	$30,000

Salaries and Interest on Capital. Sometimes both the investments of the individual partners and the value of personal services contributed by each may be quite different. In these situations, partners may agree to take into consideration both salaries and interest on capital investments in determining the division of income. Any remaining profit or loss may then be allocated on any agreed-upon fractional basis.

For example, assume that Mantle and Maris agree on the following division of income:

1. Annual salaries of $6,000 to Mantle and $8,000 to Maris.
2. Eight percent interest on beginning capital balances.
3. Any remainder to be divided equally.

Under this agreement, the $30,000 net income for 19x1 would be divided as follows:

	Mantle	Maris	Total
Salaries (per agreement)	$ 6,000	$ 8,000	$14,000
Interest:			
8% × $50,000.	4,000		4,000
8% × $100,000		8,000	8,000
Remainder	2,000	2,000	4,000
Total	$12,000	$18,000	$30,000

Allowing salaries or interest on capital is simply a procedure or step in the process of dividing partnership profits. Since partners are owners, their contributions of capital and personal services are made in an attempt to earn profits. Therefore, these amounts are not considered to be expenses and do not reduce the income of the business.

Salaries And/Or Interest in Excess of Income. In the previous illustrations, partnership net income exceeded the total salary and interest allowances to the partners, and the balance was divided between the partners according to the agreed-upon percentage. If net income is less than the sum of the allowable salaries and interest, or if there is a net loss for the period, the residual after the deduction of salaries and interest will be negative in amount. This negative amount must then be divided between the partners according to the agreed-upon fractional basis.

To illustrate this situation, assume the same salary and interest allowances as in the previous example. Further, assume that the M & M partnership had net income of only $20,000 for 19x1. The salary and interest allowances total $10,000 for Mantle and $16,000 for Maris. The total interest and salary allowances of $26,000 exceed the net income of the partnership for the period by $6,000. This excess must be deducted in determining the partners' share of the income as follows:

	Mantle	Maris	Total
Salaries.	$ 6,000	$ 8,000	$14,000
Interest.	4,000	8,000	12,000
Remainder (divided equally).	(3,000)	(3,000)	(6,000)
Total	$ 7,000	$13,000	$20,000

Partnership Financial Statements

The income statement of a partnership is very similar to that of either a sole proprietorship or a corporation. The statement does not reflect income tax expense, however, because the partnership is not subject to an income tax on its earnings. (Partners are taxed as individuals on their share of the partnership income.) In addition, the allocation of the net income among the partners is often included in the income statement as a final item below the net income figure.

The balance sheet of a partnership differs from that of a sole proprietorship or a corporation primarily in the owners' equity section. The equity section of a partnership reflects the end-of-period capital balances of each individual partner.

A statement disclosing the nature and amount of changes in the partners' capital balances during a period is often prepared for a partnership. For example, the Statement of Partners' Capital for the M & M partnership might appear as follows:

M & M
Statement of Partners' Capital
For the Year Ended December 31, 19x1

	Mantle	Maris	Total
Balances, January 1, 19x1	$50,000	$100,000	$150,000
Add: Additional investments.	20,000	60,000	80,000
Net income	15,000	15,000	30,000
Total	$85,000	$175,000	$260,000
Less: Withdrawals	(5,000)	(15,000)	(20,000)
Balances, December 31, 19x1	$80,000	$160,000	$240,000

Thus, the December 31, 19x1 balance sheet for M & M would include capital balances of $80,000 for Mantle and $160,000 for Maris.

Admission of a Partner

Although the admission of a new partner to a partnership legally dissolves the existing partnership, a new agreement may be created without disruption of business activities. An additional person may be admitted by purchasing an interest directly from one or more of the current partners or by making an investment in the partnership. When a new partner purchases his share of the partnership from a current partner, the payment is made directly to the selling partner(s). Therefore, there is no change in either the total assets or the total capital of the partnership. When a new partner invests in the partnership by contributing assets to the partnership, however, both the total assets and total capital of the partnership are increased.

Purchase of an Interest from Current Partner(s). When a new partner acquires his interest by purchasing all or part of the interest of one or more of the existing partners, the purchase price is paid directly to the selling partner(s). Therefore, the amount paid is not recorded in the partnership records. The only entry which is required in the accounts of the partnership is to transfer the interest sold from the selling partner's capital account(s) to a capital account for the new partner.

For example, assume that Mantle and Maris have capital balances of $80,000 and $160,000, respectively. Mantle agrees to sell one-half of his $80,000 interest in the partnership directly to Berra for $50,000. The entry to record this transaction on the partnership books is as follows:

```
Mantle, Capital . . . . . . . . . . . . . . . . . . . . . . . . . . . . . .   40,000
    Berra, Capital . . . . . . . . . . . . . . . . . . . . . . . . . . . . . .          40,000
```

The effect of this transaction is to transfer one half of Mantle's current capital balance ($\frac{1}{2} \times $80,000$) to the new capital account created for Berra. The total capital of the partnership, $240,000, is not affected by the transaction. The entry which was made was not affected by the amount paid by the incoming partner to the selling partner. The $50,000 payment made by Berra to Mantle reflects a bargained transaction between the two men acting as individuals, and as such does not affect the assets of the partnership.

Purchase of Interest by Investment in the Partnership. When the incoming partner contributes assets *to* the partnership for his interest, both the assets and the capital of the partnership are increased. To illustrate, again assume that Mantle and Maris are partners in the M & M Partnership with capital accounts of $80,000 and $160,000 respectively. They agree to admit Berra as a new partner with a one-fourth interest in the partnership for an investment of $80,000. The admission of Berra would be recorded by the following journal entry:

```
Cash . . . . . . . . . . . . . . . . . . . . . . . . . . . . . . . . . . . . . .   80,000
    Berra, Capital . . . . . . . . . . . . . . . . . . . . . . . . . . . .              80,000
```

After the admission of Berra, the total capital of the new partnership is as follows:

Maris, Capital.	$160,000
Mantle, Capital	80,000
Berra, Capital.	80,000
Total Capital	$320,000

Berra's capital balance of $80,000 represents a one-fourth interest in the total partnership capital of $320,000. It does not necessarily follow, however, that the new partner is entitled to a one-fourth share in the division of partnership income. Instead, the division of income or loss must be specified in the new partnership agrement.

Because balances in the asset accounts usually are not equal to their current values, the investment of the new partner may be more or less than the proportion of total assets represented by his agreed-upon capital interest. However, since the agreement concerning the new partner's relative capital interest should be reflected in the capital accounts, adjustments to the capital accounts will be necessary if the amount invested is not equal to the book value of the capital interest acquired. The adjustment required in recording the investment of the new partner is accomplished by using either the bonus method or the goodwill method.

When a new partner invests more than book value for his relative capital interest, a bonus or goodwill may be allocated to the old partners. To illustrate these two different methods, assume that Mantle and Maris, who share profits equally and have capital balances of $80,000 and $160,000 respectively, agree to admit Berra to a one-fourth interest in the new partnership for $120,000.

Bonus to Old Partners. The total net assets of the partnership after the $120,000 investment by Berra will be $360,000 ($240,000 + $120,000). In order to acquire a one-fourth interest in the net assets of the partnership, or $90,000 ($\frac{1}{4}$ × $360,000), Berra was required to invest $120,000. The excess of the investment over the amount of capital allocated to Berra may be regarded as a bonus to the old partners. The old partners share the bonus in their agreed-upon profit and loss ratio. Each partner's share of the bonus is credited to his capital account. The entry to record Berra's investment in the partnership (assuming an equal distribution of profits and losses between Mantle and Maris) is:

Cash	120,000	
Berra, Capital		90,000
Mantle, Capital		15,000
Maris, Capital		15,000

Thus, after the investment, Berra has a capital balance of $90,000 which represents one fourth of the total capital of $360,000.

Goodwill to Old Partners. Alternatively, if the new partner's investment exceeds his relative share of the net assets of the new partnership, it may be assumed that the old partnership had goodwill. The amount of goodwill is determined by the initial investment of the new partner. To illustrate, the $120,000 investment made by Berra represented a one-fourth interest in the partnership. The fact that a one-fourth interest required an investment of $120,000 implies that the business is worth $480,000 ($120,000 ÷ ¼). The amount of goodwill is computed as follows:

Investment by Berra for a ¼ interest		$120,000
Implied value of Business ($120,000 ÷ ¼)		$480,000
Net asset value exclusive of goodwill:		
Capital of old partners	$240,000	
Investment by Berra	120,000	360,000
Goodwill		$120,000

As was the case with the bonus, the goodwill is divided between the old partners in the same proportion as their profit and loss ratios unless a specific agreement is made to the contrary. The entries which are required in order to record the admission of the new partner (again assuming an equal distribution of profits and losses) are as follows:

Cash	120,000	
Berra, Capital		120,000
Goodwill	120,000	
Mantle, Capital		60,000
Maris, Capital		60,000

The capital balances of the partners after the admission of Berra are as follows:

Mantle, Capital	$140,000
Maris, Capital	220,000
Berra, Capital	120,000
	$480,000

It can be seen that Berra's share of the total capital is the agreed-upon one-fourth interest in the partnership ($120,000/$480,000).

Note that the choice between the bonus and goodwill methods results in different account balances (but the same relative capital interests). The goodwill method causes the total capital of the partners to be larger by the amount of the goodwill recorded. Thus, the choice between methods results in different financial statements.

When the new partner invests less than the book value of his relative capital interest, a bonus or goodwill may be allocated to the incoming partner. To illustrate, assume that Mantle and Maris agree to admit Berra with a one fourth interest in the partnership for an investment of only $60,000.

Bonus to New Partner. Based on this method, the excess of the new partner's share of total capital over his investment is allocated as a bonus to the new partner. The amount of the bonus is calculated as follows:

Total capital prior to admission:		
Mantle, Capital	$ 80,000	
Maris, Capital	160,000	$240,000
Investment by Berra		60,000
Total capital		$300,000
Berra's one-fourth interest		$ 75,000
Investment by Berra		60,000
Bonus to Berra		$ 15,000

The bonus may be treated as a reduction of the old partners' capital accounts on the basis of their profit and loss ratio and as a credit to the new partner's capital. The entry to record the admission of the new partner assuming an equal distribution of profits and losses between Mantle and Maris is:

Cash	60,000	
Mantle, Capital	7,500	
Maris, Capital	7,500	
Berra, Capital		75,000

Goodwill to New Partner. If the new partner's investment is less than his agreed-upon capital interest, the difference may be due to goodwill brought to the partnership by the incoming partner. This goodwill may be attributable to the reputation or special skills of the new partner which might be imparted to increase the earning power of the partnership entity. The goodwill is recorded as an asset with a corresponding credit to the new partner's capital account in order to allow him the agreed-upon capital interest in the partnership. There is no change in the capital accounts of the old partners.

To illustrate, assume that Mantle and Maris had capital balances of $80,000 and $160,000 respectively prior to the admission of Berra with a one-fourth interest in the partnership. Since the total capital of Mantle and Maris, $240,000, represents a three-fourths interest in the total capital of the partnership after Berra is admitted, the implied value of the partnership is $320,000 ($240,000 ÷ ¾). However, the actual tangible assets of the firm after Berra's investment are $300,000, consisting of net assets of $240,000 prior to the admission of Berra plus the $60,000 investment. Therefore, the implied goodwill is $20,000 ($320,000 − $300,000). The entry required to record the admission of the new partner under the goodwill method is as follows:

```
Cash . . . . . . . . . . . . . . . . . . . . . . . . . . . . . . . . . . . .   60,000
Goodwill. . . . . . . . . . . . . . . . . . . . . . . . . . . . . . . . . .   20,000
    Berra, Capital . . . . . . . . . . . . . . . . . . . . . . . . . . .            80,000
```

After his admission, Berra has the agreed-upon one-fourth interest in total capital ($80,000/$320,000).

Withdrawal of a Partner

When one partner withdraws from a partnership, he may dispose of his partnership interest in any one of several ways:

1. Sell his interest to a new partner.
2. Sell his interest to one or more of the remaining partners with the payment coming from the personal resources of the purchasing partner(s).
3. Sell his interest to the partnership with the payment from partnership funds.

In the first two cases, the sale and purchase is made among the partners themselves acting as individuals. Therefore, the accounting treatment is the same as for the admission of a new partner through the purchase of an interest from the existing partners. The journal entry required on the partnership books is simply to transfer the capital account balance by debiting the capital account of the retiring partner and crediting the capital account(s) of the purchasing partner(s). There is no effect on either the assets or the total capital of the partnership.

If the withdrawing partner is paid from partnership assets, both the total assets and total capital of the firm are decreased. Because the current value and the recorded book values of the partnership assets probably differ, the withdrawing partner may be paid either more or less than the amount of his capital balance. The difference may be attributable, for example, to the change in value of certain specific assets or alternatively to the existence of goodwill or to a combination of both factors. The change in the asset values or goodwill may be recorded in the accounts and shared by the partners in their profit and loss ratios.

For example, assume that Mantle, Berra, and Maris have capital balances of $100,000, $120,000, and $180,000 respectively, and share profits and losses on a one-fourth, one-fourth, and one-half basis. Further, assume that it is agreed to pay Mantle $120,000 from partnership funds upon his withdrawal from the partnership, and that the fair value of the partnership at that time is $480,000. Assuming that specific assets cannot be identified to account for the increase in value, the entries required in order to record the goodwill and the withdrawal of Mantle are as follows:

Goodwill.	80,000	
Mantle, Capital		20,000
Berra, Capital		20,000
Maris, Capital		40,000
Mantle, Capital	120,000	
Cash		120,000

Instead of an increase in the value of specific assets or the existence of goodwill, the difference between the payment to the withdrawing partner and his capital balance may be regarded as a bonus paid to the withdrawing partner by the remaining partners. This bonus is charged to the capital accounts of the old partners in the relative profit and loss ratios of the remaining partners. Under this assumption, the withdrawal of Mantle would be recorded as follows:

Mantle, Capital	100,000	
Maris, Capital	13,333	
Berra, Capital	6,667	
Cash		120,000

The $20,000 bonus to the retiring partner was deducted from the remaining partners' capital balances on the basis of their relative profit and loss ratios of ⅔ for Maris (50%/75%) and ⅓ for Berra (25%/75%).

If the payment made to the withdrawing partner is less than his capital balance, the difference may be attributable either to specific assets that have fair values which are less than their recorded book values or to a bonus paid by the retiring partner to the remaining partners in order to retire from the partnership without undergoing a liquidation of the business. Again, the revaluation of the assets of the partnership or the bonus is divided among the partners according to their profit and loss sharing ratio.

For example, if Mantle agrees to retire for a payment of $85,000, and it is agreed that the assets of the partnership are not overvalued, the entry to record the withdrawal would be as follows:

Mantle, Capital 100,000	
Maris, Capital	10,000
Berra, Capital	5,000
Cash	85,000

Again, Maris and Berra would share the $15,000 difference ($100,000 — $85,000) on the basis of their relative profit and loss ratios of ⅔ and ⅓ (as above).

LIQUIDATION OF THE PARTNERSHIP

When a partnership goes out of business, its assets are sold, its liabilities are paid, and any remaining cash is distributed to the partners. This process is referred to as a liquidation.

As a basis for illustration, assume that Mantle, Maris, and Berra agree to liquidate their partnership. Profits and losses are allocated one-fourth to Mantle, one-fourth to Berra, and one-half to Maris. The balance sheet of the partnership just prior to the liquidation process appeared as follows:

M, M & B
Balance Sheet
As of December 31, 19x1

Cash	$ 20,000	Liabilities	$ 50,000
Noncash assets	430,000	Mantle, Capital	100,000
		Maris, Capital	180,000
		Berra, Capital	120,000
	$450,000		$450,000

Assume that all of the noncash assets of the partnership are sold for $330,000, a loss of $100,000 ($430,000 — $330,000).

Any gain or loss on the sale of the partnership assets must be divided among the partners according to their agreed-upon profit and loss ratios before any cash is distributed to the partners. Thus, the $100,000 loss on the sale of the noncash assets of the partnership would be distributed among the partners as follows:

	Total	Mantle	Maris	Berra
Capital balance	$400,000	$100,000	$180,000	$120,000
Distribution of loss	(100,000)	(25,000)	(50,000)	(25,000)
Capital balance after sale	$300,000	$ 75,000	$130,000	$ 95,000

The entries required in order to record the sale of the assets and the distribution of the loss would be as follows:

Cash	330,000	
Loss on sale	100,000	
Noncash assets		430,000
Mantle, Capital	25,000	
Maris, Capital	50,000	
Berra, Capital	25,000	
Loss on sale		100,000

After the noncash assets of the partnership have been sold and the gain or loss has been divided among the partners, the cash will be distributed first to creditors and then to the partners. The amount of cash to be distributed to each partner is reflected in the capital balances after all gains or losses on the sale of noncash assets have been recorded. The balance sheet prior to the distribution of cash appears as follows:

M, M & B
Balance Sheet
January 10, 19x2

Cash	$350,000	Liabilities	$ 50,000
		Mantle, Capital	75,000
		Maris, Capital	130,000
		Berra, Capital	95,000
	$350,000		$350,000

The distribution of the cash, first to the creditors of the partnership and then to the partners, is recorded by the following entries:

Liabilities	50,000	
Cash		50,000
Mantle, Capital	75,000	
Maris, Capital	130,000	
Berra, Capital	95,000	
Cash		300,000

In the previous example, the capital account of each partner had a credit balance after the loss on the sale of noncash assets was distributed. In some instances, one or more of the partners may have a debit balance in his capital account as a result of losses on the disposal of the assets. This debit balance is referred to as a capital deficit since the partnership has a legal claim against the partner. If this claim cannot be collected by the partnership, the deficit must be divided among the remaining partners' capital balances according to their profit and loss ratios.

To illustrate, assume that the M, M & B partnership has the same assets and liabilities as in the preceding example. Further assume that the capital balances prior to liquidation are Mantle, $40,000; Maris, $210,000; and Berra, $150,000; and that the noncash assets are sold for $230,000 (a loss of $200,000). The capital accounts after the distribution of the loss would be as follows:

	Total	Mantle	Maris	Berra
Capital balances.	$400,000	$40,000	$210,000	$150,000
Loss on sale of noncash assets	(200,000)	(50,000)	(100,000)	(50,000)
Capital balance	$200,000	($10,000)	$110,000	$100,000

After payment of the $50,000 of liabilities, the balance sheet of M, M & B would appear as follows:

M, M & B
Balance Sheet
January 10, 19x2

Cash	$200,000	Mantle, Capital	$ (10,000)
		Maris, Capital.	110,000
		Berra, Capital.	100,000
	$200,000		$200,000

If Mantle is able to pay his capital deficiency to the partnership, the following entry would be made:

Cash 10,000
    Mantle, Capital 10,000

At this point Mantle would have a zero capital balance, and the $210,000 cash on hand would be distributed to Maris and Berra in amounts equal to the balances in their capital accounts.

If the partnership is unable to collect the capital deficiency from Mantle, this loss would be absorbed by the remaining partners. Since the partnership agreement provides that Maris had a one-half share and Berra a one-fourth share of profits and losses, their current interest in profits and losses is Maris's two-thirds (50%/75%) and Berra's one-third (25%/75%). The loss should be written off against the capital accounts of the remaining partners as follows:

Maris, Capital 6,667
Berra, Capital 3,333
    Mantle, Capital 10,000

Accordingly, the distribution of the $200,000 cash would be based on the amount of the partners' capital balances after allowances for the loss on the noncollection of the capital deficiency. These amounts are as follows:

	Mantle	Maris	Berra
Capital balances	($10,000)	$110,000	$100,000
Capital deficiency	10,000	(6,667)	(3,333)
	–0–	$103,333	$ 96,667

The entry to record the distribution of the cash would be:

Maris, Capital	103,333	
Berra, Capital	96,667	
Cash		200,000

In the event that any cash is subsequently received from the deficient partner, it would be divided between the remaining partners in their profit and loss sharing ratio, since that is how they shared the deficiency.

SUMMARY

The simplest and most common form of business organization is the sole proprietorship. A single individual owns, controls, and usually manages the firm's assets and receives the profits from its operations. The sole proprietorship is not considered a separate entity for income tax purposes and the owner is taxed on all earnings of the business, whether or not the owner withdraws them. Investments and earnings are generally recorded in the capital account and withdrawals in the drawing account. The drawing account, if used, is then closed to the capital account at the end of the period.

Accounting for the partnership form of business organization is considerably more complex in that more than a single owner is involved. A partnership is an association of two or more persons organized to carry on, as co-owners, a business for profit. The partnership agreement serves as the basis for the formation and operation of the partnership and should include all essential data. Significant characteristics of a partnership include the ease of formation, the applicability of the mutual agency concept, the existence of unlimited liability of each partner and limited life of the enterprise, and the co-ownership of the assets and earnings. The partnership has certain advantages, such as the ability to combine the skills and capital of several individuals, and certain disadvantages, such as unlimited liability of the partners. Of course, these (and other relevant) factors should be evaluated and weighed in each case.

A separate individual capital and drawing account is maintained for each partner. Upon the formation of the partnership, each capital account is credited for that individual's cash contibution or an agreed-upon value of property contributions. At the end of each period, profits or losses are divided among the partners according to the terms of the partnership agreement. When a new partner is admitted to an existing partnership, either by the purchase of an interest from a current partner or by a direct investment in the partnership, the old partners may receive a bonus which is credited to their capital accounts. In addition, if the new partner's investment differs from his relative share of the net assets of the new partnership, goodwill may need to be allocated to either the old partners or the new partner. When an existing partner withdraws from the partnership, the exact nature of the necessary entries to record the withdrawal will depend on whether it is accomplished by a sale to a new partner, by a sale to existing partners as individuals, or by a sale to existing partners with payment from partnership funds. When and if the partnership is liquidated, its assets are sold, its liabilities are paid, and any remaining cash is distributed to the partners.

KEY DEFINITIONS

Capital account The capital account of a partnership consists of a separate account for each partner which reflects the investments by the partners plus each partner's share of the earnings or losses from the operations of the business less any withdrawals made by the partners.

Division of profits and losses The agreement determines the method of dividing partnership profits or losses among the partners. In the absence of such an agreement, the law provides that profits or losses shall be divided equally among the partners.

Drawing account Cash or other assets withdrawn by a partner during the period are reflected in the partner's drawing account. The drawing accounts are closed to the partners' capital accounts at the end of the period.

Interest on capital This is a method which provides for partners' capital interests as a factor in the distribution of the partnership earnings.

Limited life A partnership is legally dissolved upon the withdrawals, death, incapacity, or bankruptcy of any of its partners.

Liquidation The process of terminating a business in which its assets are sold, its liabilities are paid, and any remaining cash or other assets are distributed to its owners.

Mutual agency Each partner may act as an agent of the partnership, with the power to enter into contracts within the scope of the normal business operations.

Partnership An association of two or more persons to carry on a business under a contractual arrangement.

Partnership agreement This written contract of partnership sets forth the agreement between the partners as to the conditions for the formation and operation of the partnership.

Salaries to partners A method which provides for the division of a portion of the partnership income by allocating specified salaries to the partners.

Sole proprietorship A business owned by one person.

Statement of partners' capital This statement shows the nature and amount of changes in the partners' capital accounts during a period.

Uniform Partnership Act This act, which has been adopted in most states, governs the formation, operation, and liquidation of partnerships.

Unlimited liability Each partner is personally liable to the creditors of the partnership in the event that the partnership assets are insufficient to meet its obligations.

1. List the three basic types of business organizations.

2. What are the primary advantages of the partnership form of organization?

3. List and describe three important disadvantages of organizing a business as a partnership.

4. Explain the difference between admittance of a new partner to a partnership by making an investment in the partnership and admittance by purchasing an interest from a partner.

5. Smith is a partner in the Smith and Jones Partnership. At the end of the year, Smith's share of the partnership income is $20,000. During the year, Smith had withdrawals of $10,000. What amount of income should be included in Smith's taxable income for the year?

6. Upon the formation of a partnership, at what amount should the investments of noncash assets be recorded? Why is this necessary?

7. What factors are usually considered in determining the method for dividing partnership income?

8. In the absence of a specific agreement, how should the profit or loss of a partnership be allocated among the partners? If there is a specific method for allocating profits in the partnership agreement but no mention of losses, how should a net loss be divided among the partners?

9. Why does the agreement for division of partnership earnings often allow for salaries and interest on partners' capital balances?

10. When a new partner is admitted to a partnership and goodwill or a bonus is attributed to the old partners, how is the goodwill or bonus distributed to the capital accounts?

11. What is the effect of gains or losses resulting from the liquidation of a partnership on the partners' capital balances? How are the gains or losses divided among the partners?

12. After the distribution of a loss on liquidation, assume that one partner has a debit balance in his capital account. If the partner is unable to contribute any personal assets, how is the loss divided among the remaining partners?

13. Bibby and Rowe formed a partnership on January 1, 19x1. Bibby contributed $75,000 capital while Rowe contributed $50,000 capital. No additions to capital were made during the year. For the year ended December 31, 19x1, the partnership had net income of $25,000. Prepare a schedule showing the division of income in each of the following cases:

a.   Partners agree to allocate ⅓ of profits or losses to Rowe and ⅔ to Bibby.

b.   Partners agree to distribute net income on the basis of their capital balances in the partnership.

c.   Bibby and Rowe agree to allow each partner 8 percent interest on his beginning capital balance and divide the remaining profits equally.

14.   Assume that Bibby and Rowe made withdrawals of $5,000 and $7,000, respectively, during 19x1. Give the entries to record the division of income in 13(a) above and the entries to record the closing of the withdrawals account.

15.   Assume that Erickson and Goodrich, who have capital balances of $160,000 and $320,000, respectively, and who divide profits equally, agree to admit Hazard to a ¼ interest in the new partnership for $200,000. Make the entry to record Hazard's investment in the partnership under both the bonus method and the goodwill method.

16.   Martin is withdrawing from the partnership of Martin, Water, and Osmond. The capital accounts of partnership are as follows: Martin, $10,000; Water, $10,000; and Osmond, $20,000. The partners share profits and losses equally. The partners agree that Martin will be paid $12,000 cash for his interest in the partnership. Give the entries to record the retirement of Martin using the bonus method.

17.   The partnership of Jones, Clare, and Jackson is being liquidated on December 31, 19x1. The balances in the capital accounts prior to liquidation of the assets were as follows: Jones, $25,000; Clare, $20,000; and Jackson, $5,000. The partners share profits and losses equally. On December 31, partnership assets with a book value of $60,000 were sold for $39,000, and liabilities of $10,000 were paid.

Required:

How should the remaining $29,000 available cash be distributed if Jackson is unable to pay the amount he owes to the firm?

18.   Bob Billy and Thomas Sloan decided to form a partnership. Bob said he would contribute a building which he purchased three years ago for $15,000. The book value of the building now is $10,000. A real estate dealer said the building could be sold presently for $18,000. Thomas said he would contribute land worth $50,000 to the partnership. The land had a mortgage of $35,000 which was to be paid over the next 10 years.

Required:

1.   What will be the balance in Bob and Thomas' capital accounts when the partnership is formed?

2.   Make entries to record the formation of the partnership.

19. In the Bell and Grubb Partnership, Bell had a capital balance on January 1, 19x1 of $26,000 and Grubb, $32,000. On June 1, Bell made a contribution of $6,000 to the partnership and on October 1, Grubb made a $3,000 contribution. The partners both receive 6 percent interest a year on their average capital balances and also divide net income based on the capital ratio of their average capital balances. If net income for 19x1 is $12,000, calculate each partner's share of the profits.

20. The capital balances for the partners of the Kingston Company as of December 31, 19x1 are as follows: Joe Kingston, $12,000; Bill Kingston, $15,000; and Paul Kingston, $13,000. The following transactions affecting their capital accounts occurred during the year.

   a. Joe and Bill Kingston withdrew $1,000 a month from the business and Paul withdrew $1,500 a month.
   b. Bill and Paul contributed $3,000 and $5,000 to the partnership, respectively.
   c. Net income for the year ending 12/31/x2 is $35,600. The profits are divided in the following manner: Joe, 50 percent; Bill, 20 percent; Paul, 30 percent.

   Required:

   Write a statement of partners' capital for the year December 31, 19x2.

21. Assume that in the Torberg and Haddix Partnership, Torberg has a capital balance of $75,000 and Haddix has a capital balance of $60,000. Make journal entries under each of the following unrelated assumptions.

   a. Haddix sells one-half of his $60,000 interest in the partnership to Carty for $40,000.
   b. Carty is admitted with a one-third interest in the partnership for an investment of $67,500. Total capital is to be $202,500.
   c. Carty is admitted with a one-third interest in the partnership for an investment of $70,500. Bonus is allowed old partners.
   d. Carty is admitted with a one-third interest in the partnership for an investment of $66,000. Bonus to Carty is recognized.

22. Lowenstein, Manning, and Norris have decided to liquidate their partnership. The balance sheet just prior to liquidation appears as follows:

LM&N
Balance Sheet
As of September 30, 19x1

Cash..................	$ 40,000	Liabilities	$100,000
Noncash assets........	860,000	Lowenstein, Capital.....	360,000
		Manning, Capital.......	200,000
		Norris, Capital........	240,000
	$900,000		$900,000

The noncash assets were sold for $980,000. Make the journal entries to record the gain or loss on the sale of the assets, payment of liabilities, and distribution of remaining cash to the partners. The profits and losses are shared equally.

PROBLEMS

23. Vallely and Patterson form a partnership with Vallely investing capital of $70,000 and Patterson investing capital of $30,000. The partners agree to allow 8 percent interest on each partner's beginning capital balance. Also, due to differences in services rendered, Patterson·is to receive a salary of $8,000 while Vallely receives a salary of $4,500. Any remaining profits or losses are to be divided equally. Make a schedule showing the division of partnership net income assuming the partnership earned $16,000 for the first year of its operations.

24. Johnson and Kennedy formed a partnership on January 1, 19x1, with investments of $40,000 each. Kennedy made an additional investment of $20,000 on June 30, 19x1. Given each of the following assumptions, determine the division of partnership net income of $27,000 for the year:

a. No method for division of income specified in the partnership agreement.
b. Divided in the ratio of the ending capital balance.
c. Divided in the ratio of the average capital balances.
d. Interest at a rate of 10 percent on the ending capital balance and the remainder divided equally.
e. Salary allowances of $10,000 to Johnson and $5,000 to Kennedy and any remainder divided ⅓ to Johnson and ⅔ to Kennedy.
f. Interest at a rate of 10 percent on the ending capital balances, salary allowance of $12,000 to Johnson and $8,000 to Kennedy, and any remainder divided equally.

25. Taylor, Smith, and Jones are partners in the TSJ Partnership. The partnership agreement provides for the following procedures for division of income:

a. Each partner is allowed 5 percent interest on the average capital balance.
b. Salary allowances of $10,000 to Taylor and $12,000 to Smith.
c. Remainder divided 50 percent to Taylor, 30 percent to Smith, and 20 percent to Jones.

During the current year, the average capital balances were $60,000, Taylor; $40,000, Smith; and $20,000, Jones.

Calculate the division of income among the partners in each of the following cases:

a. Net income, $38,000.
b. Net income, $18,000.
c. Net loss, $2,000.

26. Able and Baker agree to admit Comer into their partnership with a one-fourth interest. Currently, Able has capital of $20,000 and Baker has capital of $10,000. They share profits and losses equally. Give the journal entries necessary to record the admission of Comer for each of the following investments by Comer:

a. $10,000.
b. $20,000 using the bonus method.
c. $20,000 using the goodwill method.
d. $ 6,000 using the bonus method.
e. $ 6,000 using the goodwill method.

27. Wilkes, Lee, and Curtis have capital balances of $60,000, $80,000, and $100,000, respectively, in their partnership. They share profits on a ¼, ¼, and ½ basis, respectively. Wilkes withdraws from the partnership, and it is agreed that he will be paid $70,000 for his share of the partnership. At the time of Wilkes's withdrawal, the fair value of the partnership is $280,000.

Required:

Make the entries to record the withdrawal of Wilkes under the goodwill and bonus methods.

28. Kemp, Killough, and Kubin agree to liquidate their partnership on January 1, 19x1. The balance sheet of the firm as of that date is as follows:

Cash		$10,000
Accounts receivable		15,000
Inventory		30,000
Equipment	$60,000	
Less: Accumulated depreciation	(30,000)	30,000
Total Assets		$85,000
Accounts payable		$ 5,000
Kemp, capital		40,000
Killough, capital		30,000
Kubin, capital		10,000
Total Liabilities and Capital		$85,000

Profits and losses are distributed 50 percent to Kemp, 30 percent to Killough, and 20 percent to Kubin. On January 1, 19x1, the noncash assets were sold as follows: Accounts Receivable, $10,000; Inventory, $20,000; and Equipment, $15,000.

Required:

Prepare a schedule showing the distribution of cash to the partners upon liquidation.

29. Brown, Gray, and White agree to liquidate their partnership. Prior to beginning the liquidation process, they have cash, $15,000; other assets, $90,000; liabilities, $20,000; and capital balances of $50,000, $25,000, and $10,000, respectively. Profits and losses are divided among the partners in the ratio of 4:4:2, respectively. None of the partners had any personal assets outside of the firm. The realization and liquidation proceeded as follows:

a. $50,000 of other assets were sold for $30,000.
b. The liabilities were paid.
c. The remaining other assets were sold for $10,000.
d. The cash was distributed to the partners.

Required:

Prepare a schedule showing the effects of the liquidation process on the partners' capital accounts and the amounts distributed to the partners upon liquidation.

30. Hawk and Dove formed a partnership on January 1, 19x1, combining their separate businesses that they had operated as sole proprietorships. The account balances of the noncash assets contributed, and their agreed-upon fair values are shown below:

Hawk	Book Value	Fair Value
Accounts receivable....................	$20,000	$20,000
Inventory	10,000	15,000
Equipment	20,000	25,000
Accounts payable.....................	10,000	10,000
Dove		
Inventory	5,000	6,000
Building	25,000	32,000
Land................................	10,000	12,000

In addition, Hawk invested $5,000 in cash and Dove contributed $25,000 in cash. They agreed to share profits and losses equally.

Required:

1. Prepare the journal entries required on the books of the partnership to record the investments in the partnerships on January 1, 19x1.
2. Prepare a balance sheet for the partnership on January 1, 19x1.
3. On December 31, 19x1, the partnership income was calculated as $20,000. Hawk and Dove had $5,000 and $8,000 debit balances, respectively, in their drawing accounts. Prepare the entries to close the Income Summary and Drawing accounts on December 31, 19x1.

31. The Lord & Davis partnership began business on January 1, 19x1, Lord and Davis were to share profits in a 2:1 ratio. Below is a list of transactions affecting the partner's capital accounts which occurred during their first year of business. Journalize these transactions in chronological order, including closing entries.

a. Initially, Lord contributed a building with a fair market value of $55,000. The building held an unpaid mortgage of $15,000. Davis contributed cash of $35,000.
b. On February 10, July 16, and November 12, Lord withdrew $7,000 and Davis withdrew $6,500 (i.e., Lord withdrew a total of $21,000 during the year).
c. On June 15, Lord contributed stock to the partnership worth $25,000.
d. On September 30, the partnership admitted a new partner, Gagnon, for a one-fourth interest. Gagnon invested $15,000 in cash and his capital balance was to equal $17,000. A bonus was recognized to Gagnon because of his knowledge and expertise in the business.
e. Net income for the year ended December 31, 19x1 was $96,000. Since Gagnon entered the partnership on September 30, he was to receive one-fourth of his pro rata share of the profits and losses.
f. Due to severe illness, Davis decided to withdraw from the partnership as of the end of the year. It is agreed upon by the other partners that the assets of the partnership are not overvalued, and that Davis should receive a payment of $40,000 with a bonus recognized to the remaining partners.

32.   Below is the trial balance for the A&M Partnership.

A&M
Trial Balance
For the Year Ended December 31, 19x1

	Dr.(Cr.)
Current assets.....................	$307,100
Fixed assets, net...................	844,180
Current liabilities..................	(157,000)
8 percent mortgage note payable......	(290,000)
Anthony, Capital...................	(515,000)
Martini, Capital...................	(150,000)
Anthony, Drawing.................	24,000
Martini, Drawing..................	16,000
Sales............................	(827,000)
Cost of sales.....................	695,000
Administrative expenses.............	16,900
Other miscellaneous expenses........	11,120
Interest expense...................	11,700
Depreciation expense...............	13,000

Anthony and Martini share profits and losses in 3:1 ratio. Anthony has a tax rate of 35 percent and Martini has a tax rate of 20 percent.

Required:

1.   What is the net income for the A&M Partnership for the year ended December 31, 19x1?
2.   After allocation of net income and closing entries, what is the balance in each partner's capital account?
3.   What income taxes must be paid by the partnership? The partners? (Disregard any other possible deductions by the partners).

33.   On July 1, 19x1, Alford and Billy combined their two potato chip businesses into a partnership. Below are the balances in their accounts at that date:

	Book Value	Fair Market Value
Alford:		
Accounts receivable...............	$ 30,000	$30,000
Inventory........................	12,000	9,000
Equipment	45,000	50,000
Accounts payable.................	18,000	18,000

	Book Value	Fair Market Value
Billy:		
Accounts receivable...............	$ 22,000	$22,000
Marketable securities..............	35,000	42,000
Buildings and land................	100,000	90,000
Accounts payable.................	23,000	23,000

The fair-market value has been agreed upon by the two partners on each item. Also, Alford and Billy each contributed $5,000 in cash. During the year, Alford withdrew $20,000 in cash and Billy, $25,000 in cash. The net profit for the year was $65,000.

Required:

Prepare journal entries to record:

1. Initial investment in the partnership on July 1, 19x1.
2. Closing entries as of June 30, 19x2, the end of the partnership's fiscal year along with a statement of Partner's Capital for the year then ended.

34. The 3C's Partnership began operations on July 1, 19x1. Each partner, Coon, Cassidy, and Candon, was to receive a one-third interest in the partnership. The following transactions occurred during the fiscal year which affected their capital accounts:

   a. On July 1, each partner contributed $25,000 in cash to the partnership. In addition to the cash, Coon contributed a building with a fair market value of $33,000 and a book value of $37,000.
   b. Each partner decided to withdraw their yearly salary at different dates. Therefore, Coon withdrew $15,000 on October 1; Cassidy withdrew $13,500 on December 15; and Candon withdrew $14,000 on February 1, 19x2.
   c. On December 30, Cassidy decided he wanted to sell his partnership interest and join the Peace Corps. Candon's brother-in-law, Casey, said he would pay Cassidy $12,000 for his one-third interest. It was decided at this time that Casey would receive Cassidy's share of the profit or loss up to December 30.
   d. On January 31, Candon contributed land to the partnership with a fair market value of $80,000. However, the land still had an outstanding mortgage of $60,000.
   e. On March 19, Casey contributed an additional $15,000 in cash.
   f. The first year ending June 30, 19x2 turned out to be rather unsuccessful, netting a loss of $27,000.
   g. Also on June 30, Coon decided to withdraw from the partnership and join Vista. The remaining partners agreed to pay Coon $36,500, and that the fair value of the partnership at this time is $81,000. The partners could not identify specific assets which had increased in values. Therefore, goodwill was recognized.

Required:

Record these transactions in journal form, including closing entries as of June 30, 19x2.

Chapter 7 considers issues relating to the formation of a corporation, the issuance of capital stock, and matters relating to the retained earnings and dividends of a corporation. Studying this chapter should enable you to:

1. Discuss the steps required to form a corporation and the accounting treatment of any related expenditures incurred in so doing.

2. Distinguish between capital stock authorized, issued, and outstanding.

3. Describe the accounting entries necessary to record issuance of or subscriptions to capital stock.

4. Provide examples of extraordinary items and discuss the two essential characteristics of an extraordinary item.

5. Describe the situation in which prior period adjustments are appropriate.

6. List and give examples of three types of accounting changes.

7. Compute earnings per share and book value per share and explain the significance of each.

8. Recognize the accounting entries required to record the declaration and payment of both cash and stock dividends.

9. Discuss the purpose of and accounting procedures for treasury stock.

7

The Corporation:
Capital Stock,
Earnings, Dividends

INTRODUCTION

A corporation is an artificial "legal" person that is both separate and distinct from its owners and, as such, is permitted to engage in any acts which could be performed by a natural person. It may hold property, enter into contracts, and engage in other activities not prohibited by law. The classic definition of a corporation was given by Chief Justice Marshall in 1819 as " . . . an artificial being, invisible, intangible, and existing only in contemplation of the law."

Although there are fewer businesses organized as corporations than as either sole proprietorships or partnerships, corporations are by far the dominant form of business organization in terms of both total assets and dollar value of output of goods and services. Because of the dominance of the corporate form of business organization and the widespread ownership interests in corporations, accounting for corporations is a very important topic

CHARACTERISTICS OF THE CORPORATION

Because it is a separate legal entity, a corporation has several characteristics which differentiate it from both partnerships and sole proprietorships. The most important of these characteristics are described in the following paragraphs.

Separate Legal Existence. A corporation, unlike both sole proprietorships and partnerships, is a legal entity which is separate and distinct from its owners. Accordingly, a corporate entity may acquire and dispose of property, enter into contracts, and incur liabilities as an individual entity separate from its owners.

Transferable Units of Ownership. Ownership of a corporation is usually evidenced by shares of capital stock. These shares permit the subdivision of ownership into numerous units which may be readily transferred from one person to another without disrupting business operations and without prior approval of the other owners.

Continuity of Life. Status as a separate legal entity provides the corporation with a continuity of life. Unlike a partnership, the life or existence of a corporation is not affected by factors such as the death, incapacity, or withdrawal of an individual owner. A corporation may have a perpetual life or in some instances, its existence may be limited by the terms specified in its charter.

Limited Liability of Owners. As a separate legal entity, a corporation is legally liable for any debts which it incurs. Usually, the creditors of a corporation may not look to the personal property of the corporate stockholders for payment of any debts which are incurred by the corporation. Thus, the maximum loss which may be incurred by an individual stockholder is normally limited to the amount of his investment in the capital stock he owns. This limited liability feature is a primary advantage of the corporate form of business organization from the viewpoint of the owners.

In addition, the absence of stockholder liability and the transferability of ownership usually increase the ability of a corporate entity to raise substantial capital by means of individual investments made by many owners. On the other hand, the limited liability feature may limit the ability of a corporation to obtain funds from creditors in those instances where solvency of the corporate entity may be questionable.

Separation of Ownership and Management. Although a corporation is owned by the individuals who hold its shares of capital stock, their control over the general management of the business is generally limited to their right to elect a board of directors. The board of directors, as representatives of individual owners or stockholders of the corporation, establishes corporate policies and appoints corporate officers who are responsible for the day-to-day management of the business and its operations. Officers of a corporation usually include a president, one or more vice presidents responsible for various functions within the business, a treasurer, a secretary, and a controller. The controller is the officer responsible for the accounting function of the business. A summary organization chart indicating the normal structure of a corporation is presented below.

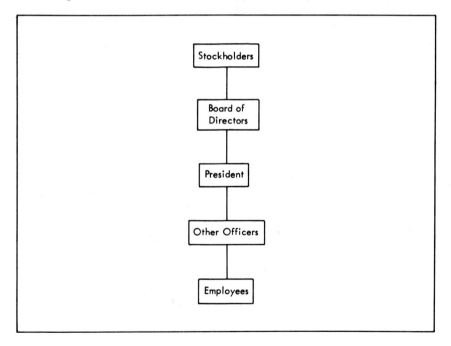

Corporate Taxation. As a separate legal entity, corporations are required to file and pay local, state, and federal income taxes on corporate earnings. In addition, when corporate earnings are distributed to shareholders as dividends, these distributions are included in the taxable income of individuals receiving the dividend. Thus, "double taxation" occurs because earnings of a corporation are taxed twice—initially as corporate income and subsequently as dividend income when distributed to stockholders.

Certain businesses may elect to operate as corporations without filing and paying corporate income taxes. In order to qualify for such an election, a corporation must meet certain requirements—for example, it must have only a single class of stock and ten or fewer stockholders. If this election is made, corporate income is taxed directly to the shareholders as it is earned by the corporation, just as would be the case if the business were organized as a partnership.

Government Regulation. Corporations are subject to numerous state and federal regulations and restrictions which are not imposed on either partnerships or sole proprietorships. This occurs primarily because corporations are separate legal entities and shareholders normally have limited liability for actions of the corporation.

FORMING A CORPORATION

A business corporation may be created by obtaining a charter from the state in which the business is to be incorporated. Although requirements for establishing a corporation vary, most states require a minimum of three natural persons to act as incorporators. An application for a corporate charter is usually made by filing articles of incorporation with the appropriate state official. Some of the more important information usually included in the articles of incorporation are:

1. Name of the corporation.
2. Location of its principal offices.
3. Nature of the business to be conducted by the corporation.
4. Identity and addresses of incorporators.
5. A detailed description of the capital stock authorized to be issued.
6. Identity of, and the amounts paid by, the original subscribers for the corporation's capital stock.
7. Names of the initial directors.

If the articles of incorporation are approved, the state issues a corporate charter which includes the general corporation laws of the state as well as any specific provisions of the articles of incorporation. The state usually charges a fee or organization tax for the privilege of incorporation.

Upon approval of the corporate charter, a corporation is authorized to begin its operations. Incorporators are required to hold a meeting in order to elect a board of directors and to adopt a set of bylaws which provide detailed operating regulations for the corporation. Directors of the corporation then elect appropriate corporate officers and authorize the issuance of capital stock certificates to the original stockholders.

Various expenditures such as those for state taxes and charter fees, legal costs, and other organizational costs are necessary in order to establish a corporation. These costs are normally accumulated in an intangible asset account referred to as organization costs. Since organization costs are expenditures which are necessary in order to provide for the creation and continued existence of a business, benefits obtained from these costs extend over the entire life of a corporation. Therefore, from a theoretical viewpoint, organization costs should be amortized over the life of the business. However, except when otherwise specified in the corporate charter, the life of a corporation is considered to be indefinite. Consequently, two different methods have evolved for accounting for organization costs. One is to simply retain organization costs as an intangible asset for an indefinite period of time without any amortization or charge to expense. The other alternative is to amortize these costs over a selected reasonable, but somewhat arbitrary, period of time. Although this alternative is certainly not justified in theory, it is usually acceptable in practice since organization costs are normally immaterial in amount and since this procedure is acceptable for income tax purposes.

CAPITAL OF A CORPORATION

Owners' equity of a corporation is commonly referred to as stockholders' equity and is accounted for in separate classifications according to the source of capital. Two primary sources of equity capital are: (1) contributed capital—amounts invested directly by shareholders; and (2) earned capital—amounts which are provided by profitable operations and retained in the business. A third major source of corporate capital, amounts obtained from creditors through borrowing, is discussed in Chapter 8.

Corporate capital provided by operations of the corporation is referred to as Retained Earnings. At the end of each period, any income or loss from operations of the corporation is transferred from the income summary account to retained earnings. The dividends account, which is used to record the dividends declared during the period, is also closed out to retained earnings during the closing process. Therefore, the balance in retained earnings at any point in time is equal to the total accumulated earnings of the business (net of any losses) less the total distributions which were paid to the stockholders in the form of dividends since the corporation's inception. If losses and dividends paid to stockholders exceed the cumulative earnings of the corporation, the resulting debit balance in retained earnings is referred to as a deficit. This deficit is deducted from invested capital in order to determine total stockholders' equity of the corporation.

NATURE OF CAPITAL STOCK

The investments made by stockholders in a corporation are represented by shares of ownership referred to as Capital Stock. Ownership of corporate stock is evidenced by a stock certificate. This certificate usually includes such information as the name of the corporation, rights of the shareholders, and the number of shares owned by each individual shareholder.

The maximum number of shares of stock *authorized* for issuance by the corporation is specified in the corporate charter. The number of shares *issued* refers to the total number of shares of stock which have been issued to stockholders since the formation of the corporation. Under certain circumstances, a corporation may reacquire shares of stock which were originally issued to its stockholders. Therefore, the remaining shares held by stockholders are referred to as *outstanding* shares. A current listing of the stockholders who own outstanding shares is maintained by the corporation's registrar or by the firm itself in a stockholders' ledger.

A corporation with a large number of shares outstanding which are traded regularly on an organized stock exchange must assign the function of transferring stocks and maintaining stock records to a stock transfer agent and a registrar. Banks or trust companies usually fulfill these functions for corporations. When a stockholder wishes to sell his stock, he endorses the stock certificate and forwards it to the transfer agent. The transfer agent cancels the certificate which was sold and prepares a new certificate which he sends to the registrar. The registrar records the stock transfer and issues a new stock certificate to the purchaser(s). Independent records maintained by the independent transfer agent and registrar provide additional controls which are intended to decrease the possibility of error or fraud in a corporation's ownership records.

RIGHTS OF STOCKHOLDERS

Many corporations issue only a single class of stock. In this instance, each shareholder possesses identical ownership rights and privileges. For an individual stockholder, these rights are proportionate to the number of shares of stock owned. Among these basic rights are:

1. The right to vote in stockholders' meetings. This includes the right to vote for directors and on decisions requiring stockholder approval as specified by the terms of the corporate charter. A stockholder has one vote for each share of stock that he owns. For example, if a stockholder owns 1,000 shares of stock, he is entitled to 1,000 votes. If a shareowner does not wish to attend a stockholders' meeting, he may assign his votes to a specified representative through a proxy statement.

2. The right to share in corporate earnings through dividends declared by the board of directors.

3. The right to maintain a proportionate interest in the ownership of

the corporation whenever any additional shares of stock are issued by the corporation. This right, referred to as the preemptive right, provides that each stockholder may purchase a percentage of the number of new shares to be issued which is equal to his ownership percentage in the number of shares outstanding prior to the new issuance. To illustrate, assume that Aaron owns 100 (10 percent) of the 1,000 outstanding shares of stock of Matthews Co. If Matthews Co. decides to issue an additional 100 shares of stock, Aaron has a right to purchase 10 percent (100/1,000), or 10 of the new shares issued. Therefore, Aaron will be permitted to maintain his 10 percent interest (110/1,100) in the corporation. Thus, by exercising his preemptive right, a stockholder is able to maintain his relative interest or ownership in the corporation. However, a shareholder is not required to exercise his preemptive right; he may elect to do so at his option.

4. The right to a proportionate share in assets upon the liquidation of the corporation. Shareholders, however, are entitled only to those assets which remain after all corporate creditors have been paid in full.

When a corporation issues only a single class of stock, its shares are referred to as common stock and the four basic rights described above apply to all shares issued and outstanding. In certain circumstances, a corporation may issue additional types of capital stock in order to satisfy management objectives and to appeal to investors who may have various investment objectives. These additional classes of stock usually grant certain preferential rights to the holders of these shares. Accordingly, such shares are usually referred to as preferred stock. Ordinarily, preferred stockholders either have no voting rights or only limited voting rights under certain conditions specified by the corporate charter. Preferred stock usually has one or more of the following preferences or privileges:

1. *Dividend preference.* Stock which is preferred as to dividends entitles its owner to receive a stated dividend *before* any distributions are made to owners of common stock. Dividends on preferred stock are normally limited to a fixed amount per share. However, this dividend preference does not assure the stockholder that he will receive a dividend. Thus, if the board of directors of a corporation chooses not to declare a dividend, neither common nor preferred shareholders will receive any distribution from the corporation.

2. *Cumulative preference.* Cumulative preferred stock provides that if all or part of the required dividend on preferred stock is not paid during a given year, the unpaid dividend accumulates and carries forward to succeeding years. The accumulated amount of unpaid dividends as well as current dividends must be paid before any dividends can be paid on common stock. Unpaid dividends on cumulative preferred stock are referred

to as dividends in arrears. To illustrate, assume that a corporation has 10,000 shares of cumulative preferred stock outstanding and a $5 stated dividend per share was not paid in the preceding year. In the current year, no dividends may be paid on the common stock until preferred dividends of $50,000 ($5 × 10,000) from the preceding year and the dividend of $50,000 for the current year are paid. Dividends in arrears are not considered to be a liability of the corporation until they are declared by the board of directors. However, because this information is important to the users of financial statements, any dividends in arrears on preferred stock should be disclosed, usually by means of a footnote to the balance sheet.

Preferred stock not having cumulative rights is referred to as noncumulative. Dividends omitted in any one year on noncumulative preferred stock do not carry forward. Therefore, dividends may be paid on common stock if preferred stock dividends are paid for the current year. Since a dividend preference is usually one of the most important rights or features of preferred stock, noncumulative preferred stock is normally not considered to be a very desirable investment under most circumstances. Consequently, most preferred stock issues provide for cumulative dividends.

3. *Participating preference.* Preferred stock is usually entitled to receive a dividend of a specified amount each year. Preferred stock is nonparticipating when preferred stockholders receive only this amount regardless of the dividends paid to common stockholders. In some cases, however, certain types of preferred stock also provide for the possibility of dividends in excess of the normal amount. This preferred stock, referred to as participating, has the right to participate with common stockholders in dividends in excess of a specified amount paid to common shareholders. The preferred stock contract must indicate the extent to which preferred shares will participate with common shares. Fully participating preferred stock is entitled to dividends at an amount which is equal to the excess of the common dividend over the regular amount for preferred. Partially participating preferred stock is entitled to participate with common stock, but it is limited to a maximum rate or amount. Issues of preferred stock normally do not include participation rights.

4. *Liquidation preference.* Preferred stock is normally preferred as to assets upon liquidation of the corporation. That is, owners of such preferred stock are entitled to receive the stated liquidation value for their shares before any payments may be made to common stockholders.

5. *Convertible preferred stock.* Preferred stock is convertible when it includes a privilege which allows stockholders to exchange their preferred shares for a specified number of common shares of the corporation at the shareholders' option. A conversion privilege allows the owner of preferred stock the option of obtaining common stock on which there is no dividend limitation in exchange for his preferred stock.

6. *Callable preferred stock.* Preferred stock contracts frequently allow corporations to repurchase outstanding shares from preferred stockholders at a fixed price in excess of the issue price of the stock. When a corporation has this option, the preferred stock is referred to as callable.

PAR VALUE AND NO-PAR VALUE

The par value of a share of capital stock is an arbitrary value established by the corporate charter. It is usually printed on the stock certificate and may be any amount decided upon by the corporation. The par value specified has no relationship whatsoever to the actual market value of the stock. Market value, which is the price at which a share of stock can be bought or sold, is dependent upon factors such as expected earnings and dividends, financial condition of the corporation, and general economic conditions. It is not unusual for a stock with a par value of $5 per share to be traded at a market value of $50, $100 or more.

The primary significance of par value is that it is used in many states in order to establish the corporation's "legal capital." The concept of legal capital was used by state laws to protect corporate creditors from possible dishonest actions of stockholders or corporate directors. In the absence of such a provision, corporate assets could be distributed to stockholders prior to the final liquidation of a corporation. Since stockholders have no liability for corporate debts, creditors would be unable to obtain satisfaction of their claims. Therefore, the concept of legal capital limits the assets that may be distributed to stockholders prior to the liquidation of the corporation and the settlement of its debts. Consequently, dividends cannot be declared by a corporation if such payments would decrease the owners' equity to an amount which is below the specified minimum legal capital—that is, the par value of the outstanding shares or, in some instances, par value plus a certain additional amount. Most state laws also provide that if the amount invested by individual stockholders is less than the established par value of the stock purchased, the stockholders may be held liable to the corporation's creditors for any difference between the amount paid and par value in the event the corporation is unable to meet its debts.

Laws requiring that stock have a par value were originally intended to protect the creditors of a corporation by restricting the distribution of a portion of corporate capital. However, the existence of a par value for capital stock has also caused certain problems. In some instances, investors have confused an arbitrary par value with the actual value of the ownership interest in the corporation. Also, if the market value of the stock falls below the par value established by the corporate charter, a potential liability to the investor may prevent the sale of additional[1] shares of stock by

---

[1] This liability applies only to the original issue of stock, not to stock purchased and then resold by investors.

the corporation unless or until the corporate charter is amended to change the par value of the stock. Consequently, some states have enacted legislation permitting the issuance of stock without par value, referred to as no-par stock. In these states, the legal capital of the corporation may be the total amount paid for the shares by the stockholders, or a stated value per share may be established by the board of directors.

ISSUANCE OF PAR VALUE STOCK

The primary significance of par value from an accounting viewpoint is that the capital stock account is credited with the par value of shares issued regardless of the amount received when the stock is sold. For example, if 1,000 shares of $10 par value common stock are sold at par value for cash, the entry would be as follows:

```
Cash ....................................... 10,000
    Common  stock  ...........................        10,000
```

When stock is sold for more than its par value, the amount received in excess of the par value is recorded as "additional paid-in capital." To illustrate, assume that 1,000 shares of $10 par value common stock were sold for $12 per share. The entry to record the issuance is as follows:

```
Cash ....................................... 12,000
    Common  stock  ...........................        10,000
    Additional paid-in capital in excess of par value  ........        2,000
```

The additional paid-in capital account is added to the capital stock account in reporting the total invested or contributed capital of the corporation. Contributed capital of the corporation in the above example would be shown in the stockholders' equity section of the balance sheet as shown below:

STOCKHOLDERS' EQUITY:

```
Common stock, $10 par value, 5,000 shares authorized,
    1,000 shares issued and outstanding .................  $10,000
Additional paid-in capital on common stock .............    2,000
    Total Contributed Capital .......................  $12,000
```

If capital stock is issued for an amount less than its par value, the difference is charged or debited to a "discount on capital stock" account. This account would be shown as a deduction from the capital stock account in the balance sheet. Since selling stock at a discount is illegal in many states and usually represents a contingent liability to the creditors of the corporation in the remaining states, it is seldom encountered in practice.

The par value of stock will normally be set at an amount which is less than its anticipated selling price, thus avoiding this problem.

ISSUANCE OF STOCK FOR NONCASH ASSETS

Sometimes a corporation may issue shares of its capital stock in exchange for assets such as land, buildings, or equipment. In such a case, the transaction may be recorded at the market value of the shares issued or at the market value of the assets acquired, whichever is a better indicator of market value. The market value of stock may be determined by reference to recent cash purchases and sales of the same class of stock by investors. Often, many shares of a large, publicly held corporation are traded daily through stock exchanges. Alternatively, if the market value of the shares issued cannot be determined, recent cash sales of similar assets or an independent appraisal of the asset may be used in order to record the transaction. Usually, the board of directors is given the responsibility by law for establishing a proper valuation for the issuance of stock for assets other than cash. To illustrate, assume that a corporation acquired land in exchange for five hundred shares of its $10 par value common stock. If the stock is traded on an established stock exchange and the current market price was $20, the transaction would be recorded as follows:

Land	10,000	
Common stock		5,000
Additional paid-in capital		5,000

If there is no established market for the stock, the market value of the asset acquired may be used in recording the exchange. For example, if similar acreage had recently sold for $11,000, the entry to record the transaction would be:

Land	11,000	
Common stock		5,000
Additional paid-in capital		6,000

ISSUANCE OF NO-PAR STOCK

At one time, all states required that stocks have a specified par value. However, to eliminate problems such as the liability for issuance discount and potential confusion over the meaning of par value, many states now permit the issuance of stock without par value.

The accounting entries which are necessary in order to record the issuance of no-par capital stock depend upon the specific laws of the state in which the shares are sold. Some states require that the entire issue price of no-par stock be regarded as legal capital. In these states, the capital account is credited for the entire amount received when the stock is issued.

To illustrate, assume that a corporation issues 1,000 shares of its no-par common stock for $12 per share. This transaction would be recorded as follows:

Cash	12,000	
Common stock		12,000

Other states allow the corporation to specify a stated value for no-par shares. When a stated value has been established, that amount is credited to Capital Stock and any excess is credited to Additional Paid-in Capital in Excess of Stated Value. For example, assume that the board of directors established a stated value of $10 per share for its stock. Issuance of 1,000 shares at a price of $12 would be recorded as follows:

Cash	12,000	
Common stock		10,000
Additional paid-in capital		2,000

The additional paid-in capital in excess of stated value account is reported as a part of contributed capital in the stockholders' equity section of the balance sheet.

SUBSCRIPTIONS FOR CAPITAL STOCK

In some instances, a corporation may make an agreement with an investor to sell a number of shares of stock to him at a stipulated price. If the purchaser agrees to pay for the stock at some future date or with installment payments over a period of time, the sale of stock is referred to as a subscription. Subscriptions are an asset to the corporation since they represent cash or other assets to be received from the investor at some future date. Therefore, an account entitled subscriptions receivable is debited when subscriptions are accepted. Although shares are not actually issued until they are paid for, a corporation accepting stock subscriptions is committed to issue the shares upon receipt of the total specified purchase price. Accordingly, a common stock subscribed account is credited for the par value of the stock subscribed. The difference between the specified subscription price and par value is credited to additional paid-in capital (or discount). For example, assume that a corporation accepts subscriptions for 1,000 shares of its $10 par value common stock at a price of $18 per share. The subscription contract requires payment in two equal installments due in 60 and 90 days. This transaction would be recorded as follows:

Subscriptions receivable	18,000	
Common stock subscribed		10,000
Additional paid-in capital		8,000

When subscribers make payments on their subscriptions, the amount collected by the corporation is credited to the subscriptions receivable account. For example, upon receipt of the first installment of the subscription illustrated above, the following entry would be made:

```
Cash ........................................ 9,000
    Subscriptions receivable   .....................        9,000
```

When the subscription price has been collected in full, shares of stock are issued to the investor by the corporation. For example, when the second installment is collected, stock certificates for 1,000 shares of stock will be issued. Collection of the installment payment and issuance of the shares would be recorded as follows:

```
Cash ........................................ 9,000
    Subscriptions receivable   .....................        9,000
Common stock subscribed  ...................... 10,000
    Common stock ............................       10,000
```

During the period in which subscriptions are outstanding, subscriptions receivable from investors are reported as an asset on the balance sheet and common stock subscribed is shown as a part of contributed capital in the stockholders' equity section of the balance sheet.

STOCKHOLDERS' EQUITY IN THE BALANCE SHEET

The stockholders' equity section of the balance sheet should report adequate information concerning each class of corporate stock outstanding. If more than a single class of stock is issued, the nature, special rights, and dollar amounts outstanding should be shown for each. Presentation of stockholders' equity in the balance sheet might appear as follows:

STOCKHOLDERS' EQUITY:

6% preferred stock, $100 par value, 10,000 shares authorized,		
6,000 shares issued and outstanding		$ 600,000
Common stock, $10 par value, 100,000 shares authorized,		
50,000 shares issued and outstanding		500,000
Common stock subscribed, 1,000 shares...............		10,000
Additional paid-in capital:		
Common stock issued and subscribed	$130,000	
Preferred stock	60,000	190,000
Total Contributed Capital......................		$1,300,000
Retained earnings...........................		450,000
Total Stockholders' Equity		$1,750,000

RETAINED EARNINGS

The stockholders' equity section of a corporation is divided into two major segments, contributed capital and retained earnings. Retained earnings represent accumulated earnings which were retained in the business. The retained earnings account is increased by the net income of the business and reduced by net losses and distributions to shareholders in the form of dividends. In the end-of-period closing entries, revenue and expense accounts are closed to the income summary account. When revenues exceed expenses, the credit balance which remains in the income summary account is equal to the firm's net income for the period. Conversely, a debit balance in the income summary account indicates a net loss for the accounting period. The balance in the income summary account is closed to retained earnings. Similarly, the debit balance in the dividends account is transferred or closed out as a reduction in retained earnings. This chapter considers the accounting for transactions affecting retained earnings and discusses various issues which are related to both corporate earnings and dividends.

NATURE OF EARNINGS

A primary purpose of reporting corporate earnings is to provide useful information to stockholders, potential investors, creditors, and other interested users of financial statements. The net income or loss of a corporation is determined in basically the same manner as that of a partnership or sole proprietorship.

There are several special problems which are related to the preparation of the income statement that have not been discussed previously. These include (1) accounting for transactions which are not related to the normal business activities and which occur infrequently; (2) accounting for discontinued operations; (3) prior period adjustments; (4) recording the effects of accounting changes; and (5) determination of earnings on a per share basis.

EXTRAORDINARY ITEMS

The net income of a corporation as reported in its income statement includes earnings from normal operations of the business as well as certain infrequently occurring transactions which are not related to the ordinary activities of the business. As a result of *Opinions No. 9* and *No. 30* of the Accounting Principles Board, transactions which occur infrequently and which do not result from the normal operations of the business, referred to as extraordinary items, are reported as a separate amount in the income statement.

To be classified as an extraordinary item in the income statement, an item must be both unusual in nature and not reasonably expected to recur in the foreseeable future. Determining the degree of abnormality and the probability of recurrence of a particular transaction should take into account the environment in which the business operates. Examples of potential extraordinary items include the effects of major casualties (e.g., an earthquake, if rare in the area, and an expropriation of assets by a foreign government). In addition, the effect of an extraordinary event should be classified separately only if it is considered to be material in amount in relation to income from normal operations. To illustrate, assume that in 19x1 the Dolphin Company had income after taxes from normal operations of $100,000 and a $20,000 gain (net of taxes)[2] which meets the criteria for classification as an extraordinary item. A simplified income statement for the Dolphin Company might appear as follows:

Dolphin Co.
Income Statement
For the Year Ended December 31, 19x1

Net sales	$400,000
Cost of goods sold	100,000
Gross margin.	$300,000
Expenses.	200,000
Income before extraordinary items.	$100,000
Extraordinary gain, net of tax.	20,000
Net Income	$120,000

As indicated above, special consideration is given to the reporting of gains and losses. The FASB has defined gains and losses as follows:

> Gains are increases in equity (net assets) from peripheral or incidental transactions of an entity and from all other transactions and other events and circumstances affecting the entity during a period except those that result from revenues or investments by owners.
> Losses are decreases in equity (net assets) from peripheral or incidental transactions of an entity and from all other transactions and other events and circumstances affecting the entity during a period except those that result from expenses or distributions to owners.[3]

Certain gains or losses should not be classified as extraordinary items, even if material in amount, because they could be expected to occur in the normal or ordinary operations of the business. For example, a loss resulting from a write-down made to recognize a decline in the value of inventory due to obsolescence should not be reported as an extraordinary item. Such an item should be included in the computation of income before extraordinary items. Other examples of items that would not normally be considered extraordinary items regardless of their amount include:

---

[2] See Chapter 12 for a discussion of the allocation of income tax within a period.

[3] "Elements of Financial Statements of Business Enterprises," FASB Statement No. 3 (Stamford, Conn. FASB, 1980), p. xii.

1. The write-down or write-off of receivables, inventories, equipment leased to others, or intangible assets.
2. The gains or losses from exchanges or translation of foreign currencies, including those relating to major devaluation or revaluations.
3. The gains or losses on the disposal of a segment of a business.
4. Other gains or losses from the sale or abandonment of property, plant, or equipment used in the business.
5. The effects of a strike.
6. The adjustments or accruals on long-term contracts.

Items which are either unusual in nature or occur infrequently, but do not meet both criteria, should not be classified as extraordinary items. However, if such items are material in amount, they should be separately disclosed by reporting them as separate components in income before extraordinary items or by including a description of the item and its effect as a footnote to the income statement.

DISCONTINUED OPERATIONS

The term "discontinued operations" refers to the operation of any subsidiary, division, or department of a business that has been or will be sold, abandoned, or otherwise disposed of. In APB *Opinion No. 30,* the Board concluded that the results of continuing normal operations should be reported separately from discontinued operations. Any gain or loss from the disposal of a segment of a business along with the results of operations of the segment should be reported in a separate section of the income statement. The purpose of reporting on the continuing operations of a business separately from the discontinued operations is that it allows financial statement users to make better judgments about the future earnings prospects of the business. Accordingly, an income statement of a firm that has discontinued operations would appear as follows:

Kingsberry Company		
Income Statement		
For the Year Ended December 31, 19x1		
Sales		$10,000
Less: Cost of goods sold		4,000
Gross profit		$ 6,000
Operating expenses		4,000
Income from continuing operations before		
income taxes		$ 2,000
Provision for income taxes		800
Income from continuing operations		$ 1,200
Discontinued operations (Footnote):		
Income from operations of discontinued		
division (less taxes of $300)	$500	
Loss on disposal of division (less tax		
effect of $200)	(300)	200
Net Income		$ 1,400

PRIOR PERIOD ADJUSTMENTS

    The provisions of FASB *Statement No. 16* indicate that, with two exceptions, all items of profit or loss recognized in a given year should be included in the determination of net income for that year. The only exceptions are corrections of errors in previous financial statements and adjustments that result from realization of income tax benefits of preacquisition loss carry forwards on purchased subsidiaries. Errors may result from computational mistakes, omission of data, incorrect application of accounting principles, or the use of unacceptable accounting principles. Corrections of errors of prior periods are not included in the income statement of the year in which the error is discovered. Instead, these items are shown as direct adjustments to beginning retained earnings.[4]

ACCOUNTING CHANGES

    Changes in accounting occur because of the uncertainty involved in the preparation of periodic financial reports. Subsequent to the preparation of financial statements, additional information may be obtained which necessitates an adjustment of the accounting records. Prior to the issuance of APB *Opinion No. 20* on accounting changes, there were various practices and procedures for reporting the effects of accounting changes on financial statements. In *Opinion No. 20*, the Board clarified the different types of changes and provided guidelines for the reporting procedures to be employed. Three types of changes may be involved: (1) a change in accounting principle; (2) a change in accounting estimate; and (3) a correction of an error of a prior period.[5] These three types of changes will be illustrated and discussed in the paragraphs that follow.

    Change in Accounting Principle. As previously indicated, the consistency principle requires that the same accounting methods be used from one accounting prior to the next. However, as an exception to this principle, a change in accounting methods is allowed if the new method used can be justified as being preferable to the previously used method, and the effects of the change are adequately disclosed in financial statements. Thus, a change in accounting principle results from the adoption of a generally accepted accounting method which differs from the one that was previously used. An example would be a change from the sum-of-the-years'-digits method of depreciation to the straight-line method. For most types of changes in accounting methods, the cumulative effect which the use of the new method would have had on income in all prior periods that the old method was used must be included in the income statement in the year in which the accounting change is made.[6]

---

    [4]*Statement on Financial Accounting Standards No. 16*, "Prior Period Adjustments" (Stamford, Conn.: Financial Accounting Standards Board, 1977).

    [5] A fourth type of accounting change, a change in reporting entity, is not applicable to this discussion.

    [6] Certain specific types of accounting changes are disclosed by revising the financial statements of prior periods to reflect the effects of the use of the new method.

To illustrate, assume that a company acquired a truck on January 1, 19x1, at a cost of $4,000. The useful life of the truck was estimated to be 4 years with a salvage value of $400. At the date of acquisition, the company decided to use the sum-of-the-years'-digits depreciation method. Further assume that the company decided to switch to the straight-line method at the end of 19x3. At the time of the change in methods, the cumulative difference between the old and the new methods of depreciation must be determined. The amount of this difference would be computed as follows:

Year	Sum-of-the-Years' Digits	Straight-Line	Difference to December 31, 19x2
19x1	$1,440	$ 900	$540
19x2	1,080	900	180
	$2,520	$1,800	$720

The $720 difference in depreciation between the two methods would be adjusted during 19x3 as follows:

Accumulated Depreciation 720
    Depreciation Adjustment, Change in Accounting Principle   720

This entry reduces the balance in the accumulated depreciation account to what it would have been had the straight-line method been used from the time the asset was purchased. The depreciation adjustment would appear in the income statement in the year of the change. After the adjustment is made, the depreciation expense for 19x3 and 19x4 would be recorded at $900 per year on the straight-line method.

The effect of this change on the current and prior years' income should be explained by a footnote to the financial statements. A change in accounting principle is appropriate only when it can be demonstrated that the new method is preferable.

Change in Accounting Estimate. Changes in the estimates used in accounting may occur as additional information regarding the original estimate is obtained. An example of such a change would be a change in the estimated salvage value or service life of an asset. The procedure used in adjusting for this change is to spread the remaining undepreciated cost of the asset over its remaining useful life. This procedure will allocate the remaining book value of the asset, less the new estimated salvage value, to expense over the revised estimated remaining useful life of the asset.

To illustrate, assume the company in the previous example decided in 19x4 that while the straight-line method should be used, the useful life of the asset should have been six (rather than four) years and the salvage value should have been $100 (instead of $400). The amount of depreciation expense for 19x4 would be computed as follows:

Original cost..	$4,000
Less: Accumulated depreciation to December 31, 19x3..................	2,700
Book value at December 31, 19x3......................................	1,300
Less: Estimated salvage value	100
Amount to be depreciated...........................	$1,200
Divide by: Estimated remaining useful life...................	3 years
Depreciation per year	$ 400

At the end of 19x4, 19x5, 19x6, the following entry would be made to record the depreciation expense:

Depreciation expense....................	400	
Accumulated depreciation..............		400

Errors.   Accounting errors may result from mistakes in the application of accounting principles, oversights, misuse of facts, or mistakes in mathematics. To illustrate, assume that the truck acquired on January 1, 19x1, had been incorrectly recorded as an expense rather than as an asset. This error was discovered on December 31, 19x2, at which time it was decided that the asset should have been assigned an estimated useful life of four years and a $400 salvage value. The company uses the straight-line method of depreciation. The entry at December 31, 19x2, to record the correction of the error would be:

Asset................................	4,000	
Accumulated depreciation..............		900
Prior period adjustment................		3,100

This entry records the asset at its cost of $4,000, the accumulated depreciation of $900 that should have been recorded in 19x1, and an adjustment of the prior year's earnings of $3,100 ($4,000 asset expenditure erroneously recorded as an expense less $900 depreciation expense which should have been recorded in 19x1). The prior period adjustment would be a correction of retained earnings and would not appear in the income statement. Depreciation for 19x2 would be recorded in the normal manner:

Depreciation expense....................	900	
Accumulated depreciation..............		900

EARNINGS PER SHARE

An amount referred to as earnings per share is basically the net income of a company per share of common stock outstanding for a given period. Data on earnings per share of a corporation probably receive more attention than any other single item of financial information. Earnings per share ratios are included in annual reports issued by corporations and receive extensive coverage in the financial press and the investment services. Earnings per share is often considered to be an important indicator of the market price of common stock and, in some cases, an indication of expected dividends per share.

Because of the widespread attention given to earnings per share data, it was recognized that such information should be computed on a consistent and meaningful basis by all companies. Accordingly, *Opinion No. 15* of the Accounting Principles Board provided detailed procedures for the computation and presentation of earnings per share figures under different circumstances.[7] Further, the APB concluded that earnings per share data should be disclosed in income statements for all periods covered by the statement. If extraordinary items and gains or losses from discontinued operations are included in net income for the period, separate earnings per share figures would normally be provided for: (1) income from continuing operations; (2) discontinued operations; (3) extraordinary items; and (4) net income. This data is usually presented in the income statement following the net income figure.

The computation of earnings per share is relatively simple when the capital structure of the corporation includes only common stock and the number of shares outstanding have not changed during the period. In this case, earnings per share of common stock is computed by dividing net income by the number of shares of common stock outstanding. To illustrate, assume that Dolphin Co. had 40,000 shares of common stock outstanding during 19x1 and earnings as shown below. Its earnings per share information would be computed as follows:

$$\text{Ordinary income} \dots \dots \dots \quad \frac{\$100,000}{40,000} = \$2.50$$

$$\text{Extraordinary gain} \dots \dots \dots \quad \frac{\$20,000}{40,000} = \$ .50$$

$$\text{Net income} \dots \dots \dots \quad \frac{\$120,000}{40,000} = \$3.00$$

When there are both common and preferred stock outstanding, the net income must be reduced by the preferred dividend requirements to determine the net income available to common stockholders. If the firm issues or acquires shares of stock during the period, the divisor in the calculation is the average number of shares outstanding during the year. In such circumstances, the earnings per share is computed as follows:

---

[7] *Opinions of the Accounting Principles Board, No. 15*, "Earnings Per Share" (New York: American Institute of Certified Public Accountants, 1969).

$$\text{Earnings Per Share} = \frac{\text{Net Income} - \text{Preferred Dividends}}{\text{Average Number of Common Shares Outstanding}}$$

The capital structures of many corporations include convertible securities, stock options, and other securities which may include rights that can be converted into shares of common stock at the option of the holder. A capital structure is considered to be complex when it includes securities and rights that could potentially decrease earnings per share by increasing the number of common shares outstanding. The existence of a complex capital structure results in significant complications in computations of earnings per share data. Essentially, they involve the calculation of hypothetical earnings per share figures which assume conversion of certain securities into common stock. The details of these considerations, however, are beyond the scope of this text.

DIVIDENDS

Dividends are distributions made by a corporation to its shareholders. Such distributions are paid in proportion to the number of shares owned by each stockholder. Dividends may be in the form of cash, other assets, or shares of the corporation's own stock. Unless otherwise specified, a dividend represents a distribution of cash. Payment of dividends is provided by action of the board of directors. The board has complete control of the type, amount, and timing of any and all dividend payments. However, once dividends are declared, they become a legal liability of the corporation to its stockholders.

In most cases, dividends represent a distribution of accumulated corporate earnings. It is ordinarily illegal to declare dividends in excess of the balance in the retained earnings account. In other words, an ordinary dividend usually may not be paid from any amounts which were invested by stockholders. The existence of a credit balance in the retained earnings account, however, does not necessarily indicate that there is cash available for the payment of dividends. Retained earnings is unrelated to the balance in the cash account because funds obtained from the accumulated income of the business may have been used to increase noncash assets or to decrease liabilities. Thus, a corporation with a large retained earnings balance may be unable to distribute cash dividends to its stockholders. On the other hand, a corporation with a substantial amount of cash may decide to pay little or no dividends to its stockholders so that the cash may be retained and used for other corporate objectives.

Because dividends are important to investors and therefore have an effect on the market price of the stock, most corporations attempt to adhere to a well formulated or established dividend policy. Although the percentage of earnings paid out in dividends varies widely according to the objectives of the firm, most corporations usually attempt to maintain a stable or increasing record of dividend payments.

While ordinary dividends are usually limited to the amount of retained earnings, a corporation may pay a liquidating dividend in order to return to the stockholders a portion of their original investment. Such a dividend is normally paid in conjunction with a permanent reduction in the size of a business or, alternatively, upon liquidation of a firm. Accordingly, such distributions are recorded by reducing capital stock and additional paid-in capital accounts.

Important Dates Related to Dividends

There are three important dates related to dividends:

1. Date of declaration.
2. Date of record.
3. Date of payment.

On the date of declaration, the board of directors of a corporation formally establishes a liability of a specified amount to its stockholders. The dividend and related liability, dividends payable, are recorded at that time. If financial statements are prepared after dividends are declared but before they are paid, dividends payable are classified as a current liability in the balance sheet. Following the declaration date, the corporation prepares a list of the stockholders as of the date of record—these are the stockholders who are entitled to receive the dividends. No entry is required by the corporation on the record date.

A period of time is usually necessary between the record date and the date of payment to allow the corporation sufficient time to identify those stockholders who will receive dividends and to process the dividend checks. An entry is made on the date of payment to record the distribution of cash and to remove the liability for dividends payable.

Cash Dividends

Dividends are usually paid in cash. Such dividends result in a reduction of both the cash and retained earnings of a corporation. Dividends on common stock are usually stated as a specific amount per share, while preferred stock dividends may be stated at either a specific dollar amount or a percentage of the par value per share. For example, a dividend on $100 par value preferred stock might be specified as either $5 or as 5 percent of par value. In either case, dividends paid to each stockholder are in proportion to the number of shares owned.

To illustrate, assume that the Jet Co. has 10,000 shares of common stock and 5,000 shares of 6 percent, $100 par value preferred stock outstanding. Further assume that on December 15 the company declares the preferred dividend and a $5 per share dividend on common stock. The

$30,000 preferred dividend (.06 × $100 × 5,000 shares) and the $50,000 common dividend ($5 × 10,000 shares) are payable on January 15 to its stockholders of record on December 20. The entries which are required to record the declaration of the dividend on December 15 and its payment on January 15 are as follows:

Dec.	15	Preferred dividends..................	30,000	
		Common dividends..................	50,000	
		Dividends payable.................		80,000
	20	No entry		
Jan.	15	Dividends payable..................	80,000	
		Cash		80,000

The dividend accounts are closed to retained earnings during the normal year-end closing process. Assuming that the accounting period for the Jet Co. ends on December 31, the following entry would be made on that date:

Dec.	31	Retained earnings..................	80,000	
		Preferred dividends...............		30,000
		Common dividends...............		50,000

In some instances, the corporation may debit retained earnings directly, rather than a dividend account. In these instances, a closing entry would not be required.

Stock Dividends

A distribution made to stockholders in the form of additional shares of a company's own stock is referred to as a stock dividend. Usually, such a distribution consists of additional common stock given to common stockholders. A stock dividend results in a proportionate increase in the number of shares owned by each stockholder. For example, a ten percent stock dividend entitles a stockholder to receive one additional share for each ten shares of stock he owns.

Since a stock dividend is paid on a pro rata basis, each stockholder retains the identical percentage interest in the firm after the dividend as he owned prior to the distribution. For example, assume that a stockholder owned 100 of 1,000 outstanding shares of a corporation. Thus, the stockholder owned 10 percent (100/1,000) of the corporation's outstanding stock. Further assume that the corporation declared a 5 percent stock dividend. The stockholder would receive 5 (.05 × 100) of the 50 (.05 × 1,000) additional shares of stock issued. Consequently, the stockholder's percentage interest in the corporation remains at 10 percent (105/1,050) after the stock dividend. A stockholder, however, may benefit from a stock dividend if there is less than a proportionate decrease in the market price of the stock associated with the distribution. In this case, the market value of the total shares owned by the stockholder would increase.

Unlike a cash dividend, a stock dividend does not result in a decrease in either the corporation's assets or its total stockholders' equity. If a stock dividend has no effect on either the assets or the equity of the corporation, or in the relative ownership interests of the shareholders, why do corporations distribute such dividends? A primary purpose of issuing stock dividends is to enable the corporation to give its stockholders some evidence of increased retained earnings without actually distributing cash. Thus, although a stock dividend does not affect corporate assets or increase the individual stockholder's relative interest in the corporation, it is perceived to be a distribution of earnings by many shareholders.

Another reason for distributing a stock dividend is to reduce the selling price of the corporation's stock. Because a stock dividend of a sizable amount increases the number of shares outstanding with no change in corporate assets, the market price of the stock normally decreases. A corporation may desire to reduce the market price of its stock so that it will be more readily marketable among investors.

Since a stock dividend increases the number of shares outstanding, many states require an associated increase in the legal capital of the corporation. Therefore, even though such a dividend has no effect on total stockholders' equity, an entry is required in order to transfer a portion of retained earnings to contributed capital if such capitalization is required by the state. This is referred to as "capitalizing" a part of retained earnings. Consequently, the retained earnings "capitalized" is no longer available for distribution to stockholders in the form of cash dividends.

In many states, the minimum amount which must be transferred from retained earnings to contributed capital is an amount equal to the par or stated value of the shares issued. In other states, there is no such requirement. However, because it is generally believed that most shareholders regard a stock dividend as something of value, the American Institute of CPAs has recommended that in certain circumstances an amount equal to the fair market value of the shares to be issued as a stock dividend should be capitalized. This reasoning was explained by the Committee on Accounting Procedure of the AICPA as follows:

> . . . many recipients of stock dividends look upon them as distributions of corporate earnings and usually in an amount equivalent to the fair value of the additional shares received. Furthermore, it is presumed that such views of recipients are materially strengthened in those instances, which are by far the most numerous, where the issuances are so small in comparison with the shares previously outstanding that they do not have any apparent effect upon the share market price and,

consequently, the market value of the shares previously held remains substantially unchanged.[8]

The Committee further suggested that these circumstances exist with the issuance of a small stock dividend. A small stock dividend is defined as an increase of less than 20 percent to 25 percent of the number of shares previously outstanding.

To illustrate the entries for the issuance of a small stock dividend, assume that the stockholders' equity of a corporation on May 1 was as follows:

Common stock, $5 par value, 20,000 shares outstanding $100,000
Additional paid-in capital 20,000
  Total Contributed Capital $120,000
Retained earnings 80,000
  Total Stockholders' Equity $200,000

Assume further that on May 2 the company declares a 10 percent stock dividend, or a dividend of 2,000 shares (.10 × 20,000), which is to be distributed on June 1. Assuming that the shares are selling in the market on the declaration date at a price of $20 per share, an amount equal to the fair value of the shares to be issued, or $40,000 (2,000 × $20), would be transferred from retained earnings to the appropriate contributed capital accounts. The capital stock account is credited for the par value of the shares issued and the remainder is added to additional paid-in capital. The following entries would be made to record the declaration and distribution of the stock dividend:

May 2 Retained Earnings. 40,000
           Stock Dividend Distributable   10,000
           Additional Paid-in Capital   30,000

June 1 Stock Dividend Distributable 10,000
           Common Stock   10,000

If financial statements are prepared between the date of declaration and the date of distribution of a stock dividend, the stock dividend distributable account should be included in the stockholders' equity section of the balance sheet. It is not classified as a liability because the corporation has no obligation to distribute cash or any other asset.

As previously indicated, the distribution of a stock dividend has no

---

[8] *Accounting Research Bulletin No. 43*, "Restatement and Revision of Accounting Research Bulletins" (New York: American Institute of Certified Public Accountants, 1953), Ch. 7, par. 10.

effect on either the assets or the total stockholders' equity of a corporation. In the illustration above, the only effect on the corporation was a transfer of $40,000 from retained earnings to contributed capital. The stockholders' equity after payment of the stock dividend on June 1 would appear as follows:

Common stock, $5 par value, 22,000 shares outstanding	$110,000
Additional paid-in capital	50,000
Total Contributed Capital	$160,000
Retained earnings	40,000
Total Stockholders' Equity	$200,000

The Committee on Accounting Procedure further indicated that stock dividends in excess of 20% to 25% would be expected to materially reduce the market value per share of stock. Accordingly, the Committee recommended that if capitalization is required by the state, such stock dividends should be recorded by capitalizing retained earnings only to the extent of the par or stated value of the shares issued. Under these circumstances, the entry to record the stock dividend would be a debit to retained earnings and a credit to capital stock for the par value of the shares issued. Again, there is no effect on the total stockholders' equity of the corporation.

STOCK SPLITS

A corporation may desire to reduce the selling price of its stock in order to facilitate purchases and sales of its shares by investors. Reducing the price of shares to a reasonable amount normally increases the number of investors who are willing to purchase a corporation's stock. This may be accomplished by increasing the number of shares outstanding and decreasing the par or stated value of the stock by a proportionate amount. This procedure is referred to as a stock split.

For example, assume that a corporation has 20,000 shares of $10 par value common stock outstanding with a current market price of $200 per share. The company might declare a two-for-one stock split in which each current stockholder receives two new shares with a $5 par value for each share of $10 par stock he owned prior to the split. This action would tend to cause the market price to decrease to approximately $100 per share because there would be twice as many shares outstanding after the split with no change in the value of the corporation.

In a stock split there is a significant increase in the number of shares outstanding without a change in total stockholders' equity. A basic difference between a stock split and a stock dividend is the magnitude of the increase in the number of shares outstanding. Also, a stock split never requires any capitalization of retained earnings. Consequently, only a memorandum entry to the common stock account to indicate the change in par value and the new number of shares outstanding is required upon a stock split.

TREASURY STOCK

Corporations often acquire shares of their own stock from its stockholders. If the corporation does not cancel these shares but instead holds the stock, it is referred to as treasury stock. A corporation may desire to reacquire shares of its stock which have been previously issued in order to have stock available for employee stock purchase plans, for stock options, for bonuses, or for some other legitimate reason. Unissued stock may not be used for these purposes because of the preemptive right of the existing stockholders. Purchases of treasury stock are limited to the amount of retained earnings if the corporation is to maintain its legal capital. This occurs because the purchase of treasury stock results in the distribution of cash to certain stockholders. If assets are distributed to stockholders in excess of the retained earnings, the corporation is returning a portion of the invested capital. Therefore, the purchase of treasury stock reduces the amount available for subsequent distributions to the stockholders.

Although the stock of another corporation is an asset of the firm which owns it, treasury stock is generally not considered to be an asset because a corporation cannot have an ownership interest in itself. Instead, the purchase of a corporation's own shares represents a return of capital to the selling shareholder and, thus, a reduction in the stockholders' equity of the corporation. Consequently, treasury stock is shown as a deduction in the stockholders' equity section of the balance sheet.

There are several different methods for recording treasury stock transactions. However, one approach, referred to as the cost method, is a method commonly used in practice for recording the acquisition of treasury stock. For this reason, the cost method will be discussed in the paragraphs which follow.

When a corporation acquires its own shares, treasury stock is debited for the cost of the shares purchased. Note that neither the par (or stated) value of the stock nor the amount originally received for the shares when they were issued is used to record the acquisition of treasury stock. If treasury shares are subsequently reissued, the difference between the cost of the shares and their selling price does not represent a gain or a loss to the corporation. Instead, the corporation has simply changed the amount of invested capital by acquiring and reissuing treasury shares. Consequently, any difference between the acquisition cost and the resale price of treasury stock is credited to additional paid-in capital if the selling price exceeds cost. If the shares are sold below cost, additional paid-in capital is reduced. If this account is not sufficient to absorb the excess of the cost over the selling price, any remainder may be charged or debited to retained earnings. To illustrate, assume that the stockholders' equity of a corporation appeared as follows on January 1:

```
Common stock, $10 par value, 10,000 shares authorized,
    issued, and outstanding .................................  $100,000
Additional paid-in capital .....................................    20,000
        Total Contributed Capital............................  $120,000
Retained earnings..............................................    30,000
        Total Stockholders' Equity ..........................  $150,000
```

Further assume that the corporation purchased 300 of its outstanding shares on January 15 at a price of $20 per share. The following entry would be necessary to record the purchase:

```
Treasury Stock .................................. 6,000
    Cash ......................................         6,000
```

To illustrate the reissuance of treasury stock, assume that the corporation subsequently sold 100 of the treasury shares on March 15 for $25 per share and another 100 shares on April 15 for $18 per share. The entries to record these transactions are as follows:

```
March 15  Cash ................................. 2,500
              Treasury Stock .....................         2,000
              Additional Paid-in Capital from Treasury
                  Stock Transactions..................          500
April 15  Cash ................................. 1,800
          Additional Paid-in Capital from Treasury
              Stock Transactions ..................    200
              Treasury Stock .....................         2,000
```

When the treasury shares were sold, the treasury stock account was credited for the acquisition cost and carrying value of the shares, or $20 per share. Further, note that the $200 excess of cost over the resale price in the April 15 sale was debited to an "additional paid-in capital from treasury stock transactions" account. If the balance in the "additional paid in capital from treasury stock transactions" account is not sufficient to absorb the difference between cost and resale price, any remaining amount is normally charged against retained earnings.

If a company holds treasury shares at the time financial statements are prepared, any balance in the treasury stock account should be shown as a deduction from total stockholders' equity. In addition, any restriction on the amount of retained earnings available for dividends should be disclosed. Additional paid-in capital from treasury stock transactions is reported in the contributed capital section of stockholders' equity. For example, the stockholders' equity of the corporation on April 15 would appear as follows:

Common stock, $10 par value, 10,000 shares authorized and issued of which 100 shares are in the treasury.		$100,000
Additional paid-in capital:		
From stock issuances.	$20,000	
From treasury stock transactions.	300	20,300
Total Contributed Capital.		$120,300
Retained earnings (of which $2,000 is not available for dividends because of the purchase of treasury stock).		30,000
Total.		$150,300
Less: Treasury stock at cost (100 shares).		2,000
Total Stockholders' Equity		$148,300

For various reasons, stockholders may donate shares of stock to the corporation. Since there is no cost to the corporation, no entry is required for the receipt of the donated stock. When these shares are resold, the entire proceeds would be credited to the additional paid-in capital from treasury stock transactions account. An alternative treatment is to record donated treasury stock at its fair market value as of the date of donation with a corresponding credit to a donated capital account. If this procedure is followed, subsequent entries affecting treasury stock would be recorded in the same manner as if the treasury stock had been purchased.

RETAINED EARNINGS

Retained earnings is that portion of stockholders' equity which results from the total net earnings of the firm less any dividends paid to stockholders since its inception. Accumulated earnings include income from normal operations and discontinued operations, extraordinary gains or losses, and prior period adjustments. Thus, the following types of transactions all affect retained earnings, either directly or indirectly.

1. Transfer of the net income or loss for the period to retained earnings (including discontinued operations and extraordinary gains or losses).
2. Reduction in retained earnings for dividends declared during the period.
3. Increase or decrease in retained earnings for prior period adjustments.
4. Transfer from or to appropriation accounts.

The first three types of entries have been discussed previously. The appropriation of retained earnings is discussed below.

**Appropriation of
Retained Earnings**

In general, the balance in the retained earnings account of a corporation is the amount which is legally available for dividend distribution to stockholders. However, in some cases the board of directors may restrict the amount of retained earnings that can be used to pay dividends. Such restrictions may be required either by law or by contract, or they may be made at the discretion of the board of directors. For example, retained earnings available for dividends are often legally limited by the cost of any treasury stock held by the company. In addition, contractual agreements with creditors or certain classes of stockholders may also impose limitations on the amount of retained earnings which is available for dividends. On the other hand, the board of directors may desire to voluntarily restrict dividends in order to provide for a future use of the assets represented by accumulated earnings. For example, a firm may wish to retain assets generated from profitable operations for future expansion of the business.

There are several methods which may be used for disclosing such restrictions on the amount of the retained earnings available for distribution to shareholders. The simplest, and probably the most logical method, is to indicate the amount and nature of the restriction by footnote or parenthetical disclosure in the financial statements. However, because many stockholders may not readily understand such disclosures, an alternative is to reclassify a portion of the retained earnings in order to indicate the amount of earnings which is unavailable for dividends. This reclassification, referred to as an appropriation, is accomplished by transferring the desired amount of retained earnings to an appropriation account.

To illustrate an appropriation of retained earnings, assume that the directors of a corporation with retained earnings of $300,000 decide that $100,000 of retained earnings should be restricted for future plant expansion. The following entry is necessary to record this appropriation:

Retained Earnings	100,000	
Appropriation for Plant Expansion		100,000

This appropriation does not affect either the assets or liabilities of the corporation. The appropriation account is not an asset to be used for expansion nor does it guarantee that cash or other assets will actually be available for this purpose. Instead, it merely restricts the assets that may be distributed to shareholders. Further, the appropriation does not change the total retained earnings; it simply divides it into appropriated and unappropriated segments. The retained earnings of the corporation in the example would appear as follows after the appropriation was made:

Retained earnings:	
Appropriated for plant expansion	$100,000
Unappropriated	200,000
Total Retained Earnings	$300,000

When the purpose for the appropriation ceases to exist, the amount of the appropriated retained earnings account should be transferred back to unappropriated retained earnings. Since an appropriation represents a segregation of retained earnings, no other entry may be made to this account. For example, assume that the corporation in the previous illustration completed the desired expansion of the business. The appropriation would be restored to unappropriated retained earnings by means of the following entry:

Appropriation for Plant Expansion.	100,000	
Retained Earnings		100,000

In recent years, the formal appropriation of retained earnings has been recognized as potentially confusing or misleading to the users of financial statements. Consequently, there has been a trend to disclose both voluntary and required restriction of retained earnings in the notes accompanying the financial statements.

Statement of Retained Earnings

Normally, the periodic financial statements issued by a corporation include a statement of retained earnings as well as a balance sheet, income statement, and statement of changes in financial position. The retained earnings statement indicates all changes which have occurred in that account during the period. The format of the statement varies considerably; sometimes the changes in retained earnings are included with income data in a combined statement of income and retained earnings. The general form of the statement is illustrated below.

Redskins Company
Statement of Retained Earnings
For the Year Ended December 31, 19x1

Balance at beginning of the year:		
As originally reported		$200,000
Prior period adjustment—correction of an error applicable to 19x0.		(50,000)
As Restated		$150,000
Add: Net income for the year		90,000
		$240,000
Less: Cash dividends:		
$6 per share on preferred	$30,000	
$5 per share on common	50,000	(80,000)
Balance at end of the year		$160,000

BOOK VALUE PER SHARE OF COMMON STOCK

The book value of a share of stock is the amount of stockholders' equity which is applicable to a single share of stock. Since the stockholders' equity is equal to total assets minus total liabilities, book value also represents the net assets per share of stock. Data on book value per share of a corporation's common stock is often included in corporate annual reports and in the financial press.

If a corporation has only common stock outstanding, book value per share is computed by dividing total stockholders' equity by the number of shares outstanding. When a corporation has both preferred and common stock outstanding, the stockholders' equity must be divided between or among the various classes of stock. This allocation depends on the nature of the preferred stock. Generally, if preferred stock is nonparticipating, the equity allocated to the preferred shares is an amount equal to the liquidation or redemption value of the preferred stock plus any cumulative dividends in arrears. To illustrate, assume that a corporation has the following stockholders' equity:

5% cumulative preferred stock, $100 par value, 1,000 shares authorized and outstanding, (callable at $106)		$100,000
Common stock, $10 par value, 20,000 shares authorized, issued, and outstanding		200,000
Additional paid-in capital:		
On preferred stock	$40,000	
On common stock	10,000	50,000
Total Contributed Capital		$350,000
Retained earnings		56,000
Total Stockholders' Equity		$406,000

If there are no unpaid dividends on the preferred stock, equity equal to the call price or redemption value of the preferred stock ($106 per share) is allocated to the preferred shares, and the remainder applies to the common stock. Thus, the book value per share of common stock is computed as follows:

Total stockholders' equity	$406,000
Less: Amount allocated to preferred	106,000
Equity to common stock	$300,000

$$\text{Book value per share of common stock} = \frac{\$300,000}{20,000} = \underline{\$15}$$

If there are unpaid preferred dividends, an additional amount equal to the arrearage is allocated to the preferred stock. For example, assume that the preferred stock mentioned in the previous illustration had one year of dividends in arrears. In that situation, the unpaid preferred dividends of $5,000 would also be allocated to the preferred stock, and the book value per share of common stock would be computed as follows:

Total stockholders' equity $406,000
Less: Amount allocated to preferred:
  Redemption value $106,000
  Dividends in arrears   5,000   111,000
Equity to common stock $295,000

$$\text{Book value per share of common stock} = \frac{\$295,000}{20,000} = \underline{\$14.75}$$

Because the market value of the assets may differ from book values based on generally accepted accounting principles, the book value per share does not indicate the amount that would be distributed to the owner of each share of stock if the assets of the corporation were sold and its liabilities were paid. That is, any gains or losses from the disposal of assets or the settlement of liabilities, and any expenses involved in the liquidation process, would affect the shareholders' equity. As noted above, book value per share is not necessarily equal to the market price of the stock. Although book value per share may have some effect on the market price, market price is much more likely to be influenced by factors such as current and expected future earnings, dividend prospects, and general economic conditions. Depending upon the specific circumstances, book value per share may be more or less than market price per share. Therefore, book value data should be used with extreme caution in making decisions concerning the value of a corporation's stock.

SUMMARY

A corporation is a separate legal entity permitted to engage in activities in a manner similar to those performed by a natural person. Other important characteristics of a corporation include the transferability of ownership, continuity of life, limited liability of owners, separation of ownership and management, corporate taxation, and government regulation.

Forming a corporation includes obtaining a state corporate charter, electing a board of directors, adopting bylaws, and issuing capital stock to shareholders. The expenses incurred in this process are referred to as organization costs and are accumulated in an intangible asset account and either retained as an asset indefinitely or amortized over a reasonable but arbitrarily selected period of time.

The two primary sources of the equity capital of a corporation are contributions by shareholders and earnings retained in the business. In exchange for their contributions, the shareholders receive stock certificates and certain basic rights. Common stock usually entitles its owners to vote in stockholders' meetings, to share in corporate earnings through dividends, to maintain a proportionate interest in the firm when additional shares are issued, and to share in the distribution of remaining assets upon liquidation. Preferred stock usually has limited or no voting rights but does have preference in dividend and liquidation distributions. In addition, preferred stock may be cumulative, participating, convertible, and/or callable.

Capital stock may have an arbitrary value established by the corporate charter (referred to as par value) or established by the corporate directors (referred to as stated value). This value generally has no relationship to the selling price of the stock, but a firm may be required to retain a corresponding amount in the business to protect corporate creditors. Upon issuance of stock, the corporation credits the Capital Stock account for the par or stated value and credits Additional Paid-in Capital for any excess. If the stock has no par or stated value, the entire proceeds of the sale are usually credited to Capital Stock.

When common stock subscriptions are taken by a corporation, receivables are created and a Common Stock Subscribed account is credited. The actual stock is not issued until the payment is received, at which time Common Stock Subscribed is debited and Common Stock is credited.

The retained earnings of a corporation reflect the accumulated net income and losses of the firm less all dividend distributions to shareholders. The net income of the firm is usually presented on the income statement in a manner that separates earnings related to the normal operations of the business from other income-related items. Such other items include extraordinary items and discontinued operations. Prior period adjustments are direct adjustments to the beginning balance of Retained Earnings resulting from error correction and other adjustments stipulated in FASB *Statement No. 16.*

The income statement will also include information regarding the earnings per share of the firm. This amount is basically the net income per share of common stock outstanding for a given period. Where preferred stock or convertible securities are outstanding, certain adjustments must be made to either the net income or number of shares of common stock outstanding to compute the earnings per share of the firm. In addition, if there are extraordinary items or gains or losses from discontinued operations it will be necessary to compute several earnings per share figures.

Certain accounting changes may necessitate an adjustment of the accounting records and/or mention in the corporation's financial statements. Included in this category are changes in accounting principles, changes in accounting estimates, and corrections of errors made in prior periods.

A corporation may distribute a portion or all of its accumulated earnings to the stockholders in the form of ordinary dividends. Additionally, the firm may return a portion of the original investment in the form of a liquidating dividend. The important dates to be noted in relation to a dividend distribution are the dates of declaration, record, and payment. Although dividends are usually paid in cash, the corporation may choose to issue a stock dividend. A stock dividend has no effect on the amount of stockholders' equity, but does require a transfer of an appropriate amount from the retained earnings account to the capital accounts. Stockholders may also be issued additional shares in a stock split. In this case, no capitalization of retained earnings is required although a memorandum is made to indicate the change in the number of shares outstanding and in the par value of the stock.

A firm may wish to purchase its own stock from shareholders and retain the shares for future reissuance or cancellation. The purchase and resale of such stock is referred to as treasury stock transactions. Treasury stock held by a corporation when financial statements are prepared is shown on the balance sheet as a deduction from total stockholders' equity.

In reporting financial position to its stockholders, a firm may wish to indicate that the entire balance of retained earnings is not available for distribution as dividends, because certain amounts have been appropriated for special purposes. This is commonly accomplished by segregating the unappropriated retained earnings from the appropriated amount on the balance sheet. Additional detail regarding the retained earnings account is provided by the statement of retained earnings, which is normally included as one of the periodic financial statements issued by a corporation.

The book value per share of common stock represents the amount of stockholders' equity or net assets applicable to a single share of common stock. If preferred stock is outstanding, an appropriate amount of equity must first be allocated to those shares before computing book value.

KEY DEFINITIONS

Additional paid-in capital   Additional paid-in capital is the amount received on the issuance of capital stock in excess of its par or stated value.

Appropriation of retained earnings   An appropriation of retained earnings is the reclassification of a portion of retained earnings by transfer to an appropriation account.

Articles of incorporation   Articles of incorporation are included in the application made to the state for a corporate charter and include information concerning the corporation.

Book value per share   Book value per share is the amount of stockholders' equity (i.e., net assets) applicable to each share of common stock outstanding.

Capital stock   Capital stock is transferable shares of stock which evidence ownership in a corporation.

Capitalization of retained earnings   The capitalization of retained earnings is an amount which is transferred from retained earnings to contributed capital at the time a stock dividend is declared.

Cash dividend A cash dividend is a distribution of cash to stockholders in the form of a dividend.

Change due to accounting errors Changes due to accounting errors may result from errors in the application of accounting principles, oversights, misuse of facts, or mistakes in mathematics.

Change in accounting estimate A change in accounting estimate occurs as additional information modifying an original estimate is obtained.

Change in accounting principle A change in accounting principle results from the adoption of a generally accepted accounting principle which differs from one that was previously used.

Charter A charter is a contract between the state and the corporation which includes the general corporation laws of the state and the specific provisions of the articles of incorporation.

Common stock Common stock is stock which has the basic rights of ownership and represents the residual ownership in the corporation.

Continuity of life Status as a separate legal entity gives the corporation a perpetual existence.

Contributed capital Contributed capital is capital invested directly by the shareholders of the corporation.

Controller The controller is an officer who is responsible for the accounting function of the business.

Convertible preferred stock Convertible preferred stock is stock which includes the privilege of allowing the shareholder to exchange preferred shares for a specified number of common shares at his option.

Corporation A corporation is an association of persons joined together for some common purpose, organized in accordance with state laws as a legal entity, separate and distinct from its owners.

Cumulative preferred stock Cumulative preferred stock is backed by a provision that if all or part of the specified dividend on preferred stock is not paid during a given year, the amount of the unpaid dividends accumulates and must be paid in a subsequent year before any dividends can be paid on common stock.

Date of declaration The date of declaration is the date on which the board of directors formally establishes a liability for a dividend of a specified amount to the stockholders.

Date of payment The date of payment of a dividend is the date on which the dividends are paid to the stockholders of record.

Date of record The date of record of a dividend is the date on which the corporation prepares a list of stockholders who are to receive the dividends.

Deficit A deficit is a debit balance in the retained earnings account.

Discontinued operations Discontinued operations refers to the operations of any subsidiary, division, or department of a business that has been, or will be sold, abandoned, or disposed of.

Dividends Dividends are distributions which are made by a corporation to its shareholders.

Earned capital   Earned capital includes amounts provided by profitable operations and retained by the business.

Earnings per share   The earnings per share is the amount of net income per share of the common stock outstanding during a period.

Extraordinary item   An extraordinary item is a gain or loss which is both unusual in nature and not reasonably expected to recur in the foreseeable future. As a result of *Opinions No. 9* and *No. 30* of the Accounting Principles Board, these items are reported as separate amounts in the income statement.

Gains   Gains are increases in equity (net assets) from peripheral or incidental transactions of an entity and from all other transactions and other events and circumstances affecting the entity during a period except those that result from revenues or investments by owners.

Incorporators   Incorporators are the persons who legally form a corporation.

Legal capital   Legal capital is a limit on the amount of assets that can be distributed to the stockholders of a corporation prior to liquidation and settlement of the corporate debts.

Limited liability   The creditors of the corporation have a claim against the assets of the corporation and not against the personal property of the stockholders.

Losses   Losses are decreases in equity (net assets) from peripheral or incidental transactions of an entity and from all other transactions and other events and circumstances affecting the entity during a period except those that result from expenses or distributions to owners.

No-par stock   No-par stock is stock without a par value.

Organization costs   Organization costs are the costs which are necessary to form the corporation.

Par value   Par value is an arbitrary value which is established in the corporate charter and printed on the stock certificate. It establishes the legal capital of the corporation in many states.

Participating preferred stock   Participating preferred stock is preferred stock which has the right to participate in some specified manner with common stockholders in dividends in excess of a stipulated amount paid to the common shareholders.

Preferred as to dividends   Stock which is preferred as to dividends is entitled to receive a stated dividend each year before any dividend is paid on the common stock.

Preferred stock   Preferred stock is a class of stock which has different rights from those associated with common stock.

Prior period adjustment   Prior period adjustments are items of gain or loss which represent material corrections of reported earnings of prior periods and are shown as direct adjustments of retained earnings.

Retained earnings   Retained earnings represent the accumulated earnings of the corporation, increased by net income and reduced by net losses and distributions to shareholders.

Stock dividend   A stock dividend is a distribution of additional shares to the stockholders in proportion to their existing holdings.

Stock split A stock split is a proportionate increase in the number of shares outstanding, usually intended to effect a decrease in the market value of the stock.

Stock subscriptions Stock subscriptions involve an agreement by the corporation to sell a certain number of shares at a specified price to an investor with the payment at some future date(s). Upon full payment, the purchaser gains control of the stock.

Treasury stock Treasury stock consists of shares of stock which have been previously issued and are reacquired by the corporation but not formally retired.

QUESTIONS

1. What are some of the main advantages of organizing a business as a corporation rather than as a sole proprietorship or partnership?

2. Describe the following characteristics of a corporation:

   a.   separate legal entity
   b.   limited liability
   c.   transferability of ownership interest
   d.   continuity of existence

3. Explain the meaning of the term "double taxation" as it applies to a corporation.

4. Explain what is meant by the number of shares of stock authorized, issued, and outstanding.

5. What are four basic rights of a stockholder?

6. Describe the following features which may be applied to an issuance of preferred stock:

   a.   cumulative
   b.   participating
   c.   preferred as to assets
   d.   callable
   e.   convertible

7. Explain the meaning of par value. Describe the accounting treatment of stock issued for more or less than par value.

8. Distinguish between par value and no-par stock.

9. What is the primary disadvantage of issuing stock for an amount less than par value?

10. What are organization costs? Describe two alternative accounting treatments for such costs.

11. Indicate the nature and balance sheet classification of the subscriptions receivable and common stock subscribed accounts.

12. What information regarding preferred stock should be disclosed in the balance sheet?

13. How should preferred dividends in arrears be reported in the balance sheet?

14. Distinguish between an ordinary item and an extraordinary item on an income statement. How is an extraordinary item presented in the income statement?

15. What is a prior period adjustment? Where is a prior period adjustment shown in the financial statements?

16. Define earnings per share of common stock. Where is this information shown in the financial statements?

17. What is the effect on earnings per share presentation when a company has extraordinary gains or losses?

18. Describe the nature of the following three dates related to dividends: (a) date of declaration, (b) date of record, and (c) date of payment. What is the accounting significance of each of these dates?

19. Distinguish between a cash dividend and a stock dividend.

20. Why does a corporation normally declare (a) a stock dividend and (b) a stock split?

21. Why is a portion of retained earnings capitalized upon the issuance of a stock dividend?

22. What is the difference between a stock dividend and a stock split? How does the accounting for a large stock dividend and a stock split differ?

23. For what purposes might a company purchase shares of its own stock?

24. What is treasury stock? How does it affect the ability of the corporation to pay dividends? How does it differ from authorized but unissued stock?

25. What is the effect on stockholders' equity when treasury stock is reissued for (a) more than the original cost, (b) less than its cost to the corporation?

26. What is the purpose of an appropriation of retained earnings? How does a company provide for and eliminate an appropriation of retained earnings?

27. What is the significance of the book value per share of common stock? Does the book value equal the amount of assets which would be distributed to each share of stock upon liquidation? Explain.

28. How is the book value per share of common stock computed when there is preferred stock outstanding?

EXERCISES

29. Give the journal entries required to record each of the following stock transactions:

    a.   Issuance of 1,000 shares of $10 par value common stock at $14 per share.

    b.   Issuance of 100 shares of $100 par value preferred stock for a total of $12,000.

    c.   Issuance of 500 shares of no-par common stock for $20 per share.

    d.   Issuance of 2,000 shares of $10 par value common stock for land. Recent sales and purchases of the stock have been made at a price of $20 per share. The value of the land is not readily determinable.

30. Make the journal entries necessary to record the issuance of stock in each of the following independent cases.

    a.   One hundred shares of $25 par value stock are sold at par for cash.

    b.   Eighty shares of $15 par value stock are sold at $17 each for cash.

    c.   One thousand shares of no-par capital stock are issued at $14 per share.

    d.   Five hundred shares of no-par capital stock with a stated value of $10 per share are sold for $11 per share.

31. Jeffry Company was organized on March 1, 19x1. The authorized capital was 20,000 shares of $50 par value, 6 percent, cumulative preferred stock and 50,000 shares of $10 par value common stock. At the date of organization, all the common stock was issued at $20 per share and 10,000 shares of the preferred stock were sold at par.

Required:

Prepare the stockholders' equity section of the balance sheet for Jeffry Co. on March 1, after the issuance of the stock.

32. Niblet Corporation was organized on January 1, 19x1. On that date, the corporation issued 1,000 shares of $100 par value, 6 percent preferred stock and 20,000 shares of $10 par value common stock. During the first five years of its life, the corporation paid the following total dividends to its stockholders.

19x1	$ 0
19x2	6,000
19x3	20,000
19x4	15,000
19x5	18,000

Determine the total dividends paid to each class of stockholders assuming that the preferred stock is:

    a.   cumulative and nonparticipating.

    b.   noncumulative and nonparticipating.

33. Loggins Music Stores, Inc. accepted subscriptions for 250 shares of its no-par, $10 stated value capital stock on January 1, 19x1, at a price of $13 per share. On March 1, the firm collected $1,625 as a partial payment on the subscriptions. Then, on April 1, the balance in the subscriptions account was paid and all the shares were issued.

Required:

Prepare the journal entries necessary to record the above transactions on the books of Loggins Music Stores, Inc.

34. Monte Carter owns 300 of the 30,000 outstanding shares of stock in the MNX Company, which allows preemptive rights to all its existing stockholders. If MNX Company decides to issue an additional 6,000 shares of stock, how many of the new shares may Carter purchase? What would be his percent interest in the company?

35. The Drinkwater Corporation, still in its preliminary stages of organization, is trying to decide in which state they should incorporate. They have selected two possible states (fictitious names) in which to incorporate: Atokad and Odaroloc. Atokad requires that the entire issue price of no-par stock be regarded as legal capital. Odaroloc allows the corporation to specify a stated value for no-par shares. If Drinkwater Corporation issues 3,000 shares of no-par capital stock for a price of $40 and a stated value of $35, what would be the entries for this transaction in each of these two states?

36. Gung-Hoe contributed land to the Howdy-Handy Corporation in exchange for 3,600 shares of its $12 par value stock. Journalize this transaction under each of the following assumptions:

   a. For the past 2 weeks, Howdy-Handy's stock has traded for about $33 a share on the American Stock Exchange.
   b. Howdy-Handy's stock is not traded on any stock exchange and therefore has no established market. However, Gung-Hoe did receive an offer from a broker a week ago to buy the land for $130,000.

37. Hoagland, Inc. accepted subscriptions for 3,000 shares of its $20 par value common stock at a price of $21 a share. However, because of the large quantity of stock being issued, Hoagland required the subscriber to pay a downpayment of 20 percent and the remainder in two months.

Required:

Prepare the journal entries to record these transactions assuming the downpayment was made on June 30, 19x1 and the remainder was paid when due.

38.   A junior accountant for the Fetters Company is unsure as to how to complete the following stockholders' equity section of the balance sheet.

Stockholders' Equity:

5 percent preferred stock *(1)* par value, 15,000 shares authorized, 9,000 shares issued and outstanding..........................	$ 810,000
Common stock, $20 par value, 200,000 shares authorized, *(2)* shares issued and outstanding........	3,000,000
Common stock subscribed, 1,500 shares..............	*(3)*
Additional paid-in capital:	
Common stock issued and subscribed................	*(4)*
Preferred stock................................	80,000
Total Contributed Capital.....................	*(5)*
Retained earnings.................................	*(6)*
Total Stockholders' Equity...................	$4,099,000

Additional information:

Earnings for the corporation over its life were $18,000 a year. No dividends had ever been paid.

Required:

Complete this stockholders' equity section by filling in the numbers 1-6.

39.   The Fabian Co. is organized on January 1, 19x1, with authorized stock of 30,000 shares of $5 par value common and 5,000 shares of $100 par value preferred. Give the entries required to record each of the following transactions:

a.   Assets are accepted as payment for 10,000 shares of common stock. The assets are valued as follows: land, $50,000; buildings, $130,000; and equipment, $20,000.

b.   The 5,000 preferred shares are sold at $105 per share.

c.   Subscriptions are received for 5,000 shares of common stock at $25.

d.   A payment of $50,000 is received on the subscribed stock.

e.   Subscriptions receivable of $75,000 are collected and the stock is issued.

f.   The remaining common stock is sold for $30 per share.

40.   Consider each of the following independent cases.

a.   Kanoch, Inc. issues 50 shares of $25 par value stock in exchange for land appraised at $1,500. The shares are not actively traded. Record the issuance of the stock on the books of Kanoch, Inc.

b.   Red Rider Stables, Inc. acquired 100 acres of prime grazing land in exchange for 200 shares of no-par capital stock. It was found that a similar

100-acre tract had sold the previous year for $11,000. The company's stock has not been registered with a major exchange but the company's balance sheet reveals a book value of $50 per share. Record the issuance of the stock on the books of Red Rider Stables, Inc.

c.   Monzingo Grocers, Inc. obtained a new store site in exchange for 400 shares of its $15 par value capital stock. The store site is in a recently developed area. Ten years ago wooded lots of similar size sold for $8,000. The latest New York Stock Exchange quotation for the stock was $30 per share. Record the issuance of the stock on the books of Monzingo Grocers, Inc.

41.   Assume that Ham Farm Supplies, Inc. had income after taxes from normal operations for 19x1 of $200,000. Also, the firm had an extraordinary loss of $40,000 (net of tax). The firm had 25,000 shares of stock outstanding throughout 19x1. Compute the earnings per share figures required by APB *Opinion No. 15*.

42.   Make the journal entries necessary to record the declaration and payment of dividends in each of the following situations:

a.   Bruin Company has 8,000 shares of common stock and 3,000 shares of 7 percent, $100 par value preferred stock outstanding. On June 15 the company declares a preferred dividend and a $3.50 per share dividend on the common stock. The dividends are payable on July 15 to the stockholders of record on June 30.

b.   Wolfpack Company has 10,000 shares of $15 par value common stock outstanding. On May 1, the company declares a 10 percent stock dividend to be distributed on May 15. At the time, the market price of a share is $19.

43.   On March 15, the board of directors of Gunsmith Corporation declared a cash dividend of $1 per share to the stockholders of record on March 20. The dividend is payable on April 1. The corporation had 10,000 shares of common stock outstanding.

Required:

Prepare the journal entries required on the date of declaration, the date of record, and the payment date.

44.   The Robinson Corporation was organized in 19x0. The company was authorized to issue 5,000 shares of $50 par value common and 1,000 shares of $100 par value, cumulative preferred stock. All of the preferred and 4,000 shares of common were issued at par. The preferred shares were entitled to dividends of 6 percent before any dividends were paid to common. During the first 5 years of its existence, the corporation earned a total of $120,000 and paid dividends of 50 cents per share each year on common stock.

Required:

Prepare *in good form* the stockholders' equity section as of December 31, 19x4.

45.   Shown below is the stockholders' equity section of the balance sheet of Falcon Company at December 31, 19x1.

Common stock, 10,000 shares issued and outstanding, $10 par value...............	$100,000
Additional paid-in capital......................	50,000
Retained earnings..............................	75,000
Total Stockholders' Equity....................	$225,000

On January 1, 19x2 the company reacquired 500 shares of its stock at $15 per share.

Required:

1.   Prepare the entry to record the purchase of the stock.
2.   Prepare the entry to record the reissuance of the treasury stock at $18 per share.
3.   Prepare the entry to record the reissuance of the stock at $13 per share.

46.   Arnold Company had a $100,000 balance in its retained earnings account on January 1, 19x1. On January 2, 19x1, by action of the Board of Directors, $25,000 of retained earnings was appropriated for future plant expansion. The plant expansion was completed on December 31, 19x2, and the appropriation of retained earnings was released.

Required:

1.   Give the journal entry necessary to record the appropriation.
2.   Give the entry necessary to release the appropriation.

47.   The stockholders' equity section of the balance sheet of Park Company on December 31, 19x1, is shown below:

6% preferred stock, $100 par value (callable at $105) 5,000 shares authorized, issued, and outstanding...........................	$ 500,000
Common stock, $5 par value, 60,000 shares, authorized and 50,000 shares issued and outstanding....	250,000
Additional paid-in capital...........................	400,000
Retained earnings..................................	75,000
Total Stockholders' Equity........................	$1,225,000

Required:

Compute the book value per share of common stock.

48. By using the following code, indicate each transaction's effect on the respective columns.

+ = increases	0 = no effect
− = decreases	? = cannot be determined

The market value of the company's common stock exceeds par value.

		Common Stock	Retained Earnings	Stockholders' Equity	Book Value Per Share of Common Stock
a.	Company declared a cash dividend payable in the next fiscal year to persons holding shares of preferred stock.				
b.	Company received shares of its own common stock, donated by a wealthy shareholder.				
c.	Company purchased shares of its own common stock through a broker at the New York Stock Exchange.				
d.	Company declared and issued a stock dividend on the common stock.				
e.	A cash dividend was declared and paid.				
f.	Retained Earnings were appropriated for plant expansion.				
g.	Treasury shares of common stock were sold at an amount in excess of the purchase price to the corporation.				

49. Jones Co. had the following stock outstanding from January 1, 19x0, to December 31, 19x5.

   a. Common stock, $10 par value, 20,000 shares authorized and outstanding.
   b. Preferred stock, $100 par value with a $6 stated dividend, 10,000 shares authorized, 5,000 shares issued and outstanding.

During that period, Jones Co. paid the following dividends:

19x0	$ 0
19x1	80,000
19x2	0
19x3	30,000
19x4	70,000
19x5	20,000

Compute the amount of preferred dividends and common stock dividends in each year assuming that:

1. The preferred stock is noncumulative.
2. The preferred stock is cumulative.

50. Smith Corporation was organized on January 1, 19x1, with 100,000 shares of $10 par value common stock and 10,000 shares of $50 par value preferred stock authorized. During 19x1, Smith Corporation had the following stock transactions:

Jan. 1	Issued 5,000 shares of common stock for $60 per share.
Oct. 1	Accepted subscriptions for 1,000 shares of common stock at a price of $16 per share. Payment is to be made in two equal installments payable in 60 and 120 days.
Nov. 30	Collected the first installment on the subscribed stock but issued no stock at this time.

Required:

   a. Prepare the journal entries to record the stock transactions.
   b. Prepare the stockholders' equity section of the balance sheet for Smith Corporation as of December 31, 19x1. (Assume that retained earnings are $64,000 on December 31, 19x1.)

51. Akens Co. was organized on January 1, 19x1. A portion of the December 31, 19x2, balance sheet of Akens Co. appeared as follows:

Stockholders' Equity:

6 percent preferred stock, $100 par value, 20,000 shares authorized............		$ 500,000
Preferred stock subscribed..................		100,000
Common stock, $10 par value, 100,000 shares authorized................		400,000
Common stock subscribed..................		50,000
Additional paid-in capital:		
On common stock issued..................	$200,000	
On common stock subscribed..............	50,000	
On preferred stock issued.................	25,000	
On preferred stock subscribed.............	10,000	285,000
Retained earnings..........................		$ 330,000
Total Stockholders' Equity..............		$1,665,000

Required:

1. How many shares of preferred stock are outstanding?
2. How many shares of common stock are outstanding?
3. How many shares of preferred stock are subscribed?
4. How many shares of common stock are subscribed?
5. What were the average issue prices of the common and the preferred shares outstanding?
6. What were the average subscription prices of the common stock and the preferred stock?
7. What is the total contributed capital of Akens Co.?

52. In examining the accounts of Longhorn Steel Company, you discover the following information pertaining to the stockholders' equity of the company at December 31, 19x1.

a. 3,000 shares of $100 par value preferred stock issued, 9,000 shares authorized.
b. The preferred dividend requirement for the year was met by paying dividends of $18,000.
c. 16,000 shares of $10 par value common stock issued and outstanding.
d. 20,000 shares of $10 par value common stock authorized.
e. 2,000 shares of common stock subscribed.
f. The average issue price of the common stock was $17.
g. The average issue price of the preferred stock was $106.
h. The average subscription price of the common stock was $19.
i. Retained earnings were $219,000.

Required:

Prepare the stockholders' equity section of Longhorn Steel Company's balance sheet at December 31, 19x1.

53.   The Babson Corporation began business on January 1, 19x1. During the first year of operations, the following transactions were completed that affected stockholders' equity.

a.   Sold for cash 300,000 shares of capital stock for $13 per share. The charter for the corporation authorized 1,000,000 shares of capital stock.

b.   Sold 5,000 shares of capital stock to the president of the company for $14 per share. Collected 35 percent of the subscription immediately and the balance is due at the end of 11 months.

c.   Exchanged 30,000 shares for a plant site. The seller had recently had an offer to sell the plant site for $380,000 and the site was carried on the seller's books at $420,000.

d.   Collected 25 percent on the subscription contract in (b).

Required:

Give entries for the above transactions using each of the following assumptions:

1.   The stock has a par value of $8 per share.
2.   The stock has no par value and no stated value.
3.   The stock has no par value but has a stated value of $10 per share. State any necessary assumptions of your own.

54.   The Auburn Corporation earned income of $33,000, $25,000, $15,000, $12,000 and $55,000 during the last five years. The common stock consisted of 200,000 shares outstanding for the first three years and 250,000 shares for the last two years. Common stock has a par value of $1 per share. The preferred stock is 7 percent cumulative and nonparticipating. There were 50,000 shares of preferred stock issued and outstanding for the first two years and 75,000 shares the last three years. Preferred stock has a par value of $5 per share.

Required:

Calculate the dividends which each class of stock would receive over each of the last five years assuming (1) the entire net income was distributed each year, and (2) only 80 percent of the reported net income was distributed in the first three years, 90 percent in the last two years.

55.   Record the following transactions on the books of the El Paso Corporation.

a.   The El Paso Corporation accepted subscriptions for 2,500 shares of its $15 par value common stock at a price of $23 per share. The subscription contract requires three installments, ½ now, ¼ in 60 days and the remainder in 90 days.

b.   The second installment was made on time.

c.   The subscriber didn't pay for the third installment when it became due. It is the policy of the corporation to issue to a forfeiting subscriber the number of shares actually paid for rather than the total number contracted.

56. The Charles Brothers Company has decided to dissolve their partnership on January 1, 19x2, and incorporate their company in order to obtain additional capital. The new company will be called Charles Manufacturing Corporation. There were three brothers in the partnership, Joe, Jim, and Dick. Joe had an adjusted capital balance on December 31, 19x1 of $135,000, Jim's balance was $129,000, and Dick's balance was $141,000. Record the following transactions dealing with the incorporation of the Charles Manufacturing Corporation and prepare the stockholders' equity portion of the balance sheet for the newly-formed company.

a.   100,000 shares of common stock with a par value of $5 per share were authorized and 20,000 shares were issued to the public for cash at $8 per share on January 1, 19x2.

b.   Each partner received 20,000 shares of stock in exchange for his share of the partnership's total capital. Goodwill was recognized.

c.   Dick Charles also contributed 500 shares of Lakeview Company stock to the corporation in exchange for 300 shares of the new corporation's stock. Dick had purchased the stock several years earlier for $10 a share.

57. Below is the stockholders' equity portion of Corpos Company's balance sheet.

Stockholders' Equity:

6 percent preferred stock, $200 par value, 25,000 shares authorized..........................	$1,000,000
Class A common stock, $12 par value 200,000 shares authorized................................	1,800,000
Class B common stock, $15 stated value, 150,000 shares authorized.........................	1,500,000
Class B common stock subscribed.....................	45,000
Additional paid-in capital:	
Preferred stock issued.............................	210,000
Class A common stock issued.......................	865,000
Class B common stock issued.......................	125,000
Class B common stock subscribed....................	12,000
Retained earnings..................................	$ 216,000
Total Stockholders' Equity......................	$5,773,000

a.   What is the total contributed capital of Corpos Company?
b.   How many shares of preferred stock are outstanding?
c.   How many shares of Class A common stock are outstanding?
d.   How many shares of Class B common stock are outstanding?
e.   How many shares of Class B common stock are subscribed?

f.   What are the average prices for which the common stock, Classes A and B, were issued?

g.   What is the average subscription price for the Class B common stock subscribed?

58.   In order to obtain additional capital and limited liability, the Star Street Partnership decided to dissolve on January 1, 19x1, in order to form the Star Street Corporation. The newly-formed corporation was issued a charter from the state which authorized them to issue 60,000 shares of $8 par value common stock. The adjusted balances in the four partners' capital accounts before incorporation was Ott, $65,000; Sinclair, $45,000; Hanscom, $96,000; and Shute, $21,000. Each partner received one share of the new corporation's stock for every $10 in their capital account. Goodwill was recognized. In addition, 30,000 shares of the corporation's stock was issued to the public for $12 a share. Also, a building with a book value of $58,715 was contributed in exchange for 4,900 shares of capital stock.

Required:

Record the above transactions in journal form and prepare the stockholders' equity portion of the balance sheet for the newly-formed corporation.

PROBLEMS

59.   Certain account balances of the Gobbler Company as of December 31, 19x2, are shown below:

Sales	$1,000,000
Cost of goods sold	500,000
Gain on sale of Meat Packing Division (net of tax)	100,000
Loss from earthquake (net of tax)	50,000
Operating expenses	350,000
Cash dividends:	
Common stock	250,000
Preferred stock	100,000
Correction of an error—prior period (income overstated)	100,000
Taxes on income from normal operations	75,000

The retained earnings balance on December 31, 19x1, was $850,000. The sale of the Division should be treated as a discontinued operation.

Required:

1.   Prepare an income statement for 19x2.

2.   Prepare a statement of retained earnings for the year ended December 31, 19x2.

60. The income statement for Bonko Company for the year ending December 31, 19x1, is shown below:

Bonko Company
Income Statement
For the Year Ended December 31, 19x1

Sales	$200,000
Cost of goods sold..........................	100,000
Gross profit................................	$100,000
Operating expenses..........................	80,000
Income before extraordinary items..............	$ 20,000
Extraordinary gain (net of tax).................	10,000
Net income................................	$ 30,000

Bonko Company had 60,000 shares of common stock outstanding during 19x1.

Required:

Compute earnings per share for 19x1.

61. The stockholders' equity of Billy, Inc. appears as follows on its December 31, 19x1 balance sheet.

Common stock, $9 par value, 25,000 shares outstanding................................	$225,000
Additional paid-in capital.......................	125,000
Total contributed capital......................	$350,000
Retained earnings.............................	195,000
Total Stockholders' Equity.....................	$545,000

Required:

Make the journal entries necessary to record the transactions in the following independent cases:

1. Billy, Inc. declares and distributes a 60 percent stock dividend on July 1 when the stock is selling for $30 per share.
2. Billy, Inc. declares a 3-for-1 stock split on July 1 when the market price of its stock is $60 per share.
3. Billy, Inc. declares and distributes a 5 percent stock dividend on July 1 when the market price of the stock is $15 per share.

62.   The stockholders' equity section of the Buckeye Company appeared as follows on January 1:

> Common stock, $15 par value, 20,000
>   shares authorized, issued, and outstanding........ $300,000
> Additional paid-in capital.......................   75,000
> Total contributed capital........................ $375,000
> Retained earnings..............................   80,000
>   Total Stockholders' Equity.................... $455,000

On February 1, the company purchased 800 of its outstanding shares at $25 per share. On June 15, the company reissued 500 of these shares at $29 per share. Then, on July 15, the company resold the other 300 shares for $24 per share.

Required:

Prepare the journal entries necessary to record the above transactions on the books of the Buckeye Company. Also, prepare the stockholders' equity section of their balance sheet as of July 15.

63.   The stockholders' equity section of the X Corporation as of December 31, 19x1 shows:

> 6% preferred, cumulative capital stock,
> $100 par value, 50,000 shares
>   authorized, 20,000 shares issued
>   and outstanding......................... $2,000,000
> Common stock, no par, $10 stated
>   value, 400,000 shares authorized,
>   260,000 shares issued and outstanding.......   2,600,000
> Additional paid-in capital:
>   On preferred stock...................... $ 80,000
>   On common stock......................   1,560,000   1,640,000
> Retained earnings..........................   1,200,000
>   Total Stockholders' Equity............... $7,440,000

Note: Dividends on preferred stock are three years in arrears.

Required:

Compute the book value per share of the common stock at December 31, 19x1.

64. The Texan Co. had the following stockholders' equity on January 1, 19x1.

Common stock, $5 par value, 100,000
  shares authorized, 50,000 shares issued
  and outstanding................................. $250,000
Additional paid-in capital.......................... 150,000
  Total Contributed Capital........................ $400,000
Retained earnings.................................. 100,000
  Total Stockholders' Equity....................... $500,000

During 19x1, the company had the following transactions related to the stockholders' equity.

Jan. 20   Issued 5,000 shares of stock for $10 per share.
Feb. 15   Purchased 3,000 shares of Texan Co. common stock for $11 per share.
May 10   Declared a $.20 per share cash dividend to the stockholders of record on May 15. The dividend is payable on June 1.
June 1   Paid the cash dividend.
     15   Sold 1,000 shares of treasury stock for $13 per share.
Aug. 15   Sold 1,000 shares of treasury stock for $10 per share.
Sept. 10 Declared a 10 percent stock dividend for the stockholders of record on September 15 to be distributed on October 1. The market price of the stock was $11 per share on September 15.
Oct. 1   Distributed the stock dividend.
Nov. 1   The Board of Directors decided to appropriate $20,000 of retained earnings for future plant expansion.
Dec. 31   Net income for the year was $35,000. The income summary and dividend accounts were closed to retained earnings.

Required:

1.   Give the necessary journal entries to record the transactions.
2.   Prepare a statement of retained earnings at December 31, 19x1.

65.   The stockholders' equity of the National Company at December 31, 19x1, was as follows:

6% noncumulative preferred stock, $100 par value, call price per share $110, authorized 70,000 shares, issued 10,000 shares..............................	$1,000,000
$5 noncumulative preferred stock, $100 par value, call price per share $105, authorized 100,000 shares, issued 5,000 shares..............................	500,000
Common stock, $50 par value, authorized 100,000 shares, issued 40,000 shares, of which 1,000 shares are held in the treasury.......................	2,000,000
Additional paid-in capital:	
On 6% preferred stock............................	100,000
On common stock.................................	255,000
Total Contributed Capital.......................	$3,855,000
Retained earnings (of which $60,000, an amount equal to the cost of the treasury stock purchased, is unavailable for dividends).......................	1,500,000
	$5,355,000
Deduct: Cost of treasury stock (1,000 shares)...........	60,000
Total Stockholders' Equity......................	$5,295,000

Note: Preferred dividends for 19x0 and 19x1 have not been paid.

During 19x2, National Company had the following transactions affecting the stockholders' equity:

Jan.	5	Sold 11,000 shares of the common stock at $55 per share.
Feb.	1	Declared a 10 percent stock dividend on the common stock; the market value of the stock on that date was $60 per share.
	28	Paid the stock dividend declared on February 1.
May	1	Purchased 500 shares of the common stock for the treasury at a cost of $65 per share.
	5	Sold all of the treasury stock held for $70 per share.
	9	Stockholders voted to reduce the par value of common stock to $25 per share and increase authorized shares to 200,000. The company issued the additional shares to effect this stock split.
June	30	The Board of Directors declared a $1 per share dividend on common stock and the regular annual dividend on both classes of preferred stock. All dividends are payable on July 20 to shareholders of record as of July 10.

Required:

1.   Prepare the necessary journal entries to record the preceding transactions.

2.   Prepare the stockholders' equity section of the balance sheet at June 30, 19x2.

66. Below is data relating to the income statement of the Benjamin Corporation:

    a.   Sales for the year ended September 30, 19x1 were $850,000. Cost of goods sold were $600,000 and expenses were $260,000.

    b.   In addition to the above, certain other revenue and expense items were incurred during the year:

        1.   Benjamin Corporation discontinued the operations of a segment of its firm. There was no income from that segment for the current year and the segment was sold at a gain of $30,000.

        2.   A write-down of inventory totaling $1,500 was recorded because of a decline in demand for the inventory due to obsolescence.

        3.   An earthquake occurred during the year which caused a total loss in corporate property valued at $75,000. Earthquakes are not a usual occurrence in the corporation's geographic area.

        4.   The average number of shares of common stock for the year was 80,000. The corporation does not have preferred stock.

Required:

Ignoring income taxes:

    1.   Calculate the total amount of extraordinary items.

    2.   Prepare an income statement in proper form including all appropriate earnings per share calculations.

67. On January 2, 19x0, the White Company purchased a building for $178,000. At that time, it was estimated that the building would have a useful life of 32 years and a salvage value of $18,000. The company decided to use the straight-line depreciation method. Calculate the effect in the financial statements of each of the following unrelated accounting changes and give journal entries to record current depreciation and any other necessary adjusting entries.

    a.   On December 31, 19x3, before the depreciation adjustment for the year had been made, it was decided that the building should be depreciated by the sum-of-the-years'-digits method.

    b.   On December 31, 19x3, the building was found to have a remaining useful life of only 22 years and a salvage value of $20,000.

    c.   Depreciation was inappropriately calculated for three years because the asset was recorded on the books at an original cost of $78,000 (i.e., the building was debited for $78,000 and cash was credited for $78,000).

68. The accountant for the Sloan Manufacturing Corporation has provided you with the following data:

    a.   Average common shares outstanding during 19x1, 60,000 shares, par $3; outstanding December 31, 19x1, 70,000 shares.

   b.   6 percent cumulative preferred stock outstanding December 31, 19x1, 10,000 shares; redemption value, $120 per share; par value, $100 per share.

   c.   Cash dividends declared on December 31, 19x1—$420,000 to common stockholders and $60,000 to preferred stockholders. There are no dividends of preferred stock in arrears.

   d.   Net income for the year was $560,000.

   e.   Total stockholders' equity as of December 31, 19x1 was $2,600,000.

Required:

   1.   What is the earnings per share for common stock?
   2.   What is the dividend declared per share of common stock?
   3.   What is the dividend declared per share of preferred stock?
   4.   What is the book value of common stock?

69.   The Peterson Company was organized on January 1, 19x0, with 10,000 shares of $10 par value common stock authorized, issued, and outstanding. Journalize the following transactions which took place in 19x4:

Jan.	1	The corporation purchased 100 shares of its common stock for $15 a share.
Feb.	1	The corporation sold the 100 shares purchased on January 1 for a total price of $1,750.
Mar.	1	Mrs. Moneybags, a stockholder, donated 100 shares of the X Corporation's common stock to the corporation.
	5	The corporation sold the 100 donated shares for a total price of $2,500.
Apr.	1	The corporation purchased 100 shares of its own stock for $9 a share.
May	1	The corporation sold the 100 shares purchased on April 1 for a total price of $500.
Dec.	15	A $.50 per share dividend on common stock was declared, to be paid on January 15, 19x5.

70.   The Jones Co. was organized on January 1, 19x0, with 20,000 shares of $10 par value common stock and 5,000 shares of $100 par value, 6 percent preferred stock authorized. The balances in the stockholders' equity accounts on December 31, 19x3, were as follows:

Preferred stock............................	$100,000
Common stock............................	120,000
Additional paid-in capital:	
On preferred stock.......................	5,000
On common stock........................	60,000
Retained earnings.........................	$190,000

During 19x4, the company had the following transactions that affected the stockholders' equity:

		Number	Amount
a.	Issuance of common stock..................	5,000	$ 20 per share
b.	Purchase of its own shares of common stock....	4,000	$ 22 per share
c.	Reissuance of treasury stock................	1,000	$ 24 per share
d.	Issuance of preferred stock................	1,000	$ 102 per share
e.	Payment of dividend on common stock........		$ .50 per share
f.	Payment of dividend on preferred stock........		$ 6 per share
g.	Appropriation of retained earnings for future plant expansion....................		$100,000
h.	Net income for the year....................		$ 60,000
i.	Stock split on common stock with par value reduced to $5 per share..............	2 for 1	

Required:

Prepare the stockholders' equity section of the balance sheet for Jones Co. on December 31, 19x4.

71. On July 1, 19x0, the Morehouse Company purchased two pieces of equipment: a tractor for $11,000 and a truck for $9,000. On that date it was estimated that the tractor would have a life of eight years with a salvage value of $300 and the truck would have a life of ten years with a salvage value of $500. The company decided to use the double-declining balance method to depreciate both assets. Calculate the effect on the financial statements of each of the following unrelated accounting changes. Also, give journal entries to record any necessary adjusting entries and current depreciation expense. The company's fiscal year ends on June 30.

   a. On June 30, 19x3, the company realized the truck only had a remaining life of four years. Salvage value was expected to remain at $500.

   b. On June 30, 19x4, the accountant found an error in the calculation of the tractor's depreciation expense. The bookkeeper had erroneously subtracted out the salvage value in the first year when calculating depreciation on the declining balance method.

   c. On June 30, 19x3, it was decided that the tractor should be depreciated using the straight-line method.

Refer to the Annual Report included in the Appendix at the end of the text:

72. At the end of the most recent year, what is the total equity?

73. At the end of the most recent year, which account(s) represent(s) the major portion of equity?

74. At the end of the most recent year, where is net income reflected in the stockholders' equity section of the balance sheet?

75. Comparing the two years, what is the increase/decrease in the common stock account?

76. What factors cause an increase in the common stock account? What factors cause a decrease?

77. What is the EPS for the most recent year?

78. On which financial statement can the EPS amount be located?

79. In which statement would a prior period adjustment be reflected?

80. What amount of stock was issued? What amount of common stock?

81. In either year, was there an accounting change? If so, what type of change was it and how did it affect net income?

Chapter 8 discusses the accounting procedures used to record and control cash and account for receivables and payables. Studying this chapter should enable you to:

1. Describe the basic procedures for controlling cash receipts and disbursements and receivables.

2. Discuss the steps involved in preparing a bank statement reconciliation.

3. Describe the procedures used to control and account for imprest funds.

4. Illustrate the use of control and subsidiary accounts for recording receivables.

5. Discuss the purposes and mechanics of estimating bad debt expense.

6. Make the entries necessary to record the issuance and payment of a note and the related interest on the books of both the borrower and the lender.

7. Describe the process of discounting a note and the effect it has on a firm's accounts.

8. Calculate and prepare the entry to record the payroll taxes levied on an employer.

8

Cash, Receivables
and Current
Liabilities

INTRODUCTION　　　　Cash includes currency, coins, checks, money orders and monies on deposit with banks. On the balance sheet, cash is classified as a current asset. Usually, the total of all cash on hand and cash on deposit in multiple bank accounts will be shown as a single amount in the balance sheet.

Almost every transaction of any business organization will eventually result in either the receipt or disbursement of cash. The accounting procedures which enable a business to establish effective control over its cash transactions are among the most important, if not *the* most important, "controls" necessary for the operation of a business. While it is certainly true that cash is no more important than any of the other individual assets of the business, cash is more susceptible to misappropriation or theft because it can easily be concealed and because it is not readily identifiable. It is essential, therefore, that the company institute procedures or controls throughout every phase of its operations in order to safeguard cash from the time of its receipt until the time it is deposited in the company's bank account.

A good system of internal control over cash transactions should provide adequate procedures for protecting both cash receipts and cash disbursements. Such procedures should include the following elements:

1.　Responsibilities for handling cash receipts, making cash payments, and recording cash transactions should be clearly defined.
2.　Employees who handle cash transactions should not maintain the accounting records for cash.
3.　All cash receipts should be deposited daily in a bank account and all significant cash payments should be made by check.
4.　The validity and amount of cash payments should be verified, and different employees should be responsible for approving the disbursement and for signing the check.

The application of these procedures in developing an adequate system of internal control over cash transactions varies from company to company depending upon such factors as the size of the company, the number of its employees, its sources of cash, etc. However, the following discussion illustrates typical procedures which may be used effectively in the control of cash receipts and cash disbursements.

CASH RECEIPTS　　　　The effective control of cash transactions begins at the moment cash is received by the business. Among the basic principles to be followed in controlling cash receipts are the following:

1.　A complete record of all cash receipts should be prepared as soon as cash is received. This involves the listing of all cash items received by mail (often accomplished by the use of EDP equipment) and the use of devices such as cash registers to record "over-the-counter" sales. The immediate recording of each cash transaction is important because the likelihood of misappropriations of cash receipts occurring is usually greatest before a record of the receipt has been prepared. Once the receipt of cash has been properly recorded, misappropriation or theft is much more difficult to accomplish and conceal.

2. Each day's cash receipts should be deposited intact in the company's bank account as soon as possible. Disbursements should never be made directly from cash receipts; each and every cash item received should be promptly deposited in the bank. All major disbursements should be made by check, while outlays of smaller amounts may be made from controlled petty cash funds (described in a later section of this chapter). Adherence to these procedures will provide the firm with a valuable test of the accuracy of its cash records since every major cash transaction will be recorded twice: by the firm in its accounting records and by the bank. The periodic comparison or reconciliation of the accounting records of the business with those maintained by an independent, external source (the bank) is an important control feature in itself and will be discussed in detail in a later section of this chapter.

3. The employees charged with the responsibility of handling cash receipts should not be involved in making cash disbursements. This is a normal procedure employed by most firms of any size. Insofar as possible, the internal functions of receiving and disbursing cash should be kept separate in order to prevent the possible misappropriation or theft of cash. The employees handling cash receipts should not have access to the other accounting records of the firm for the same reasons.

"Over-The-Counter Sales."   The cash proceeds received at the time a sale is made should be recorded by means of a cash register. In larger firms, it may be preferable to have all sales recorded by a cashier at a centrally located cash register. One employee may "make the sale" and prepare a pre-numbered sales slip which is given to the cashier who then records the sale on the cash register and accepts the customer's payment. Involving two (or more) employees in each sales transaction, rather than permitting a single employee to handle a transaction in its entirety, increases the control over cash. The use of a cash register also provides certain other benefits. Customers will observe that their purchases are recorded at the proper amount (another form of control). You may recall making a purchase where your money was refunded "if a star appears on your receipt" or where your drink was free if the waiter failed to give you a receipt. These are simple, yet effective examples of control procedures which are intended to encourage customers to note whether the sale has been properly recorded at the correct amount. The cash register may

also be used as a means of classifying the sources of receipts, such as sales by departments.

At the end of each day, or more often if necessary (for example at the end of each cashier's shift), the cash in the register should be counted and recorded on a cash register summary or other report by an employee who does not have access to the sales slips. A second employee should total the sales slips and reconcile the total of the sales slips to the cash register total. As previously indicated, all cash received should be deposited intact in the bank and the receipts recorded in the accounting records.

In certain circumstances, it may not be feasible to use prenumbered sales slips. If this is the case and a cash register is used, the above procedures should still be followed to the extent applicable. The major difference will be that the cash in the register will be reconciled to the totals contained in the register rather than to totals obtained from sales slips.

Receipts from Charge Sales. Remittances from customers for sales which were made on account may be received either by mail or by payment in person. In either case, procedures should be employed so that the receipt and the recording of the cash is performed by different employees whenever it is possible and practical to do so. If this separation of duties can be effectively maintained, the misappropriation of cash would require the collusion of two or more employees, thus diminishing the likelihood of the occurrence of any irregularity.

The employee who opens the mail should immediately prepare a listing of all cash items received. Of course this can be done "automatically," such as by the use of punched cards as remittance forms and EDP equipment. This listing, along with a summary of over-the-counter receipts described previously, may be used to record each day's receipts in the cash receipts summary. Mail remittances are then combined with over-the-counter receipts, and the daily bank deposit is prepared and made. The amount deposited will be equal to the total cash receipts for the day. The employee making the bank deposit should obtain a duplicate deposit slip or other receipt from the bank for subsequent comparison to the cash receipts book.

The advantages of the procedures described above are many. The most important of these benefits may be summarized as follows:

1. The possibility of irregularities with respect to cash transactions are reduced, since any misappropriation will generally require the collusion of two or more employees.
2. The prompt deposit of each day's receipts intact (along with the disbursement procedures described in a later section of this chapter) provides the basis for an independent, external check on the internal records of the firm by reconciliation with bank statements.

3. Frequent deposits of receipts minimizes the idle cash and thereby reduces interest or other carrying charges which might otherwise be incurred by the business.

Several sections of this chapter have discussed the possible misappropriations of cash and outlined certain procedures which are intended to minimize these occurrences. It is obvious that the owners and/or management of any organization are naturally concerned with establishing effective controls that will prevent irregularities, but it may not be as apparent that every employee of the business also has a definite interest in these safeguards. If, for example, cash is misappropriated in an instance where the control procedures are ineffective or not in existence, any employee who might possibly be involved will be under suspicion. Although it may not be possible to identify the guilty person, no employee will be able to prove his (or her) innocence. Employee morale and efficiency will be adversely effected. An effective system of internal control avoids this situation; responsibilities are well-defined, definite, and fixed. Internal control is often an excellent preventive measure, as it often removes the temptation which might cause an otherwise good employee to succumb.

Cash Over and Short. Regardless of the care exercised in handling cash transactions, employees may make errors which cause cash overages or shortages. These differences will normally be detected when the cash on hand is counted and reconciled to the beginning cash balance plus any inflows of cash less any cash outlays.

Assume, for example, that total "over the counter" cash sales for the day are shown as $1,500 on the cash register while cash on hand after deducting the $100 beginning balance, is counted and found to be $1,505. The following journal entry would be made to record the cash sales for the day:

```
Cash ................................. 1,505
    Sales ...............................        1,500
    Cash over and short.................           5
```

The cash over and short account is credited for any cash overages and debited for any cash shortages. At the end of the accounting period, the net balance in the cash over and short account is treated as miscellaneous revenues if there is a net credit balance or as a miscellaneous expense if there is a net debit balance.

CASH DISBURSEMENTS

As previously indicated, one of the basic rules of effective internal control over cash transactions is that each day's receipts should be deposited intact in the bank and that all disbursements should be made by check. The functions of handling cash receipts and cash disbursements should be separated or divided among employees to the greatest extent practical. Other procedures which may be used to establish effective control over cash disbursements include the following:

1. All checks should be prenumbered consecutively and should be controlled and accounted for on a regular basis. Checks which are voided or spoiled should be retained and mutilated to prevent any possible unauthorized use.
2. Each disbursement should be supported or evidenced by an invoice and/or voucher which has been properly approved. The procedures which identify that obligations for which checks are prepared are proper obligations and in the appropriate amount are often referred to as a voucher system. The details of a voucher system will be discussed later in this chapter.
3. Invoices and vouchers should be indelibly marked as "paid" or otherwise cancelled in order to prevent duplicate payments.
4. The bank statement and returned checks should be routed to the employee charged with the preparation of the bank reconciliation statement (described below). This employee should be someone other than the person who is responsible for making cash disbursements.

THE BANK RECONCILIATION STATEMENT

As indicated earlier, if all receipts are deposited intact in the bank and all major disbursements are made by check, each cash transaction will be recorded twice: by the business in its accounting records, and in the records of the bank. It might seem logical, then, that at any given time the cash balance obtained from the accounting records of the firm should be identical to (i.e., equal to) the balance in the business's checking account at the bank. This is very seldom the case, however. Comparison of the balance shown in the firm's records with the balance shown at the same date by the bank statement usually reveals a difference in the two amounts. One reason for the difference could, of course, be erroneous entries made either by the firm or by the bank. A more frequent cause for the difference is, however, attributable to the difference in the timing of the recording of the transactions by the firm and the bank. If all transactions were recorded simultaneously by the business and by the bank no differences would result (except in the case of errors), but this is almost never the case. The firm, for example, will write a check and immediately deduct the amount of the expenditure from the cash balance in its checkbook. The bank will not deduct this same disbursement from the firm's account until the check is presented to the bank for payment, perhaps several days later. Until the disbursement is deducted by the bank, the balance in the firm's account at the bank will exceed the firm's cash balance in its checkbook by the amount of the check. Similarly, the bank may levy a service charge against the firm's bank account from time to time. The business is usually unaware of the amount of this charge until it receives its monthly statement from the bank. Until the bank statement is received and the service charge is deducted, the balance on the firm's records will exceed the bank statement balance by the amount of the service charge.

The above examples are but two of the many items which may cause a difference between the bank statement balance and the cash balance as shown on the accounting records of the business. Other items which are often reflected in the bank statement but which have not yet been recorded by the depositor include:

1. N.S.F checks—checks that were received from the depositor's customers and which were deposited in the bank, but for which the bank on which the check was written refuses payment (usually because of insufficient funds in the customer's account).
2. Deductions for bank service charges, printing of checks, safe deposit box rentals, etc.
3. Collections by the bank in acting as a collecting agent for the depositor.

A bank reconciliation is prepared to identify and account for all items which cause a difference between the cash balance as shown on the bank statement and the balance as it appears in the firm's accounting records. One format of this statement which is often used is such that both the book and bank balances are adjusted to the actual amount of cash which is available to the business. This amount is often referred to as the "adjusted cash balance" or "true cash." This is the amount which should appear on the balance sheet. A typical bank reconciliation statement is presented in Illustration 1.

The initial step in preparing a bank reconciliation statement is to examine the bank statement and any debit and credit memoranda accompanying it. A debit memorandum is evidence of a deduction made by the bank from a depositor's account which arises from a transaction other than the normal payment of a check by the bank. Likewise, a credit memorandum is an addition to the depositor's account which arises from a transaction other than a normal deposit. These documents should be compared with the firm's accounting records in order to determine whether or not they have been previously (and properly) recorded by the business. If these transactions have not been recorded, they will be included as additions or deductions in the bank reconciliation statement and then recorded at a subsequent time. Examples of these types of reconciling items which were included in Illustration 1 are as follows:

Illustration 1

Carol's Bakery
Bank Reconciliation Statement
June 30, 19x1

Balance per the bank statement, June 30, 19x1	$4,590
Add: Deposit in transit	500
Bank error, check drawn by Carrol's Tavern	
charged to the account of Carol's Bakery	10
Less: Outstanding checks:	
Number 95—$50	
Number 101— 15	
Number 106— 30	
Number 110— 5	(100)
"True" cash balance, June 30, 19x1	$5,000
Balance per the books, June 30, 19x1	$4,000
Add: Note collected by the bank	1,000
Error made by the accountant in recording check #100	45
Less: Bank charges	(5)
N.S.F. check	(40)
"True" cash balance, June 30, 19x1	$5,000

1. The $1,000 addition to the book balance represents the proceeds from a note payable to Carol's Bakery which was collected by the bank and added to Carol's bank account.
2. The bank charges of $5 for the month of June were deducted from Carol's account by the bank.
3. The N.S.F. (Not Sufficient Funds) check of $40 represents a check received from a customer and deposited by Carol. The check was returned unpaid by the customer's bank.

The second step in preparing the reconciliation is to arrange the paid checks returned with the bank statement in numerical sequence. The checks returned by the bank are then compared with the checks issued as listed in the business checkbook or cash disbursements journal. Distinctive "tick marks" or symbols (such as a $\sqrt{}$) may be used in the checkbook in order to indicate those checks which have been returned by the bank. The amount of each check should be compared to the amount listed in the checkbook during this process. The outstanding checks are those which have been issued but not yet returned by the bank.

Checks which were outstanding at the beginning of the month and which cleared the bank during the month may be traced to the bank reconciliation statement prepared at the end of the previous month. Any checks which were outstanding at the beginning of the month and which did not clear the bank will, of course, still be included as outstanding in the current month's reconciliation. In the example, the $100 total of outstanding checks included in the bank reconciliation statement was determined by comparing the cancelled checks returned with the bank statement with the checkbook and the listing of outstanding checks included in the previous month's bank reconciliation.

In our example, examination of the cancelled checks returned with the bank statement disclosed the fact that the bank had deducted a check of Carrol's Tavern in the amount of $10 from the Carol's Bakery account. This item is shown as an addition to the balance per bank in the reconciliation and would be called to the attention of the bank for correction.

The next step in the reconciliation process is to ascertain whether or not there are any deposits in transit. A deposit in transit is a receipt which has been included in the cash balance per books and deposited in the bank (for example, in a night depository or by mail) but which has not yet been processed by the bank and credited to the depositor's account. In the illustration, the total receipts of $500 for June 30th were deposited in the bank's night depository on that date. The bank, however, did not credit the firm's account until the next day, July 1st. The $500 amount is therefore shown as a deposit in transit in the June 30, 19x1, bank reconciliation statement.

An excellent test of the accuracy of the firm's cash receipts records is to reconcile the total receipts for the month (or other period) to the total deposits credited to the bank account in the bank statement. In order to perform this test, the following information would be required:

1. The total deposits which are included in the bank statement for the month of June [including a deposit in transit at the beginning of the month (May 31, 19x1) of $700] $15,000
2. The total cash receipts shown in the firm's accounting records for the month of June (including the receipts of June 30th of $500) $14,800

The receipts as per the books for the month of June would be reconciled with the deposits as per the June 30, 19x1, bank statement as follows:

Deposits per bank statement	$15,000
Less: Deposit in transit at the end of the prior month	700
	$14,300
Add: Deposit in transit at the end of the current month	500
Cash receipts per the books	$14,800

In many instances, deposits in transit, outstanding checks, service charges, and errors will be the only reconciling items between the book and the bank balances. Omissions from, or errors in, the accounting records of the firm should, of course, be corrected immediately. If errors made by the bank are discovered in the reconciliation process (such as a check charged to the wrong account), they should be called to the attention of the bank for immediate correction.

In the example, several adjusting or correcting entries would be required. These are as follows:

Note collected by the bank

Cash	1,000	
Notes Receivable		1,000

Error

Cash	45	
Accounts Receivable		45*

Bank service charges

Service charge expense	5	
Cash		5

N.S.F. check

Accounts Receivable	40	
Cash		40

* The receipt of a payment on account of $572 was erroneously recorded as $527 by the firm. This entry reduces the customer's account in order to reflect the actual amount which was paid and increases cash to the proper amount.

The effect of these three entries will be to adjust the balance per books as of June 30, 19x1, to the "true cash" balance as of that date. This adjustment procedure may be illustrated as follows:

Cash	
4,000	
1,000	5
45	40
5,000	

It should be noted that only those items which are adjustments of the "balance per books" in the bank reconciliation statement will require adjusting or correcting entries. This is because these items have either not been previously recorded on the books of the firm (in the example, the note collected by the bank, the bank charges, and the check which was returned N.S.F.) or have been recorded erroneously (in the example, the receipt of $572 which was recorded by the firm as $527[1]). Items which

[1] Transposition errors (i.e. $572 − $527) are always divisible by nine. This fact may be helpful in locating differences, errors, etc.

are included as adjustments of the "balance per the bank statement" do not require adjustment on the firm's books since these items are either transactions which have been already recorded by the firm but not by the bank (in the example, the deposit in transit and the outstanding checks) or errors which were made by the bank (in the example, the check of Carrol's Tavern which was erroneously charged to the account of Carol's Bakery).

The bank reconciliation procedure may be summarized as follows:

Balance per the bank statement—Adjust for:

1. Transactions recorded by the firm but not by the bank (deposits in transit, outstanding checks, etc.).
2. Errors made by the bank.

Balance per the books—Adjust for:

1. Transactions recorded by the bank but not by the firm (collections made for the firm by the bank, service charges, N.S.F. checks, etc.).
2. Errors made by the firm.

PETTY CASH FUNDS

A basic principle of control over cash is that all cash disbursements should be made by check. This is not practicable, however, in instances where small expenditures are required for items such as postage, freight, carfare, employees' "supper money," etc. In circumstances such as these, it is usually more convenient and cost effective to make payments in currency and/or coin. This can be accomplished and effective control over cash still maintained by the use of an imprest fund called petty cash.

A petty cash fund is established by drawing a check on the regular checking account, cashing it, and placing the proceeds in a fund. The amount of the fund depends upon the extent to which petty cash will be used and how often it will be reimbursed. As a practical matter it should be large enough to cover petty cash disbursements for a reasonable period of time—for example, a week. A single employee should be placed in charge of the fund and made responsible for its operation.

A major difference between making disbursements from a petty cash fund and from a regular checking account is that disbursements from petty cash funds are recorded in the accounting records not as they are made, but when the fund is reimbursed. At the time each expenditure is made from the fund, a petty cash voucher, such as the one illustrated below is prepared. If an invoice or other receipt is available in support of the

Petty Cash Voucher #53

TO _Vince Brenner_   DATE _May 1_   19x1

EXPLANATION	ACCOUNT	AMOUNT
Postage	119	$5.00

APPROVED BY _PD_   RECEIVED PAYMENT _V. B._

disbursement, it should be attached to the voucher. In any event, the person receiving the cash should always be required to sign the petty cash voucher as evidence of his or her receipt of the disbursement. If this procedure is followed, at any given time the total of the cash on hand in the petty cash fund plus the total of the unreimbursed receipts should be exactly equal to the original amount of the fund.

The fund would be reimbursed on a periodic basis or whenever necessary. In order to obtain reimbursement of the fund, the employee acting as petty cashier would bring the paid petty cash vouchers to the person who is authorized to write checks on the firm's bank account and exchange them for a check equal to the total of the vouchers. At this point, the petty cash vouchers would be separated and summarized according to the appropriate expense category for recording in the firm's accounting records. Before the check is issued, the vouchers would be reviewed in order to ascertain that all the expenditures made were for valid business purposes. After the petty cash vouchers are approved and the fund replenished, the vouchers and the underlying support should be marked as "paid" or otherwise mutilated in order to prevent their reuse, either intentionally or unintentionally.

To illustrate the operation of a petty cash fund, assume that Barney Company establishes a $100 petty cash fund on January 1, 19x1, by cashing a check in the amount of $100 and placing the proceeds in the fund. The entry to record this transaction would be as follows:

January 1   Petty Cash 100
　　　　　　　 Cash 100

Assume further that during the month of January, disbursements from the fund (supported by vouchers) totaled $85. In order to replenish the fund on January 31, the employee responsible for the fund would exchange the vouchers for a check drawn on the regular cash account for $85. This check would be cashed and the $85 proceeds would be used to restore the fund to its original cash balance of $100. This transaction would be recorded by the following entry:

January 31 Various Expenses	85	
Cash		85

Note that no entry is made to the "petty cash" account after the fund is established (unless the firm wishes to increase or decrease the fund balance).

Effective control over petty cash operations is accomplished in two ways: at any time the cash on hand in the fund plus the unreimbursed petty cash vouchers must be equal to the fund balance, and the expense vouchers must be examined and approved upon reimbursement by a person other than the employee who made the disbursement. If considered necessary or desirable, surprise counts of the petty cash fund also may be made in order to insure that the fund is operating according to its intended purpose.

RECEIVABLES

The extension of credit is a significant factor in the operation of many businesses. Most businesses are both grantors of credit (creating receivables) and receivers of credit (creating payables). Receivables are assets representing the claims that a business has against others. While receivables may be generated by various types of transactions, the most common sources of receivables are the sale of merchandise or services on a credit basis. Normally these assets will be realized or converted into cash by the business. Payables are obligations of a firm which arise from past transactions and which are to be discharged at a future date by payment of cash, transfer of other assets, or performance of a service.

Typically claims against a firm originate from transactions such as purchases of merchandise or services on credit, purchases of equipment on credit, and loans from banks. In an economic system such as ours, which is based so extensively on credit, almost all business concerns incur liabilities. The purpose of this chapter is to describe and discuss the procedures which are necessary to establish effective control over receivables and payables, and to illustrate the accounting practices and procedures which are employed with regard to these assets and liabilities.

CLASSIFICATION OF RECEIVABLES AND PAYABLES

Receivables are classified according to the timing of their expected realization (i.e.—as current assets if realization is anticipated within a year, or as noncurrent assets if collection is expected subsequent to the current period). Receivables are also classified according to their form. Notes receivable are claims against others which are supported by "formal" or written promises to pay. These may or may not be negotiable instruments, depending on such factors as the terms, form, and content of the note. An example of a note receivable would be the written promise by a borrower to repay a loan with interest, at a stated date. Accounts receivable, on the other hand, are not supported by "formal" or written promises to pay. An example of an account receivable would be the claim of a business against a customer who makes a purchase on account.

Creditors of a business have claims against the assets of the firm. Depending upon the nature of the particular liability, a claim may either be against specific assets or against assets in general. In any case, claims of creditors have priority over the claims of owners. Thus, in the event of the liquidation of a business, all debts must be satisfied before any payments are made to owners.

Amounts shown in the balance sheet as liabilities may be classified as either current or noncurrent liabilities. A proper distinction between current and noncurrent liabilities is essential because comparison of current assets with current liabilities is an important means of evaluating the short-run liquidity or debt-paying ability of the firm.

Current liabilities are those debts or obligations of a firm that must either be paid in cash or settled by providing goods or services within the operating cycle of the firm or one year, whichever is longer. The operating cycle of a business is the average period of time that elapses between purchase of an inventory item and conversion of the inventory into cash. This cycle includes the initial purchase of the inventory, the sale of the item on credit, and the collection of the receivable. The most common current liabilities include accounts payable, notes payable, and accrued liabilities.

CONTROL OVER RECEIVABLES

At the time an over-the-counter sale is made, it should be recorded by means of a cash register whether it is a cash sale or a charge sale. The controls over cash previously described apply to both charge or credit sales as well as to cash sales. If a sale is made on account, a prenumbered sales ticket should be prepared and signed by the customer making the purchase. As a minimum, this charge ticket should include the following information:

1. The date.
2. The customer's name and account number.
3. A description of the item(s) purchased by the customer.
4. The total amount of the sale.
5. The customer's signature.

Effective control procedures require that the sales slip be prepared in triplicate: one copy would be given to the customer; a second copy would be placed in the cash register; and a third copy would be retained by the salesperson. An invoice dispenser which automatically retains a copy in a locked container is an ideal control device for this purpose.

At the end of each day, or more often if necessary, the charge slips accumulated in the register would be used in the reconciliation of the cash register receipts as previously described.

The charge slips will serve as the basis for recording credit purchases in customers' accounts. A "control" account, trade accounts receivable for example, would be used to record the total charge sales and the total payments which are received from customers. Individual ledger accounts, referred to as "subsidiary" accounts, would be maintained for each customer. The amount of each charge sale would be recorded individually in the particular customer's account, and the total sales would be recorded in the control account. Bills would be prepared from the individual customers' ledger accounts and mailed out periodically, usually on a monthly basis. As payments are received from customers, the remittances would be recorded individually in the customer's account and in total in the "control" account. Cash receipts, received either by mail or "over-the-counter," would be controlled according to the procedures outlined previously. At any point in time, the balance in the "control" account should be equal[2] to the total of the balances in the individual customers' accounts. Therefore, a periodic reconciliation should be made of the control and the subsidiary accounts.

ACCOUNTS RECEIVABLE

As credit sales are made, entries are recorded in both the "control" and the "subsidiary" accounts. For purposes of illustration, assume that a department store makes the following sales during the month of June:

To Larry Killough.	$ 100
To Gene Seago	150
To Pat Kemp.	200
To all other charge customers	10,000
	$10,450

These sales would be recorded in the "control" account, trade accounts receivable, by the following entry:

Accounts Receivable	10,450	
Sales		10,450

---

[2] If a special journal is used, they may be equal only at the end of the period.

At the same time, these sales would also be recorded in the individual customers' accounts, so that at all times the balance in the "control" account (accounts receivable) would be equal to the total of all the balances in the "subsidiary" accounts (individual customers' accounts). Using T-accounts, this process is illustrated as follows:

	Control Accounts		*Subsidiary Accounts*	

	Accounts Receivable	=	**Killough**	**Seago**
	100		100	150
	150			
	200			
	10,000		**Kemp**	**All Others**
Bal. 10,450			200	10,000

Sales

	100
	150
	200
	10,000
	10,450 Bal.

Now assume that the collections received from customers are as follows:

From Killough. . . . . $ 100
From Seago 100
From other customers 8,000
$8,200

These collections would also be recorded in the control account by the following entry:

Cash 8,200
    Accounts Receivable 8,200

At the same time, the collections would also be recorded in the subsidiary accounts, thereby maintaining a balance with the control account. This procedure is illustrated as follows:

	Control Account			*Subsidiary Accounts*		

	Accounts Receivable		**Killough**		**Seago**	
Bal. 10,450	8,200	100	100	150	100
2,250		0		50	

	Kemp		**All Others**	
	200		10,000	8,000
			2,000	

BAD DEBT EXPENSE

One of the costs of making sales on a credit basis is the expense that results from the fact that some of the customers who make purchases on account may never pay the amounts which are owed to the firm. This is to be expected and should be considered a normal cost of doing business. Obviously, if a firm were able to identify the particular customers who would ultimately fail to pay their accounts, it would not sell to them on a credit basis. Unfortunately, although credit investigations of varying degrees of effectiveness are made by firms, some bad debts will still result. In fact, if a firm had no bad debts whatsoever, this might be an indication that its credit department was performing unsatisfactorily. If credit standards were set so high as to eliminate *all* those potential customers whose credit rating was judged to be marginal, the revenue lost from refusing credit to these customers would no doubt exceed the potential losses, thus decreasing the firm's net income. From a theoretical viewpoint, the firm should grant credit to its customers up to that point where the marginal revenue from the granting of credit sales is exactly equal to the marginal expense, including the cost of bad debts. Of course this goal is impossible to attain in actual practice, but a firm's credit policy should attempt to approximate this objective to the extent possible and/or practical.

Bad debt expense, then, is a normal business expense which should be expected by those firms selling goods or services on a credit basis. The proper determination of income for a period requires that the revenue earned during that period be matched with the expenses which were incurred in generating that revenue. For firms that make sales or render services on a credit basis, this requires that bad debt expense be matched against revenue in the period in which the revenue is earned. Most accountants agree that this is the period in which the sale was originally made, and not the period in which a particular account is determined to be uncollectible. For example, assume that a credit sale made during the month of June is determined to be uncollectible during July, due to the bankruptcy of the customer. This would represent an expense of the month of June (when the sale was made and the revenue recognized) *not* the month of July (when the account was found to be uncollectible).

Since the particular accounts which will ultimately prove to be uncollectible are unknown, bad debt expense must be estimated using the past experience of the firm modified as necessary according to any changes in the firm's credit policies, current business conditions, etc. Two general approaches are often used to estimate bad debts: (1) an income statement approach which involves the use of a percentage of credit sales with the percentage determined by the firm's past credit experience; and (2) a balance sheet approach which is determined by an analysis of the receivable account at the end of the period. Under either method, the calculation of bad debts is necessarily an estimate, the distinction between the two methods normally is not a critical matter in practice. The important point is that a company make a good faith estimate of its probable bad debt losses for the period. The two methods of meeting this objective are explained below.

Income Statement Approach

Even though a firm makes credit sales during a period, it will normally record the estimated bad debt expense which is related to these sales on a periodic basis. Using the income statement approach, the estimate of bad debts for the period is associated directly with the current period's credit sales. Assume, for purposes of illustration, that the credit experience of a small firm has been as follows:

Year	Credit Sales	Losses from Bad Debts
19x1	$120,000	$2,300
19x2	130,000	2,650
19x3	150,000	3,050
	$400,000	$8,000

For 19x4, it might be reasonable for the firm to estimate that its losses from uncollectible accounts would be similar to its experience in prior-years. A percentage which could be used in estimating bad debts would be $8,000 divided by $400,000 or 2 percent of credit sales. In practice, of course, this percentage would be adjusted for any expected changes in general economic conditions, credit policies, etc.

Returning to the example used earlier in the chapter, recall that credit sales for the period were $10,450. Using the income statement or percentage of sales method, the estimated bad debts from these sales would be calculated by multiplying $10,450 by 2 percent or $209. This estimated bad debt expense would be recorded in the accounts by the following journal entry:

Bad debt expense	209	
Allowance for bad debts		209

Note that the credit portion of this entry is to an Allowance for Bad Debts account and not to Accounts Receivable. While the firm's best estimate of its bad debt expense, based on its past experience, indicates that approximately $209 of the receivables arising from sales made during the month of June will not be collectible, it is unable to identify the individual accounts that may not be paid at this time. Since the particular individual(s) whose account(s) may ultimately prove to be uncollectible cannot be identified at this time, a direct credit to accounts receivable is inappropriate since such a procedure would eliminate the equality of the control and the subsidiary accounts. The effect of the entry to record bad debt expense on the control and subsidiary accounts is as follows:

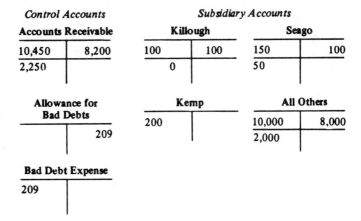

The allowance for bad debts account has a credit balance after this end-of-period entry. This credit balance is deducted from the asset account, accounts receivable, to produce the proper balance sheet value for this asset.

The income statement or percentage of sales method matches the revenue (sales) earned during the period with the expenses (bad debts) which were incurred in generating that revenue. Thus, when this method is used, the amount of the debit to bad debt expense and the credit to the allowance for bad debts is determined directly by the application of the percentage to credit sales and is not affected by the balance in the allowance account prior to the recording of bad debt expense. The income statement approach emphasizes the relationship between the credit sales and potential bad debts which arise from these sales, and does not consider any existing balance in the allowance account.

Balance Sheet Approach

An alternative approach to the estimation of bad debts is the analysis of the receivable balance at the end of a period in order to make a judgment as to which accounts are likely to prove to be uncollectible. This approach is often referred to as the balance sheet approach since it focuses on determining the proper balance in the allowance for bad debts account so that the net receivable balance is stated at its realizable value. An "aging" of the accounts is usually a part of this procedure. Aging involves the classifying or grouping of accounts according to the period of time that the accounts have been outstanding. The basic assumption is that, all other factors being equal, the collectibility of receivables decreases as the account remains outstanding. An example of the "aging" process is presented below:

Account	Balance	Number of Days Outstanding			
		0–30	31–60	61–90	91 and Older
Killough	$ 0	$ 0	$ 0	$ 0	$ 0
Seago	50	50	0	0	0
Kemp	200	200	0	0	0
All others	2,000	1,350	400	50	200
	$2,250	$1,600	$400	$50	$200

Based on the experience of the firm, different percentages may be applied to the different classifications of accounts to estimate the amount of uncollectible receivables. For example, the following calculation might be appropriate:

Number of Days Outstanding	Amount	Percentage*	Estimated to be Uncollectible
0–30	$1,600	1%	$ 16
31–60	400	10	40
61–90	50	50	25
91 and older	200	75	150
	$2,250		$231

* The percentage used would be determined by the credit experience of the firm, adjusted as considered necessary for such factors as changes in economic conditions, credit policies, etc.

The older accounts, as well as those which are known to be in financial difficulty, should also be reviewed on an individual basis as an additional test of the amount which is estimated to be uncollectible. Assume that, after this review, the firm decided that the calculation of the amount estimated to be uncollectible using the analysis of receivables by age was appropriate. The balance in the allowance for bad debts account should be increased to $231, the amount estimated to be uncollectible at the end of June. Since this approach is based on the question of how large of an allowance account is needed to reduce the net receivables balance to the amount which is expected to be collected, it is necessary to consider any balance in the allowance account before making the adjusting entry. The allowance account will have a debit or credit balance at the end of the period, prior to the adjustment if the receivables which were actually determined to be uncollectible during the period were not exactly equal to the balance in the allowance account at the beginning of the period. The procedure for writing-off an uncollectible receivable will be discussed in the next section. Assuming that the allowance for bad debts account had a debit balance of $20 prior to this determination, the following journal entry would be required:

Bad debt expense........................	251	
Allowance for bad debts...............		251

After this entry has been posted to the allowance account, the balance in the account would be $231.

Allowance for Bad Debts

20	251
	231

Note that when the balance sheet analysis of the receivable balance method is used, the total amount which is estimated to be uncollectible is determined. This amount is then compared to the existing balance in the allowance for bad debts account and the journal entry required to adjust the allowance for bad debts account to the appropriate amount is made.

The income statement or percentage of sales method focuses upon the determination of income by emphasizing the matching of revenue (sales) with the expenses (bad debts) which were incurred in generating this revenue. The balance sheet or analysis of the receivable balance method emphasizes the valuation of the receivable balance at the net realizable amount. Again, since the allowance for bad debts is necessarily an estimate, a firm may decide to use one or the other or may choose to employ both in combination. For example, the percentage of sales method might be used in preparing interim financial statements on a monthly or quarterly basis and the analysis or aging of the receivable balance method in preparing annual or year-end financial statements.

Balance Sheet Presentation

In the balance sheet, the allowance for bad debts would appear as an off-set to, or deduction from, accounts receivable. For example, the receivables of the firm would be shown as follows:

ASSETS

Cash		$ 5,000
Accounts receivable...............	$2,250	
Less: Allowance for bad debts........	231	2,019
Other assets		10,000
Total Assets		$17,019

Writing-off an Uncollectible Account

When a particular account balance is determined to be uncollectible, an entry is made in the accounts to recognize this fact. Returning to the example used earlier in the chapter, assume that the $50 balance owed by Seago proves to be uncollectible. The following entry would be required:

```
Allowance for Bad Debts  . . . . . . . . . . . . . . . . . . . . . . . . . . . . .    50
    Accounts Receivable . . . . . . . . . . . . . . . . . . . . . . . . . . . . .         50
```

After this entry has been posted to the accounts, the control[3] account would appear as follows:

	Accounts Receivable			Allowance for Bad Debts	
2,250	50		50	231	
2,200				181	

In the balance sheet, the receivables would appear as follows:

```
Accounts receivable  . . . . . . . . . . . . . . $2,200
Less:  Allowance for bad debts . . . . . . . .    181     $2,019
```

It is important to note that the entry for the write-off of the uncollectible receivable affects neither expense nor total assets. The net receivable balance (accounts receivable less the allowance for bad debts) remains the same since both accounts receivable and the allowance for bad debts are reduced by the same amount. The expense related to bad debts is recorded when the estimated bad debts are recorded (i.e., when the provision for bad debts is made). The entry to record bad debts expense is normally made during the year-end adjustment process.

Even though a company writes off an account as uncollectible, it will still attempt to collect the balance due. In some instances, it may continue its own efforts to collect the account; in others, it may turn the account over to a collection agency. In any event, if the collection efforts prove to be successful, the company will receive cash; two entries are required in order to record this receipt. The first entry reinstates the balance which has been written off by reversing the original entry made at the time of the write-off. The second entry records the collection of the account balance.

To illustrate the recovery of an account which had previously been written off, we will return to the example used above. Assume now that the $50 balance owed by Seago which was written off as uncollectible is subsequently collected. The collection would be recorded by the following entries:

---

[3] The effect on the subsidiary accounts would be to reduce the balance in Seago's account from $50 to zero, thus maintaining the equality between the control and the subsidiary accounts.

Accounts receivable......................	50	
Allowance for bad debts...............		50
Cash	50	
Accounts receivable..................		50

Again, note that the first entry simply reverses the previous write-off. The second entry records the collection of the balance.

Direct Write-off Method

In circumstances where receivables are not material in amount, a company may choose not to record its estimated bad debt expense. In this approach, the company debits bad debt expense and credits accounts receivables in the period in which the individual receivable is determined to be uncollectible. The total accounts receivable will be listed in the balance sheet at its gross amount; no allowance account is used. This method does not state accounts receivable at their expected collectible amount; it makes no attempt to match the costs of bad debts with the related sales. Theoretically, the allowance method is superior, but the direct write-off approach is acceptable if receivables are not significant in amount.

ACCOUNTS PAYABLE

The major source of accounts payable are debts to trade creditors for goods or services purchased on a credit basis by the business. Other accounts payable may consist of various debts, such as advances from officers, employees, or stockholders, or refundable deposits which were made by customers. Accounts payable are normally classified in terms of their origin in the balance sheet. An account payable does not usually involve the payment of interest, and there is no formal written promise to pay signed by the debtor.

NOTES RECEIVABLE AND PAYABLE

As previously indicated, notes receivable are claims against others which, unlike accounts receivable, are supported by formal or written promises to pay. A typical note is shown below.

The note shown above is an interest-bearing note: Don Sutton (the maker of the note) agrees to pay Willie Davis (the payee) $1,000 (the principal amount of the note) plus interest at eighteen percent on July 1, 19x1 (the maturity date). The eighteen percent annual interest is the charge that Sutton pays for the use of Davis' funds. Interest, which is an expense for Sutton and income for Davis, is calculated by the following formula:

$$\text{Principal} \times \text{Rate} \times \text{Time} = \text{Interest}$$
$$\$1{,}000 \times .18 \times \tfrac{2}{12} = \$30$$

The maturity value of this note is $1,030 (the principal amount of $1,000 plus interest at $30); this is the amount that Sutton must pay Davis on July 1, 19x1, when the note becomes due and payable (matures).

Note that for ease of calculation, the eighteen percent interest rate was expressed as a decimal, .18. Alternatively, a fraction ($\tfrac{18}{100}$) could have been used in the computation. The interest rate stated in a note is usually expressed in terms of an annual or yearly rate. Since the note used in the illustration was for a duration of two months, time was expressed as a fraction of year, $\tfrac{2}{12}$. In some instances, time may be stated in days. If this is the case, a year is usually considered to have 360 days in order to simplify the computation of interest. For example, if the note in the illustration was for a period of 30 days, the calculation of interest would be as follows:

$$\$1{,}000 \times .18 \times \tfrac{30}{360} = \$15$$

To illustrate the accounting for notes receivable, the entries necessary to record the transactions regarding the Sutton-Davis note will be presented in the sections which follow.

Issuance of the Note

On May 1, 19x1, when Sutton borrowed the $1,000 from Davis, the following entry would be made on Davis' books to record the loan:

Notes receivable	1,000	
Cash		1,000

This entry indicates that Davis has exchanged one asset (cash of $1,000) for another asset of equal value (a note receivable of $1,000).[4]

The following entry would be made by Sutton:

Cash	1,000	
Notes payable		1,000

---

[4] In some instances, a note may be taken in settlement of an open account receivable (dr. note receivable, cr. accounts receivable) or at the time of sale (dr. notes receivable, cr. sales). Except for the initial entry, these circumstances do not change the accounting or recording considerations illustrated and discussed.

This entry indicates that Sutton has incurred a liability (a note payable of $1,000) in order to obtain an asset (cash of $1,000).

Accrual of Interest

Interest is the cost of borrowing to the maker of the note or, from the payee's (lender's) viewpoint, the income which is earned. In the example, Davis' earnings during the month of May would be calculated as follows:

$$\$1,000 \quad \times \quad .18 \quad \times \quad \tfrac{1}{12} \quad = \quad \$15$$

If Davis wished to accrue the interest earned during the month of May, (i.e., record it on his books) the following entry would be necessary:

Interest receivable.....................	15	
Interest earned......................		15

This entry recognizes the fact that Davis' assets have increased by $15 because of the interest earned during the month of May. This entry would be necessary only if Davis prepares financial statements as of the end of May.

If Sutton wished to record the interest expense incurred during May, the following entry would be required:

Interest expense.......................	15	
Interest payable.....................		15

This entry recognizes that Sutton has incurred an expense of $15 for the use of the money borrowed from Davis for the month of May. Again, an entry is necessary only if financial statements are prepared as of the end of May.

Payment of the Note

On July 1, 19x1, the maturity date of the note, it becomes due and payable. As previously indicated, the interest for the two-month period was:

$$\$1,000 \quad \times \quad .18 \quad \times \quad \tfrac{2}{12} \quad = \quad \$30$$

The maturity value, (i.e., the total amount that Sutton should pay to Davis), is $1,000 plus $30 or $1,030. Since we have assumed that Davis had previously recorded or accrued the $15 of interest earned during the month of May, the entry which would be required on Davis' books in order to record the receipt of the $1,030 from Sutton at the maturity date of the note would be as follows:

Cash	1,030	
Notes receivable.....................		1,000
Interest receivable...................		15
Interest earned......................		15

Analyzing this entry, the debit to cash of $1,030 records the total proceeds of the note (i.e., its maturity value). This maturity value includes both the principal amount and the total interest earned by Davis during the two-month period that he held the note. The credit to notes receivable removes the note balance from Davis' books since it has been paid at maturity. The credit of $15 to interest receivable eliminates the receivable which had been set up at the end of May when Davis accrued the interest earned for that month. The $15 credit to interest earned is made in order to record the interest income on the note for the month of June.

The entry that would be required on Sutton's books to record the payment by Sutton to Davis would be:

```
Notes  payable.........................  1,000
Interest payable.......................     15
Interest expense.......................     15
   Cash ...............................            1,030
```

The debit to notes payable of $1,000 removes the note balance from Sutton's books since it has been paid at maturity. The debit to interest payable of $15 eliminates the payable which had been recorded at the end of May when Sutton accrued the interest expense for the month. The $15 debit to interest expense is made to record the interest expense for June. The credit to cash of $1,030 records the payment of the maturity value of the note (i.e., principal and interest) by Sutton.

Dishonored Note

If Sutton had not paid the note at maturity, the note would be said to be dishonored. Of course, Davis would continue his efforts to collect the amount due him and Sutton would still be liable for his obligation. In the event that the note was not paid at maturity, Davis would make an entry to remove the note from the notes receivable account as follows:

```
Receivable from dishonored note..........  1,030
   Notes receivable.....................           1,000
   Interest receivable..................             15
   Interest earned......................             15
```

This entry would remove the note from the notes receivable account and place it in a separate receivable classification—receivable from dishonored notes. If Sutton subsequently pays the note, Davis would record the receipt by debiting cash and crediting "receivable from dishonored note." If Davis is unable to collect the $1,030 from Sutton, he would eventually write off the receivable as an uncollectible account against the allowance for bad debts account.

**Notes Issued
at a Discount**

In some circumstances, the interest on notes is deducted in advance (i.e., at the time the note is issued). The difference between the amount due at maturity and the amount loaned is classified as unearned interest at the date of issuance on the books of the lender. As the note matures, this unearned interest is earned and is reclassified as interest income. For example, assume that on November 1, 19x1, Wynn Company borrows $1,000 from Osteen Company on a three-month note with an eighteen percent rate of interest. The entry made on November 1, 19x1, by Osteen Company to record the loan of $955 [$1,000 − ($1,000 × .18 × $\frac{3}{12}$)] would be as follows:

```
Notes receivable........................ 1,000
    Unearned interest....................        45
    Cash ................................        955
```

Wynn Company would record the transaction with the following entry:

```
Cash ................................  955
Discount on notes payable...............   45
    Notes payable.......................        1,000
```

Since interest accrues over time, the $45 which is shown as a discount on notes payable at the date the note is issued is not interest expense at that point in time. The actual net liability to Osteen at the date of the loan is equal to the amount of cash received, or $955. Therefore, a balance sheet prepared at the time of the loan would include discount on notes payable as a contra-liability deducted from notes payable as follows:

```
Notes payable........................ $1,000
Less:  Discount on notes payable.........   (45)
                                        $  955
```

At December 31, the following adjusting entry is necessary in order for Osteen to record the interest earned of $30 ($1,000 × .18 × $\frac{2}{12}$) for the months of November and December:

```
Unearned interest......................   30
    Interest income.....................        30
```

Wynn Company would record its interest expense for the two-month period with the following adjusting entry:

```
Interest expense........................   30
    Discount on notes payable.............        30
```

At December 31, Wynn Company's liability would appear in its balance sheet as follows:

```
Notes  payable...........................  $1,000
Less:   Discount on notes payable..........    (15)
                                            $  985
```

Note that the original amount of $45 in the discount on notes payable has been reduced by $30 (interest expense for the months of November and December) to $15 (which represents the amount to be charged to interest expense in January).

When the note matures and is paid, the entry to record the receipt is as follows:

```
Cash ...............................  1,000
Unearned  interest.......................      15
    Notes receivable.......................              1,000
    Interest  income.......................                 15
```

The total interest income earned on the note and recorded in the accounts is $45 ($30 in 19x1 and $15 in 19x2). Although a rate of 18 percent was used in determining the original discount on the note, the effective interest rate is actually 18.8 percent since the borrower paid $45 for the use of $955 (not $1,000) for a period of three months.

Wynn Company would make the following entry to record its payment:

```
Notes  payable.........................  1,000
Interest  expense........................      15
    Cash ...............................              1,000
    Discount on notes payable.............                 15
```

This entry records the payment of the note at maturity by Wynn and the interest expense for the month of January.

Discounting Notes Receivable

Notes receivable are sometimes sold by the payee to a third party in order to obtain funds prior to the maturity date of a note. The process of selling a note in this manner is referred to as discounting a note. The payee endorses the note, delivers it to the purchaser (usually a bank) and receives his funds. The payee discounting the note is usually contingently liable on the note, i.e., he must pay the note at the maturity if the maker fails to do so.

The calculation of the discount charged by the purchaser is somewhat similar to the calculation of interest:

$$\begin{array}{c}\text{Maturity} \\ \text{Value}\end{array} \times \begin{array}{c}\text{Discount} \\ \text{Period}\end{array} \times \begin{array}{c}\text{Discount} \\ \text{Rate}\end{array} = \text{Discount}$$

As previously indicated, the maturity value is the total amount, both principal and interest, due at the maturity of a note. The discount period is the period of time from the date a note is discounted to the maturity date of the note. The discount rate is the rate charged by the purchaser to discount a note. The amount received by the payee, referred to as the proceeds of the note, is calculated as follows:

$$\text{Maturity Value} - \text{Discount} = \text{Proceeds}$$

To illustrate the procedures which are involved in discounting a note, we will assume that *before* recording the interest earned for the month of May, Davis sold or discounted the Sutton note on May 31 and was charged a discount rate of twenty percent. The calculation of the amount of the discount and the net proceeds to Davis from the note would be as follows:

$$\$1,000 \times .18 \times \tfrac{2}{12} = \$30 \text{ (interest)}$$
$$\$1,000 + \$30 = \$1,030 \text{ (maturity value)}$$
$$\$1,030 \times .20 \times \tfrac{1}{12} = \$17.17 \text{ (discount)}$$
$$\$1,030 - \$17.17 = \$1,012.83 \text{ (proceeds)}$$

The discounting of the note will be recorded in the accounts by Davis as follows:

Cash	1,012.83	
Interest expense	2.17	
Interest revenue		15.00
Notes receivable discounted		1,000.00

The debit of $1,012.83 to cash records the proceeds received from the sale of the note. The charge to interest expense of $2.17 was calculated as follows:

Principal		$1,000.00
Interest earned during May		15.00
Book value of the note at the date of sale		$1,015.00
Principal	$1,000.00	
Total interest for the note to maturity	30.00	
Maturity value of the note	$1,030.00	
Discount	17.17	
Net proceeds		1,012.83
Interest expense		$ 2.17

As the above calculation indicates, interest expense represents the difference between the cash proceeds and the total of the: (1) face or principal amount of the note; and (2) interest earned up to the date the note was discounted.[5] The credit to interest receivable removes the interest which had been previously accrued at the end of May from the accounts. It should be noted that the credit in the entry is to notes receivable *discounted,* rather than to notes receivable. The credit to notes receivable discounted indicates that Davis is contingently liable for the note—i.e., in the event that Sutton fails to pay the note at maturity, Davis must pay it. On Davis' balance sheet the notes receivable would appear as follows:

Cash		$10,000
Notes receivable	$1,000	
Less: Notes receivable discounted	1,000	0
Other assets		50,000
Total Assets		$60,000

Offsetting the notes receivable discounted account against the notes receivable account discloses the contingent liability of Davis with regard to the Sutton note. An alternative to this presentation would be to disclose the contingent liability by means of a footnote to the balance sheet. Such a footnote might be worded as follows: "Davis is contingently liable for notes receivable discounted in the amount of $1,000."

If Sutton pays the note at its maturity, Davis would be notified of this payment and the following entry would be made on Davis' books:

Notes receivable discounted	1,000	
Notes receivable		1,000

By removing both the notes receivable discounted and the notes receivable balances from the accounts, the effect of this entry is to recognize the fact that the contingent liability for the note no longer exists.

If Sutton fails to pay the note at maturity, Davis' *contingent* liability becomes a *real* liability that he must now pay. He would recognize this fact by the same entry as that which was made above:

Notes receivable discounted	1,000	
Notes receivable		1,000

---

[5] Had the discount rate been ten percent, the entry would have been as follows:

Cash	1,021.42	
Notes receivable discounted		1,000.00
Interest revenue		21.42

In this instance the credit of $21.42 to interest income represents the excess of the proceeds over the principal amount of the note including the interest of $15.00 earned in May.

It should be noted that both the contingent liability and the notes receivable balance are removed from the books at the maturity date of the note whether or not it is paid by the maker. If it is paid, that is all that is required—no further action on the part of Davis is necessary. If it is not paid, Davis must pay the full amount due (principal plus interest, or full maturity value) to the holder of the note. This payment would be recorded as follows:

Receivable from dishonored note.......... 1,030
  Cash   1,030

Davis would then attempt to recover the $1,030 from Sutton.

STATEMENT PRESENTATION OF RECEIVABLES

Receivables are classified first according to their form: notes receivable and accounts receivable. Generally, those which are expected to be converted into cash within a year are classified as current assets while those which will be realized in subsequent periods are included in a noncurrent category. Any interest receivable from interest-bearing notes will also be classified according to the timing of its expected collection. The income from interest appears on the income statement, usually as an addition to net income from operations, as follows:

Davis Company
Income Statement
For the Year Ended December 31, 19x1

Sales	$100,000
Cost of sales	60,000
Gross profit on sales	$ 40,000
Expenses	25,000
Income from operations	$ 15,000
Other income:	
Interest income	100
Net income	$ 15,100

If there are receivables from sources other than normal operations, such as from officers, employees, affiliated companies, etc., these would be shown as separate items rather than included as a part of regular accounts or notes receivable in the balance sheet.

PAYROLL ACCOUNTING

An employer incurs certain liabilities to the Federal and state governments for taxes related to its payroll—both for the taxes levied on the business itself and for taxes withheld from the earnings of its employees.

The employer may also deduct from employees' salaries and wages amounts withheld for such items as union dues, insurance premiums, pension plans, and investment plans.

An employer incurs a number of liabilities relating to state and Federal payroll taxes. These include the following taxes:

1. Federal old-age, survivors, disability, and hospital insurance (Social Security)
2. Federal unemployment insurance
3. State unemployment insurance
4. Income taxes withheld

Social Security Taxes. The Federal Insurance Contributions Act (FICA) imposes equal taxes on both employers and employees. This Act provides for old age, disability, hospitalization, and survivors' benefits for qualified employees and members of their families. The tax rate is applied to the employee's gross wages up to a designated maximum. Both the rate and the maximum earnings to which the tax is applied have been increased frequently over the years. The rate for 1983 was 6.70 percent of the initial $35,700 of salaries and wages paid to each employee. The employee's share of this tax is withheld from the wage payment, and employers periodically remit the amounts withheld together with the amounts matched by the employer.

Federal Unemployment Tax. The Federal Unemployment Tax Act (FUTA) provides for a system of unemployment insurance with joint participation of the Federal and state governments. Employers are also required to pay state and Federal unemployment taxes for their employees. No tax is levied on the employee. Under current provisions, the Federal rate is currently 3.4 percent of the initial $6,000 in salaries and wages paid to each employee during the year. However, the employer is allowed a credit against the Federal unemployment tax for state unemployment tax payments.

State Unemployment Tax. The provisions of the unemployment programs of the various states differ in certain respects. All states levy a payroll tax on employers and a few states levy a tax on employees as well. The basic rate in most states is 2.7% of the first $6,000 in salaries and wages paid to each employee.

Income Tax Withholding. Employers of one or more persons are required to withhold income taxes from their employees and remit these withholdings to the Federal government. A number of states and cities also levy income taxes which are required to be withheld by the employer from the earnings of the employees. The amounts to be withheld by the employer may be computed by formulas provided by the law or from tax withholding tables made available by the government. The Federal income tax withheld and the FICA taxes (both employer's and employee's shares) are remitted to the Federal government at regular intervals.

Recording the Payroll. To illustrate the accounting for wages and salaries and the related taxes, assume that the gross salaries of a small business total $10,000 for the month of January. Assume that the FICA rate is 6.70 percent for the employer and employee, and that the State unemployment tax is 2.7 percent of gross salaries. The Federal unemployment tax (net of the credit for state unemployment taxes) is .7 percent, and Federal income taxes withheld for the month total $710. The employer's taxes would be computed as follows:

FICA (.067 × $10,000)............................	$ 670
State unemployment (.027 × $10,000)..............	270
FUTA (.007 × $10,000).........................	70
Total employer's taxes........................	$ 1,010

The cash paid to employees would be:

Salaries earned.................................		$10,000
Withholding		
FICA...........................	$670	
Income taxes.....................	710	1,380
Net amount paid to employees.....................		$ 8,620

The journal entries to record the payroll and the employer's payroll taxes follow:

Payroll tax expense...................... 1,010		
FICA taxes payable....................		670
State unemployment taxes payable.......		270
Federal unemployment taxes payable.....		70
Salaries expense......................... 10,000		
FICA taxes payable....................		670
Income taxes payable.................		710
Cash		8,620

The liabilities recorded in the above entries are eliminated when the employer remits the taxes to the appropriate governmental units.

SUMMARY

The proper recording and controlling of cash receipts and disbursements is a concern common to all firms. Certain basic control procedures must be followed to eliminate the probability that cash will be lost or misappropriated. Control procedures applicable to the receipt of cash include preparing a complete record immediately upon the receipt of cash, depositing the cash intact in the company's bank on a daily basis, and involving more than one employee in the handling and recording of cash transactions. In addition, employees involved in handling cash receipts should not also be authorized to make cash disbursements. Cash disbursement control measures include using pre-numbered checks to make payments for all items not paid for from petty cash, supporting each disbursement with an invoice or voucher, and having an employee that does not make cash disbursements reconcile the bank statement at frequent intervals.

Receivables are assets representing the claims that a business has against others. The two principal forms of receivables are accounts receivable and notes receivable. Accounts receivable generally arise from a company's normal course of trade or business and are normally not supported by formal written promises to pay. Notes receivable, on the other hand, are claims that are supported by formal written promises to pay.

Liabilities are claims against the business by its creditors. As such, they represent obligations which must be discharged at some future date. Current liabilities are those obligations which must be discharged within the operating cycle of the firm or one year, whichever is longer. The two major types of current liabilities are accounts payable that arise from transactions with trade creditors and short-term notes payable. A note payable is supported by a written promise to pay and requires the accrual and payment of interest.

Accounting for receivables requires the use of both a control account and individual subsidiary accounts. At the end of a period, the total of the subsidiary balances should equal the balance in the control account. In addition, bad debt expense must be estimated for each period to match this cost of selling on a credit basis with the appropriate revenues. Two common methods of estimating the bad debt expense (often used in combination) are (1) the use of a percentage based on the firm's past credit sales and (2) the analysis of the receivables balance at the end of the period. An allowance for bad debts account is used to record and report the resulting offset to accounts receivable.

Accounting procedures for notes receivable include recording the initial issuance of the note at either face or discounted value, accruing the interest income earned on the note, and recording the collection of the principal and interest. In addition, firms may wish to sell notes receivable to a third party to obtain funds prior to the maturity dates of the notes. This process is referred to as discounting the notes. Generally the firm discounting the note is contingently liable if the maker fails to pay it at maturity.

Receivables are classified on the balance sheet as accounts receivable or notes receivable and according to their status as current or noncurrent assets. Current receivables are those that are expected to be converted into cash within a year.

KEY DEFINITIONS

Accounts receivable Accounts receivable are receivables not supported by formal or written promises to pay.

Accrued interest expense Accrued interest expense is interest that has been incurred on a note payable but not paid.

Aging of accounts receivable Aging of accounts receivable is the process of classifying accounts according to the period of time that the accounts have been outstanding.

Allowance for bad debts Allowance for bad debts is a contra account to accounts receivable that reflects the portion of the total dollar amount of accounts receivable that is expected to be uncollectible.

Bad debt expense Bad debt expense is the expense that occurs from customers' failure to pay debts to the firm.

Balance per bank statement This balance is the amount in the cash account of the business according to the bank's records.

Balance per books This amount is the balance in the cash account according to the firm's records.

Bank reconciliation A bank reconciliation is an analysis made to identify and account for all items which cause differences between the cash balance as shown on the bank statement and the cash balance as it appears in the firm's accounting records.

Cash Cash consists of currency, coins, checks and certain other forms of negotiable paper.

Cash disbursement A cash disbursement is an outlay of cash made by the firm.

Cash over and short The cash over and short account is an account which is credited for any cash overages and debited for any cash shortages. The net balance in this account at the end of a period is treated as miscellaneous revenue or expense.

Cash receipt A cash receipt is an inflow of cash into the firm.

Cash transaction A cash transaction is an accounting transaction that involves either a cash receipt or a cash disbursement.

Charge sales Charge sales are sales in which the firm provides a customer with goods or services in exchange for the customer's promise to pay at a later date.

Contingent liability A contingent liability is an amount which may become a liability at some future date, depending on the occurrence of some future event. For example, the payee who discounts a note is contingently liable if the maker of the note fails to pay it at maturity.

Contra account A contra account is an account which is offset against or deducted from another account in the financial statements.

"Control" account A "control" account is used to record the total charge sales and the total payments which are received from customers.

Credit memorandum This memorandum is an addition which is made by the bank to a depositor's account. The addition arises from a transaction other than a normal deposit.

Current liability   Current debts of a firm which must be paid within the operating cycle of the firm or one year, whichever is longer.

Debit memorandum   This memorandum is a deduction which is made by the bank from a depositor's account. The deduction arises from a transaction other than the normal payment of a check by the bank.

Deposit in transit   This deposit is a receipt which has been included in the cash balance per books and deposited in the bank, but not yet processed by the bank and credited to the depositor's account.

Discount (D)   Discount is the charge made by the purchaser of a note prior to its maturity. (MV $\times$ DR $\times$ DP = D)

Discount period (DP)   The discount period is the period from the date a note is discounted until its maturity.

Discount rate (DR)   The discount rate is the rate charged to discount a note. This percentage is expressed in an annual rate and is used to calculate a discount.

Discounting   Discounting is the sale of a note by the payee prior to its maturity date.

Discounted note   On discounted notes payable, the interest is deducted from the maturity value of the note at the time the note is issued.

Dishonored notes receivable   Dishonored notes receivable are notes which are not paid at their maturity.

Effective interest rate   The effective interest rate is the actual rate of interest that the issuing corporation pays on the bond as evidenced by the relationship between the periodic interest payment and the issue price of the bonds.

Interest expense (I)   Interest expense is the cost to the borrower of borrowing funds. (P $\times$ R $\times$ T = I)

Interest income   Interest income is the income to the lender from the lending of funds. (P $\times$ R $\times$ T = I)

Interest receivable   Interest receivable is interest earned but not yet received.

Liability   A liability is an obligation which arises from a past transaction and which is to be discharged at a future date by the transfer of assets or the performance of services.

Maker   A maker is the borrower of funds on a note receivable.

Maturity date   The maturity date is the date a note becomes due and payable.

Maturity value (MV)   Maturity value is the value of a note at its maturity, i.e., principal plus interest.

Note payable   A note payable represents a written promise to pay a definite amount of money on demand or at some specified future date to the holder of the note.

Note receivable   A note receivable is a receivable supported by a formal or written promise to pay.

Outstanding check   This is a check which has been issued by the business but not yet presented to the bank for payment.

Over-the-counter sales   These sales are consummated by the immediate payment of cash for the goods or services purchased.

Payee   The payee is the lender of funds on a note receivable.

Petty cash fund   The petty cash fund is a fund established to make cash disbursements for small expenditures.

Petty cash voucher   This voucher is an authorization to disburse cash from the petty cash fund and is usually retained as a receipt for the expenditure.

Principal (P)   The principal is the face amount of a note receivable.

Proceeds   Proceeds are the net amount received by a payee selling or discounting a note prior to its maturity. Maturity value less discount equals proceeds.

Rate (R)   Rate is the percentage usually expressed as an annual rate used to calculate interest.

Receivable   A receivable is an asset representing the claim that a firm has against others.

Receivable from dishonored note   This receivable is equal to the maturity value of a note arising from the failure of the maker to pay it at maturity.

Time (T)   Time is the period usually expressed in years or a fraction thereof used to calculate interest. It is normal to assume a 360-day year when calculating simple interest.

True cash   True cash is the amount of cash that is actually available to the entity. One format for the bank reconciliation statement adjusts both the book and bank balances to true cash.

QUESTIONS

1. Why is control over cash transactions considered to be more important than other assets of a business?

2. List a few basic principles in connection with cash control. You may wish to organize your discussion along the line of the normal cash flow.

3. What are the principal advantages of maintaining a separation of duties involving cash transactions?

4. In order to establish control over the cash receipts from over the counter sales, a small firm installs a cash register with each sales clerk responsible for ringing up his or her own sales. Discuss.

5. List some procedures other than separation of duties which may be employed in order to establish effective control over cash disbursements.

6. What is the purpose of a bank reconciliation statement?

7. What are the necessary adjustments in the bank reconciliation statement to the balance per the bank statement? To the balance per the books?

8. The petty cash account has a debit balance of $300. At the end of the accounting period there is $35 in the petty cash fund along with petty cash vouchers totaling $265. Should the fund be replenished as of the last day of the period? Discuss.

9. What are some of the steps necessary to achieve effective control over cash disbursements?

10. Compare and contrast accounts receivable and notes receivable.

11. Distinguish between current and long-term liabilities.

12. Why is control over receivables important? How can control be achieved?

13. Explain how the control account, accounts receivable, is related to the individual subsidiary ledger accounts. What could make the two be out of balance?

14. Theoretically, when should a firm cease to grant credit to its customers?

15. Another method for handling bad debt expense—called the direct write-off method—is to wait until the account is known to be uncollectible. The journal entry then is a debit to bad debt expense and a credit to accounts receivable. Compare and contrast this with the allowance method. Which method is theoretically correct? Why?

16. What accounting principle does the allowance method rest upon?

17. What are the two methods for estimating bad debts?

18. Could an allowance method be used with notes receivable? Would it be feasible?

19. What is the entry to increase Allowance for Bad Debts? To decrease it?

20. Suppose an account is written off as uncollectible, but later the customer remits payment. What would the entry be?

21. Calculate the interest on a $10,000, 6-month note, with interest at 6 percent.

22. What adjusting entries may be required with regard to notes receivable at the end of the period?

23. Smith Co. borrowed $5,000 from the bank and signed a 60-day, 6 percent note dated June 1. (1) What is the face amount of the note? (2) What is the amount of interest on the note? (3) What is the maturity value of the note?

24. What is the nature of the notes receivable discounted account?

25. Why is an entry on the books of the payee necessary whether or not a discounted note is paid by the maker at maturity?

26. Explain how the proceeds from the discounting of a note receivable are calculated.

EXERCISES

27. State whether the following bank reconciliation items would need an adjusting or correcting entry on the *depositor's* books:

a. Checks totaling $1,850 were issued by the depositor but not paid by the bank.
b. A $1,000 note was collected for the depositor by the bank and was deposited in his account. Notice was sent to the depositor with the bank statement.
c. The last day's receipts ($1,750) for the month were not recorded as a deposit by the bank until the following month.
d. The depositor issued a check for $180 but entered it in his records as $810.
e. The bank paid a check for $150 but entered it as $510 on their records.
f. The bank charged a bad check that it received in a deposit back against the depositor's account. Notice to the depositor was made by the bank with the bank statement.
g. The bank charged $21 for service charges and notified the depositor with the bank statement.
h. The bank had erroneously charged a check, drawn by another depositor with a similar name, to the depositor's account.

28. Prepare the journal entries that are necessary to adjust the cash account on the depositor's books, based on the information included in Exercise 27 above.

29. The following information is taken from the books and records of the Terp Company.

Balance per the cash account (before adjustment)...	$2,860
Outstanding checks...........................	820
Deposit in transit............................	208
Bank service charges.........................	18
Cash on hand—unrecorded on the books and not yet deposited in the bank..................	180
Balance per the bank statement.................	unavailable

Required:

Prepare a bank reconciliation showing the "true" cash balance.

30. Prepare, in general journal form, the entries that Terp Company should make to adjust its cash balance as a result of the bank reconciliation in Exercise 29 above.

31. Test the accuracy of Willard Company's cash receipts records for August given the following information:

Total cash receipts as shown in the firm's records were $14,910.
Payment of $1,110 was received on August 31 but the deposit was not yet recorded by the bank.
Total deposits included in the August bank statement were $14,700.
Deposit in transit at end of July was $900.

32. The Gibbons Company reconciles its one bank account on a monthly basis. The company follows the procedure of reconciling the balance as reported on the bank statement and the balance per books *to a corrected balance.* The corrected balance appears on the balance sheet.

The facts stated in items 1 through 10 below are involved in a reconciliation for the month of December. Decide which of the five answer choices best indicates how each fact should be handled in the December 31 bank reconciliation.

Answer choices for items 1 through 9:

(1)   An addition to the balance per books.
(2)   A deduction from the balance per books.
(3)   An addition to the balance per bank.
(4)   A deduction from the balance per bank.
(5)   Should not appear in the reconciliation.

1. A deposit of $100 made on December 31 did not appear in the December bank statement..................... (   )

2. A deposit of $130 made on November 30 was recorded by the bank on December 1.......................... (   )

3. Three checks totalling $180 drawn in December did not clear the bank..................................... (   )

4. A check from customer Kay for $75 was returned by the bank marked N.S.F................................ (   )

5. The bank statement was accompanied by a credit memo dated December 30 for the proceeds of a note ($198) which Gibbons Company had left with the bank for collection..................................... (   )

6. Gibbons Company discovered that a December check recorded in the check register as $150 was actually drawn for $105. This check was cleared by the bank in December..................................... (   )

7. Two checks totalling $120 drawn in November had cleared the bank in December.......................... (   )

8. Accompanying the December bank statement was a cancelled check for $60 of Gibson Company............... (   )

9. The bookkeeper of Gibbons Company had recorded a $90 check received from customer Fay on December 29 as $190.................................... (   )

10. Which of the facts disclosed in items 1 through 9 above require adjusting entries on the books of the Gibbons Company?

(1)	1, 3, 8	(2)	6, 8, 9
(3)	1, 2, 3, 7	(4)	4, 5, 6, 9
(5)	Some other group		

33. Show in general journal form all entries that should be made to reflect the operation of the Eljon Corporation's petty cash fund.

May 10 The company established a petty cash fund of $225.
12 Paid miscellaneous office expenses amounting to $52.
14 Paid $15 to messengers for cab fares.
19 Paid telephone bill of $63.
25 Paid $21 in postage.
30 The petty cash fund was reimbursed for the first time.
31 Eljon Corporation increased its petty cash fund to $300.

34. Determine the "true cash" balance after the following adjustments or corrections have been made to the Cash account. The cash balance per books was $3,650. (Use a T-account to do this.)

    a.   A deposit in transit at the end of the period was $350.
    b.   Check #501 for $89 was still outstanding at the end of the period.
    c.   An account receivable of $110 was collected by the bank.
    d.   The service charge for the period was $47.
    e.   Check #101 for $680 which had been outstanding for 10 years was cancelled.
    f.   The bank paid $20 more on Check #509 than was written on the face of the check.
    g.   Check #513 was incorrectly entered in the books by the bookkeeper for $315 instead of $513.
    h.   A stop payment was placed on Check #507 for $265.

35. By reviewing their past credit experience, Brown Company estimated that its losses from uncollectible accounts would be three percent of credit sales for 19x1. Sales for 19x1 amounted to $360,000, of which $100,000 were in cash. Make the entry recording bad debt expense for the year in the books of the Brown Company.

36. Based on an aging of receivables, Blue Company estimated doubtful accounts to be a total of $5,000. Give the adjusting entry for bad debts under each of the following independent situations:

    a.   The Allowance for Bad Debts has a zero balance.
    b.   The Allowance for Bad Debts has a debit balance of $400.
    c.   The Allowance for Bad Debts has a credit balance of $700.

37. Bobby Mitchell's 6%, 60-day note for $600 (principal amount) was discounted by the Washington Deadskunks to the Second National Bank after it was held for 30 days. The Deadskunks received $603.96 as proceeds from the sale.

Required:

    1.   Calculate the discount rate on the sale.
    2.   Prepare the journal entry to record the sale of the note on the books of the Washington Deadskunks.
    3.   Prepare the entry necessary if Mitchell fails to pay the note at maturity.

38. On February 1, 19x1, Alex Grammas borrowed $700 from Vic Wertz and signed a note in evidence of the loan. Grammas agreed to pay Wertz $700 plus 10 percent interest on August 31, 19x1. Wertz's accounting period ends June 30. Make all entries related to the note on the books of Wertz (assume Grammas does not default on payment).

39. Dallas Company discounted three separate notes receivable at a bank on August 1, 19x1. Each note is in the amount of $1,000. The bank charged a discount rate of 10 percent. Compute the proceeds of each note from the following data.

	Date Note Received	Interest Rate	Life of Note
1.	July 1	8%	3 months
2.	June 1	6%	6 months
3.	July 15	9%	1 month

40. Give the journal entries to record the following transactions:

Mar. 15 — Accepted a $2,000, 3-month, 10% note from Bob Hanson in settlement of a past due account.

Apr. 15 — Discounted the Hanson note at the bank at a discount rate of 12%.

June 15 — Received notice from the bank that the Hanson note was in default. Paid the bank the maturity value of the note.

July 15 — Received a check from Hanson for the maturity value of the note plus 10% interest on the maturity value of the note for the 30-day period subsequent to maturity.

41. Determine the maturity value of the following notes receivable held by Staubach Company.

a. $1,000 principal, 4 percent interest, matures in 6 months.
b. $ 800 principal, 7 percent interest, matures in 60 days.
c. $ 600 principal, 3 percent interest, matures in 100 days.
d. $ 500 principal, 5 percent interest, matures in 1 month.
e. $ 900 principal, 6 percent interest, matures in 3 months.
f. $ 200 principal, 7 percent interest, matures in 30 days.
g. $ 400 principal, 4 percent interest, matures in 10 days.

42. The Dorsett Company borrowed $500 from the Pearson Company and issued a note at an 8 percent rate of interest. The interest was deducted in advance and the note was issued on October 1, 19x1 and matures February 1, 19x2. Make the necessary journal entries on Pearson Company's books for the date of issuance, December 31, 19x1, and the maturity date.

43. Prepare the necessary journal entries in Henderson's books for the following events.

a. On March 1, Sam Donaldson agreed to pay David Henderson $2,000 plus 7 percent interest on August 1.
b. Henderson accrued interest earned on June 30 for the months of March, April, May, and June.
c. Donaldson did not pay the note at maturity.

44. Prepare the necessary journal entries in Martin's books for the following events.

    a.   Mike Mason purchased merchandise on credit from Martin's Retail Outlet for $150.

    b.   Mason's account proves to be uncollectible. (Assume an allowance for bad debts account already exists.)

    c.   Mason's account was subsequently collected.

45. Determine the interest on each of the following notes:

	Face Amount	Interest Rate	Days to Maturity
a.	$1,000	6%	60
b.	$5,000	8%	90
c.	$4,000	4%	180
d.	$2,500	5%	36

46. On December 1, King, Inc. issued a 90-day, 6 percent note for $3,000 to Miller Co. to replace an account payable. Give the journal entries necessary to record the following on the books of King, Inc.

    a.   Issuance of the note by King, Inc.

    b.   Adjusting entry on December 31.

    c.   Payment of the note at maturity.

47. Assume that Richardson Company borrows $1,500 on a 6-month note bearing a 9 percent rate of discount. Three months later, the company closes its books. In the next accounting period, the note matures and is paid by Richardson Company. Prepare the necessary journal entries for Richardson Company related to this note.

48. Thompson Co. issues a 180-day, non-interest-bearing note for $10,000 to First National Bank on May 1. The bank discounts the note at 8 percent. Give the necessary journal entries for Thompson Co. to record the issuance of the note and the payment of the note at maturity.

49. On May 1, 19x1, the Bucks Company borrowed $600 on a 120-day note payable bearing an interest rate of 7 percent. This note was used to purchase equipment costing $1,000; the balance of which was paid in cash. On June 15, the company borrowed $800 on a non-interest-bearing 90-day note with a discount rate of 7 percent. The proceeds from the note were used entirely to pay for office supplies. The Bucks Company closes its year on June 30.

Required:

Give journal entries to record the issuance of the loans, adjusting entries on June 30, 19x1, and entries to record their payments when due.

PROBLEMS

50. Red, Inc.'s bank statement for the month ending June 30 shows a balance of $231. The cash account as of the close of business on June 30 indicates a credit balance or overdraft of $123. In reconciling the balances, the auditor discovers the following:

> Receipts on June 30 of $1,860 were not deposited until July 1.
> Checks outstanding on June 30 were $2,215.
> The bank has charged the depositor $10 for service charges.
> A check payable to S.S. Dohr for $56 was entered in Red's cash payments journal in error as $65.

Required:

Prepare a bank reconciliation.

51. The following refers to Ginger's Floral Shop:

a. Prepare a bank reconciliation showing the "true" cash balance for July 31 given the following information:

1. Balance per bank statement at July 31, $4,610.
2. Balance per books at July 31, $3,900.
3. Deposits in transit not recorded by banks, $445.
4. Bank error, check drawn by the Ginger Bread Shop debited to account of Ginger's Floral Shop, $20.
5. Note collected by bank, $1,025.
6. Debit memorandum for bank charges, $10.
7. N.S.F. check returned by bank, $35.
8. Accountants credited cash account for $175 rather than the correct figure of $100 in recording check #55.
9. Outstanding checks of $120 on July 31.

b. Prepare the adjusting or correcting entries required.

52. You have been engaged to audit the Able Company. In the course of your examination, you gather the following information:

a. Balance per cash account, July 31, 19x1, $2,750.
b. Bank service charges for the month included as a debit memo with the bank statement, $22.
c. Outstanding checks at June 30, $195.
d. Deposits received on July 31 and sent to bank but not yet recorded by bank, $216.
e. Checks written in month of June and returned with July statement, $135.
f. Checks written in July but not returned with July 31 bank statement, $535.

Required:

Compute the balance reported on July 31, 19x1 bank statement.

53. In connection with an examination of the cash account you are given the following worksheet:

Bank Reconciliation
December 31, 19x1

Balance per books at December 31, 19x1.............		$17,174.86
Add: Collections received on the last day of December and charged to "cash in bank" on books but not deposited.........		2,662.25
Debit memo for customer's check returned unpaid (check is on hand but no entry has been made on the books).......		200.00
Debit memo for bank service charge for December...........................		5.50
		$20,142.61
Less: Checks drawn but not paid by bank (see detailed list below)....................	$2,267.75	
Credit memo for proceeds of a note receivable which had been left at the bank for collection but which has not been recorded as collected................	400.00	
Check for an account payable entered on books as $240.90 but drawn and paid by bank as $419.....................	178.10	2,945.85
Computed balance..............................		$17,196.76
Unlocated difference.............................		200.00
Balance per bank................................		$16,996.76

Checks Drawn but Not Paid by Bank

No.	Amount
573.............................	$ 67.27
724.............................	9.90
903.............................	456.67
907.............................	305.50
911.............................	482.75
913.............................	550.00
914.............................	366.76
916.............................	10.00
917.............................	218.90
	$2,267.75

Required:

1. Prepare a corrected reconciliation.
2. Prepare journal entries for items which should be adjusted prior to closing the books.

(AICPA adapted)

54. The Backward Company decided to create a petty cash fund because of the increase in small cash disbursements such as supplies and postage. The following transactions took place in the month of May.

Postage..........................	$13
Delivery costs......................	9
Supplies	25
Tapes for recorder..................	3

The petty cash fund was established at $300 on May 1. It was replenished on May 30 and then increased by $50 on May 31.

Required:

Prepare all journal entries related to the petty cash fund for the month of May.

55. The Medich Company's petty cash fund for the first month of operations was as follows:

a. $1,000 was placed in the fund on April 1.
b.   Petty cash record for April:

	April 1-15	April 16-30
Postage.........................	$ 50	$ 60
Supplies	400	600
Miscellaneous expenses............	90	70
Total.......................	$540	$730

c.   On April 16 the fund was replenished.
d.   On April 30 the fund was replenished and decreased by $100.

Required:

Prepare all entries.

56. The Ellis Company's bank reconciliation at March 31 was as follows:

Balance per bank statement.................	$7,000
Deposits outstanding......................	400
Checks outstanding........................	(75)
	$7,325
Balance per books.........................	$7,332
Unrecorded service charge..................	(7)
	$7,325

April data are as follows:

	Bank	Books
Checks recorded......................	$5,750	$5,900
Deposits recorded.....................	5,050	5,500
Service charges recorded................	6	7
Collection by bank....................	410	0
N.S.F. check returned..................	25	0
Balances April 30.....................	6,679	6,925

Required:

1. What are the amounts of the unrecorded deposits and outstanding checks at April 30?
2. Prepare a bank reconciliation for April.
3. Prepare the needed entries at April 30.

57. The balance reported on the bank statement of Harrah Corporation on April 30, 19x1 was $65,978.40. The bookkeeper found the following by comparing the bank and the book balances:

a. Checks totaling $10,798.50 had not cleared the bank.
b. A check was recorded in the books at $730 when the correct amount was $370. The check was for the purchase of office supplies.
c. No entry was made in the books for an N.S.F. check of $210.
d. The bank had not recorded a deposit of $2,432.
e. $3 was charged for printing checks.

Required:

1. Determine the balance per books before any corrections or adjustments are made.
2. Prepare a bank reconciliation and any necessary journal entries.

58. Prepare a bank reconciliation for the May Company for September 30, 19x1.

a. Book cash balance on September 30 was $230.80.
b. On August 31 outstanding checks totaled $1,394.80. By September 30, only two of these checks had not cleared. Because of the amount of time it had been outstanding, one of the checks for $100 had a stop payment put on it. The other outstanding check was for $57.10.
c. Checks drawn and still outstanding in September amount to $1,733.48 (assume this figure is correct).
d. A check was written for $472, but was recorded as $652. It is among the outstanding checks at the end of September.
e. The September service charge of $6.80 has not been recorded by the company.
f. Receipts of $236.30 were deposited by mail on September 30.

g. The bank statement showed the collection of a note by the bank in the amount of $406.

h. Included in the checks accompanying the September bank statement was a check drawn by Moy Company but charged to May Company for $114.32.

59. Use the following data concerning King Company to prepare a bank reconciliation statement.

Balance per bank....................................	$10,500
Balance per books...................................	9,250
Deposit in transit....................................	1,015
Refund of cash for damaged material (not deposited)........	35
Outstanding checks..................................	175
Bank service charge..................................	3
N.S.F. check received by bank from the Goodman Company (a customer).............................	62
Interest collected by the bank for King Company on a note receivable.................................	1,111
$400 deposit from King Company recorded as $410 by bookkeeper.	

Hint: Watch for cash overage or shortage.

60. On December 31, 19x1, the accounting records of the Cavilier Sales Company showed a cash balance of $6,600. A review of its bank reconciliation as of that date disclosed that a deposit of $7,200 was in transit and that checks of $6,350 were outstanding. Cavilier's books showed cash receipts of $108,700 and cash disbursements of $115,250 during the year. The company's bank paid checks totaling $121,000 during 19x1. A deposit of $9,000 was in transit at the beginning of the year.

Required:

Reconstruct the December 31, 19x0 bank reconcilation of the Cavilier Sales Company.

61. The Patrick Company had poor internal control over its cash transactions. Information about its cash position at November 30, 19x1 was as follows:

The cash books showed a balance of $18,901.62, which included undeposited receipts. A credit of $100 on the bank's records did not appear on the books of the company. The balance per bank statement was $15,550. Outstanding checks were: No. 62 for $116.25, No. 183 for $150, No. 284 for $253.25, No. 8621 for $190.71, No. 8623 for $206.80, and No. 8632 for $145.28.

The cashier embezzled all undeposited receipts in excess of $3,794.41 and prepared the following reconciliation:

Balance, per books, November 30, 19x1..		$18,901.62
Add: Outstanding checks:		
8621.....................	$190.71	
8623.....................	206.80	
8632.....................	145.28	442.79
		$19,344.41
Less: Undeposited receipts............		3,794.41
Balance per bank, November 30, 19x1...		$15,550.00
Deduct: Unrecorded credit..........		100.00
True cash, November 30, 19x1.........		$15,450.00

(AICPA adapted)

Required:

1. Prepare a supporting schedule showing how much the cashier embezzled.
2. How did he attempt to conceal his theft?
3. Taking only the information given, name two specific features of internal control which were apparently missing.

62. When aging their accounts receivable, the Wingfoot Company drew up the following schedule:

Accounts Receivable Balance	Number of Days Outstanding			
	0-30	31-60	61-90	91 and older
$5,250	$3,450	$900	$650	$250
	Estimated % Uncollectible			
	1%	5%	15%	50%

Required:

Prepare a table calculating the estimated bad debt expense for the period and make the appropriate journal entry on the books of the Wingfoot Company, assuming that there is a credit balance of $100 in the Allowance for Bad Debts before adjustment.

63.   During 19x1, Squeeze, Inc. had $800,000 of sales on credit. Also, during 19x1 the company wrote off $14,000 of accounts receivable as definitely uncollectible and collected $700 from individuals whose accounts had been written off during previous years. The company estimates its bad debts each year to be 2% of credit sales. On January 1, 19x1, the accounts receivable balance was $60,000. Collections on account for 19x1 totaled $775,000 and customers returned goods for credit in the amount of $20,000. The company offers no cash discounts. On December 31, 19x1, after all adjustments and accruals, accounts receivable net of the allowance for uncollectible accounts amounted to $45,400.

Required:

1.   Prepare journal entries for *all* transactions during 19x1 involving accounts receivable and the related allowance account.
2.   The balance in the allowance account at:

    a.   January 1, 19x1.
    b.   December 31, 19x1 (after all adjustments).

64.   Charlie Tuna, owner of Tuna's Fish Wholesalers, has instructed his accountant, Jack D. Ripper, to make sure the Allowance for Bad Debts account is at least 10 percent of total accounts receivable at the end of each calendar year. The January 1, 19x1, balance in Allowance for Bad Debts is $10,000.
    During 19x1, the following transactions took place:

Jan. 13   Notice was received that I.M. Acrook, who owed the company $4,000, was in bankruptcy and no payment could be expected.

May 13   Wheel & Deal, Inc. paid $14,000 applicable to its account which totaled $20,000. Its treasurer was last seen boarding a steamer for South America (with all the company's funds), so no other payments would be forthcoming.

July 10   Received a check for $2,000 from A. Lincoln whose account had been written off as uncollectible in 19x0.

Oct. 13   H.E. Asucker, a customer, notified Charlie that his partner had absconded with all the company funds. Asucker stated that their business had folded and he was unable to pay Charlie the $8,000 he owed him.

Dec. 31   The balance of accounts receivable, as of the close of today's business, was $200,000.

Required:

Prepare general journal entries to record the above transactions.

65. On January 1, 19x1, H.E. Asucker made a loan of $1,000 to S.H. Esacrook. Asucker accepted a one (1)-year, 6 percent note as evidence of this transaction. On July 1, 19x1, Asucker, in need of funds, sold (discounted) Esacrook's note to the Piggy Bank. Piggy charged a discount rate of 10 percent. On January 1, 19x2, Piggy notified Asucker that the note had not been paid by Esacrook. Asucker paid the note.

Required:

Prepare journal entries for H.E. Asucker to record all of the above information.

66. The Marrion Company purchases and sells merchandise on account. The following transactions occurred in 19x1.

Apr.	1	Sold $2,000 worth of merchandise to Jack Palmer on account.
May	17	Purchased $275 of merchandise from the Colonial Company on account.
June	1	Jack Palmer signed a 12 percent two-month note in payment on his account.
	15	Paid for merchandise purchased from Colonial Company.
July	15	Discounted Palmer's note at the Republic Bank. The discount rate was 18 percent.
Aug.	1	Palmer dishonors his note. Marrion Company pays the bank the required amount.

Required:

Prepare journal entries to record the above transactions on the books of Marrion Company.

67. Listed below are selected transactions of Eastern Company for a six-month period ending March 31, 19x1. Eastern's accounting period ends on December 31.

Oct.	1	Sold merchandise on account to Ed Jackson for $1,600. The terms of the sale were n/30.
Nov.	1	Loaned $4,000 to Roger Herman on a three-month, 10 percent note.
	5	Accepted a $1,600, 90-day, 10 percent note from Ed Jackson in settlement of his past due account.
Dec.	5	Discounted the Jackson note at 12 percent at the bank.
	15	Sold merchandise on account to Bill Martin for $400; the terms of the sale were n/30.
	31	Determined by aging of accounts receivable that a $6,500 credit balance in the allowance for bad debts is required. There was a $300 debit balance in the allowance account prior to an adjusting entry.
	31	Made an adjusting entry to record the accrued interest on the note receivable from Roger Herman.
Jan.	24	Determined that the account receivable from Bill Martin was uncollectible, and it was then written off.

Feb. 5 Received notice from the bank that the Jackson note was in default. Paid the bank the maturity value of the note plus a $10 protest fee.

Mar. 5 Collected from Jackson the maturity value of the dishonored note plus 10 percent interest on that amount since the date of default and the protest fee.

20 Full payment of $400 was received from Bill Martin on an account previously written off.

Required:

Prepare general journal entries to record the transactions and adjustments listed above.

68. Calculate the proceeds and the interest expense from discounting the notes described below.

a. A two-month, 8 percent, $1,500 note discounted one month before maturity at a 10 percent discount rate. One month of interest income had been recorded.

b. A four-month, 9 percent, $2,500 note discounted two months before maturity at a 12 percent discount rate. Two months of interest income had been recorded.

Refer to the Annual Report included in the Appendix at the end of the text:

69. What were the total collections from accounts receivable during the most recent year, assuming that all sales were made on account?

70. Comparing the two years presented, what was the increase in current liabilities?

71. What are the total current liabilities in the most recent year?

Chapter 9 presents information relating to the determination and presentation of bonds payable and investments in corporate securities. This chapter also discusses and illustrates the use of consolidated financial statements. Studying this chapter should enable you to:

1. Describe the various classes of bonds.

2. Explain the concepts of bond discount and bond premium and how they are handled for accounting purposes.

3. Record the early retirement of bonds, including either a gain or loss if applicable.

4. Identify the elements of cost of stocks and bonds purchased as investments.

5. Discuss the methods of accounting for long-term and temporary investments subsequent to acquisition.

6. Describe the criteria used to determine when to prepare consolidated financial statements.

7. Illustrate the procedures and necessary worksheet adjustments for preparing consolidated financial statements.

8. Differentiate between the purchase and pooling of interests methods in accounting for business combinations.

Long-Term Liabilities Investments and Consolidated Financial Statements

INTRODUCTION

When a corporation desires to raise additional capital for long-term purposes, it has several alternatives. It may borrow funds by issuing bonds, or it may obtain funds by issuing additional stock to shareholders. Each source of funds has its particular advantages and disadvantages to the issuing corporation. A bondholder is a creditor of a corporation while a stockholder is an owner. As creditors, bondholders normally do not participate in the management of the firm. Therefore, by issuing bonds, a corporation does not spread or dilute control of management over a larger number of owners. Interest expense is deductible for federal income tax purposes while dividends are not a tax deduction.

The interest expense on a bond is a fixed obligation to the borrower. If the interest is not paid on the dates specified by the contract, legal action may be brought by the bondholders. Dividends on stock, on the other hand, are declared at the discretion of the board of directors of the issuing corporation.

BOND OBLIGATIONS

Bonds are issued as a means of borrowing money for long-term purposes. The desired funds are obtained by issuing a number of bonds with a certain denomination (usually $1,000). Normally, a corporation sells all of its bonds to an investment firm, referred to as an underwriter. The underwriter then resells the bonds to investors. For accounting purposes, only the amount received from the underwriter is relevant to the issuing firm. Individual bonds are sold to investors with a promise to pay a definite sum of money to the holder at a fixed future date and periodic interest payments at a stated rate throughout the life of the liability. Since bonds usually do not name individual lenders, they may be bought and sold by investors until their maturity.

When funds are borrowed by issuing bonds, interest payments and the timing of the repayment of the principal of the debt to bondholders are obligations which are fixed in amount and must be paid at specified dates regardless of the amount of income earned by the firm. If the rate of earnings on invested funds exceeds the interest rate on the bonds, it is usually to the owners' advantage for the firm to issue bonds. However, if the expected rate of earnings is less than the interest rate, it would not be to the advantage of the owners to borrow funds. Furthermore, interest payments must be made when due regardless of whether or not sufficient income is earned. If interest payments are not made, the bondholders may bring action in order to foreclose against the assets of the corporation in the settlement of their claims. Bondholders are creditors and their claims for interest and the repayment of principal have priority over the claims of owners. Therefore, the feasibility of obtaining funds by issuing bonds depends upon factors such as the expected rate of interest and the stability of the earnings of the firm.

Bond interest payments are a deductible expense in the computation of taxable income, while dividends paid to owners are not deductible for tax purposes. Because of the magnitude of corporate income taxes (up to 46 percent of net income), the effect of taxes is often an important factor in determining the source which will be used by the business to obtain its long-term funds.

Approval of the board of directors and stockholders of the corporation is normally required prior to issuance of bonds. In addition, the firm issuing bonds selects a trustee to represent the bondholders. The trustee acts to protect the bondholders' interests, and takes legal action if the pledged responsibilities of the corporation are not satisfied.

CLASSES OF BONDS

Bonds may be either secured by specific assets or unsecured. Unsecured bonds are referred to as debenture bonds. Debenture bonds have as "security" the general credit standing of the issuing corporation. Therefore, debenture bonds are usually issued successfully only by companies with a favorable financial position.

A secured bond gives the bondholder a prior claim against specific assets in the event that the issuing corporation is unable to make the required interest or principal payments as they become due. Secured bonds differ as to the type of assets pledged. Real estate mortgage bonds are secured by a mortgage on specific·land or buildings. Equipment trust bonds are secured by mortgages on tangible personal property such as equipment. Collateral trust bonds are secured by stocks and bonds of other companies owned by the corporation issuing the bonds.

A bond issue that matures on a single date is referred to as a term bond. Bonds that mature on several different dates and are retired in installments over a period of time are called serial bonds. Bonds that may be retired before maturity at the option of the issuing corporation are referred to as callable bonds. Bonds which may be exchanged for a specified amount of stock at the option of the bondholder are termed convertible bonds.

Bonds may also differ as to the method of interest payment. Registered bonds require that the bondholders' names be registered with the issuing corporation. The corporation issuing bonds is required to maintain a record of the current owners; periodic interest payments are mailed directly to the registered owners. Other bonds, called coupon bonds, have interest coupons attached which call for the payment of the required amount of interest on specified dates. A bond coupon is similar to a note payable to the holder at the date specified on the coupon. At each interest date, the appropriate coupon may be detached by the bondholder and presented at a bank for payment.

Despite the wide variety of bonds offered, it should be noted that the value of bonds to the investor depends to a significant degree on the financial condition and long-term earning prospects of the issuing corporation. While the various optional provisions that may be included in a bond issue may affect the issue price of the bonds, it would be difficult for a company in poor financial condition to issue bonds regardless of the provisions.

When a corporation issues bonds, it is obligated to pay the principal or face amount of the bonds at a specified maturity date and to make periodic interest payments as well. The interest rate specified on the bonds is referred to as the coupon rate. The interest rate which investors are willing to accept on a bond at the time of its issue depends upon factors such as the market evaluation of the quality of the bond issue as evidenced by the financial strength of the business, the firm's earnings prospects and the particular provisions of the bond issue. This rate is referred to as the market or effective interest rate. If the effective interest rate exceeds the coupon rate, the issue price of the bonds will fall below the face amount of the bonds. When the issue price is less than face value, the difference is referred to as a discount. For example, if Pearson Co. offers bonds with an interest rate of 7 percent when the market rate is 8 percent for similar bonds, the selling price of the bonds will be less than their face value. Since annual interest payments on each $1,000 of bonds will be $70 (.07 × $1,000), the issue price of the bonds will fall to the point where the interest received will yield an effective rate of 8 percent. Similarly, if the coupon rate exceeds the market interest rate for comparable bonds at the time of the issue, the price of the bonds will exceed the face amount. That is, the bonds will be issued at a premium. The bonds will sell at their face amount only when the coupon rate is exactly equal to the market rate.[1]

Bonds Issued at Face Value

If the coupon rate offered on bonds is identical to the market rate, the bonds will be issued at their face value. To illustrate, assume that Dascher Co. had authorization to issue $100,000 of 25-year, 18 percent debenture bonds on January 1, 19x1, with interest payable semiannually on June 30 and December 31. If $50,000 of the bonds are issued at face value on January 1, 19x1, the entry for the issuance would be:

Cash 50,000
Bonds payable...................... 50,000

No journal entry is made for the authorization of the bonds. The balance sheet, however, should disclose all of the pertinent facts with respect to the bond issue. For example, a balance sheet for Dascher Co. on January 1, 19x1, would include the following information:

[1] The procedures for computing the selling price for a bond are presented in the appendix to this chapter.

Long-term liabilities:
18% debenture bonds payable, due on December 31, 19x25 . . . . $50,000

After the bonds are issued, Dascher Co. must make semiannual interest payments of $4,500 on each June 30 and December 31 that the bonds remain outstanding ($50,000 × $\frac{18}{100}$ × $\frac{1}{2}$). The entry to record each payment would be as follows:

Interest expense	4,500	
Cash		4,500

If the accounting period used by the firm ends between interest dates, an adjusting entry must be made to accrue the interest expense from the last interest date to the end of the period. For example, if the accounting period of Dascher Co. ended on September 30, the following adjusting entry would be necessary in order to record the accrued interest expense of $2,250 ($50,000 × $\frac{18}{100}$ × $\frac{3}{12}$) from June 30 to September 30.

Interest expense	2,250	
Interest payable		2,250

Interest expense will be closed to the Income Summary account, and interest payable will remain as a liability until the next regular semiannual interest payment. The entry to record the interest payment on December 31 would be:

Interest expense	2,250	
Interest payable	2,250	
Cash		4,500

Issuance Between Interest Dates

Once authorized, bonds may be issued at any time. Bonds are often issued at a time between the interest dates. Since the corporation will pay the full semiannual interest on all bonds outstanding at an interest date, the bondholder is usually required to purchase the interest that has accrued from the previous interest date to the date of sale. This interest paid by the bondholder is returned as part of the first interest payment after issuance. To illustrate, assume that the Dascher Co. bonds from the previous example were issued at face value plus accrued interest on March 1, 19x1. The issue price would be $50,000 plus two months' interest of $1,500 ($50,000 × $\frac{18}{100}$ × $\frac{2}{12}$). The entry to record the issuance is:

Cash	51,500	
Bonds payable		50,000
Interest payable		1,500

On the first semiannual interest payment date, June 30, which occurs four months after issuance, a full six months' interest ($4,500) will be paid. Of this amount, $1,500 is a return to the investor of accrued interest paid at the time of the purchase of the bonds and the remaining $3,000 represents the interest expense for the four months since the issuance. Therefore, the entry for the interest payment on June 30, 19x1, would be as follows:

Interest payable........................	1,500	
Interest expense........................	3,000	
Cash		4,500

Issuance of Bonds at a Discount

When the coupon rate on a bond issue is less than the prevailing market interest rate for similar bonds, the bonds will sell at a discount. For example, assume the prevailing market interest rate exceeds 18 percent when Dascher Co. offers $50,000 face value of 18 percent, 25-year debenture bonds. As a result, assume that the $50,000 of Dascher Co. bonds are issued at a price of $47,500 on January 1, 19x1. The $2,500 excess of the face value over the issue price represents a discount. Normally bonds are carried in the accounts at face value with the discount recorded in a separate contra account. The issuance of the bonds would be recorded by the following entry:

Cash	47,500	
Discount on bonds payable..............	2,500	
Bonds payable.......................		50,000

Although the issuing corporation receives less than the face amount of the issue when bonds are sold at a discount, the entire face amount must be repaid at maturity. Therefore, the total cost of borrowing includes the discount as well as the interest payments. To illustrate, the total interest cost to Dascher Co. for the bonds issued at a discount is computed as follows:

Amount to be repaid at maturity.........................	$ 50,000
Amount received at issuance............................	47,500
Excess of cash to be paid over cash received (discount).....	$ 2,500
Cash interest payments ($9,000 annually for 25 years)........	225,000
Total Interest Cost...............................	$227,500

The average yearly interest expense over the period until the maturity of the bonds is $9,100 ($227,500 ÷ 25). Therefore, in order to reflect the total interest cost of the bonds, bond discount should be allocated to expense over the 25-year life of the bonds as additional interest expense. The process of transferring a portion of bond discount to interest expense during each period is referred to as amortization. One common method of amortizing discount is to transfer or write off equal amounts at each interest payment date. This process is referred to as straight-line amortization.[2] In the illustration above, application of the straight-line method would yield amortization of $100 ($\frac{1}{25}$ × $2,500) each year, or $50 on each semiannual interest date. The following entry would be made at each interest payment date.

Interest expense............................	4,550	
Discount on bonds payable...............		50
Cash		4,500

Because of the amortization of the discount, total interest expense recorded over the life of the bond issue will be equal to the cash interest payments plus the bond discount. Further, amortization reduces the balance in the Discount of Bonds Payable account to zero at the maturity date of the bonds.

Unamortized discount on bonds payable should be classified as a deduction from the related Bonds Payable account. To illustrate, the Dascher Co. bonds in the preceding example were issued at a discount of $2,500 on January 1, 19x1. After two years, on December 31, 19x2, a total of $200 ($2,500 × $\frac{2}{25}$) of the original discount would have been amortized, and the balance sheet would include the following amounts in the long-term liabilities section:

Long-term liabilities:		
18% debenture bonds payable, due on		
December 31, 19x25..............................	$50,000	
Less: Unamortized discount on bonds payable........	2,300	$47,700

If the accounting period of the firm falls between interest dates, amortization of bond discount must be included in the adjusting entry which is made for the accrual of interest expense. For example, if the accounting period of Dascher Co. ends on September 30, the following adjusting entry would be required in order to record the interest expense for the period from June 30 (the last regular interest payment date) to September 30.

Interest expense............................	2,275	
Discount on bonds payable...............		25
Interest payable..........................		2,250

The interest payable of $2,250 ($50,000 × $\frac{18}{100}$ × $\frac{3}{12}$) and the discount amortization of $25 ($\frac{1}{4}$ × $100) is the interest expense for the three-month period since the last interest payment was made.

---

[2] The interest method of discount amortization is discussed in the appendix to this chapter.

Issuance of Bonds at a Premium

If the coupon rate on a bond issue exceeds the prevailing market interest rate for comparable bonds, the bonds will sell at an amount above their face value. The excess of the issue price over the face value is referred to as premium. For example, assume that $50,000 of Brenner Co. 25-year, 18 percent debenture bonds are issued on January 1, 19x1, when the market rate is less than 18 percent. As a result, assume that the bonds are sold for $55,000. The entry to record the issuance of the bonds would be:

Cash	55,000	
Bonds payable		50,000
Premium on bonds payable		5,000

When a premium is received on the issuance of bonds, the total cost of borrowing funds is equal to the cash interest payments made reduced by the amount of the premium. The total interest cost for Brenner Co. over the life of the bonds is calculated as follows:

Amount received at issuance	$ 55,000
Amount to be repaid at maturity	50,000
Excess of cash received over cash paid (premium)	($ 5,000)
Cash interest payments ($9,000 × 25)	225,000
Total Interest Cost	$220,000

The average yearly interest cost over the life of the bond issue is $8,800 ($220,000/25). Consequently, in order to reflect the actual interest cost of the bond issue, the premium should be periodically written off or amortized as a reduction of the interest cost over the life of the issue. The procedures for the amortization of premium are similar to those used for bonds issued at a discount. In the Brenner Co. example, application of the straight-line method would result in premium amortization of $200 ($\frac{1}{25}$ × $5,000) each year and, therefore, $100 on each semiannual interest date. The entry to record each semiannual interest payment and premium amortization would be as follows:

Interest expense	4,400	
Premium on bonds payable	100	
Cash		4,500

The unamortized balance in the premium account would be reported as an addition to bonds payable on the balance sheet.

As indicated with respect to bond discount, if the firm's accounting period falls between interest payment dates, an adjusting entry is required in order to record the accrued interest expense and amortization of premium for the period since the last interest date.

Convertible Bonds

In certain circumstances, a company may issue bonds which are convertible at a specific rate into the common stock of the corporation at the option of the bondholder. This provision may be attached to a bond in order to enhance the marketability of the bond issue. The holder initially has the right of a creditor, but he may later convert to common stock and share in the earnings of the business.

The entries to record the issuance of convertible bonds are similar to those which were discussed previously. At the date of conversion, the carrying value of the bond (face value plus any premium or less any discount) is normally transferred to the stockholder equity accounts which are associated with the new shares of stock issued in the conversion. To illustrate, assume that a corporation had issued a $1,000, 10-year, convertible bond for $1,100 on January 1, 19x1. The bond is convertible into 20 shares of $10 par value common stock at the option of the holder. Further assume that the holder converted the bond into common stock on December 31, 19x5. At the time of the conversion, there is unamortized premium of $50. The entry to record the conversion would be as follows:

Bonds payable........................	1,000	
Premium.............................	50	
Common stock.......................		200
Additional paid-in capital.............		850

RETIREMENT OF BONDS

Bonds may be retired by the issuing corporation at maturity or before the maturity date either by redeeming callable bonds or by repurchasing bonds in the open market. If bonds are retired at their maturity, any premium or discount will have been completely amortized and the entry to record the retirement of the bonds would be a debit to bonds payable and a credit to cash for an amount equal to the face or maturity value of the bonds.

Callable bonds may be redeemed at the option of the issuing corporation within a specified period and at a stated price referred to as the call price. The call price is usually an amount which is in excess of face value, with the excess referred to as call premium. In the absence of a call provision, the issuing corporation may retire its bonds by purchasing them in the open market at the prevailing market price.

If bonds are repurchased by the issuing corporation at a price less than their book value (i.e., maturity value less discount or plus premium), the corporation realizes a gain on the retirement of the bonds. The carrying value of the bonds is equal to the face value plus any unamortized premium or less any unamortized discount. Similarly, if the purchase price is greater than the carrying value, a loss is incurred on the retirement of the debt.[3]

To illustrate a redemption prior to maturity, assume that the Carpenter Co. has a $50,000 bond issue outstanding with $2,000 of unamortized premium. Further assume that the corporation has the option of calling the bonds at 105 (i.e., 105 percent of the face value) and that the company exercises its call provision. The entry to record the redemption of the bonds for $52,500 ($50,000 × 1.05) would be as follows:

Bonds payable	50,000	
Premium on bonds payable	2,000	
Loss on redemption	500	
Cash		52,500

If the bonds do not include a call provision, the corporation could purchase the bonds in the open market. For example, assume that Carpenter Co. purchased one fifth of the $50,000 face value bonds outstanding for $9,800. The carrying value of the bonds purchased is $10,400 (face value plus one fifth of the unamortized premium), while the purchase price is $9,800. Therefore, the company would realize a $600 gain on the retirement. The entry to record the retirement of the bonds would be as follows:

Bonds payable	10,000	
Premium on bonds payable	400	
Gain on retirement		600
Cash		9,800

BOND SINKING FUND

In order to offer additional security to the investor, a provision may be included in the bond indenture which requires the issuing corporation to set aside funds for repayment of the bond at maturity by periodic accumulations over the life of the issue. These funds may be accumulated by periodically depositing cash in a bond sinking fund. The cash deposited in the fund is usually invested in income producing assets. Therefore, the total deposits made by the issuing corporation over the life of the bond issue are normally less than the total maturity value of the bonds. At maturity, the securities in the fund are sold and the proceeds are used to retire the bonds.

Cash and securities included in a sinking fund are not available for the retirement of current liabilities; they are normally shown as a single total and included under the caption of investments. Similarly, earnings on the sinking fund assets are shown as a separate item in the income statement.

---

[3] According to FASB *Statement No. 4*, "Reporting Gains and Losses From Extinguishment of Debt," (1975), gains or losses from retirement of bonds should be aggregated and, if material in amount, classified in the income statement as an extraordinary item (net of the related income tax effect).

**RESTRICTION
ON DIVIDENDS**

Another means of increasing the security of the bondholder is a provision whereby dividend payments by the issuing company will be restricted during the life of the bond issue. The actual restriction on dividends may vary. For example, a restriction may limit the payment of dividends during a given year to the excess of net income over the sinking fund requirements for the period. There are various methods for disclosing this restriction in the financial statements. Such a restriction could be shown by a footnote or parenthetically in the balance sheet. Alternatively, the restriction could be indicated by appropriating retained earnings each year. To illustrate, assume that the sinking fund requirement for the year is $20,000 and that net income is $35,000. If dividends are limited to the excess of net income over the sinking fund requirement, an appropriation of retained earnings could be made with the following entry:

Retained earnings......................	20,000	
Appropriation for bonded debt..........		20,000

**BALANCE SHEET
PRESENTATION**

The presentation of long-term liabilities in the balance sheet should disclose all information which is relevant to the debt including the maturity dates, interest rates, conversion privileges, etc. In addition, if a liability is secured by specific assets, or restricts the payment of dividends, such information should also be disclosed in the financial statements. To illustrate, the long-term liabilities section of the balance sheet might appear as follows:

Long-term liabilities:		
25-year, 16% mortgage bonds due on		
December 31, 19x9............................	$100,000	
Less: Unamortized discount......................	4,000	$ 96,000
20-year, 18% debenture bonds, convertible		
into 15 shares of common stock, due on		
December 31, 19x4............................	$ 50,000	
Add: Unamortized premium......................	1,000	51,000
Total Long-Term Liabilities......................		$147,000

**INVESTMENTS IN
CORPORATE
SECURITIES**

Corporations frequently acquire the stocks and bonds of other corporations as investments. If the securities are readily marketable and if a firm intends to hold these securities for a relatively short period of time, the investments are normally classified as a current asset, Marketable Securities. On the other hand, investments in stocks and bonds which do not meet the criteria for temporary investments are classified as a noncurrent asset, long-term investments.

INVESTMENTS IN BONDS

Bonds may be purchased as a long-term investment or as a temporary investment. The purpose for acquiring bonds must be determined on the basis of management's intention. Bonds held as temporary investments are classified as current assets, and bonds acquired for long-term purposes are reported as noncurrent assets. The primary difference in the accounting for bonds classified as temporary versus long-term is in the treatment of the premium or discount on the purchase. Companies making long-term investments in bonds must amortize the difference between the cost of the investment and its maturity value over the life of the bonds. This parallels the treatment used for the issuance of bonds discussed earlier in the chapter. Companies acquiring bonds for temporary purposes, however, are not required to amortize premium or discount. Instead, a short-term investment in bonds is normally carried in the investor's accounts at the acquisition cost, and any gain or loss is recognized in the period the investment is sold. The logic for not amortizing premium or discount is that since it is a temporary investment, the company does not expect to hold the bond until it matures. The following dicussion deals with the accounting treatment for long-term investments in bonds.

The cost of a bond includes the quoted price of the bond plus brokerage commissions, transfer taxes, etc. When bonds are purchased between interest dates, the purchase price of the bonds usually includes payment for the interest which has accrued since the previous interest payment date. To illustrate, assume that on June 1, 19x0, Edwards Co. purchases $10,000 face value of 12 percent bonds of the Bell Co. at 111½ plus accrued interest. The bonds pay interest on June 30 and December 31 and mature on December 31, 19x9. The entry to record the purchase would be:

Investment in bonds.....................	11,150	
Bond interest receivable..................	500	
Cash		11,650

The debit to the Investment in Bonds account records the cost of the bond—the face value of $10,000 × 111.5 percent or $11,150. This indicates that the bonds were purchased at a premium. Note that this premium is not recorded in a separate account, but instead is included as a part of the Investment in Bonds account. The debit to bond interest receivable records the fact that Edwards Co. purchased five months accrued interest along with the bonds ($10,000 × .12 × $\frac{5}{12}$ = $500). The credit to cash is for the total amount paid by Edwards.

Amortization of Premium

On June 30, 19x0, Edwards Co. will receive its first interest payment which will be recorded as follows:

Cash..................................	600	
Bond interest receivable...............		500
Investment in bonds..................		10
Interest income.....................		90

This entry records the receipt of the $600 interest payment ($10,000 × .12 × 5/12 = $600). Of this amount, $500 is the return of the accrued interest that was purchased when the bonds were acquired. Recall that the bonds were purchased at a premium of $1,150 ($11,150 purchase − $10,000 face value). This premium is amortized as a reduction of interest income over the life of the bonds (June 1, 19x0 to December 31, 19x9 = 115 months). The amortization is $10 per month ($1,150 ÷ 115 months). Since Edwards Co. had held the bonds for one month (June 1 to June 30) when the first interest payment was received, $10 of the purchase premium was amortized at that time. Note that the amortization is recorded by a credit to the bond investment account. The income for June is $90, one month's interest of $100 ($10,000 × .12 × 1/12 = $100) minus $10 amortization of premium.

On December 31, 19x0, Edwards Co. will receive its second interest payment of $600. The entry to record the receipt of this interest and the amortization of premium is:

Cash..................................	600	
Investment in bonds....................		60
Interest income.......................		540

Again, the debit to cash records the receipt of six months' interest ($10,000 × .12 × 5/12 = $600). The credit to the bond investment account is for six months' amortization of premium ($1,150/115 months = $10 per month × 6 months = $60). The interest income is the receipt of $600 less the $60 amortization. The total interest income recognized over the life of the bonds will be equal to the total cash interest received minus the amount of the premium.

At December 31, 19x0, the bond investment account would appear in the balance sheet as follows:

Investment in bonds.......................	$11,080

This represents the original cost of the bonds, $11,150 less $70 for seven months' amortization of premium.[4] The investment in bonds account will decrease each period by the amount of the premium amortized and, therefore, at maturity will be equal to the face amount of the bonds.

---

[4] Premium or discount on bonds held as long-term investments is amortized over the life of the bonds. If bonds are held as a temporary investment, no amortization is required.

**Amortization
of Discount**

When bonds are purchased at less than their face value, the discount is not shown separately, but as a part of the investment in bonds account. Discount is amortized as an increase in the interest income earned over the life of the bonds. The interest income recognized on bonds that were acquired at a discount and held to maturity is equal to the total of the cash interest payments received plus the amount of the purchase discount. The carrying value of the investment will increase each period by the amount of the discount amortized and at maturity will equal the face amount of the bonds.

Sale of Bonds

If bonds are sold prior to maturity, accrued interest from the last interest payment date to the date of sale should be recorded. Any difference between this accrued interest plus the carrying value of the bond investment account and the net cash proceeds of the sale represents a gain or loss on the sale and is recorded as such. For example, assume that the bonds used in the above illustration were sold on January 1, 19x1, for $12,000. The entry to record the sale would be as follows:

```
Cash...................................  12,000
    Investment in bonds....................           11,080
    Gain on the sale of bonds...............              920
```

Alternatively, had the selling price on January 1, 19x1, been $11,000, the entry would have been:

```
Cash...................................  11,000
Loss on sale of bonds.....................      80
    Investment in bonds....................           11,080
```

**INVESTMENTS
IN STOCK**

Investments in stock are the temporary or long-term conversion of cash into productive use by the purchase of securities. Such investments are found among the assets of almost all businesses. In general, investments are classified as either temporary or long-term depending on the nature of the security and the intention of the investor firm.

It should be noted that when stock is purchased as an investment, the seller of the stock receives the money paid. Most investment transactions in stock are between two individual investors, one who already owned the stock and then sells it to the new investor who purchases it. The corporation whose stock is traded in the transaction becomes involved directly only if the shares exchanged are a part of a new issue of securities it sold to raise funds.

**Temporary
Investments**

Temporary investments, usually referred to as marketable securities, normally arise from seasonal excesses of cash and represent its conversion to productive use (earning interest or dividends) on a short-term basis. In order to be classified as a temporary investment, a security must be readily salable and the volume of trading of the security should be such that the sale does not materially affect the market price. In addition, there is general agreement that there should be an intention on the part of the investor firm to sell the securities in the short run as the need for cash arises.

Control Over Investments

The effective control over marketable securities includes the physical safeguarding of the certificates. This usually means that the securities should be kept in a safe if they are retained by the firm, and access to the certificates controlled. In many instances, the firm will leave its investments in the custody of its broker. The authority to purchase and sell is usually vested in the Board of Directors of the firm or in a specifically designated investments committee. In either case, requiring written authorization in order to either acquire or dispose of investments is another important control feature. Finally, the accounting records themselves are important in establishing control over investments. The periodic reconciliation of the accounting records to the securities on hand or in the custody of the broker and the reconciliation of the recorded income to the income which should have been earned (as determined by calculation and reference to sources such as *Standard & Poor's Dividend Record*) help to provide effective control over investments.

Accounting for Acquisition of Temporary Investments

The basis for recording temporary investments in the accounts is the cost of the investment. Cost includes all outlays which are required to acquire the investment including the quoted price of the security, brokerage commissions, transfer taxes, etc. To illustrate the accounting for the acquisition of marketable securities, assume that Jones Company purchased 100 shares of the stock of IBM Corporation at a price of $200 per share on January 1, 19x1. The entry to record this purchase would be as follows:

Investment in stock	20,000	
Cash		20,000

When a temporary investment is sold, the difference between the selling price and the cost of the investment is recorded as a gain or loss of the period in which the sale took place.

Valuation of Temporary Investments

Temporary investments are classified as either debt securities (government and corporate bonds) or equity securities (preferred and common stock). Prior to 1976 there was considerable diversity in the accounting for temporary investments. However, a significant degree of uniformity in practice resulted from the issuance of FASB *Statement No. 12* which was concerned with the accounting for certain marketable securities. This statement requires that marketable equity securities be accounted for at the lower of aggregate cost or market value. Other marketable securities may be valued either at cost or at lower of cost or market.

If a company owns more than a single kind of marketable equity security, the lower of cost or market procedure is applied to the securities as a group. In applying this method, the *total cost* of the group (often referred to as the portfolio) of securities is compared to the *total current market value* of the securities, and the *lower* of these two amounts is reported as the balance sheet valuation. A decline in value of the aggregate marketable equity securities is recorded as a debit to an unrealized loss account and a credit to a valuation allowance account. The unrealized loss is included in the income statement and the valuation allowance account is deducted from the original cost of the marketable securities in the balance sheet. The loss from decline in value is referred to as an *unrealized* loss to differentiate it from a loss which is realized upon the sale of the securities.

The balance in the valuation allowance account must be adjusted at the end of every period so that the portfolio of marketable equity securities will be reflected in the balance sheet at the *lower* of cost or current market value. Thus, if there are further declines in market value, the adjusting entry will recognize an additional unrealized loss. On the other hand, if the excess of aggregate cost over market value decreases (or is eliminated) in a subsequent period, a gain on recovery is recognized to the extent of previously recognized unrealized losses. The entry to record a recovery in value is a debit to the valuation allowance account and a credit to an unrealized gain account which is included in the income statement. The limitation on unrealized gains to the extent of unrealized losses previously recognized requires that the valuation allowance account must either have a credit or a zero balance. For income tax purposes, the lower of cost or market method is not acceptable, and taxable gain or loss is determined in the period of sale as the difference between original cost and the selling price.

To illustrate the use of the lower of cost or market method, assume that during 19x1 Carol Company acquires 100 shares of IBM stock for $20,000 and 100 shares of AT&T stock for $10,000. On December 31, 19x1, the company determined the carrying amount of its portfolio to be:

	Cost	Market
IBM stock	$20,000	$19,000
AT&T stock	10,000	10,500
	$30,000	$29,500

The following entry would be required in order to record the unrealized loss (i.e., $30,000 − $29,500):

```
Unrealized loss on marketable equity securities . . . . . . . . . . . . . . . . 500
    Allowance for decline in value . . . . . . . . . . . . . . . . . . . . . . . .        500
```

The $500 loss would be reported in the 19x1 income statement, and the allowance account would be deducted from marketable securities at cost in the December 31, 19x1 balance sheet.

An increase in aggregate market value in a subsequent period reduces or eliminates the allowance account. For example, assume that Carol Company had no transactions relating to marketable securities during 19x2, and that the aggregate market value of the securities held at December 31, 19x2 was $29,750. The adjustment to the valuation allowance account at December 31, 19x2, would be recorded as follows:

```
Allowance for decline in value . . . . . . . . . . . . . . . . . . . . . 250
    Unrealized gain on marketable equity securities . . . . .        250
```

The gain of $250 ($29,750 − $29,500) would be included in the income statement for 19x2. If the aggregate market value had increased to $30,000 or more, the amount of the unrealized gain would be limited to $500 (the amount required to eliminate the allowance account). If the market value of the temporary investments in marketable equity securities had decreased below $29,500 during 19x2, an unrealized loss account would have been debited and the allowance account credited in order to increase the balance in the allowance for decline in value account to the aggregate difference between the original cost and the current market value of the securities.

Because the allowance for decline in value is based on a comparison of the total portfolio cost and its market value, there is no effect upon the gain or loss recognized when an investment is sold. When a specific temporary investment in marketable equity securities is sold, the total difference between the net proceeds of the sale and the original cost is recorded as a realized gain or loss. For example, assume that Carol Company sold the 100 shares of IBM stock on June 30, 19x3 for $20,600 (net of commissions). This sale would be recorded as follows:

```
Cash . . . . . . . . . . . . . . . . . . . . . . . . . . . . . . . . . . . . . . . . . . 20,600
    Investment in stock . . . . . . . . . . . . . . . . . . . . . . . . . . . .        20,000
    Gain on sale of marketable equity securities . . . . . . . .         600
```

Note that the entry made at the time of sale makes no adjustment for previously recorded unrealized gains or losses or for the allowance account. These accounts are adjusted at the end of the period when the aggregate cost and market values of the securities held are compared.

**Long-Term
Investments
in Stock**

Investments in stocks which are not held as temporary investments are classified as long-term assets. Such investments are recorded at their cost as of the date of acquisition. This cost includes the purchase price of the shares plus all brokerage fees, transfer costs, and excise taxes paid by the purchaser. The accounting treatment for long-term investments subsequent to acquisition is generally a function of the degree of ownership interest one corporation (investor) acquires in the other corporation (investee). For purposes of determining the appropriate accounting treatment, long-term investments in common stock may be classified according to the percentage of stock owned by the investor: (1) more than 50 percent ownership; (2) ownership of between 20 percent and 50 percent; (3) ownership of less than 20 percent. When an investor corporation acquires more than 50 percent of the common stock of another corporation, *Consolidated Financial Statements* which treat the investor and investee corporations as a single business entity are normally prepared. The details involved in the preparation of such statements are presented and discussed later in this chapter. However, whether or not consolidated statements are prepared, the investment must still be accounted for in the investor corporation's books. Depending upon the particular circumstances of the investment, there are three methods which may be used in accounting for long-term investments in stock: (1) *the cost method*—the investment is valued at the original acquisition cost; (2) *the lower of cost or market method*—similar to the cost method except the investments are reflected in the balance sheet at the lower of the aggregate cost or market value of the securities; (3) *the equity method*—the investment is valued so as to reflect changes in the underlying net assets of the investee corporation.

The cost method is based on the fact that the two corporations are separate legal entities. Therefore, the carrying value of the investment included in the accounts of the investor remains at the original cost. Any changes in the underlying net assets of the investee corporation which may have occurred as a result of its operations are ignored under this method. The logic underlying the lower of cost or market method is similar to that of the cost method—that is, since both the investor and investee are viewed as separate entities, dividends are recorded as income when received and a gain or loss on the investment is not recognized until the time of disposition. The difference in the methods is that in the lower of cost or market method a year-end adjustment is used to reflect the investment at the lower of aggregate cost or aggregate market value. The equity method, on the other hand, is intended to reflect the economic relationship which exists between the two companies. This method recognizes that an investment in stock which allows the investor company to exercise significant control or influence over the operations of the investee company should be accounted for in such a way that changes in the underlying net assets of the investee company are reflected in the accounts of the investor company.

The choice between the methods was, for all practical purposes, optional prior to the issuance of *Opinion No. 18* of the Accounting Principles Board in 1971. However, the Board stated in this Opinion that the equity method should be used if the investment in stock enables the investor company to exercise significant influence over the operating and financial policies of an investee. The Board assumed that, in the absence of evidence to the contrary, ownership of 20 percent or more of the voting stock of an investee represented evidence of the ability of the investor company to exercise significant influence over the activities of the investee firm. Thus, the cost method or the lower of cost or market method would normally be used for an investment of less than 20 percent of the voting common stock and the equity method would be used for an investment of 20 percent or more of the voting stock of an investee. Most investments in preferred stocks (regardless of the percentage ownership) would also be accounted for by either the cost method or lower of cost or market method because preferred stock does not normally have voting rights. For investments of less than 20 percent of the common stock or investments in preferred stock, the lower of cost or market method must be used to account for investments in marketable equity securities. Generally, a security is classified as "marketable" if there is a currently available sales price in the securities market. The cost method is appropriate for investments in nonmarketable securities which are not required to be accounted for under the equity method. In summary, long-term investments in stock are accounted for as follows:

Investment	*Method*
Ownership of 20 percent or more of the common stock............................	Equity
Ownership of less than 20 percent of the common stock and ownership of preferred stock in the form of marketable equity securities......................	Lower of Cost or Market
Ownership of less than 20 percent of the common stock and ownership of preferred stock in the form of non-marketable securities............................	Cost

To illustrate the use of the lower of cost or market method, assume that Winston Company made the following long-term investments in marketable equity securities during 19x1:

1. Purchased 100 shares of IBM Common Stock at a price of $20,000 including commissions.
2. Purchased 100 shares of AT&T Common Stock at a price of $10,000 including commissions.

On December 31, 19x1, Winston Company determined the following information regarding its investments:

Investment	Cost	Market Value	Difference
IBM Stock	$20,000	$19,000	($1,000)
AT&T Stock	10,000	10,500	500
	$30,000	$29,500	($500)

As is the case with the application of the lower of cost or market rule to temporary investments in marketable equity securities, when market value is less than cost, this difference is recorded in an allowance account which is offset against the investment account on the balance sheet. However, unlike temporary investments, this decrease is not reflected as an "unrealized loss" in the income statement. Rather, a separate allowance account with a debit balance is used and this account is shown as a deduction from stockholders' equity in the balance sheet. The following journal entry would be required at December 31, 19x1:

Allowance for net unrealized loss on long-term investments......... 500
    Allowance for decline in value of long-term investments..........   500

If the market value of the Winston Company portfolio of long-term investments in marketable equity securities increases in a subsequent period, the above entry would be reversed to the extent of the increase or to bring the allowance accounts to zero, whichever is less. That is, if market value should exceed cost in a future period, the allowance accounts are eliminated. The procedures which are employed in accounting for each of these two methods are summarized below.

Cost Method. Under the cost method, the investment account is carried at the original cost of the investment. Any increases or decreases in the net assets of the investee company resulting from earnings or losses do not affect the investor company's investment account. Dividends received by the investor company are recorded as dividend income.

Equity Method. Under the equity method, the investment is initially recorded at its original cost. After acquisition, the investment account is adjusted for any increases or decreases in the net assets of the investee company which have occurred since the stock was acquired. Net income of the investee results in an increase in its net assets. Therefore, the investor company increases the carrying value of its investment and recognizes investment income to the extent of its share (determined by the percentage of the investee's stock owned by the investor company) of the net income of the investee. For example, assume that an investor firm owned 20 percent of the outstanding voting stock of an investee. If the investee reported earnings of $50,000, the investor would increase the carrying value of its investment by $10,000 and simultaneously recognize investment income of $10,000. Similarly, a net loss incurred by the investee company would result in a reduction of the investment account and the recognition of a loss on investments by the investor firm. Since dividends also reduce the net assets of the investee, any dividend distributions made to the investor are recorded by a decrease in the investment account balance. The effect of the equity method is to value the investment at the original cost plus the investor's share of the undistributed retained earnings (net income less dividends) of the investee company since its acquisition of the stock.

To illustrate the difference between the cost and the equity methods, assume that Stolle Company purchases 1,000 of the 5,000 outstanding shares of Most Company stock on January 1, 19x1, at a cost of $10 per share. During 19x1, Most Company reports net income of $20,000 and pays dividends of $10,000, and during 19x2 Most Company reports a net loss of $5,000 and pays no dividends. The journal entries of Stolle Company under both the cost and the equity methods are shown on the following page.

These entries have the following effect on the financial statements of Stolle Company as of the end of 19x2.

	Cost Method	Equity Method
Investment in Most Company		
December 31, 19x2..................	$10,000	$11,000
Income Statement:		
19x1	2,000	4,000
19x2	0	(1,000)

Under the cost method, Stolle Company would report its investment in Most Company at December 31, 19x2, at its original cost of $10,000. Under the equity method the investment would be carried at $11,000. The $1,000 increase in the investment account under the equity method reflects Stolle Company's share (20 percent) of the $5,000 increase in the net assets of Most Company since the time the Most Company stock was acquired by Stolle.

Under the cost method, the investor recognizes income only to the extent of assets received from the investee (i.e., dividends). The equity method, on the other hand, recognizes income to the extent of the investor's share of the net income of the investee company, whether or not dividends were received.

Event	Cost Method	Equity Method
January 1, 19x1 Acquisition of 1,000 shares of the common stock of Most Company	Investment in Most Company.... 10,000 Cash.......................... 10,000	Investment in Most Company... 10,000 Cash.......................... 10,000
December 31, 19x1 Net income of $20,000 reported by Most Company	No Entry	Investment in Most Company.... 4,000 Investment income........... 4,000 To record Stolle Company's $4,000 share (20% × $20,000) of Most Company's net income.
June 30, 19x2 Stolle Company received dividends of $2,000. (20% of $10,000 dividend paid by Most Company.)	Cash........... 2,000 Dividend income.......... 2,000	Cash............. 2,000 Investment in Most Company...... 2,000
December 31, 19x2 Net loss of $5,000 reported by Most Company	No Entry	Investment loss............. 1,000 Investment in Most Company... 1,000 To record Stolle Company's $1,000 share (20% × $5,000) of Most Company's $5,000 net loss.

When the long-term investment is in the form of marketable equity securities and the use of the equity method is not appropriate, the lower of cost or market method must be used. The application of this method to the aggregate long-term equity securities is basically similar to the procedures used for short-term investments which were discussed previously. The major difference is that the changes in the valuation allowance account for the noncurrent investment in marketable equity securities is recorded as a contra account (reduction) in stockholders' equity rather than as an unrealized loss or gain to be reported in the income statement.

CONSOLIDATED FINANCIAL STATEMENTS

In many instances, investments in stock are made to secure ownership of a controlling interest in the voting stock of another company. A firm owning a majority of the voting stock of another company is usually referred to as a *parent company*; the company whose stock is owned is called the *subsidiary company*. A parent company and one or more of its related subsidiary companies are usually referred to as *affiliated companies*. Since a parent and its subsidiary are separate legal entities, separate financial statements are prepared for the stockholders and creditors of each company.

The relationship between a parent and its subsidiary is disclosed in the parent company's financial statements in the investment in stock account. However, parent company statements do not reflect the complete economic effect of the parent's ownership of the subsidiary. Therefore, it is often useful to prepare financial statements based on the financial position and operating results of the combined affiliated companies as if they were a single economic entity. The combined financial statements of two or more affiliated companies are called *consolidated statements*. Consolidated statements provide the stockholders and creditors of the parent company with an overall view of the combined financial position and operating activities of the parent company and its subsidiaries.

There are a variety of economic, legal, and tax advantages which encourage large organizations to operate through a group of affiliated corporations, rather than a single legal entity. For example, the financial statements of General Motors Corporation, which are reproduced in the appendix, are consolidated financial statements.

Two basic criteria are used in deciding whether or not to prepare consolidated statements. The subsidiary company must be under the continuing control of the parent and the activities of the affiliated companies must be similar. There is no general agreement among accountants as to the percentage ownership which gives the parent company sufficient control to influence the activities of a subsidiary. In many cases, however, ownership of a majority of the voting stock of a subsidiary is considered to be adequate evidence of the ability to control a subsidiary for the purpose of deciding whether or not to prepare consolidated statements. If the operations of the parent and subsidiary companies are unrelated (for example, a bank owning a manufacturing concern), consolidated statements should not be prepared even if the parent owns a majority of the voting stock of the subsidiary. An evaluation of the relationship between the operations of the two firms is based primarily upon the nature of the business activities and the structure of their respective financial statements. For example, consolidated statements prepared for a retail firm that held a controlling interest in an insurance company would normally be of little value to the user of such statements.

From a legal standpoint, a subsidiary company is a separate entity. Accordingly, the subsidiary maintains its own accounting records and prepares separate financial statements. However, since the parent owns a majority of the voting stock of its subsidiary, the parent and subsidiary companies are a business entity under common control. Therefore, individual financial statements of the parent and subsidiary do not provide a comprehensive view of the financial position of the affiliated companies as a single economic unit. Consolidated financial statements, which ignore the legal distinction between the parent and its subsidiary, serve this purpose by reflecting the financial position and results of operations of the affiliated companies as a single economic entity.

Consolidated Balance Sheet at Date of Acquisition

In preparing a consolidated balance sheet, the accounts which are included in the individual parent and subsidiary company records are combined. In the process of this combination, however, certain adjustments must be made to avoid duplication or double-counting in determining the balances to be used. For example, the investment account of the parent company reflects its equity in the net assets of the subsidiary. Including both the parent company's investment account and the net assets of the subsidiary in a consolidated statement would result in double-counting the net assets of the subsidiary. Therefore, the parent's investment account should not be included in the consolidated statements. Since the stockholder's equity of the subsidiary is represented by the investment account, it should also be excluded from the consolidated financial statement. The investment of the parent company is referred to as the reciprocal of the stockholders' equity of the subsidiary. Therefore, these accounts and any other reciprocal accounts which may exist as a result of transactions between the parent and its subsidiaries must be eliminated in combining the accounts of the parent and subsidiary companies.

Separate financial records are not maintained for the consolidated entity. The amounts reported in consolidated financial statements are determined using a worksheet and combining the amounts of like items from the financial statements of the affiliated companies. Entries included on the consolidation worksheet are made for the sole purpose of preparing consolidated financial statements. Consequently, consolidating adjustments and eliminations are not posted to the books of either the parent or its subsidiary.

Preparation of consolidated balance sheets under varying circumstances is illustrated by the following examples. First, let us consider the process of consolidating two balance sheets at the time a parent company initially acquired the stock of a subsidiary company.

Complete Ownership Acquired at Book Value. Assume that the parent company, P, acquired 100 percent of the common stock of a subsidiary company, S, at a price of $20,000 on December 31, 19x1. Separate balance sheets of P Company and S Company immediately following the acquisition are presented in Illustration 1.

Illustration 1

P Company and S Company
Balance Sheets
At December 31, 19x1

	P Company	S Company
Cash	$ 10,000	$ 5,000
Accounts receivable	10,000	5,000
Fixed assets	60,000	20,000
Investment in S Company	20,000	-0-
Total Assets	$100,000	$30,000
Accounts payable	$ 10,000	$10,000
Capital stock	60,000	15,000
Retained earnings	30,000	5,000
Total Liabilities and Equities	$100,000	$30,000

P Company paid an amount equal to the stockholders' equity (common stock and retained earnings) of the subsidiary for 100 percent ownership of S. This indicates that the acquisition was made at the book value of the subsidiary's net assets. Since no transactions have occurred between the companies, the only adjustment required is to eliminate the investment account of the parent against the stockholders' equity accounts of the subsidiary, as shown in Illustration 2.

As previously indicated, the elimination entry is made on a worksheet which is used in order to facilitate the preparation of the consolidated balance sheet. No entries are made in the accounting records of either the parent or the subsidiary.

Complete Ownership Acquired at More than Net Asset Value. In most cases when the parent acquires stock in a subsidiary, the cost of the investment will differ from the recorded value of the net assets (assets less liabilities) of the subsidiary. From a consolidated standpoint, the purchase

Illustration 2

P Company and S Company
Consolidation Worksheet
At December 31, 19x1

	P Co.	S Co.	Eliminations Dr.	Eliminations Cr.	Con-solidation
Cash	$ 10,000	$ 5,000			$ 15,000
Accounts receivable	10,000	5,000			15,000
Fixed assets	60,000	20,000			80,000
Investment in S Company	20,000			$20,000 (a)	
Total Assets	$100,000	$30,000			$110,000
Accounts payable	$ 10,000	$10,000			$ 20,000
Capital stock	60,000	15,000	$15,000 (a)		60,000
Retained earnings	30,000	5,000	5,000 (a)		30,000
Total Liabilities and Equity	$100,000	$30,000			$110,000

a Elimination of the investment account against book value of the subsidiary's stock.

of subsidiary stock may be regarded as similar to the purchase of the subsidiary's net assets (i.e., its assets less liabilities). Consequently, subsidiary assets should be recorded at an amount equal to the price paid by the parent for its 100 percent interest in the subsidiary. To adjust the carrying values of subsidiary assets to reflect the price paid by the parent for the stock, information concerning the fair values of the subsidiary assets at the time of acquisition must be obtained.

The amount paid by the parent company for the subsidiary's stock may differ from the net asset value of the subsidiary for two primary reasons. First, subsidiary assets may have a fair market value which differs from their recorded book value. This may occur because the accounting methods used for recording assets are normally not intended to reflect the fair value of the assets of the firm. Thus, if the parent company pays an amount which is in excess of book value, this excess may exist because the net assets of the subsidiary are undervalued (that is, the book value of the assets determined on the basis of proper accounting methods is less than their fair market value). Also, the excess may be due to the existence of unrecorded intangible assets of the subsidiary or from anticipated advantages which are expected because of the affiliation. If the assets of the subsidiary are undervalued, any specific tangible or intangible assets with fair market values in excess of recorded book values should be restated at fair market value in the consolidation worksheet. Thus, identifiable assets will be reported in the consolidated balance sheet at an amount equal to their fair market values at the date of acquisition. If the cost of the subsidiary stock still exceeds the amount assigned to the net assets of the subsidiary in the consolidation worksheet, this excess is assigned to an intangible asset, Goodwill or "Excess of Cost Over Book Value." Therefore, the total excess of the cost of the subsidiary stock over the book value of the subsidiary's net assets is included among consolidated assets—either as increases in the value of specific assets or alternatively as goodwill. Again, it is important to note that these adjustments are made only in the consolidation worksheet.

To illustrate, assume the same facts as in the previous illustration except that P Company acquired all of the stock of S Company at a cost of $25,000. Thus, the cost of investment ($25,000) exceeds the stockholders' equity of the subsidiary ($20,000) by $5,000. Apparently the management of P Company believes that the fair value of specific assets of S Company is greater than their recorded book value or that there are advantages of affiliation, such as future earnings prospects, which justify payment of $5,000 in excess of book value for S Company's net assets. In this illustration, assume that the excess of cost over book value existed because the fair market value of S Company's land exceeded its recorded book value by $5,000. Therefore, this excess would be assigned to land (which is summarized in fixed assets in this example) in the consolidation worksheet. The consolidation worksheet would be as shown in Illustration 3. The eliminating entries on the consolidation worksheet would be:

(a)	Fixed Assets–S Company	5,000	
	Investment in S Company		5,000
(b)	Capital Stock–S Company	15,000	
	Retained Earnings–S Company	5,000	
	Investment in S Company		20,000

Again, it is important to note that these entries would not appear in the accounts of either P Company or S Company. These are worksheet entries that would be used to facilitate the consolidation of the financial reports of the parent and subsidiary company.

If the excess cannot be assigned to any specific assets (that is, the recorded book values of the subsidiary assets are equal to their fair values at acquisition), the $5,000 excess would have been reported in the consolidated balance sheet as Goodwill or "Excess of Cost Over Book Value." This is a new account which is introduced in the consolidated worksheet—it does not appear in the accounts of either P or S.

Complete Ownership Acquired for Less than Net Asset Value. If the cost of the stock acquired by the parent company is less than book value, a similar problem exists. When specific overvalued assets can be

---

Illustration 3

P Company and S Company
Consolidation Worksheet
At December 31, 19x1

	P Co.	S Co.	Eliminations Dr.	Eliminations Cr.	Con-solidation
Cash	$ 5,000	$ 5,000			$ 10,000
Accounts receivable.	10,000	5,000			15,000
Fixed assets	60,000	20,000	$ 5,000(a)		85,000
Investment in S Company	25,000			{$ 5,000(a) 20,000(b)	
Total Assets	$100,000	$30,000			$110,000
Accounts payable.	$ 10,000	$10,000			$ 20,000
Capital stock.	60,000	15,000	15,000(b)		60,000
Retained earnings.	30,000	5,000	5,000(b)		30,000
Total Liabilities and Equity	$100,000	$30,000			$110,000

ᵃ Adjustment for undervaluation of Subsidiary's assets.
ᵇ Elimination of the investment against the book value of the Subsidiary's stock.

---

identified, the excess would be reflected on the balance sheet by reducing the value of specific assets of the subsidiary. Thus, subsidiary assets would be reported at their fair values in the consolidated balance sheet. When specific assets which are overvalued cannot be identified, the excess is used to reduce noncurrent assets. If the allocation reduces the noncurrent assets to zero, the remainder of the excess is credited to an account referred to as "Excess of Book Value of Subsidiary Interest Over Cost." This account is shown as a reduction of assets on the consolidated balance sheet. For example, assume P Company purchased 100 percent of the stock of S Company at a price of $18,000 on December 31, 19x1. At that date the stockholders' equity of S Company was $20,000, consisting of $15,000 capital stock and $5,000 retained earnings. Eliminating entries on the con-solidation worksheet would be as follows:

(a)	Investment in S Company	2,000	
	Specific Assets of S Company.		2,000
(b)	Capital Stock –S Company.	15,000	
	Retained Earnings—S Company.	5,000	
	Investment in S Company (from P's books).		20,000

Less Than Complete Ownership.   A parent company may obtain control of a subsidiary by acquiring less than 100 percent of the capital stock of the subsidiary. When a parent owns less than 100 percent of the stock, the remainder of the stock held by stockholders outside the affiliated companies is classified as a *minority interest* in the consolidated balance sheet. The existence of a minority interest does not affect the amount at which the assets and liabilities of the affiliated companies will ultimately appear on the consolidated balance sheet. However, only a portion of the equity in the net assets of the subsidiary company is owned by the parent since a portion of the owners' equity is held by minority stockholders. Equity held by minority stockholders, or minority interest, is a part of the stockholders' equity of the consolidated entity.

To illustrate, assume that P Company acquired only 90 percent of the capital stock of the subsidiary at a cost of $18,000. The remaining 10 percent of the subsidiary's stock represents the minority interest in S Company. The only change required in the elimination entries is that only 90 percent of the capital stock and retained earnings of S Company is eliminated. The remaining 10 percent of S Company stockholders' equity represents the minority interest in the subsidiary and is classified as such in the consolidated balance sheet. The consolidated worksheet used to prepare the consolidated balance sheet is shown in Illustration 4.

The initial consolidation entry (a) eliminated 90 percent of the capital stock and retained earnings of S Company against the investment account of the parent. The remaining 10 percent of the stockholders' equity of S Company was then reclassified as a minority interest in entry (b).

It should be noted that, in this example, the parent company paid an amount which was equal to book value for its interest in the subsidiary. Therefore, the investment account was exactly equal to 90 percent of the stockholders' equity of S Company at acquisition. The existence of a minority interest, however, would not affect the procedures which are required when the investment is acquired at either more or less than book value. Any difference between the cost of the investment and the amount representing the parent company's interest in the stockholders' equity of the subsidiary increases consolidated assets if cost exceeds book value, and reduces consolidated assets if cost is less than book value.

Consolidated Balance Sheet after the Date of Acquisition

Net assets of a subsidiary change subsequent to the date of affiliation as a result of the difference between the net income earned and the dividends paid by the subsidiary since the date the parent acquired its interest in the subsidiary. If the parent company carries its investment using the equity method, the parent's share of such changes in the net assets of a subsidiary is reflected in the investment account. This occurs because the parent company increases the investment account and records investment

Illustration 4

P Company and S Company
Consolidation Worksheet
At December 31, 19x1

	P Co.	S Co.	Eliminations Dr.	Eliminations Cr.	Con-solidation
Cash	$ 12,000	$ 5,000			$ 17,000
Accounts receivable.	10,000	5,000			15,000
Fixed assets	60,000	20,000			80,000
Investment in S Company	18,000			$18,000(a)	
Total Assets	$100,000	$30,000			$112,000
Accounts payable.	$ 10,000	$10,000			$ 20,000
Capital stock.	60,000	15,000	$ 1,500(b) / 13,500(a)		60,000
Retained earnings.	30,000	5,000	500(b) / 4,500(a)		30,000
Minority interest	–0–	–0–		2,000(b)	2,000
Total Liabilities and Equity	$100,000	$30,000			$112,000

a Elimination of investment against 90 percent of the Subsidiary's stockholders' equity.
b Adjustment to reclassify 10 percent of the Subsidiary's stockholders' equity as minority interest.

income for its share of subsidiary earnings and reduces the investment account for any dividends which it receives from the subsidiary. Similarly, a loss incurred by the subsidiary is recorded by the parent as a decrease in the investment account and a corresponding decrease in the parent company's earnings. At any time subsequent to the date of affiliation, the change in the parent's investment account for each year must be equal to the parent company's share (that is, the parent company's percentage ownership of the voting stock of its subsidiary) of the change in the retained earnings of the subsidiary company. The eliminations which are required in order to prepare a consolidated balance sheet are basically the same as those which were required at the date of acquisition except that the amount eliminated from the investment account of the parent and the stockholders' equity of the subsidiary will change each year. Since the two entries which are made in the elimination of the parent's investment account against the stockholders' equity of the subsidiary will change by the same amount, the original difference between the cost of the investment and the book value of the subsidiary will be the same for each period.

To illustrate the procedures required for the preparation of a worksheet for a consolidated balance sheet, assume that P Company purchases 90 percent of the outstanding stock of S Company on December 31, 19x1, at a price of $21,000. At that time, S Company had capital stock of $15,000 and retained earnings of $5,000. Therefore, the cost of the investment exceeded the book value of the subsidiary stock by $3,000 (the book value of the net assets purchased was 90% × $20,000 or $18,000). It was determined that this excess of cost over book value was attributed to the excess of the market value of land owned by the subsidiary over the book value of the land. Further, assume that the subsidiary company had net income of $20,000 and paid dividends totaling $10,000 during 19x2. The effect of these transactions is to increase the retained earnings of the subsidiary by $10,000, from $5,000 to $15,000 (retained earnings on December 31, 19x1, of $5,000 plus 19x2, net income of $20,000 minus 19x2 dividends of $10,000). Similarly, net income and dividends paid by the subsidiary will cause a net increase of $9,000 in the parent company's investment account (90% of $20,000 net income minus 90% of the $10,000 dividends). The remaining 10 percent of the increase in the subsidiary's retained earnings represents an increase in the equity of the minority stockholders and would be classified as such. The worksheet (Illustration 5) for consolidation illustrates the procedures which are required in preparing a consolidated balance sheet (Illustration 6) one year after the date of acquisition of the subsidiary.

OTHER RECIPROCAL ACCOUNTS

In preparing a consolidated balance sheet, the investment account of the parent company must be eliminated against the stockholders' equity accounts of its subsidiary. If any transactions occurred between the parent and subsidiary companies, there might be additional reciprocal accounts which would also be eliminated in the consolidation worksheet in order to avoid the double counting of assets and liabilities.

One of the most common of these additional reciprocal accounts involves intercompany receivables and payables. If one affiliated company borrows from another, the debtor firm incurs a liability (payable) equal to an asset (receivable) of the creditor company. From a consolidated standpoint, the payable does not represent an amount owed to an entity outside the affiliated group, nor does the related asset represent a receivable from an outside group. Therefore, in the consolidation worksheet, both the reciprocal asset and liability should be eliminated.

To illustrate this point, assume that the parent company owes the subsidiary company $5,000 as of December 31, 19x2. The following entry would be made on the consolidation worksheet in order to eliminate the reciprocal accounts:

Accounts payable—P Company	5,000	
Accounts receivable—S Company		5,000

Illustration 5

P Company and S Company
Consolidation Worksheet
At December 31, 19x2

	P Co.	S Co.	Eliminations Dr.	Eliminations Cr.	Consolidations
Cash	$ 10,000	$ 7,000			$ 17,000
Accounts receivable.........	10,000	6,000			16,000
Fixed assets	70,000	20,000	$ 3,000 (a)	$ 3,000 (a)	93,000
Investment in S Company	30,000			27,000 (b)	
Total Assets...........	$120,000	$33,000			$126,000
Accounts payable..........	$ 15,000	$ 3,000			$ 18,000
Capital stock...........	60,000	15,000	1,500 (c) / 13,500 (b)		60,000
Retained earnings.........	45,000	15,000	1,500 (c) / 13,500 (b)		45,000
Minority interest				3,000 (c)	3,000
Total Liabilities and Equity	$120,000	$33,000			$126,000

ᵃ Adjustment for undervaluaton of Subsidiary's assets.
ᵇ Elimination of investment against 90% of the Subsidiary's Stockholders' equity.
ᶜ Adjustment to reclassify 10% of the Subsidiary's stockholders' equity as minority interest.

Illustration 6

P Company and S Company
Consolidated Balance Sheet
At December 31, 19x2

Current assets:		
Cash	$17,000	
Accounts receivable	16,000	
Total current assets		$ 33,000
Fixed assets		93,000
Total Assets.................		$126,000
Liabilities:		
Accounts payable.................		$ 18,000
Minority interest in S Co.		3,000
Stockholders' equity:		
Capital stock	$60,000	
Retained earnings..................	45,000	$105,000
Total Liabilities and Equities		$126,000

POOLING OF INTEREST

In the discussion of consolidated statements included in the preceeding section of this chapter, it was assumed that the parent company purchased the stock of the subsidiary with cash or other assets. The consolidated statements were prepared on the premise that the purchase of stock represented a purchase of the underlying net assets of the subsidiary. Therefore, in the consolidated statements, the cost of the acquisition was allocated to the individual assets of the subsidiary with any excess reported as "excess of cost over book value."

A subsidiary may also be acquired by the exchange of the parent's stock for the stock of the subsidiary. Under certain circumstances, this combination may be accounted for as a *pooling of interests*. Because the stockholders of the subsidiary become stockholders of the parent company, one group has not acquired the interests of the other. Rather, both have "pooled" their interests in a combined entity. A pooling of interests unites the ownership interests of two or more firms by the exchange of stock. A purchase transaction is not recognized because the combination is accomplished without disbursing the assets of either company. A key feature of a pooling is that the former ownership interests continue and the basis of accounting remains the same.

Since no purchase is recognized and basically the same ownership interests continue, there is no justification for revaluing assets in a pooling of interests. All assets and liabilities of the companies are carried forward to the consolidated statements at their recorded book value. The parent company records the acquisition by debiting the investment account for the par value of the stock issued. Since assets and liabilities are combined at their recorded amounts, there is no excess of cost over book value to be accounted for in the consolidated statements. In addition, retained earnings of the subsidiary at acquisition may be combined with the parent's retained earnings in determining consolidated retained earnings.

To illustrate, assume that P Company issued 1,000 shares of its $50 par value stock in exchange for all of the stock of S Company. Assume that S Company has 6,000 shares of $10 par value stock outstanding. The parent company records the acquisition at the par value of the stock issued as follows:

Investment in S Company.....................	50,000	
Capital stock.............................		50,000

Under the pooling of interests method, the fair values of the subsidiary's assets are not considered to be relevant for purposes of consolidation. Therefore, the entry required on the worksheet eliminates the investment account of the parent company against the capital stock of the subsidiary. The consolidation worksheet at the date of acquisition is shown in Illustration 7. Since the par value of the stock issued by the parent ($50,000)

Illustration 7

P Company and S Company
Consolidation Worksheet
At January 1, 19x2

	P Co.	S Co.	Eliminations Dr.	Eliminations Cr.	Con-solidations
Other assets	$250,000	$120,000			$370,000
Investment in S Co..	50,000	-0-		$50,000(a)	-0-
Total	$300,000	$120,000			$370,000
Liabilities	$ 30,000	$ 20,000			$ 50,000
Capital stock—					
P Co. ($50 par value). . . .	150,000	-0-			150,000
S Co. ($10 par value). . . .	-0-	60,000	$60,000(a)		-0-
Capital in excess of					
par value	50,000	-0-		10,000(a)	60,000
Retained earnings	70,000	40,000			110,000
Total	$300,000	$120,000			$370,000

ª Elimination of investment account against an equal amount of stockholders' equity.

is less than the par value of the shares acquired ($60,000), the difference was shown as an addition to capital in excess of par value in the consolidated balance sheet. If the par value of the stock issued exceeds the par value of the shares acquired, the difference may be charged or debited to capital in excess of par value. If capital in excess is insufficient to absorb the difference, the remainder may be charged against retained earnings.

Note that combining the parent and subsidiary retained earnings accounts is allowable under the pooling method. In the example, consolidated retained earnings at acquisition ($110,000) was equal to the sum of the parent's and subsidiary's retained earnings balances. Consolidated retained earnings may be less than the sum of the retained earnings balances if the par value of the stock issued by the parent is more than the par value of the shares acquired and if there is insufficient capital in excess of par value to absorb this difference.

Prior to 1970, accountants often considered the purchase and pooling of interests method to be acceptable alternatives for accounting for any given business combination. The pooling of interests method was popular because in circumstances where the fair value of the subsidiary assets exceeds the recorded book values, the pooling treatment results in higher future net income and earnings per share to be reported than does the purchase method. In addition, pooling normally causes higher retained earnings than the purchase method. The Accounting Principles Board, however, attempted to resolve this problem by issuing *Opinion No. 16*. With respect to the purchase versus pooling issue, the Board concluded that ". . . the purchase method and the pooling of interests method are both acceptable in accounting for business combinations, although not as alternatives in accounting for the same business combinations." The Board specified the conditions under which each of the two methods is applicable to a business combination.[5]

USEFULNESS OF CONSOLIDATED STATEMENTS

In a situation where one corporation owns a majority of the voting stock of one or more other corporations, financial statements which are prepared for the separate legal corporate entities may not provide the most useful information to management, stockholders, and potential investors of the parent company. Instead, these users are interested in the financial position and results of operations of the combined entity, i.e., the parent company and all other companies under the control of the parent.

On the other hand, minority stockholders of a subsidiary company ordinarily have little use for consolidated financial statements. Since minority stockholders are primarily concerned with their ownership in the subsidiary company, separate financial statements of the subsidiary are usually more useful to them. Similarly, creditors of either the parent or a subsidiary are primarily concerned with their individual legal claims. Therefore, separate financial statements based on the individual entities concerned are of primary interest to these creditors.

CONSOLIDATED INCOME STATEMENT

A consolidated income statement is prepared by combining the revenues and expenses of the parent and subsidiary companies. If the parent company owns 100 percent of the subsidiary stock and there have been no transactions between the parent and its subsidiary, consolidation is simply a combination of revenues and expenses resulting from the parent and subsidiary companies' operations. The only adjustment necessary is that which is required in order to eliminate the investment income of the parent company (the parent company's share of the subsidiary's net income). This amount must be eliminated in order to avoid duplication or double-counting of earnings in the consolidated income statement.

As in the case of the consolidated balance sheet, elimination of reciprocal accounts may be necessary in order to avoid duplication or double-counting of revenues and expenses resulting from transactions which have

---

[5] Discussion of the specific criteria for purchase vs. pooling is beyond the scope of this text.

occurred between the parent and its subsidiary. For example, interest expense of one company and interest income of the other resulting from an intercompany loan are eliminated because they do not change the net assets of the total entity from a consolidated viewpoint.

MINORITY INTEREST

If the parent owns less than 100 percent of the subsidiary stock, an additional adjustment is required in the consolidated worksheet in order to allocate the net income of the subsidiary between the parent company and the minority stockholders of the subsidiary. This division of the consolidated income is based on the percentage of the subsidiary stock owned by the parent company and the minority stockholders.

To illustrate the consolidation procedure for the income statement, again assume that P Company purchased 90 percent of the stock of S Company on December 31, 19x2. The 19x2 income statement for P Company is presented in Illustration 8. Also, assume that the parent rents a building to its subsidiary at a rental of $5,000 per year. The procedures which are necessary in order to prepare a consolidated income statement are illustrated in the consolidated worksheet in Illustration 9. It should be noted that the worksheet has a self balancing format. That is, the net income figures have been included along with the expenses so that the revenues are equal to income plus expenses.

Elimination (a) removes the duplication or double-counting effect of the intercompany building rental. This entry has no effect on consolidated net income since it simply offsets rent revenue of P Company against an

---

Illustration 8

P Company and S Company
Income Statements
For the Year Ended December 31, 19x2

	P Company	S Company
Revenues:		
Sales	$195,000	$100,000
Rent revenue	5,000	0
Investment income	18,000	0
Total Revenues	$218,000	$100,000
Expenses:		
Cost of goods sold	$150,000	$ 70,000
Other expenses	20,000	10,000
Total Expenses	$170,000	$ 80,000
Net Income	$ 48,000	$ 20,000

Illustration 9

P Company and S Company
Consolidation Worksheet
At December 31, 19x2

	P Co.	S Co.	Eliminations Dr.	Eliminations Cr.	Consolidations
Sales	$195,000	$100,000			$295,000
Rent revenue	5,000	0	$ 5,000(a)		
Investment income	18,000	0	18,000(b)		
Total revenues.	$218,000	$100,000			$295,000
Cost of goods sold	$150,000	$ 70,000			$220,000
Other expenses	20,000	10,000		$ 5,000(a)	25,000
Net income—P Co.	48,000				48,000
Net income—S Co.		20,000		{ 2,000(c) 18,000(b)	
Minority interest in net income			2,000(c)		2,000
Total expenses and net income	$218,000	$100,000			$295,000

a Elimination of intercompany rent revenue and rent expense.
b Elimination of investment income against 90 percent of subsidiary net income.
c Adjustment to reclassify 10 percent of the subsidiary's net income as minority interest.

equal amount of rent expense of S Company. Elimination (b) cancels the investment income which P Company records as its share of the net income of S Company under the equity method. This entry corrects the double-counting of S Company's net income. Elimination (c) allocates 10 percent of S Company's net income to the minority stockholders of the subsidiary company.

The amounts in the consolidation column of the worksheet are used in order to prepare the consolidated income statement in Illustration 10. Notice that the minority interest in net income is treated as a reduction of net income of the consolidated entity to arrive at consolidated net income.

PROFIT ON INTERCOMPANY SALES

An additional problem occurs if the assets which were transferred in intercompany sales were sold at a price which differed from the cost to the selling affiliate. If these assets were not resold by the end of the period, the gain or loss on the sale between the affiliates must be eliminated in

---

Illustration 10

P Company and Subsidiary
Consolidated Income Statement
For the Year 19x2

Sales	$295,000
Cost of goods sold	220,000
Gross profit	$ 75,000
Other expenses	25,000
Combined net income	$ 50,000
Less minority interest in net income	2,000
Consolidated Net Income	$ 48,000

---

the consolidation process. To illustrate this point, assume that the following transactions take place between a parent company (P) and its subsidiary (S):

1. P purchases two ten-speed bicycles for $100.
2. P sells the two bicycles to S for $120 on account.
3. S sells one of the bicycles to an outsider for $80 in cash.

These entries would be recorded on the books of P and S as follows:

"P" Books			*"S" Books*		
1. Inventory	100		No Entry		
Cash		100			
2. Accounts Receivable	120		Inventories	120	
Sales		120	Accounts Payable		120
Cost of Goods Sold	100				
Inventories		100			
3. No Entry			Cash	80	
			Sales		80
			Cost of Goods Sold	60	
			Inventories		60

As a result of these transactions, there is a receivable of $120 from S on P's books and a payable of $120 to P on S's books. Also, P's books show sales of $120 (to S) and a related cost of goods sold of $100, while S's books show the cost of the bicycle sold to the outsider as $60. The unsold bicycle is carried in S's inventory at a cost of $60.

The problem, in terms of preparing consolidated financial statements, is that the intercompany receivables and payables and the effects of the intercompany sales must be eliminated. Also, the cost of the bicycle remaining in S's inventory must be reduced from $60 to $50 (the cost to P) and the $10 profit on the "sale" of this bicycle by P to S must be eliminated from the net income of P Company. The worksheet entries required to accomplish these objectives are as follows:

Accounts payable......................	120	
Accounts receivable...................		120
Sales................................	120	
Cost of goods sold....................		120
Cost of goods sold....................	10	
Inventories..........................		10

The first entry eliminates the intercompany receivables and payables. The second entry eliminates the intercompany sale and the related cost of goods sold, while the final entry corrects the cost of goods sold (and therefore net income) by eliminating the intercompany profit in the ending inventory.

SUMMARY

To raise additional funds for long-term purposes, a firm may borrow by issuing bonds. Bonds require the firm to pay a definite amount (the face value) at a specified date (the maturity date) and may be traded by the investors until that date. In addition, the firm agrees to make periodic interest payments at a stated rate throughout the life of the liability. Bonds may either be secured by specific assets or, in the case of debenture bonds, by only the general credit rating of the issuing corporation.

Since bonds may be traded by investors, the actual selling price received by the issuing corporation may vary from face value. If the selling price is less than the face value of the bond, it is said to be selling at a discount and if the selling price is greater than face value, at a premium. This discount or premium is amortized over the life of the bond and results in either an increase or a decrease in the interest expense incurred on the bond issue.

Bonds may be retired prior to maturity, either by redeeming callable bonds or by repurchasing bonds on the open market. In either case it may be necessary for the firm to recognize either a gain or loss on the early retirement of the debt, depending on the repurchase price. A firm may be required to provide investors with a degree of security, either by periodically setting aside funds in a sinking fund or by making an appropriation of retained earnings.

Companies often make temporary investments in marketable securities to obtain productive use of seasonal excesses of cash. Temporary investments are considered current assets and include both stocks and bonds that are readily salable. Because of this liquidity, careful control should be exercised over the investment documents. Marketable securities are typically valued at cost, but FASB *Statement 12* requires that marketable equity securities be valued in the aggregate at the lower of cost or market for financial reporting purposes.

Corporations often make long-term investments in the stocks and bonds of other corporations. Since bonds may be purchased for an amount greater or lesser than face value, the acquiring company will amortize the resulting bond premium or discount. This amortization is recorded as an adjustment to the interest income earned on the bond. When bonds are purchased or sold between interest dates, the firm must calculate the amount of interest receivable being purchased or sold. In the case of a sale, the firm may also recognize a resulting gain or loss.

Investments in the securities of other corporations are recorded at the purchaser's cost. If there is no significant relationship between the investor and investee corporations, this acquisition cost will remain as the carrying value of the investment. However, if the investor company may exercise significant control or influence over the investee company (for example, as evidenced by an ownership of 20 percent or more of its voting stock) subsequent increases and decreases in the net assets of the investee must be reflected in the carrying value of the investment on the investor's books.

If two firms are associated in such a manner that one owns a controlling interest in the other, the firms are referred to as affiliated companies. Since these firms remain separate legal entities, separate financial statements are prepared for each company. However, if the subsidiary company is under the continuing control of the parent company and their activities are similar, it may be desirable to prepare consolidated financial statements. When a consolidated balance sheet is prepared at the date of acquisition (unless the purchase price equals the book value of the subsidiary's stock) the subsidiary's assets must be adjusted prior to being combined with the value of the parent's assets. In addition, elimination entries must be made on the worksheet for the parent's investment account and the subsidiary's owners' equity accounts to avoid duplication of information. The elimination entries are varied slightly if the parent company acquires less than complete ownership of the subsidiary. In addition, such a situation will require adjustments to the entries recording changes in the net assets of the subsidiary after acquisition. Regardless of the percentage of ownership by the parent, certain elimination entries may be required on the consolidation worksheet if the affiliated companies engage in business transactions with each other.

A business combination may also be affected by one company exchanging its stock for the stock of another corporation. The former ownership interests continue and the basis for accounting remains the same. Such a situation is referred to as a pooling of interests and requires appropriate worksheet elimination entries prior to final preparation of consolidated statements.

KEY DEFINITIONS

Affiliated companies   A parent company and one or more related subsidiary companies are said to be affiliated.

Amortization of premium or discount   Amortization is the process of allocating a portion of the discount or premium on bonds payable (investment in bonds) to interest expense (revenue).

Bond   A bond is an issuance of debt used as a means of borrowing money for long-term purposes.

Bond discount   The discount is the amount by which the face value of a bond payable exceeds the issue price. A discount occurs when the coupon rate on the bonds is less than the market interest rate at the time the bonds are issued.

Bond premium   The premium is the amount by which the issue price of a bond payable exceeds the face value. A premium occurs when the coupon rate of interest on a bond is higher than the market interest rate at the time of issuance.

Bond sinking fund   A sinking fund is accumulated by the issuing corporation specifically for the repayment of bonds at maturity. A sinking fund may be created voluntarily or required by provisions of the bond issue.

Callable bonds   Callable bonds may be repurchased at the option of the issuing corporation within a specified period at a specified price.

Consolidated statements   Consolidated financial statements present the combined assets, equities, and results of operations of affiliated corporations.

Consolidation worksheet   Consolidation working papers are used in the preparation of consolidated statements for two or more companies. The consolidating adjustments and eliminations are never posted to the books of the individual companies involved, only to the worksheet.

Convertible bonds   Convertible bonds may be exchanged for a specified amount of capital stock at the option of the bondholder.

Cost method   The cost method of accounting is used for an investment in the stock of another company in which the investment account is carried at the original cost and income is recognized when dividends are received.

Coupon bonds   Coupon bonds have interest coupons attached which call for the payment of a specified amount of interest on the interest dates.

Coupon rate   The interest rate specified on the bond is the coupon rate. Periodic interest payments equal the coupon interest rate multiplied by the face amount of the bond.

Debenture bonds   Debenture bonds are not secured by any specific assets of the corporation. Their security is dependent upon the general credit standing of the issuing corporation.

Equity method The equity method of accounting is used for an investment in the stock of another company in which the investment account is adjusted for changes in the net assets of the investee, and income is recognized by the investor company as the investee earns profits or incurs losses.

Long-term investment in stock This involves the acquisition of stock of other corporations as long-term, income-producing investments. Such purchases are often made for the purpose of obtaining a controlling interest in a company or for some other continuing business advantage.

Minority interest Shares held by stockholders of a subsidiary company when the parent acquires less than 100 percent of the subsidiary stock are referred to as a minority interest.

Mortgage A mortgage is a conditional conveyance or transfer of property to a creditor as security for a loan.

Parent company A firm owning a majority of the voting stock of another company is called a parent company.

Pooling of interests Pooling of interests is a method used for recording a business acquisition where the assets and liabilities of the combining companies are combined at their existing book values.

Purchase The purchase method for recording a business acquisition is the use of the cost to the acquiring corporation in valuing the assets of the subsidiary.

Registered bonds Registered bonds have the name of the owner registered with the issuing corporation. Periodic interest payments are mailed directly to the registered owner.

Retirement of bonds Retiring bonds is the process of redeeming bonds or repurchasing bonds in the open market.

Secured bond Secured bonds are secured by prior claim against specific assets of the business in the event that the issuing corporation is unable to make the required interest or principal payments.

Serial bonds Serial bond issues are bonds which mature on several different dates.

Subsidiary company A subsidiary company is a firm which has a majority of its voting stock owned by a parent company.

Temporary investments A temporary investment is a security that is readily salable, and the volume of trading of the security should be such that the sale does not materially affect the market price. In addition, there should be an intention on the part of the investor firm to sell the security in the short run as the need for cash arises.

Term bonds A term bond is a bond issue that matures on a single date.

QUESTIONS

1. Define each of the following terms related to the issue of bonds: (a) debenture, (b) secured, (c) callable, (d) convertible, (e) serial bonds.

2. How are interest payments made to the holders of (a) coupon bonds, and (b) registered bonds?

3. How can bonds be sold when the market interest rate for comparable bonds is higher than the stated contract rate on the bond certificate?

4. How does a discount on the issuance of bonds affect the total cost of borrowing to the issuing corporation?

5. What is the effect of a premium on the interest expense of the company issuing bonds? Explain.

6. What is the effect of a discount on the interest expense of the company issuing bonds? Explain.

7. Give the journal entries required for the amortization of (a) Discount on Bonds Payable and (b) Premium on Bonds Payable.

8. How should Discount on Bonds Payable and Premium on Bonds Payable be classified and presented on the balance sheet?

9. If bonds are issued at a time between interest payment dates, why does the issuing company receive an amount of cash equal to the issue price of the bonds plus the accrued interest?

10. Differentiate between long-term (permanent) and short-term (temporary) investments in stocks.

11. Explain the essential characteristics of the cost method.

12. Explain the essential characteristics of the equity method.

13. Under what circumstances would each of the following methods of accounting for long-term investment in stocks be used: (a) cost method? (b) equity method?

14. Define: (a) parent company, (b) subsidiary company, and (c) affiliated companies.

15. Describe the two essential conditions for the preparation of consolidated financial statements.

16. A consolidated balance sheet prepared for a parent company that owns less than 100 percent of the common stock of the subsidiary shows an item called "minority interest." What is the nature of this balance sheet account, and where does it appear on the consolidated balance sheet?

17. How is the difference between the cost of the subsidiary stock and the book value of the stock at the date of acquisition reported on the consolidated balance sheet?

18. Explain why intercompany debts and receivables should be eliminated in preparing consolidated balance sheets.

19. Why is the investment account of the parent company eliminated in preparing a consolidated balance sheet?

20. What types of users of financial statements are primarily interested in consolidated financial statements?

21. If the parent owns less than 100 percent of the subsidiary stock, the consolidated income statement shows an item called "minority interest in subsidiary income." What does this item represent?

22. Where are the entries recorded for the eliminations that are made in the process of preparing consolidated statements?

EXERCISES

23. Stengel Company has authorization to issue $200,000 of 10-year, 7 percent bonds on January 1, 19x1, with semiannual interest payments on June 30 and December 31. Stengel Company issues $100,000 of the bonds on January 1 at face value. Another $100,000 of bonds are issued on August 1, 19x1, at face value plus accrued interest. Assume Stengel Company's accounting period ends March 31.

Required:

Give the firm's journal entries with respect to the bonds for 19x1.

24. Terry Tractors, Inc., has outstanding a $100,000, 10-year bond issue which was sold on January 1, 19x0, at a price of $110,000. The following liability, shown below, appeared on the balance sheet on December 31, 19x4.

Bonds payable................	$100,000	
Premium....................	5,000	$105,000

Make the entry necessary to record the retirement of the bonds in each of the following two situations:

a. The firm calls the bonds at 106 on January 1, 19x5.
b. Terry Tractors, Inc., purchases half of the outstanding bonds in the open market for $51,000 on January 1, 19x5.

25. Boyer, Inc., issued 100, $1,000, 20-year convertible bonds at a price of $1,020 each on January 1, 19x1. Each of the bonds is convertible into 20 shares of $20 par value common stock. On December 31, 19x7, 50 of these bonds were converted into common stock. Make the journal entry necessary to record the conversion on the books of Boyer, Inc.

26. The Trail Blazers Company issued a $70,000, 7 percent, 15-year debenture bond on July 1, 19x1, at a price of $68,000. Interest is to be paid on December 31 and June 30 of each year.

Required:

1. Record the journal entries with respect to the bond up to and including December 31, 19x1.
2. What is the total interest cost to the Trail Blazers Company for this bond issue?
3. Assuming the Trail Blazers Company has only this bond issue in long-term debt outstanding, prepare the long-term liabilities section of the balance sheet as of December 31, 19x1.

27. Ames Company had the following transactions relating to marketable securities during the last three months of 19x1.

Sept. 1   Purchased 100 shares of Burden Company common stock for $27 per share plus commission of $100.
Nov. 1   Received a $1 per share dividend on the Burden Company stock.
Dec. 1   Sold 50 shares of Burden Company stock at $32 per share net of commissions.

Required:

1. Prepare the journal entries necessary to record the above transactions.
2. Determine the cost basis for marketable securities at December 31, 19x1.

28. On January 1, 19x1, Lang Company acquired 25 percent of the outstanding shares of stock of Brenner Company at a cost of $250,000. On that date, Brenner Company had common stock of $750,000 and retained earnings of $250,000. Brenner Company reported net income of $100,000 during 19x1, and paid a cash dividend of $20,000. Make the necessary journal entries on Lang's books during 19x1 using the equity method.

29. Assume that Lang Company (Exercise 28) acquired only 19 percent of the shares of Brenner Company at a cost of $100,000. Prepare the necessary journal entries on Lang's books during 19x1 using the cost method.

30. On December 31, 19x1, P Company acquired a controlling interest in S Company. The balance sheets prior to acquisition were as follows:

	P Company	S Company
Current assets....................	$100,000	$ 50,000
Fixed assets (net).................	300,000	70,000
	$400,000	$120,000
Liabilities	$ 40,000	$ 20,000
Common stock....................	300,000	80,000
Retained earnings................	60,000	20,000
	$400,000	$120,000

Prepare a consolidation worksheet at the date of acquisition assuming that P Company paid $100,000 cash for all the outstanding common stock of S Company.

31. Prepare a consolidation worksheet at the date of acquisition assuming that P Company (of Exercise 30) paid $90,000 cash for 90 percent of the outstanding common stock of S Company.

32. On December 31, 19x1, the account balances of a parent and its subsidiary included the following amounts:

	Parent	Subsidiary
Notes receivable....................	$ 10,000	$ 20,000
Notes payable.....................	30,000	15,000
Sales	500,000	100,000
Purchases........................	300,000	70,000

All of the subsidiary sales were made to the parent company. All of the goods purchased from the subsidiary were sold by the parent company during the year. The parent company owed the subsidiary $10,000 as of December 31, 19x1.

a. What amounts of notes receivable and notes payable should be reported on the consolidated balance sheet?

b. What amount of sales and purchases should be reported on the consolidated income statement?

33. Walton, Inc. is a 100 percent owned subsidiary of Portland Company. The following transactions occurred in 19x1.

a. Portland Company purchased two basketballs for $10.

b. Portland Company sold the two basketballs to Walton, Inc. for $12 on account.

c. Walton, Inc. sold one of the basketballs to an outsider for $8.

Required:

1.   Prepare journal entries on the books of Portland Company and Walton, Inc., to reflect the above information.
2.   Prepare the necessary elimination entries for consolidation.

34.   Armor Company purchased a $1,000 face value, 5-year, 8 percent bond on April 1, 19x1, for $1,020 including accrued interest. Interest on the bond is paid semiannually on June 30 and December 31. Prepare the journal entries required on the books of Armor Company on April 1, June 30, and December 31, 19x1.

35.   Prepare the following *worksheet* entries which would appear on the consolidation worksheet of the Samson and Golieth Company as of December 31, 19x1. Do not prepare a consolidation worksheet.

a.   The Samson Company had purchased 90 percent of the common stock of the Golieth Company, for $38,000, on January 1, 19x1, when the stockholders' equity portion of Golieth Company's balance sheet appeared as follows:

Capital stock............................	$30,000
Retained earnings........................	10,000
	$40,000

The management of the Samson Company believes that the fair value of specific assets of Golieth Company is greater than their recorded assets.

b.   During the year, Samson sold Golieth two chariots (the company's stock-in-trade) on account for a total of $2,000. Prior to this sale, Samson had purchased the chariots for $800 each. Neither of these chariots were sold by Golieth during the remainder of the year.

c.   Golieth rented a building to Samson during the year at a rental of $300 per month.

36. On December 31, 19x1, the Brewer Company issued 2,000 shares of its $10 par value stock in exchange for all of the stock of the White Sox Company. White Sox Company has 3,000 shares of $5 par value stock outstanding. Below are their balance sheets prior to acquisition:

	Brewer Company	White Sox Company
Cash.....................................	$ 30,000	$ 12,000
Accounts receivable.........................	75,000	36,000
Fixed assets...............................	110,000	78,000
	$215,000	$126,000

	Brewer Company	White Sox Company
Liabilities	$100,000	$ 45,000
Common stock............................	65,000	15,000
Capital in excess of par value.................	35,000	0
Retained earnings..........................	15,000	66,000
	$215,000	$126,000

Required:

Prepare a consolidation worksheet at the date of acquisition assuming the pooling of interests method is used.

PROBLEMS

37. Kubek Company is authorized to issue $50,000 of 10-year, 8 percent bonds with semiannual interest payments on June 30 and December 31. Record the journal entries necessary on January 1 and June 30, 19x1, on the books of Kubek Company in each of the following independent cases.

   a. The bonds are issued at a price of $45,000 on January 1, 19x1. Interest is paid on June 30 and December 31.
   b. The bonds are issued at a price of $53,000 on January 1, 19x1. Interest is paid on June 30 and December 31.

38. Dean Co. issued $100,000 of 6 percent, 20-year debenture bonds on January 1, 19x1. Interest is payable semiannually on June 30 and December 31. The following information is given on the bonds at December 31, 19x1:

   Carrying value of bonds........................ $103,800
   Interest expense for the year.................... 5,800

   a. Were the bonds issued at a premium or discount?
   b. What was the amount of premium or discount on the issuance of the bonds?
   c. How much of the discount or premium was amortized during the year?

39. On January 1, 19x1, the stockholders of Howard Company authorized the issuance of $8,000 (par value) of 3-year bonds paying interest (8 percent) se-
miannually on June 30 and December 31. The bonds were sold on April 1,
19x1, for $8,330 plus accrued interest. On April 1, 19x2, Howard Company
retired half of the issue at 102 (plus accrued interest).

Required:

Prepare all general journal entries for:

1. Issuance of the bonds.
2. Interest payment on June 30, 19x1.
3. Interest payment on December 31, 19x1.
4. Retirement of portion of issue on April 1, 19x2.
5. Interest payment on June 30, 19x2.

40. On October 1, 19x1, the Badger Company issued $10,000 (face value) of 3 per-
cent bonds which will mature on September 30, 19x3. On December 31, 19x1,
the company's accountant made the following adjusting journal entry relative
to the bonds (Badger Company's accounting period is the calendar year):

Interest expense............................	90	
Interest payable..........................		75
Discount on bonds payable..................		15

Required:

Give the journal entry made to record the sale of the bonds on October 1,
19x1. Assume that interest is payable annually on September 30.

41. The following data related to long-term liabilities appeared on the books of
Summer Co. on December 31, 19x1 (after the payment of interest on
December 31, 19x1).

Bonds payable—6 percent, 20-year debenture bonds due on December 31, 19x25, $100,000 authorized interest payable semiannually on June 30 and December 31...............	$100,000	
Discount on bonds payable.............	3,000	$97,000

On January 1, 19x2, half of the bonds were purchased and retired at 102 percent of face value. Prepare the necessary journal entries to record the semiannual interest payment on December 31, 19x1, and the retirement of $50,000 of
bonds on January 1, 19x2.

42. Cavalier Corporation issued a $10,000, 5-year, 6 percent convertible bond for $9,280 on September 1, 19x1. Interest is to be paid semiannually on March 1 and September 1 each year. The bond is convertible into 10 shares of $20 par value common stock for each $1,000 of the bond issue.

   Required:

   Make the required journal entries to record the:

   1. Issuance of the bond.
   2. Accrual of interest on December 31, 19x1, the end of the fiscal year.
   3. Payment of interest on March 1, 19x2.
   4. Conversion of $5,000 worth of bonds payable into common stock on November 30, 19x4.
   5. Payment of interest on September 1, 19x5.
   6. Payment on the remainder of the bond principle and interest on the due date.

43. The Knick Company decided to issue a 5-year, $20,000 bond on January 2, 19x1, at a price and interest rate which has not yet been determined. Interest payments are to be made annually on December 31.

   Required:

   Prepare a table showing the cash interest payments, amortization of premium or discount, interest expense, and carrying value of the bond (as shown on the end-of-year balance sheet) over the bond's life using each of the following assumptions:

   1. The bond was issued at 6 percent interest for $19,520.
   2. The bond was issued at 8 percent interest for $20,360.

44. Jason Company issued $100,000 of 6 percent, 10-year debenture bonds at face value plus accrued interest on April 1, 19x1. Interest is payable semiannually on January 1 and July 1.

   Required:

   Prepare the journal entries necessary to record the issuance of the bonds and to record interest expense for the first interest date subsequent to issuance.

45. Dorey Co. issued $500,000 of 20-year, 8 percent bonds on April 1, 19x1, with interest payable on June 30 and December 31. The bonds were callable after January 1, 19x8 at 105 percent of face value and mature on December 31, 19x20. The fiscal year of the company ends on September 30. Give the necessary journal entries for the following transactions:

19x1

Apr.   1   Issued the bonds for $529,750 including accrued interest.
June 30   Paid interest.
Sept. 30   Recorded adjusting entry for accrued interest.
Dec. 31   Paid interest.

19x8

Jan.   1   Called the bonds.

46. Hawk Company issued $150,000, 10-year, 8 percent convertible bonds for $155,392 including four months accrued interest on April 30, 19x0. Interest is to be paid semiannually on June 30 and December 31. The bonds are convertible into 5 shares of $50 par value common stock for each $1,000 of the bond issue. (Any premium or discount on the bonds should be amortized over 116 months, the remaining life of the bonds.)

Required:

Make the required journal entries to record the

1.   Issuance of bonds.
2.   Accrual of interest on September 30, 19x0, the end of the fiscal year.
3.   Payment of interest on December 31, 19x0.
4.   Conversion of a portion of the bonds into 375 shares of common stock on August 31, 19x2.
5.   Payment of interest on June 30, 19x3.
6.   Payment on the remainder of the bond principal and interest on the due date—December 31, 19x9.

47. The transactions of Sandy Company relating to marketable securities during 19x1 are listed below.

Jan. 10   Purchased 500 shares of Smith Corporation common stock at a price of $21 per share plus a $200 commission.
Feb.   5   Purchased 100 shares of Dade Corporation common stock at a price of $40 per share plus an $80 commission.
Mar.   1   Received a cash dividend of $1 per share on Smith Corporation common stock.
Apr. 16   Purchased 200 shares of Consolidated Company common stock at $80 per share plus $120 commission.
June   1   Received a cash dividend of $2 per share on Dade Corporation common stock.
Aug. 20   Sold 100 shares of Dade Corporation stock at $42 per share, net of sales commissions.
Sept. 1   Received a $1 per share dividend on Consolidated Company common stock.

Required:

1. Prepare the journal entries necessary to record the above transactions.
2. Prepare the necessary adjusting entry at December 31, 19x1, assuming that the aggregate market value of the portfolio is $11,000.

48. Handy Company had the following transactions relating to marketable securities during 19x1:

Jan. 20 Purchased 100 shares of Bear Corporation common stock at $50 per share plus a $105 commission.
Apr. 16 Purchased 400 shares of River Corporation common stock at $10 per share plus a commission of $95.
May 1 Received a cash dividend of $1 per share on Bear Corporation common stock.
June 5 Purchased 100 shares of Gunner Corporation common stock at $75 per share plus a $160 commission.
Aug. 11 Received a cash dividend of $2 per share on River Corporation common stock.
Nov. 1 Sold 100 shares of Bear Corporation common stock at $55 per share, net of commissions.
Dec. 1 Received a $1 per share dividend on Gunner Corporation common stock.

Required:

1. Prepare the journal entries to record the above transactions.
2. Prepare the necessary adjusting entry at December 31, 19x1, assuming that the aggregate market value of the portfolio is $9,600.

49. The balance sheets of Stevens Corporation and Thomas Corporation reflected the following on December 31, 19x1:

	Stevens Corporation	Thomas Corporation
Current assets.......................	$100,000	$ 30,000
Other assets........................	500,000	100,000
Investment in Thomas...............	120,000	0
	$720,000	$130,000

	Stevens Corporation	Thomas Corporation
Current liabilities....................	$100,000	$ 10,000
Common stock......................	500,000	100,000
Retained earnings...................	120,000	20,000
	$720,000	$130,000

Stevens Corporation purchased 100 percent of the capital stock of Thomas Corporation on January 1, 19x1, for $111,000. The stockholders' equity of Thomas Corporation on that date included common stock of $100,000 and retained earnings of $11,000. Stevens Corporation had an account payable of $10,000 to Thomas Corporation at December 31, 19x1.

Required:

Prepare the December 31, 19x1, consolidated balance sheet.

50. The balances presented below were taken from the books of the Burns Co. and its subsidiary, the Gentry Co., as of December 31, 19x2. Burns Co. purchased 90 percent of the stock of Gentry Co. for $110,000 on December 31, 19x1. At the date of acquisition, Gentry Co. had common stock of $100,000 and retained earnings of $10,000. The difference between cost and book value was attributed to land owned by Gentry Co. Burns Co. uses the equity method for accounting for its investment in Gentry Co.

	Burns Co.	Gentry Co.
Cash	$ 20,000	$ 20,000
Accounts receivable	40,000	20,000
Inventories	60,000	25,000
Land	80,000	25,000
Buildings and equipment (net)	281,000	60,000
Investment in Gentry Co.	119,000	0
	$600,000	$150,000
Accounts payable	$120,000	$ 30,000
Capital stock	400,000	100,000
Retained earnings	80,000	20,000
	$600,000	$150,000

At the end of the year, Gentry Co. owed Burns Co. $10,000 on open account.

Required:

1. Prepare a worksheet for a consolidated balance sheet as of the end of 19x2.
2. Prepare a consolidated balance sheet in good form for the two companies.

51. Condensed balance sheet information of P Company and S Company at the end of 19x1 is shown below:

	P Company	S Company
Current assets	$300,000	$ 50,000
Other assets	500,000	100,000
	$800,000	$150,000
Liabilities	$100,000	$ 30,000
Capital stock ($100 par value)	500,000	100,000
Retained earnings	200,000	20,000
	$800,000	$150,000

Each of the cases described below involves a situation in which P Company acquires a controlling interest in the stock of S Company on December 31, 19x1.

Required:

Prepare a consolidated balance sheet at the date of acquisition for each of the following cases:

1. P Company purchased all of the outstanding shares of S Company for $140,000. There was evidence that the buildings and equipment of S Company were worth more than their book value.
2. P Company purchases all the outstanding shares of S Company for $110,000.
3. P Company purchases 80 percent of the outstanding shares of S Company for $105,000. The management of P Company paid more than book value because of anticipated advantages of affiliation.

52. On January 1, 19x1, Ace Co. purchased a 90 percent interest in Deuce Co. Income statement data for 19x1 are shown below:

	Ace Co.	Deuce Co.
Sales.....................................	$500,000	$ 88,000
Rental income........................	0	12,000
Interest income......................	1,000	0
Investment income....................	9,000	0
Total income.......................	$510,000	$100,000
Cost of goods sold....................	$300,000	$ 55,000
Operating expenses (including rent).......	180,000	30,000
Interest expense......................	10,000	5,000
Total expenses.....................	$490,000	$ 90,000
Net income..........................	$ 20,000	$ 10,000

Intercompany items were as follows:

a. Deuce Co. rented a building to Ace Co. for $1,000 a month during 19x1.
b. Deuce Co. paid Ace Co. $1,000 interest on intercompany notes during the year.
c. Ace Co. sold goods to Deuce Co. for $50,000 during the year. All the goods were resold by Deuce Co. to outsiders by the end of the year.

Required:

1. Prepare working papers for a consolidated income statement for 19x1.
2. Did the parent company use the cost method or equity method for accounting for its investment in the subsidiary?
3. If you had not been told that Ace Co. owned 90 percent of Deuce Co., how could you have determined this fact from the income statement data?

53. On January 1, 19x1, the Strock Co. acquired 90 percent of the common stock of the Bristow Co. for $145,000. The stockholders' equity of Bristow Co. on that date was as follows:

Common stock....................	$120,000
Retained earnings.................	30,000
	$150,000

During 19x1, the Bristow Co. earned $20,000 of net income and paid cash dividends of $12,000. The Strock Co. reported net income of $50,000 (including investment income) and paid dividends of $20,000. The Strock Co. uses the equity method for accounting for its investment in Bristow. The stockholders' equity of the Strock Co. on December 31, 19x1, was as follows:

Common stock....................	$400,000
Retained earnings.................	180,000
	$580,000

Required:

Determine the amounts at which the following items would be shown in the December 31, 19x1, consolidated statements.

a. Difference between cost and book value of subsidiary stock.
b. Consolidated net income.
c. Consolidated retained earnings.
d. Minority interest.

54. Income statement data for 19x1 for King Co. and its 100 percent owned subsidiary, Queen Co., are shown below.

	King Co.	Queen Co.
Sales...............................	$200,000	$100,000
Investment income...................	20,000	0
	$220,000	$100,000
Cost of goods sold...................	$100,000	$ 60,000
Operating expenses...................	80,000	20,000
	$180,000	$ 80,000
Net income.........................	$ 40,000	$ 20,000

During 19x1, Queen Co. sold all of its goods to King Co. An intercompany profit of $5,000 was recorded by Queen Co. on the sale of goods held in King Co.'s inventory at the end of 19x1.

Required:

Prepare the worksheet to develop a consolidated income statement at the end of 19x1.

55. Separate balance sheets for the Cat Company and Mouse Company for the years ended December 31, 19x1 and 19x2 are presented below:

| | December 31, 19x1 | | December 31, 19x2 | |
	Cat Co.	Mouse Co.	Cat Co.	Mouse Co.
Cash	$ 24,000	$10,000	$ 20,000	$14,000
Accounts receivable.........	20,000	10,000	20,000	12,000
Fixed assets...............	120,000	40,000	140,000	44,000
Investment in Mouse Co......	36,000		60,000	
Total Assets.............	$200,000	$60,000	$240,000	$70,000
Accounts payable...........	$ 20,000	$20,000	$ 30,000	$ 6,000
Capital stock..............	120,000	30,000	120,000	30,000
Retained earnings...........	60,000	10,000	90,000	34,000
Total Liabilities and				
Equities...............	$200,000	$60,000	$240,000	$70,000

Cat Company had acquired a 100 percent interest in Mouse Company on December 31, 19x1. The difference in the cost of the company versus its book value is due to a difference between the book value and market value of fixed assets. During 19x2, Mouse Company earned $35,000 in net income and paid out $11,000 in cash dividends. As of December 31, 19x2, Cat Company owes Mouse Company $5,000 and Mouse Company owes Cat Company $3,000.

Required:

1. Prepare a consolidation worksheet for December 31, 19x1 and 19x2.
2. Does the Cat Company use the cost or equity method to record its investment in the Mouse Company?

56. Below is the adjusted trial balance for the Indian Company and Tiger Company for the year ended December 31, 19x1.

	Indian Company	Tiger Company
Cash..............................	$ 10,000	$ 8,000
Accounts receivable....................	23,000	21,000
Accrued interest receivable..............	600	1,200
Accrued rent receivable.................	1,200	0
Fixed assets..........................	168,100	123,600
Investment in Tiger Company...........	72,900	0
Accounts payable.....................	(9,500)	(6,600)
Rent payable.........................	0	(1,200)
Long-term debt.......................	(126,000)	(65,000)
Capital stock.........................	(84,000)	(41,500)
Retained earnings.....................	(18,000)	(26,000)
Sales................................	(205,000)	(150,000)
Cost of goods sold....................	133,250	97,500
Other expenses.......................	60,000	39,000
Rent revenue.........................	(14,400)	0
Investment revenue...................	(12,150)	0

The Indian Company had purchased a 90 percent interest in the Tiger Company on December 31, 19x0 when Tiger Company had the following balances in its stockholders' equity accounts.

Capital stock.............................	$41,500
Retained earnings.........................	26,000
	$67,500

The Indian Company uses the equity method to record its investment in the subsidiary.

During 19x1, Tiger Company rented a building from Indian Company for $1,200 a month. Rent is paid on the first day of each month.

Required:

Prepare consolidation income statement worksheets and consolidation balance sheet worksheets for the Indian and Tiger Companies as of December 31, 19x1. Don't forget to add net income earned during the year to retained earnings for each company.

57. Jijo Co. purchased 80 percent of the outstanding stock of Eli Co. for $175,000 on January 1, 19x1. Balance sheet data for the two corporations immediately after the transaction are presented below.

	Jijo Co.	Eli Co.
Cash................................	$ 10,000	$ 5,000
Accounts receivable..................	30,000	15,000
Inventories	60,000	30,000
Fixed assets (net).....................	300,000	170,000
Investment in Eli Co..................	175,000	0
	$575,000	$220,000

Assume that the difference between the cost of the investment and the book value of the subsidiary was attributed to advantages of affiliation.

Required:

Prepare a consolidated balance sheet for Jijo Co. and Eli Co. at January 1, 19x1.

58. Below are given the trial balances of Moore Company and its 90 percent owned subsidiary, Parker Company, as of December 31, 19x1:

	Moore Company		Parker Company	
Cash.........................	$ 31,000		$ 12,750	
Accounts receivable..............	24,000		12,400	
Advances to Parker Company.....	10,000			
Investment in Parker Company....	76,500			
Inventory......................	26,000		28,100	
Other assets...................	80,840		50,000	
Accounts payable...............		$ 31,960		$ 8,250
Advances from Moore Company...				10,000
Capital stock..................		200,000		60,000
Retained earnings...............		16,380		25,000
	$248,340	$248,340	$103,250	$103,250

Additional data:

The advances are non-interest bearing. At the time of acquisition, Parker Company's equity section was as follows:

Capital stock..........................	$60,000
Retained earnings......................	15,000

Required:

1. Elimination entries.
2. Consolidated balance sheet.

59. Below is shown the condensed balance sheets of the A's and Angel Companies at the end of 19x1, before the acquisition of the stock of Angel Company.

	A's Company	Angel Company
Current assets........................	$100,000	$ 25,000
Other assets.........................	400,000	75,000
Total Assets......................	$500,000	$100,000

	A's Company	Angel Company
Liabilities	$ 50,000	$ 10,000
Capital stock ($50 par value).............	150,000	35,000
Retained earnings.....................	300,000	55,000
Total Liabilities and Equities..........	$500,000	$100,000

Required:

Prepare a consolidated balance sheet for the year 19x1, under each of the following unrelated assumptions. A's Company has acquired a controlling interest in the stock of Angel Company in each case.

1. A's Company purchased all of the outstanding shares of Angel Company for $80,000 in cash. An appraisal of land held by Angel Company determined the land to be worth less than its book value.
2. A's Company purchased all the outstanding shares of Angel Company for $100,000. They paid more for the shares than book value because the value of several assets had increased over their book value.
3. A's Company purchased 90 percent of the outstanding shares of Angel Company for $79,000. A's Company paid less than book value because the product manufactured by Angel Company was outdated.

60. On January 1, 19x1, Royals Company purchased an 80 percent interest in Twins Company. Their income statements for the year ended December 31, 19x1 are shown below.

	Royals Company	Twins Company
Sales................................	$250,000	$28,000
Rental income........................	18,000	3,000
Interest income.......................	1,500	500
Investment income....................	6,720	0
Total Revenues.....................	$276,220	$31,500
Cost of goods sold....................	$100,000	$14,000
Operating expenses....................	50,500	7,900
Interest expense......................	300	1,200
Total Expenses.....................	$150,800	$23,100
Net Income.........................	$125,420	$ 8,400

Additional data:

a.   Royals Company rented a building from Twins Company for $250 a month during 19x1.

b.   Royals Company sold $13,000 worth of goods to Twins Company and all these goods were later resold.

c.   Royals Company paid $280 interest to Twins Company during the year and Twins Company paid $1,000 interest to Royals Company.

Required:

Prepare working papers for a consolidated income statement for 19x1.

61. On January 1, 19x2, the Ranger Company purchased 80 percent of the common stock of the Blue Jay Company for $310,000. The stockholders' equity of Blue Jay Company on that date was:

Common stock..........................	$100,000
Retained earnings........................	260,000
	$360,000

The Ranger Company decided to use the equity method to account for its investment in Blue Jay Company. During 19x2, the Blue Jay Company earned $50,000 in net income and paid $30,000 in dividends. The Ranger Company reported $150,000 in net income (excluding investment income) and paid dividends of $90,000.

Required:

1.   What amount would be shown on the consolidated balance sheet as "Excess of cost over book value of subsidiary," assuming the fair value of the assets of Blue Jay Company was $10,000 above the book value?

2.   What is the amount of the consolidated net income as of December 31, 19x2?

3.   What is the amount of Ranger Company's investment in Blue Jay Company which must be eliminated at year-end using the equity method?

4.   What is the minority interest on December 31, 19x2 to be disclosed in the consolidated balance sheet?

62. Below are the income statements for Dodger and Red Companies. Red owns 100 percent of Dodger.

	Red Company	Dodger Company
Sales...........................	$56,000	$25,000
Investment income.................	6,000	0
	$62,000	$25,000
Cost of goods sold.................	$29,000	$18,000
Operating expenses...............	6,000	1,000
	$35,000	$19,000
Net Income......................	$27,000	$ 6,000

During 19x1, Red Company sold $15,000 of its goods to Dodger Company at a mark-up of 30 percent (cost to Red Company being $15,000). At the end of the year, Dodger Company still had $3,900 (cost plus mark-up) in its ending inventory.

Required:

Prepare the worksheet to develop a consolidated income statement on December 31, 19x1.

Refer to the Annual Report included in the Appendix at the end of the text:

63. Comparing the two years, did long-term liabilities increase or decrease?

64. What factors might cause an increase in long-term liabilities?

65. What factors could cause a decrease in liabilities?

66. What is the total debt due in more than one year at the end of the most recent year?

67. Was the long-term debt issued at a premium or at a discount? Where can this information be located?

68. Are current liabilities greater than long-term liabilities at the end of the most recent year?

69. Can the amount of amortization be determined from the body of the financial statements?

70. What is the highest interest paid on long-term debt? Where can this information be found?

71. Was there amortization expense in either year?

**APPENDIX
INTEREST AND
PRESENT VALUE
CONCEPTS**

The principles used in discounting cash flows due at certain future points in time by the use of compound interest concepts are discussed in this appendix. These concepts have a broad application in business decisions. For example, most business entities often make decisions to: (1) borrow funds in the current period in return for a promise to pay cash or other resources in future periods; and (2) invest resources at the current time with the expectation of receiving benefits at various future times. For both of these types of decisions, the timing of the various cash inflows and outflows has a significant effect on the desirability of the various possible investment and borrowing alternatives. Timing of the cash flows is important because of the following principle: *an amount of cash to be received in the future is not equivalent to the same amount of cash held at the present time.* This statement is true because money has a time value—it can be invested to earn a return (i.e., interest or dividends). For this reason, in both borrowing and investing decisions, consideration must be given to the time values of the various cash inflows and outflows.

In order to understand the implications of such decisions, the accountant must be able to determine the *present value* of future cash flows. Although there are a number of important applications of present value concepts in the financial accounting area, this appendix is limited to the application of these concepts to long-term liabilities.

INTEREST

Interest represents the amount received by the lender and paid by the borrower for the use of money for a given period of time. Thus, upon payment of a debt, interest is the excess of the cash repaid over the amount originally borrowed (referred to as the *principal*). Interest is normally stated as a rate for a one year period.

Simple interest is the amount of interest that is computed on the principal *only,* for a given period of time. Simple interest is computed as follows:

$$\text{Interest} = \text{Principal} \times \text{Rate} \times \text{Time}$$
$$\text{Interest} = P \times I \times T \tag{1}$$

To illustrate, interest on $1,000 for 6 months at an annual interest rate of 10 percent is:

$$\$50 = \$1,000 \times .10 \times \tfrac{6}{12}$$

Compound interest is interest that is computed for a period of time both on the principal and on the interest which has been earned but not paid. That is, interest is compounded when the interest earned in each period is added to the principal amount and both principal and interest earn interest in all subsequent periods. To illustrate, assume that $1,000 is deposited in a bank which pays interest at 10 percent annually. If the interest was withdrawn each year (simple interest), the depositor would collect $100 in interest each year (or $300 in interest over a three-year period):

$$\text{Interest Per Year} = \$1,000 \times .10 \times 1 = \$100$$
$$\text{Total Interest for 3 Years} = \$100 \times 3 = \$300$$

However, if the interest at the end of each period is added to the principal sum (compound interest), the amount earned over the three-year period is computed as follows:

Original investment.................................		$1,000
Balance at the		
End of Year:	1.	$1,000 + (.10 × $1,000 × 1)	1,100
	2.	$1,100 + (.10 × $1,100 × 1)	1,210
	3.	$1,210 + (.10 × $1,210 × 1)	1,331

Compound interest for the three-year period is $331 ($1,331 − $1,000), the difference between the balance at the end of the three-year period and the original investment. This amount exceeds simple interest because interest was earned each year both on the principal and on the interest earned in previous years.

Since compounding occurs when interest is earned on previously accumulated interest, a formula can be developed for computing the compound amount at which the principal sum will increase over a given time period. To develop this formula, consider the compound interest on one dollar invested at an interest rate of I percent. The amount accumulated at the end of the first year would be [$1 + (1 × I)] or (1 + I). If this amount is allowed to accumulate and earn interest for the second year, the amount accumulated is (1 + I)(1 + I) which is equal to $(1 + I)^2$. Similarly, the amount at the end of T periods is $(1 + I)^T$. Consequently, the amount (A) that a principal amount (P) will accumulate over a time period (T) at an interest rate (I) is expressed as:

$$A = P(1 + I)^T \tag{2}$$

For example, if $1,000 is invested for three years at 10 percent interest per year, the amount accumulated at the end of three years is computed as follows:

$$A = \$1,000 (1 + .10)^3$$
$$A = \$1,000 (1.331)$$
$$A = \$1,331$$

This computation of the sum for a single principal amount and the compound interest at a specified future time may be illustrated as follows:

$1,000 ————————————————→ $1,331

| 0 | 1 | 2 | 3 |

Time (years)

**PRESENT
VALUES OF A
FUTURE SUM**

The present value of a given amount at a specified future time is the sum that would have to be invested at the present time in order to equal that future value at a given rate of compound interest. For example, it was determined that $1,000 invested at 10 percent compound interest would accumulate to a total of $1,331 in three years. Therefore, $1,000 is the *present value* of $1,331 three years from the present time (given a 10 percent rate of interest). That is, if you could earn 10 percent on a bank deposit, you would be indifferent between receiving $1,000 now (which could be deposited to accumulate to $1,331 in three years) or $1,331 three years from now, all other factors being equal.

The present value of a future amount is determined by computing the amount that a principal sum will accumulate to over a specified period of time. Consequently, by dividing equation (2) by $(1 + I)^T$, we obtain the formula for computing the present value of a future amount (A):

$$P = \frac{A}{(1 + I)^T} \tag{3}$$

For example, the present value of $1,331 three years from now would be computed as follows:

$$P = \frac{\$1,331}{(1 + .10)^3}$$
$$P = \$1,000$$

Because of the number and variety of decisions which are based on the present value of future cash flows, tables have been developed from the formula which give the present value of $1 for various interest rates and for various periods of time. These values may be multiplied by any future amount to determine its present value. The factors for the present value of $1 are listed in Table A-1.

To illustrate the use of this table, let us compute the present value of $1,331 to be received three years from now at a compound interest rate of 10 percent. The value from the table for 3 years at 10 percent is .7513. This is the present value of $1. Accordingly, the present value of $1,331 is computed as $1,331 \times .7513 = \$999.80$, (this amount is not exactly equal to $1,000 because of the rounding error in the present value factor included in the table). The computation of the present value of a simple payment due in the future may be illustrated as follows:

440

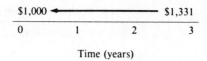

Time (years)

COMPOUND INTEREST AND PRESENT VALUE ON A SERIES OF EQUAL PAYMENTS

Business decisions involving a series of cash flows to be paid or received periodically are more common than decisions involving the accumulation of a single principal sum. It is possible to determine the present value of a series of payments (or receipts) by computing the present value of each payment or receipt and adding these values to obtain the present value for the entire series. However, if all the payments are equal, formulas or tables may be used to compute the present value of a series of payments. Such a series of equal periodic payments is normally referred to as an *annuity*. If the payments are made at the end of each period, the annuity is referred to as an *ordinary annuity*.

The accumulated amount (future value) of an ordinary annuity is the sum of the periodic payments and the compound interest on these payments. For example, the future value of an annuity of $1,000 per year (at the end of each year) for three years at 10 percent interest could be determined as follows:

The initial payment accumulates at 10 percent for two years to....................................	$1,210
The second payment accumulates at 10 percent for one year to.......................................	1,100
The third payment is due at the end of the third year.........	1,000
Amount of an ordinary annuity of $1,000 for three years at 10 percent..............................	$3,310

The computation of the future value of a series of payments may be expressed as follows:

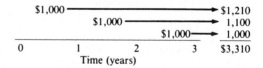

Time (years)

The present value of an ordinary annuity is the amount which, if invested at the present time at a compound rate of interest, would provide for a series of equal withdrawals at the end of a certain number of periods. The present value of an ordinary annuity may be computed as the present values of each of the individual payments. For example, the present value of an ordinary annuity of $1,000 per year for three years at 10 percent could be computed as follows (see Table A-1):

Present value of $1,000 in one year. . . . .   .9091 × 1,000 = $ 909.10
Present value of $1,000 in two years . . . .   .8264 × 1,000 =   826.40
Present value of $1,000 in three years . . . . . .   .7513 × 1,000 =   751.30

Present value of an annuity of $1,000 for
three periods at 10 percent $2,486.80

This computation indicates that if $2,486.80 is invested at an interest rate of 10 percent, it would be possible to withdraw $1,000 at the end of each year for three years.

The formula for the present value of an ordinary annuity of $R per period for T periods at I rate of interest may be stated:

$$P = R \left[\frac{1 - \dfrac{1}{(1 + I)^T}}{I} \right]$$

Table A-2 gives the present value of an ordinary annuity of $1 per period for various periods at varying rates of interest. By multiplying the appropriate value from the table by the dollar amount of the periodic payment, the present value of the payments may be calculated. For example, the present value of three annual cash payments of $1,000 made at the end of the next three years at a 10 percent interest rate would be computed as follows:

$$\$1,000 \times 2.4869 = \$2,486.90[1]$$

This amount may be interpreted as the present cash payment which would be exactly equivalent to the three future installments of $1,000 if money earns 10 percent compounded annually. The computation of the present value of a series of future payments may be illustrated as follows:

```
$  909.10  ←———— $1,000
   826.40  ←——————————— $1,000
   751.30  ←——————————————————— $1,000
$2,486.80
───────────────────────────────────────────
   0          1           2           3
```

Time (years)

APPLICATION OF PRESENT VALUE CONCEPTS TO BONDS PAYABLE

A bond is a contract between an issuing company and the purchaser of the bond. There are two types of payments that a company will have to make to bondholders. One payment is a lump-sum payment made at

---

[1] Difference of $.10 due to rounding in tables.

the end of the life of the bond, which is the return of the *face value* or *maturity value* of the bond. The other payment is for interest, which will be made at specific intervals in fixed amounts over the life of the bond. Interest is usually paid semiannually by the issuing company. Bond contracts will state the *coupon* or *nominal rate* of interest on an annual basis.

To calculate the selling price of a bond (the amount the firm will receive upon issuance of the bond), consider a company that has sold a $1,000 face value bond with a nominal rate of interest of 8 percent. The bond will mature in 5 years and the interest is payable June 30 and December 31 of each year. The company has made two promises to the purchaser of the bond:

Promise 1:   To pay $1,000 at the end of 5 years.
Promise 2:   To pay $40 semiannually for 5 years.

The price that any investor would pay for a bond would depend upon the *effective rate*[2] of interest on the date that the investor decided to buy the bond. The effective rate will be dependent upon many factors such as the prime interest rate in money markets, the risks involved in buying the bond of that specific company, and the provisions of the bond that may make it more attractive for investment purposes. In general, the effective rate will be determined by supply and demand in the bond market.

There are three possible general cases that illustrate the potential selling price of the bond. These three cases are dependent upon the earnings expectations of buyers of bonds in the market place. In the prior example, where the nominal rate is eight percent, the three possible cases are:

1.   The effective (market) rate of interest is equal to eight percent.
2.   The effective (market) rate of interest is below eight percent.
3.   The effective (market) rate of interest is greater than eight percent.

If the market is demanding an eight percent return on bonds of like kind, and the company enters the market with an eight percent coupon rate on its bond, the bond should sell at its face value of $1,000. The buyer is demanding eight percent and the seller is paying eight percent; therefore the bond would sell at *par*.

If the market is demanding a return that is less than eight percent and the company enters the market with an eight percent coupon rate on its bond, the company is paying a greater return than is demanded in the market. Therefore, the bond will sell for a price in excess of $1,000. This

---

[2] The effective rate is also referred to as the market rate or the yield.

excess is referred to as a *premium*. The investors will buy the bond at a price greater than $1,000 because the coupon rate exceeds the rate demanded by the market.

If the market is demanding a return that is greater than eight percent and the company enters the market with an eight percent coupon rate on its bond, the company is paying less than the return demanded by the market. Therefore, the bond will sell for less than $1,000. The difference between $1,000 and the selling price will be a *discount* on the bond.

To calculate the selling price of the bond, assume that the market rate of interest was either eight percent, six percent, or ten percent. Note that the bond contract provides for a lump-sum payment at maturity and semiannual interest payments over the life of the bond. Thus, in order to find the current value, or selling price, of the bond, it is necessary to determine the present value of the lump-sum payment at maturity and the present value of the periodic interest payments (an ordinary annuity). Illustration A-1 presents the calculations which are necessary to determine the selling price of the $1,000 bond at the three market rates of interest assumed above.

Illustration A-1

Selling Price of a Bond with 8% Coupon Rate,
5-Year Life, and Semiannual Payments

	Present Value Factors for 10 Periods at 4% Semiannual Interest		
	Table 1	Table 2	Totals
8% Coupon, 8% Market **Bond Sells at Par**			
Promise #1 = $1,000 – lump sum	.6756		= $ 675.60
Promise #2 = $40 – annuity		8.1109	= 324.44
		Selling price (rounded)	= $1,000.00
8% Coupon, 6% Market **Bond Sells at Premium**			
Promise #1 = $1,000 – lump sum	.7441		= $ 744.10
Promise #2 = $40 – annuity		8.5302	= 341.21
		Selling price (rounded)	= $1,085.31
8% Coupon, 10% Market **Bond Sells at Discount**			
Promise #1 = $1,000 – lump sum	.6139		= $ 613.90
Promise #2 = $40 – annuity		7.7217	= 308.87
		Selling price (rounded)	= $ 922.77

Even though the selling price of the bond will vary according to the three different market rate assumptions, it is important to remember that the bond is a fixed contract that will pay a return of $40 to the bondholder semiannually and $1,000 at its maturity date. These amounts are paid regardless of the initial selling price of the bond.

ACCOUNTING FOR PREMIUM OR DISCOUNT ON BONDS—THE INTEREST METHOD

The following example will be used to illustrate the accounting treatment of a bond issue sold at a premium or discount using the interest method. Assume that on July 1, 19x1, a company sold a $1,000,000 bond issue with a nominal interest rate of eight percent and a maturity date of July 1, 19x6. Interest will be paid on June 30 and December 31. The company's fiscal year ends on December 31.

The calculations necessary in order to compute the initial selling price of the bond are the same as the calculations in Illustration A-1, except that the entire issue, $1,000,000, is under consideration. If the market rate of interest demanded is eight percent, the bonds will sell for $1,000,000. If the market rate of interest is six percent, the bonds will sell at a premium. The selling price will be ($1,000,000 × .7441) + ($40,000 × 8.5302) = $1,085,308. If the market rate of interest demanded is ten percent, the bonds will sell at a discount. The selling price will be ($1,000,000 × .6139) + ($40,000 × 7.7217) = $922,768.

The face value of the bonds is paid to bondholders at the maturity date regardless of the original price of the bonds. The premium or discount on a bond is paid or received, respectively, to adjust the interest that will be paid on the bond to the return on the investment demanded by the market (market rate of interest) given the type of bond and the risk involved as perceived by investors.

There are two acceptable methods for amortizing bond premium or discount. One technique for amortization, the straight-line method, was discussed in the chapter. A second technique, referred to as the interest method, has been suggested by the Accounting Principles Board.[3] This method of amortization results in recognizing a constant rate of interest on the bond liability over the life of the bond. The interest expense for each period is computed by multiplying a constant rate of interest by the beginning liability for that period. The interest method is described in this appendix.

Bonds Sold at a Premium

If the market rate of interest in the prior example is six percent, the bonds will sell at a premium of $85,308 ($1,085,308 − $1,000,000). The interest method will yield a different interest expense for each interest period. To determine the interest expense, the carrying value of the liability (face value plus unamortized premium or minus unamortized discount) is multiplied by

---

[3] *APB Opinion No. 21* (New York, American Institute of Certified Public Accountants, 1972).

the semiannual effective rate of interest. Thus, the interest expense will be a constant percentage (equal to the effective semiannual interest rate on the issuance of the bonds) of six percent per year or three percent on the outstanding liability at the beginning of each semiannual interest period. The following journal entries would be made in 19x1 under the interest method:

June 30, 19x1	Cash	1,085,308.00	
	Bond premium.		85,308.00
	Bonds payable.		1,000,000.00
December 31, 19x1	Interest expense.	32,559.24	
	Bond premium.	7,440.76	
	Cash		40,000.00

(Interest expense = $1,085,308.00 × .03 = $32,559.24)

At the end of 19x1, the balance sheet presentation of the liability will include both the bonds payable and bond premium accounts. The bond premium account is rounded in the example.

Bonds payable.	$1,000,000	
Add: Bond premium.	77,867	
Total bonds payable.		$1,077,867

When bonds are issued at a premium, use of the interest method will cause the *interest* expense to decrease over the life of the bond because both the premium account and the carrying value of the liability will decrease over the life of the bonds. The bond premium amortization will increase because the cash payment to bondholders remains constant and the interest expense decreases each period. The total interest expense and premium amortization schedule is given in Illustration A-2.

Bonds Sold at a Discount

If the market rate of interest demanded by investors is ten percent, the bonds in the prior example will sell at a discount because the face rate of interest is eight percent. The discount will be the difference between the maturity value of $1,000,000 and the selling price of $922,768, or $77,232.

The concepts underlying the *interest* method for bond discount are the same as those discussed in the prior section on bonds sold at a premium. The journal entries for 19x1 for bonds sold at a discount are:

June 30, 19x1	Cash	922,768.00	
	Bond discount.	77,232.00	
	Bonds payable.		1,000,000.00
December 31, 19x1	Interest expense.	46,138.40	
	Bond discount.		6,138.40
	Cash		40,000.00

(Interest expense = $922,768 × .05 = $46,138.40)

446

Illustration A-2

Interest Expense and Premium Amortization Schedule

Date	Debit to Interest Expense*	Debit to Bond Premium	Credit to Cash	Bond Premium Balance	Total Liability
July 1, 19x1..........	0	0	0	$85,308.00	$1,085,308.00
December 31, 19x1....	$32,559.24	$ 7,440.76	$ 40,000	77,867.24	1,077,867.24
July 1, 19x2..........	32,336.02	7,663.98	40,000	70,203.26	1,070,203.26
December 31, 19x2....	32,106.10	7,893.90	40,000	62,309.36	1,062,309.36
July 1, 19x3..........	31,869.28	8,130.72	40,000	54,178.64	1,054,178.64
December 31, 19x3....	31,625.36	8,374.64	40,000	45,804.00	1,045,804.00
July 1, 19x4..........	31,374.12	8,625.88	40,000	37,178.12	1,037,178.12
December 31, 19x4....	31,115.34	8,884.66	40,000	28,293.46	1,028,293.46
July 1, 19x5..........	30,848.80	9,151.20	40,000	19,142.26	1,019,142.26
December 31, 19x5....	30,574.27	9,425.73	40,000	9,716.53	1,009,716.53
July 1, 19x6..........	30,291.47*	9,716.53	40,000	0	1,000,000.00
		$85,308.00	$400,000		

*To determine interest expense, the total liability at the beginning of the period was multiplied by the semiannual market interest rate of three percent. Any rounding errors are included in the July 1, 19x6 debit to interest expense.

At the end of 19x1, the balance sheet presentation of the liability will include both the bonds payable and the bond discount account. The bond discount account is rounded in the example.

Bonds payable..............	$1,000,000	
Less: Bond discount........	71,094	
Total bonds payable.......		$ 928,906

In the case of bonds sold at a discount, using the interest method, interest expense increases over the life of the bond because discount decreases and the carrying value of the bonds increases. The total interest expense and discount amortization schedule is given in Illustration A-3.

Illustration A-3

Interest Expense and Discount Amortization Schedule

Date	Debit to Interest Expense*	Credit to Bond Discount	Credit to Cash	Bond Discount Balance	Total Liability
July 1, 19x1..........	0	0	0	$77,232.00	$ 922,768.00
December 31, 19x1....	$46,138.40	$ 6,138.40	$ 40,000	71,093.60	928,906.40
July 1, 19x2..........	46,445.32	6,445.32	40,000	64,648.28	935,351.72
December 31, 19x2....	46,767.59	6,767.59	40,000	57,880.69	942,119.31
July 1, 19x3..........	47,105.97	7,105.97	40,000	50,774.72	949,225.28
December 31, 19x3....	47,461.26	7,461.26	40,000	43,313.46	956,686.54
July 1, 19x4..........	47,834.33	7,834.33	40,000	35,479.13	964,520.87
December 31, 19x4....	48,226.04	8,226.04	40,000	27,253.09	972,746.91
July 1, 19x5..........	48,637.35	8,637.35	40,000	18,615.74	981,384.26
December 31, 19x5....	49,069.21	9,069.21	40,000	9,546.53	990,453.47
July 1, 19x6..........	49,522.53*	9,546.53	40,000	0	1,000,000.00
		$77,232.00	$400,000		

*To determine interest expense, the total liability at the beginning of the period was multiplied by the semiannual market interest rate—in this case, five percent. Any rounding errors are included in the July 1, 19x6, debit to interest expense.

Table A-1
Present Value of $1.00

Periods (n)	1%	1½%	2%	2½%	3%	3½%	4%	4½%	5%	6%	7%	8%	10%
1	0.9901	0.9852	0.9804	0.9756	0.9709	0.9662	0.9615	0.9569	0.9524	0.9434	0.9346	0.9259	0.9091
2	0.9803	0.9707	0.9612	0.9518	0.9426	0.9335	0.9246	0.9157	0.9070	0.8900	0.8734	0.8573	0.8264
3	0.9706	0.9563	0.9423	0.9286	0.9151	0.9019	0.8890	0.8763	0.8638	0.8396	0.8163	0.7938	0.7513
4	0.9610	0.9422	0.9238	0.9060	0.8885	0.8714	0.8548	0.8386	0.8227	0.7921	0.7629	0.7350	0.6830
5	0.9515	0.9283	0.9057	0.8839	0.8626	0.8420	0.8219	0.8025	0.7835	0.7473	0.7130	0.6806	0.6209
6	0.9420	0.9145	0.8880	0.8623	0.8375	0.8135	0.7903	0.7679	0.7462	0.7050	0.6663	0.6302	0.5645
7	0.9327	0.9010	0.8706	0.8413	0.8131	0.7860	0.7599	0.7348	0.7107	0.6651	0.6227	0.5835	0.5132
8	0.9235	0.8877	0.8535	0.8207	0.7894	0.7594	0.7307	0.7032	0.6768	0.6274	0.5820	0.5403	0.4665
9	0.9143	0.8746	0.8368	0.8007	0.7664	0.7337	0.7026	0.6729	0.6446	0.5919	0.5439	0.5002	0.4241
10	0.9053	0.8617	0.8203	0.7812	0.7441	0.7089	0.6756	0.6439	0.6139	0.5584	0.5083	0.4632	0.3855
11	0.8963	0.8489	0.8043	0.7621	0.7224	0.6849	0.6496	0.6162	0.5847	0.5268	0.4751	0.4289	0.3505
12	0.8874	0.8364	0.7885	0.7436	0.7014	0.6618	0.6246	0.5897	0.5568	0.4970	0.4440	0.3971	0.3186
13	0.8787	0.8240	0.7730	0.7254	0.6810	0.6394	0.6006	0.5643	0.5303	0.4688	0.4150	0.3677	0.2897
14	0.8700	0.8118	0.7579	0.7077	0.6611	0.6178	0.5775	0.5400	0.5051	0.4423	0.3878	0.3405	0.2633
15	0.8613	0.7999	0.7430	0.6905	0.6419	0.5969	0.5553	0.5167	0.4810	0.4173	0.3624	0.3153	0.2394
16	0.8528	0.7880	0.7284	0.6736	0.6232	0.5767	0.5339	0.4945	0.4581	0.3936	0.3387	0.2919	0.2176
17	0.8444	0.7764	0.7142	0.6572	0.6050	0.5572	0.5134	0.4732	0.4363	0.3714	0.3166	0.2703	0.1978
18	0.8360	0.7649	0.7002	0.6412	0.5874	0.5384	0.4936	0.4528	0.4155	0.3503	0.2959	0.2502	0.1799
19	0.8277	0.7536	0.6864	0.6255	0.5703	0.5202	0.4746	0.4333	0.3957	0.3305	0.2765	0.2317	0.1635
20	0.8195	0.7425	0.6730	0.6103	0.5537	0.5026	0.4564	0.4146	0.3769	0.3118	0.2584	0.2145	0.1486
21	0.8114	0.7315	0.6598	0.5954	0.5375	0.4856	0.4388	0.3968	0.3589	0.2942	0.2415	0.1987	0.1351
22	0.8034	0.7207	0.6468	0.5809	0.5219	0.4692	0.4220	0.3797	0.3418	0.2775	0.2257	0.1839	0.1228
23	0.7954	0.7100	0.6342	0.5667	0.5067	0.4533	0.4057	0.3634	0.3256	0.2618	0.2109	0.1703	0.1117
24	0.7876	0.6995	0.6217	0.5529	0.4919	0.4380	0.3901	0.3477	0.3101	0.2470	0.1971	0.1577	0.1015
25	0.7798	0.6892	0.6095	0.5394	0.4776	0.4231	0.3751	0.3327	0.2953	0.2330	0.1842	0.1460	0.0923
26	0.7720	0.6790	0.5976	0.5262	0.4637	0.4088	0.3607	0.3184	0.2812	0.2198	0.1722	0.1352	0.0839
27	0.7644	0.6690	0.5859	0.5134	0.4502	0.3950	0.3468	0.3047	0.2678	0.2074	0.1609	0.1252	0.0763
28	0.7568	0.6591	0.5744	0.5009	0.4371	0.3817	0.3335	0.2916	0.2551	0.1956	0.1504	0.1159	0.0693
29	0.7493	0.6494	0.5631	0.4887	0.4243	0.3687	0.3207	0.2790	0.2429	0.1846	0.1406	0.1073	0.0630
30	0.7419	0.6398	0.5521	0.4767	0.4120	0.3563	0.3083	0.2670	0.2314	0.1741	0.1314	0.0994	0.0573
40	0.6717	0.5513	0.4529	0.3724	0.3066	0.2526	0.2083	0.1719	0.1420	0.0972	0.0668	0.0460	0.0221
50	0.6080	0.4750	0.3715	0.2909	0.2281	0.1791	0.1407	0.1107	0.0872	0.0543	0.0339	0.0213	0.0085

Table A-1 (Continued)
Present Value of $1.00

12%	14%	15%	16%	18%	20%	22%	24%	25%	26%	28%	30%	40%	50%
0.893	0.877	0.870	0.862	0.847	0.833	0.820	0.806	0.800	0.794	0.781	0.769	0.714	0.667
0.797	0.769	0.756	0.743	0.718	0.694	0.672	0.650	0.640	0.630	0.610	0.592	0.510	0.444
0.712	0.675	0.658	0.641	0.609	0.579	0.551	0.524	0.512	0.500	0.477	0.455	0.364	0.296
0.636	0.592	0.572	0.552	0.516	0.482	0.451	0.423	0.410	0.397	0.373	0.350	0.260	0.198
0.567	0.519	0.497	0.476	0.437	0.402	0.370	0.341	0.328	0.315	0.291	0.269	0.186	0.132
0.507	0.456	0.432	0.410	0.370	0.335	0.303	0.275	0.262	0.250	0.227	0.207	0.133	0.088
0.452	0.400	0.376	0.354	0.314	0.279	0.249	0.222	0.210	0.198	0.178	0.159	0.095	0.059
0.404	0.351	0.327	0.305	0.266	0.233	0.204	0.179	0.168	0.157	0.139	0.123	0.068	0.039
0.361	0.308	0.284	0.263	0.225	0.194	0.167	0.144	0.134	0.125	0.108	0.094	0.048	0.026
0.322	0.270	0.247	0.227	0.191	0.162	0.137	0.116	0.107	0.099	0.085	0.073	0.035	0.017
0.287	0.237	0.215	0.195	0.162	0.135	0.112	0.094	0.086	0.079	0.066	0.056	0.025	0.012
0.257	0.208	0.187	0.168	0.137	0.112	0.092	0.076	0.069	0.062	0.052	0.043	0.018	0.008
0.229	0.182	0.163	0.145	0.116	0.093	0.075	0.061	0.055	0.050	0.040	0.033	0.013	0.005
0.205	0.160	0.141	0.125	0.099	0.078	0.062	0.049	0.044	0.039	0.032	0.025	0.009	0.003
0.183	0.140	0.123	0.108	0.084	0.065	0.051	0.040	0.035	0.031	0.025	0.020	0.006	0.002
0.163	0.123	0.107	0.093	0.071	0.054	0.042	0.032	0.028	0.025	0.019	0.015	0.005	0.002
0.146	0.108	0.093	0.080	0.060	0.045	0.034	0.026	0.023	0.020	0.015	0.012	0.003	0.001
0.130	0.095	0.081	0.069	0.051	0.038	0.028	0.021	0.018	0.016	0.012	0.009	0.002	0.001
0.116	0.083	0.070	0.060	0.043	0.031	0.023	0.017	0.014	0.012	0.009	0.007	0.002	
0.104	0.073	0.061	0.051	0.037	0.026	0.019	0.014	0.012	0.010	0.007	0.005	0.001	
0.093	0.064	0.053	0.044	0.031	0.022	0.015	0.011	0.009	0.008	0.006	0.004	0.001	
0.083	0.056	0.046	0.038	0.026	0.018	0.013	0.009	0.007	0.006	0.004	0.003	0.001	
0.074	0.049	0.040	0.033	0.022	0.015	0.010	0.007	0.006	0.005	0.003	0.002		
0.066	0.043	0.035	0.028	0.019	0.013	0.008	0.006	0.005	0.004	0.003	0.002		
0.059	0.038	0.030	0.024	0.016	0.010	0.007	0.005	0.004	0.003	0.002	0.001		
0.053	0.033	0.026	0.021	0.014	0.009	0.006	0.004	0.003	0.002	0.002	0.001		
0.047	0.029	0.023	0.018	0.011	0.007	0.005	0.003	0.002	0.002	0.001	0.001		
0.042	0.026	0.020	0.016	0.010	0.006	0.004	0.002	0.002	0.002	0.001	0.001		
0.037	0.022	0.017	0.014	0.008	0.005	0.003	0.002	0.002	0.001	0.001	0.001		
0.033	0.020	0.015	0.012	0.007	0.004	0.003	0.002	0.001	0.001	0.001			
0.011	0.005	0.004	0.003	0.001	0.001								
0.003	0.001	0.001	0.001										

Table A-2
Present Value of Annuity of $1.00 Per Period

Periods (n)	1%	1½%	2%	2½%	3%	3½%	4%	4½%	5%	6%	7%
1....	0.9901	0.9852	0.9804	0.9756	0.9709	0.9662	0.9615	0.9569	0.9524	0.9434	0.9346
2....	1.9704	1.9559	1.9416	1.9274	1.9135	1.8997	1.8861	1.8727	1.8594	1.8334	1.8080
3....	2.9410	2.9122	2.8839	2.8560	2.8286	2.8016	2.7751	2.7490	2.7232	2.6730	2.6243
4....	3.9020	3.8544	3.8077	3.7620	3.7171	3.6731	3.6299	3.5875	3.5460	3.4651	3.3872
5....	4.8534	4.7826	4.7135	4.6458	4.5797	4.5151	4.4518	4.3900	4.3295	4.2124	4.1002
6....	5.7955	5.6972	5.6014	5.5081	5.4172	5.3286	5.2421	5.1579	5.0757	4.9173	4.7665
7....	6.7282	6.5982	6.4720	6.3494	6.2303	6.1145	6.0021	5.8927	5.7864	5.5824	5.3893
8....	7.6517	7.4859	7.3255	7.1701	7.0197	6.8740	6.7327	6.5959	6.4632	6.2098	5.9713
9....	8.5660	8.3605	8.1622	7.9709	7.7861	7.6077	7.4353	7.2688	7.1078	6.8017	6.5152
10....	9.4713	9.2222	8.9826	8.7521	8.5302	8.3166	8.1109	7.9127	7.7217	7.3601	7.0236
11....	10.3676	10.0711	9.7868	9.5142	9.2526	9.0016	8.7605	8.5289	8.3064	7.8869	7.4987
12....	11.2551	10.9075	10.5753	10.2578	9.9540	9.6633	9.3851	9.1186	8.8633	8.3838	7.9427
13....	12.1337	11.7315	11.3484	10.9832	10.6350	10.3027	9.9856	9.6829	9.3936	8.8527	8.3577
14....	13.0037	12.5434	12.1062	11.6909	11.2961	10.9205	10.5631	10.2228	9.8986	9.2950	8.7455
15....	13.8651	13.3432	12.8493	12.3814	11.9379	11.5174	11.1184	10.7395	10.3797	9.7122	9.1079
16....	14.7179	14.1313	13.5777	13.0550	12.5611	12.0941	11.6523	11.2340	10.8378	10.1059	9.4466
17....	15.5623	14.9076	14.2919	13.7122	13.1661	12.6513	12.1657	11.7072	11.2741	10.4773	9.7632
18....	16.3983	15.6726	14.9920	14.3534	13.7535	13.1897	12.6593	12.1600	11.6896	10.8276	10.0591
19....	17.2260	16.4262	15.6785	14.9789	14.3238	13.7098	13.1339	12.5933	12.0853	11.1581	10.3356
20....	18.0456	17.1686	16.3514	15.5892	14.8775	14.2124	13.5903	13.0079	12.4622	11.4699	10.5940
21....	18.8570	17.9001	17.0112	16.1845	15.4150	14.6980	14.0292	13.4047	12.8212	11.7640	10.8355
22....	19.6604	18.6208	17.6580	16.7654	15.9369	15.1671	14.4511	13.7844	13.1630	12.0416	11.0612
23....	20.4558	19.3309	18.2922	17.3321	16.4436	15.6204	14.8568	14.1478	13.4886	12.3034	11.2722
24....	21.2434	20.0304	18.9139	17.8850	16.9355	16.0584	15.2470	14.4955	13.7986	12.5504	11.4693
25....	22.0232	20.7196	19.5235	18.4244	17.4131	16.4815	15.6221	14.8282	14.0939	12.7834	11.6536
26....	22.7952	21.3986	20.1210	18.9506	17.8768	16.8904	15.9828	15.1466	14.3752	13.0032	11.8258
27....	23.5596	22.0676	20.7069	19.4640	18.3270	17.2854	16.3296	15.4513	14.6430	13.2105	11.9867
28....	24.3164	22.7267	21.2813	19.9649	18.7641	17.6670	15.6631	15.7429	14.8981	13.4062	12.1371
29....	25.0658	23.3761	21.8444	20.4535	19.1885	18.0358	16.9837	16.0219	15.1411	13.5907	12.2777
30....	25.8077	24.0158	22.3965	20.9303	19.6004	18.3920	17.2920	16.2889	15.3725	13.7648	12.4090
40....	32.8347	29.9158	27.3555	25.1028	23.1148	21.3551	19.7928	18.4016	17.1591	15.0463	13.3317
50....	39.1961	34.9997	31.4236	28.3623	25.7298	23.4556	21.4822	19.7620	18.2559	15.7619	13.8007

Table A-2 (continued)
Present Value of Annuity of $1.00 Per Period

8%	10%	12%	14%	15%	16%	18%	20%	22%	24%	25%	26%	28%	30%	40%	50%
0.9259	0.9091	0.893	0.877	0.870	0.862	0.847	0.833	0.820	0.806	0.800	0.794	0.781	0.769	0.714	0.667
1.7833	1.7355	1.690	1.647	1.626	1.605	1.566	1.528	1.492	1.457	1.440	1.424	1.392	1.361	1.224	1.111
2.5771	2.4869	2.402	2.322	2.283	2.246	2.174	2.106	2.042	1.981	1.952	1.923	1.868	1.816	1.589	1.407
3.3121	3.1699	3.037	2.914	2.855	2.798	2.690	2.589	2.494	2.404	2.362	2.320	2.241	2.166	1.849	1.605
3.9927	3.7908	3.605	3.433	3.352	3.274	3.127	2.991	2.864	2.745	2.689	2.635	2.532	2.436	2.035	1.737
4.6229	4.3553	4.111	3.889	3.784	3.685	3.498	3.326	3.167	3.020	2.951	2.885	2.759	2.643	2.168	1.824
5.2064	4.8684	4.564	4.288	4.160	4.039	3.812	3.605	3.416	3.242	3.161	3.083	2.937	2.802	2.263	1.883
5.7466	5.3349	4.968	4.639	4.487	4.344	4.078	3.837	3.619	3.421	3.329	3.241	3.076	2.925	2.331	1.922
6.2469	5.7590	5.328	4.946	4.772	4.607	4.303	4.031	3.786	3.566	3.463	3.366	3.184	3.019	2.379	1.948
6.7101	6.1446	5.650	5.216	5.019	4.833	4.494	4.192	3.923	3.682	3.571	3.465	3.269	3.092	2.414	1.965
7.1390	6.4951	5.988	5.453	5.234	5.029	4.656	4.327	4.035	3.776	3.656	3.544	3.335	3.147	2.438	1.977
7.5361	6.8137	6.194	5.660	5.421	5.197	4.793	4.439	4.127	3.851	3.725	3.606	3.387	3.190	2.456	1.985
7.9038	7.1034	6.424	5.842	5.583	5.342	4.910	4.533	4.203	3.912	3.780	3.656	3.427	3.223	2.468	1.990
8.2442	7.3667	6.628	6.002	5.724	5.468	5.008	4.611	4.265	3.962	3.824	3.695	3.459	3.249	2.477	1.993
8.5595	7.6061	6.811	6.142	5.847	5.575	5.092	4.675	4.315	4.001	3.859	3.726	3.483	3.268	2.484	1.995
8.8514	7.8237	6.974	6.265	5.954	5.669	5.162	4.730	4.357	4.033	3.887	3.751	3.503	3.283	2.489	1.997
9.1216	8.0216	7.120	6.373	6.047	5.749	5.222	4.775	4.391	4.059	3.910	3.771	3.518	3.295	2.492	1.998
9.3719	8.2014	7.250	6.467	6.128	5.818	5.273	4.812	4.419	4.080	3.928	3.786	3.529	3.304	2.494	1.999
9.6036	8.3649	7.366	6.550	6.198	5.877	5.316	4.844	4.442	4.097	3.942	3.799	3.539	3.311	2.496	1.999
9.8181	8.5136	7.469	6.623	6.259	5.929	5.353	4.870	4.460	4.110	3.954	3.808	3.546	3.316	2.497	1.999
10.0168	8.6487	7.562	6.687	6.312	5.973	5.384	4.891	4.476	4.121	3.963	3.816	3.551	3.320	2.498	2.000
10.2007	8.7715	7.645	6.743	6.359	6.011	5.410	4.909	4.488	4.130	3.970	3.822	3.556	3.323	2.498	2.000
10.3711	8.8832	7.718	6.792	6.399	6.044	5.432	4.925	4.499	4.137	3.976	3.827	3.559	3.325	2.499	2.000
10.5288	8.9847	7.784	6.835	6.434	6.073	5.451	4.937	4.507	4.143	3.981	3.831	3.562	3.327	2.499	2.000
10.6748	9.0770	7.843	6.873	6.464	6.097	5.467	4.948	4.514	4.147	3.985	3.834	3.564	3.329	2.499	2.000
10.8100	9.1609	7.896	6.906	6.491	6.118	5.480	4.956	4.520	4.151	3.988	3.837	3.566	3.330	2.500	2.000
10.9352	9.2372	7.943	6.935	6.514	6.136	5.492	4.964	4.524	4.154	3.990	3.839	3.567	3.331	2.500	2.000
11.0511	9.3066	7.984	6.961	6.534	6.152	5.502	4.970	4.528	4.157	3.992	3.840	3.568	3.331	2.500	2.000
11.1584	9.3696	8.022	6.983	6.551	6.166	5.510	4.975	4.531	4.159	3.994	3.841	3.569	3.332	2.500	2.000
11.2578	9.4269	8.055	7.003	6.566	6.177	5.517	4.979	4.534	4.160	3.995	3.842	3.569	3.332	2.500	2.000
11.9246	9.7791	8.244	7.105	6.642	6.234	5.548	4.997	4.544	4.166	3.999	3.846	3.571	3.333	2.500	2.000
12.2335	9.9148	8.304	7.133	6.661	6.246	5.554	4.999	4.545	4.167	4.000	3.846	3.571	3.333	2.500	2.000

NOTE: To convert this table to values of an annuity in advance, take one less period and add 1.0000.

1. Determine the amount that $1,000 will accumulate to in three years at an 8 percent annual interest rate.

2. Determine the present value of $1,000 due in five years at each of the following interest rates:

    a.   6 percent
    b.   8 percent
    c.   10 percent

3. An investor wishes to have $5,000 available at the end of five years. State the amount of money that must be invested at the present time if the interest rate is:

    a.   6 percent
    b.   8 percent
    c.   12 percent

4. Determine the present value of an ordinary annuity for a period of five years with annual payments of $2,000, assuming that the interest rate is:

    a.   7 percent
    b.   10 percent
    c.   12 percent

5. What is the maximum amount you would be willing to pay at the present time in order to receive 10 annual payments of $1,000 beginning one year from now? The current interest rate is 10 percent.

6. Hays Company leases a building at an annual rental of $2,000 paid at the end of each year. The company has been given the alternative of paying the remaining 10 years of the lease in advance on January 1, 19x0. Assuming an interest rate of 8 percent, what is the maximum amount that should be paid now for the advance rent?

7. Determine the selling price of the bonds in each of the following situations (assume that the bonds are dated and sold on the same date):

    a.   A 10-year, $1,000 face value bond with annual interest of 9 percent (payable annually) sold to yield 8 percent effective interest.
    b.   A 10-year, $1,000 face value bond with annual interest of 9 percent (payable annually) sold to yield 10 percent effective interest.
    c.   A 10-year, $1,000 face value bond with annual interest of 9 percent (payable annually) sold to yield 9 percent effective interest.

8. Nancy Company issued $10,000 of bonds payable on January 1, 19x1 with an 8 percent coupon interest rate, payable annually on December 31. The bonds mature in 5 years and were sold at a 10 percent effective interest rate.

    a.   Determine the selling price of the bonds.

    b.   Prepare a schedule showing the amount of discount to be amortized each year for the life of the bonds, assuming the interest method of amortization.

    c.   Give the journal entry to record the interest payment on December 31, 19x1.

9.   Joyce Company issued $10,000 of bond payable on January 1, 19x1, with an 8 percent coupon interest rate payable annually on December 31. The bonds mature in 5 years and were sold at a 7 percent effective interest rate.

Required:

    1.   Determine the selling price of the bonds.

    2.   Prepare a schedule showing the premium to be amortized each year for the life of the bonds, assuming the interest method of amortization.

    3.   Give the journal entry to record the interest payment on December 31, 19x1.

Chapter 10 discusses common techniques of analyzing information presented in financial statements. Studying this chapter should enable you to:

1. Distinguish between horizontal and vertical analyses and discuss the type of information that is provided by each.

2. Discuss the concept of ratio analysis and identify the problems that may be inherent in its use.

3. List the most commonly used standards against which a firm may be compared and explain the strengths and limitations associated with the use of these standards.

4. Describe and apply the basic techniques of financial analysis as they are used by common stockholders, long-term creditors, and short-term creditors.

10

Financial Statement Analysis

INTRODUCTION

The financial statements of a business enterprise are intended to provide much of the basic data used for decision-making and, in general, evaluation of performance by various groups such as current owners, potential investors, creditors, government agencies, and in some instances, competitors. Because general-purpose published financial statements are by their very nature issued for a wide variety of users, it is often necessary for particular user groups to extract the information in which they are particularly interested from the statements. For example, owners and potential investors are normally interested in the present earnings and future earnings prospects of a business. Similarly, short-term creditors are primarily concerned with the ability of a firm to meet its short-term obligations as they become due and payable. Consequently, a somewhat detailed analysis and interpretation of financial statements is usually required in order to obtain the information which may be relevant for the specific purposes of a particular user. In this chapter, several selected techniques which are useful in financial analysis will be described and discussed.

COMPARATIVE FINANCIAL STATEMENTS

In general, the usefulness of financial information is increased when it can be compared with related data. Comparison may be internal (i.e., within one firm) or external (i.e., with another firm). External comparisons may be difficult to make in practice since financial statements of firms may not be readily comparable because of the use of different generally acceptable accounting principles. However, some useful information may be obtained by comparison with industry averages, ratios, etc. (such as those compiled by *Moody's* and *Standard and Poor's*) or by direct comparison with the statements of another firm. Obviously, considerable caution must be exercised when making this type of analysis.

The financial statements of a particular firm are most useful when they can be compared with related data from within the current period, information from prior periods, or with budgets or forecasts. Comparative statements are useful in providing a standard which facilitates the analysis and interpretation of changes and trends which have occurred in elements of the financial statements. Generally, published annual reports of corporations provide comparative accounting statements from the previous period and often also include selected historical information for the firm for a longer period of time, such as ten years.

Assume that the income statement of a firm for the year ended December 31, 19x2, disclosed net income of $100,000. This information, in and of itself, provides a user with only a single indicator of the absolute amount of income for the year. If an income statement for 19x1, disclosing net income of $80,000 was also presented, 19x2 net income would become much more meaningful information to the user. The 25 percent increase of 19x2 income over that for 19x1 indicates a significant improvement in performance that could not be determined from the 19x2 statements alone.

BASIC ANALYTICAL PROCEDURES   Comparisons of financial statement data are frequently expressed as percentages or ratios. These comparisons may represent:

1. Percentage increases and decreases in an item in comparative financial statements;
2. Percentage relationships of individual components to an aggregate total in a single financial statement; or
3. Ratios of one amount to another in the financial statements.

Application of each of these three methods will be illustrated by the use of the comparative financial statements of Dolbey Company which follow. These comparative statements will also serve as a basis for the analysis presented in the remainder of this chapter.

Dolbey Company
Comparative Balance Sheet
December 31, 19x2 and 19x1

	19x2		19x1		Increase (Decrease)	
	Dollars	Per-cent of Total Assets	Dollars	Per-cent of Total Assets	Dollars	Per-cent
ASSETS						
Current assets:						
Cash	$ 80,000	5.0	$ 40,000	2.8	$ 40,000	100.0
Net accounts receivable	100,000	6.3	80,000	5.5	20,000	25.0
Inventories	200,000	12.5	160,000	11.1	40,000	25.0
Prepaid expenses	20,000	1.2	8,000	.6	12,000	150.0
Total Current Assets	$ 400,000	25.0	$ 288,000	20.0	$112,000	38.9
Land, buildings, and equipment						
(Net).	1,200,000	75.0	1,152,000	80.0	48,000	4.2
Total Assets	$1,600,000	100.0	$1,440,000	100.0	$160,000	11.1
LIABILITIES						
Current liabilities:						
Accounts payable.	$ 200,000	12.5	$ 130,000	9.0	$ 70,000	53.8
Notes payable	100,000	6.3	60,000	4.2	40,000	66.7
Total Current Liabilities	$ 300,000	18.8	$ 190,000	13.2	$110,000	57.9
Bonds payable.	200,000	12.5	200,000	13.9	-0-	-0-
Total Liabilities	$ 500,000	31.3	$ 390,000	27.1	$110,000	28.2
STOCKHOLDERS' EQUITY						
Common stock ($30 par)	$ 900,000	56.2	$ 900,000	62.5	-0-	-0-
Retained earnings.	$ 200,000	12.5	$ 150,000	10.4	$ 50,000	33.3
Total Liabilities and Stockholders'						
Equity	$1,600,000	100.0	$1,440,000	100.0	$160,000	11.1

Horizontal Analysis   Analysis of increases or decreases in a given financial statement item over two or more accounting periods is often referred to as horizontal analysis. Generally, this type of analysis discloses both the dollar and percentage changes for the corresponding items in comparative statements. An example of horizontal analysis is included in the comparative financial statements presented for Dolbey Company. These statements include data with regard to income, retained earnings, and financial position for a two-year period with the dollar and percentage changes for each item listed in the final two columns.

Dolbey Company
Comparative Income Statement
For the Years Ended December 31, 19x2 and 19x1

	19x2		19x1		Increase (Decrease)	
	Dollars	*Percent of Sales*	*Dollars*	*Percent of Sales*	*Dollars*	*Percent*
Net sales	$2,000,000	100.0	$1,500,000	100.0	$500,000	33.3
Cost of goods sold	1,400,000	70.0	1,080,000	72.0	320,000	29.6
Gross profit on sales	$ 600,000	30.0	$ 420,000	28.0	$180,000	42.9
Operating expenses:						
Selling expenses.	$ 300,000	15.0	$ 240,000	16.0	$ 60,000	25.0
Administrative expenses	180,000	9.0	129,000	8.6	51,000	39.5
Total Operating Expenses . .	$ 480,000	24.0	$ 369,000	24.6	$111,000	30.1
Operating income	$ 120,000	6.0	$ 51,000	3.4	$ 69,000	135.3
Interest expense.	10,000	.5	9,000	.6	1,000	11.1
Income before income taxes. . .	$ 110,000	5.5	$ 42,000	2.8	$ 68,000	161.9
Income taxes	30,000	1.5	12,000	.8	18,000	150.0
Net Income	$ 80,000	4.0	$ 30,000	2.0	$ 50,000	166.7

Dolbey Company
Comparative Statement of Retained Earnings
For the Years Ended December 31, 19x2 and 19x1

	19x2	19x1	Increase (Decrease)	
			Dollars	*Percent*
Retained earnings, January 1	$150,000	$135,000	$15,000	11.1
Net income	80,000	30,000	50,000	166.7
	$230,000	$165,000	$65,000	39.4
Less: Dividends	30,000	15,000	15,000	100.0
Retained earnings, December 31	$200,000	$150,000	$50,000	33.3

Data from the 19x0 statements:	
Total assets (December 31, 19x0).	$1,160,000
Stockholders' equity (December 31, 19x0). . . .	1,035,000
Net receivables (December 31, 19x0).	70,000
Inventory (December 31, 19x0).	110,000

Interpretation of the increases or decreases in individual statement items cannot be completely evaluated without additional information. For example, the comparative balance sheet discloses an increase in inventory during 19x2 of $40,000, to an amount 25 percent greater than in 19x1. This increase may have been required in order to support a higher sales volume as net sales increased by a third during 19x2. Alternatively, this increase could have resulted from a buildup of an obsolete inventory item. Obviously, the point to be made here is that additional information is often useful and sometimes absolutely necessary for meaningful interpretation.

Percentage changes included in the statements for Dolbey Company were stated in terms of the data for two years. When a comparison is made between statements of two periods, the earlier statement is normally used as a base in computing percentage changes. For statements which include more than two years, there are two methods which may be used in selecting a base year. One alternative is to use the earliest year as a base. If this alternative is selected, each amount on all succeeding statements will be expressed as a percentage of the base year amount. Since this procedure results in a constant base, percentage changes for more than two years can be interpreted as trend values for individual components of the financial statements. A second alternative is to compare each statement with the statement which immediately precedes it. Adoption of this procedure results in a changing base that may make comparisons of percentage changes over a period of several years more difficult.

Vertical Analysis

The percentage relationship of an individual item or component of a single financial statement to an aggregate total in the same statement often discloses significant relationships. These relationships may be useful information for decision-making purposes. For example, in reporting income data, it may be useful to indicate the relationship between sales and other elements of the income statement for a period. This analysis of the elements included in the financial statements of a single period is often referred to as vertical analysis.

Vertical analysis is also illustrated in the financial statements presented for Dolbey Company. In the comparative balance sheet, the total assets balance and the total liabilities and stockholders' equity balance for each year are used as a base. Each item in the statement is then expressed as a percentage of this base. For example, the statements indicate that current assets increased from 20 percent of total assets in 19x1 to 25 percent at the end of 19x2. An analysis of the composition of the current asset balance provides additional details of the changes in various individual categories of current assets.

Vertical analysis may also be employed in presenting a comparative income statement. In the Dolbey Company illustration, each individual item is stated as a percent of net sales for the period.

Common-Size Statements

Horizontal and vertical analyses are frequently useful in disclosing certain relationships and trends in individual elements included in the financial statements. The analysis of these relationships may be facilitated by the use of common-size statements, i.e.,—statements in which all items are stated in terms of percentages or ratios. Common-size statements may be prepared in order to compare data from the current period with that from one or more past periods for a firm. These statements may also be used to compare data of two or more business firms for the same period or periods, subject to the limitations mentioned previously.

A common-size statement comparing income statement data for Dolbey Company with that of Nutt Company is presented below. The column for Dolbey Company is prepared by using the percentage figures that were included in the comparative income statement previously given. Net sales of each firm are set as a base of 100 percent and each individual item included in the statement is shown as a percentage of net sales. Consequently, use of this statement format provides a comparison of the relationships of the income statement items for the two firms regardless of the absolute dollar amount of sales and expenses of either company. It can be seen, for example, that Dolbey Company obtained $.04 of net income from each dollar of net sales, while Nutt Company netted only $.01 of net income from each sales dollar.

Dolbey Company and Nutt Company
Condensed Common-Size Income Statement
For the Year Ended December 31, 19x2

	Dolbey Company	Nutt Company
Net sales	100.0%	100.0%
Cost of goods sold	70.0	72.5
Gross profit on sales	30.0%	27.5%
Operating expenses:		
Selling expense	15.0%	17.5%
Administrative expense	9.	7.5
Total Operating Expenses	24.0%	25.0%
Operating income	6.0%	2.5%
Interest expense	.5	1.0
Income before income taxes.	5.5%	1.5%
Income taxes	1.5	.5
Net Income	4.0%	1.0%

RATIO ANALYSIS

A ratio is an expression of the relationship of one numerical item to another. Significant interrelationships which may be present in financial statements are often identified and highlighted by the use of ratio analysis. A simple example of such a relationship would be the ratio of cash to current liabilities for Dolbey Company at the end of 19x2. The ratio would be calculated or computed as follows:

$$\frac{\text{Ratio of Cash to}}{\text{Current Liabilities}} = \frac{\text{Cash}}{\text{Current Liabilities}}$$

$$.27 = \frac{\$\ 80,000}{\$300,000}$$

Ratios may be expressed in several different ways. Generally, ratios are stated in relation to a base of one. For example, for the ratio computed above, it could be stated that the ratio of cash to current liabilities is .27 to 1 (which is sometimes simply stated as .27 with the "to 1" omitted). In any case, a ratio is a method used to describe a relationship between two financial statement amounts. The meaningful use of ratio analysis requires that there be a logical relationship between the figures compared, and that this relationship be clearly understood by the user.

Comparison with Standards

The analytical procedures employed in computing percentage changes (horizontal analysis), component percentages (vertical analysis), and ratios convert financial statement items into a form which may be comparable to various standards. It is comparisons made among the relationships derived from the financial statements and selected standards that allow the user to draw meaningful conclusions concerning the firm. Among the most commonly used standards of comparison against which the position of a particular firm may be measured are the following:

1. Past performance of the firm.
2. Financial data of similar or competing firms.
3. Average performance of a number of firms in the industry.

A major deficiency of comparison with the past performance of the firm is that there is no indication of what *should* have occurred given the nature of the firm, the economy of the period, etc. For example, the fact that the net income of a firm increased by 3 percent from the previous year may initially appear to be favorable. However, if there is evidence that net income *should* have increased by 6 percent, the performance for the current year would be regarded as unfavorable.

The weakness of comparisons with past performance of the firm may be overcome somewhat by using the performance of a similar firm or firms or an industry average as an additional standard for comparison. A problem with this approach, however, is that it is often difficult to identify firms which are truly comparable, both because of the nature of the firms themselves and because of the use of alternative "generally accepted accounting principles." In spite of these limitations, a careful analysis of comparative performance, both internal and external, often provides meaningful input for use in decision-making.

ANALYSIS FOR COMMON STOCKHOLDERS

Common stockholders and potential investors purchase securities of a firm in an attempt to earn a return on their investment through increases in the market price of the stock and by dividends. Because each of these factors is influenced by net income, the analysis of financial statements made by, or on behalf of, an investor is focused primarily on the company's record of earnings. Certain of the more important relationships which are of interest to the stockholder-investor are discussed in the following sections of this chapter.

Rate of Return on Total Assets

The rate of return on total assets provides a measure of management's ability to earn a return on the firm's assets. The income figure used in this computation should be income before the deduction of interest expense, since interest is the return to creditors for the resources that they provide to the firm. Thus, the rate of return on total assets is computed by dividing net income plus interest expense by the average investment in assets during the year.

$$\frac{\text{Rate of Return}}{\text{on Total Assets}} = \frac{\text{Net Income (after taxes)} + \text{Interest Expense}}{\text{Average Total Assets during the Year}}$$

Although assets are continually acquired and disposed of throughout a period, an average of asset balances at the beginning and end of the period is generally used for this calculation. The calculation for Dolbey Company would be as follows:

	19x2	19x1
Net income	$ 80,000	$ 30,000
Add interest expense	10,000	9,000
Net income before interest expense.	$ 90,000	$ 39,000
Total assets		
Beginning of year	$1,440,000	$1,160,000
End of year	1,600,000	1,440,000
Total	$3,040,000	$2,600,000
Average total assets	$1,520,000	$1,300,000
Rate of return on assets	5.9%	3.0%

This ratio indicates that the earnings per dollar of assets invested have almost doubled in 19x2. It appears that the management of Dolbey Company has increased its efficiency in the use of the firm's assets to generate income.

Rate of Return on Common Stockholders' Equity

The rate of return on common stockholders' equity is a measure of a firm's ability to earn a profit for its residual owners, the common stockholders. Because interest paid to creditors and dividends paid to preferred stockholders are normally fixed in amount, the return on common stockholders' equity may not be equal to the return on total assets. If management is able to earn a higher return on assets than the cost (i.e., interest expense) of assets contributed by the creditors, the excess benefits the owners. This is often referred to as using debt as favorable "leverage" in order to increase the owners' rate of return or as "trading on equity." Of course, if the cost of borrowing funds exceeds the return on assets, leverage will be unfavorable and will reduce the rate of return to the residual owners. The rate of return on common stockholders' equity is computed by dividing net income, less preferred dividends, by the average equity of the common stockholders.

$$\frac{\text{Rate of Return}}{\text{on Common}} = \frac{\text{Net Income (after taxes)} - \text{Preferred Dividends}}{\text{Average Common Stockholders' Equity}}$$

Since Dolbey Company has no preferred stock, the rate of return on common stockholders' equity would be computed as follows:

	19x2	19x1
Net income	$ 80,000	$ 30,000
Common stockholders' equity:		
Beginning of the year	$1,050,000	$1,035,000
End of the year	1,100,000	1,050,000
Total	$2,150,000	$2,085,000
Average common stockholders' equity	$1,075,000	$1,042,500
Rate of return on common stockholders' equity	7.4%	2.9%

The rate of return on the common stockholders' equity is higher than the rate of return on assets for 19x2 because the cost of funds contributed by creditors is less than the rate earned on assets. Thus the company is experiencing favorable "leverage," using borrowed funds to earn a return in excess of their cost.

Earnings Per Share of Common Stock

Since the owners of a business invest in shares of stock, they are usually interested in an expression of earnings in terms of a per share amount. If a company has only a single class of common stock outstanding, the earnings per share figure is computed by dividing net income for the period by the average number of common shares outstanding.[1] If the firm has other securities outstanding which have certain characteristics similar to

---

[1] The calculation of earnings per share was discussed in Chapter 6.

those of common stock (such as convertible bonds), the usefulness of earnings per share data is enhanced if these other securities are also considered in the computation of earnings per share. These securities are often referred to as common stock equivalents. While a discussion of the inclusion of common stock equivalents in the computation of earnings per share is beyond the scope of this text, the basic principle involved is that earnings per share figures are calculated so as to indicate the effects of the conversion of these securities into common stock.

When there is both common and preferred stock outstanding, net income must be reduced by preferred dividend requirements in order to determine net income available to common stockholders.

$$\text{Earnings Per Share} = \frac{\text{Net Income} - \text{Preferred Dividends}}{\text{Average Number of Common Shares Outstanding}}$$

In the case of Dolbey Company, which has no preferred stock, the earnings per share of common stock would be calculated as follows:

	19x2	19x1
Net income	$80,000	$30,000
Number of common shares outstanding	30,000	30,000
Earnings per share of common stock	$ 2.67	$ 1.00

Earnings per share is a ratio frequently mentioned in the financial press in relation to the earnings performance of business firms. In addition, earnings per share data is reported on the income statement, and usually in various other sections of corporate annual reports. Although the concept of earnings per share has received a great deal of attention, particularly in recent years, it should be viewed with some caution. As a minimum, it should be recognized that all of the significant aspects of a firm's performance simply cannot be reduced to a single figure. This point cannot be overemphasized.

Price-Earnings Ratio on Common Stock

Each investor must allocate his limited resources among various investment opportunities which are available to him. For this reason the rate of earnings in relation to the current market price of his investment often provides a useful basis for comparing alternative investment opportunities. This ratio is commonly referred to as the price-earnings ratio. It is computed by dividing the current market price per share of common stock by earnings per share.

$$\text{Price-Earnings Ratio} = \frac{\text{Market Price Per Share of Common Stock}}{\text{Earnings Per Share}}$$

Assuming that the market price per common share of Dolbey Company at the end of 19x2 was $24 and at the end of 19x1 was $8, price-earnings ratios would be calculated as follows:

	19x2	19x1
Market price per share at the end of the year	$24.00	$8.00
Earnings per share.	$ 2.67	$1.00
Price-earnings ratio	9	8

The price-earnings ratio may be interpreted as the value that investors in the stock market place on every dollar of earnings for a particular firm. An investor may compare the price-earnings ratio of a firm to that of other companies in an attempt to estimate whether a firm's stock is overpriced or underpriced.

Debt-to-Equity Ratio

The debt-to-equity ratio measures the proportion of funds supplied to the firm by its stockholders as opposed to funds provided by creditors. It is computed by dividing total debt by stockholders' equity.

$$\text{Debt-to-Equity Ratio} = \frac{\text{Total Debt}}{\text{Stockholders' Equity}}$$

The debt-to-equity ratio provides a measure of the risk incurred by common stockholders. Since debt consists of fixed obligations, the larger the debt-to-equity ratio, the greater is the chance that a firm may face a situation in which it is unable to meet its obligations. At the same time, however, a high debt-to-equity ratio can increase the rate of return on stockholders' equity through the use of favorable financial leverage. This can occur because interest on debt is fixed in amount, regardless of the amount of earnings. Consequently there is no ideal debt-to-equity ratio. Rather, each investor must define a satisfactory debt-to-equity ratio based on his desired degree of risk.

For Dolbey Company, the debt-to-equity ratios are calculated as follows:

	19x2	19x1
Total debt	$ 500,000	$ 390,000
Stockholders' equity	$1,100,000	$1,050,000
Debt-to-equity ratio	45.5%	37.1%

ANALYSIS FOR LONG-TERM CREDITORS

Bondholders and other long-term creditors, like stockholders and investors, are also concerned with measures of the profitability of a business. In addition, however, long-term creditors are particularly interested in a firm's ability to meet its interest requirements as they become due and payable. A good indicator of a firm's ability to pay interest is the margin between income and interest payments. A common measure of this margin is the ratio of net income available for interest payments to annual interest expense. This ratio, which is referred to as the number of times interest earned, is computed by dividing net income before interest expense and income taxes by the interest requirement for the period. Income taxes are added back to net income because interest charges are an expense which is deducted in computing income taxes. Similarly, interest charges are added back to net income because the ratio provides a measure of the ability of the firm to pay fixed interest charges.

$$\frac{\text{Number of Times}}{\text{Interest Earned}} = \frac{\text{Net Income } + \text{ Interest Expense } + \text{ Income Taxes}}{\text{Interest Expense}}$$

The computation for Dolbey Company would be as follows:

	19x2	19x1
Net income	$ 80,000	$30,000
Add back:		
Income taxes	30,000	12,000
Interest expense	10,000	9,000
Amount available for interest requirements	$120,000	$51,000
Number of times interest earned	12.0	5.7

The increase in the ratio from 5.7 times in 19x1 to 12.0 times in 19x2 would appear to be favorable with respect to a long-term creditor of Dolbey Company.

ANALYSIS FOR SHORT-TERM CREDITORS

Short-term creditors are also concerned with the earnings prospects of a firm. Of primary importance to the short-term creditor, however, is a firm's ability to pay its current debt on a timely basis and to meet its current operating needs. This is often referred to as the current position of the firm.

The ability of a firm to pay its current debts as they fall due depends largely upon the relationship between its current assets and its current liabilities. The excess of a firm's current assets over its current liabilities is termed working capital. Adequate working capital enables a firm to meet its current needs and obligations on a timely basis. However, an analysis of the components of working capital and the flow of working capital is necessary in order to determine the adequacy of the working capital position of a specific firm.

Current Ratio

The absolute amount of working capital may be an inadequate measure of a firm's ability to meet its obligations. As an illustration, consider the following data for two companies:

	Reed Company	Frazier Company
Current assets	$20,000	$50,000
Current liabilities	10,000	40,000
Working capital	$10,000	$10,000

In this example, both companies have $10,000 of working capital. However, the current assets of Reed Company could be reduced by 50 percent and still be equal to the current liabilities, while the current assets of Frazier Company could only shrink by 20 percent and remain equal to current liabilities.

Another means of evaluating working capital is to evaluate the relationship between current assets and current liabilities. This ratio is referred to as the current ratio.

$$\text{Current Ratio} = \frac{\text{Current Assets}}{\text{Current Liabilities}}$$

The use of the current ratio for the example given would disclose a ratio of 2 to 1 for Reed Company and 1.25 to 1 for Frazier Company. This clearly indicates the stronger current position of Reed Company.

The current ratio for Dolbey Company is calculated as follows:

	19x2	19x1
Current assets	$400,000	$288,000
Current liabilities	300,000	190,000
Current ratio.	1.3	1.5

Although the working capital of Dolbey Company increased from $98,000 in 19x1 to $100,000 in 19x2, current assets per dollar of current liabilities declined from $1.50 to $1.30. This is an unfavorable trend from the viewpoint of short-term creditors because the margin of safety has declined.

A satisfactory current ratio for a particular firm depends, of course, upon the nature of its business. Although short-term creditors generally feel safer as the current ratio increases in amount, this may not be efficient from a business standpoint. For example, a firm with excess cash in relation to its current needs is inefficient since cash is a nonproductive asset. A good measure of the adequacy of a firm's current ratio is often a comparison with the current ratios of similar firms or industry averages.

Acid-Test or Quick Ratio

In analyzing the ability of a firm to meet its obligations, the distribution of current assets is also important. For example, a firm with a large proportion of cash to current assets is better able to meet its current debts than a firm with a larger proportion of inventories. This is because inventories usually require more time for conversion into cash than do other current assets. Assets with a longer conversion period are usually referred to as being less liquid. For this reason, a ratio which excludes the less liquid assets is often used as a supplement to the current ratio. The ratio of the highly current assets—cash, marketable securities, and receivables—to current liabilities is known as the acid-test or quick ratio.

$$\text{Acid-Test Ratio} = \frac{\text{Cash} + \text{Marketable Securities} + \text{Receivables}}{\text{Current Liabilities}}$$

Since Dolbey Company owns no marketable securities, its acid-test ratio would be calculated as follows:

	19x2	19x1
Cash	$ 80,000	$ 40,000
Net accounts receivables	100,000	80,000
Total	$180,000	$120,000
Current liabilities	$300,000	$190,000
Acid-test ratio	.60	.63

In evaluating the acid-test ratio, again the nature of the business must be considered. The .6 acid-test ratio for Dolbey Company in 19x2 may indicate a serious problem as there may not be sufficient liquid assets to meet current liabilities as they become due.

Analysis of Accounts Receivable

It is obvious that the rate at which non-cash current assets may be converted into cash is an important determinant of the firm's ability to meet its current obligations. Because neither the current nor the acid-test ratio considers this movement in current assets, short-term creditors should use additional tests in considering the liquidation of two significant working capital items, receivables and inventories.

An approximation of the average time which is required by a firm in order to collect its receivables may be determined by first computing the turnover of accounts receivable. Receivables turnover is computed by dividing net credit sales by the average accounts receivable balance. Ideally, a monthly average of receivables should be used, but generally only the balances at the beginning and end of the year are available to the user of the financial statements.

$$\frac{\text{Accounts Receivable}}{\text{Turnover}} = \frac{\text{Net Sales on Account}}{\text{Average Accounts Receivable}}$$

The accounts receivable turnover is an approximation of the number of times accounts receivable were converted into cash during the period. Therefore, the higher the turnover, the more liquid are the firm's receivables.

Accounts receivable turnover of Dolbey Company is computed below. Assume that all sales were made on a credit basis and that only the beginning and end of the year balances of receivables are available.

	19x2	19x1
Net sales on account	$2,000,000	$1,500,000
Net receivables:		
Beginning of year	$ 80,000	$ 70,000
End of year	100,000	80,000
Total	$ 180,000	$ 150,000
Average	$ 90,000	$ 75,000
Accounts receivable turnover per year	22.2 times	20.0 times

This increase in the receivables turnover for Dolbey Company during 19x2 indicates that the average collection period for receivables has decreased. This could be a result of more successful collection practices or a change in credit policies, or a combination of both factors.

The receivables turnover may be used to determine the average collection period, which can be readily compared with the firm's credit terms. The average number of days to collect receivables is computed by dividing 365 days by the receivables turnover.

$$\text{Average Number of Days to Collect Receivables} = \frac{365 \text{ Days}}{\text{Accounts Receivable Turnover}}$$

If the average number of days required to collect receivables significantly exceeds the credit terms of the firm, this would indicate that the credit department may be ineffective in its credit granting and collecting activities.

The average number of days to collect receivables is calculated for the Dolbey Company as follows:

	19x2	19x1
Receivables turnover	22.2 times	20.0 times
Average number of days to collect receivables	16.4 days	18.3 days

Analysis of Inventories

A procedure similar to that used for evaluating receivables may be employed in evaluating the inventories of a firm. One indication of the liquidity of inventories is obtained by determining the relationship between the cost of goods sold and the average balance of inventories on hand during a period. Cost of goods sold is used because it represents the cost (rather than selling price) of goods that have been sold from the inventories during the period.

Inventory turnover is calculated by dividing cost of goods sold by the average inventory. Again, if possible, monthly figures should be used to determine average inventory. Usually, however, only the beginning and end of the year inventory balances are available.

$$\text{Inventory Turnover} = \frac{\text{Cost of Goods Sold}}{\text{Average Inventory}}$$

A low inventory turnover may indicate management inefficiency in that excess cash has been committed to the investment in inventory. Although inventories are necessary to meet the demands of a firm, there are advantages in maintaining the investment in inventory at the minimum level necessary to service customers, thus minimizing carrying costs, risks of loss or obsolescence, etc.

Assuming that only the beginning and ending inventories are available, the computation of inventory turnover for Dolbey Company is as follows:

	19x2	19x1
Cost of goods sold	$1,400,000	$1,080,000
Inventory:		
Beginning of the year.	$ 160,000	$ 110,000
End of the year	200,000	160,000
Total.	$ 360,000	$ 270,000
Average inventory	$ 180,000	$ 135,000
Inventory turnover	7.8 times	8 times

It appears that the trend of the inventory turnover for Dolbey Company is somewhat unfavorable, since inventories were turned over more slowly in 19x2 than in 19x1. Again, the analyst would want to obtain additional information before making a definitive judgment.

INTERPRETATION OF ANALYSES

The user must exercise considerable caution in the use of ratios in order to analyze the financial statements of a business enterprise. Some of the problems inherent in ratio analysis are summarized below:

1. Comparisons of items for different periods or for different companies may not be valid if different accounting practices have been used. For example, one firm may use straight-line depreciation and the Fifo inventory method while a similar company may use accelerated depreciation and Lifo for its inventories.

2. Financial statements represent only one source of financial information

concerning a firm and its environment. Consequently, other information not disclosed in financial statements may have an impact on the evaluation of the statements.

3. Most financial statements are not adjusted either for changes in market values or in the general price level. This may seriously affect comparability between firms over time.

4. As ratio analysis has increased in popularity, there has sometimes been a tendency to develop ratios which have little or no significance. A meaningful ratio can be developed only from items which have a logical relationship.

All of the ratios and measurements developed in this chapter need not be used as input in a particular decision. In determining the financial strengths and weaknesses of a particular firm, relevant measurements need to be selected, developed, and interpreted in view of the conditions relating to the business.

SUMMARY   Financial statements provide a variety of external users with essential data regarding a firm's financial position and the results of its operations. However, most users of financial statements must make a detailed analysis and interpretation of the data presented to obtain evaluative information useful in making decisions.

The actual evaluative techniques used by an individual will vary according to personal preference and the nature of the individual's relationship to the reporting firm. Most techniques involve some type of comparison with related data. The data may relate to the firm's past performance, to similar or competing firms, or to an industry average. Comparisons are often expressed in terms of percentages or ratios, although there are certain problems inherent in ratio analysis.

Firms may present a horizontal or vertical analysis of relevant data along with their regular financial statements. A horizontal analysis usually presents both the dollar and percentage changes for corresponding items for two or more accounting periods. Vertical analysis discloses the percentage relationship of an individual item or component of a single financial statement to an aggregate total included in the same statement. Presentation of these analyses may be facilitated by the use of common-size statements in which all items are stated in terms of percentages and ratios.

Since current and potential stockholders are primarily interested in earning an acceptable return on their investments through increases in the market price of the stock and by dividends, their analyses focus on the company's record of earnings. Examples of earnings relationships of interest to the stockholder-investor are the rate of return on total assets, the rate of return on common stockholders' equity, the earnings per share of common stock, and the price-earnings ratio on common stock. The stockholders may also be interested in the debt to equity ratio as a measure of the risk incurred by the common stockholders as opposed to the risk incurred by creditors.

In addition to their interest in the profitability of the business, bondholders and other long-term creditors are concerned with the firm's ability to meet its interest requirements as they become payable. A common measure of such ability is the ratio of net income available for interest payments to annual interest expense. This measure is generally referred to as the number of times interest is earned.

Short-term creditors are primarily interested in the firm's ability to pay its current debt on a timely basis and to meet its current operating needs. Although the absolute amount of working capital available to a firm may provide useful information to a creditor, the ratio of current assets to current liabilities (referred to as the current ratio) is generally thought to provide better evaluative data. If only the more liquid current assets are used in the ratio, it is referred to as an acid-test ratio. Other evaluation methods used by short-term creditors include the analysis of accounts receivable and the analysis of inventories.

KEY DEFINITIONS

Accounts receivable turnover Accounts receivable turnover is an approximation of the number of times accounts receivable were converted into cash during the period. It is defined as net sales on account divided by average accounts receivable.

Acid-test ratio This ratio is a measure of a firm's ability to pay its current liabilities as they come due with the more liquid current assets. It is usually the ratio of cash, marketable securities, and receivables to total current liabilities.

Average collection period This is a measure of the average time required by a firm to collect a receivable. Collection period is computed by dividing 365 days by the receivables turnover.

Common-size statements In common-size financial statements, all items are stated in terms of percentages or ratios.

Current ratio This ratio measures a firm's ability to pay current liabilities as they come due. It is defined as the ratio of current assets to current liabilities.

Debt-to-equity ratio Debt-to-equity measures the proportion of funds supplied by stockholders as opposed to the funds provided by creditors. It is computed by dividing total debt by total stockholders' equity.

Horizontal analysis The analysis of the increase or decrease in a given financial statement item over two or more accounting periods.

Inventory turnover Inventory turnover gives an indication of the liquidity of inventories. Its computation involves dividing cost of goods sold by the average inventory.

Number of times interest earned This measure of a firm's ability to pay interest is computed by dividing net income before interest expense and income taxes by the interest expense.

Price-earnings ratio The current market price of a share of stock divided by the earnings per share.

Rate of return on common stockholders' equity This measure of the firm's ability to earn a profit for its common stockholders is computed by dividing net income after taxes and preferred dividends by the average common stockholders' equity.

Rate of return on total assets This measure of the ability of the firm's management to earn a return on the assets without regard to variations in the method of financing is computed by dividing net income plus interest expense by the average investment in assets during the year.

Ratio analysis The analysis of items in a financial statement expressing the relationship of one numerical item to another.

Vertical analysis The percentage relationship between an individual item or a component of a single financial statement to an aggregate total in the statement.

QUESTIONS

1. How is the financial statement analysis related to the needs of the various users of financial statements?

2. Distinguish between vertical analysis and horizontal analysis.

3. What are common-size statements?

4. How are each of the following computed?

   a. Rate of Return on Total Assets.
   b. Rate of Return on Common Stockholders' Equity.
   c. Earnings per Share of Common Stock.
   d. Price-Earnings Ratio on Common Stock.
   e. Debt-to-Equity Ratio.
   f. Number of Times Interest Earned.
   g. Current Ratio.
   h. Acid-Test Ratio.
   i. Accounts Receivable Turnover.
   j. Average Number of Days to Collect Receivables.
   k. Inventory Turnover.

5. Each of the ratios (in Question 4 above) are utilized by one user group more than others. Indicate whether each item is utilized most by (1) common shareholders (or investors), (2) long-term creditors, or (3) short-term creditors.

6. What are the most commonly used standards against which to measure the position of a particular firm? What are the weaknesses inherent in these standards?

7. Business corporations usually provide comparative statements in their annual reports. What is a comparative statement? How do they enhance the usefulness of financial information?

8. What will be the effect (increase, decrease, none) on the rate of return on assets of each of the following?

   a. Cash purchase of a new machine.
   b. Increase in the tax rate.
   c. Reduction of accounts payable.
   d. Cash sale of a fully depreciated machine.

9. What is indicated if the average number of days to collect receivables significantly exceeds the credit terms of the firm?

10. What are the principal limitations that should be considered in evaluating ratios?

11. When percentage changes are given in comparative statements for more than two years, there are two methods for selecting the base year. What are they?

12. Which of the methods in Question 11 makes comparison of percentage changes over several years more difficult? Why?

13. The acid-test ratio at the beginning of 19x0 was 2 to 1 for the Gilly Company.

Required:

How would the following transactions affect the acid-test or quick ratio?

1. Collection of note receivable from Silly Co. The note was due in 19x3.
2. Collection of accounts receivable.
3. Sales on account.
4. Purchase of inventory on account.
5. Payment of accounts payable.
6. Collection of an account receivable.
7. Cash purchase of common stock of ABC Co. as a temporary investment.
8. Purchase of a new machine on a credit basis, the purchase price payable in 6 months.

14. The following information has been extracted from the financial statements of Cozeb Corp.

Common stock, $5 par......................	$ 5,000,000
Common stock, $10 par.....................	5,000,000
Preferred stock, $100 par....................	10,000,000
Net income...............................	3,000,000
Preferred dividends........................	1,000,000

Required:

Compute earnings per share assuming the number of shares outstanding did not change during the year.

15. The December 31, 19x1 financial statement of Flunkart Company included the following data:

Cash.....................................	$ 60,000
Accounts receivable.......................	200,000
Marketable securities......................	100,000
Prepaid expenses..........................	25,000
Accounts payable..........................	200,000
Notes payable (current)....................	85,000
Inventory.................................	115,000
Bonds payable (due in 5 years)..............	300,000
Wages payable............................	15,000

Required:

1. What is the current ratio? Acid-test ratio? Working capital?
2. Comment on the significance of this current ratio.

16. Using the information given, complete the balance sheet below.

a. The "quick" ratio is 2:1.

b. Notes payable are long-term liabilities and are four times the dollar amount of the marketable securities.

c. Accounts receivable are $2,000 and are one-half of the "quick" assets, one-fourth of the current assets, and equal to plant and equipment.

d. Total stockholders' equity is equal to the working capital and contributed capital is twice the dollar amount of the net accumulation of earnings.

Assets		Liabilities and Stockholders' Equity	
Cash	_____	Accounts payable	_____
Marketable securities	_____	Notes payable	_____
Accounts receivable	_____		
Inventories	_____	Capital stock	_____
Plant and equipment	_____	Retained earnings	_____

17. Consider the following information concerning the 19x1 and 19x2 operations of ABC Co.

	19x1	19x2
Sales	$800,000	$1,000,000
Purchases	400,000	450,000
Beginning inventory	80,000	90,000
Ending inventory	90,000	90,000
Selling expense	40,000	50,000
Administrative expenses	10,000	40,000
Income taxes	100,000	200,000

Required:

Prepare a comparative income statement for the years ending December 31, 19x1 and 19x2. Indicate the changes both in percentages and dollars.

18. Small Company is a manufacturer of widgets. Industrywide averages (expressed in percentages of sales) for the production and sale of widgets are as follows:

Sales	100%
Cost of goods sold	70%
Selling expenses	10%
Administrative expenses	7%

In order to compare its own performance with industrywide standards, the Small Company has computed the following percentages:

Sales	100%
Cost of goods sold	60%
Selling expenses	20%
Administrative expenses	15%

Required:

1. Comment on the performance of Small Company.
2. What are the problems relating to the use of industrywide standards as a basis for evaluating an individual company's performance?

19. The current ratio of Lap Co. on December 31, 19x1 was 2 to 1 ($200,000 to $100,000). In 19x2 the following transactions occurred:

   a. Payment of accounts payable, $125,000.
   b. Collection of accounts receivable, $50,000.
   c. Sales of $200,000, ¾ of which was cash; cost of goods sold was $125,000.
   d. Purchase of goods, all on credit, $150,000.
   e. A loan for $100,000, due in 5 years.
   f. Cash purchase of marketable securities, $10,000.

   Required:

   On the basis of the preceding information, compute the current ratio at December 31, 19x2.

20. The Hawks Company decided to change its credit policy in 19x3, from 2/10, n/30, the policy in effect during 19x2, to 5/10, n/30. Using the information given below, evaluate whether or not this was a beneficial change.

	19x2	19x3
Total sales	$350,000	$400,000
Cash sales	75,000	85,000
Accounts receivable, 12/31/x1	25,000	
Accounts receivable, 12/31/x2	28,000	
Accounts receivable, 12/31/x3	18,000	

21. The ending inventory for each month of 19x1 is listed below for the Expo Company:

1/31	$21,998	7/31	$35,000
2/28	33,000	8/31	40,000
3/31	28,000	9/30	47,000
4/30	29,500	10/31	48,600
5/31	34,200	11/30	47,300
6/30	29,000	12/31	49,100

   During the last half of the year, the company decided to order inventory in larger quantities to take advantage of a quantity discount. The company was able to pass this discount on to its customers in the form of a price decrease. Cost of goods sold for the first half of the year was $224,000 and for the last half of the year was $410,000, reflecting an increase in demand.

   Required:

   Compute inventory turnover for both halves of the year and decide whether this new inventory policy is beneficial.

22. What would Phillie Company's working capital be after the occurrence of *each* of the following consecutive transactions during March? Working capital as of March 1 was ($10,000).

Mar. 2 Sold $15,000 of merchandise. Cost of goods sold was $13,500.
      8 Paid $11,000 on accounts payable.
     10 Purchased $6,000 of inventory for cash.
     15 Collected $3,000 on accounts receivable.
     18 Issued a $10,000, 8 percent bond for $12,000.
     21 Purchased a building with the proceeds from the bond.
     26 Issued 25 shares of $10 par value capital stock for $13.
     31 Adjustment for $200 accrued interest payable.
     31 Adjustment for $500 accrued rent receivable.

PROBLEMS

23. The comparative income statement for Joe Company and John Company is presented below.

Joe Company and John Company
Comparative Income Statement
For the Year Ending December 31, 19x1

	Joe Company	John Company
Net sales	$500,000	$250,000
Cost of goods sold	350,000	150,000
Gross profit on sales	$150,000	$100,000
Operating expenses:		
Selling expense	$ 50,000	$ 10,000
Administrative expense	10,000	7,000
Total Operating Expenses	$ 60,000	$ 17,000
Operating income	$ 90,000	$ 83,000
Interest expense	30,000	5,000
Income before income taxes	$ 60,000	$ 78,000
Income taxes	20,000	25,000
Net income	$ 40,000	$ 53,000

Required:

Using the above information, prepare a common-size statement comparing income data for Joe Company and John Company.

24. The income statements for 19x2 for Spahn Company and Sain Company are presented below.

Spahn Company
Income Statement
For the Year Ended December 31, 19x2

Sales		$225,000
Cost of goods sold		140,000
Gross profit from sales		$ 85,000
Expenses:		
Selling expense	$18,000	
Administrative expense	20,000	
General expenses	15,000	
Total Expenses		53,000
Income from operations		$ 32,000
Interest expense		2,000
Income before taxes		$ 30,000
Income taxes		7,000
Net Income		$ 23,000

Sain Company
Income Statement
For the Year Ended December 31, 19x2

Sales		$300,000
Cost of goods sold		195,000
Gross profit from sales		$105,000
Expenses:		
Selling expense	$15,000	
Administrative expense	30,000	
General expenses	21,000	
Total Expenses		66,000
Income from operations		$ 39,000
Interest expense		6,000
Income before taxes		$ 33,000
Income taxes		4,000
Net Income		$ 29,000

Required:

Prepare a common-size income statement comparing Spahn Company with Sain Company.

25. The following information was taken from the financial statements of Maker Company on December 31, 19x2.

Cash	$ 75,000
Accounts receivable	125,000
Inventory	100,000
Fixed assets (net)	500,000
	$800,000
Accounts payable	$100,000
Bond payable (due December 31, 19x27)	300,000
Capital stock ($10 par)	300,000
Retained earnings	100,000
	$800,000
Net income	$ 50,000

Required:

Compute the following:

1. Current ratio
2. Working capital
3. Acid-test ratio
4. Earnings per share
5. Debt-to-equity ratio

26. Following is the condensed common-size income statement for Francis Co.:

Francis Company
Condensed Common-Size Income Statement
For the Year Ended December 31, 19x2

Net sales	100.0%
Cost of goods sold	68.0
Gross profit on sales	32.0%
Operating expenses:	
Selling expense	16.0%
Administrative expense	6.0
Total Operating Expense	22.0%
Operating income	10.0%
Interest expense	0.5
Income before income taxes	9.5%
Income taxes	2.0
Net income	7.5%

Net sales for the period were $3,000,000.

Required:

Prepare the income statement for Francis Company.

27.   Your examination of the balance sheet for Reswarts Corp. on December 31, 19x1, 19x2, and 19x3 reveals the following information:

	19x1	19x2	19x3
Cash	$ 50,000	$ 75,000	$100,000
Accounts receivable (net)	150,000	100,000	150,000
Inventory	175,000	200,000	225,000
Prepaid expenses	25,000	25,000	40,000
Land	45,000	45,000	45,000
Buildings (net)	170,000	155,000	200,000
Machinery and equipment (net)	70,000	60,000	50,000
Accounts payable	120,000	140,000	130,000
Notes payable	50,000	40,000	50,000
Capital stock	400,000	400,000	400,000
Retained earnings	115,000	80,000	230,000

Required:

Prepare comparative balance sheets for the three years using (1) the first year presented as a base and (2) the previous year as a base. Include both percentage and dollar changes.

28.   Given below are the balance sheets for Meyers, Inc., for 19x1 and 19x2.

Meyers, Inc.
Comparative Balance Sheet
December 31, 19x2 and 19x1

	19x2	19x1
ASSETS		
Current assets:		
Cash	$ 20,000	$ 17,000
Accounts receivable (net)	45,000	60,000
Supplies inventory	8,000	6,000
Prepaid expenses	7,000	5,000
Total Current Assets	$ 80,000	$ 88,000
Land	120,000	70,000
Buildings (net)	200,000	100,000
Total Assets	$400,000	$258,000
LIABILITIES		
Current liabilities:		
Accounts payable	$ 10,000	$ 7,000
Taxes payable	9,000	3,000
Total Current Liabilities	$ 19,000	$ 10,000
Bonds payable	115,000	70,000
Total Liabilities	$134,000	$ 80,000
STOCKHOLDERS' EQUITY		
Common stock ($5 par)	$ 50,000	$ 45,000
Additional paid-in capital	125,000	80,000
Retained earnings	91,000	53,000
Total Liabilities and Stockholders' Equity	$400,000	$258,000

Required:

Prepare a horizontal and vertical analysis of the balance sheets of Meyers, Inc. for 19x1 and 19x2.

29. Shown below are partially completed comparative financial statements of Neil Company.

Required:

1. Complete the statements.
2. Compute the following for 19x2:

   a. Rate of Return on Total Assets
   b. Rate of Return on Common Stockholders' Equity
   c. Earnings per Share of Common Stock
   d. Debt-to-Equity Ratio
   e. Number of Times Interest Earned
   f. Working Capital
   g. Current Ratio
   h. Acid-Test Ratio
   i. Inventory Turnover
   j. Average Number of Days to Collect Receivables

Neil Company
Comparative Balance Sheet
December 31, 19x2 and 19x1

	19x2		19x1		Increase (Decrease)	
	Dollars	Percent of Total Assets	Dollars	Percent of Total Assets	Dollars	Percent
ASSETS						
Current assets:						
Cash......................	$ 55,000		$ 50,000			
Net accounts receivable........	200,000		175,000			
Inventories.................	300,000		225,000			
Prepaid expenses.............	45,000		50,000			
Total Current Assets........	$ 600,000		$ 500,000			
Land, buildings and						
equipment (net).............	1,400,000		1,250,000			
Total Assets.................	$2,000,000		$1,750,000			
LIABILITIES						
Current liabilities:						
Accounts payable.............	$ 300,000		$ 350,000			
Notes payable...............	200,000		100,000			
Total Current Liabilities.....	$ 500,000		$ 450,000			
Bonds payable.................	500,000		500,000			
Total Liabilities...............	$1,000,000		$ 950,000			
STOCKHOLDERS' EQUITY						
Common stock ($20 par)........	$ 600,000		$ 600,000			
Retained earnings.............	400,000		200,000			
Total Liabilities and						
Stockholders' Equity..........	$2,000,000		$1,750,000			

Neil Company
Comparative Income Statement
For Years Ended December 31, 19x2 and 19x1

	19x2		19x1		Increase (Decrease)	
	Dollars	Percent of Sales	Dollars	Percent of Sales	Dollars	Percent
Net sales....................	$3,000,000		$2,000,000			
Cost of goods sold............	2,100,000		1,500,000			
Gross profit on sales...........	$ 900,000		$ 500,000			
Operating expenses:						
Selling expenses..............	$ 400,000		$ 200,000			
Administrative expenses.......	100,000		50,000			
Total Operating Expenses........	$ 500,000		$ 250,000			
Operating income..............	$ 400,000		$ 250,000			
Interest expense................	40,000		30,000			
Income before income taxes......	$ 360,000		$ 220,000			
Income taxes..................	90,000		45,000			
Net Income...................	$ 270,000		$ 175,000			

Neil Company
Comparative Statement of Retained Earnings
For Years Ended 12/31/x2 and x1

	19x2	19x1	Increase (Decrease)	
			Dollars	Percent
Retained earnings, January 1..........	$200,000	$ 75,000		
Net income........................	270,000	175,000		
	$470,000	$250,000		
Less: Dividends...................	70,000	50,000		
Retained earnings, December 31.......	$400,000	$200,000		

30. Met Wholesale Company has in recent prior years maintained the following relationships among the data on its financial statements:

1.	Gross profit rate on net sales...................	35%
2.	Net profit rate on net sales....................	5%
3.	Rate of selling expenses to net sales.............	25%
4.	Accounts receivable turnover..................	8 per year
5.	Inventory turnover...........................	6 per year
6.	Times interest earned in 19x4..................	2
7.	Current ratio...............................	2.5
8.	Rate of return on total assets.................	3%
9.	Quick-asset composition:	
	Cash....................................	10%
	Marketable securities......................	30%
	Accounts receivable.......................	60%

The company has a net income of $240,000 for 19x4. The resulting earnings per share was $0.48 per share on common stock. Additional information follows:

a.   Capital stock issued (all in 19x2) and outstanding:

> Common, $20 per share par value, issued at 2 percent premium.
> Preferred, 8 percent nonparticipating, $100 per share par value,
> issued at an 8 percent premium.

b.   Long-term debt issued at par value in 19x0 has an interest rate of 5 percent and is due in 19x10. Total debt is $5,408,000.

c.   The company owns no depreciable assets.

d.   All sales were on account. Assume the ending accounts receivable, fixed assets, and inventory balances are the average for the year.

e.   The preferred dividend's obligation for 19x4 totaled $8,000 and was paid on December 31, 19x4. There had been no dividends in arrears for years prior to 19x4.

Required:

1.   Prepare an income statement.

2.   Prepare a balance sheet for the Met Wholesale Company for the year ending December 31, 19x4 from the ratios and information given above. Ignore taxes. The two statements will only include the accounts divulged in this problem. (Hint: Retained Earnings is a balancing figure in this problem.)

31.   Joe Stockholder is contemplating buying stock in one of the following companies, both in the same business. Below is financial data relating to each company:

	Pirate Company	Cardinal Company
Sales	$ 6,000	$18,000
Cost of goods sold	3,800	13,884
Depreciation expense	800	1,400
Interest expense	200	800
Other expenses	44	110
Income taxes	480	600
Cash	1,000	4,000
Accounts receivable	3,500	10,000
Inventory	800	1,900
Fixed assets	10,000	38,000
Accumulated depreciation	4,000	14,000
Accounts payable	1,800	4,000
Income taxes payable	480	600
Bonds payable	200	3,600
Common stock ($20 par value)	6,000	36,000
Retained earnings	2,820	(4,300)
Current market value per share	$ 33	$ 5.35

Required:

Compute the ratio that would best give the answer to each of the following questions, then answer the question. Make all necessary assumptions.

1. Which company has the best current position?
2. Which company has the most effective credit department?
3. Which company is doing the best job at keeping the most appropriate inventory level?
4. Which firm has the best ability to make their interest payments?
5. Which firm is earning the best return on the firm's assets?
6. Which stock is the best buy?

32. From the following stockholders' equity portion of the balance sheet and additional information calculate these ratios for the year ended December 31, 19x2:

a. Earnings per share.
b. Rate of return on common stockholders' equity.
c. Price-earnings ratio.

| | December 31 | |
	19x1	19x2
Stockholders' Equity:		
6 percent preferred stock, $90 par value, 10,000 shares authorized, 5,000 shares issued and outstanding in 19x1; 6,000 in 19x2 (callable at $110)	$ 450,000	$ 540,000
Common stock, $8 par value, 100,000 shares authorized, 45,000 shares issued and outstanding in 19x1; 54,000 in 19x2	360,000	432,000
Additional paid-in capital:		
Common stock issued	135,000	270,000
Preferred stock issued	105,000	126,000
Total contributed capital	$1,050,000	$1,368,000
Retained earnings	48,000	89,000
Total Stockholders' Equity	$1,098,000	$1,457,000

Additional information:

No dividends were paid during 19x2. Preferred stock has no dividends in arrears from previous years and is nonparticipative. The market price per share of common stock at the end of 19x2 is $13.50.

33. The following are financial statements of ZYX Corporation for 19x1.

ZYX Corporation
Balance Sheet
December 31, 19x1

ASSETS

Current assets:

Cash	$100,000	
Accounts receivable (net)	200,000	
Prepaid expenses	50,000	
Inventory	110,000	
Total Current Assets		$ 460,000

Fixed assets:

Land	$ 50,000	
Machinery (net)	100,000	
Building (net)	250,000	
Total Fixed Assets		400,000
Total Assets		$ 860,000

LIABILITIES AND STOCKHOLDERS' EQUITY

Accounts payable	$ 50,000
Wages payable	5,000
Interest payable	2,000
Bonds payable (due December 31, 19x6)	200,000
Capital stock ($2 par value)	400,000
Retained earnings	203,000
Total Liabilities and Stockholders' Equity	$ 860,000

ZYX Corporation
Income Statement
For the Year Ended December 31, 19x1

Sales (net)		$1,000,000
Cost of goods sold:		
Beginning inventory	$ 90,000	
Purchases	600,000	
Goods available for sale	$690,000	
Ending inventory	110,000	
Cost of goods sold		580,000
Gross profit on sales		$ 420,000
Operating expenses:		
Sales salaries expense	$ 75,000	
Depreciation expense	20,000	
Insurance expense	5,000	
Interest expense	10,000	
Total operating expense		110,000
Income before taxes		$ 310,000
Income taxes		100,000
Net Income		$ 210,000

January 1, 19x0 data:

Common shares outstanding	200,000

Required:

Compute the following:

1. Earnings per Share of Common Stock
2. Debt-to-Equity Ratio
3. Number of Times Interest Earned
4. Current Ratio
5. Acid-Test or Quick Ratio
6. Inventory Turnover

34.   Orioles Retail Company has maintained the following relationships in recent years among the data on its financial statements:

1.	Gross profit rate on net sales............	30%
2.	Net profit rate on net sales...............	6%
3.	Rate of selling expenses to net sales......	6%
4.	Accounts receivable turnover...........	10 per year
5.	Inventory turnover....................	7 per year
6.	Times interest earned in 19x4...........	4 times
7.	Current ratio.........................	3.2
8.	Rate of return on total assets............	5%
9.	Quick-asset composition:	
	Cash.............................	15%
	Marketable securities................	25%
	Accounts receivable.................	60%
10.	Tax rate.............................	40%

The company has a net income after taxes of $450,000 for 19x4. The resulting earnings per common share was $2.50. Additional information follows:

a.   Capital stock issued (all in 19x2) and outstanding:

> Common, $10 per share par value, issued at 10 percent premium.
> Preferred, 7 percent nonparticipating, $100 per share par value, issued at a 10 percent premium.

b.   Preferred dividends were paid up through 19x3; 19x3 dividends of $4,900 were paid on July 1, 19x4.

c.   The only long-term debt, an 8 percent bond payable, was issued at par in 19x0 and is due in 19x10. Total debt is $3,750,000.

d.   All sales were on account. Assume that accounts receivable and inventory balances were the same on January 1, 19x4 as they are on December 31, 19x4.

e.   Fixed assets have been owned for five years and are depreciated at a rate of 5 percent on their original cost per year.

Required:

1. Prepare an income statement.
2. Prepare a balance sheet for the Orioles Retail Company for the year ending December 31, 19x4. The two statements will only include the accounts divulged in this problem. (Hint: Retained Earnings is a balancing figure.)

Refer to the Annual Report included in the Appendix at the end of the text:

35. Compute the accounts receivable turnover for the most recent year.

36. Compute the average collection period for the most recent year.

37. Compute the current ratio for the most recent year.

38. Compute the acid-test ratio for the most recent year.

39. Compute the debt-to-equity ratio for the most recent year.

40. Compute the average inventory for the most recent year.

41. Compute the number of times interest was earned in the most recent year.

42. Compute the return on total assets in the most recent year.

Chapter 11 illustrates the procedures used in preparing the statement of cash flows. Studying this chapter should enable you to:

1. Understand and give examples of the types of information an analysis of cash flows will provide.

2. Identify the primary sources and uses of cash.

3. Describe the procedures involved in preparing the statement of cash flows.

4. Prepare a statement of cash flows using both the indirect and the direct methods of computing net cash flows from operating activities.

11

The Statement of Cash Flows

INTRODUCTION

An important consideration in the decision process of many users of financial statements is the amount of, and the changes in, the resources of a business. Comparative balance sheets indicate the resources available at the beginning and the end of a period. These statements do not, however, explain the causes of any changes in the resources. While a part of the change in resources may result from the operations of the business, the net income as reported in the income statement may not be accompanied by an equivalent increase in resources. Consequently, the combination of the balance sheet and income statement may not provide an adequate indication of the flow of the various liquid resources which takes place during the business cycle. For this reason, a statement which discloses the analysis of the funds flows of a firm is required along with the balance sheet and income statement as a part of a firm's report "package." This statement, the statement of cash flows, is a significant measure of the effectiveness of the financing activities of a firm. This analysis and the information that it provides is considered to be of sufficient importance that it is now included as a formal statement in the published annual reports of firms.

IMPORTANCE OF CASH FLOWS

Investors are interested in receiving dividends, creditors are concerned about receiving periodic interest payments and principal payments, suppliers want to be assured that they will receive payments for merchandise sold, and employees depend on being able to receive paychecks when due. The critical issue for all these groups is cash flow.

Although some information about cash flows can be derived from comparative balance sheets and income statements, neither of these statements provides a complete picture of a company's cash flows. An income statement discloses the results of operations for a period of time, but does not indicate the cash provided by operations or the cash provided by other activities. Comparative balance sheets show net changes in assets, liabilities, and owners' equity, but do not indicate the specific causes of these changes. A third statement is needed—a statement of cash flows.

The statement of cash flows explains the causes of changes in cash plus highly liquid marketable securities and provides a summary of the investing and financing activities of an enterprise during a period of time. While the basic purpose of this statement is to provide information concerning the changes in cash plus highly liquid marketable securities, the statement also is useful in appraising other factors such as the firm's financing policies, dividend policies, ability to expand productive capacity, and ability to satisfy future debt requirements.

A BRIEF HISTORY

Prior to the 1960s, many firms voluntarily prepared statements of changes in financial position for their annual reports. The statement of changes usually provided information on the sources and uses of working capital (current assets minus current liabilities) during the accounting period. The statement of changes in financial position was not provided to replace the balance sheet or income statement, but was intended to provide information that was not available directly from the other statements.

While the basic objective of the statement of changes in financial position was to summarize the financing and investing activities of the firm, in practice the form and content of these statements varied considerably. The statement was designed to allow users to analyze the flow of funds. Funds were usually defined as working capital, but some companies defined funds as cash.

Due to increasing attention placed on funds-flow analysis, the AICPA published *Accounting Research Study No. 2*, " 'Cash Flow' Analysis and the Funds Statement," in 1961.[1] This study recommended that the funds statement be presented in annual reports. In 1963, *APB Opinion No. 3*, "The Statement of Source and Application of Funds," recommended, but did not require, that a statement of sources and applications of funds be presented as supplementary information in financial reports.[2] Since the issuance of *APB Opinion No. 3*, there was a substantial increase in the number of firms presenting funds-flow data. However, the nature of the funds statement varied widely in practice, because *APB Opinion No. 3* allowed considerable latitude as to the form, content, and terminology of the statement.

In 1971, the APB issued its *Opinion No. 19*,[3] which required the presentation of funds flow in annual reports. In this *Opinion*, the APB stated that a statement of changes in financial position is essential for financial statement users and must be presented as a basic financial statement for each period for which an income statement is presented.

The objective of the statement of changes in financial position was to provide information on all of the financing and investing activities that occurred during an accounting period. This statement did not replace the income statement or balance sheet. Rather, it was intended to provide information that the other statements did not provide concerning the flow of funds and changes in financial position.

---

[1] Perry Mason, " 'Cash Flow' Analysis and the Funds Statement," *Accounting Research Study No. 2* (New York: AICPA, 1961).

[2] *APB Opinion No. 3*, "The Statement of Source and Application of Funds" (New York: AICPA, 1963).

[3] *APB Opinion No. 19*, "Reporting Changes in Financial Position" (New York: AICPA, 1971), para. 7.

In July 1986, the FASB issued an Exposure Draft entitled "Statement of Cash Flows," requiring a statement of cash flows. The statement should be in terms of cash plus cash equivalents (such as Treasury bills, commercial paper, and money market funds).

In recent years, many companies had switched from defining funds as working capital to defining funds as cash or cash plus cash equivalents. The change can be seen from data provided in the 1986 edition of *Accounting Trends & Techniques* for its survey of 600 companies. In 1980, funds were defined as working capital by 541 of the 600 companies; in 1985, funds were defined as working capital by only 220 companies and as cash or cash plus cash equivalents by 380 companies.

ALL FINANCIAL RESOURCES CONCEPT

Most financing or investing activities involve a net change in cash or working capital—that is, an increase or decrease in cash or another current asset or a current liability. In some cases, however, a significant financial transaction may affect only noncurrent accounts. For example, the issuance of capital stock or long-term debt in exchange for a long-term asset has no effect on either cash or working capital. This type of exchange would be excluded from the statement of cash flows if only cash transactions were included.

APB Opinion No. 19 broadened the concept underlying the statement of changes in financial position to include all important aspects of an entity's financing and investing activities regardless of whether cash or other elements of working capital are affected directly. In this approach, referred to as the "all financial resources" concept, a material transaction involving changes in noncurrent accounts must be disclosed in the statement of changes in financial position. Of course, including this type of transaction has no effect on the reported increase or decrease in cash or working capital, but it does provide the user with a comprehensive view of the total inflow and outflow of all financial resources during a period. The FASB has continued this practice by requiring entities to report the effects of investing and financing activities that do not directly affect cash.

THE STATEMENT OF CASH FLOWS

The statement of cash flows consists of three major sections: the cash effects of an entity's operations, its investing activities, and its financing activities. Grouping cash flows into these categories enables significant relationships within and among these activities to be analyzed and provides useful information to users of financial statements.

Previously, the statement of changes in financial position (either on a cash or working capital basis) was in the format of a listing of the sources and then the uses of cash or working capital. However, sources can include such dissimilar transactions as the issuance of bonds and the proceeds on the sale of plant and equipment; similarly, uses can include transactions such as the payment of dividends and the repayment of long-term debt. The new format required by the FASB should be more useful and understandable.

The three sections of the statement of cash flows are as follows:

1. *Operating activities*—Operating activities include selling, purchasing, and producing goods; providing services; and paying suppliers, employees, and lenders.

2. *Investing activities*—Investing activities include receipts from loans, acquiring and selling securities (except for cash equivalents), and acquiring and selling plant assets.

3. *Financing activities*—Financing activities include proceeds from the issuance of the entity's bonds or stocks, outlays to pay the maturity value of bonds, outlays to purchase the entity's stock, and the payment of dividends.

In addition, there may be a separate schedule for noncash investing and financing activities (for example, acquiring land by issuing common stock).

A format for the statement of cash flows is as follows:

Cash flows from operating activities:		
Net income	$X	
Noncash expenses, revenues, losses,		
and gains included in income:		
Depreciation and amortization	X	
Increase in receivables	(X)	
Increase in inventories	(X)	
Increase in payables	X	
Net cash flow from operating activities		$X
Cash flows from investing activities:		
Proceeds from sale of plant assets	$X	
Purchase of plant assets	(X)	
Net cash provided by investing activities		X
Cash flows from financing activities:		
Proceeds from issuance of bonds payable	$X	
Proceeds from issuance of common stock	X	
Payment of cash dividends	(X)	
Net cash provided by financing activities		X
Net increase (decrease) in cash		$X

This format uses the indirect method to obtain net cash flow from operating activities.

An alternative format for the statement of cash flows is as follows:

Cash flows from operating activities:

Cash received from customers	\$X	
Dividends received	X	
Cash provided by operating activities		\$X
Cash paid to suppliers	(X)	
Cash paid to employees	(X)	
Cash paid for interest and taxes	(X)	
Cash paid for operating activities		(X)
Net cash flow from operating activities		\$X
Cash flows from investing activities:		
Proceeds from sale of plant assets	\$X	
Purchase of plant assets	(X)	
Net cash provided by investing activities		X
Cash flows from financing activities:		
Proceeds from issuance of bonds payable	\$X	
Proceeds from issuance of common stock	X	
Payment of cash dividends	(X)	
Net cash provided by financing activities		X
Net increase (decrease) in cash		\$X

This format uses the direct method to obtain net cash flow from operating activities.

The purpose of the second Exposure Draft, issued in 1987, was to determine which of these two formats, the indirect method or the direct method, to use in the body of the statement of cash flows and which to use as a supplementary schedule.

Cash From Operations

The net income of a firm for a particular period has been defined as the excess of its revenues over its related expenses. Revenues generally result in an increase in current assets. For example, sales usually cause an increase in either cash or accounts receivable. Similarly, most expenses require either that a current outlay of cash be made or that a current liability be incurred.

The reported net income of a firm, however, is not always equal to the net cash flow from operating activities. Not all expenses or revenues result in a corresponding outflow or inflow of cash.

Indirect Method. Certain types of expenses enter into the determination of net income but do not affect cash. For example, depreciation on plant assets is an expense that reduces income but does not require an outlay of cash during the current period. Therefore, depreciation expense does not affect cash. Consequently, to determine the net cash flow from operating activities, it is necessary to include only those expenses that required an outflow of cash during the period. An important factor in determining net cash flow from operating activities under the indirect method is to add back to (or subtract from) net income all those items that did not result in an outflow (inflow) of cash.

Examples of items that are added to net income include depreciation expense, amortization expense, bond interest expense due to the amortization of a bond discount, and the reduction to interest revenue due to the amortization of a premium on a bond investment. Examples of items that are subtracted from net income include the reduction to interest expense due to the amortization of a bond premium and interest revenue due to the amortization of a discount on a bond investment.

Additional adjustments are required to convert revenues and expenses to cash receipts and disbursements, because income statement data are based on the accrual method of accounting. To determine net cash flow from operating activities under the indirect method, net income must be adjusted for changes in current assets (other than cash) and for changes in current liabilities (other than those which are not related to operations, such as non-trade notes payable and dividends payable).

These additional adjustments essentially convert the funds provided by operations from the accrual to the cash basis. Some of the most common adjustments under the indirect method to net income to obtain net cash flow from operating activities are as follows:

Add	*Subtract*
Decrease in net accounts receivable	Increase in net accounts receivable
Decrease in inventories and prepaid expenses	Increase in inventories and prepaid expenses
Increases in accounts payable, trade notes payable, and accrued liabilities	Decreases in accounts payable, trade notes payable, and accrued liabilities

Net income is adjusted by the change in net accounts receivable to convert sales on an accrual basis to sales on a cash basis. Assume that sales on an accrual basis are $50,000, beginning accounts receivable are $10,000, and ending accounts receivable are $8,000. Then sales on a cash basis are as follows:

Sales on an accrual basis	$50,000
Beginning accounts receivable	10,000
	$60,000
Less: Ending accounts receivable	8,000
Sales on a cash basis	$52,000

The decrease in accounts receivable ($10,000 − $8,000 = $2,000) results in sales on a cash basis exceeding sales on an accrual basis. Therefore, a decrease in accounts receivable is added to net income to obtain net cash flow from operations. Conversely, an increase in accounts receivable would be subtracted from net income to obtain net cash flow from operations.

In a similar fashion, net income is adjusted by the change in accounts payable, trade notes payable, and accrued liabilities to convert expenses on an accrual basis to expenses on a cash basis. A decrease in these payables results in expenses on a cash basis being higher than expenses on an accrual basis. Therefore, a decrease to these payables is subtracted from net income to obtain net cash flow from operations. Conversely, an increase in these payables would be added to net income to obtain net cash flow from operations.

The change in inventories is an adjustment to net income in order to convert cost of goods sold, which has no potential to affect cash, to purchases, which has the potential to affect cash. An increase in inventories means that purchases exceed cost of goods sold; a decrease in inventories means that purchases are less than cost of goods sold. Therefore, an increase in inventories is subtracted from net income to obtain net cash flow from operations and a decrease in inventories is added to net income to obtain net cash flow from operations.

A firm that experiences a net loss during a period still may generate cash from its operations if: (1) the total expenses that did not require the use of cash exceed the amount of the loss, or (2) adjustments for current assets (other than cash and cash equivalents) and current liabilities convert a net loss on an accrual basis to net income on a cash basis. For example, a firm may have a net loss of $10,000 and have included depreciation expense of $15,000 among its expenses.

Additional adjustments may be required in order to obtain net cash flow from operating activities if net income includes extraordinary gains or losses. The disclosure of cash provided by operations is most useful if the effects of extraordinary items, net of tax, are reported separately from the effects of normal items.

The net cash flow from operating activities may begin with the net income or loss from continuing operations. Any items that did not use or provide cash during the period and were included in the net income or loss from continuing operations should be added or deducted. Cash provided or used by extraordinary items, net of tax, should be reported immediately following cash provided or used in operations. Of course, adjustments are necessary for any of these items that did not provide or use cash during the period.

Similarly, other nonoperating gains or losses should be excluded from cash provided by operations. These amounts should be included as a part of the investing or financing activities. For example, if land that had an original cost of $10,000 is sold for $9,000 in cash, a $1,000 loss on the sale of land is included in the net income for the period. The $9,000 received from the sale represents the cash provided and is shown in the statement as a separate item. Therefore, the $1,000 loss should not be included in determining the net cash flow from operating activities. Thus, to determine the net cash flow from operating activities, it is necessary to add back any nonoperating losses and to deduct any nonoperating gains.

Direct Method.   Alternatively, the statement of cash flows may show cash receipts and payments from operations directly. Such a format could appear as follows:

Cash flows from operating activities:		
Cash received from customers	$X	
Dividends received	X	
Cash provided by operating activities		$X
Cash paid to suppliers	(X)	
Cash paid to employees	(X)	
Cash paid for interest and taxes	(X)	
Cash paid for operating activities........................		(X)
Net cash flow from operating activities		$X

Cash received by customers is equal to sales on an accrual basis plus the decrease in accounts receivable or minus the increase in accounts receivable. An example of this was shown earlier in this chapter.

Cash paid to suppliers of merchandise is equal to cost of goods sold: (1) plus the increase in inventories or minus the decrease in inventories, and (2) plus the decrease in accounts payable for merchandise or minus the increase in accounts payable for merchandise. For example, assume that cost of goods sold is $40,000, beginning inventories are $7,000, ending inventories are $9,000, beginning accounts payable for inventories is $6,000, and ending accounts payable for inventories is $5,000. Then cash paid to suppliers is as follows:

Cost of goods sold..............................	$40,000
Ending inventories	9,000
Cost of goods available..........................	$49,000
Less: Beginning inventories.....................	7,000
Purchases	$42,000
Beginning accounts payable	6,000
	$48,000
Less: Ending accounts payable	5,000
Cash paid to suppliers...........................	$43,000

Cash paid for other expenses is equal to the expense on an accrual basis plus the decrease in the related payable or minus the increase in the related payable. For example, cash paid to employees is equal to salaries on an accrual basis plus the decrease in salaries payable or minus the increase in salaries payable.

Both the indirect and the direct methods will be used in this chapter to compute net cash flow from operating activities.

**Preparation of
the Statement
of Cash Flows**

The change in cash (including cash equivalents) during the period must be equal to the change in the noncash accounts during the period, because the accounting equation must always balance. Based on this relationship, the increase or decrease in cash may be explained by examining the changes in the noncash accounts for the period.

The primary sources of information used in preparing the statement of cash flows are comparative balance sheets, the statement of retained earnings, the income statement, and certain supplementary data concerning the transactions affecting specific noncash accounts during the period. The basic data that will be used to present the required steps for the preparation of a statement of cash flows are shown in the financial statements of the Kraton Company presented below.

Kraton Company
Income Statement
For the Year Ended December 31, 19x1

Net sales		$1,000
Cost of goods sold		400
Gross margin		$ 600
Operating expenses:		
Depreciation	$100	
Wage expense	100	
Other expenses	200	400
Net income from operations		$ 200
Gain on sale of land		100
Net income		$ 300

Kraton Company
Retained Earnings Statement
For the Year Ended December 31, 19x1

Retained earnings at beginning of year	$250
Add: Net income	300
	$550
Subtract: Cash dividends	100
Retained earnings at end of year	$450

Kraton Company

Comparative Balance Sheet

| | *December 31* | | |
	19x1	*19x0*	*Change*
Assets:			
Cash	$ 250	$ 100	+ 150
Accounts receivable	350	200	+ 150
Inventories	200	250	− 50
Building	600	400	+ 200
Accumulated depreciation—			
building	(200)	(100)	+ 100
Land	100	200	− 100
Total assets.....................	$1,300	$1,050	
Liabilities and Stockholders' Equity:			
Accounts payable	$ 300	$ 200	+ 100
Accrued wages payable...............	50	100	− 50
Bonds payable—long-term............	100	200	− 100
Capital stock	400	300	+ 100
Retained earnings	450	250	+ 200
Total liabilities and equities	$1,300	$1,050	

Assume that the following additional information is available:

1. During the year, a building was purchased for $200 and land was purchased at a cost of $100.

2. Land with a cost of $200 was sold at a gain of $100.

3. All capital stock was issued for cash.

4. A long-term bond was retired for $100.

5. A $100 dividend was paid during the year.

6. The other expenses of $200 were paid in cash.

Change in Cash   The change in the cash account is an increase of $150. The cash balance was $100 at the end of 19x0, but increased to $250 at the end of 19x1.

**Changes in
Noncash Accounts**

Once the change in cash has been determined, the next step is to compute the changes in all of the noncash accounts. All changes in the noncash accounts of Kraton Company from December 31, 19x0 to December 31, 19x1 are summarized below:

Kraton Company
Changes in Noncash Accounts

	December 31			
	19x1	*19x0*	*Increase*	*Decrease*
Accounts receivable, net	$350	$200	$150	
Inventories.....................	200	250		$ 50
Buildings	600	400	200	
Accumulated depreciation—				
buildings	200	100	100	
Land........................	100	200		100
Accounts payable	300	200	100	
Accrued wages payable	50	100		50
Bonds payable—long-term	100	200		100
Capital stock	400	300	100	
Retained earnings	450	250	200	

Once the amount of these changes has been determined, it is necessary to consider the effect that each change had on cash. If more than one transaction caused the change in a particular account, the effect of each transaction must be analyzed separately. Let us consider the changes in the noncash accounts of Kraton Company.

Retained Earnings. An examination of the comparative balance sheets reveals that retained earnings increased by $200 during 19x1. An analysis of the statement of retained earnings indicates that net income for 19x1 was $300 and that dividends of $100 were declared and paid during the year. These two transactions account for the net change in retained earnings. The effect of the net income of the period on cash is included in the calculation of net cash flow from operating activities using the indirect method.

Cash flow from operating activity:
Net income $300

The payment of the cash dividend affected cash as follows:

Cash flow from financing activity:
Cash dividend............................. ($100)

As previously indicated, the net income of Kraton Company is not equivalent to net cash flow from operating activities. Depreciation expense that is included in the income statement did not require an outflow of cash. Therefore, it is necessary to add back depreciation expense of $100 to the net income of the period in computing net cash flow from operating activities.

A second adjustment is required to eliminate the nonoperating gain on the sale of land from net income. The $100 gain is included in the proceeds from the sale of land as an investing activity and must be excluded from net cash flow from operating activities.

The increase in accounts receivable of $150 must be subtracted from net income in calculating net cash flow from operating activities. The decrease in inventories of $50 must be added to net income in calculating net cash flow from operating activities. The increase in accounts payable of $100 must be added to net income in calculating net cash flow from operating activities. The decrease in accrued wages payable of $50 must be subtracted from net income in calculating net cash flow from operating activities. Therefore, the net cash flow from operating activities is determined as follows:

Cash flows from operating activities:	
Net income	$300
Noncash expenses, revenues, losses, and gains included in income:	
Depreciation	100
Nonoperating gain	(100)
Increase in accounts receivable	(150)
Decrease in inventories	50
Increase in accounts payable	100
Decrease in accrued wages payable	(50)
Net cash flow from operating activities	$250

Alternatively, net cash flow from operating activities under the direct method is equal to cash receipts from operations minus cash payments from operations. Cash receipts from operations are equal to net sales less the increase in accounts receivables. Cash payments to suppliers are equal to cost of goods sold less the decrease in inventories less the increase in accounts payable. Cash payments to employees are equal to wage expense plus the decrease in accrued wages payable. Cash payments for other expenses are given at $200. Therefore, net cash flow from operating activities using the direct method is as follows:

Cash flows from operating activities:

Cash receipts from operations ($1,000 − $150)		$850
Cash paid to suppliers ($400 − $50 − $100)	$250	
Cash paid to employees ($100 + $50)	150	
Cash paid for other expenses	200	
Cash paid for other operating activities		600
Net cash flow from operating activities		$250

Accumulated Depreciation. The $100 increase in accumulated depreciation—buildings resulted from recording the depreciation expense for the year (see the income statement). The amount of depreciation expense is added to net income in determining net cash flow from operating activities under the indirect method and is not considered under the direct method, because it does not result in a decrease in cash.

Buildings. The increase in the buildings account was the result of a single transaction in which a building was acquired at a cost of $200. The effect of this purchase on cash is as follows:

Cash flow from investing activity:
Purchase of building .... ($200)

Land. The comparative balance sheet indicates that the land account decreased by $100 during 19x1. This decrease was a result of the sale of land during the year exceeding the purchase of land during the year. The cash flow from the sale of land is the proceeds received from the sale. The entry to record the sale was as follows:

Cash	300	
Gain on sale of land		100
Land		200

Thus, $300 of cash was provided by the sale. As indicated previously, the $100 gain on the sale must be subtracted from net income in the calculation of net cash flow from operating activities under the indirect method and not considered under the direct method. The effect of the sale on cash is as follows:

Cash flow from investing activity:
Sale of land $300

The purchase of land for $100 affected cash as follows:

Cash flow from investing activity:
Purchase of land .... ($100)

Bonds Payable.   Bonds payable, decreased by $100 during the year. An analysis of the additional information provided indicates that this decrease resulted from the retirement of the bonds. The effect on cash is as follows:

> Cash flow from financing activity:
> Retirement of bonds payable .... ($100)

Capital Stock.   The increase in the capital stock account resulted from the issuance of additional stock for $100 in cash during the year. This amount would be included in the statement as follows:

> Cash flow from financing activity:
> Issuance of capital stock $100

The Statement of Cash Flows

All information that is necessary to prepare the statement of cash flows now has been analyzed. Kraton Company's statement of cash flows for the year ended December 31, 19x1 is shown below using: (1) the indirect method, and (2) the direct method to obtain net cash flow from operating activities:

---

(1)

Kraton Company
Statement of Cash Flows
For the Year Ended December 31, 19x1

Cash flows from operating activities:		
Net income	$300	
Noncash expenses, revenues, losses, and gains included in income:		
Depreciation	100	
Gain on sale of land	(100)	
Increase in accounts receivable......................	(150)	
Decrease in inventories	50	
Increase in accounts payable	100	
Decrease in accrued wages payable	(50)	
Net cash flow from operating activities		$250
Cash flows from investing activities:		
Sale of land	$300	
Acquisition of land	(100)	
Acquisition of building	(200)	
Net cash used by investing activities		0
Cash flows from financing activities:		
Sale of capital stock	$100	
Retirement of long-term bonds	(100)	
Payment of dividends	(100)	
Net cash provided by financing activities		(100)
Increase in cash		$150

(2)

Kraton Company
Statement of Cash Flows
For the Year Ended December 31, 19x1

Cash flows from operating activities:		
Cash receipts from operations		$850
Cash paid to suppliers	$250	
Cash paid to employees	150	
Cash paid for other expenses	200	
Cash paid for operating activities		600
Net cash flow from operating activities		$250
Cash flows from investing activities:		
Sale of land	$300	
Acquisition of land	(100)	
Acquisition of building	(200)	
Net cash used by investing activities		0
Cash flows from financing activities:		
Sale of capital stock	$100	
Retirement of long-term bonds.......................	(100)	
Payment of dividends	(100)	
Net cash provided by financing activities		(100)
Increase in cash...................................		$150

Worksheet Approach

In a relatively uncomplicated situation such as that of the Kraton Company described above, it is possible to prepare a statement of cash flows by simply sequentially examining the changes in each account. In a more realistic situation, however, a worksheet often is used to facilitate the analysis and preparation of the statement. Although it is not necessary to use a worksheet, its use normally aids in the preparation of the statement when there are a large number of transactions and various complicating factors.

The following is a worksheet for Kraton Company. The indirect method is used to obtain net cash flow from operating activities.

Kraton Company
Worksheet for Statement of Cash Flows
For the Year Ended December 31, 19x1

	Balance December 31, 19x0	Adjustments Debit	Adjustments Credit	Balance December 31, 19x1
Debits:				
Cash	$ 100			$ 250
Accounts receivable (net)	200	$ 150 (9)		350
Inventories	250		$ 50 (10)	200
Buildings....................................	400	200 (4)		600
Land	200	100 (7)	200 (5)	100
	$1,150			$1,500
Credits:				
Accumulated depreciation	$ 100		100 (3)	$ 200
Accounts payable............................	200		100 (11)	300
Accrued wages payable	100	50 (12)		50
Bonds payable	200	100 (6)		100
Capital stock	300		100 (8)	400
Retained earnings	250	100 (1)	300 (2)	450
	$1,150			$1,500
Statement of cash flows:				
Cash flows from operations:				
Net income		300 (2)		
Adjustments:				
Depreciation expense......................		100 (3)		
Gain on sale of land......................			100 (5)	
Increase in accounts receivable..............			150 (9)	
Decrease in inventories		50 (10)		
Increase in accounts payable		100 (11)		
Decrease in accrued wages payable			50 (12)	
Sale of land................................		300 (5)		
Purchase of land			100 (7)	
Sale of capital stock........................		100 (8)		
Purchase of building			200 (4)	
Retirement of bonds payable			100 (6)	
Payment of dividends			100 (1)	
		$1,650	$1,650	

The explanation of the adjustments is as follows:

1. The declaration and payment of a cash dividend ($100) that decreased retained earnings is recorded as a financing activity.

2. Net income included in the ending retained earnings balance is reported as the initial component of net cash flow from operating activities. This amount will be adjusted below in determining the net cash flow from operating activities.

3. The increase in accumulated depreciation ($100) is added to net income in determining the net cash flow from operating activities, because the depreciation expense did not decrease cash.

4. The purchase of the building for $200 is recorded as an investing activity.

5. The sale of land for $300 is shown as an investing activity; the $100 gain is subtracted from net income in determining net cash flow from operating activities.

6. The retirement of long-term bonds payable ($100) at face value is recorded as a financing activity.

7. The purchase of land for $100 is recorded as an investing activity.

8. The sale of capital stock for cash is recorded as a financing activity.

9. The increase in accounts receivable ($150) is subtracted from net income in determining net cash flow from operating activities.

10. The decrease in inventories ($50) is added to net income in determining net cash flow from operating activities.

11. The increase in accounts payable ($100) is added to net income in determining net cash flow from operating activities.

12. The decrease in accrued wages payable ($50) is subtracted from net income in determining net cash flow from operating activities.

The following is an alternative worksheet for Kraton Company. The direct method is used to obtain net cash flow from operating activities.

Kraton Company
Worksheet for Statement of Cash Flows
For the Year Ended December 31, 19x1

	Balance December 31, 19x0	Adjustments Debit	Adjustments Credit	Balance December 31, 19x1
Debits:				
Cash	$ 100			$ 250
Accounts receivable (net)	200	$ 150 (3)		350
Inventories	250		$ 50 (11)	200
Buildings................................	400	200 (5)		600
Land	200	100 (8)	200 (6)	100
	$1,150			$1,500
Credits:				
Accumulated depreciation	$ 100		100 (4)	$ 200
Accounts payable............................	200		100 (12)	300
Accrued wages payable	100	50 (14)		50
Bonds payable	200	100 (7)		100
Capital stock	300		100 (9)	400
Retained earnings	250	100 (1)	1,000 (2)	450
		100 (4)	100 (6)	
		400 (10)		
		100 (13)		
		200 (15)		
	$1,150			$1,500
Statement of cash flows:				
Cash flows from operations:				
Net sales		1,000 (2)		
Increase in accounts receivable.................			150 (3)	
Cost of goods sold			400 (10)	
Decrease in inventories		50 (11)		
Increase in accounts payable		100 (12)		
Wages expense			100 (13)	
Decrease in accrued wages payable			50 (14)	
Other expenses			200 (15)	
Sale of land................................		300 (6)		
Purchase of land			100 (8)	
Sale of capital stock		100 (9)		
Purchase of building			200 (5)	
Retirement of bonds payable			100 (7)	
Payment of dividends			100 (1)	
		$3,050	$3,050	

The explanation of the adjustments is as follows:

1. The declaration and payment of a cash dividend ($100) that decreased retained earnings is recorded as a financing activity.

2. Net sales ($1,000) is included in net income and retained earnings and is a component of net cash flow from operating activities.

3. The increase in accounts receivable ($150) is subtracted from net sales in determining cash received from customers.

4. The increase in accumulated depreciation ($100) is due to depreciation expense, which is included as a negative element in net income and retained earnings but is not considered in determining net cash flow from operating activities.

5. The purchase of the building for $200 is recorded as an investing activity.

6. The sale of land for $300 is shown as an investing activity; the $100 gain is included in net income and retained earnings but is not considered in determining net cash flow from operating activities.

7. The retirement of long-term bonds payable ($100) at face value is recorded as a financing activity.

8. The purchase of land for $100 is recorded as an investing activity.

9. The sale of capital stock for cash is recorded as a financing activity.

10. Cost of goods sold is a negative element in net income and retained earnings and is a negative component of net cash flow from operating activities.

11. The decrease in inventories ($50) is an adjustment to cost of goods sold to determine purchases.

12. The increase in accounts payable ($100) is subtracted from purchases in determining cash paid to suppliers.

13. Wage expense is a negative element in net income and retained earnings and is a negative component in net cash flow from operating activities.

14. The decrease in accrued wages payable ($50) is added to wage expense in determining cash paid to employees.

15. Other expenses is a negative element in net income and retained earnings and is a negative component in net cash flow from operating activities.

The procedures used in preparing a worksheet are summarized below:

1. The account balances appearing on the previous year's balance sheet are entered in the first column of the worksheet. All accounts with debit balances are listed first, followed by all accounts with credit balances.

2. Adjustments are entered into the adjustment columns to account for all noncash items from the upper section and to list all of the separate increases and decreases to cash in the lower section of the worksheet. The worksheet adjustments are not entered in any journal; their purpose is solely to facilitate the analysis and classification of the data for the statement of cash flows.

3. The account balances appearing on the current year's balance sheet are entered in the last column of the worksheet. These account balances are used as a check to determine whether the change in the balance of each noncash item has been explained completely—that is, whether the beginning balance plus or minus the change equals the ending balance.

Additional Problems in the Analysis of the Statement of Cash Flows

Many of the problems that occur in the preparation of the statement of cash flows were discussed in the preceding sections of this chapter. However, additional problems may arise that require special analysis to determine the effect on cash of a change in an asset (excluding cash and cash equivalents), a liability, or an owners' equity account. Some of these special problems are examined in the following paragraphs.

Uncollectible Accounts.   A change in the balance in the allowance for bad debts account resulting from either a charge to bad debt expense for the current period or a write-off of uncollectible accounts does not require any adjustment in determining the changes to cash. The allowance for bad debt account is a contra account to a current asset, accounts receivable. Therefore, the change in the allowance account is a part of the increase or decrease to net accounts receivable for the period. The debit to bad debt expense represents a deduction from revenues in determining net income. The decrease to net accounts receivable from the credit to the allowance account is added to net income in determining net cash flow from operating activities under the indirect method. Therefore, the bad debt expense is a deduction in net income and the corresponding decrease to net accounts receivable is added to net income so that there is no effect on cash. A write-off of an uncollectible account reduces both the receivable and the related contra account; it does not affect the balance of net accounts receivable. Accordingly, the write-off has no effect on cash.

Dividends.   A reduction in retained earnings resulting from the declaration of a cash dividend to be paid during the following period has no effect on cash. The subsequent payment of the dividend does affect cash and would be a financing activity in the period in which the disbursement is made.

Income Tax Expense.   If the amount of income tax expense exceeds the income tax payable, resulting in a credit to a deferred income tax liability, then the difference should be added to net income in arriving at net cash flow from operating activities under the indirect method. Similarly, if the amount of income tax is less than income tax payable, resulting in a debit to a deferred income tax asset, then the difference should be subtracted from net income in arriving at net cash flow from operating activities under the indirect method. In addition, net cash flow from operating activities has to be adjusted for the increase or decrease in income taxes payable. Under the direct method, income tax expense is decreased by a credit to deferred taxes and increased by a debit to deferred taxes and is then adjusted by the change in income tax payable to determine cash paid for income taxes. The amount of the income tax expense is debited to retained earnings.

Stock Dividends and Conversions.   When a corporation declares a stock dividend, a transfer is made from retained earnings to one or more contributed capital accounts. Such a transfer does not affect either total stockholders' equity or assets. Therefore, the resulting changes in the stockholders' equity items would not be included on the statement of cash flows.

Changes of substance in the individual components of owners' equity should be reported in the statement of cash flows even though these changes do not involve either a receipt or disbursement of cash. Accordingly, the conversion of long-term debt or preferred stock to common stock should be reflected in the statement of cash flows.

Significant Noncash Transactions.   The statement of cash flows should report all financing and investing activities, including those that do not involve a receipt or disbursement of cash. Among the most common of these transactions are the following:

1.   The issuance of noncurrent debt or capital stock for noncurrent assets.

2.   The issuance of capital stock to retire noncurrent debt.

3.   Refinancing of long-term debt.

4.   Conversion of long-term debt or preferred stock to common stock.

To illustrate, assume that a firm issued 50,000 shares of its $5 par value common stock in exchange for land with a fair market value of $380,000. This transaction would have been recorded in the accounts as follows:

Land	380,000	
Common stock...............................		250,000
Additional paid-in capital......................		130,000

Although this transaction did not affect cash, the transaction should be viewed as being comprised of two parts—the sale of stock for $380,000, and the purchase of a building for the same amount. Thus, the transaction would be reported on the statement of cash flows as follows:

Schedule of noncash investing and financing activities:
Issuance of common stock to purchase a building $380,000

Multiple Changes Affecting Specific Accounts.   Frequently, there may be several transactions that cause a net change in a noncurrent account. In these circumstances, it normally is helpful to analyze the individual transactions affecting the account in order to identify the effect on cash.

For example, assume that the following information is available regarding equipment.

	End of Year	Beginning of Year
Equipment	$212,000	$200,000
Accumulated depreciation	55,000	90,000
Depreciation expense...........................	15,000	
Gain on sale of equipment	7,000	

Equipment with a cost of $70,000 and a book value of $20,000 was sold for $27,000 during the year. Equipment was acquired at a cost of $82,000. The individual transactions that caused the changes in the equipment and the accumulated depreciation accounts may be summarized as follows:

	Equipment	Accumulated Depreciation
Beginning of year............................	$200,000	$90,000
Acquisition of equipment	82,000	
Sale of equipment	(70,000)	(50,000)
Depreciation expense..........................		15,000
End of year	$212,000	$55,000

The journal entries recorded at the time of each event and the resulting effect on cash are summarized below:

Sale of equipment:

Cash	27,000	
Accumulated depreciation	50,000	
Equipment		70,000
Gain on sale of equipment		7,000

        Cash inflow of $27,000 as an investing activity;
          the $7,000 gain is subtracted from net income
          in determining net cash flow from operations
          under the indirect method and is not considered
          under the direct method

Acquisition of equipment:

Equipment	82,000	
Cash		82,000

        Cash outflow of $82,000 as an investing activity

Depreciation:

Depreciation expense............................	15,000	
Accumulated depreciation		15,000

        Depreciation expense is added to net income
          in determining net cash flow from operations
          under the indirect method and is not considered
          under the direct method

SUMMARY

The statement of cash flows is included as one of the major financial statements in annual reports. This statement explains the causes of changes in cash plus highly liquid marketable securities and provides a summary of the investing and financing activities of an enterprise during a period of time. A majority of nonfinancial companies defined funds as cash or as cash plus cash equivalents prior to the issuance in 1987 of the FASB's pronouncement requiring the presentation of a statement of cash flows. Under the "all financial resources" concept, a material transaction involving changes in noncash accounts must be disclosed in the statement of cash flows.

The sections of the statement of cash flows are as follows: (1) cash flows from operating activities, (2) cash flows from investing activities, and (3) cash flows from financing activities. Investing activities include collections on loans, proceeds from the sale of plant assets, and purchases of plant assets; financing activities include proceeds from the issuance of bonds and stock and the payment of cash dividends.

KEY DEFINITIONS

All financial resources   This concept modifies "funds" to include not only those transactions affecting cash or working capital, but also those transactions of significant amount that affect the financing and investing activities of the firm, even though they involve only noncurrent accounts.

Cash concept of funds   This concept defines funds in terms of cash or near-cash, and utilizes the funds statement to point out changes in the cash flow of the firm.

Cash disbursement   Any outflow of cash by the firm is a cash disbursement.

Cash flow   Any transaction that increases or decreases the cash balance of the firm is a cash flow.

Cash receipt   Any transaction that increases the cash account of the firm is a cash receipt.

Direct method   Computing net cash flow from operations as the difference between cash receipts from operating activities and cash disbursements from operating activities.

Financing activities   The section of the statement of cash flows which includes proceeds from the issuance of the entity's bonds or stocks, outlays to pay the maturity value of bonds, outlays to purchase the entity's stock, and the payment of dividends.

Funds   According to *APB Opinion No. 19*, funds were either cash, near cash, or working capital.

Funds from operations   The effect on funds caused by the normal operating activities of the firm.

Indirect method   Computing net cash flow from operations by adjusting net income for noncash items included in income.

Investing activities   The section of the statement of cash flows which includes receipts from loans, acquiring and selling securities (except for cash equivalents), and acquiring and selling plant assets.

Noncurrent account   An account that is neither a current asset nor a current liability.

Operating activities   The section of the statement of cash flows which includes selling, purchasing, and producing goods; providing services; and paying suppliers, employees, and lenders.

Sources of funds   Sources of funds involve any transaction that has caused funds to flow into a firm (i.e., any transaction that has increased working capital or cash, depending upon the definition of funds).

Statement of cash flows   A statement which explains the causes of changes in cash plus highly liquid marketable securities and provides a summary of the investing and financing activities of an enterprise during a period of time.

Statement of changes in financial position   A statement of changes in financial position is a statement summarizing the financing and investing activities of the firm and disclosing changes in financial position.

Uses of funds   Any transaction that has caused funds to flow out of the firm (i.e., any transaction that has decreased working capital or cash).

Working capital   Working capital is the excess of current assets over current liabilities.

Working capital concept of funds   This concept defines funds in terms of working capital, and utilizes the funds statement to point out changes in the working capital of the firm.

QUESTIONS

1. Why is a statement of cash flows necessary?

2. What is the all-financial-resources concept and why is it important?

3. What are the three major sections of a statement of cash flows?

4. Give examples for each of the three major sections of a statement of cash flows.

5. Explain how income affects cash. Is reported net income always equal to the amount of cash flows from operations? Explain.

6. List items that may be included in the determination of net income but that have no effect on cash.

7. Compare and contrast the direct and indirect methods of preparing the statement of cash flows.

8. What steps are needed in preparing a statement of cash flows?

9. What is the purpose of a worksheet in preparing a statement of cash flows?

10. State how the following are presented on a statement of cash flows.

    a. Dividends paid.
    b. Conversions of bonds to common stock.
    c. Amortization of discount on bonds payable.
    d. Loss on the sale of equipment.

11. Explain how each of the following are treated in a statement of cash flows.

    a. Bad debt expense.
    b. Purchasing land by issuing common stock.
    c. Reclassifying a note payable from long-term to current.
    d. Loss on sale of current marketable equity securities.
    e. Increase in inventories.
    f. Amortization of patents.
    g. Increase in accounts payable.
    h. Conversion of bonds to common stock.

12. What are two types of financial transactions that would be disclosed under the "all-financial-resources" concept that would not be disclosed without this concept?

EXERCISES   **13.**   Consider the following income statement for Wills Company.

Sales	$1,000,000
Cost of goods sold	750,000
Gross margin	$ 250,000
Selling and administrative expenses:	
Salary expense........................... $50,000	
Depreciation expense 25,000	
Administrative expense 25,000	100,000
Net income	$ 150,000

Additional information:

Decrease in inventories	$9,000
Increase in accounts receivable.........................	5,000
Increase in accounts payable	6,000

Required:

Compute the cash flows from operating activities.

14.   Below is the income statement for Lopes Company for the year ending December 31, 19x2.

Lopes Company
Income Statement
For the Year Ended December 31, 19x2

Sales (net)		$500,000
Cost of goods sold:		
Beginning inventory.....................	$ 50,000	
Purchases	300,000	
Goods available for sale	$350,000	
Ending inventory	40,000	
Cost of goods sold		310,000
Gross margin		$190,000
Expenses:		
Wages	$ 35,000	
Depreciation	30,000	
Advertising	15,000	
Administrative	5,000	85,000
Income from operations		$105,000
Gain on sale of equipment.................		50,000
Net income		$155,000

The following balances were derived from the balance sheet.

| | December 31 | |
	19x2	19x1
Accounts receivable	$100,000	$90,000
Accounts payable	30,000	50,000
Prepaid advertising expense................	5,000	3,000
Wages payable..........................	5,000	4,000

Required:

Prepare a schedule showing cash flows from operating activities.

15. Your examination of the financial statements of Russell Company reveals the following data:

	19x2		19x1	
Sales (net)		$100,000		$75,000
Cost of goods sold:				
Beginning inventory	$17,000		$12,000	
Purchases (net)................	58,000		55,000	
Goods available	$75,000		$67,000	
Ending inventory	15,000		17,000	
Cost of goods sold		60,000		50,000
Accounts payable................		20,000		25,000
Accounts receivable..............		50,000		45,000

Required:

Compute the following for 19x2:

1. Cash receipts from sales.
2. Cash disbursements for purchases.

16. Consider the following information for the period ending December 31, 19x1, concerning the Cey Company.

a. Net income for 19x1 was $250,000.
b. Depreciation expense on its buildings was $25,000. Accumulated depreciation on the buildings is $200,000.
c. Extraordinary (non-operating) gains and losses included a loss of $50,000 on an uninsured building destroyed by fire.
d. Dividends paid during the year in cash—$50,000.

Required:

Compute the cash flows from operating activities.

17.   Indicate how each of the items presented below would appear in a statement of cash flows.

1. Declaration of a cash dividend.
2. Payment of cash dividend after above declaration.
3. Depreciation expense for the year.
4. Fully depreciated equipment written off the books.
5. Amortization of premium on long-term bonds payable.
6. Semiannual coupon *payments* on bonds mentioned in item (5) above.
7. Sale of common stock at a discount.
8. Purchase of treasury stock at a price above the original issue price.
9. Payment of wages accrued at the end of the prior year.
10. Sale of fixed assets at a loss.
11. Discounting the company's own 90-day note at a bank.
12. Sale of ten-year bonds at a discount.
13. Three for one (3-1) split of the preferred stock.
14. Sale of machinery at a price in excess of its book value.
15. Amortization of goodwill.

18.   Wynn, Inc., hired you as an independent accountant to analyze the reasons for their unsatisfactory cash position. The company earned $42,000 during the year (19x1) but their cash balance is lower than ever. Your assistant prepared a worksheet providing you with the following information:

a.   Additional capital stock was sold in 19x1; the proceeds of the sale were $40,000.
b.   Vacant land purchased in 19x0 at a cost of $27,000 was sold in 19x1 for $30,000.
c.   A payment of $22,000 was made in 19x1 on a long-term mortgage.
d.   Equipment costing $89,000 was purchased during the year.
e.   Included in the firm's expenses for 19x1 were depreciation charges of $7,500.
f.   The firm's accounts receivable increased by $4,000 and their accounts payable decreased by $4,500 during the year.

Required:

Prepare a statement of cash flows for the year ended December 31, 19x1, which reflects the reasons for the firm's unsatisfactory cash position.

19. Indicate how each of the following items would be presented in a statement of cash flows.

   1. Net income from operations.
   2. Purchase of treasury stock by company.
   3. Sale of bonds payable.
   4. Issuance of bonds payable for land.
   5. Sale of equipment at a gain.
   6. Declaration (but not payment) of cash dividends.

20. From the following information prepare a statement of cash flows for the Sabre Company for 19x1.

   a. Net income for 19x1 was $6,000.
   b. Dividends paid during 19x1 were $1,000.
   c. Captital stock was sold for $2,500.
   d. Depreciation for the year was $1,500.
   e. Long-term bonds of $1,000 were retired at par.
   f. Land was purchased for $3,000.
   g. Land was sold for $6,000, resulting in a gain of $1,000.
   h. A building was purchased for $4,000.

21. Determine the amount of purchase, the cash disbursements for rent expense, and the cash applied to dividends for the Maple Leaf Company for the month of March from the information given below.

Cost of goods sold	$2,579
Increase in prepaid rent	864
Dividends	4,953
Rent expense	970
Increase in inventory	1,240
Decrease in dividends payable	691

22.   Condensed financial statements for the Billy Company are as follows:

Billy Company
Balance Sheet

	December 31	
	19x2	*19x1*
Cash	$ 7,500	$ 6,000
Accounts receivable	9,000	11,000
Inventories	15,000	12,500
Fixed assets	30,000	25,000
Accumulated depreciation	(12,500)	(10,000)
	$49,000	$44,500
Accounts payable	$18,000	$15,000
Bonds payable	10,000	15,000
Common stock	15,000	10,000
Retained earnings	6,000	4,500
	$49,000	$44,500

Billy Company
Income Statement
For the Year Ending December 31, 19x2

Sales		$35,000
Cost of goods sold		17,000
Gross margin		$18,000
Depreciation	$ 2,500	
Operating expenses	11,000	13,500
Net income		$ 4,500

Required:

Prepare a statement of cash flows for 19x2.

PROBLEMS   **23.**   The condensed financial statements of Buckner Corporation are as follows:

Buckner Corporation
Comparative Balance Sheet
December 31, 19x1 and 19x2

	19x2	19x1
Assets		
Current assets:		
Cash	$ 50,000	$ 35,000
Accounts receivable	100,000	90,000
Inventory	60,000	65,000
Prepaid expenses	10,000	8,000
Total current assets	$220,000	$198,000
Fixed assets:		
Building and equipment (net)	$200,000	$220,000
Land	50,000	50,000
Total assets	$470,000	$468,000
Liabilities and Stockholders' Equity		
Accounts payable	$100,000	$ 80,000
Interest payable	10,000	10,000
Notes payable (current)	50,000	40,000
Capital stock	200,000	200,000
Retained earnings	110,000	138,000
Total liabilities and stockholders' equity	$470,000	$468,000

Buckner Corporation
Income Statement
For the Year Ending December 31, 19x2

Sales		$250,000
Less: Cost of goods sold		184,000
Gross margin		$ 66,000
Operating expenses	$64,000	
Depreciation	20,000	84,000
Net loss		($18,000)

Required:

Prepare a statement of cash flows for 19x2.

24.   Below is the income statement for the Rau Company for the year ended December 31, 19x1.

Rau Company
Income Statement
For the Year Ended December 31, 19x1

Sales		$1,000,000
Cost of goods sold:		
Beginning inventory.......................	$ 20,000	
Purchases	500,000	
Goods available for sale....................	$520,000	
Ending inventory.........................	25,000	
Cost of goods sold......................		495,000
Gross margin.............................		$ 505,000
Operating expenses:		
Salaries	$ 50,000	
Depreciation.............................	20,000	
Bad debts...............................	10,000	
Advertising..............................	20,000	
Patent amortization.......................	5,000	
Total operating expenses.....................		105,000
Operating income.........................		$ 400,000
Gain on sale of equipment....................		50,000
Net Income...............................		$ 450,000

Required:

Prepare a schedule computing cash flows from operating activities.

25.   Consider the following selected account balances for Messerschmidt, Inc.

	December 31			
	19x2	*19x1*	*Increase*	*Decrease*
Cash................................	$ 175	$300		$125
Buildings...........................	1,000	800	$200	
Accumulated depreciation—				
building...........................	175	150	25	
Land	300	200	100	
Bonds payable—long-term..............	200	100	100	
Capital stock........................	200	300		100
Retained earnings.....................	300	150	150	
Cash flow (other than depreciation):	$ 100			

Required:

Prepare a statement of cash flows for Messerschmidt, Inc., for the period ending December 31, 19x2, assuming, where it is necessary, that the changes in the accounts are the result of cash transactions.

26. Given below are the balance sheets for Zahn Company for 19x1 and 19x2.

Zahn Company
Comparative Balance Sheet
December 31, 19x1 and 19x2

	19x1	19x2
Cash	$ 100	$ 300
Accounts receivable	400	350
Inventories	300	500
Fixed assets	900	1,000
Less: Accumulated depreciation	(100)	(200)
	$1,600	$1,950
Accounts payable	$ 400	$ 600
Bonds payable (due in 19x7)	400	200
Capital stock	500	700
Retained earnings	300	450
	$1,600	$1,950

Additional information:

The corporation paid a 10 percent stock dividend on January 2, 19x2, when its capital stock was selling at par. Net income for 19x2 was $200. During the year, the company sold a fixed asset with an original cost of $100 (and a book value of $25 at the date of sale) for $50. All other changes in the accounts are the results of transactions typically recorded in such accounts.

Required:

Prepare a statement of cash flows for 19x2.

27. The condensed comparative balance sheet for Marshall Company is presented below.

	December 31	
	19x2	19x1
Assets		
Cash	$ 80,000	$ 65,000
Accounts receivable (net)	100,000	90,000
Inventory	40,000	45,000
Prepaid expenses	12,000	10,000
Fixed assets	173,000	150,000
Accumulated depreciation—		
fixed assets	(35,000)	(30,000)
Total assets	$370,000	$330,000
Liabilities and Stockholders' Equity		
Accounts payable	$ 80,000	$ 60,000
Bonds payable	150,000	150,000
Capital stock	100,000	100,000
Retained earnings	40,000	20,000
Total liabilities and stockholders' equity	$370,000	$330,000

Supplemental data for 19x2.

Net income.............................	$20,000
Depreciation expense....................	5,000
A building was purchased for $23,000 cash.	

Required:

Prepare a statement of cash flows for 19x2.

28. Following are financial statements for Brewer, Inc.:

Brewer, Inc.
Comparative Balance Sheet
December 31, 19x2 and 19x1

	19x2	19x1	Increase (Decrease)
Assets			
Current assets:			
Cash	$ 5,000	$ 45,000	$(40,000)
Accounts receivable..................	100,000	75,000	25,000
Inventories........................	50,000	45,000	5,000
Prepaid expenses.....................	30,000	35,000	(5,000)
Total current assets.................	$185,000	$200,000	$(15,000)
Noncurrent assets:			
Land...............................	$100,000	$ 75,000	$ 25,000
Buildings	200,000	175,000	25,000
Accumulated depreciation—			
buildings.........................	(50,000)	(40,000)	(10,000)
Equipment	100,000	75,000	25,000
Accumulated depreciation—			
equipment	(35,000)	(15,000)	(20,000)
Patents	20,000	30,000	(10,000)
Total noncurrent assets..............	$335,000	$300,000	$ 35,000
Total assets........................	$520,000	$500,000	$ 20,000
Liabilities and Stockholders' Equity			
Current liabilities:			
Accounts payable....................	$ 50,000	$ 40,000	$ 10,000
Notes payable......................	25,000	25,000	0
Accrued expenses....................	40,000	35,000	5,000
Total current liabilities..............	$115,000	$100,000	$ 15,000
Long-term liabilities:			
Bonds payable......................	$100,000	$140,000	$(40,000)
Stockholders' equity:			
Common stock ($100 par value)........	$230,000	$200,000	$ 30,000
Additional paid-in capital.............	40,000	30,000	10,000
Retained earnings....................	35,000	30,000	5,000
Total stockholders' equity...........	$305,000	$260,000	$ 45,000
Total liabilities and stockholders' equity....	$520,000	$500,000	$ 20,000

Brewer, Inc.
Income Statement
For the Year Ended December 31, 19x2

Sales......................................		$2,000,000
Cost of goods sold.......................		1,500,000
Gross margin............................		$ 500,000
Operating expenses:		
Depreciation and amortization expense....	$ 50,000	
Selling and administrative expense........	265,000	
Miscellaneous expense..................	170,000	
Total operating expenses..............		485,000
Net income from operations..............		$ 15,000
Other revenue and expense		
Add: Gain on sale of building..........		20,000
		$ 35,000
Less: Loss on sale of land.............	$ 10,000	
Interest expense................	15,000	25,000
Net income before income taxes...........		$ 10,000
Less: Income taxes.....................		5,000
Net income...........................		$ 5,000

Supplementary data:

a.   Depreciation and amortization of patents were as follows:

Building................................	$20,000
Equipment	20,000
Patents.................................	10,000
Total	$50,000

b.   A building which cost $50,000 and had accumulated depreciation of $10,000 was sold for $60,000.

c.   Common stock with $30,000 par value was sold for $40,000.

d.   Land with a cost of $25,000 was sold for $15,000.

e.   Land was purchased for $50,000.

f.   Bonds of $40,000 were retired.

g.   A building was purchased for $75,000.

h.   Equipment was acquired for $25,000 cash.

Required:

Prepare a statement of cash flows for 19x2.

29. Below is information pertinent to John Corp. for the period ending December 31, 19x1.

   a. Sales, $50,000.
   b. Cost of goods sold, $20,000.
   c. Expenses, $10,000 (of which $2,000 was depreciation).
   d. Increase in accounts payable, $5,000.
   e. Increase in accounts receivable, $5,000.
   f. Sold land which cost $500 for $1,000 cash.
   g. Purchased a building for $10,000 cash and $10,000 par value common stock.
   h. Cash dividends paid, $5,000.
   i. Retired bond payable of $500.

   Required:

   Prepare a statement of cash flows for 19x1.

30. From the following information, prepare a statement of cash flows for 19x1.

Ferguson Company
Trial Balances
(in thousands)

	December 31, 19x1		December 31, 19x0	
Account	*Debit*	*Credit*	*Debit*	*Credit*
Cash.....................................	$ 178		$ 84	
Accounts receivable......................	300		240	
Allowance for bad debts..................		$ 13		$ 10
Merchandise inventory....................	370		400	
Building and equipment...................	420		360	
Allowance for depreciation...............		180		190
Accounts payable.........................		220		210
Mortgage bonds...........................		300		300
Unamortized bond discount................	18		21	
Capital stock............................		357		270
Retained earnings........................		125		90
Net sales................................		4,200		4,000
Cost of goods sold.......................	2,300		2,100	
Salaries and wages.......................	1,500		1,400	
Administrative expense...................	110		100	
Depreciation expense.....................	20		20	
Maintenance expense......................	10		10	
Interest expense.........................	16		15	
Bad debt expense.........................	20		20	
Loss on equipment sales*.................	6		0	
Dividends paid†..........................	127		300	
	$5,395	$5,395	$5,070	$5,070

* In 19x1, equipment costing $40,000 and having a net book value of $10,000 was sold for $4,000.
† Dividends paid in 19x1 include a stock dividend of $27,000.

31. The trial balances of Canuck Company revealed the following information.

	December 31	
Debits	*19x1*	*19x2*
Cash	$ 14,000	$ 15,400
Accounts receivable (net)................	26,600	33,600
Inventory	72,800	70,000
Prepaid expenses......................	4,200	5,600
Permanent investments..................	14,000	0
Buildings.............................	126,000	168,000
Machinery............................	56,000	86,800
Patents	7,000	5,600
	$320,600	$385,000

Credits		
Accounts payable......................	$ 16,800	$ 11,200
Notes payable—short-term (nontrade).....	12,600	18,200
Accrued wages........................	4,200	2,800
Accumulated depreciation..............	56,000	54,600
Notes payable—long-term..............	42,000	49,000
Common stock........................	168,000	210,000
Retained earnings.....................	21,000	39,200
	$320,600	$385,000

Additional data:

a. Net income for 19x2 was $33,600.
b. Recorded depreciation on fixed assets was $11,200.
c. Amortization of patents was $1,400.
d. Machinery was purchased for $21,000; one-third was paid in cash; an interest-bearing note was given for the balance.
e. Common stock was issued to purchase machinery costing $35,000.
f. Old machinery which originally cost $25,200 (one-half depreciated) was sold for $9,800; the gain or loss was reported on the income statement.
g. Cash was paid for the building addition—$42,000.
h. Common stock was issued to pay a $7,000 long-term note.
i. Cash was received for the sale of permanent investment—$16,800.
j. Paid cash dividends.
k. Credit sales were $168,000.
l. Collections of accounts receivable were $161,000.

Required:

Prepare a statement of cash flows for 19x2.

32.   The trial balances of Islander Company revealed the following information.

	December 31	
	19x1	*19x2*
Cash	$ 3,200	$ 4,000
Accounts receivable (net)................	4,000	7,200
Inventory	8,000	9,600
Permanent investments..................	1,600	0
Fixed assets...........................	24,000	37,600
	$40,800	$58,400
Accumulated depreciation...............	$ 4,000	$ 5,600
Accounts payable.......................	2,400	4,000
Notes payable—short-term..............	3,200	2,400
Notes payable—long-term..............	8,000	14,400
Common stock.........................	20,000	23,200
Retained earnings.....................	3,200	8,800
	$40,800	$58,400

Additional data:

a.   Net income was $11,200.
b.   Depreciation was $1,600.
c.   Permanent investments were sold at cost.
d.   Dividends of $5,600 were paid.
e.   Fixed assets were purchased for $4,000 cash.
f.   A long-term note payable for $9,600 was given in exchange for fixed assets.
g.   Common stock was issued to pay a $3,200 long-term note payable.

Required:

Prepare a statement of cash flows for the year ended December 31, 19x2.

33. Below is the balance sheet for Ranger Company comparing the years 19x1 and 19x2.

| | December 31 | |
	19x2	19x1
Assets		
Cash	$ 25,000	$ 20,000
Accounts receivable (net).....................	90,000	75,000
Marketable securities.........................	50,000	55,000
Prepaid expenses............................	15,000	13,000
Buildings....................................	150,000	120,000
Accumulated depreciation—		
buildings...............................	(85,000)	(65,000)
Total assets.............................	$245,000	$218,000
Liabilities and Stockholders' Equity		
Accounts payable............................	$ 71,000	$ 50,000
Bonds payable..............................	100,000	80,000
Capital stock...............................	50,000	60,000
Retained earnings...........................	24,000	28,000
Total liabilities and stockholders' equity........	$245,000	$218,000

Additional information for 19x2:

Net income..................................	$ 6,000
Cash dividends paid..........................	10,000

Required:

Prepare a statement of cash flows for the year ended December 31, 19x2.

34. The 19x1 financial statements for the Alston Company are:

Alston Company
Income Statement
For the Year Ended December 31, 19x1

Net sales.....................................		$50,000
Cost of goods sold............................		30,000
Gross margin.................................		$20,000
Operating expenses:		
Depreciation.............................	$2,000	
Wage expense............................	7,000	
Other expenses...........................	1,000	10,000
Net income from operations....................		$10,000
Gain on sale of land...........................		5,000
Net income..................................		$15,000

Alston Company
Retained Earnings Statement
For the Year Ended December 31, 19x1

Retained earnings at beginning of year.......	$25,000
Add: Net income......................	15,000
	$40,000
Subtract: Dividends....................	5,000
Retained earnings at end of year............	$35,000

Alston Company
Comparative Balance Sheet

	December 31	
	19x1	*19x0*
Assets		
Cash	$ 69,000	$ 60,000
Accounts receivable....................	25,000	20,000
Inventories	15,000	10,000
Building	100,000	100,000
Accumulated depreciation—		
building..........................	(27,000)	(25,000)
Land	125,000	100,000
Total assets.......................	$307,000	$265,000
Liabilities and Stockholders' Equity		
Accounts payable......................	$ 35,000	$ 15,000
Accrued wages payable.................	7,000	5,000
Bonds payable—long-term..............	130,000	120,000
Capital stock........................	100,000	100,000
Retained earnings....................	35,000	25,000
Total equities......................	$307,000	$265,000

The following information is also available:

a. Land with a cost of $25,000 was sold for $30,000.
b. Additional land was purchased for $50,000.
c. A long-term bond was issued for $10,000.
d. $5,000 cash dividends were paid during the year.

Required:

Prepare a statement of cash flows for the Alston Company for the year ending December 31, 19x1.

35. From the following pre-closing trial balances, prepare an income statement and a statement of cash flows for the year ended December 31, 19x1.

Rockies Incorporated
Trial Balances
(in thousands)
For the Year Ended December 31, 19x1

Account	December 31, 19x1 Debit	December 31, 19x1 Credit	December 31, 19x0 Debit	December 31, 19x0 Credit
Cash	$ 373		$ 26	
Accounts receivable..............	980		589	
Allowance for bad debts...........		$ 6		$ 3
Inventory	960		612	
Buildings......................	495		560	
Allowance for depreciation........		170		100
Accounts payable................		105		86
Bonds payable, due in 19x9........		300		300
Unamortized bond premium, due in 19x2....................		19		20
Mortgage bond payable...........		0		50
Capital stock...................		250		280
Retained earnings...............		948		399
Net sales......................		3,100		3,297
Cost of goods sold...............	1,100		1,600	
Salaries expense.................	850		980	
Depreciation expense.............	135		135	
Interest expense.................	5		5	
Bad debt expense................	15		16	
Gain on sale of building...........		25		0
Dividends	10		12	
	$4,923	$4,923	$4,535	$4,535

Additional information:

a. In 19x1, a building with an original cost of $65,000 was sold for $25,000. The building had been fully depreciated.
b. Capital stock was repurchased and retired.

36. The trial balance of Canadiens Company revealed the following information.

	December 31	
	19x1	19x2
Cash	$20,400	$ 20,700
Accounts receivable (net)...............	7,200	10,200
Inventory	9,600	8,400
Permanent investments..................	3,600	0
Fixed assets..........................	48,000	55,800
Treasury stock........................	0	6,900
	$88,800	$102,000
Accumulated depreciation...............	$28,800	$ 23,400
Accounts payable......................	11,400	7,200
Bonds payable........................	6,000	18,000
Common stock........................	30,000	36,600
Retained earnings.....................	12,600	16,800
	$88,800	$102,000

Additional information:

a.   Credit sales were $42,000.
b.   Credit purchases were $24,000.
c.   Depreciation was $3,000.
d.   Cash disbursements for expenses were $10,800.
e.   Inventory decreased by $1,200.
f.   Fixed assets were sold for $3,600; their original cost was $12,600 and two-thirds of this cost had been depreciated.
g.   Fixed assets were purchased for $2,400 cash.
h.   Bonds payable were issued for $18,000 to purchase fixed assets.
i.   Permanent investments were sold for $5,400 cash.
j.   Treasury stock was purchased for $6,900.
k.   Bonds payable of $6,000 were retired by issuing common stock.
l.   Accounts receivable collections were $39,000.
m.   Accounts payable of $28,200 were paid.
n.   Unissued common stock was sold for $600.

Required:

Prepare a statement of cash flows for the year ended December 31, 19x2.

Refer to the Annual Report included in the Appendix at the end of the text:

37. What was the total current assets and current liabilities at the end of the most recent year?

38. Which current liability changed the most in the most recent year?

39. Prepare a statement of cash flows for the most recent year.

Chapter 12 presents a general discussion of the federal income tax. Studying this chapter should enable you to:

1. Identify the primary objectives of the federal income tax.

2. Discuss the process of determining an individual and corporate taxpayer's tax liability.

3. Recognize the important differences in the taxation of corporations vs. the taxation of individuals.

4. Describe the purpose of interperiod tax allocation and the accounting procedures involved.

5. Illustrate how intraperiod tax allocation is gnerally accomplished.

12

Income Tax Considerations*

*This chapter was written by Professors Steven D. Grossman and Bob G. Kilpatrick of Texas A&M University, Thomas L. Dickens of Clemson University and Kenneth R. Orbach of Louisiana State University.

INTRODUCTION

Income taxes are periodic charges levied by federal, state, and city governments on the taxable income of both individuals and business corporations. Taxable income is a statutory concept (i.e., it is defined by law and is equal to gross income minus all allowable deductions). For businesses organized as corporations, income taxes are accounted for as an expense which is deducted in computing the net income for the period. The amount of taxes owed, but not paid, is a liability which is included in the balance sheet. Because income taxes normally represent a significant cost to a business enterprise, an awareness of the tax laws and how they are applied is essential to a complete understanding of accounting information.

Data which are required for the determination of income taxes are usually found in the accounting records. Taxable income, however, may not be the same as the income reported in the income statement even though both are determined from the identical set of accounting records. This difference often occurs because income tax law is not always the same as the basic concepts which are used for financial accounting purposes.

This chapter is devoted to a general discussion of the federal income tax and its implication for the financial reporting process of a business. Although many states and cities also impose income taxes, which may differ in application from the federal income tax, the income tax liability to all governmental units is treated similarly in the accounting records. For this reason, the following discussion is limited to the federal income tax.

THE FEDERAL INCOME TAX

The modern era of federal income taxation originated in 1913 with the adoption of the Sixteenth Amendment to the Constitution. This amendment gives Congess the power to ". . . lay and collect taxes on incomes, from whatever source derived, without apportionment among the several States, and without regard to any census or enumeration." Soon after the Sixteenth Amendment was adopted, Congress enacted the Revenue Act of 1913, which provided for a general yearly income tax. Since that time, Congress has passed numerous income tax statutes amending the various Revenue Acts so that there has been a continuous development of income tax law in the United States. In 1939 the Internal Revenue Code was enacted. This code was thoroughly revised in 1954 and extensively amended and supplemented by the Tax Reform Act of 1969, the Revenue Act of 1971, the Tax Reduction Act of 1975, the Tax Reform Act of 1976, the Tax Reduction and Simplification Act of 1977, the Revenue Act of 1978, the Economic Recovery Act of 1981, the Tax Equity and Fiscal Responsibility Act of 1982, and the Deficit Reduction Act of 1984, and the Tax Reform Act of 1986. Tax law is also supplemented by interpretations of the Internal Revenue Code by both the courts and the Treasury Department. The Treasury Department, operating through a branch known as the Internal Revenue Service, is charged with the enforcement and collection of income taxes.

The original purpose of the income tax was stated as simply to obtain revenues for the use of the federal government. The income tax on individuals under the 1913 Act consisted of a flat 1 percent tax on taxable income in excess of $4,000 for married persons plus a progressive surtax of 1 to 7 percent on income in excess of $20,000. A progressive tax is one in which tax rates increase as taxable income increases.

Since 1916, both the objectives of the income tax and income tax rates have undergone a significant change. The purpose of the federal income tax today includes such diverse objectives as controlling inflation, influencing economic growth, decreasing unemployment, redistributing national income, and encouraging the growth of small businesses. All of these purposes are in addition to the original objective of raising revenue to finance the operations of the government. Similarly, there have been substantial changes in tax rates. The current rates for married taxpayers are presented in Illustration 1.

CLASSES OF TAXPAYERS

Income taxes are levied upon four major types of taxable entities: individuals, corporations, estates, and trusts. Business entities organized as sole proprietorships or partnerships are not taxable entities. Instead, their income is included in the gross income of the individual owner or owners, whether or not it is actually withdrawn from the business and distributed to these owners. A partnership, however, is required to prepare an information return which indicates the items of its gross income, deductions, and credits and how these are allocated to the partners. The partners then report these amounts in their own tax returns.

A corporation is treated as a separate entity for tax purposes and must pay taxes on its taxable income. In addition, individual corporate stockholders must include any dividends received from the corporation as a part of their taxable income. For this reason, it is often argued that the profits of a corporation are taxed twice—once to the corporation when the income is reported and again to its stockholders when dividends are distributed. Under limited circumstances, a corporation meeting certain qualifications may avoid this "double taxation" of corporate income by making an S Corporation election; the shareholders are then taxed on undistributed income on a current basis.[1]

An estate is a separate legal entity which is created to take charge of the assets of a deceased person to pay the decedent's debts and distribute any remaining assets to the heirs. A trust is a legal entity which is created when a person by gift or devise transfers assets to a trustee for the benefit of designated persons. The tax rules that apply to estates and trusts will not be discussed in this chapter, as they are beyond the scope of this text.

---

[1] These entities are referred to as "S Corporations." Numerous changes in the tax treatment of S Corporations were made in the "Subchapter S Revision Act of 1982." Subchapter S Corporations are now called S Corporations.

Illustration 1

Taxable Income Brackets—1987

Tax Rate	Married/ Joint	Head of Household	Single	Married/ Separate
11%	First $3,000	First $2,500	First $1,800	First $1,500
15	$ 3,001-28,000	$ 2,501-23,000	$ 1,801-16,800	$ 1,501-14,000
28	28,001-45,000	23,001-38,000	16,801-27,000	14,001-22,500
35	45,001-90,000	38,001-80,000	27,001-54,000	22,501-45,000
38.5	Over 90,000	Over 80,000	Over 54,000	Over 45,000

After 1987, the tax rate schedule will consist of only two brackets:

Taxable Income Brackets—1988 and After

Tax Rate	Married/ Joint	Head of Household	Single	Married/ Separate
15%	First $29,750	First $23,900	First $17,850	First $14,875
28	Over 29,750	Over 23,900	Over 17,850	Over 14,875

Filing Status	Standard Deduction	
	1987	1988
Married/joint..................	$3,760	$5,000
Head of household	2,540	4,400
Single.......................	2,540	3,000
Married/separate.............	1,880	2,500

INDIVIDUAL FEDERAL INCOME TAX

The cash basis of measuring taxable income is used by almost all individuals in preparing their tax returns. Generally, revenue is recognized upon the actual or constructive receipt of cash and expenses are recognized as cash is expended.

Individual income tax rates depend on the status of the taxpayer. There are different tax rate schedules for married taxpayers who file a joint return, married individuals who file separate returns, unmarried taxpayers, and single taxpayers qualifying as a "head of household." Generally, "head of household" status applies to certain unmarried or legally separated persons who maintain the principal residence for a relative.

The federal income tax rate structure has been changed from a structure containing 15 graduated brackets to a structure that has five brackets in 1987 and only two brackets—15 percent and 28 percent—in 1988. This change alters the previously graduated progressive structure in which each increment of taxable income is subject to a higher rate than the preceding increment of income.

The amount of federal income tax that an individual must pay is generally determined by knowledge of gross income, deductions for adjusted gross income, adjusted gross income, itemized deductions (deductions from adjusted gross income), personal exemptions, tax table income or taxable income, and credits. The relationship of these concepts and the procedures for determining taxable income are summarized in Illustration 2. A more detailed explanation of the items outlined in the determination of taxable income is given in the following paragraphs.

Gross Income. Basically, gross income is defined as all income from whatever source derived, unless expressly excluded by law or by the U.S. Constitution. This includes income from sources such as wages, dividends, interest, partnership income, rents, and numerous other items. Among the more important classes of income which are currently excludable from gross income by law are gifts, life insurance proceeds received at the insured's death, social security benefits (up to certain amounts), inheritances (but not income from trusts and life estates), workmen's compensation, and interest on certain state and municipal bonds.

Deductions for Adjusted Gross Income. The deductions for adjusted gross income are business expenses and other expenses connected with earning certain types of revenue. These include ordinary and necessary expenses incurred by the taxpayer in the operation of his unincorporated business or profession, certain business expenses of an employee, losses from the sale or exchange of certain property, expenses incurred in connection with earning rent or royalty income, payments to an individual retirement arrangement or to a Keogh retirement plan, and periodic payments of alimony made under a court decree.

Deductions From Adjusted Gross Income (Itemized Deductions). Itemized deductions include such items as a limited amount of charitable contributions, mortgage interest payments, other interest payments (deductions for consumer interest are being phased out over 1987-1990), certain taxes paid by the taxpayer, a limited amount of medical expenses, a limited amount of casualty and theft losses, and nonbusiness expenses (other than expenses incurred in connection with earning rent or royalty income). These nonbusiness expenses are the necessary expenses incurred in producing income, for the management of income-producing property, or in connection with the determination, collection or refund of any tax. These include such items as certain legal fees relating to investments, dues to professional organizations, and expenses incurred for the preparation of tax returns.

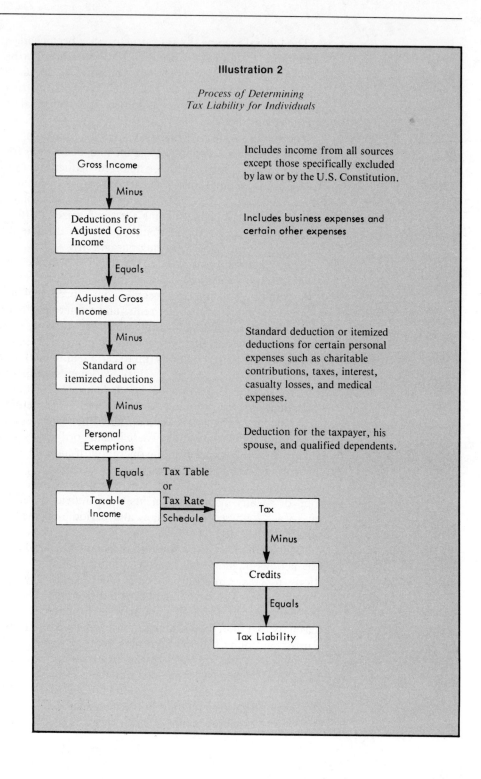

Illustration 2

*Process of Determining
Tax Liability for Individuals*

Gross Income

Minus

Includes income from all sources
except those specifically excluded
by law or by the U.S. Constitution.

Deductions for
Adjusted Gross
Income

Equals

Includes business expenses and
certain other expenses

Adjusted Gross
Income

Minus

Standard deduction or itemized
deductions for certain personal
expenses such as charitable
contributions, taxes, interest,
casualty losses, and medical
expenses.

Standard or
itemized deductions

Minus

Personal
Exemptions

Equals

Deduction for the taxpayer, his
spouse, and qualified dependents.

Taxable
Income

Tax Table
or
Tax Rate
Schedule

Tax

Minus

Credits

Equals

Tax Liability

Under prior law, a taxpayer could either deduct the sum of itemized deductions or take the standard deduction. For tax years beginning after December 31, 1976, individual taxpayers could no longer elect a standard deduction. In its place the 1977 Tax Reduction and Simplification Act substituted the zero bracket amount (this is simply that initial range of income on which there is a zero tax (e.g., 0-$3,540 for married taxpayers filing jointly). The zero bracket amount was $3,540 for married taxpayers filing jointly, $1,770 for a married taxpayer filing separately, and $2,390 for single taxpayers and heads of household. The zero bracket amount was not a deduction; rather it was incorporated into the tax tables and the tax rate schedules. As a result, a taxpayer who itemized had to deduct from adjusted gross income the excess itemized deductions (i.e., the difference between the itemized deductions and the relevant zero bracket amount). The Tax Reform Act of 1986 replaced the zero bracket amount with a new standard deduction for those taxpayers who do not itemize deductions. The zero bracket amount is no longer applicable to those who do itemize deductions.

Taxable income may now be computed. Generally, taxable income equals adjusted gross income reduced by either the standard deduction or itemized deductions and personal exemptions.

Personal Exemption. A taxpayer is allowed a deduction for each personal exemption to which he or she is entitled. The deduction is $1,900 for 1987, $1,950 for 1988, and $2,000 for 1989. After 1989, the $2,000 amount will be indexed for inflation. Personal exemptions may be taken for the following individuals:

1. *The taxpayer.*

2. *The taxpayer's spouse if a joint return is filed.*

3. *The taxpayer's spouse if a joint return is not filed, but only if the spouse has no gross income and is not a dependent of another taxpayer.*

4. *Certain dependents.* A dependent is an individual who meets all five of the following requirements:

   a. *Support.* More than one-half of whose support is provided by the taxpayer,

   b. *Income.* Dependent's gross income is less than the amount of the personal exemption (unless the dependent is the taxpayer's child and is either less than 19 years old or is a full-time student),

   c. *Relationship.* Must be related to the taxpayer or the principal place of abode is with the taxpayer,

   d. *Joint Return.* The dependent cannot file a joint return with his or her spouse, and

   e. *Citizenship.* Must be either a U.S. citizen or national or a resident of the U.S., Canada, or Mexico.

Credits.   A credit is an amount by which the tax liability is reduced. At the time of this writing, the most commonly used credits included the earned income credit, credit for the elderly, credit for child and dependent care expenses, and the foreign tax credit.

Withholding and Estimated Tax.   Taxpayers are generally required to make payments on their estimated tax liability during the year. This is accomplished by two principal procedures:

1.   Employers withhold income tax on compensation to their employees.

2.   Individuals who have income not subject to withholding (such as self-employed individuals) or who have income from which not enough is withheld should file a declaration of estimated tax. This estimated tax is generally paid in four equal installments.

In either instance, any difference between the amounts paid and the actual tax liability at the end of the year is settled when the tax return is filed.

Capital Gain and Losses.   Gains from the sale of certain property defined by the tax law as capital assets were given special treatment for income tax purposes. Capital assets most commonly held by taxpayers include stocks, bonds, personal residences, and land. To qualify for special tax treatment, capital gains had to be long-term. Long-term capital gains or losses result from the sale of capital assets held by the taxpayer for more than six months, and short-term gains or losses result from the sale of those held six months or less. Short-term capital gains did not qualify for special tax treatment and were taxed as ordinary income.

The special tax treatment applied to the taxpayer's net capital gain, i.e., the excess of the net long-term capital gain (long-term capital gains less long-term capital losses) over the net short-term capital loss (short-term capital losses less short-term capital gain); 60 percent of the net capital gain was a deduction for adjusted gross income.

To illustrate this concept, assume that a taxpayer had the following capital gains and losses:

Long-term capital gains	$11,000
Long-term capital losses	2,000
Short-term capital gains	5,000
Short-term capital losses	6,000

In this case, the taxpayer had a net long-term capital gain of $9,000 ($11,000 − $2,000) and a net short-term capital loss of $1,000 ($6,000 − $5,000). The taxpayer's net capital gain of $8,000 ($9,000 − $1,000) was included in computing adjusted gross income. In addition, the taxpayer enjoyed a $4,800 (60% × $8,000) deduction for adjusted gross income.

Therefore, there was a net increase of $3,200 ($8,000 − $4,800 or 40% × $8,000) in adjusted gross income due to the capital transactions. The Tax Reform Act of 1986 eliminated the 60 percent capital gains exclusion. Starting in 1988, net capital gains are taxed at the same rate as any other income. Capital losses are allowed to the extent of capital gains plus $3,000. Losses may offset gains and other income dollar for dollar. Losses that cannot be used in a particular year may be carried over to succeeding years.

Computation of Individual Income Tax—An Illustration. The example included in Illustration 3 details the computation of the income tax for an individual filing a joint return. This individual, who owns a drug store organized as a sole proprietorship, is married and has two minor children. In practice, the information would be reported on standard tax forms provided by the Federal government.

Illustration 3
Income Tax Computation for
Married Taxpayer Filing Jointly

Gross Income and Deductions From Gross Income

Sales		$100,000
Less:		
Cost of goods sold	$50,000	
Business expenses	30,000	80,000
Net business income		$ 20,000
Interest on savings accounts		1,000
Rents received	$ 5,000	
Less: Expenses	2,000	
Net rental income		3,000
Net capital gain		4,000
Adjusted gross income		$ 28,000
Itemized deductions:		
Charitable contributions	$ 600	
Interest paid	1,100	
Property taxes	2,000	
Casualty loss (in excess of $100)	300	4,000
Less: Exemptions (4 × $1,950)		7,800
Taxable income		$ 16,200
Total tax (at 15%)		$ 2,430
Less: Payments on estimated taxes		3,500
Amount of refund		$ 1,070

CORPORATE INCOME TAX

A corporation is a taxable entity which is separate and distinct from its stockholders. In general, the taxable income of a corporation is computed by deducting its ordinary business expenses and special deductions from its gross income. Although a corporation is taxed in generally the same manner as individuals, there are several important differences:

1. The concepts of itemized deductions and personal exemptions are not applicable to corporations.

2. Corporations may ordinarily deduct 80 percent of all dividends received on investments in stocks of other taxable domestic corporations.

3. The deduction for charitable contributions is limited to 10 percent of taxable income (before charitable contributions, before the 80% dividend deduction and before certain other deductions) in any one year.

The corporate tax rate also differs from the rate applied to individual taxpayers. A corporation pays a tax of 15 percent of the first $50,000 of taxable income, 25 percent of the next $25,000, and 34 percent of taxable income in excess of $75,000. Corporations also have available an alternative tax that is intended to ensure that a corporation with economic income pays at least some federal income tax. The calculation of the minimum tax involves increasing the corporation's taxable income by certain tax preferences and adjusting certain deductions (e.g., depreciation).

DIFFERENCES BETWEEN ACCOUNTING INCOME AND TAXABLE INCOME

The taxable income of a corporation often differs from the net income reported in its financial statements. Taxable income is determined by tax law while accounting income is based on generally accepted accounting principles. The rules and regulations comprising the income tax laws reflect the objectives of income taxation as well as administrative rulings which have been made to implement the law. Financial accounting, on the other hand, is concerned with the proper determination and matching of revenues and expenses in order to measure income.

Some differences between taxable income and accounting income occur because of special tax rules that differ from generally accepted accounting principles. Certain items of revenue are excluded by law from taxable income. For example, interest on state and municipal bonds is included in accounting income but not in taxable income. Similarly, certain expenses may not be treated as deductions for tax purposes. For example, goodwill is amortized as an expense for accounting purposes but it is not subject to amortization under current tax regulations. These items represent permanent differences between taxable and accounting income and are referred to as such.

Other differences between taxable income and accounting income are not permanent. These result from temporary differences in the timing of the recognition of revenues and expenses. Temporary differences occur because, in some instances, one method or procedure may be used for tax purposes and a different method or procedure for financial accounting purposes. The underlying reason why different methods are used is because of the differences in the objectives of accounting and taxation. The objective of financial accounting is a fair and accurate measurement of income and financial position, while the objective of a business in selecting tax methods is usually to minimize taxable income and postpone the payment of taxes. Although over a long enough period of time the temporary differences should "wash out" so that total taxable income and total accounting income are the same, the difference during any one year may be significant. Two major examples of temporary differences are as follows:

1. *Depreciation.* Prior to 1981, the tax laws allowed the use of several depreciation methods. A firm could use an accelerated depreciation method such as double-declining balance or sum-of-the-years'-digits for tax purposes, and straight-line depreciation for purposes of financial accounting. The accelerated methods resulted in larger depreciation expense than the straight-line method in the earlier years of the life of an asset, and smaller depreciation charges in the later years. Thus, the use of the different methods resulted in lower taxable income than accounting income during the early years, but had the opposite effect in later years.

   The 1981 Economic Recovery Tax Act overhauled the system of tax depreciation through the introduction of the Accelerated Cost Recovery System (ACRS). The Tax Reform Act of 1986 modified ACRS procedures.[2] Because ACRS has not been approved as a generally accepted method for financial reporting purposes, the reporting difference between accounting income and taxable income will continue.

2. *Installment basis.* Businesses that sell merchandise on the installment basis may recognize revenue for financial accounting purposes at the time of sale but report the income for tax purposes as cash is actually received.

There are also several different methods of accounting for inventories. During periods of increasing prices, the last-in, first-out (LIFO) method results in higher costs and, thus, lower net income than the other acceptable

---

[2] See Chapter 4 for a discussion of ACRS.

inventory pricing methods. Consequently, with the general increase in prices in recent years, many firms have adopted the LIFO method for tax purposes. The use of LIFO for tax purposes, however, has not resulted in significant differences between taxable and accounting income because the tax law requires generally that a business must use this method for financial accounting if it is used for tax purposes.

Interperiod Tax Allocation

When one accounting method is used for tax purposes and a different method for financial accounting, revenues or expenses may be reported on the income statement and the tax return in different periods. These are called temporary differences. Although the same total revenue and expenses (ignoring permanent differences) eventually are reported for both tax and financial accounting purposes, taxable income and accounting income during any one period may differ significantly. Therefore, as a result of temporary differences, a part of the income tax liability during one year is caused by revenues and expenses reported during some other year for financial accounting purposes. Consequently, if income tax expense reported in the income statement is based on income taxes actually paid, there is a mismatching of revenues and expenses. That is, earnings may be included in the income statement of one period and the related tax expense reported in a different period.

To illustrate this situation, assume that taxable income exceeds accounting income in earlier years. Under interperiod tax allocation, the excess of the tax liability over tax expense would be considered a prepayment of income taxes. The difference would be debited to an asset account, deferred tax asset, representing income taxes paid on accounting income that will be recognized in a later period. For example, assume that Marion Company agrees to rent a portion of its office space to Dean Company on a one-time basis for 19x2 and receives its annual rent of $3,600 for the year 19x2 on December 31, 19x1. None of this amount would be included in accounting income for 19x1 since it will not be earned by Dean Company until 19x2. For tax purposes, however, the entire amount would be included in taxable income for 19x1 since prepaid rent is taxed as it is received rather than as it is earned. Assume that the income of Marion Company from all sources other than rentals was $10,000 for both 19x1 and 19x2. Its taxable income would be $13,600 (accounting income of $10,000 plus the $3,600 rent received) in 19x1 and $10,000 in 19x2. Further assume that the tax rate in both years was 40 percent. The entries to record the tax expense for 19x1 and 19x2 would be as follows:

19x1	Tax expense	4,000	
	Deferred tax asset	1,440	
	Income taxes payable		5,440
19x2	Tax expense	5,440	
	Deferred tax asset		1,440
	Income taxes payable		4,000

In this example, the difference between accounting income and taxable income due to the temporary difference in recognizing the rental income was eliminated by the end of 19x2.

To illustrate a slightly more complex situation, assume that Ruth Company purchased several light trucks on January 1, 19x1, for $120,000. The firm plans to use the straight-line depreciation method for financial accounting purposes and ACRS depreciation for tax purposes. No salvage value is anticipated and the trucks are assigned a four year useful life for accounting purposes. For tax purposes, the trucks would be included in the five year ACRS class and depreciated using the 200 percent declining-balance method. Assume further that the income before taxes and depreciation remains constant at $100,000 for the years 19x1 through 19x7, and that the applicable tax rate is 40 percent. Under these circumstances, the depreciation expense on the income statement will be $30,000 ($120,000 ÷ 4) each year, 19x1 through 19x4 and zero for 19x5 and 19x6, since the trucks were assigned a four year life with no salvage value for accounting purposes. The deduction for depreciation on the tax return, on the other hand, would be as follows:

		Annual	Cumulative
19x1:	(2 × 20%) × ($120,000 − 0) × ½ =	$24,000	$ 24,000
19x2:	(2 × 20%) × ($120,000 − $24,000) =	38,400	62,400
19x3:	(2 × 20%) × ($120,000 − $62,400) =	23,040	85,440
19x4:	(2 × 20%) × ($120,000 − $85,440) =	13,824	99,264
19x5:	(2 × 20%) × ($120,000 − $99,264) =	8,294	107,558
19x6:	$120,000 − $107,558 =	$12,442	120,000

Note that only one-half year's depreciation is taken in 19x1, the year of acquisition, because of the half-year convention. In 19x6, the remaining undepreciated cost is charged to depreciation, also because of the half-year convention.

The firm's taxable income and actual tax liability are as follows:

	19x1	19x2	19x3	19x4	19x5	19x6	Total
Income before depreciation and taxes	$100,000	$100,000	$100,000	$100,000	$100,000	$100,000	$600,000
Deduction for depreciation	24,000	38,400	23,040	13,824	8,294	12,442	120,000
Taxable income	$ 76,000	$ 61,600	$ 76,960	$ 86,176	$ 91,706	$ 87,558	$480,000
Income tax paid (40%)	$ 30,400	$ 24,640	$ 30,784	$ 34,470	$ 36,682	$ 35,024	$192,000

Using the income tax due the government for the year as the income tax expense on the income statement would result in the following determination of accounting income.

	19x1	19x2	19x3	19x4	19x5	19x6	Total
Income before depreciation and taxes	$100,000	$100,000	$100,000	$100,000	$100,000	$100,000	$600,000
Depreciation expense	30,000	30,000	30,000	30,000	0	0	120,000
Income before taxes	$ 70,000	$ 70,000	$ 70,000	$ 70,000	$100,000	$100,000	$480,000
Income tax expense (40%)	30,400	24,640	30,784	34,470	36,682	35,024	192,000
Net income	$ 39,600	$ 45,360	$ 39,216	$ 35,530	$ 63,318	$ 64,976	$288,000

It should be noted that even though Ruth Company had identical operating results during each year, the tax expense and the net income figures vary.

To correct this improper matching of revenues and expenses, tax expense in the income statement should be matched against the income reported therein, regardless of when the income will be included in taxable income and the tax actually paid. This procedure, known as interperiod tax allocation, relates the income tax expense for the period to accounting income rather than to taxable income. Thus, the tax expense reported on the income statement is related to accounting income rather than equal to the actual tax liability (tax rate × taxable income) for the period (after adjustments to reflect permanent differences have been made). If the temporary differences cause the tax expense to exceed the taxes actually owed for the period, the excess represents a deferred liability—deferred income tax liability. With regard to a particular temporary difference, this deferred liability will eventually be eliminated in future periods when the tax liability exceeds the tax expense.

Using interperiod tax allocation, Ruth Company would report tax expense equal to the tax rate (40%) applied to the accounting income before taxes. The resulting income statements for the four year period would be as follows:

	19x1	19x2	19x3	19x4	19x5	19x6	Total
Income before depreciation and taxes	$100,000	$100,000	$100,000	$100,000	$100,000	$100,000	$600,000
Depreciation expense	30,000	30,000	30,000	30,000	0	0	120,000
Income before taxes	$ 70,000	$ 70,000	$ 70,000	$ 70,000	$100,000	$100,000	$480,000
Income tax expense (40%)	28,000	28,000	28,000	28,000	40,000	40,000	192,000
Net income	$ 42,000	$ 42,000	$ 42,000	$ 42,000	$ 60,000	$ 60,000	$288,000

Thus, under tax allocation procedures, the tax expense in the income statement is logically related to the earnings before taxes. Note that the tax expense over the period is still $192,000 and the total tax liability is also $192,000. The entries to record the tax expense for the year are:

19x1	Income tax expense	28,000	
	Deferred tax asset	2,400	
	Income taxes payable		30,400
19x2	Income tax expense	28,000	
	Income taxes payable		24,640
	Deferred tax asset		2,400
	Deferred tax liability		960
19x3	Income tax expense	28,000	
	Deferred tax liability	960	
	Deferred tax asset	1,788	
	Income taxes payable		30,748
19x4	Income tax expense	28,000	
	Deferred tax asset	6,470	
	Income taxes payable		34,470
19x5	Income tax expense	40,000	
	Deferred tax asset		4,976
	Income taxes payable		35,024
19x6	Same as 19x5		

In this example, the difference between accounting income and taxable income is eliminated over the six year period. Therefore, the deferred tax accounts, both deferred tax asset and deferred tax liability, have a zero balance at the end of the six years. In practice, the differences between accounting and taxable income may last for a considerable number of years or even indefinitely since the company is continually replacing its assets and seldom, if ever, would all assets be fully depreciated. The balance in the deferred tax liability account may, therefore, become a significant amount.

In general, interperiod tax allocation for timing differences consists of charging income tax expense for an amount equal to the accounting income tax rate, crediting income tax payable for an amount equal to taxable income tax rate, and debiting or crediting the difference to a deferred tax account. This "rule" assumes that there are only timing and not permanent differences between accounting income and taxable income.

Allocation of Income Tax Within a Period

According to Accounting Principles Board *Opinions No. 9* and *30*, the income statement should disclose separate income figures for: (1) income from continuing operations; (2) income from any segment or division of the business which has been, or is to be discontinued or sold—referred to as discontinued operations; and (3) income from unusual, nonrecurring items, referred to as extraordinary items. Income from continuing opera-tions, income or losses from discontinued operations, and extraordinary gains or losses may be included in taxable income and, hence, affect the tax liability for the period. For this reason, it is believed that allocation of the total amount of income taxes for the period among income from continuing operations, discontinued operations, and extraordinary gains or losses provides a more meaningful income statement.

This allocation, called intraperiod tax allocation, is accomplished by deducting from income from continuing operations, the taxes related to that amount showing income or losses from discontinued operations and extraordinary gains and losses net of the tax applicable to the gain or income and less the related tax reduction due to losses.

To illustrate, assume that Cobb Company, which uses the same methods for tax purposes and for financial accounting purposes (so that there are no timing difference), determined its tax liability for 19x2 as follows:

Revenues	$100,000
Operating expenses	60,000
Operating income before taxes	$ 40,000
Income from discontinued operations	20,000
Extraordinary gain	30,000
Taxable income	$ 90,000

Further, assume that the tax rate is 40 percent. The total tax liability would be $36,000 ($90,000 × 40%). Of this amount, $16,000 ($40,000 × 40%) is applicable to normal operating income; $8,000 ($20,000 × 40%) is due to discontinued operations; and $12,000 ($30,000 × 40%) is applicable to the extraordinary gain. The following statement illustrates the intraperiod tax allocation.

Cobb Company
Income Statement
For the Year Ended December 31, 19x2

Revenues	$100,000
Operating expenses	60,000
Income from continuing operations before taxes	$ 40,000
Provisions for income taxes	16,000
Income from continuing operations	$ 24,000
Discontinued operations:	
Income from discontinued operations	
(less related taxes of $8,000)	12,000
	$ 36,000
Extraordinary items:	
Extraordinary gain	
(less related taxes of $12,000)	18,000
Net income	$ 54,000

INCOME TAXES AND MANAGEMENT DECISIONS

Because money has a "time value," it is rational for corporate management to defer as long as possible the incurrence and payment of corporate income taxes. Thus, a major consideration in tax planning is the timing of income and deductions. Management will normally attempt to minimize the current tax liability by deferring income or accelerating deductions to the extent possible under the tax laws. Successful tax planning is dependent upon a timely selection of the most advantageous tax alternatives.

While a detailed review of management decision making regarding corporate income taxes is beyond the scope of this text, the following are major areas of importance in tax planning:

1. Selecting the form of business organization;

2. Acquisition, use, and disposition of fixed assets;

3. Employee compensation;

4. Corporate reorganizations; and

5. Financing arrangements.

SUMMARY

Income taxes represent a significant expense of doing business for both corporate and noncorporate business enterprises. The four major classes of taxpayers are individuals, corporations, estates, and trusts. Sole proprietorships and partnerships are not taxable entities, although the income from these enterprises is taxed as income to their owners.

The individual federal income tax is computed by appropriately utilizing the tax tables or the tax rate schedules. Before calculating one's tax liability, an individual should be aware of the amount of gross income, deductions for adjusted gross income, adjusted gross income, itemized deductions, personal exemptions, taxable income, and credits.

Although the general procedure for determining a corporation's income tax is similar to that used by an individual, the treatment of specific items may differ significantly. In addition, the tax rate structure for corporations is greatly simplified from that for individuals. Since taxable income is determined by tax law while accounting income is based on generally accepted accounting principles, the tax liabilities based on the two amounts may differ. Tax expense in the income statement should be matched against the income reported therein, regardless of when the income is included in taxable income and the tax actually paid. The process of matching tax expense to the appropriate accounting periods is referred to as interperiod tax allocation. This process is used only when the difference in tax liabilities is due to timing. If a difference is permanent, no allocation is appropriate or necessary. An additional allocation of income tax within a period is made on the income statement to income from continuing operations, from discontinued operations, and from extraordinary items. This is referred to as intraperiod tax allocation.

KEY DEFINITIONS

Accounting income   Accounting income is the amount of income determined using generally accepted accounting principles.

Adjusted gross income (for individuals)   Adjusted gross income is gross income less deductions for adjusted gross income.

Capital assets   Capital assets generally include all property except such items as trade receivables, inventories, copyrights or compositions in the hands of their creator, and government obligations issued on a discount basis and due within one year without interest. Real or depreciable property used in a trade or business may be treated as capital assets under certain circumstances.

Capital gain or loss   A capital gain or loss is a realized gain or loss incurred from the sale or exchange of a capital asset.

Deductions for adjusted gross income (for individuals)   Deductions for gross income in computing adjusted gross income include business and other expenses connected with earning certain types of revenue. These include ordinary and necessary expenses incurred by the taxpayer in the operation of his business or profession and certain employee expenses.

Deductions from adjusted gross income (for individuals) Deductions from adjusted gross income are legally allowable deductions that may be classified as either itemized deductions or personal exemptions.

Double taxation The corporation is taxed on its reported income and stockholders are taxed upon the receipt of dividends from the corporation. This is sometimes referred to as double taxation.

Estate An estate is a separate legal entity created to take charge of the assets of a deceased person, paying the decedent's debts and distributing the remaining assets to heirs.

Gross income Gross income includes all income from whatever source derived unless expressly excluded by law or the U.S. Constitution.

Head of household The title of head of household is a tax status that applies to certain unmarried or legally separated persons who maintain a residence for a relative.

Itemized deductions Deductions for certain employee business expenses and for personal expenses and losses such as charitable contributions, taxes, interest, casualty losses, and medical expenses are referred to as itemized deductions.

Interperiod tax allocation Interperiod tax allocation is a procedure used to apportion tax expense among periods so that the income tax expense reported for each period is in relation to the accounting income.

Intraperiod tax allocation Intraperiod tax allocation is the allocation of the total amount of income tax expense for a period among income from normal operations, discontinued operations, extraordinary items, and prior period adjustments.

Long-term capital gains or losses Long-term capital gains or losses are gains or losses which result from the sale or exchange of capital assets and certain productive assets of a business held by the taxpayer for more than twelve months.

Permanent difference A permanent difference is a difference between taxable income and accounting income which occurs because of tax rules which differ from generally accepted accounting principles and which will not be offset by corresponding differences in future periods.

Personal exemptions A personal exemption is a deduction of $1,000 from adjusted gross income for the taxpayer, his spouse, and qualified dependents. There are additional exemptions for the taxpayer and his spouse who are over 65 or blind.

Progressive tax This is a tax in which the tax rates increase as taxable income increases.

Taxable income Generally, taxable income is obtained by reducing adjusted gross income by the sum of: (1) the difference between the taxpayer's itemized deductions, and (2) the deduction for personal exemptions.

Temporary differences These are differences between taxable income and accounting income which occur because an item is included in taxable income in one period and in accounting income in a different period.

Trust A trust is a legal entity which is created when a person transfers assets to a trustee for the benefit of designated persons.

QUESTIONS

1. Explain how the net earnings of the following types of business entities are taxed by the federal government: (a) sole proprietorships, (b) partnerships, and (c) corporations.

2. The earnings of a corporation are subject to a "double tax." Explain.

3. Certain factors may cause the income before taxes in the accounting records to differ from taxable income. These factors may be either permanent differences or temporary differences. Explain.

4. Does a corporation electing partnership treatment for tax purposes (Subchapter S) pay federal income taxes? Discuss.

5. What are the four major classes of taxable entities?

6. What is the objective of using the interperiod tax allocation procedures?

7. Does it make any difference in computing income taxes whether a given deduction is for computing adjusted gross income or an itemized deduction? Explain.

8. How did the Tax Reform Act of 1986 change the treatment of capital gains?

9. What are some of the differences between the tax rules for corporations and those for individuals?

10. What are some of the objectives of the federal income tax?

EXERCISES

11. Indicate the income tax status for each of the items listed below. For each item, state whether it is (a) included in gross income, (b) a deduction from gross income to determine adjusted gross income, (c) an itemized deduction, or (d) none of the above.

    1. Property taxes paid on personal residence.
    2. Interest paid on mortgage on personal residence.
    3. Damages of $500 to personal residence from a storm.
    4. Capital loss on the sale of stock.
    5. Insurance on home.
    6. Sales taxes.
    7. Inheritance received upon death of a relative.
    8. Interest received on municipal bonds.
    9. Share of income from partnership.
    10. Salary received as an employee.
    11. Rental income.
    12. Expenses incurred in earning rental income.
    13. Contributions to church.

12. James and Martha Gentry, filing a joint return, are entitled to one personal exemption each and two additional exemptions for dependent children. James Gentry owns a business organized as a sole proprietorship. Additional information related to their income tax return is as follows:

Revenues	$100,000
Cost of goods sold	60,000
Business expenses	20,000
Life insurance proceeds (death of father)	10,000
Interest on city of Bowro Bonds	500
Rental income	5,000
Allowable itemized deductions	1,800
Salary—Martha Gentry	6,000

The deduction for a personal exemption is $1,950.

Determine the following:

a. Adjusted gross income
b. Taxable income
c. Income tax liability. (Use the tax rates provided in this chapter.)

13. Don Looney had the following capital gains and losses in 1988.

Long-term losses	$ 3,000
Long-term gains	12,000
Short-term losses	8,000
Short-term gains	6,000

Determine the tax on Looney's capital gain assuming that the tax rate is 28 percent.

14. The following differences enter into the reconciliation of financial net income and taxable income of A.P. Baxter Corp. for the current year:

a. Tax depreciation exceeds book depreciation by $30,000.
b. Estimated warranty costs of $6,000 applicable to the current year's sales have not been paid. (Not deductible for tax purposes until paid.)
c. Percentage depletion deducted on the tax return exceeds cost depletion by $45,000.
d. Unearned rent revenue of $25,000 was deferred on the books but appropriately included in taxable income.
e. A book expense of $2,000 for life insurance premiums on officers' lives is not allowed as a deduction on the tax return. (**Note:** This is not a timing difference.)
f. A $7,000 tax deduction resulted from expensing research and development costs for tax purposes while such costs were capitalized for financial reporting.

g. Gross profit of $80,000 was excluded from the taxable income because Baxter had appropriately elected the installment sale method for tax reporting while recognizing all gross profit from installment sales at the the time of the sale for financial reporting.

Required:

Consider each reconciling item independently of all others and explain whether each item would enter into the calculation of income taxes to be allocated. For any which are included in the income tax allocation calculation, explain the effect of the item on the current year's income tax expense and how the amount would be reported on the balance sheet. (Tax allocation calculations are not required.)

15. From the following information, calculate corporate income tax for the Brown Company.

a. Sales were $990,000; cost of goods sold was 70 percent of sales.
b. Dividends from domestic corporations totaled $30,000.
c. Selling and miscellaneous expenses were 10 percent of sales.
d. Assume that the corporate tax rates are as stated in the chapter.

16. The partial tax return is shown below for Bengal, Inc. for the year 1988.

Operating income before taxes....................	$ 80,000
Income from discontinued operations..............	45,000
Extraordinary gain (capital gain)..................	25,000
Taxable income...............................	$150,000

Assume that the tax rate is 40 percent. Bengal, Inc. uses the same methods for tax and financial accounting purposes.

Required:

Reflect the application of intraperiod income tax allocation procedures as they would be reported on the financial statements.

17. The taxable income for the Saints Corporation for 19x1 was $12,000, $15,000 for 19x2 and $10,000 for 19x3. Due to temporary differences of reporting income for book purposes and tax purposes, the following differences occurred in these three years: 19x1—Book income exceeded income per tax return by $2,000; 19x2—Income per tax return exceeded book income by $3,500; 19x3—Book income exceeded income per tax return by $5,000. Assume that the tax rate is 40 percent.

Required:

Prepare journal entries to record the tax accrual and to reflect tax allocation procedures.

18. Mary and Harry Jones have two children and file a joint return. In addition, they provide for the full support of Harry's mother and Mary's father, both over 65. Mary earns a gross salary of $10,000 a year and Harry earns $8,000. Mary received $250 in dividends and Harry received $70. Together they earned $500 interest on their joint savings account and $700 interest on municipal government bonds. On December 1, one of their children died and they received $5,000 in life insurance proceeds.

Required:

1. How many personal exemptions can the Jones' claim? (Each deduction is $1,950.)
2. What is their adjusted gross income (or gross income in this case)?
3. What is their taxable income?
4. How much must they pay in federal income taxes, using the tax rates provided in the chapter.

19. The taxable income for the Patriot Corporation is $150,000 before capital gains and losses are taken into consideration. Determine the company's corporate income tax under each of the following independent assumptions involving capital gains and losses:

a. Long-term capital gains, $10,000; long-term capital losses, $15,000.
b. Long-term capital gains, $12,000; long-term capital losses, $9,000.
c. Long-term capital gains, $13,000; long-term capital losses, $5,000; short-term capital gains, $3,000; short-term capital losses, $6,000.

Assume that the corporate tax rates are as given in the chapter.

PROBLEMS

20. Jim Simmons and his wife are both 63 years old and own a dry cleaning store. His wife has been legally blind since she was in a car accident when she was 55. In reviewing the books of his dry cleaning store, Jim finds that it had revenues of $95,000 and expenses of $80,000. During the year, Jim rented a vacant lot to a friend at an annual rental of $3,000. Jim paid property taxes of $300 on the lot.

Jim and his wife have a $7,000 savings account and earned interest at six percent compounded annually on this amount. On July 30, Jim realized a $1,000 capital gain on stocks purchased January 1 of the *preceding* year, and a $250 capital gain on other securities purchased June 1 of the *present* year. In examining his personal records, Jim found that he had made charitable contributions of $275 and had paid interest on his mortgage of $300. Also, he had paid $300 of property taxes.

Required:

Compute Jim's taxable income for 1988 assuming he filed a joint return with his wife.

21. In each of the following cases, determine the amount of capital gains to be included in adjusted gross income or the amount of capital loss to be deducted for an individual taxpayer in 1988. Assume taxpayer's taxable income from noncapital sources is $100,000.

	A	B	C
Long-term capital gains........	$20,000	$20,000	$15,000
Long-term capital losses........	15,000	15,000	20,000
Short-term capital gains........	4,000	6,000	4,000
Short-term capital losses........	6,000	4,000	6,000

22. An individual taxpayer had the following capital gains and losses during 1988:

	Gains	Losses
Short-term	$ 6,000	$11,000
Long-term.................	20,000	5,000

Required:

Compute the amount of income tax on the capital gains assuming that the taxpayer has a marginal tax rate of: (a) 15 percent, and (b) 28 percent.

23. The Hall Company uses ACRS for tax purposes and straight-line depreciation for its financial accounting records. Its taxable income and accounting income (before income taxes) for a four-year period are shown below:

	19x1	19x2	19x3	19x4
Taxable income...........	$ 70,000	$100,000	$140,000	$210,000
Accounting income........	100,000	120,000	150,000	200,000

Assume that the corporate tax rate is 40 percent.

Required:

1. Compute the net income after taxes in the financial statement for Hall Company: (a) assuming that interperiod tax allocation procedures are not used, and (b) assuming the tax allocation procedure is used.
2. Determine the balance in the "Deferred Tax Liability" account at the end of 19x4 in 1(b) above.

Refer to the Annual Report included in the Appendix at the end of the text:

24.   Are the stockholders being taxed twice?

25.   What is the amount of deferred taxes "owed" at the end of the most recent year?

26.   What was the effective tax rate for the most recent year?

27.   Was there a capital gain or loss in the most recent year?

28.   What was the amount of this gain or loss (if any)?

Chapter 13 introduces management and cost accounting systems. Studying this chapter should enable you to:

1. Understand the nature and purpose of both financial and management accounting.

2. Trace the information flows in a typical management accounting system.

3. Discuss how cost accounting is related to both financial and management accounting.

4. Identify the different cost classifications.

5. Distinguish between product costs and period costs, and explain the importance of this distinction in determining income.

6. Define a cost behavior pattern and discuss the relationship of cost behavior to a relevant range of activity.

7. Identify, discuss, and give examples of each of the primary and related cost behavior patterns.

8. Distinguish between the various categories of costs, such as committed fixed costs and managed fixed costs.

13

Management Accounting: An Introduction

INTRODUCTION

The remaining chapters of this text will emphasize management or managerial accounting. Accounting may be thought of as consisting of two basic segments: financial accounting and managerial accounting. Although there is considerable overlap between these two segments, the primary difference lies in the basic orientation of each. Financial accounting is primarily concerned with users who are *external* to the firm and managerial accounting is concerned with *internal* users. Financial accounting attempts to provide external user groups (such as current or potential owners, creditors, government agencies, and other interested parties) with information concerning the status of the firm and the results of its operations. Managerial accounting, on the other hand, attempts to provide internal user groups with data and information which serve as a basis for internal decision making.

A definition of managerial or management accounting and the key terms found in that definition was developed in *Statements on Management Accounting, Statement Number 1A*:[1]

> Management accounting is the process of identification, measurement, accumulation, analysis, preparation, interpretation, and communication of financial information used by management to plan, evaluate, and control within an organization and to assure appropriate use of and accountability for its resources. Management accounting also comprises the preparation of financial reports for non-management groups such as shareholders, creditors, regulatory agencies, and tax authorities.

A further distinction in accounting is between managerial accounting and cost accounting. But in today's complex business environment the nature and purpose of the different accounting systems are difficult to distinguish. Management uses cost accounting and cost accumulating systems for gathering data and for making management decisions. In addition, cost accounting also serves the purposes of financial accounting by providing a system for accumulating cost information. This cost information is used as the basis for much of the financial information needed for financial reports to stockholders, compliance with government requirements for financial information, and many other users' needs. In a sense then, cost accounting may be regarded as a subdivision of both financial and managerial accounting.

---

[1] *Definition of Management Accounting, Statements on Management Accounting, Statement Number 1A* (New York, National Association of Accountants, 1981), pg. 4-5.

BASIC DIFFERENCES BETWEEN FINANCIAL AND MANAGEMENT ACCOUNTING— FURTHER COMMENTS

Financial and management acccounting methods were developed for different purposes and for different users of financial information. There are, however, numerous similarities and areas of overlap between financial and managerial accounting methods. It is difficult to classify a particular technique or approach as belonging exclusively to financial or managerial accounting.

Financial accounting is primarily intended to provide external user groups with information concerning the current status of the firm and the results of its operations. The accounting system of a company, therefore, accumulates and communicates financial information that is basically historical in nature. Of course, this information is usually presented in the form of financial statements, tax returns, and other formal reports distributed to various external users. The same information may also be used internally to provide a basis for financial analysis by management.

Financial accounting is required for many firms organized as corporations because of the regulations of the Securities and Exchange Commission (SEC). The SEC is an agency of the federal government which regulates companies whose stock is sold publicly and traded on organized stock exchanges. Most of the large corporations and many medium-sized corporations fall within the jurisdiction of the SEC.

The Internal Revenue Service also requires financial accounting information for compliance with the nation's tax laws. Many state governments require this data for compliance with the various state tax laws. Information based on accounting data is required for all firms without regard to their size.

Interested third parties without substantial influence over the firm, such as individual stockholders of a large corporation, must use the general purpose financial statements made available to them by management. Financial statements prepared for users (other than governmental regulatory agencies that are authorized to establish their own disclosure laws by legislation) must be prepared in accordance with what are known as generally accepted accounting principles. Generally accepted accounting principles serve as guidelines which are used by accountants in disclosing the financial information which is made available to the general public. Knowledgeable users of general financial information can then interpret the data presented in financial statements with some assurance as to consistency of methodology underlying the data. The auditors' report also adds to the reliability of general purpose financial statements.

Managerial accounting has developed over time to meet the need of management for quantitative information to be used internally for planning, control, performance evaluation and internal decision making. The emphasis of management accounting is then directed toward the internal user of information; therefore, the structure of the managerial accounting system is not nearly as rigid as that of the financial accounting system. The best data available are used as the basis for the information which management relies upon to make its decisions. It is important to note that management accounting is by no means separate and distinct from financial accounting. Financial accounting data are used in the managerial accounting system. Management decisions made today will affect the financial statements of future periods. Managerial accounting does not utilize generally accepted accounting principles per se, but there are general practices that should be followed to maximize the benefits of planning, control and performance evaluation. There is no requirement or legislation that mandates the format or use of managerial accounting. Rather, managerial accounting methods are tools that are available for use to management.

Financial accounting attempts to present some degree of precision in reporting historical information while at the same time emphasizing verifiability and freedom from bias in the information, relevance to the general user and some element of timeliness in reporting. The presentation of historical financial information which is precise, verifiable and free from bias is not as critical for managerial accounting. The timing of information and its relevance to the decision at hand has greater significance to the internal decision maker. If the information is useful in making a good internal decision, management is not *primarily* concerned with precision, verifiability or the bias which might be built into the data on hand. Obviously, management cannot wait until tomorrow for information that is required for today's decision.

Theoretically, a managerial accounting system could provide individualized or tailor-made information which is relevant for each user or for each decision. As a practical matter, however, this simply cannot be done because of the high cost involved. The accounting reports that are prepared should include relevant information for that user's segment of the organization.

The measuring base used in management accounting does not necessarily have to be restricted to dollars. Various bases may be appropriate to report managerial information. Examples include: (1) an economic measure such as dollars, (2) a physical measure such as pounds, gallons, tons, or units, and (3) a relationship measure such as ratios. If all of these and other measures are appropriate to management's needs, then this information should be presented in the same report. Relevance to the decision or to the user is a primary consideration when deciding which measurement technique to use.

The Objectives of Management Accounting[2]

The objectives of management accounting are to provide information and participate actively in the process of management. Illustration 1 depicts the hierarchical relationships among these objectives and the responsibilities, principal activities and processes of management accountants in meeting these goals. Each of the items included in the illustration are briefly described on the following page.

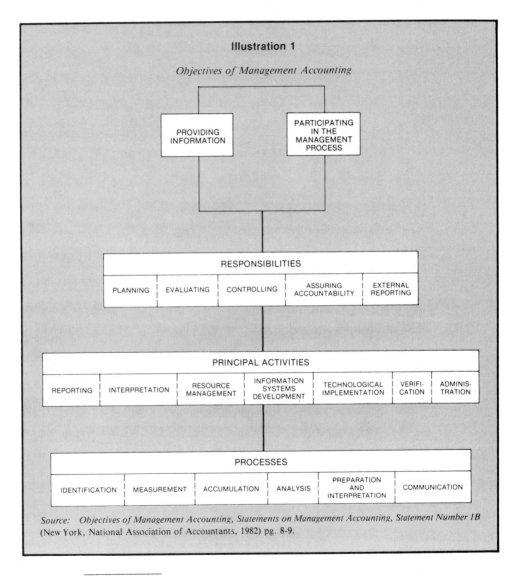

Illustration 1

Objectives of Management Accounting

PROVIDING INFORMATION

PARTICIPATING IN THE MANAGEMENT PROCESS

RESPONSIBILITIES

| PLANNING | EVALUATING | CONTROLLING | ASSURING ACCOUNTABILITY | EXTERNAL REPORTING |

PRINCIPAL ACTIVITIES

| REPORTING | INTERPRETATION | RESOURCE MANAGEMENT | INFORMATION SYSTEMS DEVELOPMENT | TECHNOLOGICAL IMPLEMENTATION | VERIFI-CATION | ADMINIS-TRATION |

PROCESSES

| IDENTIFICATION | MEASUREMENT | ACCUMULATION | ANALYSIS | PREPARATION AND INTERPRETATION | COMMUNICATION |

Source: Objectives of Management Accounting, Statements on Management Accounting, Statement Number 1B (New York, National Association of Accountants, 1982) pg. 8-9.

[2] This section is taken from *Objectives of Management Accounting, Statements on Management Accounting, Statement Number 1B* (New York, National Association of Accountants, 1982) pg. 1-9.

Providing Information

Management accountants select and provide, to all levels of management, information needed for (a) planning, evaluating, and controlling operations; (b) safeguarding the organization's assets; and (c) communicating with interested parties outside the organization, such as shareholders and regulatory bodies.

Participating in the Management Process

Management accountants at appropriate levels are involved actively in the process of managing the entity. This process includes making strategic, tactical, and operating decisions and helping to coordinate the efforts of the entire organization. The management accountant participates, as part of management, in assuring that the organization operates as a unified whole in its long-run, intermediate, and short-run best interests.

RESPONSIBILITIES

To fulfill the objectives, management accountants accept certain major responsibilities. They establish and maintain the necessary practices and techniques to provide essential information to management, and they fulfill external reporting requirements. The responsibilities of management accountants, which are set forth in *Statement No. 1A*, are as follows:

1. *Planning*—Quantifying and interpreting the effects on the organization of planned transactions and other economic events. The planning responsibility, which includes strategic, tactical, and operating aspects, requires that the accountant provide quantitative historical and prospective information to facilitate planning. It includes participation in developing the planning system, setting obtainable goals, and choosing appropriate means of monitoring the progress toward the goals.
2. *Evaluating*—Judging implications of historical and expected events and helping to choose the optimum course of action. Evaluating includes translating data into trends and relationships. Management accountants must communicate effectively and promptly the conclusions derived from the analyses.
3. *Controlling*—Assuring the integrity of financial information concerning an organization's activities and resources; monitoring and measuring performance and inducing any corrective actions required to return the activity to its intended course. Management accountants provide information to executives operating in functional areas who can make use of it to achieve desirable performance.

4. *Assuring accountability of resources*—Implementing a system of reporting that is aligned with organizational responsibilities. This reporting system will contribute to the effective use of resources and measurement of management performance. The transmission of management's goals and objectives throughout the organization in the form of assigned responsibilities is a basis for identifying accountability. Management accountants must provide an accounting and reporting system that will accumulate and report appropriate revenues, expenses, assets, liabilities, and related quantitative information to managers. Managers then will have better control over these elements.

5. *External reporting*—Preparing financial reports based on generally accepted accounting principles, or other appropriate bases, for nonmanagement groups such as shareholders, creditors, regulatory agencies, and tax authorities. Management accountants should participate in the process of developing the accounting principles that underlie external reporting.

ACTIVITIES

Management accountants discharge their responsibilities by organizing and implementing activities in seven principal categories: reporting, interpretation, resource management, information systems development, technological implementation, verification, and administration.

Reporting

Reporting relates to both internal and external needs for information about past or future events and circumstances. Management accountants make available to managers timely reports that provide the information and perspective necessary for them to make decisions in a goal-congruent manner. The reports may concern financial, physical, and human resources and the markets and regulatory environments in which entities operate. In addition to reporting internally, management accountants make appropriate information available to shareholders, creditors, and governmental regulatory agencies and tax authorities.

Interpretation

Management accountants interpret all forms of internal and external information pertinent to the various segments of the organization and communicate the implications of the information being reviewed, including its relevance and reliability. Management accountants thus must understand both the sources and uses of the information.

Resource Management

Management accountants must establish systems which facilitate planning and control of the organization's resources to ensure that their use is consistent with established policies. These systems also should meet the needs of management, investors, creditors, and other interested parties. Some of these needs are:

- Custody and management of working capital, including credit and collections and inventory management
- Creating and maintaining the most appropriate debt and equity capital structure
- Developing and implementing a system to control plant, property, and equipment
- Administering a pension or similar plan
- Tax planning and compliance
- Insurance management
- Creating and operating a system of internal accounting control that can detect misuses of assets, taking into account the cost/benefit aspects of the control system

Information Systems Development

Design and development of the overall management information system implies:

- Determining the output required by users
- Specifying the data inputs needed to obtain the required output
- Developing the requirements for a processing system that converts input to output
- Managing and securing the data bases

Technological Implementation

Modern equipment and techniques should be employed to facilitate the selection, accumulation, transmission, analysis, and safeguarding of information. Management accountants therefore should be familiar with current technology relative to information processing and the accounting techniques appropriate to controlling and using the information. Some examples are:

- Computer applications
    - basic accounting functions and data-base management
    - techniques in financial planning and decision making, such as models for optimizing asset utilization and resource allocation

- Network and communications systems.

Verification

Management accountants assure the accuracy and reliability of information derived from the accounting system or related sources that is used throughout the organization. They also must be satisfied that actions taking place throughout the entity are consistent with policies of the organization. Both of these activities use the internal control system and are reviewed by internal audit.

Administration

Administration includes development and maintenance of an effective and efficient management accounting organization. This organization addresses and resolves issues relevant to the accounting and financial structure such as:

- Assignment of management accounting responsibilities
- Interface between accounting and other operations
- Delegation of authority and determinations relevant to centralization or decentralization
- Recruiting, training, and developing personnel in the various areas of responsibility
- Separation of duties

Other important administrative activities performed by management accountants include the development and maintenance of:

- Accounting policy and procedure manuals
- A cost-effective records management program
- Records adequate to meet the requirements of tax laws, other laws and regulatory agencies, and independent auditors

PROCESSES

Certain operational processes are inherent throughout the range of activities described in the preceding section. These processes are articulated in *Statement No. 1A* and include:

1. *Identification*—recognition and evaluation of business transactions and other economic events for appropriate accounting action.
2. *Measurement*—quantification, including estimates, of business transactions or other economic events that have occurred or forecasts of those that may occur.

3. *Accumulation*—disciplined and consistent approaches to recording and classifying appropriate business transactions and other economic events.

4. *Analysis*—determination of the reasons for the reported activity and its relationship with other economic events and circumstances.

5. *Preparation and Interpretation*—meaningful coordination of accounting and/or planning data to provide information, presented logically, and including, if appropriate, the conclusions drawn from those data.

6. *Communication*—reporting pertinent information to management and others for internal and external uses.

COST CLASSIFICATIONS

The cost classifications which are used in accounting are generally determined by the purpose for which the cost information is intended. Four major cost classification categories defined by purpose are discussed in this text:

1. Income determination
2. Planning
3. Control and performance evaluation
4. Special decisions requiring accounting information

For purposes of income determination, costs are normally classified on a functional basis, that is, according to the type of function, i.e., salaries, rent, depreciation, etc. The general functional cost classifications which are used for income determination purposes are product costs and period costs.

PRODUCT COSTS: FOR INCOME DETERMINATION

Product costs are those costs that can be directly identified with the purchase or production of those goods made available for sale by the firm. These costs are recorded and inventoried as assets until the goods are sold. For example, the inventory purchased by a retailer is considered an asset until the time that it is sold. When the sale takes place, the cost of the asset (inventory) becomes an expense (cost of goods sold) and is reported as such on the income statement.

The cost flows of a manufacturing firm differ substantially from those of a retail business. In a manufacturing company, the process of producing a marketable product for sale causes the accounting process to be somewhat more complex than it is for the retailer. The manufacturer acquires raw materials and converts these materials into a finished product. During this production process, the manufacturer purchases labor and services, utilizes manufacturing facilities, and usually employs a unique process.

Thus, value is added to the raw materials by the manufacturing process which ultimately results in a product that is marketable at a price in excess of its cost. The manufacturer must accumulate all of the production costs incurred, along with the cost of raw materials used during a period, in order to determine the cost of goods manufactured during that period.

PRODUCT COST FLOWS IN MANUFACTURING

The three basic elements of product cost incurred by a manufacturing company are: (1) direct materials, (2) direct labor, and (3) manufacturing overhead. *Direct materials* are those raw materials used in the production process which can be directly identified with the finished products. For example, lumber is a direct material used in the production of furniture. *Direct labor* includes the wages of production employees who work directly with a product and whose efforts may be directly traced to specific units or batches of production output. Thus, the wages of an employee who applied paint or varnish to furniture would be a direct labor cost in the production of that furniture. Manufacturing costs which are associated with the production process but which are not directly traceable to specific units of output either as direct materials or direct labor are classified as *manufacturing overhead*. Examples of manufacturing overhead include depreciation on plant, building, and equipment; maintenance costs; indirect labor costs; costs of factory supplies; salaries of production foremen; etc.

As a product is manufactured, the direct materials, direct labor and manufacturing overhead costs used in the process are accumulated and combined in a special inventory account called work-in-process. When the production process is completed, the costs associated with the resulting goods are transferred from the work-in-process inventory account to the finished goods inventory account. These costs remain as assets in this inventory account until the goods are sold. When the sale is made, the cost of the inventory is transferred to the cost of goods sold account for income determination purposes.

PERIOD COSTS: FOR INCOME DETERMINATION

Those expenses incurred by the company which are associated with the passage of time are normally referred to and classified as period costs. In contrast to product costs, period costs are costs which generally cannot easily be traced to either the purchase or the manufacture of a particular product. Period costs are not considered to be assets because these expenses normally do not yield benefits to the firm beyond the current accounting period or because the possibility of such benefits is not readily measureable. For these reasons, period costs are treated as expenses of the period in which they are incurred. Examples of period costs include

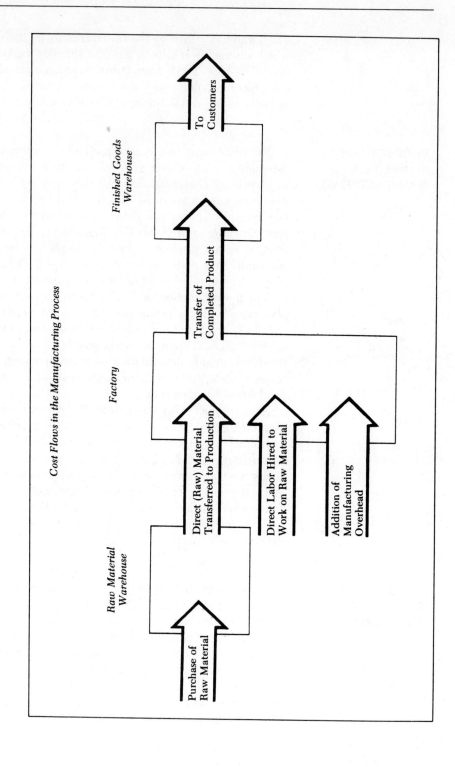

Cost Flows in the Manufacturing Process

such costs as interest expense, salaries of administrative employees, depreciation on non-manufacturing facilities, sales, salaries, advertising expense, and insurance expense for non-manufacturing facilities.

IMPORTANCE OF THE DISTINCTION BETWEEN PRODUCT AND PERIOD COST

The distinction between product costs and period costs is essential for purposes of income determination. A brief example may add insight to this important distinction.

Pete Rose and Joe Morgan are both employed by Redleg Manufacturing Company, and each earns an annual salary of $25,000. Rose works as a salesman while Morgan is employed as a department head in a manufacturing area. Last year, Redleg Manufacturing Company produced a single product. In all, 10,000 units of this product were manufactured and, of these, 8,000 units were sold. Under these circumstances, Rose's salary is considered a period cost and is classified as an expense on the income statement. Morgan's salary is considered to be a cost of manufacturing the product, since he is directly involved with producing the product. Only $20,000 of Morgan's earnings is considered a part of the cost of goods sold included on the income statement, since Morgan is involved in the manufacturing process and only 80 percent (8,000 of the 10,000 units produced) of the current period's production was sold. The remaining portion of Morgan's salary ($5,000 or 20 percent) is considered a part of the ending inventory asset value. Therefore, the importance of the distinction between product costing and period costing is obvious in that the classification of the costs directly impacts on the reported profitability of the firm.

COSTS FOR PLANNING: COST BEHAVIOR

Planning is, by its very nature, essentially a future-oriented process. A basic objective of management is to employ the available resources of the firm in the most efficient and effective manner possible. In order to achieve this objective, management must utilize the best information available, irrespective of the source of the data in making its plans for the future. Some of the most important information used in the planning process is concerned with the behavior of costs.

In any analysis of cost information, management accounting makes the basic assumption that most cost behavior may be associated with measures of activity within a relevant range. For our purposes, the relevant range may be defined as that operating range or span over which a firm finds it practical to operate in a short-run time period. There is, of course, an upper limit of operating capacity when some short-run constraining factor prevents the firm from operating at a higher level. There is also a lower limit of operating capacity below which it would be impractical for the firm to operate.

Generally, the total cost function for a given range of output is not linear (see Illustration 2). The economic nature of costs suggests that at some point in time economies of scale occur. These economies occur when the firm is able to produce higher quantities of output without a proportionate increase in costs. In the relevant range of a firm's operating capacity, the curve representing total cost is approximately equal to a linear curve. Therefore, for planning convenience, managerial accounting frequently assumes linear cost functions within the relevant range of activity. Of course, the estimate of the linear cost function is not precise, but then neither is the planning process.

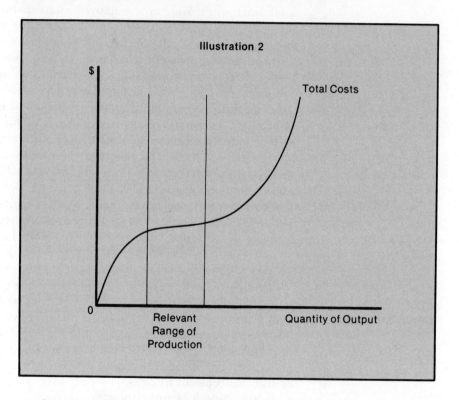

Illustration 2

The activity base or quantity of output within the relevant range depends on the particular cost being measured. A few selected examples may help to illustrate and explain the concept of activity measures.

1. The total cost of raw materials in a manufacturing process is directly related to the number of units which are produced. The activity measure in this instance would be units produced.
2. The total cost of gasoline for a truck is directly related to the number of miles driven. The activity measure in this case would be miles driven.

3. The total cost of meals in a hospital is directly related to the number of beds occupied by patients. The activity measure in this circumstance would be the number of beds occupied.

4. If the firm uses a billing service to mail out its accounts receivable billings and the charge is twenty-five cents per billing, the total cost is related to the number of customers billed. The activity measure in this situation would be the number of customers billed.

In establishing an activity base, a firm attempts to identify those causal relationships that explain fluctuations in costs. In this regard, it is important to note that certain costs will not appear to change in relation to any particular activity measure. For example, rent or interest costs are normally related to the passage of time rather than to some level of activity.

VARIABLE COSTS   Variable costs are those costs which vary directly and proportionately with some measure of activity within the relevant range. If, for example, the base activity increases by five percent, the *total* variable cost will also increase by five percent. Total variable costs increase and decrease as the level of activity changes within the relevant range. Illustration 3 provides a graphic example of two different variable costs.

In Example 1 of Illustration 3, the indicated relevant range of production is from 75,000 to 150,000 units, and the variable cost of raw materials is $4 for each unit produced. If the production for the period was scheduled at a level of 100,000 units, the planned raw material cost would total $400,000 (100,000 × $4). At a production level of 120,000 units, the anticipated raw material cost would total $480,000 (120,000 × $4). At production levels of fewer than 75,000 units or more than 150,000 units, the total variable cost cannot be as readily estimated since these levels of output are outside the relevant range of activity.

The relevant range of miles driven in Example 2 of Illustration 3 is from 20,000 to 50,000 miles. The variable cost of gasoline is assumed to be $.10 per mile driven. If it were anticipated that the truck would be driven a total of 30,000 miles, the projected gasoline cost would be $3,000 (30,000 × $.10). At 40,000 miles, the planned gasoline cost would total $4,000 (40,000 × $.10).

Of course, the variable costs per unit could change over time due to such factors as inflation or evolving technology. Naturally, any changes which may be foreseen should be taken into consideration in formulating the budget plan.

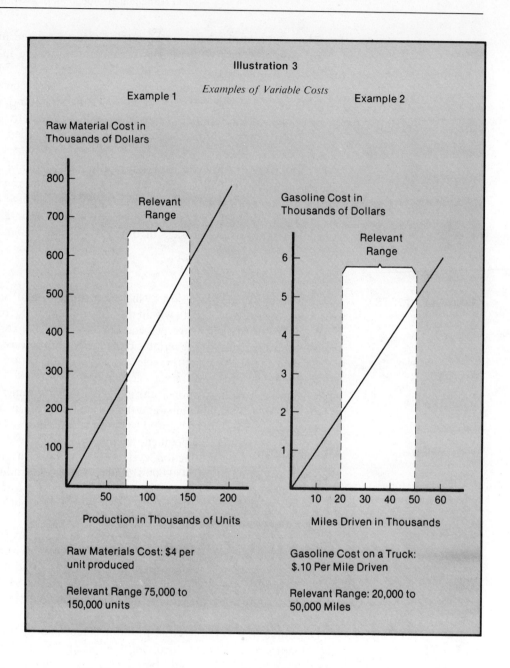

Illustration 3

Examples of Variable Costs

Example 1   Example 2

Raw Material Cost in
Thousands of Dollars

Production in Thousands of Units

Miles Driven in Thousands

Raw Materials Cost: $4 per
unit produced

Relevant Range 75,000 to
150,000 units

Gasoline Cost on a Truck:
$.10 Per Mile Driven

Relevant Range: 20,000 to
50,000 Miles

FIXED COSTS   Fixed costs are those costs which are not related to activity within the relevant range. As the name implies, fixed costs are those expenditures which remain fixed or constant for a given period of time. Changes in fixed costs may be expected, however, and do occur either over long periods of time or outside the relevant range of activity. Fixed costs provide the capacity required to sustain a planned volume of activity within a given time period. Total fixed costs and their relationship to activity are presented graphically in Illustration 4.

The fixed costs identified in Illustration 4 will remain at $1,500,000 at production levels anywhere within the relevant range, which is assumed to be from 75,000 to 150,000 units. Below 75,000 units or above 150,000 units, the total fixed cost may change.

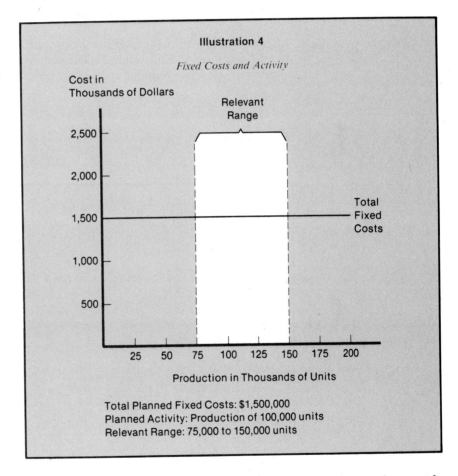

Illustration 4

Fixed Costs and Activity

Total Planned Fixed Costs: $1,500,000
Planned Activity: Production of 100,000 units
Relevant Range: 75,000 to 150,000 units

Per Unit Fixed Cost

The fixed cost per unit of activity is an amount which must be considered and used with some degree of caution. In the previous discussions of variable cost included in this chapter, it was noted that the variable cost per unit was constant, and that the total variable cost within the relevant range increased and decreased according to the level of activity.

Total fixed costs, by definition, remain constant within the relevant range for a given time period, irrespective of the level of activity. At higher levels of activity, the fixed cost per unit will be lower than the fixed cost per unit at lower levels of activity simply because the identical amount of cost is being allocated or spread over additional units of activity. For example, in Illustration 4, at 75,000 units of production the fixed cost is $1,500,000 or $20 per unit ($1,500,000 ÷ 75,000). At 100,000 units of production, the total fixed cost remains at $1,500,000, but the fixed cost per unit is reduced to only $15 per unit ($1,500,000 ÷ 100,000).

Total Costs

Economics identifies the traditional cost function as being very similar to the one presented in Illustration 5. The component parts of total cost include fixed costs plus variable costs. Therefore the total cost equation is:

$$\text{Total Cost} = \text{Total Fixed Costs} + \text{Total Variable Costs}$$

Within the relevant range of production capacity, total cost and its components parts—fixed costs and variable costs—are assumed to be linear.

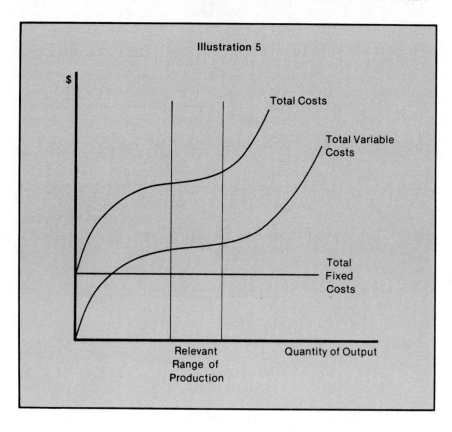

Illustration 5

COMMITTED AND MANAGED FIXED COSTS

For purposes of planning, fixed costs may be conveniently classified into two distinctly different categories. These categories are committed fixed costs and managed fixed costs.

Committed Fixed Costs

Committed fixed costs represent those fixed costs which the firm will incur because of the past decisions or commitments made by management. This type of fixed cost relates to the capacity of the firm to engage in its operations at a planned volume or level of activity. Of the two classifications of fixed costs, committed fixed costs are less responsive than are managed costs to the short-term decision-making process.

Committed fixed costs essentially represent the long-term costs of maintaining a given capacity to produce. It is therefore expected that these costs will be associated with the ownership of an organization as well as the related long-term resources or assets that are required to operate the business. Committed fixed costs are those costs which are related to acquiring and maintaining the organization and its long-term assets. Costs such as depreciation on fixed assets, lease or rental costs of buildings, equipment or other assets, property taxes, salaries of key personnel, and insurance are all examples of committed fixed costs.

Managed Fixed Costs

Managed fixed costs (also referred to as discretionary, programmed or planned fixed costs) are those fixed costs incurred on a short-term basis in accordance with an established objective of management. This type of fixed cost does not necessarily relate to the anticipated level of activity. Rather, management will decide on the expenditures it considers necessary to attain a specific objective at some future date. The funds are then spent, unless the objective or economic climate varies and causes a change in management plans.

Examples of managed fixed costs include research and development costs, product improvement costs, public relations costs, advertising costs, sales promotion costs, major plant rearrangement costs, outlays for cost reduction programs, costs of employee training programs and charitable donations. Theoretically, managed fixed costs could be substantially reduced by management decisions in any given period and the profits for that period would be increased (since expenses would have been decreased without a corresponding reduction of revenues). Any adverse impact of reducing a managed fixed cost would probably not be realized until some future time period, assuming that the expenditure would, in fact, have ultimately yielded future benefits.

Illustration 6 identifies the two major fixed cost classifications and the relationship of each to production levels. Total fixed costs are projected in the amount of $1,500,000, consisting of a committed cost element of $1,000,000 and a managed cost element of $500,000. Assuming a level of

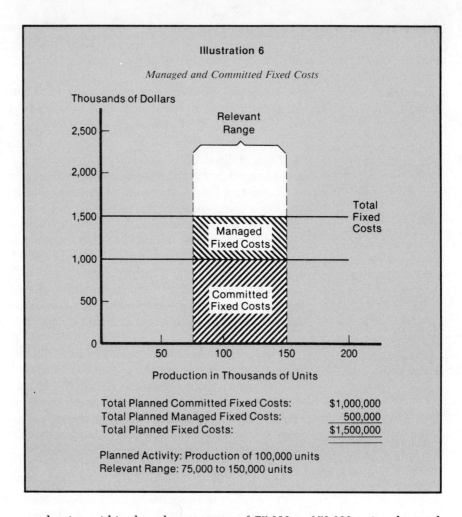

Illustration 6

Managed and Committed Fixed Costs

Thousands of Dollars

Relevant Range

Total Fixed Costs

Managed Fixed Costs

Committed Fixed Costs

Production in Thousands of Units

Total Planned Committed Fixed Costs:	$1,000,000
Total Planned Managed Fixed Costs:	500,000
Total Planned Fixed Costs:	$1,500,000

Planned Activity: Production of 100,000 units
Relevant Range: 75,000 to 150,000 units

production within the relevant range of 75,000 to 150,000 units, the total fixed cost could be any amount between $1,000,000 (committed costs only) and $1,500,000 (committed costs plus all managed costs), depending on which managed fixed costs management chooses to incur.

SEMIVARIABLE COSTS

Semivariable costs, also referred to as mixed costs, are those costs which are comprised of both a fixed and a variable component. As the level of activity increases, the total cost will also increase, but the increase will be less than proportional in amount. A typical example of the variation which occurs with this type of cost is a rental car.

The cost for a short-term rental car has two components. There is a basic charge, usually a daily or weekly amount. The total rental charge can never fall below this fixed base even if the vehicle is not used. A charge on a per mile driven basis plus this basic per day or week charge are the components of the total charge. The total cost for the car for the time period used will therefore be a semivariable cost, a cost which is comprised of both a fixed (the basic per day or per week charge) and a variable (the charge on a per mile driven basis).

A hypothetical rental charge is presented graphically in Illustration 7. To simplify this illustration, assume that the basic charge for the car is $10.00 per day with an additional charge of $.10 per mile for every mile driven. In other words, the basic charge of $10.00 simply makes the use of the car available to the renter and does not entitle the renter to drive any miles (without paying the additional charge of $.10 per mile for each mile driven).

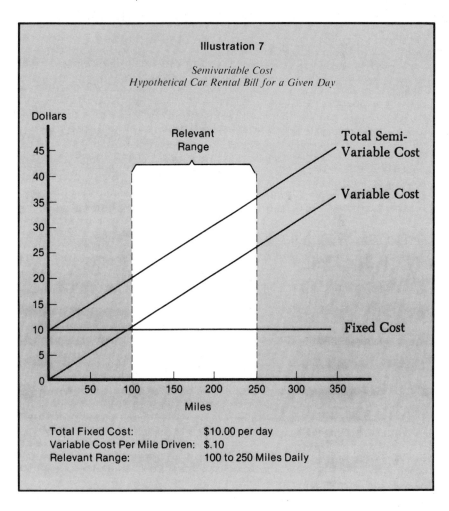

Illustration 7

Semivariable Cost
Hypothetical Car Rental Bill for a Given Day

Total Fixed Cost: $10.00 per day
Variable Cost Per Mile Driven: $.10
Relevant Range: 100 to 250 Miles Daily

As indicated above, the rental charge for any given day can never be less than $10.00. If a hundred miles were driven in one day the total bill for that day would be $20 [$10 + (100 miles × $.10)]; and if 200 miles were driven in a day the bill would be $30 [$10 + (200 × $.10)].

Graphically, the slope of the total semivariable cost line is identical to the slope of the variable cost line portion of the semivariable cost. These two lines are parallel because the slope of the lines is based entirely on the variable cost component of the total charge. Each mile driven would cause the variable cost component of the semivariable cost to increase in total by $.10. Consequently, the total semivariable cost would also increase by $.10 for every mile driven in a given day.

Other possible examples of semivariable costs include repair costs for most types of equipment (normally the greater the usage, the higher the cost), power costs, clerical costs, telephone costs, and delivery costs.

STEP COSTS

Step costs are those costs which must be incurred in a series of fixed amounts. Generally, a cost behaving as a step cost remains constant over a given range of activity and then increases or decreases in a fixed incremental amount. Although step costs are said to vary according to the level of activity, it should be noted that their relationship to activity is not necessarily a proportionate one.

The salary of a supervisor, such as a foreman, is a typical example of a step cost. The cost of supervisory personnel will remain fixed over a broad range of activity; but when a certain level of production is reached, it will be necessary to hire an additional supervisor and the total cost will increase to a new level. The cost will then remain fixed at this new level for another range of activity.

SUMMARY

Financial accounting is primarily concerned with accumulating historical data and communicating this data to interested external users that require the data. Management accounting, on the other hand, is primarily concerned with providing information for internal planning, control, performance evaluation, and decision making. Therefore, management accounting information is generally more future-oriented than is financial accounting information.

Cost accounting is a segment of accounting that accumulates cost information used in external financial reporting (usually as inventory costs) and in managerial decision making and control.

In a manufacturing firm, those costs used for determining income are further classified into product costs (direct material, direct labor, and manufacturing overhead costs which are directly identifiable with the production or purchase of goods made available for sale) and period costs (costs associated with the passage of time). Distinguishing between product and period costs is necessary for proper income determination. This is because period costs are considered expenses in the period incurred, but product costs are carried in inventory valuations and are charged to expense only as the associated products are sold.

Effective planning for the future requires that a firm accumulate certain basic information regarding the behavior patterns of its costs. A cost behavior pattern is the typical manner in which a particular cost behaves in relation to a change in a given level of activity. Cost behavior is generally associated with activity within a relevant range; that is, the operating range over which the firm finds it practical to operate in the short-run. In establishing an activity base for a particular cost, the firm attempts to identify those causal relationships that explain the fluctuations in the cost under consideration.

For planning purposes, costs are commonly classified into two major categories according to behavior patterns. These classifications are fixed costs and variable costs. Variable costs are those costs that vary directly and proportionately with the associated activity measure. Fixed costs, on the other hand, generally do not vary according to activity, but instead remain fixed or constant within the relevant range over a given period of time. Fixed costs may be further classified into committed fixed costs (those costs that must be incurred because of past management decision) and managed fixed costs (those costs over which management has the short-run ability to change).

Although the variable and fixed dichotomies are the major categories used for cost classification according to cost behavior patterns, many costs simply cannot be identified as either entirely variable or entirely fixed. Therefore, other related cost categories are required to accurately describe all of the cost behavior patterns of a firm. Semivariable costs are those costs that include both a fixed and a variable component. A step cost is a cost that must be incurred in a series of fixed amounts.

KEY DEFINITIONS

Committed fixed costs—fixed costs which the firm will incur because of the past decisions or commitments made by management, such as those costs related to acquiring and maintaining the organization and its long-term assets.

Cost accounting—a system of accumulating cost information for external financial reporting and internal management accounting.

Direct labor—a product cost which includes the wages of production employees whose effort may be traced directly to specific units or batches of output.

Direct materials—a product cost which includes the cost of raw materials used in the production process and directly identified with the finished products.

Financial accounting—a method of accounting which provides external user groups with information concerning the status of the firm and the results of its operations.

Finished goods—a special inventory account where the production costs of goods already completed but not yet sold remain as assets until the point of sale.

Fixed costs—costs which do not change in relationship to an activity within a relevant range and which are fixed or constant for a given period of time.

Managed fixed costs—discretionary, programmed, or planned fixed costs. These are fixed costs incurred on a short-term basis in accordance with an established management objective.

Management or managerial accounting—a type of accounting which is concerned with providing information for internal uses of management such as planning, control, performance evaluation and other decision-making activities. Management accounting utilizes financial accounting data as well as other internal and external information which may be available.

Manufacturing overhead—a product cost that includes manufacturing costs associated with the production process, but not directly traceable to specific units of output either as direct materials or direct labor.

Period costs—costs that are associated with the passage of time and are usually not easily identified with either the purchase or the manufacturing of products. Period costs are recorded as expenses in the period incurred.

Product costs—all costs that can be directly identified with the purchase or production of goods made available for sale by the firm. These costs are inventoried and carried as assets and then expensed as cost of goods sold when the product is sold.

Relevant range—range of operating capacity where the firm finds it practical to operate in the short-run. Total fixed costs remain constant within this range.

Semi-variable costs—costs which have both a fixed and a variable component so that as the level of activity increases the total cost will increase, but in a less than proportional amount.

Step costs—costs which are constant over a given range of activity, but which increase or decrease in a fixed incremental amount as the level of activity changes.

Variable costs—costs which vary directly and proportionally with the level of activity.

Work-in-process—a special inventory account where the costs of direct materials, direct labor and manufacturing overhead are accumulated as the product is manufactured.

QUESTIONS

1. What differences exist between financial accounting and management accounting? Is management accounting separate and distinct from financial accounting?

2. How does management accounting serve both external financial reporting purposes and the internal needs for management information?

3. Define product cost. What three general elements make up a product cost? Define them.

4. Define period cost. Give examples.

5. Define manufacturing overhead. Give examples.

6. Define relevant range.

7. List two examples which help to explain the concept of activity measures.

8. Define variable costs. Give examples.

9. (a) Define fixed costs. (b) Give two categories into which fixed costs may be classified. Define each and give examples.

10. Define semi-variable costs. Give examples.

EXERCISES

11. Classify each of the following items as either a period cost (P) or a product cost (PR).

    a. Direct materials
    b. Depreciation on office building
    c. Property taxes on office building
    d. Direct labor
    e. Sales salaries
    f. Indirect materials for manufacturing
    g. Rent on administrative building
    h. Power for manufacturing machines
    i. Administrative salaries
    j. Office building maintenance

12. The Small Manufacturing Company employs only six people. There are Max Small, President; Tony Brown, salesman; Bill Russel, foreman; and three people on the assembly line. The salaries for these people in 19x1 were $28,000, $16,000, $17,000, and $10,000, respectively. In 19x1 the company produced 20,000 units of product and sold 18,000 units.

    Required:

    Determine whether each person's salary is a period cost or a product cost. If it is a product cost, determine how the salary should be allocated.

13. The following are employed by the Randolph Manufacturing Company in New York:

	Annual Salary
John Smith — President	$50,000
Lewis Clark — Vice President	30,000
David Jones — Manufacturing Department Head	20,000
Paul Frey — Manufacturing Department Head	20,000
Jerry Lawson — Sales Manager	15,000
James Ryan — Salesman	10,000
Joe Phillips — Production Foreman	10,000

Last year the Randolph Manufacturing Company produced a total of 100,000 units of their product of which 60,000 units were sold.

Required:

How would each of the above salaries be recorded on the income statement? In other words, which would be classified as cost of goods sold and which as salary expense?

14. From the following scattergraphs, state the type of cost each represents.

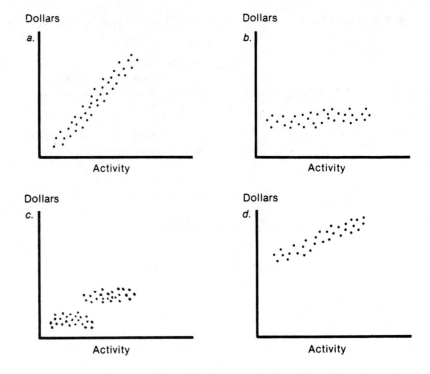

15. The Weinberg Company is in the process of developing and marketing a new product. From the list of fixed costs listed below, categorize each cost according to whether it is a committed or managed fixed cost as it relates to this new product.

   a. Research and development costs
   b. Building modifications
   c. Depreciation on existing building
   d. Market tests
   e. Initial training expenses of sales people
   f. Salary of the vice president of the new product department
   g. Product samples distributed by sales people.

PROBLEMS

16. Jeff Sims and Jim Ryan are employed by the Ace Manufacturing Company. Mr. Sims, the production manager, and Mr. Ryan, the sales manager, each earn an annual salary of $30,000. During the year, 10,000 units of the company's product were produced of which 6,000 units were sold and 4,000 units remained in inventory as finished goods.

   Required:

   Using only the above data, calculate the following:

BALANCE SHEET	
Finished goods inventory.....................	*(a)*
INCOME STATEMENT	
Cost of goods sold........................	*(b)*
Expense	*(c)*

17. During the year, the Texas Plastics Company produced 20,000 units of the company's products. Of this amount, 12,000 units were sold with 8,000 units remaining in finished goods inventory. The following information shows the components of major cost items for the company:

Salaries and Wages:	
Executive salaries..........................	$ 50,000
Sales salaries and commissions................	30,000
Office salaries..............................	21,000
Production employees wages..................	65,000
Factory maintenance employee wages...........	15,000
	$181,000

Depreciation Expense:	
On office building and equipment..............	$ 15,800
On factory building and equipment.............	9,500
	$ 25,300

Supplies Expense:	
Supplies used in offices......................	$ 2,200
Supplies used in production...................	1,600
	$ 3,800

Required:

Using the above information only (ignoring direct materials), calculate the finished goods inventory, cost of goods sold and operating expenses for Texas Plastics.

18. John and Frank Ryan are both salesmen for the Brown Manufacturing Corporation. They each make a salary of $20,000. Bill Snow, the production manager, has a salary of $22,000; John Adams, a production foreman, makes $10,000. During the year of 19x1, the corporation produced 100,000 units of its product and sold 75,000 units.

Required:

Which of the salaries above would be classified as product costs and which as period costs? Give the total amount of product costs and the total period costs that would appear on the income statement.

19. The Royal Corporation has just added a new product and wants to know what it should charge for the product. They will have $250,000 fixed costs and $5.25 per unit in variable costs. The marketing research department feels that Royal can expect the sales volume given below by using the suggested prices.

Expected sales (in units)......	450,000	625,000	730,000	1,000,000
Unit sales price.............	$12.00	$10.30	$8.25	$5.50

Required:

Using the information given above, what should Royal use as its selling price? (Base your answer on the highest expected profit.)

20. Terry Company has collected the following production cost data:

	0 Units Produced	100 Units Produced	200 Units Produced
Depreciation	$500	$700	$ 900
Supplies	0	950	1,900
Property taxes..............	600	600	600
Labor	0	425	850

In addition, the company has found that maintenance expense exhibits the following "step" behavior:

For   0- 75 units, maintenance costs = $ 800
For 76-150 units, maintenance costs = 1,600
For 151-225 units, maintenance costs = 2,400

Required:

What would you expect the total production costs to be if Terry Company produced 125 units?

Chapter 14 describes job order and process cost accounting and illustrates how costing systems are used to accumulate inventory costs. Studying this chapter should enable you to:

1. Discuss and give examples of each of the basic elements of product costs.

2. Describe a "full" product cost and explain its derivation.

3. Calculate a predetermined overhead rate.

4. Explain the basics of job order cost accounting and job order costing systems.

5. Identify and illustrate alternative methods of handling overapplied and underapplied manufacturing overhead.

6. Discuss the cost of goods manufactured statement.

7. Discuss a process costing system and give examples of situations in which its use may be desirable.

8. Describe the format and purpose of the production cost report.

9. Explain and illustrate the concept of equivalent units and calculate equivalent units of production.

10. Derive unit costs in given situations.

14

Cost Accounting for Inventories

INTRODUCTION

This chapter emphasizes manufacturing cost accumulation systems used for inventory costing purposes. Inventory costing, on either a per unit or a per batch basis, is necessary to determine a valuation for inventory which is used for planning and control purposes. This inventory is also used as an input in preparing the balance sheet and in determining the cost of goods sold for income statement purposes.

There are two fundamental systems of cost accumulation: job order costing and process costing. Each of these cost systems provides a product cost for inventory on a physical measure basis. Examples of physical measures used as bases for product costing purposes include units, pounds, gallons, and tons.

THE ELEMENTS OF PRODUCT COST

The basic elements of product cost for a manufacturing firm were identified as direct materials, direct labor, and manufacturing overhead. Accounting for product costs is based on the assumption that each of these basic elements of product cost attaches to, or can be matched or identified with, specific units or batches of production.

For income determination purposes, the product cost to be used will, of course, represent the full or total cost of manufacturing. The use of this full or total cost implies that the total manufacturing costs for a given accounting period are allocated or assigned to those units produced during that period. The full costing method requires that a portion of the manufacturing overhead costs incurred during the period, as well as the costs of direct labor and direct materials used in the production process, be allocated or assigned to each unit or batch of products produced.

Direct Materials Cost

As previously indicated, direct materials are those materials which are used in the production process and which can be directly traced to, or identified with, specific units of product or batches of production. In certain instances, direct materials may include certain materials acquired in a semi-finished state from a supplier as well as those materials normally regarded as raw materials. By definition, the total cost of the direct materials introduced and used in the production process will be proportional to the number of units produced, i.e., the amount of goods manufactured. Therefore, the cost of direct materials is, by its very nature, a variable cost of production.

In practice, certain raw materials may be traced directly to units of product or batches of production. However, the cost of doing so exceeds the additional benefits or accuracy which would be derived from this allocation process. The cost of the raw materials which fall into this category are usually classified as indirect materials simply as a matter of convenience. Examples of indirect materials include: lubricants, sandpaper, wiping rags, packing materials, etc. The costs of indirect materials are considered to be a part of manufacturing overhead costs and are allocated to production as such.

Direct Labor Cost

Direct labor costs include expenses incurred for, and related to, the activities of those employees who are involved in the production process and whose efforts may be directly traced to the manufacturing of specific units of product or batches of production. Direct labor cost is a variable manufacturing cost. As is the case for materials, it may not be efficient to trace certain types of labor costs related to production (such as the salaries of foremen, maintenance personnel, janitors, etc.) to units of product or batches of production. Therefore, such expenditures are normally classified as indirect labor costs. Consistent with the treatment suggested for indirect materials costs, indirect labor costs are considered to be a part of manufacturing overhead costs and are accounted for as such as a matter of convenience.

Manufacturing Overhead Cost

Manufacturing overhead includes all manufacturing costs *other* than direct materials and/or direct labor costs which are incurred in order to manufacture the product. Examples of cost items considered part of manufacturing overhead include: depreciation on plant and equipment; heat, light and power pertaining to the factory; factory supplies; insurance and property taxes on the plant; costs of service departments such as maintenance for the plant; and indirect materials and labor.

Any other costs incurred by the firm not related to the production process are considered to be period costs, not manufacturing overhead. Expenses such as depreciation on the administrative and sales facilities, salaries of sales people, utilities expense for administrative and sales facilities, office supplies expense, rental expense for administrative or sales facilities, and property taxes on administrative buildings are all examples of expenditures classified as period costs. As such, they are included as expenses in the income statement in the time period in which they were incurred. Period costs are not included in computing the cost of manufacturing the product.

Manufacturing overhead includes both fixed and variable cost components. The fixed component of overhead normally includes such costs as insurance, property taxes, and depreciation on plant facilities. Variable cost components usually include costs such as indirect materials, indirect labor, and utilities.

FLOW OF MANUFACTURING COSTS

Manufacturing costs are accumulated for purposes of inventory costing on what is referred to as a full cost basis. The use of "full costing" indicates that the cost of the products produced during a period should include the costs of all direct materials and direct labor used as well as a *normal* share of both variable and fixed manufacturing overhead incurred. The overhead that should be included as a portion of the cost of the products manufactured is that overhead which is incurred under normal operating conditions.

The product cost flows generally experienced by a manufacturing firm may be traced in the following diagram:

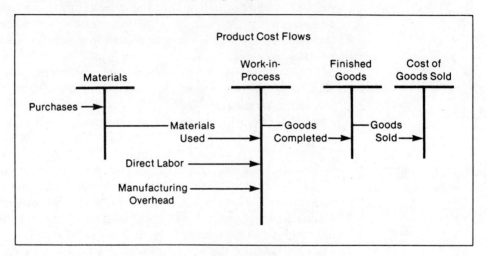

These cost flows may also be summarized in the form of a statement referred to as the cost of goods manufactured and sold statement, as follows:

Cost of Goods Manufactured and Sold Statement

Raw Materials
    Beginning Inventory .... $ xx
    Add: Purchases x

    Raw Material Available for Use .... $xxx
    Less: Ending Inventory .... (xx)

    Cost of Raw Materials Used .... $xxx
Direct Labor xx
Manufacturing Overhead xx

Total Current Manufacturing Costs .... $xxx
    Add: Beginning Work-in-Process Inventory xx

Total Manufacturing Costs. .... $xxx
    Less: Ending Work-in-Process Inventory .... (xx)

Total Cost of Goods Manufactured, Completed and
    Transferred during the Period .... $xxx
    Add: Beginning Finished Goods Inventory xx

Goods Available for Sale .... $xxx
    Less: Ending Finished Goods Inventory .... (xx)

Cost of Goods Sold During the Period .... $xxx

The cost of the direct materials, direct labor, and manufacturing overhead incurred are combined and accumulated in a work-in-process inventory account. As goods are completed, the production costs of these goods are determined and transferred to a finished goods inventory account. It is important to note that the raw materials, work-in-process, and finished goods accounts are *all* inventory accounts. The raw materials inventory account reflects the cost of all direct materials on hand which are available for use in the manufacturing process, but which have not yet been used in production during the period. The work-in-process inventory represents the cost of partially completed products on hand at the close of the period and, as such, is composed of transfers from the direct materials, direct labor, and manufacturing overhead accounts. The finished goods inventory indicates the cost of the inventory which has been completed, but which is unsold and remains on hand at the end of the period. These three inventory accounts are all classified as current assets on the balance sheet. As sales are made from the finished goods inventory, the related cost of the products sold is transferred from the asset account to the cost of goods sold expense account.

PREDETERMINED OVERHEAD RATES

As previously indicated, overhead cost includes both variable and fixed cost components. The benefits which may be derived from a precise or exact accounting for certain of the variable components of overhead are usually not justified in terms of the cost of doing so. The fixed cost component of overhead represents, in general, the long-range commitment that management has made to both obtain and retain the firm's ability to produce. These fixed costs are incurred whether production is at the lower or at the upper end of the relevant range.

For example, if the actual fixed overhead costs of $1,000 incurred during January were assigned by a firm to the production of that month when a total of 200 units of product were manufactured, then the fixed overhead per unit would be $5 ($1,000 divided by 200 units). If the production during June increased to 500 units while the fixed overhead remained constant at $1,000, then fixed overhead per unit would be only $2 ($1,000 divided by 500 units). Under these circumstances, this firm would experience fluctuating monthly production costs per unit (product costs) because a constant amount of fixed overhead ($1,000 per month) is allocated to a different number of units produced each month. The variable cost per unit is normally relatively constant within the relevant range since variable costs, by definition, are incurred in proportion to activity.

To eliminate certain problems which might be encountered in the direct allocation of fixed overhead over a short time span, a *predetermined overhead rate* may be established and used. The use of this rate is implemented under the concept of *normal costs*. The overhead rate used for product costing purposes is determined before the production process is completed, thus the rate is identified as predetermined. This rate is based on the total normal overhead cost expected to be incurred for the time period under consideration assuming usual operating conditions.

The time period chosen for "normalizing" overhead should be sufficiently long to eliminate the effects of any seasonal aspects of production. Even if no seasonal fluctuations exist, the time period chosen must be long enough to eliminate any unusual events which might occur during a given period. For purposes of illustration in this text, a year will normally be considered a sufficient period for use in establishing an overhead rate. One should note that both the fixed and the variable overhead cost components are included in the predetermined rate. For example, assume that a firm anticipates the production of 40,000 units for 19x1 and that total overhead costs (i.e., both fixed and variable overhead) of $100,000 are expected for the year. The predetermined overhead per unit is calculated as follows:

$$\frac{\text{Planned total overhead costs}}{\text{Planned production}} = \frac{\$100,000}{40,000 \text{ units}} = \$2.50 \text{ of overhead per unit produced}$$

Each unit produced during 19x1 includes the actual costs of the direct materials and direct labor used and, in addition, an allocation of $2.50 per unit produced for manufacturing overhead. This $2.50 allocation for overhead is considered the normal overhead cost applied to each unit without regard to the actual level of production that may take place within any given period—for example, a week or month during the year.

It should be noted that units of production are not always the best measure or denominator for calculating a predetermined overhead rate. In fact, the use of units as a base frequently poses certain problems, as in the case of a firm which produces a number of different products. If the production process for each product differs in such a firm, then the firm might wish to use different overhead rates for each of its products or product groups.

APPLICATION BASES FOR OVERHEAD RATES

There are many bases that may be used for *allocating, absorbing* or *applying* overhead costs to the production of a period. The criteria for selecting a base should emphasize ease of measurability and a causal relationship to the incurrence of variable overhead.

Planned production was used as the application base in calculating the predetermined overhead rate in the previous illustration. Direct labor hours could also have been used. If the firm were a multiple product company, and if the incurrence of variable overhead were related to the number of direct labor hours worked, then the rate could have been established on the basis of planned direct labor hours. Under these circumstances, the product costs for each unit or batch of units produced would absorb an amount of predetermined overhead based on the actual number of direct labor hours worked. Thus, in order to calculate the predetermined overhead rate, the direct labor hours per unit must be computed.

The predetermined rate could also have been based on other factors which have a causal relationship to overhead. If direct labor cost is closely related to the incurrence of overhead, it is not uncommon to use a percentage of this labor cost as a basis for the application of overhead, rather than using an overhead rate based on labor hours. In a firm where there is limited use of labor and extensive use of equipment, machine hours used might be an appropriate base for applying or allocating overhead costs to products. Whatever basis is used for applying overhead, the concept is to have each unit of product produced absorb into its cost its proportional share of the predetermined manufacturing overhead cost.

INVENTORY COST ACCUMULATION: JOB ORDER COSTING

As the title "job order costing" implies, costs are accumulated by individual jobs or job lots under a job order costing system. A job is defined as either a single unit or as a batch of units. The costs of direct materials and direct labor traced to the specific job become a part or component of the cost of that job. Normal overhead is assigned to the job using a predetermined overhead rate.

The application of normal overhead is the basis for the term normal costs. Actual costs of direct labor and direct materials are charged to each job, but a normal or a "fair share" of overhead costs is also allocated to the individual jobs. If the causal basis of variable overhead is also the application base for product costing, then normalization is related to the fixed portion of overhead. The projected portion of overhead which is fixed is usually allocated over the projected activity base to develop a cost per unit of activity. Through the use of a predetermined overhead rate, the allocated cost is charged to individual jobs as if it were a variable cost. The total or full cost overhead application rate will be comprised of both the fixed and variable components of overhead.

INVENTORY LEDGERS

The inventory records used in a job order costing system include both the control and the underlying subsidiary ledger accounts. The control accounts used include the following general ledger accounts: raw materials inventory, work-in-process inventory, and finished goods inventory. The subsidiary accounts include the detail which underlies or supports

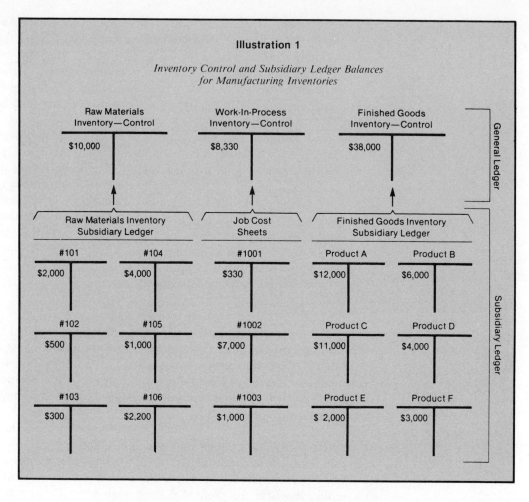

Illustration 1

*Inventory Control and Subsidiary Ledger Balances
for Manufacturing Inventories*

the control account balances. Illustration 1 presents the inventory account relationships in "T"-account format. Illustration 2 is a typical example of the format of the subsidiary ledger inventory accounts.

The relationships of the subsidiary and control accounts in the manufacturing inventory accounting system do not differ either in purpose or in use from those used in a retailing concern. In both cases, subsidiary accounts are updated on a periodic basis and the balances of the subsidiary accounts are posted to the control accounts at appropriate intervals.

JOB COST SHEET

The basis of a job order cost system is the job cost sheet. This subsidiary ledger is the cost accumulation device for each job. In other words, each job has its own job cost sheet which serves as the subsidiary

Illustration 2

Sax Company
Subsidiary Ledger Accounts for Manufacturing Inventories
Raw Materials Inventory Card in Subsidiary Ledger

Material __101 1″ Copper Bushing__   Reorder Point __2,000__
Location __Aisle 29__   Maximum Order __7,000__

Date	Issue Requisition Number	Quantity Received	Quantity Issued	Unit Cost	Balance Quantity	Balance Total Cost
1/1 Bal.				.25	2,000	500
2/10		7,000		.25	9,000	2,250
2/16	1704		1,000	.25	8,000	2,000

JOB COST SHEET

Manufactured For   Job No. __1001__
Customer __John Doe__   Due Date __2/26__
Stock __✓__   Date Started __2/16__
Product __E__   Date Finished __2/26__
Quantity in Job __500 units__

Direct Material Date	Requisition Number	Amount Q	Amount $	Direct Labor Date	Hours	Cost	Overhead Rate 100% of Direct Labor Cost
2/16	1704	1,000	250	2/16	10	40	40
Totals							

Cost Summary
Direct Material __$250__   Total Cost __$330__
Direct Labor __40__   Units __500__
Overhead __40__   Cost Per Unit __$.66__
Total __$330__

Finished Goods Inventory Card in Subsidiary Ledger

Product __A__   Restock Point __3,000__
Location __Aisle 51__   Production Run __6,000__

Date	Order Number	Job Cost Number	Quantity Received	Quantity Shipped	Unit Cost	Balance Quantity	Balance Total Cost
1/1 Bal.					3.00	6,000	18,000
1/15	1055			4,000	3.00	2,000	6,000
1/25		760	6,000		3.00	8,000	24,000
1/28	2010			4,000	3.00	4,000	12,000

ledger account on which costs are accumulated for that specific job. Direct material and direct labor costs are traced to the individual job, and overhead costs are applied or allocated to that job. Per unit costs are calculated directly from the job cost sheet.

If you have had your automobile repaired, you have no doubt dealt with a job cost sheet, perhaps without realizing it. The garage prepares a cost sheet which also serves as your bill. Generally, this cost sheet includes the cost of both parts and labor. In the case of a garage, the overhead charge is usually included in the labor charge for billing purposes. The profit earned by the garage is added to the cost of the parts and the combined labor and overhead rate. In this case, the job cost sheet also serves as a pricing mechanism and invoice for the customer.

MANUFACTURING OVERHEAD CONTROL ACCOUNT

The predetermined overhead rate is assigned to jobs as they are completed or as the accounts are closed. In order to achieve a full cost valuation of work-in-process inventory accounts for reporting purposes, it is necessary to maintain the overhead on the job cost sheets on a current basis.

The amount of overhead applied to a particular job is recorded by a debit to the work-in-process control account and a credit to the manufacturing overhead control account. This entry is normally made when the control accounts are updated.

The actual overhead costs for the period are recorded in the accounts by debits to the manufacturing overhead control account and credits to the other appropriate accounts. For example, if the depreciation expense related to the manufacturing equipment is $1,000 for a particular month, then the manufacturing overhead control account is debited $1,000, and accumulated depreciation—manufacturing equipment is credited $1,000. If actual factory supplies of $200 are used during the month, then the manufacturing overhead control account is debited $200, and factory supplies inventory is credited $200.

The inflows and outflows associated with the manufacturing overhead control account are presented in Illustration 3. Any balance remaining in the manufacturing overhead control account at the end of an accounting period represents either an *over* or an *under application* of predetermined overhead. If the overhead applied to the production for the period is greater than the actual overhead incurred, the firm will have overapplied its overhead and the manufacturing overhead control account will have a credit balance at the end of the period. If the overhead applied to production is less than the actual overhead incurred, then the firm will have underapplied overhead and the manufacturing overhead control account will have a debit balance at the end of the period.

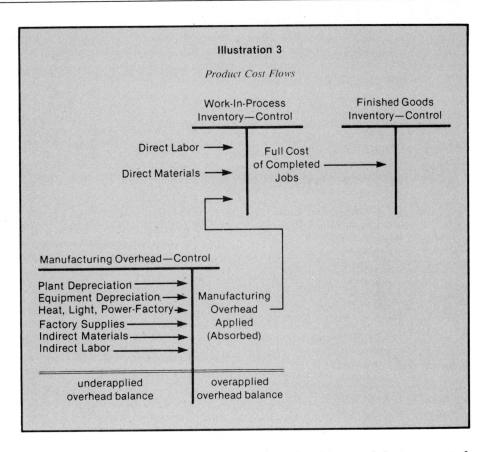

Illustration 3

Product Cost Flows

Theoretically, the amount of actual overhead incurred during a period should be equal to the overhead applied during that period. In practice, this perfect matching will rarely, if ever, be the case and will only occur if the predetermined overhead rate is exactly equal to the actual overhead rate for the period and if actual production is exactly equal to planned production. Of course, this equality is extremely unlikely. If the over or underapplied overhead is an immaterial amount, then an adjustment is made to cost of goods sold in order to close out the overhead account and adjust the cost of goods sold amount. A debit balance in the manufacturing overhead control account (actual overhead costs exceed the overhead applied to the jobs) indicates an increase (debit) in the cost of goods sold, because the manufacturing overhead account must be credited in order to close the account. Alternatively, a credit balance in the manufacturing overhead control account represents overapplied overhead and therefore a decrease in cost of goods sold for the period.

If the balance of over or underapplied overhead for the period is considered to be a significant amount, this balance should be allocated to or prorated among the cost of goods sold, finished goods, and work-in-process accounts. The pro rata allocation to these accounts is necessary to eliminate a distortion of the reported income for the period and the financial position of the company at the end of that period.

A COMPREHENSIVE EXAMPLE: BASIC DATA

The Sax Company uses a job order cost system. The company also uses a predetermined overhead rate for applying overhead costs to its manufactured products. Sax Company has found that there appears to be a cause and effect relationship between the direct labor hours worked during a period and the manufacturing overhead incurred for that same period. Last November, Sax's accountant prepared an estimate of the total manufacturing overhead costs anticipated for the current year. This analysis is presented in Illustration 4 which indicates that Sax will include an overhead allocation of $10 per direct labor hour worked as a part of the product cost of each job worked on this year.

January is an ideal time to follow a job through Sax's manufacturing process and accounting records since the firm closes for two weeks at the end of December for employee vacations. Each January, the firm begins its operations without any work-in-process inventory since all jobs are completed during December prior to the shut-down of the plant. The company uses a perpetual inventory system for all of its inventories. Indirect materials and factory supplies are accounted for in terms of dollars only, and not units.

Sax's production schedule for January consists of a single production run of metal shafts for power turbines, a standard inventory product for the company. Normally, Sax would also engage in other transactions during January, but for purposes of illustration we will focus on tracing Job Number 3032, a production run of 7,000 power turbine shafts, through the manufacturing process and the accounts. We will assume that the transactions which are identified and discussed in this example are the only transactions which occurred in January.

A summarized post-closing trial balance as of December 31, 19x0 for Sax Company is presented in Illustration 5.

The normal cost to produce a power turbine shaft is $19, calculated as follows:

One Direct Labor Hour	$ 5
One Round Steel Billet (Shaft)	4
Overhead Applied (One Hour @ $10.00) . .	10
Total Cost of One Shaft	$19

The transactions of the Sax Company for the month of January, 19x1 are presented and discussed in the remainder of this chapter.

Illustration 4

Sax Company
Projected Manufacturing Overhead Rate

Projected Activity: 60,000 Direct Labor Hours
Projected Total Manufacturing Overhead Costs: $600,000

	Variable Costs Per Direct Labor Hour	Fixed Costs	Total Costs
Indirect Material and Supplies	$3.10	$ 14,000	$200,000
Indirect Labor	1.00	40,000	100,000
Electricity	.10	34,000	40,000
Heat	0	8,000	8,000
Equipment Depreciation	0	48,000	48,000
Plant Depreciation	0	144,000	144,000
Factory Property Taxes	0	60,000	60,000
	$4.20	$348,000	$600,000

Predetermined Manufacturing Overhead Rate:

$$\frac{\text{Total Projected Manufacturing Overhead Cost}}{\text{Total Projected Activity}} = \frac{\$600,000}{60,000 \text{ hours}} = \$10 \text{ Per Direct Labor Hour}$$

Illustration 5

Sax Company
Post-Closing Trial Balance
December 31, 19x0

	Debit	Credit
Cash	$ 60,000	
Accounts receivable	20,000	
Indirect materials and factory supplies	30,000	
Raw materials inventory	40,000	
Work-in-process inventory	–0–	
Finished goods inventory	70,000	
Equipment	300,000	
Accumulated depreciation—equipment		$ 184,000
Plant	1,082,000	
Accumulated depreciation—plant		600,000
Accounts payable		34,000
Federal income taxes payable		–0–
Property taxes payable		–0–
Long-term debt		400,000
Common stock		250,000
Retained earnings		134,000
Total	$1,602,000	$1,602,000

A COMPREHENSIVE EXAMPLE: MANUFACTURING JOURNAL ENTRIES

During the month of January, 19x1, the Sax Company planned to begin and complete Job Number 3032, which consisted of 7,000 power turbine shafts. A summary of the manufacturing transactions that occurred during the month of January follows:

January 2. Materials with a cost of $49,000 were issued to production. Of this amount, $28,000 (representing the cost of 7,000 units of materials) was direct materials and was issued from raw materials. The balance, $21,000, was the cost of indirect materials and factory supplies and was issued from that account. The raw materials requisition number was 1012, and the indirect materials and factory supplies requisition number was 1013.

Work-in-process inventory—control..................	28,000	
Manufacturing overhead—control....................	21,000	
Raw materials inventory—control..................		28,000
Indirect materials and factory supplies..............		21,000

The issue of direct materials to the production process was recorded by a debit of $28,000 to the work-in-process inventory—control account and a corresponding credit to the raw materials inventory—control account. The indirect materials and supplies represent *actual* overhead costs so the manufacturing overhead—control account is increased to reflect these costs. The normal costs of these indirect materials and supplies have been considered in determining the overhead rate, and are therefore components of the rate applied to Job Number 3032 when this job is completed. If a separate inventory account is not maintained for the inventory or indirect material and supplies, the raw materials account is also credited for the $21,000 cost of the indirect material and supplies which were transferred to the work-in-process inventory, thus making the total credit $49,000.

January 15. Paid wages to manufacturing employees totaling $25,000. Of this amount, $20,000 (representing the cost of 4,000 hours of direct labor) was incurred for direct labor and the balance, $5,000 was for indirect labor.

Work-in-process inventory—control..................	20,000	
Manufacturing overhead—control....................	5,000	
Cash		25,000

All Sax Company employees are paid on the fifteenth and on the final day of each month. The direct labor cost for the first fifteen days of January was $20,000, while indirect labor costs for the same period totaled $5,000. The indirect labor cost represents an actual overhead cost and is recorded as a debit in the manufacturing overhead—control account, just as indirect materials and supplies were recorded in the entry made on January 2.

January 31. Paid wages of $19,000 to manufacturing employees. Of this amount, $15,000 (for 3,000 hours of direct labor) was for the cost of direct labor incurred and the balance, $4,000, was incurred for indirect labor.

Work-in-process inventory—control...................	15,000	
Manufacturing overhead—control....................	4,000	
Cash		19,000

This entry represents the cost of employee wages for the latter half of January. Again, the indirect labor costs are recorded by a debit to manufacturing overhead—control and not to work-in-process inventory—control, because these indirect costs are part of the predetermined manufacturing overhead rate which is applied to the job upon its completion.

January 31. Manufacturing overhead of $70,000 (7,000 direct labor hours multiplied by the overhead rate of $10 per direct labor hour) was applied to the production of 7,000 power turbine shafts.

Work-in-process inventory—control..................	70,000	
Manufacturing overhead—control..................		70,000

This journal entry recognizes the normal overhead for January using the predetermined overhead rate of $10 per direct labor hour for each hour worked on Job Number 3032. The normal portions of all of the manufacturing overhead costs identified in Illustration 4 are included in the overhead rate of $10 per direct labor hour.

January 31. The units that were completed were transferred to finished goods.

Finished goods inventory—control....................	133,000	
Work-in-process inventory—control................		133,000

The full cost of the completed inventory includes the direct material cost of $28,000 (January 2), direct labor cost of $35,000 (January 15 and 31), and the manufacturing overhead applied of $70,000 (January 31). The preceding journal entry transferred the accumulated costs of Job Number 3032 from the work-in-process—control account to the finished goods inventory—control account.

January 31. The plant electricity bill of $3,700 for the month of January was paid.

Manufacturing overhead—control....................	3,700	
Cash		3,700

This journal entry records the electricity expense incurred for the month, at its actual cost, as a component of manufacturing overhead. The anticipated cost of electricity had been used in establishing the predetermined manufacturing overhead rate just as the indirect labor and indirect materials and supplies were considered. Therefore, the normal cost of electricity had already been absorbed as a part of the cost of the job when the overhead was applied.

January 31. The plant heating bill of $2,000 for the month of January was paid.

Manufacturing overhead—control....................	2,000	
Cash		2,000

This entry recognizes the actual factory heating cost for January. As was the case with indirect materials and supplies, indirect labor costs, and electricity costs, the normally expected costs of heating were considered in determining the predetermined overhead rate and were thus absorbed into the job. Consequently, the actual heating expense for January is recorded by a debit to the manufacturing overhead—control account.

January 31. Sold 2,000 of the power turbine shafts which were produced during January at a sales price of $50 per shaft. The proceeds of the sale were received in cash. The entry for cost of goods sold was made.

Cash	100,000	
Sales revenue.....................................		100,000

Sax sold 2,000 of the power turbine shafts produced during January at a sales price of $50 per shaft for a total selling price of $100,000. The proceeds of the sale were received in cash.

Cost of goods sold................................	38,000	
Finished goods inventory..........................		38,000

Sax uses a perpetual inventory system. Therefore, the cost of goods sold is recognized at the time the sale is made. Cost of goods sold, as may be seen in the following calculation, is $19 per unit for 2,000 units or a total of $38,000. A total of $133,000 was transferred to the finished goods—control account on January 31. This amount represented the full cost of the 7,000 units completed during January. The full cost per unit would be $19 ($133,000 divided by 7,000 units).

January 31. The selling and administrative expenses for January totaled $28,000 and were paid in cash.

Selling and administratives expenses....................	28,000	
Cash		28,000

The total selling and administrative costs for January were $28,000, and these amounts were paid in cash.

January 31.   Depreciation expense for the month (from Illustration 4) is calculated as follows (assuming the straight-line method of depreciation is used):

$$Equipment: \quad \$\,48,000 \times \tfrac{1}{12} = \$\,4,000$$
$$Plant: \quad\quad\ \$144,000 \times \tfrac{1}{12} = \$12,000$$

Accrued property taxes on the factory for January (from Illustration 4 are as follows:

$$\$\,60,000 \times \tfrac{1}{12} = \$\,5,000$$

Manufacturing overhead—control....................	21,000	
Accumulated depreciation—equipment..............		4,000
Accumulated depreciation—plant....................		12,000
Accrued property taxes payable.....................		5,000

Other actual overhead costs, which have not yet been recognized but which were included in the job as part of the overhead applied, include depreciation expense of $4,000 on equipment and $12,000 on plant. Accrued property taxes of $5,000 on the plant also have not previously been recognized in the accounts. The above adjusting journal entry brings the manufacturing overhead—control account up to date as of January 31.

The depreciation expense and accrued taxes are considered as a part of the overhead costs which were included in determining the predetermined overhead rate. Even if this entry were not made—and in most cases it is likely that it would not be made for purposes of the monthly management reports—the inventory values would reflect the normal cost of depreciation and property taxes. These costs are reflected in the inventory values because they are included as a part of the predetermined manufacturing overhead application rate which was used to apply overhead to production.

A COMPREHENSIVE EXAMPLE: GENERAL AND SUBSIDIARY LEDGERS

The general ledger accounts are presented in "T"-account format in Illustration 6, and the related subsidiary ledger inventory accounts are presented in Illustration 7. All beginning balances were taken from the post-closing balance which was included in Illustration 5. To fully understand the concept of manufacturing cost flows, the reader should trace the general journal entries through both the general ledger and the subsidiary ledger accounts.

Illustration 6

Sax Company
General Ledger Accounts

Cash

1/1	60,000	25,000	1/15
1/31	100,000	19,000	1/31
		3,700	1/31
		2,000	1/31
		28,000	1/31
1/31	82,300		

Indirect Materials and Factory Supplies

1/1	30,000	21,000	1/2
1/31	9,000		

Raw Materials Inventory—Control

1/1	40,000	28,000	1/2
1/31	12,000		

Work-In-Process Inventory—Control

1/1	–0–	133,000	1/31
1/2	28,000		
1/15	20,000		
1/31	15,000		
1/31	70,000		
1/31	–0–	–0–	

Finished Goods Inventory—Control

1/1	70,000		
1/31	133,000	38,000	1/31
1/31	165,000		

Manufacturing Overhead—Control

1/1	–0–	–0–	
1/2	21,000	70,000	1/31
1/15	5,000		
1/31	4,000		
1/31	3,700		
1/31	2,000		
1/31	21,000		
		13,300	1/31

Accumulated Depreciation—Equipment

		184,000	1/1
		4,000	1/31
		188,000	1/31

Accumulated Depreciation—Plant

		600,000	1/1
		12,000	1/31
		612,000	1/31

Property Taxes Payable

		–0–	1/1
		5,000	1/31
		5,000	1/31

Sales Revenue

		–0–	1/1
		100,000	1/31
		100,000	1/31

Cost of Goods Sold

1/31	38,000		
1/31	38,000		

Selling and Administrative Expenses

1/31	28,000		
1/31	28,000		

Illustration 7

Sax Company

Subsidiary Ledger Accounts for Manufacturing Inventories

Material __Round Steel Billet 2″ diameter__   Reorder Point ____500____
Location __Aisle 84__   Maximum Order __9,000__

Date	Issue Requisition Number	Quantity Received	Quantity Issued	Unit Cost	Balance Quantity	Balance Total Cost
1/1 Bal.				4	10,000	40,000
1/2	1012		7,000	4	3,000	12,000

Material __Ind. Mat. & Fac. Supp.__   Reorder Point __Visual Inspection__
Location __Aisle 29: Bins 40-50__   Maximum Order __Marked in Bin__

Date	Issue Requisition Number	Received	Issued	Balance
1/1 Bal.				30,000
1/2	1013		21,000	9,000

Job Cost Sheet

Manufactured for
Customer __John Doe__   Job No. __3032__
Stock __✓__   Due Date __1/31__
Product ____   Date Started __1/2__
Quantity in Job __7,000__   Date Finished __1/31__

Date	Direct Material Requisition Number	Amount Q	Amount $	Date	Hours	Cost	Overhead Rate $10 Per Direct Labor Hour
1/2	1012	7,000	28,000	1/15	4,000	20,000	7,000 hours
				1/31	3,000	15,000	X $10
							$70,000
Totals		7,000	28,000		7,000	35,000	70,000

Cost Summary
Direct Material __$28,000__   Total Cost __$133,000__
Direct Labor __35,000__   Units __7,000__
Overhead __70,000__   Cost Per Unit __$19__
Total __$133,000__

Product __Power Turbine Shafts__   Restock Point ____500____
Location __Aisle 76__   Production Run __7,000__

Date	Order Number	Job Cost Number	Quantity Received	Quantity Shipped	Unit Cost	Balance Quantity	Balance Total Cost
1/1 Bal.					19	3,684	70,000
1/31		3032	7,000		19	10,684	203,000
1/31	2051			2,000	19	8,684	165,000

The manufacturing overhead—control account included in the general ledger and the job cost sheet in the subsidiary ledger deserve special attention. Manufacturing overhead—control serves as an account that is used to accumulate the actual overhead costs as a debit amount. When overhead is allocated or applied to jobs, the application of the overhead is recorded by a credit to the manufacturing overhead—control account. A credit balance in the manufacturing overhead account at the end of an accounting period represents overapplied overhead, while a debit balance represents underapplied overhead.

The job cost sheet, which is the subsidiary ledger account for the work-in-process—control account, deserves special consideration because of the important role it plays in accumulating costs by specific jobs. This cost sheet is the basic cost accumulation instrument used in the job order costing system.

A COMPREHENSIVE EXAMPLE: THE MANUFACTURING OVERHEAD— CONTROL ACCOUNT

The manufacturing overhead—control account used in Illustration 6 reflects the overhead applied or absorbed into production (the credit entry of $70,000) and actual overhead costs for January (the debit entries totaling $56,700). In this example, manufacturing overhead for the month was *overapplied* by a total of $13,300. The $70,000 of manufacturing overhead costs accumulated for inventory valuation purposes using the predetermined overhead rate exceeded the actual costs of $56,700 incurred during January by $13,300.

This overapplication of manufacturing overhead may have been caused by a change in the anticipated volume of activity during January when manufacturing overhead was applied to production. Alternatively, the actual costs of the various components of manufacturing overhead may have differed from the costs which were planned for by the Sax Company when it computed its predetermined overhead rate. The overapplication could also have been the result of a combination of these, as well as other factors.

Theoretically, assuming a reasonable prediction is made for the overhead rate, at the end of each year the difference between actual and applied overhead should be negligible. This is because overapplications in some months will be offset in other months when overhead is underapplied. In our example, Sax Company must now decide how to treat the overapplied manufacturing overhead of $13,300 in its January financial reports. Remember that the predetermined rate is based on normal overhead for an entire year, so that one would usually expect either an overapplied or underapplied amount in any given month.

A COMPREHENSIVE EXAMPLE: TREATMENT OF OVERAPPLIED OR UNDERAPPLIED OVERHEAD

When a periodic closing of the accounts occurs, the over or underapplied overhead is normally immaterial in amount if the costs and level of anticipated activity for the period have been reasonably forecasted. If indeed the amount is immaterial, the procedure usually accepted as most expedient in general practice is to adjust the amount of cost of goods sold by the amount necessary to close out any debit or credit balance in the manufacturing overhead—control account. If overhead were overapplied, using the 13,300 from the illustration of Sax's January operations, this adjusting entry would be made as follows:

Manufacturing overhead—control..............	13,300	
Cost of goods sold.........................		13,300

The effect of this entry would be to close out the manufacturing overhead—control account and to decrease the cost of goods sold for the period by the amount of the overapplied overhead.

Alternatively, if manufacturing overhead were underapplied, the following adjusting entry would be required:

Cost of goods sold...........................	XX	
Manufacturing overhead—control............		XX

The effect of this entry would be to increase the cost of goods sold by the amount of the underapplied overhead and to close out the balance in the manufacturing overhead—control account.

The normal treatment of over or underapplied overhead used by the Sax Company at its year-end is to make a direct adjustment to cost of goods sold assuming that the amount is not significant. In view of this annual treatment, we will assume for purposes of illustration that management has provided for the use of a monthly worksheet closing that is equivalent to the annual closing process. In practice, this procedure may cause a distortion of income on a monthly basis, but we will assume that management uses the financial reports only for internal purposes and is aware of this potential distortion.

A COMPREHENSIVE EXAMPLE: THE WORKSHEET FOR FINANCIAL STATEMENT PREPARATION

Illustration 8 presents the worksheet used by Sax Company at the end of January. The adjusted trial balance was developed from the post-closing trial balance at December 31 (Illustration 5), and from the general ledger accounts (Illustration 6). The general ledger accounts included in Illustration 6 reflect the January 31 balances for all accounts that were affected by the transactions for January. If an account is not found in Illustration 6, it is because the January 31 ledger account balance is unchanged from the December 31 balance presented in Illustration 5.

Illustration 8

Sax Company
Worksheet
For the Month Ended January 31, 19x1

	Trial Balance Before Adjustments		Adjustments		Trial Balance After Adjustment		Income Statement		Statement of Capital		Balance Sheet	
Cash	82,300				82,300						82,300	
Accounts receivable	20,000				20,000						20,000	
Indirect materials and factory supplies	9,000				9,000						9,000	
Raw materials inventory	12,000				12,000						12,000	
Work-in-process inventory	–0–				–0–						–0–	
Finished goods inventory	165,000				165,000						165,000	
Equipment	300,000				300,000						300,000	
Accumulated depreciation—equipment•		188,000				188,000						188,000
Plant	1,082,000				1,082,000						1,082,000	
Accumulated depreciation—plant•		612,000				612,000						612,000
Accounts payable		34,000				34,000						34,000
Federal income taxes payable		–0–		(b) 22,704		22,704						22,704
Property taxes payable•		5,000				5,000						5,000
Long-term debt		400,000				400,000						400,000
Common stock		250,000				250,000						250,000
Retained earnings 1/1		134,000				134,000				134,000		
Manufacturing Overhead	13,300			(a) 13,300	–0–						–0–	
Sales revenue		100,000				100,000		100,000				
Cost of goods sold	38,000		(a) 13,300		24,700		24,700					
Selling and administrative expenses	28,000				28,000		28,000					
Federal income taxes (48%)			(b) 22,704		22,704		22,704					
	1,736,300	1,736,300	36,004	36,004	1,745,704	1,745,704	75,404	100,000				
Net income after taxes							24,596			24,596		
							100,000	100,000		158,596		
Retained earnings 1/31									–0–	158,596		158,596
									158,596	158,596	1,670,300	1,670,300

Key to Adjustments:

* Adjustments were made in the example directly to facilitate discussing overapplied and underapplied manufacturing overhead.
• Adjustments were made to adjust cost of goods sold for overapplied manufacturing overhead.
(a) To adjust cost of goods sold for overapplied manufacturing overhead.
(b) To adjust for income taxes. The before tax income was 47,300. The income tax rate used by Sax's management is forty-eight percent.

The only adjusting entry required on the worksheet at the end of January, besides the closing of the manufacturing overhead-control account, is the accrual of income taxes assuming a rate of 48 percent. The calculations for this accrual are presented in Illustration 9. The adjusting entry is as follows:

Federal income taxes........................... 22,704
Federal income taxes payable.................   22,704

COST OF GOODS MANUFACTURED STATEMENT

Sax Company maintains its inventories on a perpetual system so that a Cost of Goods Manufactured Statement can be prepared for the month of January from these records. If this were year-end, a physical inventory of work-in-process and finished goods might also be taken in order to verify and, if necessary, adjust the inventory records to reflect the cost of the goods that are actually on hand.[1]

A cost of goods manufactured statement may be regarded as an analysis of the work-in-process—control account, or, alternatively, as a summary of the job cost sheets for the accounting period. The usual format employed in the cost of goods manufactured statement is a chronological analysis of the work-in-process—control account. Illustration 9 presents the cost of goods manufactured statement for the Sax Company for January.

OTHER FINANCIAL STATEMENTS

The cost of goods sold statement, the income statement, the statement of retained earnings for January and the balance sheet as of January 31 for Sax Company are also presented in Illustration 9. These statements were prepared directly from the worksheet in Illustration 8, except as noted on the statements.

INVENTORY COST ACCUMULATION: PROCESS COSTING

A process costing system is normally used for the accumulation of costs in those manufacturing situations characterized by the continuous production of a uniform product. Typical examples of industries where a process costing system may be appropriately used include petroleum refining, chemical manufacturing, paint manufacturing, flour milling and cement manufacturing.

---

[1] Alternatively, physical inventories may be taken throughout the year and the accounts adjusted as considered necessary to reflect any differences detected.

Illustration 9

Sax Company
Cost of Goods Manufactured
For the Month Ended January 31, 19x1

Raw materials used:

Beginning raw materials inventory............................	$ 40,000
Add: Purchases...	0
Raw materials available for use..............................	$ 40,000
Less: Ending raw materials inventory........................	12,000
Raw materials used in production............................	$ 28,000
Direct labor used in production.............................	35,000
Manufacturing overhead costs applied.......................	70,000
Total manufacturing costs....................................	$133,000
Add: Work-in-process inventory, January 1..................	0
Less: Work-in-process inventory, January 31................	0
Cost of goods manufactured in January......................	$133,000

Sax Company
Cost of Goods Sold Statement
For the Month Ended January 31, 19x1

Beginning finished goods inventory...........................	$ 70,000
Cost of goods manufactured.................................	133,000
Goods available for sale......................................	$203,000
Ending finished goods inventory..............................	165,000
Cost of goods sold before over or underapplied manufacturing overhead...................................	$ 38,000
Less: Overapplied manufacturing overhead (adjusting entry)...	13,300
Costs of goods sold for January..............................	$ 24,700

Sax Company
Income Statement
For the Month Ended January 31, 19x1

Sales Revenues..	$100,000
Less: Costs of goods sold (from cost of goods sold statement)...	24,700
Gross margin..	$ 75,300
Less: Selling and administrative expenses.....................	28,000
Operating income before taxes...............................	$ 47,300
Less: Federal Income Taxes (at 48%—adjusting entry)............	22,704
Operating income after taxes.................................	$ 24,596

Illustration 9 continued:

Sax Company
Statement of Retained Earnings
For the Month Ended January 31, 19x1

Retained earnings balance, January 1	$134,000
Add: Operating income after taxes	24,596
	$158,596
Less: Dividends	–0–
Retained earnings balance, January 31	$158,596

Sax Company
Balance Sheet
January 31, 19x1

ASSETS
Current Assets:

Cash			$ 82,300
Accounts receivable			20,000
Indirect materials and factory supplies			9,000
Raw materials inventory			12,000
Work-in-process inventory			–0–
Finished goods inventory			165,000
Total Current Assets			$288,300
Long-Term Assets:			
Equipment	$ 300,000		
Less: Accumulated depreciation—equipment . .	188,000	$112,000	
Plant	$1,082,000		
Less: Accumulated depreciation—plant	612,000	470,000	
Total Long-Term Assets			$582,000
TOTAL ASSETS			$870,300

LIABILITIES AND STOCKHOLDERS' EQUITY
Current Liabilities:

Accounts payable		$ 34,000
Federal income taxes payable		22,704
Property taxes payable		5,000
Total Current Liabilities		$ 61,704
Long-Term Liabilities:		
Long-term Debt		400,000
Total Liabilities		$461,704

STOCKHOLDERS' EQUITY

Common stock		$250,000
Retained earnings		158,596
Total Stockholders' Equity		$408,596
TOTAL LIABILITIES AND STOCKHOLDERS' EQUITY		$870,300

In a process cost accounting system, costs are accumulated by process rather than by individual job or job lots. At the conclusion of each reporting period, usually a month, *a production cost report* is prepared for each manufacturing department or process. The total output or production for the period is determined, and the costs of the direct materials and direct labor used as well as the overhead applied are accumulated and summarized. The unit cost of the production for the period is then calculated by dividing the total manufacturing costs (direct materials, direct labor and overhead applied) for the period by the number of units produced during that period.

At this point, it should be noted that a job order costing system could also be used under process costing conditions. In practice, however, the expense of maintaining a job order cost system under such circumstances would probably be prohibitive since job order costing requires numerous supporting source documents and extensive detail. These sources and details are normally considered unnecessary in a typical process costing situation. For example, accumulating costs by individual jobs or job lots requires maintaining detailed records of the direct labor applicable to each job; therefore, employee time tickets for each job are necessary. Also, materials must be requisitioned for a specific job and accounted for accordingly.

In a process cost system, however, direct labor cost is simply accumulated and assigned to the work in that particular process or department. Therefore, daily timecards for payroll are usually considered to be sufficient documentation for use in establishing and accumulating the cost of the direct labor incurred in that process. Since the production process is both continual and repetitive in a process costing situation, raw materials flow into the process continuously. Thus, the need for multiple purpose requisitions for materials, such as those required for job order costing, is substantially reduced. The resultant input-output relationships of raw materials to the finished product can usually be fairly well defined and documented in a process costing situation. A degree of control over materials is also available because of the well defined input-output production relationships.

All of these economies are directly related to the nature of the production process. Job order cost systems are established to account for the production of a number of different products with varying inputs of raw materials, direct labor, and overhead. Process costing is used in those circumstances where a limited number of products are produced in large volume by continuous production runs.

THE PRODUCTION COST REPORT

The production cost report serves as the basic document for inventory cost accumulation in a process costing system. A production cost report may be prepared and presented in the same general format as the Cost of Goods Manufactured Statement. The beginning work-in-process inventory plus the additions (materials, labor and overhead) made to work-in-process during the period, less the ending balance in the work-in-process inventory—is the cost of goods manufactured for the period. This relationship or flow is valid for the accountant working with either dollar amounts of cost or units of production. For purposes of process costing, this relationship must be defined in terms of units in order to derive the number of units which were produced during the period. The number of units produced is then divided into the total manufacturing costs for that period to arrive at a cost-per-unit figure. Of course, if there is neither a beginning nor an ending work-in-process inventory, the procedure is greatly simplified. All of the units started during the period would also have been completed. No partially completed units would exist to complicate the computation of number of units produced during the period.

In actual practice, however, the problem of accounting for beginning and ending work-in-process inventories exists in most, if not all, manufacturing situations. In order to deal with this problem, the accountant must calculate the production for the period in terms of the number of *equivalent units* produced. Thus both the beginning and the ending work-in-process inventories must be considered in order to determine the total production for the period.

EQUIVALENT UNITS OF PRODUCTION

Equivalent units of production are measured in terms of the number of whole or completed units of product that could have been produced at the expended cost if every unit worked on had been started and completed during the period. The assumption is made that the effort and cost required to complete one unit, for example, is *equivalent* to that which is necessary to have three units which are each one-third complete, hence the term equivalent units. For example, assume that the Regan Manufacturing Company began its January, 19x1 operations with no work-in-process inventory. During January it started and completed a total of 100 units and had an ending work-in-process inventory of 10 units at January 31. The ending work-in-process inventory was fully complete as to materials (all materials are added at the beginning of the process) but only 60 percent complete as to labor and overhead. The equivalent production for the month of January would be calculated as follows:

	Total	Materials	Labor and Overhead
Units Completed	100	100	100
Add: Ending Work-in-Process	10	10 (10 × 100%)	6 (10 × 60%)
Total Equivalent Units	110	110	106

Note that the equivalent units of the ending work-in-process inventory were added to the units which were started and completed (which were, of course, 100 percent completed as to materials, labor and overhead since these units were finished) in order to determine the total equivalent units for the month. Note also that the number of equivalent units for materials (110) differs from that for labor and overhead (106). This is not at all unusual and is to be expected. In our example, all material is added at the time a unit is put into production, so all units will be 100 percent complete as to materials. On the other hand, it is to be expected that units will be at various stages of completion as to labor and overhead. At the end of each period, estimates will be made as to the completion status of the inventories on hand and still in process, and these estimates will be used to determine the equivalent units of production in the ending work-in-process inventories.

To continue our example, assume that Regan Manufacturing completed a total of 200 units during the month of February. Its ending work-in-process inventory at the end of February consisted of 20 units which were 100 percent complete as to materials and 40 percent complete as to labor and overhead. The equivalent production for the month of February would be calculated as follows:

	Total	Materials	Labor and Overhead
Units Completed	200	200	200
Add: Ending Work-in-Process	20	20 (20 × 100%)	8 (20 × 40%)
Total Equivalent Units	220	220	208

Again, note that the number of units completed were combined with the equivalent units of the ending work-in-process inventory in order to determine the total equivalent units of production for the month. Note also that the equivalent units included in the beginning work-in-process inventory (which is, of course, the ending work-in-process inventory for January) was ignored in this computation. This is because we used the *weighted average* technique for calculating equivalent units; beginning equivalent units are not used with this method.

An alternative to the use of the weighted average method is the first-in, first-out (FIFO) method. We will now illustrate the calculation of equivalent units under the FIFO technique using the data for the Regan Manufacturing Company for February.[2]

	Total	Materials		Labor and Overhead	
Units Completed...................	200	200		200	
Less: Beginning Work-in-Process....	10	10	(10 × 100%)	6	(10 × 60%)
Units Started and Completed........	190	190		194	
Add: Ending Work-in-Process......	20	20	(20 × 100%)	8	(20 × 40%)
Total Equivalent Units.............	210	210		202	

Using the FIFO method, we start with the units completed, deduct the equivalent units included in the beginning work-in-process inventory to obtain the number of units which were started and completed. We then add the equivalent units included in the ending work-in-process inventory to the units started and completed to obtain the total equivalent production for the period.

The purpose of calculating equivalent units of production is to measure in terms of the number of completed units of product the number of units that could have been produced during a period if every unit started had been worked on until it was fully completed. Again, the assumption that we make is that the effort and cost required to fully complete one unit is the same as that required to have five units which are each 20 percent complete, ten units which are each 10 percent complete, etc. Equivalent unit calculations are used for such purposes as evaluating production activities and determining costs of production.

In order to further illustrate the calculation of equivalent units and the determination of production costs, we will assume that the Jackson Company completed a total of 500 units during a period and had 100 units in its ending work-in-process inventory. We will also assume that there was no work-in-process inventory at the beginning of the period, and that sufficient materials had been applied those units included in the ending work-in-process inventory to manufacture exactly 100 complete units of a product (in other words all units were fully complete as to materials). Also assume that if the labor and overhead which was applied to all 100 units included in the ending work-in-process inventory had been used to fully complete units at the normal cost for the period, 40 complete units could have been produced. Given these two assumptions, we can now calculate the number of equivalent units and the production cost per unit for this period.

---

[2] Since there was no beginning work-in-process inventory at January 1, the total equivalent units for January will be the same for the weighted average and FIFO methods.

To calculate these unit costs, we must first determine the equivalent number of units of production which were included in the ending work-in-process inventory. The number of equivalent units in the ending work-in-process inventory is then added to the number of fully-completed units of production for the period to arrive at the total production for the period stated in terms of equivalent whole units of production.

Therefore, in the example cited above, the equivalent units that would be used for the ending work-in-process inventory cost calculation for inventory valuation are 100 units for raw materials, 40 units for direct labor and 40 units for manufacturing overhead calculated as follows:

Manufacturing Cost Component	Number of Units that Could be Completed	Percent of Completion in terms of Cost Incurred at the End of the Period	Number of Equivalent Units
Raw Materials	100	100%	100 Units
Direct Labor	100	40	40
Manufacturing Overhead	100	40	40

Remember, there are a total of 100 units in the ending work-in-process that could have been completed. To date, however, these units are fully complete only as far as materials are concerned. In terms of direct labor and manufacturing overhead, the 100 units are only 40% complete.

To illustrate the complete calculation of both the equivalent units of production and the cost per unit produced during the period, assume that the following costs were incurred during the current accounting period.

Cost Calculation

Total Direct Material Costs	$ 6,000
Total Direct Labor Costs	4,320
Manufacturing Overhead Applied	2,160
Total Costs of Production	$12,480

Data regarding the units produced are as follows:

Unit Calculation	Equivalent Units
Beginning Work-In-Process	–0–
Units Completed During the Period	500
Ending Work-In-Process:	
Direct Material 100 Units, 100% Complete	100
Direct Labor 100 Units, 40% Complete	40
Manufacturing Overhead 100 Units, 40% Complete	40

The calculation of cost per unit is presented below:

Per Unit Cost Calculation

	Direct Materials	*Direct Labor*	*Manufacturing Overhead*
Total Cost	$6,000	$4,320	$2,160
Finished Units	500	500	500
Equivalent Units Included in Ending Work-In-Process . . .	100	40	40
Total Equivalent Units	600	540	540

Total Cost ÷ Total Equivalent
Units . . . .   ($6,000 ÷ 600)   ($4,320 ÷ 540)   ($2,160 ÷ 540)
                                          = $10   = $ 8   = $ 4

Cost Per Equivalent Unit . . . $10 (materials) + $8 (labor) + $4 (overhead) = $22

Cost of Goods Completed (500 Units @ $22) $11,000
Cost of Ending Work-In-Process:
    Raw Materials (100 Units @ $10) $1,000
    Direct Labor (40 Units @ $8)   320
    Manufacturing Overhead (40 Units @ $4)   160   1,480
Total Cost Accounted For $12,480

The calculations which are made under a process costing system to compute the number of equivalent units included in the work-in-process inventory are usually not complex. Remember, the intent is to arrive at a unit cost for the production of an equivalent number of fully completed units.

In many firms, manufacturing overhead is applied using some predetermined base, such as direct labor hours or direct labor cost. In this situation, the costs associated with direct labor and manufacturing overhead are usually combined and referred to as *conversion costs*. Under these circumstances, the equivalent units for both direct labor and manufacturing overhead are identical.

SUMMARY

Job order costing is one of two fundamental systems of cost accumulation employed by manufacturing firms. Inventory values provided by the cost accounting system of a firm are used to determine inventory valuation on the balance sheet and the cost of goods sold on the income statement. They are, therefore, instrumental in determining the financial position and the profitability of the firm. It follows, then, that the total or full cost of manufacturing the product must be used as the product cost. This "full" cost includes the total costs of the direct materials and direct labor used as well as an allocated share of manufacturing overhead including indirect costs incurred in the period.

Overhead costs are allocated using a predetermined overhead rate. This rate is determined by relating the expected or planned normal overhead costs to a planned level of activity. In this "normalizing" process, a time period is selected which is sufficiently long to avoid the effect of seasonal fluctuations in activity or cost levels. There are many activity bases that may be used to allocate costs. The basis selected should be easily measurable and should be the primary factor related to the incurrence of variable overhead. Some of the common bases used include: units of production, direct labor hours used, and machine hours used.

Under a job order costing system employing normal costs, product costs are usually accumulated in the work-in-process inventory account and transferred to the finished goods inventory account upon completion of the job. The costs are expensed and included as cost of goods sold when the products are sold. The same product cost information contained in the work-in-process inventory account is generally reflected in a specialized subsidiary ledger known as the job cost sheet. Each job will have its individual job cost sheet, and unit costs for inventory costing are often calculated directly from this sheet.

Since manufacturing overhead under a normal cost system is applied using a predetermined rate, it is necessary to accumulate actual overhead costs in a manufacturing overhead control account. Unless the actual costs incurred during a period coincide exactly with the costs used in calculating the predetermined application rate for that period (assuming the planned level of activity is achieved), then the firm will have either over or underapplied overhead at the end of the period. If the over or underapplication is immaterial in amount, a direct adjustment can be made to the cost of goods sold on the income statement. However, if the amount is significant, then the balance in the control account should be prorated to the cost of goods sold, finished goods, and work in process accounts.

The cost of goods manufactured statement is a specialized financial statement prepared by manufacturing firms. This statement can be regarded as an analysis of the work-in-process control account for the reporting period. It is usually presented along with the firm's regular cost of goods sold statement, income statement, statement of retained earnings, and balance sheet.

Process costing systems are used to accumulate costs in those firms that manufacture uniform products in continuous production runs. Costs are normally accumulated for each process and a production cost report is then prepared at the end of the accounting period for each process. Unit costs are generally calculated using information from these reports.

The basic format of the production cost report resembles the cost of goods manufactured statement. Where no beginning or ending work-in-process inventories exist, the unit cost calculation simply involves dividing total costs by units completed. However, in most process manufacturing systems, beginning and ending inventories do exist and this fact complicates the unit cost calculation significantly.

In calculating the unit cost in a process costing system, it is normally necessary to determine the equivalent units of production. This represents the number of whole or completed units that could have been entirely processed with the materials, labor, and overhead that were actually expended or used up. This computation involves adding the equivalent units in the ending work-in-process to the equivalent units of completed production. The equivalent units of completed production are equal to the actual units completed less the equivalent units in the beginning work-in-process inventory.

Generally, it is necessary to calculate equivalent units for each element of product cost (i.e., direct material, direct labor, and manufacturing overhead). The total cost for each element is then divided by the number of equivalent units for that element to determine the unit element cost. The three unit element costs are then summed to yield a unit cost per equivalent unit of product. Once the unit cost per equivalent is derived, the firm's normal inventory valuation method is employed to arrive at ending inventory values.

KEY DEFINITIONS

Conversion costs—the costs of direct labor and manufacturing overhead incurred in a production process.

Cost data worksheet—summarizes the costs which are accumulated in the work-in-process account for each element of manufacturing cost described in the quantity data worksheet.

Cost of goods manufactured statement—a statement which summarizes total manufacturing costs for the period. As such, the statement is regarded as an analysis of the work-in-process control account or as a summary of the job cost sheets for the accounting period.

Equivalent units of production—a measure in terms of the number of whole or completed units of a product which could have been produced at the actual expended cost.

Full cost basis—full costing of the products produced during a period includes the costs of direct materials, direct labor, and a normal share of both variable and fixed overhead incurred.

Job cost sheet—the job cost sheet serves as the subsidiary ledger account for each job. All costs applicable to the job are accumulated on the job cost sheet.

Job order costing system—under this system, costs are accumulated by individual jobs or job lots. These costs include actual costs of direct materials and direct labor and a normal or fair share of overhead costs applied to each job.

Manufacturing overhead-control account—a subsidiary ledger asset account which accumulates actual overhead costs. When overhead is applied or allocated to a job, the application of the overhead is recorded by a credit to this account.

Overapplied overhead—occurs when more overhead costs are allocated to production during a period than were actually incurred. Overapplied overhead is indicated by a credit balance in the manufacturing overhead control account at the end of the period.

Predetermined overhead rate—an overhead burden rate used to apply overhead costs to production. The predetermined overhead rate is based on the total normal overhead cost that is expected to be incurred for the time period (normally a year) in which the rate is to be used. The base selected for calculating the rate should be easily measurable and should be the factor which causes or is related to the incurrence of variable overhead.

Process costing system—a cost accounting system in which costs are accumulated by the production process. This system is normally used in manufacturing situations characterized by continuous productions runs of a uniform product.

Production cost report—a report prepared at the end of an accounting period for each production process. It summarizes the amounts of production, total costs of direct materials, direct labor and applied overhead so that the unit cost of production may be calculated.

Quantity data worksheet—summarizes, in terms of units, the work-in-process account and the percentage of completion of each element of manufacturing cost for beginning and ending inventories.

Underapplied overhead—occurs when more overhead costs are actually incurred by the firm than were allocated to production during the period. Underapplied overhead is indicated by a debit balance in the manufacturing overhead-control account at the end of the period.

QUESTIONS

1. Give some examples of fixed and variable manufacturing overhead costs.

2. What are the three inventory accounts of a manufacturing firm? What functions do they serve?

3. Describe the flow of product costs for a manufacturing firm.

4. What is meant by "normalizing" overhead?

5. How are application bases for overhead selected? Name three bases.

6. What do the control and subsidiary ledger accounts include when accounting for the inventories in manufacturing?

EXERCISES

7. You are presented with the inventory ledger accounts for one year of the ABC Company. You are called upon by the president of ABC Company to help determine what the various entries in the ledger accounts pertain to.

Materials & Supplies		Work-in-Process		Finished Goods	
30,000	35,000	50,000	76,000	40,000	90,000
40,000	4,000	(1) 35,000		(4) 76,000	
		(2) 40,000			
		(3) 22,000			
31,000		71,000		26,000	

Manufacturing Overhead	
(5) 4,000	22,000
(6) 8,000	
(7) 6,000	
(8) 10,000	
6,000	

The president tells you that indirect labor during the year was 20% of direct labor and that factory supervision costs were 60% of other factory costs.

Required:

1. What does the entries (1)-(8) represent in the inventory ledger accounts?
2. What was the amount of cost of goods sold for the year?

8. A job order cost system is used by the Poland Company. The company has no beginning or ending inventory in work-in-process or finished goods, and manufacturing overhead is applied at $4.50 per direct labor hour. Actual results for this year are:

```
Indirect labor  . . . . . . . . . . . . . . . . . $  120,000
Direct labor cost . . . . . . . . . . . . . . .      600,000
Direct labor hours used . . . . . . . . . . .        225,000
Raw materials used . . . . . . . . . . . . . .       300,000
Electricity used in factory . . . . . . . . . . .    210,000
Indirect supplies used . . . . . . . . . . . .        37,500
Miscellaneous overhead . . . . . . . . . . . .       240,000
Cost of goods sold . . . . . . . . . . . . . . $  1,912,500
```

Required:

1. How much manufacturing overhead was applied to production during the year?
2. How much manufacturing overhead was actually incurred during the year?
3. Was manufacturing overhead under or overapplied during the year and by how much?

9. Below are the balances in selected accounts of the Mustang Company:

```
Direct labor used in production. . . . . . . . . . . . . . . . . .   $ 38,000
Finished goods inventory, January 1. . . . . . . . . . . . .        10,200
Finished goods inventory, December 31. . . . . . . . . . .          3,200
Manufacturing overhead used in production. . . . . . .             41,000
Raw materials inventory, January 1. . . . . . . . . . . . .          2,000
Raw materials inventory, December 31. . . . . . . . . . .           4,000
Raw materials purchased. . . . . . . . . . . . . . . . . . . . .    23,000
Sales . . . . . . . . . . . . . . . . . . . . . . . . . . . . . . . . . . .   200,000
Selling expenses. . . . . . . . . . . . . . . . . . . . . . . . . . .   60,000
Work-in-process inventory, January 1. . . . . . . . . . . .          4,800
Work-in-process inventory, December 31. . . . . . . . .             8,800
```

Required:

Prepare the following:

1. A statement of goods manufactured.
2. An income statement.

10. During its first month of operation, the Phoenix Company had the following transactions:

a. Purchased raw materials for $20,000.
b. $15,000 of raw materials were transferred to production.
c. Direct labor costs totaling $10,000 were paid in cash and total manufacturing overhead costs incurred and applied to work-in-process was $5,000.
d. Total cost of goods completed was $25,000.
e. Total cost of the goods sold was $17,000.

Required:

1. Make journal entries for the above transactions.
2. Determine the cost of the work-in-process inventory at the end of the month and the cost of the finished goods inventory at the end of the month.

11. The following information is available from the records of the Park Manufacturing Company for the month of December:

Work-in-process, December 31....................	$ 2,000
Raw materials, December 1.......................	1,000
Labor	5,000
Purchases of raw material.......................	10,000
Manufacturing overhead applied and actual..........	2,000
Raw materials, December 31......................	2,000
Work-in-process, December 1....................	1,000

Required:

Determine the cost of goods manufactured for December.

12. Compute the equivalent units produced in each of the following independent situations.

		Units
a.	Beginning inventory—50% complete..........................	15,000
	Ending inventory—50% complete............................	15,000
	Units started...	120,000
b.	Beginning inventory—30% complete..........................	72,000
	Ending inventory—75% complete............................	90,000
	Units transferred out.....................................	300,000
c.	Ending inventory—75% complete............................	42,000
	Units transferred out.....................................	78,000
	Units started...	102,000
	Beginning inventory—80% complete..........................	?
d.	Units transferred out.....................................	108,000
	Beginning inventory—75% complete........................	33,000
	Units started...	90,000
	Ending inventory—45% complete............................	?

13. During 19x1, the Ace Company completed and transferred to finished stock 100 widgets. The inventory of widgets in process at January 1, 19x1 totaled 40—they were 75% complete as to materials, 50% complete as to labor and overhead. The company began work on 80 new widgets in 19x1; at the end of the year, the widgets on hand were 80% complete as to materials; 50% complete as to labor and 40% complete as to overhead. Calculate the equivalent production of widgets (as to materials, labor and overhead) for 19x1.

14. During 19x1, the Diamond Company completed and transferred to finished goods a total of 100 widgets. The inventory of widgets-in-process on January 1, 19x1 was 20 widgets; they were 60% complete as to conversion costs (all materials are added at the beginning of the process). The company began work on 130 new widgets in 19x1. At the end of the year, the widgets on hand were 40% complete as to conversion costs.

Required:

Compute the equivalent units for 19x1.

PROBLEMS

15. The Vice President of Park Manufacturing Corporation has given you the following information:

1.	Sales	$130,000
2.	Raw materials, January 1	12,000
3.	Raw materials, December 31	20,000
4.	Work-in-process, January 1	18,000
5.	Work-in-process, December 31	14,000
6.	Finished goods, January 1	20,000
7.	Finished goods, December 31	28,000
8.	Raw materials purchased	30,000
9.	Direct labor	32,000
10.	Manufacturing overhead applied and actual	26,000
11.	Administrative expenses	16,000
12.	Selling expenses	24,000

Required:

You have been asked to obtain the answers to the following questions for the December meeting of the Board of Directors.
What is:

1. The cost of raw materials available?
2. The cost of raw materials used?
3. The cost of goods manufactured during the year?
4. The cost of goods sold during the year?
5. The net profit on sales?

16. From the information below, prepare (a) a cost of goods manufactured statement, and (b) an income statement.

Drippy Pipe Company
Before Closing Trial Balance
December 31, 19x1

Assets	$1,800	
Inventory—raw materials (beginning).	100	
Inventory—work-in-process (beginning).	300	
Inventory—finished goods (beginning).	500	
Liabilities		$ 100
Capital stock.		600
Retained earnings.		550
Sales		3,000
Expenses.	550	
Raw materials purchases.	1,000	
	$4,250	$4,250

December 31, 19x1 Ending inventories:
    Raw materials—$200
    Work-in-process—$400
    Finished goods—$600
Direct labor costs for 19x1 was $800.
Manufacturing overhead actual and applied for 19x1 was $400.

17. You are given information concerning the production cost accounts of Which Company for 19x1.

Raw materials purchased.	$ 75,000
Direct factory labor.	35,000
Factory overhead applied.	28,000
Raw materials inventory December 31.	5,500
Cost of goods sold.	143,000
Finished goods inventory January 1.	21,000
Finished goods inventory December 31.	19,600
Work-in-process January 1.	10,000
Work-in-process December 31.	11,500

(**Hint:** Construct a cost of goods sold statement before attempting to answer the questions. Assume that there is not any over- or underapplied overhead.)

Required:

Compute the following:

1. The maximum amount of finished goods that could have been sold during 19x1.
2. The amount of goods manufactured during 19x1.
3. The total production costs incurred in 19x1.
4. Raw materials used during 19x1.
5. Raw materials inventory on January 1, 19x1.

18. The Do-Little Company manufactures scratch pads using a job order cost system. It assigns actual factory overhead to individual jobs at the end of each month in proportion to the direct machine hours required of each job during the month.

The August 1 inventories consist of the following:

Materials and supplies inventory.............	$3,400
Work-in-process inventory (Job #203).........	200
Finished goods inventory (Job #202)...........	4,500

Given below is information pertaining to the jobs worked on in August.

Job#	Materials Issued from Inventory	Labor	Machine Time (hrs.)
203........................	$ 200	$ 300	50
204........................	1,100	1,450	500
205........................	980	1,200	450
	$2,280	$2,950	1,000

Other costs incurred during the month were:

Factory maintenance salaries.................	$1,200
Factory heat, light and power expense.........	2,300
Factory supplies...........................	850
Depreciation of factory equipment...........	900
	$5,250

Job #202 was shipped to the customer. He was billed $5,260. Job #203 and #204 were completed on August 28 and transferred to finished goods.

Required:

Complete the following:

1. The gross margin on Job #202 was $ _____.
2. The work-in-process inventory as of August 31 was $ _____.
3. The finished goods inventory as of August 31 was $ _____.

19. The following income summary "T"-account was given to you by the bookkeeper of Backwards, Inc. for May.

Income Summary

Raw materials purchases......	$15,000	Sales........................	$51,000
Direct labor.................	15,000	Gain on the sale of land.......	4,000
Manufacturing overhead......	10,000	Closing inventories:	
Selling expenses.............	25,000	Raw materials (at cost)......	3,000
Loss on fire.................	1,000	Work-in-process (at	
Opening inventories:		cost)..................	5,000
Raw materials (at cost)......	4,000	Finished goods (at	
Work-in-process (at		selling price)...........	27,000
cost)..................	4,000	Net loss to balance for	
Finished goods (at		the year.................	2,000
selling price)...........	18,000		
	$92,000		$92,000

Required:

1. Prepare a statement of cost of goods manufactured (in *proper* form).
2. Prepare an income statement (in *proper* form).

(**Hint:** Use the ratio of cost of goods manufactured at cost and at sales price in your calculations to arrive at the cost of goods sold.)

20. The beginning and ending inventories of Stapleton, Inc. for 19x1 are:

Inventories	January 1	December 31
Raw materials..................	$38,600	$36,500
Work-in-process................	9,800	10,600
Finished goods.................	18,000	23,400

The cost of goods sold for 19x1 is $216,300. Direct labor for the year is $83,200 and factory overhead costs are $60,700.

Required:

Compute to following:

1. Cost of goods manufactured.
2. Total manufacturing costs incurred this period.
3. Cost of raw materials used this period.
4. Cost of raw materials purchased this period.

21. Below is the post-closing trial balance for the Fairfield Company as of December 31, 19x1:

	Debits	Credits
Cash.............................	$ 160,000	
Accounts receivable................	40,000	
Indirect materials...................	2,500	
Raw materials inventory.............	16,000	
Finished goods inventory...........	35,000	
Factory equipment..................	500,000	
Accumulated depreciation—		
equipment......................		$ 25,000
Plant	800,000	
Accumulated depreciation—		
plant...........................		400,000
Office equipment...................	40,000	
Accumulated depreciation—		
office equipment................		36,000
Accounts payable...................		11,000
Federal income taxes payable.........		100,000
Long-term debt.....................		400,000
Common stock......................		381,500
Retained earnings..................		240,000
	$1,593,500	$1,593,500

The following transactions occurred during the month of January 19x2:

1. Raw materials worth $22,000 were purchased on account.
2. Indirect materials costing $6,000 were purchased for cash.
3. Direct labor amounting to $65,000 and indirect labor totaling $30,000 were paid.
4. Electricity and heat bills for the month, amounting to $4,500, were received but not paid.
5. Raw materials worth $26,000 and indirect materials worth $5,400 were issued to production.
6. $26,000 was paid on accounts payable.
7. Depreciation is calculated at 0.5 percent a month on plant and equipment and 1 percent a month on office equipment.
8. Manufacturing overhead is applied to production at a rate of 65 percent of direct labor cost.
9. Units completed and transferred to finished goods totaled $125,000.
10. Sales on account for the month totaled $360,000 and the cost of those sales amounted to $140,000.
11. $250,000 was received on accounts receivable.
12. Selling and administrative expenses totaled 3 percent of sales.
13. Federal income taxes of $100,000 were accrued.

Required:

1. Journalize the above transactions.
2. Post the beginning balances and journal entries to "T"-accounts.
3. Prepare a worksheet for the month of January.

22. Given the following information for Stacy, Inc., compute the equivalent units and the cost per equivalent unit for the month of June.

Production:
Beginning—work-in-process . . . . 20 units
  Direct materials . . . . 80% complete
  Direct labor . . . . 50% complete
  Manufacturing overhead . . . . 40% complete
Units completed . . . . 4,000 units
Ending—work-in-process . . . . 40 units
Direct material . . . . 60% complete
Direct labor . . . . 30% complete
Manufacturing overhead . . . . 25% complete

Costs:
Beginning—work-in-process
  Direct material $96
  Direct labor 40
  Manufacturing overhead 24
Cost added this month:
  Direct material $24,048
  Direct labor 16,008
  Manufacturing overhead 12,006

23. The Hansen Company uses process costing accounting to determine their cost of goods manufactured.

Below is production data for the year ended December 31.

Beginning work-in-process—3,500 units—100% complete for material and 70% complete for conversion costs (labor and overhead).

Finished and transferred to finished goods—32,000 units.

Ending work-in-process—2,100 units—100% complete for material and 60% complete for conversion costs.

Cost Summaries for the Year

Material:		
Beginning work-in-process.........	$ 7,350.00	
Current costs....................	68,160.00	$75,510.00
Conversion:		
Beginning work-in-process.........	$ 5,414.50	
Current costs....................	73,280.00	$78,694.50

Required:

Compute the cost of goods manufactured.

24. On December 31, 19x1, Sudsy Floors, Inc., which manufactures commercial and home floor care products, took an inventory of its Wax Division. In particular, they were interested in the Mixing Department. They found that there were 400 gallons of wax in work-in-process. The wax was 100% complete as to materials, 60% complete as to labor, and 60% complete as to manufacturing overhead. Costs accumulated at that time were $200, $144, $72, respectively. During 19x2, 21,000 gallons of wax were completed and transferred to the Bottling Department. Costs incurred during 19x2 were $10,520 of direct materials, $12,588 of direct labor, and $6,294 of manufacturing overhead. At the end of the year, the 550 gallons in work-in-process were 80% complete as to direct materials and 40% complete as to direct labor and manufacturing overhead.

Required:

Your job is to determine the equivalent units produced in 19x2, the cost per equivalent unit, and the total cost transferred to the Bottling Department.

25. The Ludwig Company uses a process costing system. At the beginning of the period, it had 10 units in process which were 40% complete as to labor and overhead (all material is added at the beginning of the process). The costs associated with the beginning work-in-process were $10 as to materials, $6 as to labor and $10 as to overhead. During the period, 100 units of product were completed and transferred to finished goods. The current period's costs were $110 for materials, $165 for labor and $275 for overhead. The ending work-in-process consisted of 20 units which were 70% complete as to labor and overhead.

Required:

Compute the following:

1. Equivalent units as to materials for the current period were... _____.
2. Equivalent units as to labor and overhead in the rent period were...................................... _____.
3. The unit cost (total) for the current period was.............. _____.
4. The unit cost (total) for the prior period was................ _____
5. The unit cost of the units finished and transferred to finished goods during the period was................. _____.
6. The number of units started during the period were......... _____.

Refer to the Annual Report included in the Appendix at the end of the text:

26. How is inventory classified in the financial statements?

27. If more than one type of inventory is maintained, which is the largest component?

28. What factors can explain the differences observed above?

29. What is the cost of goods manufactured expense for the most recent year?

30. In which statement would direct materials and direct labor appear?

31. Which is used, a process cost system or a job order cost system?

Appendix:

Cost Accounting
for Inventories:
Joint and By-Products

DUE To the nature of a number of products and/or production processes involved, it is impossible to manufacture certain products without obtaining additional products from the production process. For example, when crude oil is processed the refiner obtains a combination of gasoline, kerosene, fuel oil, naptha, lubricating oil and numerous additional products. It is important to note that the refiner does not have a choice in deciding which of these products will be produced; they are all generated in the refining process. Under most circumstances, gasoline is the most profitable of these products, but in order to obtain gasoline, the other products must also be produced. However, the product mix or proportion of the products may be—and is—altered by the refiner within limitations.

When a packing house slaughters a steer, various cuts of meat with different sales values are obtained. These assorted cuts are basically different products. In addition, other products, such as hides, bone meal, glue, and grease, are also obtained from the steer.

The cost accumulation problem which results when more than a single major product is obtained from a manufacturing process is referred to as a joint or common cost problem. It is important to note that, of necessity, joint costs are assigned or allocated to products for inventory costing purposes by the use of an arbitrarily selected basis for the allocation. This allocation process is discussed in this appendix.

**NATURE OF
THE PRODUCTS
OBTAINED FROM
A JOINT PROCESS**

Outputs of a joint cost manufacturing process, either in the form of joint raw materials, joint processing or both, are categorized for accounting purposes as either joint products or as by-products. Joint products are the *major* products which are obtained from a joint cost production process. It is anticipated that these products will make a significant contribution to the revenues of the firm. In general, joint products are those products usually considered to be the most desirable ones obtained from the production process. If it were possible, only joint products would be produced in most circumstances.

By-products represent those products obtained from the manufacturing process which are not usually of major importance or significance to the firm. Therefore, by definition, by-products are less important than joint products. The production of by-products is the natural result of the process undertaken to obtain the joint products. In comparison to the revenues generated by the sale of the joint products, by-product sales make a relatively minor contribution to revenues. This characteristic is helpful in classifying by-products. Such factors as small quantities of production, low per unit sales prices, or a combination of these and other factors are also measures considered in classifying a by-product. It is possible, however, in some circumstances that the total revenues which are realized from the sale of by-products of the production process may be substantial.

The exact point at which a distinction is made between a joint product and a by-product cannot always be identified or defined with precision. For inventory costing purposes, a manufacturing concern with substantial joint costs must make this distinction using the best judgment available, given the circumstances at hand.

**JOINT
PRODUCT COSTS**

In every joint manufacturing process, there is some point where two or more co-products are physically identifiable as separate and distinct products. This point is usually referred to as the split-off point or the point of separation. In practice, there are numerous split-off points where various products become identifiable at different stages or points in the manufacturing process.

The costs incurred prior to the split-off point cannot be directly traced to any single product. Therefore, they are handled or accounted for as joint costs. Costs incurred after the split-off point which are attributable to the further processing of a physically identifiable product are not considered joint costs. Rather, these costs are treated as separate costs or further processing costs traceable to the specific product involved.

JOINT COST ALLOCATION TO JOINT PRODUCTS

The costs incurred in manufacturing products are *entirely* absorbed by those products produced in the manufacturing process. If all of the output produced from a multiple product process is sold in the period in which it is produced, no allocation of costs is necessary for inventory costing purposes. Because all of the products were sold in the period in which they were produced there are no finished goods inventories on hand at the end of the period. However, this is not usually the case.

The allocation techniques used for distributing costs fall into two major categories: (1) allocation based on physical measures and (2) allocation based on relative sales value measures. Remember that only joint costs are allocated; any separable costs that may be identified with the further processing of a specific product are absorbed into the cost of that particular product.

In order to illustrate the basic considerations which are involved in the allocation of costs to multiple products, we will begin with a simple example. Assume that a manufacturing company is able to produce 2 units of X, 3 units of Y and 10 units of Z by incurring processing costs of $60. The selling price of X is $30 per unit, Y sells at a price of $10 per unit and Z has a selling price of $1 per unit.

As indicated above, one technique which may be used for allocating costs is an allocation based upon physical measures. In our example, 2 units of X, 3 units of Y and 10 units of Z were obtained at a cost of $60. If this $60 in processing cost is allocated to the three products based upon physical measures (in this case, the number of units), the allocation would be as follows:

Product	Units Produced	Proportion to Total Units		Processing Cost		Allocated Joint Cost	Cost Per Unit*
X	2	$2/15$	×	$60	=	$ 8	$4
Y	3	$3/15$	×	60	=	12	4
Z	10	$10/15$	×	60	=	40	4
	15					$60	

*Allocated joint cost divided by number of units.

Note that allocating processing costs to products by the use of physical measures assigns the same cost to each unit of product ($60 divided by 15 units or $4). This technique ignores any differences between and among products, including the relative values of the products.

An alternative method which may be used is to allocate costs based upon the relative sales values of the products. This approach assumes that each product should absorb a share of production costs which is proportionate to the ability of that product to generate revenues. This approach assigns a proportionately higher amount of costs to those products with higher sales values. Using the information presented above, the $60 of processing costs would be allocated to the three products as follows using the relative sales values approach:

Product	Units Produced		Selling Price		Total Sales Value	Sales Value to Total Sales	Processing Cost		Allocated Joint Cost	Cost Per Unit*
X	2	×	$30	=	$ 60	$60/$100	× $60	=	$36	$18.00
Y	3	×	10	=	30	$30/$100	× 60	=	18	6.00
Z	10	×	1	=	10	$10/$100	× 60	=	6	.60
	15				$100				$60	

*Allocated joint cost divided by number of units.

Both of the methods illustrated above assume that all three products are joint products. This assumption may be somewhat unrealistic in this case because of the relatively low selling price and total sales value of product Z, relative to X and Y. A more appropriate allocation might consider X and Y to be joint products and Z a by-product. If Z is considered to be a by-product, one method of allocating costs would be to allocate the processing costs of $60 between the two joint products, X and Y, and consider any revenues from the sale of by-product Z as (1) other income or (2) a reduction of the cost of goods sold for the period. Using the information employed in the examples above, the $60 of processing costs would be allocated as follows:

Product	Units Produced		Selling Price		Total Sales Value	Sales Value to Total Sales	Processing Cost		Allocated Joint Cost	Cost Per Unit*
X	2	×	$30	=	$60	$60/$90 ×	$60	=	$40	$20.00
Y	3	×	10	=	30	$30/$90 ×	60	=	20	6.67
	5				$90				$60	

*Allocated joint cost divided by number of units.

Using this method, all of the $60 in processing costs are allocated to the two joint products, X and Y. Product Z is considered to be a by-product and the revenues received from the sale of Z (10 units × $1) may be considered as either (1) other income or (2) a reduction of the cost of goods sold for the period.

An alternative method of accounting for production costs when there are both joint products and by-products is to consider the sales value of the by-product as a reduction of the processing cost of the joint products. Using this method, the allocation would be made as follows:

Product	Units Produced		Selling Price		Total Sales Value	Sales Value to Total Sales	Net Processing Cost*	Allocated Joint Cost	Cost Per Unit**
X	2	×	$30	=	$60	$60/$90 × ($60 − $10)	$33.33	$16.67
Y	3	×	10	=	30	$30/$90 × ($60 − $10)	16.67	5.56
	5				$90		$50.00	
							$50	

*Total processing cost less the sales value (10 units × $1) of the by-product.
**Allocated joint cost divided by the number of units.

The costs allocated to X, Y and Z under the various methods described above may be summarized as follows:

Method	Allocated Unit Cost		
All Joint Products	X	Y	Z
Physical measures......................	$ 4.00	$4.00	$4.00
Relative sales values....................	18.00	6.00	.60
Joint and By-Products			
Relative sales values with by-product other income or a reduction of cost of goods sold.........................	20.00	6.67	1.00*
Relative sales values with by-product treated as a reduction of processing costs	16.67	5.56	1.00*

*Under these methods, the unit "cost" of the by-product is its selling price, if there is a "certain" market.

As can easily be seen from the above table, the allocated cost per unit varies widely depending upon the techniques used. It should be noted that any method of allocating costs among multiple products is at least somewhat arbitrary. Further, if all of the output produced from a multiple product process is sold, no allocation of cost for inventory costing purposes is necessary since all processing costs will be included in cost of goods sold. Of course, it is rare that all production will be sold every period, so some method of allocation must be selected and used for inventory costing purposes.

QUESTIONS

1. Define joint products and by-products.

2. Explain the split-off point.

3. How are costs treated before and after the split-off point?

4. What allocation techniques can be used for distributing joint costs?

5. Explain what is meant by allocating joint costs using a physical measure.

6. Explain what is meant by allocating joint costs using relative sales value.

7. Which technique, the relative sales value or the physical method, is more frequently used in practice to allocate joint costs? Why?

8. What three approaches are used in accounting for the revenues realized from the sale of by-products?

EXERCISES

9. Stevenson Company produces three products: Alpha, Beta, and Gamma. All three products are initially put into process at the same time in Department A, and in this process, joint costs of $5,600 are incurred. Alpha is further processed in Department B, incurring $2,400 in additional costs. Beta and Gamma are further processed in Department C, incurring joint costs of $3,200. Beta and Gamma are then finished in separate departments (Departments D and E) where they incur additional costs of $300 and $500, respectively. In the month of April, 2,000 gallons of Alpha, 2,500 gallons of Beta, and 3,200 gallons of Gamma were produced. Alpha sells for $1.50 per gallon; Beta, $3.25 per gallon; and Gamma, $2.75 per gallon.

Required:

Diagram the costs and outputs of this total process for the month of April.

10. ABC Company produces two joint products: Alpha and Beta, and a by-product Gamma. Alpha sells for $20,000, Beta sells for $30,000 and Gamma sells for $1,000. The production process costs $15,000.

Required:

Using the relative sales value, allocate the joint costs.

11. Samson Oil, Inc. uses a manufacturing process from which three products are obtained. The joint costs incurred to produce 24,000 gallons of Product One, 18,000 gallons of Product Two, and 18,000 gallons of Product Three are $141,000. The products sell for $2.80, $3.60, and $2.30, respectively.

Required:

Allocate the joint costs using the physical measures. Is this a good method of allocation? Why?

12. Gree-Dee, Inc. has two products, Gamma and Sigma which sell for $28 and $35, respectively. These two products are the natural result of one production process. The company incurs joint cost of $22,400 to produce 5,000 units of Gamma and 4,000 units of Sigma.

Required:

Allocate the joint cost using the relative sales value method.

13. Yason and Sons Chemical Company has two joint products, XYZ and JXL, and a by-product, ABC. During 19x0, 25,000 units of XYZ, 30,000 units of JXL and 400 units of ABC were produced. Allocated joint costs for XYZ were $3.30 per unit and $4.80 for JXL. Selling prices were $5.50, $8.00, and $.75, respectively. Selling costs for ABC were $.12 per unit. During 19x0, 18,900 units of XYZ, 26,200 units of JXL, and 400 units of ABC were sold.

Required:

Determine the gross margin by treating the net revenues from the by-product as (a) a reduction of cost of goods sold, and (b) other income.

14. The Starnes Chemical Company has two products, R and S, which are the natural output of their production process. This process, which costs $42,000, produces 10,000 gallons of R and 11,000 gallons of S. They sell for $35,000 and $49,000, respectively.

Required:

1. Allocate the production costs to R and S using the relative sales value.
2. Assume that S can be further processed for $15,000 to produce T and U which sell for $40,000 and $70,000, respectively. Use the relative sales value approach to allocate these costs.

15. The Cogwell Company produces two products in a joint process. Material, labor, and overhead for the month of October in this process were $2,025, $2,592, and $2,349, respectively. Product J sold for $4,500 and Product N sold for $3,600.

Required:

Allocate material, labor, and overhead joint costs to products J and N using the relative sales value method.

Appendix:

Allocation of Service Department Costs to Producing Departments

All manufacturing overhead costs must be allocated to products produced under the full or absorption costing approach to product costing. For purposes of simplicity, the prior chapters assumed a plant-wide overhead rate and ignored service departments and the allocation of the costs of the service departments to the producing departments. The allocation of service department costs to producing departments is necessary if the departmental manufacturing overhead rate applied to products is to reflect the *full* or *total* manufacturing overhead costs. Some general examples of service departments in a manufacturing plant that would serve as support for production departments are as follows:

Cost Accounting   Maintenance
General Building Services   Power Plant
General Supervision   Production Planning
Plant Cafeteria   Purchasing
Plant Engineering   Toolroom

Allocating Service Department Costs— General Concepts

Any allocation of the costs of the service departments to producing departments in an equitable manner is complicated by the fact that some service departments will serve other service departments. The basis for the allocation of the costs of the service departments to the producing departments should be that basis which best reflects the services rendered to the producing departments. This basis will usually be different for different service departments. The interrelationship of the service departments in rendering service to each other would distort the allocation because some of the cost of service is caused by the needs of other service departments and not the producing departments.[1]

The concept of reciprocal services between service departments and the allocation of the costs of the departments to the producing departments in establishing an overhead rate is presented in Illustration 1.

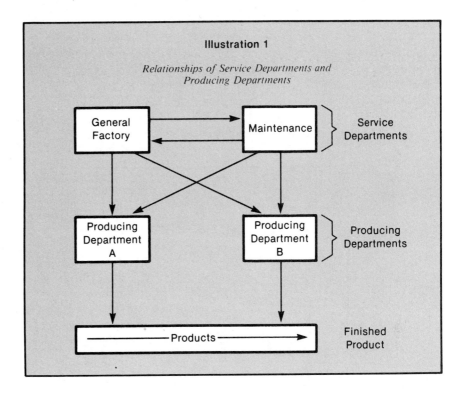

Illustration 1

*Relationships of Service Departments and
Producing Departments*

In Illustration 1 there are two service departments, Maintenance and General Factory. To keep the example simple, assume that the General Factory Department does everything associated with service except maintenance. General Factory and Maintenance provide service to each other and to the producing departments. In order to pass the total overhead cost on to the products which are produced, the service department costs will have to be allocated in total to the producing departments. The service department allocations will be added to the overhead costs in the

---

[1] This problem of reciprocal services can be solved using linear algebra or simultaneous equations. The step method of allocation, which is covered in this chapter, is an approximation of the linear algebra solution when reciprocal services are involved.

producing departments to arrive at the total overhead projection for each producing department. These overhead projections and the basis for the allocations will serve to establish the predetermined overhead rate to be used in applying overhead costs to production. As the products pass through the producing departments, the manufacturing overhead will be applied using the predetermined overhead rate.

METHODS FOR ALLOCATING COSTS OF SERVICE DEPARTMENTS TO PRODUCING DEPARTMENTS

The two methods covered in this appendix for allocating the costs of the service departments to the producing departments are the direct method of allocation and the step method of allocation. The major difference between the two approaches is the recognition given to reciprocal services between service departments.

The basic data that will be used in illustrating both the direct method of allocation and the step method of allocation is presented in Ilustration 2.

Illustration 2

Projected Overhead Costs for Service Departments and Producing Departments

	Service Departments		Producing Departments		
	General Factory	Maintenance	Machining	Finishing and Pressing	Total
Departmental Identifiable (Traceable) Overhead Costs	$5,000	$4,000	$3,500	$2,500	$15,000
Services Furnished:					
1. General Factory Based on Square Feet	–0–	400	1,000	1,000	2,400
2. Maintenance Based on Projected Maintenance Hours Worked in Each Department	100	–0–	3,000	1,000	4,100
Basis For Allocation To Production:					
Projected Machine Hours			2,000		
Projected Direct Labor Hours				1,000	

In the example in Illustration 2, there are two service departments: General Factory and Maintenance, and two producing departments: Machining and Finishing and Pressing. The projected overhead costs for the General Factory Department are $5,000. This would be the total projected cost of this department for the period under consideration. The basis for the allocation of the $5,000 will be square feet of plant used in the other departments. This is the basis that is the most common denominator that can be used to measure the services provided by the General Factory Department to all other service departments and producing departments.

The projected cost of the Maintenance Department is $4,000. The basis of allocation of maintenance costs for the projected overhead rate will be projected maintenance hours to be worked in each service and production department. Maintenance hours are considered to be the common denominator in the other departments that provides a causal relationship with costs in the maintenance department.

The overhead directly identifiable with the producing departments is $3,500 for Machining and $2,500 for Finishing and Pressing. The basis that will be used to apply overhead to production in the Machining Department is machine hours. The basis in Finishing and Pressing will be direct labor hours. These bases for application are felt to be the most meaningful because of their relationship to overhead cost incurrence. The final predetermined manufacturing overhead rates will include the total $15,000 of projected costs when the rates for both producing departments are considered. That is, the combined application rates will attempt to pass the $15,000 of overhead to the products produced during the time period under consideration.

The Direct Method of Allocation

The direct method of allocation of service department costs allocates the projected costs of each service department directly to the producing departments. The interaction between service or support departments and the related costs that are incurred in one service department because of the needs of another service department is ignored.

Of the costs of the General Factory Department, $5,000 will be allocated directly to the producing departments on a square foot basis. The $4,000 of projected costs of the Maintenance Department will be allocated to the producing departments on the basis of projected maintenance hours to be worked in each producing department. Of the projected costs of all the service departments a total of $9,000, therefore, will be allocated to the producing departments and included in the final predetermined overhead rate.

The direct method of allocation using those projected overhead costs for service departments and producing departments from Illustration 2, is presented in Illustration 3. Using the direct method of allocation, the order of the allocation of the costs of the service departments to the producing departments does not make any difference. Each of the producing departments uses 1,000 square feet of factory and the Maintenance Department uses 400 square feet. The Maintenance Department's use will be

---

Illustration 3

*Direct Method of Allocation of
Projected Service Department Costs*

| | Service Departments | | Producing Departments | | |
	General Factory	Maintenance	Machining	Finishing and Pressing	Total
Overhead Costs Before Allocation	$5,000	$4,000	$3,500	$2,500	$15,000
Allocation:					
1. General Factory Based on Square Feet $\frac{1,000}{2,000} \quad \frac{1,000}{2,000}$ *	(5,000)		2,500	2,500	
2. Maintenance Based on Projected Maintenance Hours Worked in Each Department $\frac{3,000}{4,000} \quad \frac{1,000}{4,000}$ †		(4,000)	3,000	1,000	
Total Overhead to be Applied to Production			$9,000	$6,000	$15,000

Predetermined Departmental Overhead Rates:

Projected Overhead Costs in Machining	$9,000	
Projected Machine Hours in Machining	2,000	=
Overhead Application Rate Per Machine Hour	$4.50	

Projected Overhead Costs in Finishing and Pressing	$6,000	
Projected Direct Labor Hours in Finishing and Pressing	1,000	=
Overhead Application Rate Per Direct Labor Hour	$6.00	

* Each producing department uses 1,000 square feet (from Illustration 2).
† The projected maintenance hour usage is 3,000 hours for Machining and 1,000 hours for Finishing and Pressing (from Illustration 2).

ignored in the allocation because the costs of the General Factory Department will be allocated directly to the producing department. The Machining Department and the Finishing and Pressing Department both use equal amounts of square feet of factory space; therefore, each will be allocated one-half of the cost of the General Factory Department or $2,500.

The costs of the Maintenance Department are allocated on the basis of projected maintenance hours to be worked in each department. Total projected maintenance hours are 3,000 hours for the Machining Department and 1,000 hours for the Finishing and Pressing Department. The appropriate allocation of the projected costs of the Maintenance Department is three-quarters (3,000 hours ÷ 4,000 hours) to Machining and one-quarter (1,000 hours ÷ 4,000 hours) to Finishing and Pressing. Therefore, $3,000 will be allocated to the Machining Department and $1,000 to the finishing and Pressing Department. The projected manufacturing overhead rate that will be applied to products produced in the two production departments will include the allocated costs of the service departments and the manufacturing overhead costs of the production departments.

The predetermined manufacturing overhead rate for the Machining Department will include $3,500 of manufacturing overhead identified directly with the Machining Department, $2,500 allocated from the General Factory Department, and $3,000 allocated from the Maintenance Department, or $9,000 in manufacturing overhead in total. The manufacturing overhead application basis for the Machining Department in Illustration 3 is machine hours. Two thousand machine hours are projected; therefore, the predetermined overhead rate for the Machining Department will be $9,000 ÷ 2,000 hours or $4.50 per machine hour worked on a job. If a job uses 2 hours of machine time, the applied overhead on that job will be $4.50 × 2 hours or $9.00.

The Finishing and Pressing Department has $2,500 of manufacturing overhead identified directly with itself (Illustration 3). Twenty-five hundred dollars of manufacturing overhead is allocated from the General Factory Department. The Maintenance Department allocation is $1,000. In total, the projected manufacturing overhead that will be applied to products being worked on in the Finishing and Pressing Department is $6,000 ($2,500 + $2,500 + $1,000). The basis for the application of overhead in the Finishing and Pressing Department is direct labor hours. There are 1,000 direct labor hours projected. The predetermined manufacturing overhead rate will be $6.00 ($6,000 ÷ 1,000 direct labor hours) per direct labor hour worked. If a job uses two direct labor hours in Machining and Finishing, that job will absorb $6.00 × 2 hours or $12.00 in manufacturing overhead.

If a job used 5 hours of machine time in the Machining Department and 3 hours of direct labor time in the Finishing and Pressing Department, the job would absorb ($4.50 × 5 hours) + ($6.00 × 3 hours) or $40.50 in manufacturing overhead.

The Step Method of Allocation

Direct allocation of the costs of the service department to the production departments is the most popular approach for service department cost allocations. Some accountants would argue that cost inequities result when using the direct method if there are reciprocal services between service departments. If some service departments serve other service departments, and if the use of service departments is different for different production departments, an unequitable allocation of service department costs, and thus overhead allocation to products, could result.

For example, a maintenance department would normally provide more service to a producing department that is machine intensive than to one that is labor intensive. If another service department is a large user of the Maintenance Department but provides a greater proportion of its resources to the labor intensive production department, that production department may be getting the benefits of maintenance expenditures without a proportional share of the maintenance costs if a direct method of allocation is used. The maintenance-using machine intensive department would be allocated a share of the maintenance cost based on its proportional use of the maintenance department. However, a large part of maintenance cost would be caused by the other service department that provides a greater share of its resources to the labor intensive production department.

To solve the allocation equitably, simultaneous equations would have to be used in making the allocation.[2] An approximation of an equitable solution using simultaneous equations can be achieved by using the step method of allocation. The step method of allocation is only an approximation to the extent that costs are allocated on a sequential basis starting with the service department that provided the most service to other service departments. The costs of this service department will be allocated to the remaining service departments and all production departments. Then, in turn, all costs of the service department that provided the next most service are allocated to the remaining service and production departments. The costs of the second service department would include an allocated portion of the costs of the first service department. This sequential system will continue until all service department costs are allocated

---

[2] This approach will not be covered in this text. The practical application of service department allocations using simultaneous equations is not common and would probably be done using a computer.

to the production departments. Once a service department's costs are allocated, that service department will not be allocated any costs from the subsequent cost allocations of other service departments.

The Step Method of Allocation— An Illustration

Illustration 4 is an example of the step method of allocation using the data presented in Illustration 2. Assume that the costs of the General Factory Department will be allocated first because it provides more

---

Illustration 4

Step Method of Allocation of Projected Service Department Costs

	Service Departments		Producing Departments		
	General Factory	Maintenance	Machining	Finishing and Pressing	Total
Overhead Costs Before Allocation	$5,000	$4,000	$3,500	$2,500	$15,000
Allocation:					
1. General Factory Based on Square Feet $\frac{400}{2,400}$ $\frac{1,000}{2,400}$ $\frac{1,000}{2,400}$ °	(5,000)	834	2,083	2,083	
2. Maintenance Based on Projected Maintenance Hours Worked in Each Department $\frac{3,000}{4,000}$ $\frac{1,000}{4,000}$ †		(4,834)	3,625	1,209	
Total Overhead to be Applied to Production			$9,208	$5,792	$15,000

Predetermined Departmental Overhead Rates:

Projected Overhead Costs in Machining
Projected Machine Hours in Machining
Overhead Application Rate Per Machine Hour

$\dfrac{\$9,208}{2,000} =$
$\$4.60$

Projected Overhead Costs in Finishing and Pressing
Projected Direct Labor Hours in Finishing and Pressing
Overhead Application Rate Per Direct Labor Hour

$\dfrac{\$5,792}{1,000} =$
$\$5.79$

---

* Maintenance uses 400 square feet, Machining 1,000 and Finishing and Pressing 1,000 (from Illustration 2).

† The projected maintenance hour usage is 3,000 hours for Machining and 1,000 hours for Finishing and Pressing (from Illustration 2).

services to the Maintenance Department than the Maintenance Department provides to it. The General Factory Department costs will be allocated to the Maintenance Department, the Machining Department, and the Finishing and Pressing Department on the basis of square feet.

The Maintenance Department will be allocated $834 [(400 square feet ÷ 2,400 square feet) × $5,000] of the General Factory Department's costs. Each of the producing departments will be allocated an equal amount of the remaining General Factory Department's costs based on their proportional square feet of use (1,000 square feet ÷ 2,400 square feet) × $5,000, or $2,083.

The second step in the sequential allocation will be to allocate the Maintenance Department's costs to the producing departments. The Maintenance Department's costs to be allocated are $4,834 which is the cost of providing $4,000 of manufacturing overhead directly identifiable with the Maintenance Department in Illustration 4 plus the $834 of costs allocated from the General Factory Department. The Maintenance Department's costs of $4,834 will be allocated based on the projected usage of maintenance hours by the producing departments. No maintenance costs will be allocated back to the General Factory Department.

The projected usage of maintenance hours is 3,000 hours for the Machining Department and 1,000 hours for the Finishing and Pressing Department. The allocation of the $4,834 will be three-fourths to the Machining Department (or $3,625) and one-fourth (or $1,209) to the Finishing and Pressing Department.

The total projected manufacturing overhead to be applied to production in the Machining Department is $9,208 of the $15,000 of manufacturing overhead for the entire plant. The basis for manufacturing overhead application for the Machining Department of Illustration 4 is 2,000 hours of projected machine usage. The appropriate application rate for applying manufacturing overhead to production will be $9,208 ÷ 2,000 projected machine hours, or $4.60 per machine hour worked on a job.

The total projected manufacturing overhead that will be applied to production in the Finishing and Pressing Department is $5,792. The basis for manufacturing overhead application for the Finishing Pressing Department is the projected 1,000 hours of direct labor time usage. The manufacturing overhead rate per direct labor hour will be $5,792 ÷ 1,000 projected direct labor hours, or $5.79 per direct labor hour.

QUESTIONS

1. Why are the costs of service departments allocated to the producing departments in a manufacturing company?

2. Discuss the concept of reciprocal services. How may reciprocal services present a problem in the allocation of service department costs?

3. Identify and briefly describe two approaches for allocating the costs of several service departments to more than one producing department.

4. What does the step method of allocation specifically take into account that the direct method does not?

5. Which department has its costs allocated first in the step method of allocation? Which department is allocated next? Last?

EXERCISES

6. Service Department 1 provides maintenance to Production Departments 2 and 3. Service department costs are allocated according to projected usage of direct labor hours. Given the following information:

    Department 1 projected costs $100,000.
    Department 2 projected usage is 2,500 hours of Department 1 labor.
    Department 3 projected usage is 3,500 hours of Department 1 labor.

    How much of the projected service department costs are to be allocated to each production department?

7. Ajax Company has two service departments, Maintenance and Power, and two production departments, Powders and Liquids. Budgeted costs for Maintenance and Power are $60,000 and $200,000, respectively. Service costs are allocated to production according to the number of labor hours of maintenance and the number of machine hours of power used. Powders and Liquids are expected to use the following:

	Expected Usage of Labor Hours of Maintenance	Expected Usage of Machine Hours of Power
Powders	500 hours	2,500 hours
Liquids	750 hours	7,500 hours

    Allocate the service costs to the production departments.

8. Atlas Corporation has two service departments (A and B) providing services to three production departments (I, II and III). All service department costs are allocated to the production department based on the projected amount of labor cost expected to be incurred by the respective service departments for each of the production departments. Expected service department costs are $10,000 for A and $20,000 for B. The wage rate for A is $5 per hour and for B is $4 per hour. The service departments are expected to be needed as follows:

Expected Departmental Requirements for Service Labor Hours					
Dept.	*A*	*B*	*I*	*II*	*III*
A		10	20	30	40
B	50		60	70	80

By using a direct method of allocation, determine the amount of service costs allocated to each production department.

9. Redetermine the amount of service costs allocated to each production department in Exercise 8 by using a step method of allocation. Allocate A first.

10. Given the following information:

	Service Departments		Production Departments	
	1	*2*	*1*	*2*
Application Basis	Square Footage Used	Direct Labor Hours Used	Machine Hours Used	Units Finished
Expected use of Service Dept. 1		100 sq. ft.	2,000 sq. ft.	1,200 sq. ft.
Expected use of Service Dept. 2	10 hrs.		120 hrs.	130 hrs.
Expected machine hours	55 hours	75 hrs.	2,000 hrs.	370 hrs.
Expected number of units finished				4,000 units
Expected service costs	$15,000	$40,000		
Expected manufacturing overhead			$20,000	$350,000

Service Department 1 provides more service to Service Department 2 than Service Department 2 does to Service Department 1. Determine the amount of service cost allocated to each of the production departments from Service Department 2 if a direct allocation method is used.

11. Redetermine the amount of service cost allocated to each of the production departments from Service Department 2 in Exercise 10 if a step method of allocation is used.

12. The Clinton Company has two Production Departments, X and Y, and two Service Departments, I and II. Projected overhead amounted to $305,000 for X, $428,000 for Y, $298,000 for I and $367,000 for II. Overhead in Department X is allocated in accordance with the number of physical units of projected production, which is 350,000. Department Y allocates overhead based upon projected direct labor hours which totaled 293,000. Department I allocates its overhead based upon the projected number of machine hours used for other departments which amounted to 30,000 for X, 47,500 for Y and 20,450 for II. Department II allocates overhead based upon the projected units of direct materials that it handles for the various departments. These amounted to 29,000 units for X, 56,000 units for Y and 13,000 units for I.

a. Assume Department I provides Department II with the greater amount of service.

b. Assume Department II provides Department I with the greater amount of service.

13. The Zepher Company has two service departments and two production departments. The costs of operating the various departments are as follows:

	Service Departments		Production Departments		
	A	B	Y	Z	Total
Overhead	$30,000	$44,000	$75,000	$51,000	$200,000
Dept. A (allocation base is sq. ft. of area).Proportion allocable to each of the other Depts.		16%	39%	45%	100% of 350,000 sq.ft.
Dept. B (allocation base is direct labor hours). Proportion allocable to each of the other depts.	20%		45%	35%	100% of 210,000 direct labor hours

Department Y's allocation base is labor cost. The projected labor cost is $390,000. Department Z's allocation base is direct labor hours. The projected direct labor hours are 130,000.

Required:

Assuming Department A provides the greater amount of services to B, compute the predetermined overhead rate for each department using the step method of allocation for service department overhead.

14. The Clark Company has three service departments which provide services to two factory departments. The following annual costs have been budgeted for the various departments:

	Service			Production		
	I	II	III	Y	Z	Total
Overhead	$30,000	$50,000	$90,000	$25,000	$55,000	$250,000

The following amounts have been budgeted with regard to the services expected to be provided by the three service departments to the other departments:

Dept.	Allocation Base	I	II	III	Y	Z	Total
I	Machine Hrs.		70,000	80,000	100,000	100,000	350,000
II	Sq. ft. of space	40,000		60,000	80,000	120,000	300,000
III	Labor Cost	$100,000	$100,000		$250,000	$350,000	$800,000

Required:

Using the step method, allocate the budgeted costs of the service departments to the factory departments, assuming III renders the greatest service to the other service departments, followed by I and then II.

15. The Birdsong Company manufactures cuckoo clocks. It has three service departments which serve three production departments. Annual fixed overhead of the various departments is budgeted as follows:

	Service			Production			
	I	II	III	X	Y	Z	Total
Overhead	$200,000	$300,000	$100,000	$500,000	$400,000	$600,000	$2,100,000

The following proportional breakdowns have been budgeted to the various departments:

Service Dept.	Allocation Base	I	II	III	X	Y	Z
I	Labor Hrs.		10%	5%	30%	25%	30%
II	Machine Hrs.	15%		15%	20%	30%	20%
III	Number of Orders	10%	12%		28%	25%	25%

Required:

Using the step method, allocate service department overhead to the various production departments assuming Department II provides services to the greatest number of other service departments, followed by I and then III.

Chapter 15 discusses and illustrates the use of a standard cost system. Studying this chapter should enable you to:

1. Distinguish between standard costs and normal costs.

2. Discuss the uses and advantages of a standard cost system.

3. Identify and explain the basic types of standards in general use.

4. Calculate the standard manufacturing overhead cost per unit.

5. Explain the sources of the direct materials and direct labor variances and how these variances are calculated.

6. Understand the concept of the flexible budget.

7. Understand the underlying concepts of manufacturing overhead variance analysis.

8. Determine why the variances could occur.

9. Calculate the volume and budget variances for manufacturing overhead costs.

15

Standard Costs

INTRODUCTION

Prior to this chapter, the inventory costing systems used by manufacturing firms have been discussed and illustrated using actual historical costs for the accounting for both direct materials and direct labor. In these examples, manufacturing overhead was applied or absorbed into production using a predetermined overhead rate. Therefore, the inventory produced, absorbed or included a normal amount of overhead without regard to the actual level of production. These procedures are used in an attempt to smooth out the expected overhead costs over a sufficiently long time period in order to eliminate any distortions of cost. For example, distortions in per unit costs could be caused by fluctuations in the production schedule. These distortions are possible because the allocated fixed overhead remains relatively constant for each period, while the number of units produced varies according to production which is scheduled considering the anticipated demand for products.

It should be noted, however, that the inventory cost determined using the predetermined overhead rate introduced previously is not a standard cost. Rather, the overhead rate is a measure based upon the *expected* future costs that are allocated over the anticipated production and expressed per a selected unit of activity. The activity base chosen was used as the basis for applying or allocating the anticipated overhead costs to the production for the period. Standard costs, on the other hand, are based on the level of costs which *should* be incurred under efficient and effective operations. Thus standard costs do not necessarily reflect the costs which are expected to occur or actually do occur in a particular period. Standard costs are regarded as cost guidelines, or benchmarks, for the input factors of production and the related outputs resulting from the processing of these inputs.

When standard costs are used in accounting for the factors of production, the inventory cost system is referred to as a standard cost system. Standard costs may be used with either a job-order or a process cost system or with a combination and/or variation of these two basic methods for accumulating the costs of production.

PHYSICAL STANDARDS AND STANDARD COSTS

Physical standards for the production process relate to the standard requirements necessary to manufacture a product. These standards are stated or expressed in terms of quantities of raw materials, hours of direct labor, hours of processing time and similar measures. There is a general relationship between these input factors and the quantity or amount of output that may be expected or anticipated at standard levels of production. The standard costs of manufacturing are these physical standards expressed in terms of dollars of costs.

TYPES OF STANDARDS

The types of standards in general use in standard cost systems fall into three basic categories or classifications:

1. Standards based on historical or past performance.
2. Standards based on ideal performance.
3. Standards based on attainable performance.

Any standard based on historical or past performance will, by definition, include the efficiencies and inefficiencies of the period(s) of time used as the base in determining the standard. At best, this type of standard can be considered only a very rough benchmark or estimate of what may be anticipated or expected in the future. However, this does not indicate that historical performance should be ignored, but rather that it should not be used as the sole basis for establishing a standard cost for a specific cost factor for future periods.

Any standard based on ideal or engineering performance may not consider factors such as waste, downtime, fatigue, breakdowns, reworking, idle time or other similar inefficiencies. An "ideal" standard, therefore, represents perfection. All factors in the production process are assumed to interact perfectly. This type of standard cannot be ignored completely because it does represent what is possible under ideal or optimum conditions. In actual practice, an ideal standard is usually impossible·to attain for all of the input factors of production for any sustained time period.

An attainable standard is an ideal or engineering standard which has been modified or adjusted for tolerable inefficiencies. Attainable standards represent a level of efficiency and effectiveness that can be attained over a sustained production period if all of the factors of production are operating and interacting at a satisfactory level. Theoretically, attainable standards are normally considered the proper standards to be applied to the many facets of management accounting.

AN IMPORTANT ADVANTAGE OF STANDARD COSTS FOR INVENTORY COSTING

For inventory costing purposes, a simple yet important advantage realized by using standard costs is clerical convenience. The raw materials inventory subsidiary ledgers can be maintained in terms of physical quantities, but without pricing these quantities at actual input prices. Material requisitions may be costed at their standard cost. When the manufacturing process is completed, the finished goods are costed and recorded at their standard cost. Historical costs are not traced to either specific units or to batches of product. Although it may seem to be somewhat unusual at first, these record keeping conveniences may make a standard cost system worthwhile even without considering the other advantages which the use of a standard cost system affords.

OTHER USES OF STANDARD COSTS

A standard cost system usually is not limited to a single primary use. Rather, standards have many and varied applications in any type of organization. Standards are useful aids to management in planning, control, performance evaluation, cost reduction programs, pricing studies, cost interpretation studies, and other types of special studies made to assist management in the decision-making process. Well designed and accepted standards enhance employee motivation, because practical guidelines or benchmarks for performance measurement are identified, communicated, and may be attained under efficient and effective operating conditions.

A SIMPLE EXAMPLE: USING STANDARD COSTS

In order to illustrate the use of standard costs, a simple example will be used. We will assume that the Sherrill Manufacturing Company produces a single product that requires the use of 2 pounds of material (at a cost of $3 per pound) and 3 hours of direct labor (at a cost of $5 per hour). During the month of January, Sherrill purchased and used 23 pounds of materials (at $2 per pound) and employed 26 hours of direct labor (at a cost of $6 per hour). A total of 10 units of product were produced during the month. Sherrill uses a standard cost system.

Standard cost data for a unit of product for the Sherrill Manufacturing Company may be summarized as follows:

Standard cost of one unit of product:		
Materials:	2 pounds @ $3..................	$ 6
Labor:	3 hours @ $5..................	15
Standard Cost Per Unit...................		$21

Based upon this standard cost data, Sherrill's cost of producing 10 units during January should have been $210 (10 units @ $21). The actual cost of the 10 units produced by Sherrill during January was $202 (23 pounds of materials × $2 + 26 hours of labor × $6). The comparison of standard and actual costs for January may be summarized as follows:

Cost of producing 10 units of product:

	at Standard	at Actual		Difference
Materials (10 units × 2 lbs. × $3)..	$ 60	(23 × $2)	$ 46	$(14)
Labor (10 units × 3 hrs. × $5).....	150	(26 × $6)	156	6
Total	$210		$202	(8)

The actual costs of production for January ($202) were $8 less than the standard costs; this $8 difference ($202 vs. $210) is referred to as a variance. Variances are due to two factors: (1) the actual prices paid for materials and labor may differ compared to the standard prices established for these inputs, and (2) the actual quantities of materials (pounds) and labor (hours) used may differ from the standard quantities allowed for these items. For example, the price variance experienced by Sherrill Manufacturing Company during January would be calculated as follows:

$$\text{Price Variance} = \left(\begin{array}{c} \textit{Standard} \\ \textit{Price} \\ \textit{Per} \\ \textit{Unit} \end{array} - \begin{array}{c} \textit{Actual} \\ \textit{Price} \\ \textit{Per} \\ \textit{Unit} \end{array} \right) \times \begin{array}{c} \textit{Actual} \\ \textit{Number} \\ \textit{of Units} \end{array}$$

Using this approach, the material price variance is:

$$\$23 = (\$3 - \$2) \times 23 \text{ pounds}$$

This variance is favorable since the actual price paid per pound was less than the standard price per pound.

The labor price variance would be calculated as follows:

$$(\$26) = (\$5 - \$6) \times 26 \text{ hours}$$

This variance is unfavorable because the actual price paid per labor hour was more than the standard price per direct labor hour.

Note that in calculating both the material price variance and the labor price variance, the total *actual* number of units (pounds of materials purchased and hours of labor paid) for the period was used. Actual units are used because the objective of a price variance is to isolate the entire effect (for all inputs acquired) of any differences between the standard cost and the actual cost during the period.

The quantity variance experienced by Sherrill Manufacturing Company for the month of January would be computed as follows:

$$\text{Quantity Variance} = \left(\begin{array}{c} \textit{Standard} \\ \textit{Quantity} \\ \textit{Allowed} \end{array} - \begin{array}{c} \textit{Actual} \\ \textit{Quantity} \\ \textit{Used} \end{array} \right) \times \begin{array}{c} \textit{Standard} \\ \textit{Price} \\ \textit{Per} \\ \textit{Unit} \end{array}$$

Using this approach, the material quantity variance would be calculated as follows:

$$(\$9) = [(10 \times 2) - 23] \times \$3$$

The material quantity variance is unfavorable since the actual quantity of materials used during January (23 pounds) exceeded the standard quantity that should have been used in order to produce 10 units of product (10 units @ 2 pounds).

The labor quantity variance would be:

$$\$20 = [(10 \times 3) - 26] \times \$5$$

The labor quantity variance for January is favorable since the actual hours worked (26) were less than the standard hours allowed for January production (10 units × 3 hours).

Note that in calculating the quantity variances for both materials and labor the difference between the standard quantity allowed for the number of units produced and the actual quantity used is multiplied by the *standard* price per unit. The standard, rather than actual, price is used in calculating the quantity variance in order to isolate the effect of the quantity difference only (the difference between standard and actual prices were already isolated when the price variances were computed).

The variances between standard cost and actual cost for Sherrill Manufacturing Company for the month of January may be summarized as follows:

	Cost for January			Variance Due to	
	Standard	*Actual*	*Variance*	*Price*	*Quantity*
Materials	$ 60	$ 46	$14	$23	$(9)
Labor	150	156	(6)	(26)	20
Total	$210	$202	$ 8	$(3)	$11

Note that the $8 difference between the standard costs of $210 and the actual costs of $202 is explained by the calculation of the variances. The total price variance was $3 (unfavorable) — consisting of a $23 favorable material price variance and a $26 unfavorable labor price variance. The total quantity variance was $11 (favorable) — consisting of a $9 unfavorable material quantity variance and a $20 favorable labor quantity variance. Likewise, the $14 favorable variance for materials may be explained by the combination of the $23 (favorable) materials price variance and the $9 (unfavorable) materials quantity variance. The unfavorable labor variance of $6 consists of the $26 (unfavorable) labor price variance and the $20 (favorable) labor quantity variance.

A COMPREHENSIVE EXAMPLE: USING STANDARD COSTS

In September 19x1, the management of Sax Company decided that a standard cost system would assist the company in its planning, control, performance evaluation, and inventory costing activities. Prior to this time, the management of Sax Company had no experience in implementing a standard cost system. Therefore, it was decided that standard costs should first be introduced in the manufacturing area where the firm had the greatest production experience—the production of power turbine shafts. Power turbine shafts had become such a high volume item for Sax Company that the firm was scheduled to move into new production facilities for this product line during November. The company wished to have its standard cost job order inventory system on-line as of January 1, 19x2.

Sax Company established a team for developing its standard cost system that included at least one representative from each of the basic areas involved: production management, engineering, personnel, purchasing and cost accounting. The task of this group was to develop physical standards for manufacturing from which the company's cost accounting department could determine standard costs for inventory costing and control purposes.

The team viewed its assignment as being comprised of four distinct steps:

1. Developing a standard operations routing sheet.
2. Developing a standard bill of materials.
3. Developing manufacturing overhead standards at a defined level of capacity.
4. Converting all of the manufacturing cost factors into a format that the cost accounting department could use in developing a standard cost sheet.

Operations Routing Sheet

The new facility has modern equipment and the capacity for manufacturing almost any type of turbine shaft. However, Sax's management anticipates a demand for only power turbine shafts which have been manufactured from a two-inch diameter steel shaft or billet. Sax Company also presses ball bearings onto the ends of the turbine shafts to conform to the orders of specific customers. Since the difference in size is minor, there is no difference in the cost of the bearings because of this added feature.

Two departments were established in the new facility. The machining department is charged with the responsibility for all of the initial machining work performed on the shafts. The finishing and pressing department does all of the finishing work and presses on the bearings as ordered by customers. Although many different turbines can be produced, separate operations are not necessary for the production of any of the versions currently manufactured.

The initial decision required of the standards team was to determine whether or not rework time, waiting time and setup time should be included in the operations routing sheet. After careful consideration and study, it was decided that these cost factors should be considered in determining the manufacturing overhead rate that is charged to specific jobs. There are simply too many uncontrollable variables to assume that these factors are associated with or caused by any one specific job. By including rework time, waiting time, and setup time in the manufacturing overhead charge, these costs would be allocated or spread over all of the production of any given time period instead of affecting just a few units or batches of production.

The final operations routing sheet developed by Sax's standards team is presented in Illustration 1.

The standard time required for processing a power turbine shaft in the machining department is 20 minutes. Sax Company wishes to use attainable standards; therefore, based on their prior experience, an 11 percent allowance for delays is built into the standard time. Remember, all rework time, waiting time, and setup time is included in the manufacturing overhead rate.

The standard time for the finishing and pressing operation is 10 minutes. Again, based on prior experience, an 11 percent allowance for delays is built into the standard time to arrive at an attainable standard.

Standard Bill of Materials

Sax Company employs two basic materials in manufacturing its power turbine shafts: a two-inch diameter steel billet and various sizes of ball bearings. As previously indicated, the ball bearings are fitted to order, but most of the production is accomplished using off-the-shelf items with standard size ball bearings. There is little or no cost differential for the materials. However, because of market conditions, Sax Company commands a higher selling price for its made-to-order power turbine shafts.

Certain indirect materials and supplies are also used in producing the power turbine shafts. The standards team felt that these items should be included in the manufacturing overhead standard, because the cost of accounting for these indirect materials and supplies probably exceed any benefits that might be derived from a separate accounting for these items as direct materials.

Illustration 2 presents the standard bill of materials that was prepared for the power turbine shaft production.

After preparing the standard bill of materials, the standards team had to decide on an appropriate capacity measure to be used for developing the standard manufacturing overhead rate. It was also necessary to select a base for applying the overhead to the products produced.

Manufacturing Overhead Costs

The standards team decided to use the practical capacity of the new facility in determining a standard for overhead. Practical capacity is that capacity that can be attained under efficient and effective operating conditions. The practical output that can be expected from the new production facility is 1,800 power turbine shafts per month. Standard direct

Illustration 1

Sax Company
Operations Routing Sheets

Operations Routing Sheet		

Department <u>Machining</u>
Product Name <u>Power Turbine Shafts</u>
Materials <u>Round Steel Billet 2″ Diameter</u>

Operation	Minutes	Tools
Initial materials handling......	2	
Put into lathe.................	3	Lathe
Machining	3	Lathe
Check machining.............	2	Micrometer
Machining	1	Lathe
Check machining.............	2	Micrometer
Final machining	3	Lathe
Materials handling...........	2	
Allowance for delays (11%)....	<u>2</u>	
Standard Time	20	

Operations Routing Sheet		

Department <u>Finishing and Pressing</u>
Product Name <u>Power Turbine Shafts</u>
Materials <u>Round Steel Billet from Machining</u>
        <u>Ball Bearings</u>

Operation	Minutes	Tools
Initial materials handling......	2	
Finishing	3	Lathe and Polisher
Pressing	2	Hydraulic Press
Materials handling...........	2	
Allowance for delays (11%)....	<u>1</u>	
Standard Time	10	

Illustration 2

Sax Company
Standard Bill of Materials

Standard Bill of Materials		
Product Power Turbine Shafts		
Location	Required Number	Description
Aisle 84	1	Round Steel Billet 2″ Diameter
Aisle 85	2	Ball Bearings — Size Varies by Order

---

labor hours were chosen as the base to be used for the application of overhead. Direct labor hours were considered the factor most closely related to the variable portion of manufacturing overhead in the past, and management anticipates that this relationship will hold in the new facilities. The standards team estimated that 900 direct labor hours are required to produce a total of 1,800 power turbine shafts.

The standards team made an analysis of the overhead factors and related costs that are anticipated in the new facility during 19x2. The results of this study are presented in Illustration 3.

The standards teams based its analysis of overhead costs on an output measure, the production of 1,800 units, which represents the practical capacity of the new facilities. Standard manufacturing overhead at this level of production is determined to be $3.40 per unit produced. As previously indicated, standard direct labor hours were the input measure chosen and used as the basis for applying manufacturing overhead to the products produced. The relationship between the input and output measures is known. Two power turbine shafts can be produced, at standard, for each direct labor hour worked. Overhead per direct labor hour is twice the overhead rate per unit produced since one direct labor hour is required to produce every two units of product. The standard variable overhead rate per standard direct labor hour is $2.80, and the standard fixed manufacturing overhead per standard direct labor hour totals $4.00.

The Standard Cost Sheet

After the standards team prepared a standard operations routing sheet, a standard bill of materials, and the manufacturing overhead cost standards, the entire study was forwarded to the cost accounting department.

Illustration 3

Sax Company
Developing the Standard Manufacturing Overhead

Projected Practical Capacity: 1,800 Units
Standard Direct Labor Hours at Practical Capacity: 900 Hours

Standard Manufacturing Overhead Per Unit

	Variable per Unit Produced	Fixed	Total
Rework Time..........................	$ .10	0	$ 180
Waiting Time.........................	.06	0	108
Setup Time...........................	.08	0	144
Indirect Materials and Supplies...........	.60	$ 88	1,168
Indirect Labor........................	.46	272	1,100
Electricity...........................	.10	240	420
Heat................................	0	100	100
Equipment Depreciation.................	0	600	600
Plant Depreciation.....................	0	1,500	1,500
Factory Property Taxes..................	0	800	800
Totals.........................	$1.40	$3,600	$6,120

Standard Manufacturing Overhead per Unit:

Standard Variable Manufacturing Overhead per Unit................. $1.40

Standard Fixed Manufacturing Overhead per Unit........ $\dfrac{\$3,600}{1,800 \text{ units}}$ = 2.00

Standard Total Manufacturing Overhead per Unit................... $3.40

The cost accounting department made a further analysis of the data and developed the standard cost sheet for power turbine shaft production that is presented in Illustration 4.

A COMREHENSIVE EXAMPLE: ACCOUNTING FOR STANDARD COSTS

The actual process of recordkeeping for standard costs varies from company to company. To illustrate both the accounting for standard costs for purposes of inventory costing and the analysis of the related variances, assume that Sax Company wishes to integrate its standard costing system into its accounts as of January 1, 19x2.

Illustration 4

Sax Company
Standard Cost Sheet

Standard Cost Sheet
Product: <u>Power Turbine Shafts</u>
Basis for Cost Sheet: <u>One Unit</u>

Materials

Location	Standard Quantity	Standard Price per unit	Total
Aisle 84	1	$4.00	$4.00
Aisle 85	2	1.00	<u>2.00</u>
			<u>$6.00</u>

Labor

Department	Standard Hours	Standard Hourly Rate	Total
Machining	1/3	$6.00	$2.00
Finishing and Pressing	1/6	6.00	<u>1.00</u>
			<u>$3.00</u>

Manufacturing Overhead

Variable Overhead Per Unit	$1.40
Fixed Overhead Per Unit	<u>2.00</u>
Total Overhead Per Unit	<u>$3.40</u>

Cost Summary Per Unit

Materials @ Standard	1 Steel Billet @ $4.00	=	$ 4.00
	2 Ball Bearings @ 1.00	=	2.00
Direct Labor @ Standard	½ hour @ $6.00/hour	=	3.00
Variable Manufacturing Overhead @ Standard*		=	1.40
Fixed Manufacturing Overhead @ Standard*		=	<u>2.00</u>
Total Manufacturing Cost @ Standard			<u>$12.40</u>

*Basis of Application to Product is Standard Direct
Labor Hours. Application Rate is $6.80 Per Standard
Direct Labor Hour.

Sax Company decided that its standard cost system should be developed such that:

1. All inventories (raw materials, work-in-process, and finished goods) are accounted for at standard costs in preparing its internal monthly financial reports.
2. Any variances from standard costs are analyzed on a monthly basis, but the inventories will remain at standard costs. Variances are also analyzed and closed to the cost of goods sold account, **provided that** in so doing, the financial position and results of operations of Sax Company will not be materially distorted.

During January, 19x2, Sax Company entered into numerous transactions with regard to its power turbine shaft manufacturing operation. For purposes of this comprehensive example, these transactions are presented in summarized form along with the corresponding general journal entries. The related ledger accounts are also presented in "T"-account format.

Recording Raw Material Purchases

Since Sax Company wishes to maintain all of its inventory balances at standard costs, any inventory increases or withdrawals that affect raw materials, work-in-process, or finished goods must be recorded in the accounts at standard costs. This procedure permits all of the subsidiary accounts to be maintained in terms of physical units without including the corresponding dollar amounts in these records.

As raw materials are purchased, an unfavorable price variance is recognized if the price actually paid for the materials exceeds the standard price. Alternatively, if the price paid is less than the standard price, a favorable price variance is recognized at the point of the purchase.[1]

Transaction 1. During the month, Sax Company purchased a total of 1,850 steel billets at an average price of $4.02 per billet. Assuming that all of these purchases were paid for in cash during the year, the summary journal and "T"-account entries necessary to record the steel billet purchase transactions are as follows:

Raw Materials Inventory—Steel Billets ($4.00 X 1,850)....	7,400	
Raw Materials Price Variance [($4.02-$4.00) X 1,850].....	37	
Cash ($4.02 X 1,850)................................		7,437

---

[1] In some instances, companies record their raw material inventories at actual cost. Under such a system, price variances are not recognized until the raw materials are introduced into the production process.

	Cash		Raw Materials Inventory Steel Billets		Raw Materials Price Variance
1/1 Bal. 20,000		7,437 (1)	(1) 7,400		(1) 37

The raw materials price variances can also be calculated at this point using the following formula:

$$\begin{array}{l}\text{Raw Materials} \\ \text{Purchase Price} \\ \text{Variance}\end{array} = \left(\begin{array}{c}\text{Standard Price} \\ \text{Per Unit}\end{array} - \begin{array}{c}\text{Actual Price} \\ \text{Per Unit}\end{array}\right) \times \begin{array}{c}\text{Number of} \\ \text{Units} \\ \text{Purchased}\end{array}$$

$$= (\$4 - \$4.02) \times 1,850$$
$$= \$37 \text{ unfavorable price variance}$$

Another method which may be used to calculate this variance is one which utilizes the total purchases of steel billets as follows:

Actual purchases at standard prices (1,850 × $4)....	$7,400
Actual purchases at actual prices (1,850 × $4.02)....	7,437
Excess of total actual prices over standard prices.....	($ 37)

Both methods arrive at the identical answer.

Since all inventories are carried in the accounts at standard cost, the price variance is determined entirely within the accounting system. The debit to raw materials inventory or purchases will be at standard cost and the credit to accounts payable or cash will be at actual cost. The offsetting debit or credit will be the raw materials price variance. If the Sax Company had used actual costs in their accounting records, the formula approach could have been used for an analysis of the raw materials price variance. Both standard and actual costs must be analyzed in order to determine if the variance is favorable or unfavorable. In this case, an average price of $4.02 was actually paid for the steel billets. The standard price is $4.00. The price differential between the actual price ($4.02) and the standard price ($4.00) caused the price variance. If the standard price had been paid, any quantity could have been purchased and a price variance would not have been incurred. When standard costs are incorporated in an accounting system, an unfavorable variance is always recorded by a debit to a variance account while a favorable variance is indicated by a credit to a variance account. An unfavorable variance indicates that actual costs exceeded standard costs, while a favorable variance indicates that actual costs were less than standard costs.

Transaction 2. Sax Company purchased 4,000 ball bearings during the month and paid an average price of $.98 per ball bearing. These purchases of ball bearings caused a favorable material price variance since the price paid ($.98) was less than the standard price ($1.00).

Raw materials inventory—Ball Bearings ($1 × 4,000)..... 4,000
    Raw materials price variance [($1 − $.98) × 4,000].....   80
    Cash ($.98 × 4,000)...............................   3,920

Cash		Raw Materials Inventory—Ball Bearings	Raw Materials Price Variance	
1/1 Bal. 20,000	7,437 (1)	(2) 4,000	(1) 37	80 (2)
	3,920 (2)			

Again, the raw materials price variance could have been calculated using the formula as follows:

$$\begin{array}{l}\text{Raw Materials}\\\text{Purchase Price}\\\text{Variance}\end{array} = \left(\begin{array}{l}\text{Standard Price}\\\text{Per Unit}\end{array} - \begin{array}{l}\text{Actual Price}\\\text{Per Unit}\end{array}\right) \times \begin{array}{l}\text{Actual Number}\\\text{of Units}\\\text{Purchased}\end{array}$$

$$= (\$1 - \$.98) \times 4,000$$
$$= \$80 \text{ Favorable price variance}$$

If the total ball bearing purchases were used in the calculation, the variance would be computed as indicated below:

Actual purchases at standard prices (4,000 × $1)............ $4,000
Actual purchases at actual prices (4,000 × $.98)............. 3,920
Excess of standard prices over actual prices................ $ 80

Again, both of these methods will provide the same answer since the only difference is that the first calculation is made on a per unit basis while the second uses total figures.

When standard costs are incorporated into the accounting system, a favorable variance is reflected by a credit balance in a variance account. The term favorable when used in this regard indicates that the standard cost anticipated exceeded the actual cost incurred.

Recording Raw Material Transfers to Work-in-Process

Before a production run is initiated, a requisition is prepared for the standard amount of raw materials required to produce the goods. If the production run ultimately requires the use of additional raw materials, the foreman or other supervisory personnel in the production department must make a formal request for the additional raw materials needed. This request would, of course, ultimately cause an unfavorable raw materials quantity or usage variance. If less than the standard quantity of raw materials is used, then the excess materials are returned to the raw materials inventory. This return causes a favorable raw materials quantity or usage variance.

During January, Sax had formal production runs totaling 1,760 power turbine shafts. The materials requisitions, at standard quantities, were for 1,760 steel billets and 3,520 ball bearings. Additional requests for raw materials made by production foremen totaled 40 steel billets and 30 ball bearings. Therefore, the usage or quantity variances for both steel billets and ball bearings were unfavorable since the actual quantities used during the period exceeded the standard amounts.

Transaction 3. A total of 1,800 steel billets was transferred from the raw materials inventory to the work-in-process inventory. Of these billets, 1,760 were transferred by standard materials requisitions and 40 were transferred by excess materials requisitions. The summary journal entry necessary to record the transfer of all of the steel billets (both regular and excess) to work-in-process is as follows:

Work-in-process ($4 × 1,760)......................	7,040	
Raw materials quantity variance ($4 × 40).............	160	
Raw materials inventory—Steel Billets		
($4 × 1,800)..................................		7,200

Raw Materials Inventory Steel Billets		Work-in-Process		Raw Materials Quantity Variance	
(1) 7,400	7,200 (3)	(3) 7,040		(3) 160	

As was the case with raw materials, the work-in-process inventory account is recorded at standard costs. The raw materials quantity or usage variance can be calculated using the following formula:

$$\begin{array}{c}\text{Raw}\\\text{Materials}\\\text{Quantity}\\\text{Variance}\end{array} = \left(\begin{array}{ccc}\text{Standard}&&\text{Actual}\\\text{Quantity}&-&\text{Quantity}\\\text{Allowed}&&\text{Used}\end{array}\right) \times \begin{array}{c}\text{Standard}\\\text{Price}\\\text{Per}\\\text{Unit}\end{array}$$

= (1,760 − 1,800) × $4
= $160 Unfavorable materials quantity variance

Alternatively, if total amounts are used, the variance calculation is made as follows:

Standard quantity allowed at the standard price	
(1,760 × $4)...	$7,040
Actual quantity used at the standard price (1,800 × $4).......	7,200
Excess of quantity used at the standard price...............	($ 160)

Again, both methods yield the identical result.

A quantity variance measures the deviation of actual from standard usage. The variance experienced by Sax Company in January was caused by the fact that an excess of 40 steel billets over the standard quantity was used during the year. The standard price is employed in calculating the variance for both the actual quantities used and the standard quantities that should have been used. Of course, a variance is introduced into the analysis only if the standard and actual quantities differ.

Transaction 4.   A total of 3,550 ball bearings was transferred from raw materials inventory to the work-in-process inventory. Of these, 3,520 ball bearings were transferred by standard materials requisitions and 30 by excess materials requisitions. The summary transaction for the month would be recorded as follows:

Work-in-process ($1 × 3,520)............................	3,520	
Raw materials quantity variance ($1 × 30)..............	30	
Raw materials inventory—Ball Bearings		
($1 × 3,550).................................		3,550

Raw Materials Inventory Ball Bearings		Work-in-Process	Raw Materials Quantity Variance
(2) 4,000	3,550 (4)	(3) 7,040 (4) 3,520	(3) 160 (4) 30

Again, both the raw materials account and the work-in-process account are maintained at standard cost. The transfer to work-in-process can be calculated at standard in either of two ways. Since 1,760 power turbine shafts were produced in January, the amount of the standard inventory transfer should have been $2 × 1,760 or $3,520. Alternatively, as was presented in the previous journal entry, 3,520 bearings should have been transferred at the standard price of $1.

The variance is calculated using the following formula:

$$\begin{matrix} \text{Raw} \\ \text{Materials} \\ \text{Quantity} \\ \text{Variance} \end{matrix} = \left(\begin{matrix} \text{Standard} \\ \text{Quantity} \\ \text{Allowed} \end{matrix} - \begin{matrix} \text{Actual} \\ \text{Quantity} \\ \text{Used} \end{matrix} \right) \times \begin{matrix} \text{Standard} \\ \text{Price} \\ \text{Per} \\ \text{Unit} \end{matrix}$$

$$= (3,520 - 3,550) \times \$1$$
$$= \$30 \text{ Unfavorable materials quantity variance}$$

If total amounts are used, the variance calculation is made as follows:

Standard quantity allowed at the standard price	
(3,520 × $1)..	$3,520
Actual quantity used at the standard price (3,550 × $1).......	3,550
Excess of quantity used at the standard price...............	($ 30)

This unfavorable material quantity variance was caused by the fact that 30 ball bearings in excess of the standard amount were used in the production process during the month.

Recording Direct Labor Costs

All direct labor costs are charged to jobs at the standard labor rate using the standard time established for performing a particular job or operation. However, employees are paid based on their actual pay rate and the actual amount of time that they work. Given these two statements, it is apparent that two types of direct labor variances are possible. A rate of pay either greater or lesser than the standard wage rate may be paid. This would cause Sax Company to recognize a rate variance for direct labor. In addition, the amount or quantity of direct labor worked may be more than or less than the standard amount. This would cause an efficiency or usage variance for direct labor.

Transaction 5. During January, a total of 890 direct labor hours was used by Sax Company to produce the 1,760 power turbine shafts. This amount, as per standard, *should* have been 880 hours. The actual payroll for this direct labor totaled $5,251. This amount represented an average cost of $5.90 for each direct labor hour worked. There were no wages payable at the end of the year.

When the standards team developed the standard for labor time (Illustration 1), it established the basis for recording the standard labor on the job cost sheets. As jobs progress through the factory, the actual time for each job is also recorded on the job cost sheets. The standard time at the standard rate is recorded by a debit to the work-in-process inventory account. Remember, all manufacturing inventory accounts are maintained at standard costs by Sax Company. Any difference between the standard time (recorded at the standard rate) and the actual time (recorded at the standard rate) is reflected in the labor efficiency or usage variance. The difference between the actual labor rates which were paid and the standard rates is multiplied by the actual hours worked to determine the labor rate variance.

The summary entry for January to record direct labor costs is as follows:

Work-in-process ($6 × 880)............................	5,280	
Direct labor efficiency variance [$6 × (890 − 880)].......	60	
Cash..		5,251
Direct labor rate variance [($6 − $5.90) × 890]........		89

Cash		
1/1 Bal. 20,000	7,437 (1)	
	3,920 (2)	
	5,251 (5)	

Work-in-Process	
(3) 7,040	
(4) 3,520	
(5) 5,280	

Direct Labor Efficiency Variance	
(5) 60	

Direct Labor Rate Variance	
	89 (5)

The debit to the work-in-process account reflects the standard rate per hour ($6) multiplied by the standard number of hours (880) allowed to produce 1,760 power turbine shafts.

The debit to the direct labor efficiency variance account reflects the difference between the actual direct labor hours worked (890) and the standard hours that should have been worked (880) at the standard rate ($6). Since actual hours worked exceeded the standard established for hours worked, the direct labor efficiency variance is unfavorable. The credit to cash of $5,251 represents the actual direct labor wages paid to employees. The standard wage rate is $6 per hour, and employees were paid an average rate of $5.90 per hour for the 890 hours worked during January. Therefore, the direct labor rate variance was favorable and is recorded by a credit of $89 [($6 − $5.90) × 890] to the direct labor rate variance account.

Alternatively, the labor efficiency and rate variances could have been calculated using the following formula:

$$\begin{matrix} Direct \\ Labor \\ Efficiency \\ Variance \end{matrix} = \left(\begin{matrix} Standard \\ Hours \\ Allowed \end{matrix} - \begin{matrix} Actual \\ Hours \\ Used \end{matrix} \right) \times \begin{matrix} Standard \\ Wage \\ Rate \\ Per\ Hour \end{matrix}$$

$$= (880 - 890) \times \$6$$
$$= \$60\ \text{Unfavorable direct labor efficiency variance}$$

Or, if total amounts are used, the calculation is:

Standard hours allowed at the standard rate (880 × $6)	$5,280
Actual hours used at the standard rate (890 × $6)	5,340
Excess of quantity used at the standard price	($ 60)

$$
\begin{array}{c}
\textit{Direct} \\
\textit{Labor} \\
\textit{Rate} \\
\textit{Variance}
\end{array}
=
\left(
\begin{array}{c}
\textit{Standard} \\
\textit{Rate}
\end{array}
-
\begin{array}{c}
\textit{Actual} \\
\textit{Rate}
\end{array}
\right)
\times
\begin{array}{c}
\textit{Actual} \\
\textit{Quantity} \\
\textit{of Labor} \\
\textit{Used}
\end{array}
$$

= ($6 − $5.90) × 890

= $89 Favorable direct labor rate variance

Or, if total amounts are used:

Standard rate at the actual hours worked (890 × $6).............	$5,340
Actual rate at the actual hours worked (890 × $5.90)............	5,251
Excess of standard rate at the actual hours worked..............	$ 89

The above computations indicate that the method for calculating the labor efficiency or usage variance follows the same principles used to calculate the raw materials usage variance. The principles underlying the computation of the labor rate variance and the raw materials price variance are also identical.

Applying Manufacturing Overhead to Production

Sax Company has decided to use standard direct labor hours as a basis for applying manufacturing overhead to its products. At this point it should be noted that since all inventories are carried at standard costs, Sax Company uses standard direct labor hours rather than actual direct labor hours because to do otherwise would allow the efficiencies or inefficiencies of labor to affect the amount of overhead absorbed by a specific job. By using standard direct labor hours, the inventories are maintained at standard costs. The use of standard direct labor hours provides the same absorption of overhead by products as the output measure, units finished, would provide. Standard direct labor hours are relatively easy to calculate and are homogeneous in that one standard direct labor hour is identical to all other standard hours.

The manufacturing overhead applied at standard for Sax Company is determined by multiplying the total standard direct labor hours for January (880) by the manufacturing overhead rate at standard (obtained from the standard cost sheet presented in Illustration 4). The standard manufacturing overhead rate is $6.80 per standard direct labor hour.

Transaction 6. The manufacturing overhead applied to the 1,760 power turbine shafts produced in January totaled $5,984 ($6.80 × 880). The summary journal and "T"-account entries required to record the overhead for January are as follows:

Work-in-process ($6.80 × 880)........................	5,984	
Manufacturing overhead—control ($6.80 × 880).......		5,984

Work-in-Process	Manufacturing Overhead—Control
(3) 7,040	5,984 (6)
(4) 3,520	
(5) 5,280	
(6) 5,984	

Recording Transfers from Work-in-Process

As goods are completed, they are transferred from the work-in-process inventory to the finished goods inventory at their standard cost.

Transaction 7. During January, a total of 1,760 power turbine shafts were completed and transferred to the finished goods inventory. The standard cost of one power turbine shaft is $12.40, according to Sax Company's standard cost sheet (Illustration 4). The total transferred to finished goods is therefore 1,760 × $12.40 or $21,824. The summary journal and "T"-account entries required to recognize the transfers from work-in-process to finished goods are:

Finished goods inventory ($12.40 × 1,760)............. 21,824
    Work-in-Process ($12.40 × 1,760)................... 21,824

Work-in-Process		Finished Goods	
(3) 7,040	21,824 (7)	(7) 21,824	
(4) 3,520			
(5) 5,280			
(6) 5,984			

For any goods sold during January, the cost of goods sold associated with these sales would also be recognized at standard cost. (Sales for the period will be recorded in Transaction 9.)

Recording Actual Manufacturing Overhead Costs

Sax Company's actual manufacturing overhead costs for January totaled $6,320. An analysis of the subsidiary records revealed the following components of the actual manufacturing overhead for January:

Rework Time.........................	$ 160
Waiting Time........................	100
Setup Time..........................	140
Indirect Materials and Supplies..........	1,100
Indirect Labor......................	1,160
Electricity..........................	700
Heat...............................	60
Equipment Depreciation...............	600
Plant Depreciation....................	1,500
Factory Property Taxes.................	800
	$6,320

The rework time, waiting time, setup time and indirect labor were all labor costs which were paid but which were not reflected in the direct labor payroll recorded in Transaction 5. The indirect materials and supplies were obtained from the materials and supplies inventory. The electricity, heat, and property taxes were all paid. The total cash outlay for the manufacturing overhead items for the period was $3,120.

Transaction 8. Actual manufacturing overhead costs incurred during the period are $6,320. The summary entry necessary to record the actual manufacturing overhead for January is as follows:

Manufacturing Overhead—Control	6,320	
Cash		3,120
Indirect Materials and Supplies Inventory		1,100
Accumulated Depreciation—Equipment		600
Accumulated Depreciation—Plant		1,500

Manufacturing Overhead—Control		Cash	
(8) 6,320	5,984 (6)	1/1 Bal. 20,000	7,437 (1)
			3,920 (2)
			5,251 (5)
			3,120 (8)

Indirect Materials and Supplies Inventory	
1/1 Bal. 2,000	1,100 (8)

Accumlated Depreciation—Equipment		Accumulated Depreciation—Plant	
	600 (8)		1,500 (8)

Manufacturing overhead of $5,984 at standard cost was applied to the products during the month in Transaction 6. As indicated in Transaction 8, however, the actual manufacturing overhead for the year was $6,320. Manufacturing overhead costs were, therefore, underapplied by a total of $336. This difference will be analyzed later in this chapter.

Recording Cost of Goods Sold at Standard

The finished goods inventory is recorded and accounted for at standard cost. As the goods are sold, any cost of goods sold is also recognized at standard cost.

Transaction 9. A total of 1,600 power turbine shafts were sold during January at an average selling price of $50 per shaft. All but $2,000 of these sales had been collected by month-end.

The summary entry to record this transaction is as follows:

Cash [($50 × 1,600) − $2,000]...................... 78,000
Accounts receivable................................   2,000
    Sales revenue ($50 × 1,600)........................   80,000

Cash			Accounts Receivable	
1/1 Bal. 20,000	7,437 (1)		(9) 2,000	
(9) 78,000	3,920 (2)			
	5,251 (5)			
	3,120 (8)			

Sales Revenue	
	80,000 (9)

The cost of goods sold for January is recorded by the following entry:

Cost of goods sold ($12.40 × 1,600)................... 19,840
    Finished goods inventory ($12.40 × 1,600)............   19,840

Cost of Goods Sold		Finished Goods Inventory	
(9) 19,840		(7) 21,824	19,840 (9)

The cost of goods sold account represents the standard cost of the goods sold during the period. For income statement purposes, the management of Sax Company wishes to close out all of the variance accounts to the cost of goods sold account at the end of the month.

Closing the Variance Accounts

At the end of January, Sax Company decided to adjust the amount of cost of goods sold used for income statement purposes to include the net effect of all of the variances from standard costs which were experienced during the month. This means that the cost of goods sold account will absorb all of the differences between standard and actual costs that were recognized during the month. In effect, closing all the variance accounts to the cost of goods sold account will convert Sax's standard cost system to an actual cost system for income statement purposes.

The balances in the cost of goods sold account and the individual variance accounts at the end of January are as follows:

Raw Materials Price Variance	
(1) 37	80 (2)
	43

Raw Materials Quantity Variance	
(3) 160	
(4) 30	
190	

Direct Labor Efficiency Variance	
(5) 60	
60	

Direct Labor Rate Variance	
	89 (5)
	89

Manufacturing Overhead— Control	
(8) 6,320	5,984 (6)
336	

Cost of Goods Sold	
(9) 19,840	
19,840	

Transaction 10.   *The variance accounts should be closed to the cost of goods sold account.* The following journal entry is necessary:

Cost of Goods Sold........................	454	
Raw Materials Price Variance..............	43	
Direct Labor Rate Variance................	89	
Raw Materials Quantity Variance..........		190
Direct Labor Efficiency Variance..........		60
Manufacturing Overhead—Control........		336

Raw Materials Price Variance	
(1) 37	80 (2)
(10) 43	43

Raw Materials Quantity Variance	
(3) 160	
(4) 30	
190	190 (10)

Direct Labor Efficiency Variance	
(5) 60	
60	60 (10)

Direct Labor Rate Variance	
	89 (5)
(10) 89	89

Manufacturing Overhead— Control	
(8) 6,320	5,984 (6)
336	336 (10)

Cost of Goods Sold	
(9) 19,840	
(10) 454	
20,294	

By adopting this procedure, the management of Sax Company is assuming that the net variance of $454 is immaterial for purposes of financial reporting. This does not imply, however, that the individual variances are immaterial or insignificant for purposes of managerial analysis. Management will decide which variances to investigate in detail.

CONTROLLING MANUFACTURING OVERHEAD WHEN COMPARED TO OTHER PRODUCT COSTS

Manufacturing overhead is a major production cost. In fact, the total manufacturing overhead costs may be as large or larger than the direct material or direct labor costs. But the individual cost items in the total overhead cost may not justify the in-depth analysis and control techniques that can be justified for direct materials and direct labor. That is, the amount of cost at risk for the individual items may not be worth an item-by-item analysis on a continual basis. As a general statement, it can be said that direct material and direct labor costs and the effectiveness and efficiency of their use may be reviewed on a daily or hourly basis, but manufacturing overhead costs are reviewed and analyzed on a basis covering a longer time period such as a week or a month.

Direct materials and direct labor are considered to be variable costs within the relevant range of production. Total manufacturing overhead is a mixed cost (semi-variable) with both a fixed and variable component of cost within the relevant range of production. The directly variable relationship between the financial and physical aspects of both direct materials and direct labor make controlling and analyzing variances from these production costs easier and more meaningful than a similar analysis of manufacturing overhead. Standard costs can be used as a tool in controlling direct materials and direct labor costs on a daily basis. Standard costs in conjunction with departmental overhead budgets are used in controlling manufacturing overhead.

Concept of a Flexible Budget

A major underlying assumption of standard costs for manufacturing is that a known relationship exists between the production inputs and output. This relationship can be expressed in physical measures or in dollars when the physical inputs are multiplied by their respective costs. For example, the standard cost sheet for one power turbine shaft for Sax Company is presented in Illustration 4.

It takes one steel billet and two ball bearings to manufacture one power turbine shaft. The quantity of steel billets necessary to meet the January production of 1,760 power turbine shafts is 1,760 steel billets. The input to output relationship at standard is defined. The standard cost of a steel billet is $4. The standard cost of the steel billets needed to output 1,760 power turbine shafts is 1,760 billets $\times$ $4 or $7,040. The input to output relationship for ball bearings in Illustration 4 is a standard input of two ball bearings, at a standard cost of $1 per ball bearing, for every power turbine shaft produced.

Input to output relationships for labor and overhead from Illustration 4 could also be identified. The critical factor in identifying the relationships is a knowledge of the input to output factors and the cost per unit of the input factor. The knowledge of the cost behavior patterns and costs within the relevant range of production permits the use of the *flexible budget* in analyzing both the efficiency and effectiveness of the use of input factors in producing the required output at the required quality and cost. With a flexible budget, a budget can be established for any level of activity.

The Flexible Budget— An Example

If the production standards from Illustration 4 are used as the basis for a flexible standard cost budget for power turbine production, a budget could be prepared for any level of activity. Illustration 5 has the flexible budget prepared at production levels of 1,700, 1,760, and 1,800 power turbine shafts. Once the output level of power turbine shafts is determined, the production input factors in Illustration 4 are used to develop the flexible budget.

Illustration 5

Sax Company
Flexible Budget for Power Turbine Shaft Production

Input Cost Factors	Budget Formula per Unit of Activity	Fixed Costs	Variable Costs Budgeted Activity Level		
			1,700 Units	1,760 Units	1,800 Units
Direct Material:					
Billets	$ 4.00 per Unit		$ 6,800	$ 7,040	$ 7,200
Bearings	2.00 per Unit		3,400	3,520	3,600
Direct Labor	3.00 per Unit		5,100	5,280	5,400
Manufacturing Overhead:					
Variable Costs	1.40 per Unit		2,380	2,464	2,520
Fixed Costs	-0-	$3,600			
	$10.40 per Unit	$3,600	$17,680	$18,304	$18,720

As can be seen from Illustration 5, the flexible portion of the flexible budget for production costs is caused by the variable cost components. The fixed cost component of the flexible budget is the *static* component of the budget. The flexible budget formula for total production cost is:

$$\begin{pmatrix} Total \\ Production \\ Costs \end{pmatrix} = \begin{pmatrix} Standard \\ Budgeted\ Fixed \\ Production\ Costs \end{pmatrix} + \begin{pmatrix} Standard\ Variable \\ Production\ Cost\ Per \\ Unit\ of\ Activity \end{pmatrix} \times \begin{pmatrix} Level \\ of \\ Activity \end{pmatrix}$$

This formula can provide the standard production cost in total for any projected activity level within the relevant range. For an after-the-fact analysis of what production costs should have been given the level of activity attained, the formula can be used by introducing the actual level of activity in the calculations. For example, using the data in Illustration 5, if 1,770 power turbine shafts were the projected (or actual production), the total manufacturing costs should be (or should have been), respectively:

$$\begin{aligned} \text{Total manufacturing costs} &= \$3,600 + (\$10.40 \times 1,770 \text{ Power turbine shafts}) \\ &= \$3,600 + \$18,408 \\ &= \$22,008 \end{aligned}$$

Each of the individual cost items can also be calculated using the concept of the flexible budget. This concept was implicitly assumed in this chapter when analyzing the variances from direct materials and direct labor. The flexible budget concept and its use must be explicitly used to perform the necessary calculations in analyzing manufacturing overhead costs.

A COMPREHENSIVE EXAMPLE THE FLEXIBLE MANUFACTURING OVERHEAD BUDGET

At the close of January, Sax Company knew the actual total overhead for the year was $6,320. The company also knew that the amount of manufacturing overhead that had been applied to production totaled $5,984. The difference between these two amounts, $336, represents the total overhead variance for the month. Sax's management is interested in an analysis of this variance and wishes to identify its underlying causes.

Recall that the standard costs used for the application of overhead were developed for a practical production level of 1,800 units, or 900 standard direct labor hours. Actual production in January totaled 1,760 units, or 880 standard direct labor hours. For any meaningful analysis of overhead, a concept not normally encountered in the accounting records must be introduced, that is, the concept of the flexible budget. With regard to manufacturing overhead, the flexible budget indicates the amount of overhead which should have been incurred at standard rates if Sax Company had known in advance that 1,760 rather than 1,800 units were going to be produced during January.

The total flexible budget for Sax Company may be developed after-the-fact from the information provided in Illustration 6. The standard variable manufacturing overhead cost was $1.40 per unit produced for a total of

---

Illustration 6

Sax Company
Developing the Standard Manufacturing Overhead

Projected Practical Capacity: 1,800 Units
Standard Direct Labor Hours at Practical Capacity: 900 Hours

Standard Manufacturing Overhead

	Variable per Unit Produced	*Fixed*	*Total*
Rework Time...............................	$ .10	0	$ 180
Waiting Time..............................	.06	0	108
Setup Time................................	.08	0	144
Indirect Materials and Supplies................	.60	$ 88	1,168
Indirect Labor.............................	.46	272	1,100
Electricity	.10	240	420
Heat.....................................	0	100	100
Equipment Depreciation......................	0	600	600
Plant Depreciation.........................	0	1,500	1,500
Factory Property Taxes......................	0	800	800
Totals................................	$1.40	$3,600	$6,120

Standard Manufacturing Overhead per Unit:
Standard Variable Manufacturing Overhead per Unit.................. $1.40
Standard Fixed Manufacturing Overhead per Unit $\frac{\$3,600}{1,800 \text{ units}} =$ 2.00

Standard Total Manufacturing Overhead per Unit..................... $3.40

($1.40 × 1,760 power turbine shafts) or $2,464 in January. Fixed manufacturing overhead *at standard* totaled $3,600. At 1,760 units, or 880 standard direct labor hours, the flexible budget is derived as follows:

$$\text{Flexible Budget} = \begin{array}{c}\text{Standard Fixed}\\\text{Manufacturing}\\\text{Overhead}\\\text{Costs}\end{array} + \left(\begin{array}{c}\text{Standard Variable}\\\text{Manufacturing}\\\text{Overhead Cost}\\\text{Per Unit}\end{array} \times \begin{array}{c}\text{Actual}\\\text{Units}\\\text{Produced}\end{array}\right)$$

= $3,600 + ($1.40 × 1,760 units)
= $3,600 + $2,464
= $6,064

If the variable overhead costs are in fact variable and the fixed overhead costs are indeed fixed, at 1,760 units or 880 standard direct labor hours, Sax Company's planned total overhead cost would be $6,064. A flexible budget could have been prepared for each specific overhead

Illustration 7

Sax Company
The Flexible Budget

	Variable* per Unit Produced	Fixed*	Total Budgeted Cost at 1,760 Units or 880 Standard Hours
Rework Time...................	$ .10	0	$ 176.00
Waiting Time...................	.06	0	105.60
Setup Time....................	.08	0	140.80
Indirect Materials and Supplies.....	.60	$ 88	1,144.00
Indirect Labor.................	.46	272	1,081.60
Electricity.....................	.10	240	416.00
Heat.........................	0	100	100.00
Equipment Depreciation..........	0	600	600.00
Plant Depreciation..............	0	1,500	1,500.00
Factory Property Taxes...........	0	800	800.00
Total......................	$1.40	$3,600	$6,064.00

*From Illustration 6.

cost and the total would have remained the same. Illustration 7 presents a flexible budget for manufacturing overhead costs at a production level of 1,760 units or 880 standard direct labor hours.

A COMPREHENSIVE EXAMPLE: THE VOLUME VARIANCE FOR MANUFACTURING OVERHEAD

The total underapplied overhead of $336 for Sax Company is caused, in part, by a volume variance. Sax Company based its standard overhead rates for applying manufacturing overhead on an anticipated level of production of 1,800 units or 900 standard direct labor hours (Illustration 6). Since the actual production achieved was 1,760 units or 880 standard direct labor hours, a portion of the fixed manufacturing overhead incurred was not applied to production.

An analysis of the resultant volume variance can be made based either on the number of units produced or on the standard direct labor hours. Alternatively, the total flexible budget may be compared to the total overhead applied to production. Remember, the volume variance relates to the absorption of fixed manufacturing overhead—*not* variable manufacturing overhead—into the cost of production.

Volume Variance Based on Units Produced

Standard Fixed Overhead per Unit Produced...................	$ 2 *
Practical Capacity (units).....................................	1,800
Actual Production (units).....................................	1,760
	40
Unfavorable volume variance = 40 units × $2 =	$ 80

Volume Variance Based on Standard Direct Labor Hours Used

Standard Fixed Overhead per Standard Direct Labor Hour.......	$ 4 *
Practical Capacity (Standard Direct Labor Hours)..............	900
Actual Production (Standard Direct Labor Hours)..............	880
	20
Unfavorable volume variance =	
20 Direct labor hours × $4 =	$ 80

*Volume Variance Based on Applied Manufacturing
Overhead and the Flexible Budget*

Manufacturing Overhead Applied to Products..................	$5,984
Flexible Budget..	6,064
Unfavorable Volume Variance...........................	$ 80

*From Illustration 3.

Of course, each of these methods provides the identical answer because each examines the same variance. The volume variance for Sax Company is unfavorable because the company did not produce a sufficient number of units to apply all of the fixed manufacturing overhead at standard to its production. Thus, in effect, the company lost the opportunity to produce at a practical capacity level in January.

A COMPREHENSIVE EXAMPLE: THE BUDGET VARIANCE FOR MANUFACTURING OVERHEAD

The budget variance analysis determines the amount by which the total actual overhead deviated from the overhead determined by the flexible budget. For Sax Company, the budget variance represents an attempt to determine the portion of underapplied manufacturing overhead of $336 which was due to a deviation from the amount of manufacturing overhead costs that should have been incurred at standard costs and a production level of 1,760 units. Standard manufacturing overhead costs for this level of production can be determined by using the flexible budget. The actual amount of manufacturing overhead costs are obtained from the accounting records. For Sax Company, the actual manufacturing overhead costs for the year were recorded in Transaction 8.

The budget variance plus the volume variance must equal the total overhead variance. In this case, the total overhead variance is $336 (unfavorable) and the volume variance is $80 (unfavorable); thus, the budget variance must be $256 (also unfavorable). Note that there is absolutely no reason why both components of the overhead variance should be either favorable or unfavorable. One of the variances may be favorable and the other unfavorable. The budget variance is calculated using either the actual units produced or standard direct labor hours, and then determining the difference between the total flexible budget costs and the actual costs incurred.

Budget Variance Based on Units Produced

Actual manufacturing overhead costs......................	$6,320
Flexible budget $3,600 + (1,760 units × $1.40)............	6,064
Unfavorable budget variance...........................	($ 256)

Budget Variance Based on Standard Direct Labor Hours

Actual manufacturing overhead costs......................	$6,320
Flexible budget $3,600 + (880 standard direct labor hours × $2.80)............................	6,064
Unfavorable budget variance...........................	($ 256)

In this example, the budget variance is unfavorable because the actual manufacturing overhead costs were greater than anticipated at the actual level of 1,760 units of production, or 880 standard direct labor hours.

The cost items that caused the unfavorable variance can be identified. If the flexible budget for manufacturing overhead is calculated on an item-by-item basis and compared with the actual item costs, then the individual variances should total the budget variance. Illustration 8 presents an item-by-item analysis of the manufacturing overhead costs that caused the budget variance.

Rework time, waiting time, setup time, indirect materials and supplies and heat caused favorable cost variances totaling $106.40. Indirect labor and electricity caused unfavorable cost variances totaling $362.40. The manufacturing overhead budget variance was the net unfavorable variance of the individual items, $256.

Dividing the under or overapplied overhead into two variances is referred to as two-way analysis of overhead variances. A two-way analysis of overhead variances is presented as follows:

Actual Manufacturing Overhead Costs.........	$6,320		
		Budget Variance (Unfavorable)	($256)
Flexible Budget.............................	$6,064		
		Volume Variance (Unfavorable)	($ 80)
Applied Manufacturing Overhead Costs........	$5,984		

Illustration 8

Sax Company
Manufacturing Overhead Budget Variance

	Total Budgeted Cost * at 1,760 Units or 880 Standard Hours	Total Actual † Cost at 1,760 Units	Manufacturing ‡ Overhead Budget Variance
Rework Time	$ 176.00	$ 160.00	$ 16.00
Waiting Time	105.60	100.00	5.60
Setup Time	140.80	140.00	.80
Indirect Materials and Supplies	1,144.00	1,100.00	44.00
Indirect Labor	1,081.60	1,160.00	(78.40)
Electricity	416.00	700.00	(284.00)
Heat	100.00	60.00	40.00
Equipment Depreciation	600.00	600.00	0
Plant Depreciation	1,500.00	1,500.00	0
Factory Property Taxes	800.00	800.00	0
Totals	$6,064.00	$6,320.00	($256.00)

* From Illustration 7.

†From information for Transaction 8.

‡( )'s indicate an unfavorable variance.

SUMMARY

A standard cost system is often used in conjunction with a job order or process costing system to facilitate the costing of inventory. In a standard cost system, products are costed at that cost which should have been incurred under efficient and effective operations. Any deviations from the standard cost are reflected as variances at the end of the period.

Standard costs differ from normal costs in that normal costs are a combination of actual and expected costs, whereas standard costs are entirely based on costs expected under a given set of conditions. In addition to the obvious clerical convenience resulting from their use, standard costs are useful aids in planning, control, performance evaluation, and other management activities. If well-designed, standard costs may also be an effective means of employee motivation.

Standard costs are based on the physical standards of production. Physical standards relate to the quantities of materials, labor, processing time, etc., that are required under standard conditions to produce the product. Several types of standard costs are in general use. These types include standards based on (1) historical or past performance, (2) ideal or engineering performance, and (3) attainable performance. Of these, standard costs based on attainable performance are preferred for management accounting purposes.

The variance in direct materials cost and in direct labor cost can usually be explained by two factors: (1) the actual price paid differing from the standard price (referred to as the price or rate variance) and (2) the actual quantity used differing from the standard quantity (referred to as the quantity or efficiency variance).

Total manufacturing overhead is a semi-variable cost with both a fixed and variable component. A flexible budget can be used to determine manufacturing overhead at standard costs at any level of production within the relevant range. The flexible portion of the flexible budget is caused by the variable cost components of manufacturing overhead. The fixed cost component of the flexible budget is the static component of the budget.

The analysis of overhead variances can be done using a two-variance approach. The difference or total variance being analyzed is the difference between actual manufacturing overhead and manufacturing overhead applied to production. With a two-way analysis, this difference will be analyzed on the presumption that only two factors could have caused the variance: a volume deviation or a budget deviation. The volume variance occurs as the result of attaining a level of production other than the standard or practical capacity level, and over or under applyng fixed manufacturing overhead to products produced. The budget variance is the difference between the flexible budget, based on actual activity, and the actual manufacturing overhead costs that were incurred.

Following is a summary of the equations of the standard cost variances listed in this chapter:

1. $\text{Material Price Variance} = \left(\begin{array}{c} \textit{Standard Price Per Unit} \end{array} - \begin{array}{c} \textit{Actual Price Per Unit} \end{array} \right) \times \begin{array}{c} \textit{Actual Number of Units Purchased} \end{array}$

2. $\text{Material Quantity Variance} = \left(\begin{array}{c} \textit{Standard Quantity Allowed} \end{array} - \begin{array}{c} \textit{Actual Quantity Used} \end{array} \right) \times \begin{array}{c} \textit{Standard Price Per Unit} \end{array}$

3. $\text{Direct Labor Rate Variance} = \left(\begin{array}{c} \textit{Standard Rate Per Hour} \end{array} - \begin{array}{c} \textit{Actual Rate Per Hour} \end{array} \right) \times \begin{array}{c} \textit{Actual Number of Hours of Direct Labor Used} \end{array}$

4. $\begin{matrix} \text{Direct} \\ \text{Labor} \\ \text{Efficiency} \\ \text{Variance} \end{matrix} = \left(\begin{matrix} \text{Standard} \\ \text{Hours} \\ \text{Allowed} \end{matrix} - \begin{matrix} \text{Actual} \\ \text{Hours} \\ \text{Used} \end{matrix} \right) \times \begin{matrix} \text{Standard} \\ \text{Wage Rate} \\ \text{Per} \\ \text{Hour} \end{matrix}$

5. $\begin{matrix} \text{Volume} \\ \text{Variance for} \\ \text{Manufacturing} \\ \text{Overhead} \end{matrix} = \left(\begin{matrix} \text{Standard} \\ \text{Production} \\ \text{Capacity} \\ \text{in Units} \end{matrix} - \begin{matrix} \text{Actual} \\ \text{Production} \\ \text{in Units} \end{matrix} \right) \times \begin{matrix} \text{Standard Fixed} \\ \text{Overhead Rate} \\ \text{Per Unit} \\ \text{Produced} \end{matrix}$

(This equation may substitute direct labor hours if fixed overhead rate has also been calculated using direct labor hours.)

6. $\begin{matrix} \text{Fixed} \\ \text{Overhead} \\ \text{Rate} \end{matrix} = \dfrac{\text{Total Fixed Overhead Costs at Standard}}{\begin{matrix}\text{Projected Practical Production Capacity} \\ \text{(in Units)}\end{matrix}}$

7. $\begin{matrix} \text{Budget} \\ \text{Variance for} \\ \text{Manufacturing} \\ \text{Overhead} \end{matrix} = \begin{matrix} \text{Flexible} \\ \text{Budget} \end{matrix} - \begin{matrix} \text{Actual} \\ \text{Manufacturing} \\ \text{Overhead} \\ \text{Costs} \end{matrix}$

8. $\begin{matrix} \text{Flexible} \\ \text{Budget for} \\ \text{Manufacturing} \\ \text{Overhead} \end{matrix} = \begin{matrix} \text{Fixed Costs} \\ \text{at Standard} \\ \text{for Projected} \\ \text{Practical Capacity} \end{matrix} + \left(\begin{matrix} \text{Actual} \\ \text{Level of} \\ \text{Production} \\ \text{in Units} \end{matrix} \times \begin{matrix} \text{Variable} \\ \text{Per Unit} \\ \text{Costs} \\ \text{at Standard} \end{matrix} \right)$

(This equation may substitute standard direct labor hours allowed if variable costs are related to direct labor hours.)

KEY DEFINITIONS

Attainable standard—a satisfactory level of efficiency where the ideal standard has been modified to allow for normal tolerable inefficiencies.

Budget variance—an overhead variance which results when the actual total manufacturing overhead costs differ from the total manufacturing overhead costs budgeted for the actual level of production.

Favorable variance—a variance which occurs in a standard cost accounting system when actual costs are less than standard costs. A favorable variance is recorded by a credit to a variance account.

Flexible budget—a budget used to calculate a total budgeted manufacturing overhead cost for a given level of production.

Ideal standard—the highest level of efficiency attainable, based on all input factors interacting perfectly under ideal or optimum conditions.

Labor efficiency or usage variance—a variance occurring in a standard cost accounting system when the actual amount or quantity of direct labor used differs from the standard amount required.

Labor rate variance—a variance which occurs in a standard cost accounting system when the actual pay rate differs from the standard pay rate for direct labor.

Materials price variance—a variance which occurs in a standard cost accounting system when actual prices paid for raw materials differ from the standard prices.

Materials quantity or usage variance—a variance which occurs in a standard cost accounting system when the actual amounts of raw materials used to produce a good differ from the standard amounts required to produce that good.

Practical capacity—that level of production that can be attained under efficient and effective operating conditions.

Standard costs—costs which are assigned to the factors of production based on physical standards under efficient and effective operations required to manufacture the product, and not necessarily the costs which are expected to occur or actually do occur.

Standard cost system—an inventory cost system where standard costs are used in accounting for the factors of production.

Two-way analysis of overhead variances—a method which separates total overhead variance into volume and budget variance components.

Unfavorable variance—a variance which occurs in a standard cost accounting system when actual costs exceed standard costs. An unfavorable variance is recorded by a debit to a variance account.

Volume variance—an overhead variance which results when actual production differs from the practical capacity so that the total manufacturing overhead is under- or over-applied to the cost of production.

1. What is the purpose of using standard costs?

2. What are the three basic classifications used to determine standard costs? Theoretically, which of these standards should be applied to a standard cost system?

3. At what two times may a material price variance be recognized, and at which time do you feel it is more correct for control reasons?

4. What are the two possible variances associated with direct labor costs? Identify one reason why each could occur.

5. Which of the following variances are Favorable (F) Unfavorable (U)?

    a. Debit to direct labor efficiency variance.
    b. Credit to direct labor rate variance.
    c. Debit to raw material price variance.
    d. Credit to material quantity variance.

6. What is the purpose of the flexible manufacturing overhead cost budget?

7. Why is fixed cost considered the static component of the flexible budget?

8. What is the volume variance for manufacturing overhead cost analyzing?

9. Why does the flexible budget have to be adjusted to the actual level of outputs or standard inputs to analyze manufacturing overhead cost variances?

10. When analyzing the volume variance or the budget variance, why must standard activity instead of actual activity be used when the basis for the flexible budget is an input factor such as direct labor hours?

EXERCISES 11. You have been given the following information:

Actual labor hours used.......................... 315 hours
Standard materials price......................... $2.50 per unit
Standard labor hours used........................ 300 hours
Standard quantity of materials used.............. 450 units
Actual labor rate per hour....................... $3
Actual quantity of materials purchased and used........ 445 units
Standard labor rate per hour..................... $3.10
Actual materials price........................... $2.52 per unit

Required:

Prepare a schedule for the following variances:

1. Raw materials price variance
2. Raw materials quantity variance
3. Direct labor efficiency variance
4. Direct labor rate variance.

12. The Simons Company manufactures bolts in standard batches of 5,000 units. The standard cost for a batch is as follows:

Raw materials 200 lbs. @ $.04 per lb....................	$ 8.00
Direct labor 4 hrs. @ $5.15 per hr.....................	20.60
Overhead (including variable overhead of $4.50)........	10.00
Total standard cost.............................	$38.60

Data for the month of March is as follows:

Planning production............................	240 batches
Actual production..............................	250 batches
Cost of raw materials purchased (55,000 lbs.).........	$2,310.00
Cost of raw materials used (51,250 lbs.)..............	$2,152.50
Direct labor cost (998 hrs.)........................	$5,189.60
Actual overhead cost............................	$2,560.00
Budgeted fixed overhead cost.....................	$1,320.00

Required:

Compute the following variances, indicating whether each is favorable or unfavorable.

1. Raw materials price variance
2. Raw materials quantity variance
3. Direct labor rate variance
4. Direct labor efficiency variance

13. The Taylor Company would like you to calculate the standard costs per unit for their product, widgets. Each unit must go through two departments, processing and finishing. The hourly employees in the processing department are paid $5 an hour and $6.15 an hour in finishing. Materials used in the processing department for making widgets include wids for $20 per kilogram and gets for $6 per kilogram. Practical capacity is expected to be 50,000 units per year. From the additional information listed below provided by various departments in the Taylor Company, calculate the standard cost per unit for material, labor, and overhead. Use the high-low method to calculate the fixed and variable cost components of manufacturing overhead.

Department **Product Name**	*Processing* *Widgets* *Operation*	*Minutes* *Per Widget*
	Materials handling..............	5
	Machining.....................	6
	Check machining................	2
	Final machining................	4
	Materials handling..............	4
	Allowance for delays............	3
		24

Department **Product Name**	Finishing Widgets	Minutes
	Operation	Per Widget
	Materials handling..............	3
	Finishing.......................	6
	Final inspection................	2
	Materials handling..............	6
	Allowance for delays............	3
		20

Standard Bill of Materials

Department **Product Name**	Processing Widgets	Required
	Material	Number
	Wids......................	1 Kilogram
	Gets......................	3 Kilograms

Manufacturing Overhead Costs

Department Processing and Finishing
Product Name Widgets

Year	Units Produced	Costs
19x0	48,000	249,600
19x1	45,000	240,000

14. The Loren Company produces one product with the following standard costs per unit:

Materials, 2 lbs. @ $3.25......................		$ 6.50
Labor, 5 hrs. @ $2.05.........................		10.25
Manufacturing overhead:		
Variable $1 per hr. × 5 hrs....................	$5.00	
Fixed $120,000 = $.50 per hr. × 5 hrs........	2.50	7.50
240,000 (hours practical yearly capacity)		
		$24.25

Journalize the following transactions for the Loren Company for June. Units produced during the month totaled 3,000.

a. Purchased 6,400 pounds of material at a cost of $19,600 on account.

b. Issued 6,300 pounds of material to production to be used during June.

c. 21,500 labor hours were charged to production during June at a cost of $2 per hour.

d. Actual overhead incurred was $22,000 for variable overhead and $9,500 for fixed overhead. The variable overhead was paid for in cash and the fixed overhead was made up entirely of depreciation on plant and equipment.

e. Applied overhead was recorded based on standard direct labor hours.

f. Sales in June totaled 2,900 units at a mark-up of 40% on standard costs.

g. There were no beginning inventories on June 1. Variances are closed to the cost of goods sold on December 31.

15. During December, the Strickem Co. produced 4,000 hunting knives which required 12,380 ounces of steel and 6,000 quarts of plastic (raw material plastic in liquid form). In order to do this, Strickem purchased 15,000 ounces of steel for $6,450 and 7,000 quarts of plastic for $2,100. The payroll for December amounted to $14,895. Total hours worked were 1,960 hours. The following are the per unit standards for material and labor established by Strickem.

Material:
　Steel, 3 ozs. @ $.40/oz.
　Plastic, 1.5 qts. @ $.30/qt.
Labor:
　½ hr. at $7.50/hr.

Required:

1. Calculate the material price and quantity variances.
2. Calculate the labor rate and efficiency variances.

16. The following summarizes the standard cost for producing one metal tennis racket frame for McMullian Corp. In addition, the variances for January's production are given. Note that all inventory accounts have zero balances at the beginning of January.

	Standard Costs/Unit		*Standard Production Costs*
Materials	$4.00		$ 8,400
Direct labor, 2 hrs. @ $2.60	5.20		10,920
Manufacturing overhead:			
Variable	1.80		3,780
Fixed	5.00		10,500
			$33,600

Variances

Material price	($ 222.50)*
Material quantity	(500.00)
Direct labor rate	(750.94)
Direct labor efficiency	(2,096.25)

*Brackets indicate unfavorable variances.

Required:

Determine the following for a tennis racket frame:

1. Actual direct labor hours.
2. Actual direct labor rate.
3. Actual materials used.
4. Actual per unit price for materials.

17. Because of inflation and a new labor agreement, Miller Thunderbolt Co. is revising its standard costs of producing a toy race car. The new labor agreement increased direct labor rates $.15 per hour. In addition, Thunderbolt Co. is facing a 6 percent increase in the cost of materials. From the available information, calculate the new standard cost for material per unit produced and labor per hour. Raw materials used in production is the amount of raw materials purchased.

a. Normal production........................... 750 units.
b. Actual material purchases..................... $2,195.
c. Actual direct labor wages paid................. $6,795.
d. Actual production........................... 723 units.
e. Materials price variance...................... $46.30 favorable.
f. Actual direct labor hours..................... 2,265.
g. Direct labor rate variance.................... $135.90 favorable.

18. The Walters Manufacturing Company has established the following standards for one unit of their product, Alpha.

Material......................	6 lbs.	@ $8/lb.	=	$ 48
Labor........................	12 hrs.	@ $6/hr.	=	72
Variable overhead..............		@ $18	=	18
Fixed overhead................		@ $25	=	25
Total Standard Cost..........			=	$163

During August, the Walters Manufacturing Company purchased 7,000 pounds of material at $56,350 and incurred total labor costs of $71,248. 1,000 units of Alpha were produced. They required 6,220 pounds of material and 11,680 hours of labor. Normal capacity is 1,100 units. Actual manufacturing overhead was $45,000.

Required:

1. Compute the material price and usage variances.
2. Compute the labor rate and efficiency variances.
3. Compute the budget and volume variances for manufacturing overhead.

19. The Goodness Company uses a standard cost system with the following standard costs:

Material—5 lbs. @ $6/lb............................	$30.00
Labor—3 hrs. @ $4.50/hr...........................	13.50
Overhead—3 hrs. @ $7/hr..........................	21.00
Total Standard Cost Per Unit......................	$64.50

During the year, 10,000 units were produced. Costs incurred for material, labor, and overhead were $325,000, $136,000, and $209,000, respectively. Normal capacity is 9,000 units. Variable overhead is $4 per standard direct labor hour.

Required:

1. Calculate the total variation from standard costs of the total costs incurred this year.
2. Calculate the total material variance, labor variance, and the overhead variance from standard costs. It is not necessary to calculate price, rate, and efficiency variances.
3. Calculate the budget and volume variances for manufacturing overhead.

PROBLEMS   20. Cooper, Inc. has established the following standards for direct materials and direct labor:

	Cost Per Finished Unit
Materials, 5½ lbs. @ $1.80.................	$ 9.90
Labor, 2 hrs. @ $6.........................	12.00
	$21.90

During the month, 540 units were produced. Purchases and actual operating results were as follows:

Purchases..................	3,500 lbs. at a total cost of $6,475
Materials..................	3,000 lbs. used
Direct labor................	1,076 hrs. at a total cost of $6,542.08

Required:

Show computations for all material and labor variances.

21. A manufacturing firm produces three varieties of a basic product which are manufactured from *two* raw materials.

Finished Product	Standard Usage Per Finished Unit in Units of Raw Material		Standard Prices
	A	B	
R	1	2	Raw material A $4 per unit
S	2	2	Raw material B $3 per unit
T	2	3	

Purchases:
Material A 100,000 units $405,000
Material B 140,000 units $415,800

Usage:
Material A 75,600 units
Material B 115,000 units

Finished Units:

Variety	Amount
R	15,000 items
S	15,000 items
T	15,000 items

Required:

Make the journal entries for materials: (a) purchases and (b) usage as they would appear under an actual cost system and as they would appear under a standard cost system. Assume no previous balances in any of the accounts.

22. A clothing company has just switched from an actual cost system to a standard cost system. The following information pertains to the new standard cost system just employed.

Material, 3½ yds. @ $3.50 per yd....................	$12.25
Labor, 4 hrs. @ $3 per hr...........................	12.00
Overhead, $1.50 per direct labor hr..................	6.00
	$30.25

The manager of the plant wants to know the difference between the actual cost system previously employed, and the newly initiated standard cost system.

Required:

Prepare the journal entries as they would appear under *each* system.

1. Purchased 40,000 yards of material—$150,000.
2. Production completed 10,000 units. There was no beginning or ending work-in-process inventory; 37,000 yards of material were used in production.
3. Direct labor hours used totaled 42,500 hours at a total cost of $131,750.

23. The Hanlon Co. manufactures a product called Pattimar which has the following Standard Cost Sheet:

Standard Cost Sheet

Product: Pattimar
Basis for Cost Sheet: One Unit

Materials

#	Location	Standard Quantity	Standard Price/Unit	Total
1	Bin 57	3	$2.00	$6.00
2	Bin 72	5	.60	3.00
				$9.00

Labor

Department	Standard Hours	Standard Hourly Rate	Total
Assembly	2	$4.50	$ 9.00
Finishing	1	5.00	5.00
			$14.00

Manufacturing Overhead

Variable overhead per unit	$ 7.00
Fixed overhead per unit	9.00
Total overhead per unit	$16.00

The company's records indicate the following production cost figures:

Units produced...................	18,000
Material used	
#1...........................	56,800 units
#2...........................	91,200 units
Labor costs	
Assembly (35,980 hours)..........	$165,508
Finishing (18,200 hours)...........	$ 88,270
Materials purchased:	
#1...........................	(60,000 units) for $129,000
#2...........................	(100,000 units) for $ 55,000

Required:

Calculate materials price and quantity variances for each material and labor rate and efficiency variances for each department.

24. The Monkey Precinct Department Store has suffered a fire in its business office. Many of the records were destroyed and you have been called to piece things back together again. The store wants to know the amount and price of materials A, B, and C which were purchased and used during the past year. The following information was available from the records that were not destroyed:

   a.   Cost of goods sold was $6,030 greater due to variances.
   b.   Total variance of A was $1,000 F.
   c.   Total variance of B was $4,000 U.
   d.   Actual price of A was $3 per unit.
   e.   Actual price of B was $.75 per unit.
   f.   Actual price of C was $2 per unit.
   g.   Standard price of B was $1 per unit.
   h.   Standard amount of A needed   5,000 units.
   i.   Standard amount of B needed 10,000 units.
   j.   Standard amount of C needed   6,000 units.
   k.   4,000 units of A were purchased.
   l.   7,000 units of C were purchased.
   m.   Material price variance of A = $1,000 U.
   n.   Material price variance of B = $1,000 F.
   o.   Material price variance of C = $2,030 U.
   p.   Material quantity variance of C = $1,000 U.

Required:

  1.   Determine the standard price of A and C.
  2.   Determine the actual number of B purchased.
  3.   Determine the actual quantity of A, B, and C used.

25. Nancy Company produced 17,800 footballs during May. Material purchases amounted to 184,000 pounds at $2.10 per pound Usage of the materials amounted to 92,200 pounds. The footballs required 53,000 hours of labor at $4.20 per hour while plant capacity is 60,000 labor hours. Manufacturing overhead actually incurred was $35,000 for fixed and $66,250 for variable. Nancy Company has established the following standards for one football:

5 lbs. of material @ $2 per lb.	$10.00
3 hrs. of labor @ $4 per hr.	12.00
Fixed manufacturing overhead	
$1 per labor hr.	3.00
Variable manufacturing overhead	
$2 per labor hr.	6.00
	$31.00

Required:

Compute the material, labor, and manufacturing overhead budget and volume variances for May.

26. The Green Thing Company produces green things. The standard cost of one green thing is:

Direct materials—1 lb. @ $2./lb.	$2.00
Direct labor—1 ½ hrs. @ $3/hr.	4.50
Manufacturing overhead—variable............	1.50
Manufacturing overhead—fixed..............	.60
Total Standard Cost Per Green Thing........	$8.60

Overhead is applied to things produced on a standard direct labor hour basis. Normal capacity per month is 10,000 things. Last month, 9,800 things were produced. Actual manufacturing overhead was $21,500, of which $15,000 was variable. Fourteen thousand direct labor hours at a total actual cost of $63,000 were used to produce the things. A total of 9,900 pounds of materials was used. Raw materials purchases of 10,000 pounds at $2.05 per pound were made last month.

Required:

Calculate the materials price and usage variances, the direct labor rate and efficiency variances, and the overhead budget and volume variances.

27. The Monroe Company incorporates standard costs in their process costing system. The standard costs per unit for their only product, trinkets, are listed below:

Material: 2 lbs. @ $4.10/lb.			$ 8.20
Labor: 0.6 hrs. @ $6/hr.			3.60
Overhead: Variable @ $4.60/hr.	=	$2.76	
*Fixed @ $2/hr.	=	1.20	3.96
Total Standard Cost Per Trinket.....			$15.76

*Fixed overhead is based on a normal capacity of 132,000 trinkets.

Production statistics for this year are as follows:

Trinkets finished this year—110,000.
Costs incurred for this year were $1,037,850, $430,500, and $475,120 for material, labor, and overhead, respectively.
There was no beginning work-in-process inventory.
Ending work-in-process—15,000 trinkets; 100% complete for material, 80% complete for labor and overhead.
255,000 pounds of material and 70,000 labor hours were actually used. Monroe computes material price variances at the point of transfer to work-in-process.

Required:

Compute:

1. The material price and usage variances,
2. The labor rate and efficiency variances, and
3. The overhead budget and volume variances.

28. The Haywood Company is preparing to close their accounts. They have asked you to prepare a jounal entry to close all variance accounts to the cost of goods sold account.

Direct Materials Price Variance	Direct Materials Quantity Variance
4,000	2,000

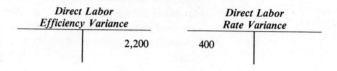

Direct Labor Efficiency Variance	Direct Labor Rate Variance
2,200	400

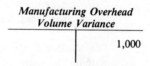

Manufacturing Overhead Volume Variance

1,000

Manufacturing Overhead Efficiency Variance

4,000

Manufacturing Overhead Spending Variance

2,000

Manufacturing Overhead Control

27,000 | 30,000

Chapter 16 discusses the variable costing format and the various approaches to cost-profit-volume analysis. Studying this chapter should enable you to:

1.   Compare and contrast variable costing and absorption costing.

2.   Understand the basic elements of short-range profit planning.

3.   Distinguish between common and traceable cost factors.

4.   Discuss and apply the general approaches to cost-profit-volume analysis.

16

Variable Costing and Cost-Profit-Volume Analysis

INTRODUCTION   Cost accumulation for inventory valuation used full costs to develop costs of production. Full costs include the costs of all direct materials, direct labor, variable manufacturing overhead used in the production process, and an allocated portion of the fixed manufacturing overhead based on normal or practical capacity. This approach stresses the accumulation of full costs in determining the cost of goods manufactured for a given accounting period. The determination of the cost of goods manufactured directly affects both the carrying value of the inventory reported on the balance sheet and the cost of goods sold included on the income statement.

Cost of goods sold is one of two broad cost categories normally included on a traditional full or absorption costing income statement. The amount which is reported as cost of goods sold represents a product cost. The other expenses included on the income statement are classified as period costs, and are normally classified and reported on a functional basis. The absorption costing income statement is generally accepted by the accounting profession for external reporting purposes.

For purposes of internal planning, control, performance evaluation, and decision-making by management, an alternative cost behavior format has been developed for the income statement which many accountants feel appears to be superior to the full or absorption costing format, at least for internal decision-making purposes. This alternative method is referred to as the variable costing or direct costing approach to income measurement.[1] The emphasis of this approach is focused on the separation of costs into their fixed and variable components on the income statement. From a managerial point of view, variable costing is considered an internal management tool. Normally a firm must prepare its external reports on an absorption costing basis for third party users. An income statement prepared under the variable costing concept includes separate classifications for variable and fixed costs. Variable costs include expenditures for such items as raw materials, direct labor, variable manufacturing overhead, and variable selling and administrative expenses. Fixed costs include the fixed portion of manufacturing overhead and fixed selling and administrative expenses. A full absorption income statement summarizes the expenses for the period in traditional product cost and period expenditure form or format. Product costs, including both fixed and variable portions, are incorporated into cost of goods sold while period costs, also including both fixed and variable elements, are included in the expense section. These two income statement formats are shown in Illustration 1.

In summary, full or absorption costing includes fixed manufacturing overhead costs as a part of the cost of goods manufactured by applying a

---

[1] Since "variable costing" describes the approach more accurately than "direct costing" we will use the term "variable costing" in this chapter.

Illustration 1

Income Statement Formats

1. Using Variable Costing Methods

Sales Revenue		$xx
Variable Costs		
Production Costs	$xx	
Selling Expenses	xx	
Administrative Expenses	xx	xx
Contribution Margin		$xx
Fixed Costs:		
Manufacturing Overhead Costs	$xx	
Selling Expenses	xx	
Administrative Expenses	xx	xx
Net Income Before Taxes		$xx

2. Using Absorption Methods

Sales Revenue		$xx
Cost of Goods Sold:		
Direct Labor	$xx	
Direct Materials	xx	
Variable Manufacturing Overhead	xx	
Fixed Manufacturing Overhead	xx	xx
Gross Margin		$xx
Expenses:		
Selling Expenses	$xx	
Administrative Expenses	xx	xx
Net Income Before Taxes		$xx

---

predetermined or standard rate for fixed manufacturing overhead. Variable costing treats fixed manufacturing overhead as a cost of the time period under consideration, i.e., a period cost. The cost of goods manufactured under absorption costing includes direct labor, direct materials, variable manufacturing overhead, and fixed manufacturing overhead. The cost of goods manufactured under variable costing will include only the variable elements of manufacturing costs: direct labor, direct materials, and variable manufacturing overhead. Fixed manufacturing overhead is a *product cost* under absorption costing, but a *period cost* under variable costing.

In order to illustrate the differences between an income statement prepared under absorption costing and one prepared under variable costing a simple example will be used. Assume that a company manufactures and sells a single product. The selling price of this product is $10 per unit and sales for the first two months of 19x1 were 8 units in January and 11 units in February. There was no beginning inventory of this product at January 1, 19x1, and 10 units were produced in both January and in February. The costs incurred by the company in producing and marketing this product were as follows:

	January	February
Fixed Production Costs (in total).....................	$30	$30
Variable Production Costs (per unit)..................	4	5
Fixed Selling and Administrative Expenses (in total)*.....	10	10

*All selling and administrative expenses are assumed to be fixed in this simplified example.

Using the above information, the income statements prepared under absorption and variable costing for the month of January are as follows:

A Company
Income Statements
For the Month Ending January 31, 19x1

		Absorption Costing		Variable Costing
Sales Revenue (8 units × $10)........................		$80		$80
Beginning Inventory.............................	$ 0		$ 0	
Cost of Goods Manufactured:				
Variable (10 units × $4)......................	40		40	
Fixed	30		—	
	$70		$40	
Ending Inventory:				
($70/10 units × 2 units).....................	$14			
($40/10 units × 2 units).....................	___		8	
Cost of Goods Sold.............................		56		32
Gross Margin or Contribution Margin................		$24		$48
Selling and Administrative Expenses..................	$10		$10	
Fixed Production Costs.............................	—	10	30	40
Net Income......................................		$14		$ 8

Note that in the absorption costing income statement the fixed production costs of $30 are considered to be a part of the cost of the units manufactured during the period. Alternatively, fixed production costs are considered to be an expense of the period in the variable costing income statement. This difference in the treatment of fixed production costs accounts for the difference ($14 vs. $8) in net income reported in the two alternative income statements. In the absorption costing income statement, these fixed costs were included in the cost of the inventory ($30 divided by 10 units produced = $3 per unit). Since 8 units were sold during the month and 2 units remain in the ending inventory at the end of January, $24 (8 units × $3) of fixed production costs were included in January expenses (as a part of cost of goods sold) and $6 (2 units × $3) were considered a part of the carrying value of the ending inventory at January 31. This $6 of fixed production costs carried as an asset accounts for the difference ($14 vs. $8) in the net income reported under the two methods since, under variable costing, all $30 of fixed production costs was treated as a January expense. The ending inventory at January 31 under variable costing consists of 2 units at a cost of $4 per unit; only variable production costs are included in the inventory carrying value when variable costing is used.

Continuing our example, the income statement for the month of February under absorption and variable costing (using the FIFO method of inventory valuation) are as follows:

A Company
Income Statements
For the Month Ending February 28, 19x1

	Absorption Costing		Variable Costing	
Sales Revenue (11 units × $10)		$110		$110
Beginning Inventory:				
($70/10 units × 2 units)	$14			
($40/10 units × 2 units)			$ 8	
Cost of Goods Manufactured:				
Variable (10 units × $5)	50		50	
Fixed	30		—	
	$94		$58	
Ending Inventory (FIFO):				
($80/10 units × 1 unit)	8			
($50/10 units × 1 unit)			5	
Cost of Goods Sold		86		53
Gross Margin or Contribution Margin		$24		$57
Selling and Administrative Expenses	$10		$10	
Fixed Production Costs	—	10	30	40
Net Income		$14		$17

Again, in the absorption costing income statement the fixed production costs of $30 are considered a part of the cost of the units produced during February. These costs are treated as expenses of the month in the variable costing income statement. The difference in the treatment of fixed production costs again accounts for the difference ($14 vs. $17) in net income reported in the two alternative income statements. Since 11 units were sold during the month of February, a total of $33 in fixed production costs was expensed in the absorption costing income statement ($6 included in the 2 units of beginning inventory sold plus $27 included in the 9 units produced and sold during February) while only $30 (the fixed production costs incurred during February) was included as an expense in the variable costing income statement. This difference ($33 vs. $30) is the reason for the difference ($14 vs. $17) in net income for February reported using the alternative methods. In January, production exceeded sales (10 vs. 8) so income calculated using absorption costing ($14) exceeded income using variable costing ($8) by the amount of fixed production cost included in the ending inventory (2 units × $30/10 units). This will always be true when production exceeds sales because inventories will increase and the carrying value of inventories is always higher under absorption costing since fixed production costs are included in inventory. In February, sales exceeded production (11 vs. 10) so income under variable costing ($17) exceeded income calculated using absorption costing ($14). This will always be the case when sales exceed production because inventories will decrease and the inventories carried under variable costing which are charged to expense will be of a lesser amount since they include no fixed production costs. Of course, if sales and production are exactly equal, income under the two methods will be the same[2] since all costs, variable and fixed, will be expensed under both methods.

Although the example discussed above is a relatively simple one, it does serve to illustrate the basic differences between absorption and variable costing. A more complex illustration will be used later in the chapter to emphasize and reinforce these differences.

THE CONTRIBUTION MARGIN AND VARIABLE COSTING

The contribution margin is defined as the difference between revenues and all variable costs associated with those revenues. The contribution margin may be calculated on a total income statement basis, on a per unit basis, or as a percentage of sales. The contribution margin is a managerial decision-making tool. Moreover, variable costing may be regarded as a contribution margin approach to the measurement of income.

As indicated in Illustration 1, the format used in the variable costing income statement first deducts all variable manufacturing costs as well as all other variable costs (selling and administrative expenses) from total revenues in order to arrive at the contribution margin. The total fixed manufacturing costs and other fixed selling and administrative expenses are then deducted from the contribution margin to arrive at net income before taxes. Since total fixed manufacturing costs are expensed each period, there is no volume variance to consider at the end of each accounting period using variable costing.

---

[2] This assumes that there are either (1) no beginning and ending inventories or, (2) no changes in costs.

EXTERNAL FINANCIAL REPORTING IMPLICATIONS

If inventory levels fluctuate during an accounting period (that is, if the beginning and ending inventory balances differ), then the variable costing and full or absorption costing techniques provide different income amounts for that period due to the different treatment of fixed costs.

The approach normally used to illustrate the different income statements is to prepare a comparative example that has no beginning or ending finished goods inventory. This permits an analysis which illustrates the fact that over the long-run, the two techniques will provide identical total income amounts when the income for all accounting periods is summed. The assumption made is that all other factors are equal. However, this is rarely, if ever, the case.

The three cases that must be considered in order to fully illustrate the impact of the two costing approaches on income are:

1. Production equals sales.
2. Production exceeds sales.
3. Sales exceed production.

AN ILLUSTRATION: ABSORPTION VERSUS VARIABLE COSTING

During January, 19x2, the president of Sax Company decided that the power turbine shaft segment of the business should be established as a separate division with its own division manager, and that a planning, control and performance evaluation system should be added to its standard cost system.

A variable cost system for cost accumulation appears to be appropriate for internal use. The company uses absorption costing for external financial reporting purposes. The president requested that an analysis be made of the differences between variable costing and absorption costing in terms of the impact that each of these methods has on income. Implicit in his request was the fact that the president did not wish to maintain the accounts on both a variable costing basis for internal purposes and on an absorption costing basis for external financial reporting purposes.

Sax Company's president asked that the standard costs of manufacturing developed in Illustration 4 of the previous chapter be used and, in addition, that a $20,000 budget for fixed selling and administrative costs be assumed. The variable selling costs are approximately $5 per unit sold. The production and sales levels which the president suggested for use in the analysis are rough estimates of the anticipated activity for the months of February, March, April and May and are presented in Illustration 2.

Factors other than volume are assumed to be constant for all months under consideration. Selling prices, standard costs of manufacturing, and selling and administrative costs should not change for any month of the

---

Illustration 2

Sax Company
Power Turbine Shaft Division
Projected Cost, Sales and Production Data

Per Unit Sales and Production Costs:
Average Sales Price $50.00

Standard Production Cost:
Direct Material @ Standard 6.00
Direct Labor @ Standard 3.00
Variable Manufacturing Overhead @ Standard 1.40

Total Variable Production Cost $10.40
Fixed Manufacturing Overhead @ Standard ° 2.00

$12.40

Projected Selling and Administrative Expense:
Variable Selling Costs. . . . . $5 per unit
Fixed Selling and Administrative Expenses. $20,000

President's Estimate of Production and Sales Volumes in Units:

	February	March	April	May	Total
Beginning inventory.	0	0	550	150	—
Production	1,800	2,200	1,250	1,500	6,750
Sales.	1,800	1,650	1,650	1,650	6,750
Ending Inventory.	0	550	150	0	—

* Total fixed overhead is budgeted at $3,600 (Illustration 3 of the preceding chapter) or $2 per unit.

---

time period under observation. For absorption costing purposes, the practical capacity of 1,800 power turbine shafts, or 900 direct labors, is used to allocate fixed overhead to production.

Illustration 2 summarizes the sales, production and cost data which the president of Sax Company wants used in the comparison of income calculations using absorption and variable costing.

The income statements prepared using absorption costing use the full cost of manufacturing, $12.40 per unit, which has been adjusted for any volume variance since Sax Company closes its variances to cost of goods sold at the end of each period. Remember, the basis for developing the fixed manufacturing overhead in Illustration 4 of the preceding chapter was 1,800 units of production or 900 standard direct labor hours. At any other level of production, a volume variance would appear in the accounts. The income statements prepared under both conventional absorption costing and variable costing for the four months are presented in Illustration 3.

To understand the computations included in Illustration 3, the absorption costing and the variable costing income statements should be reviewed

Illustration 3

Sax Company
Power Turbine Shaft Division
Comparison of Absorption and Variable Costing Income Statements
(in units)

	February	March	April	May	Total
Production (Budget)........	1,800	2,200	1,250	1,500	6,750
Sales (Budget)............	1,800	1,650	1,650	1,650	6,750
Projected Income Statements—Absorption Costing					
Sales....................	$90,000	$82,500	$82,500	$82,500	$337,500
Less: Cost of Goods Sold After Adjustment*...........	22,320	19,660	21,560	21,060	84,600
Gross Margin.............	$67,680	$62,840	$60,940	$61,440	$252,900
Less: Selling and Administrative Expenses...............	29,000	28,250	28,250	28,250	113,750
Net Income Before Taxes...........	$38,680	$34,590	$32,690	$33,190	$139,150

*Cost of Goods Sold After Adjustment for Volume Variance. Assume the entire variance is included in cost of goods sold.

February. No adjustment.
March —   (12.80 × 1,650 units sold) + [(1,800 units − 2,200 units) × $2]
           $20,460 − $800 = $19,660
April — $20,460 + [(1,800 units − 1,250 units) × $2]
           $20,460 + $1,100 = $21,560
May — $20,460 + [(1,800 units − 1,500 units) × $2]
           $20,460 + $600 = $21,060

Sax Company
Power Turbine Shaft Division
Projected Income Statements—Variable Costing

	February	March	April	May	Total
Sales.....................	$90,000	$82,500	$82,500	$82,500	$337,500
Less: Variable Costs					
Product Costs.........	18,720	17,160	17,160	17,160	70,200
Selling Expenses............	9,000	8,250	8,250	8,250	33,750
Contribution Margin.......	$62,280	$57,090	$57,090	$57,090	$233,550
Less: Fixed Costs					
Manufacturing Overhead............	3,600	3,600	3,600	3,600	14,400
Selling and Administrative Expenses	20,000	20,000	20,000	20,000	80,000
Net Income Before Taxes...........	$38,680	$33,490	$33,490	$33,490	$139,150

for a month in which there is a volume variance. For example, in March projected sales are 1,650 units at $50 per unit or a total sales revenue of $82,500. Under absorption costing, cost of goods sold at standard would be 1,650 units at $12.40 per unit for a total of $20,460. Fixed overhead applied at standard is $2 per unit produced, and is based on a practical capacity of 1,800 units. Anticipated production in March is 2,200 units. The favorable volume variance is 400 units at $2 per unit or $800. If standard direct labor hours were used in the analysis, then the volume variance would still be projected at $800 (200 hours × $4 per hour). The total selling and administrative expenses would consist of a fixed portion of $20,000 and a variable portion of $5 per unit sold or $8,250.

The sales for March in the variable costing income statement would, of course, be identical to the amount of absorption costing sales—$82,500. Under variable costing, the cost of goods sold, however, would include only the variable manufacturing costs of $10.40 per unit (Illustration 3) for 1,650 units or a total of $17,160. The variable selling expenses would be $8,250 ($5 per unit sold). Total fixed manufacturing overhead is projected at $3,600 per month. The president projected fixed selling and administrative expenses of $20,000 per month. These fixed costs would be considered period, rather than product, costs under variable costing.

A number of observations concerning the two different income statement formats are appropriate:

1. Expense classifications under absorption costing are made on a functional cost basis while variable costing classifications are made on a cost behavior pattern basis (variable vs. fixed).

2. The gross margin obtained using the absorption costing format is not the same as the contribution margin under variable costing. Sales less all product costs equals the gross margin under absorption costing. Sales less all variable costs equals the contribution margin under variable costing.

3. Income under variable costing follows the level of sales. When sales increase, income increases; when sales fall, income declines; and when sales remain constant, income remains the same (March-May). Income under absorption costing is related to *both* the level of sales and to the level of production. Sales for the months of March through May are projected at the same level. By inspecting production levels shown in Illustration 3, we note that under the absorption method, income varies in those months in relationship to the levels of production.

4. When sales and production are identical, as in February, both costing methods yield the same net income before taxes. Under either approach, the total fixed manufacturing overhead is considered an expense on the income statement when sales and production are equal,

since there is no change in the beginning or ending inventory balance. Classifications within the income statement differ, however. Cost of goods sold, including any volume variance, incorporates total fixed manufacturing overhead under absorption costing. Under variable costing, total fixed manufacturing overhead is reflected as a period cost.

5.   When production exceeds sales (as is the case in March) absorption costing yields a higher net income before taxes, because a portion of the fixed manufacturing overhead costs has been allocated to and included in the ending inventory, and thus, deferred to future periods. Under variable costing, all fixed manufacturing overhead costs are expensed during the period in which they are incurred.

6.   When production is less than sales (April and May), variable costing yields a higher net income before taxes. Under absorption costing, the cost of goods sold, after taking volume variances into consideration, includes an amount of current and past applied fixed manufacturing overhead costs exceeding the total fixed manufacturing overhead costs incurred during the current period. The inventories are reduced to match decreased sales demands; therefore, the applied fixed manufacturing overhead in ending inventories is less than the applied fixed manufacturing overhead in the beginning inventories. Using variable costing methods, total fixed manufacturing overhead is considered to be an expense in each accounting period in which it is incurred; therefore, there is no deferral of fixed costs in the finished goods inventory accounts.

7.   Over time, assuming that all factors except volume are equal, total income under the two income statement formats is the same. Furthermore, total production could not exceed total sales by a material amount in the long-run. If production did exceed sales over the long-run, the firm would have large quantities of finished goods inventories on hand.

AN ILLUSTRATION: RECONCILING ABSORPTION AND VARIABLE COSTING INCOME STATEMENTS

The differences between absorption costing and variable costing are explained by analyzing the beginning and the ending inventory amounts for each month. Alternatively, the difference in income can be calculated each month by considering the impact of fixed overhead on both production and sales levels.

The finished goods inventory levels under both absorption and variable costing from Illustration 2 are as follows:

Month	Beginning Inventory	Ending Inventory	Difference
February	0 units	0 units	0 units
March	0	550	550
April	550	150	(400)
May	150	0	(150)

The inventory values reported on the balance sheets at the end of each month are at the full standard manufacturing cost per unit ($12.40) under absorption costing, and at the variable manufacturing cost per unit ($10.40) under variable costing. The difference between these two values, $2, represents the allocated fixed manufacturing overhead cost per unit at standard cost.

In March, the president anticipates that inventory will increase by a total of 550 units. The costs accumulated for these 550 units under absorption costing are $6,820 (550 units × $12.40 per unit). The costs accumulated under variable costing are $5,720 (550 units × $10.40 per unit). The difference between the two inventory costs at the end of March is $1,100. Again, this difference of $1,100 represents the $2 per unit of fixed manufacturing overhead allocated to the 550 units which is deferred to future months under absorption costing. Since there is no beginning inventory, absorption costing shows a higher net income before taxes for March than does the variable costing method. As shown in Illustration 3, the net income under absorption costing is $34,590 and for variable costing income is $33,490; a difference of $1,100 (550 units × $2 per unit).

If the inventory differences are calculated for April and May, then the same reconciliation can be made. It is not necessary to calculate the costs accumulated for both the beginning and the ending inventories; only the amount and direction of change need to be considered. In April, the president anticipates that the finished goods inventory will decrease by 400 units. The absorption costing income statement will include fixed overhead in cost of goods sold on the income statement in an amount larger than that which was incurred because production was less than sales by 400 units. The fixed overhead at standard included in these 400 units is $800; therefore, net income before taxes under absorption costing is $800 less than the comparable net income before taxes computed using variable costing. In May, the inventory decline is 150 units, and the absorption costing net income before taxes is $300 less than the variable costing net income before taxes.

The same analysis may be used to calculate the impact on inventories and net income before taxes by considering production and sales volumes in each month. As an example of these calculations, the projected April data from Illustration 3 are presented below:

April Sales..........1,650 units
April Production.....1,250 units

Net Income Before Taxes Under Variable Costing........		$33,490
Fixed Manufacturing Costs Included in Sales (1,650 × $2)	$3,300	
Fixed manufacturing costs included in production (1,250 × $2)	2,500	
Inventory Level Impact.............................		(800)
Net Income Before Taxes Under Absorption Costing......		$32,690

Since finished goods inventory levels are projected to decrease during April, absorption costing includes fixed costs of manufacturing in cost of goods sold of $800 in excess of that incurred in April.

THE VARIABLE COSTING CONTROVERSY

For external reporting purposes, the concept of absorption costing is well entrenched and represents "generally accepted principles of accounting" as well as being the formally accepted method as required by the IRS for purposes of income tax determination. There have been many advocates of variable costing for external reporting, but the arguments for acceptance have met with very limited success to date. Generally accepted accounting principles and most, if not all, regulatory bodies require absorption costing income statements for external reporting purposes. For internal planning, control, performance evaluation, and decision-making, the variable costing approach has gained widespread managerial acceptance. For internal use, the concept of variable costing is usually adjusted to meet the particular information needs of the firm.

COST-PROFIT-VOLUME ANALYSIS

Cost-profit-volume analysis is a managerial technique which is used for analyzing profit planning information for short-range planning purposes. This technique is a modeling tool which may be used for estimating income or selecting between alternative short-run operating strategies. Cost-profit-volume analysis uses the variable costing concept of income determination, and provides a quick overview of a firm's profit structure which supplies management with estimates of limited accuracy. These estimates, however, are valuable for such purposes as analyzing potential changes in selling prices, sales mix, sales volume, variable costs, and fixed costs. These five elements represent managerial decisions which must be considered in short-range profit planning.

Cost-Profit-Volume Analysis: Common Versus Traceable Factors

Cost-profit-volume analysis may be applied to the entire firm or to one or more segments of the firm. When this technique is applied to the entire firm, all of the revenues and costs are directly traceable to the planning unit. Directly traceable costs and revenues are those costs and revenues that may be attributed to the segment under consideration on a nonarbitrary basis. Theoretically, if the segment were eliminated, the directly traceable costs or revenues would also be eliminated.

Cost-profit-volume analysis is also applied to individual segments of the firm such as product lines, divisions, or sales territories. The smaller the segment of the organization analyzed by this technique, the greater the problem of common cost allocation. Common costs are those costs which benefit more than one segment of the firm. If these costs are allocated, the allocation is usually made on an arbitrary basis. Fixed manufacturing overhead is an example of a common cost that is allocated to production. There are numerous other examples of common costs if one considers only a specific segment of the firm. The president's salary, costs, of company production planning, research and development expenditures, market research costs, advertising campaign costs, and the costs incurred in the legal department are all examples of costs common to many segments of an organization.

By definition, a common cost problem does not exist in those circumstances when the unit being analyzed using cost-profit-volume analysis is the entire firm. The firm must generate revenues which are adequate to cover its total costs, but any segment cost-volume-profit analysis should use only those costs and revenues which are traceable to that segment. Furthermore, if all segments of a firm are engaged in cost-profit-volume analysis separately, certain common costs would not be considered in the analyses.

COST-PROFIT VOLUME ANALYSIS: THE CALCULATIONS

After reviewing the absorption and variable costing income statements presented in Illustration 3, the president of Sax Company requested that a graph illustrating the cost-profit-volume relationships per month for the Power Turbine Shaft Division be prepared assuming changes in certain financial factors. These factors were: (1) a reduction in variable production costs to $10 per unit; (2) a reduction in fixed manufacturing overhead costs to $3,000 per month; and (3) a reduction to $18,000 per month in fixed selling and administrative expenses. The costs were reclassified into the following variable and fixed components:

		Amount	*Percent*
Sales Revenue Per Unit		$ 50	100%
Variable Costs:			
Production Costs	$10		
Selling Expenses	5		
		15	30
Contribution Margin		$ 35	70%
Fixed Costs:			
Fixed Manufacturing Overhead Costs		$ 3,000	
Fixed Selling and Administrative Expenses		18,000	
Total Fixed Costs		$21,000	

Illustration 4 presents the profit capabilities of the Power Turbine Shaft Division in a format which indicates areas of loss and profit and the break-even point for this division.

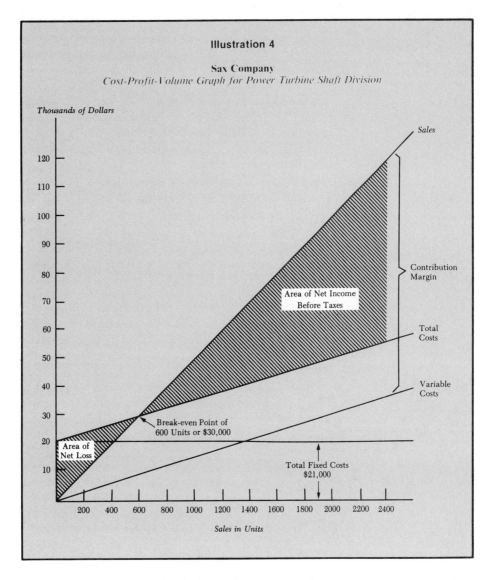

Illustration 4

Sax Company
Cost-Profit-Volume Graph for Power Turbine Shaft Division

A break-even point is that point where total revenues are exactly equal to total costs. Revenues in excess of the break-even point produce a profit, while revenues in an amount less than that stipulated by break-even analysis indicate a loss. However, the break-even formula or relationship may also be used by the firm to determine the level of profit it wishes to obtain.

Break-even relationships:

	Total Revenues	=	Total Costs
or	Total Revenues	=	Variable Costs + Fixed Costs
or	Total Revenues	=	Variable Costs + Fixed Costs + Desired Profit Level

The president was especially pleased with the margin of safety indicated by the cost-profit-volume graph. The margin of safety is the amount that budgeted sales can decline before the break-even point is reached. In the near future, the president could not foresee a loss in the Power Turbine Shaft Division.

The next factor that the president wished to consider was the level of sales required to earn $56,000 in before-tax profits each month, assuming a reduction in variable production costs to $10 per unit, and a reduction in total fixed costs to $21,000 with all other financial factors remaining constant. Four approaches may be used in cost-profit-volume analysis. Each of these approaches provides the same information, but in a different manner. The four approaches or techniques are:

1. Graphical
2. Equation
3. Contribution Margin
4. Contribution Percentage or Ratio

The graphical approach was presented in Illustration 4. The equation, contribution margin, and contribution ratio or percentage approaches may be used to respond to questions raised by management regarding changes in financial factors.

Equation Method

The equation method establishes the mathematical relationships between sales, variable costs, fixed costs, and desired net income before taxes. This approach provides a solution expressed in terms of units, which must be multiplied by the selling price per unit to obtain the solution in terms of sales dollars.

The general form of the equation, with X representing the number of units necessary to yield the desired net income before taxes is:

$$\begin{array}{l}\text{Unit} \\ \text{Sales} \ (X) = \end{array} \begin{array}{l}\text{Variable} \\ \text{Expenses} \ (X) + \text{Fixed Expenses} + \\ \text{Per Unit} \end{array} \begin{array}{l}\text{Desired Net} \\ \text{Income Before} \\ \text{Taxes} \end{array}$$

1. To break-even

$$\$50(X) = \$15(X) + \$21,000 + \$0$$
$$\$35(X) = \$21,000$$
$$X = 600 \text{ units}$$
$$\text{Sales dollars} = 600 \times \$50 = \$30,000$$

2.   To earn $56,000 net income before taxes

$$\$50(X) = \$15(X) + \$21,000 + \$56,000$$

$$\$35(X) = \$77,000$$

$$X = 2,200 \text{ units}$$

$$\text{Sales dollars} = 2,200 \times \$50 = \$110,000$$

**Contribution
Margin Method**

The contribution margin approach rearranges the equation, but also provides a solution in units. The general form of the contribution margin approach is as follows:

$$X = \frac{\text{Fixed Expenses} + \text{Desired Net Income Before Taxes}}{\text{Contribution Margin Per Unit}}$$

1.   To break-even

$$X = \frac{\$21,000 + \$0}{\$50 - \$15}$$

$$= \frac{\$21,000}{\$35}$$

$$= 600 \text{ units}$$

$$\text{Sales dollars} = 600 \times \$50 = \$30,000$$

2.   To earn $56,000 net income before taxes

$$X = \frac{\$21,000 + \$56,000}{\$50 - \$15}$$

$$= \frac{\$77,000}{\$35}$$

$$= 2,200 \text{ units}$$

$$\text{Sales dollars} = 2,200 \times \$50 = \$110,000$$

The results using the contribution margin approach are, of course, identical to those obtained under the equation approach. The contribution margin approach answers the question, "Given a $35 contribution margin, how many units must be sold in order to attain the desired profit?"

**Contribution
Percentage or
Ratio Method**

The contribution percentage or ratio approach provides an answer stated in terms of dollars of sales. If an answer in terms of units is desired, the dollars of sales must be divided by the selling price per unit.

The contribution percentage approach uses the contribution margin approach and converts the contribution margin in the denominator to a percentage of contribution margin per sales dollar. The general formulation of the contribution percentage approach is:

Let Y = Necessary dollars of sales to yield the desired net income before taxes

$$Y = \frac{\text{Fixed Costs } + \text{ Desired Net Income Before Taxes}}{\left(\dfrac{\text{Contribution Margin Per Unit}}{\text{Sales Price Per Unit}} \right)}$$

1. To break-even

$$Y = \frac{\$21,000 + \$0}{\left(\dfrac{\$50 - 15}{\$50} \right)}$$

$$= \frac{\$21,000}{\left(\dfrac{\$35}{\$50} \right)}$$

$$= \frac{\$21,000}{.70}$$

$$= \$30,000$$

In units = $\$30,000 \div \$50 = 600$

2. To earn $56,000 net income before taxes

$$Y = \frac{\$21,000 + \$56,000}{\left(\dfrac{\$50 - \$15}{50} \right)}$$

$$= \frac{\$77,000}{\left(\dfrac{\$35}{\$50} \right)}$$

$$= \frac{\$77,000}{.70}$$

$$Y = \$110,000$$

In units = $\$110,000 \div \$50 = 2,200$

The contribution margin percentage approach asks the question, "Given a contribution margin of $.70 for every $1 of sales, how many dollars of sales are necessary to cover fixed costs and attain the desired profit level?"

Summary of Methods

All of the above approaches provide identical answers because they are merely variations of the same equation and consider identical input factors. In choosing one approach as opposed to another, one must consider such factors as the purpose for which the information is intended, the form in which the information is desired, personal preference, and convenience.

COST-PROFIT-VOLUME ANALYSIS: UNDERLYING ASSUMPTIONS

Conventional cost-profit-volume analysis is a static tool in that it assumes that all factors, with the exception of the single factor that is being analyzed, will remain constant over the relevant range. The equations are mathematical; therefore, any single factor may be computed given that all the other factors are known. The examples included in this chapter have all considered sales volume in units or dollars, which is the conventional approach.

Once the relationship of the following factors to volume are determined, this analysis assumes that the relationships with the following variables do not change over the relevant range of volume.

1. Variable costs
2. Fixed costs
3. Selling prices
4. Sales mix
5. Efficiency
6. Productivity

Any projected change requires a new analysis. The linearity of the approach forces the user to consider all of the financial factors that affect profit and their relationships to volume. Note that this tool is not a precise planning tool, but it does provide an estimate of projected net income before taxes using the variable costing concept of income determination.

SUMMARY

For external reporting purposes, the use of full or absorption costing is required. However, for management accounting purposes, variable or direct costing is often more useful as a decision-making tool. Variable costing emphasizes the separation of manufacturing costs into their fixed and variable components.

From the standpoint of income determination, the primary difference between the two costing formats is in the treatment of fixed costs. Under the absorption costing format, fixed manufacturing overhead is allocated and inventoried as an element of product cost and is charged to expense only as the associated units of product are sold. In contrast, under the variable costing format, fixed manufacturing overhead is expensed as a period cost as it is incurred and the product cost includes only the variable cost elements.

This difference in the treatments of fixed manufacturing overhead means that net income under the two formats will vary whenever there is a difference between the sales and production for the period. When sales are equal to production, both formats will yield the identical net income figure, assuming no changes in the inventory balances.

The variable costing approach, although not acceptable for external financial accounting purposes, is instrumental in cost-profit-volume analysis for management purposes. Cost-profit-volume analysis is used as a tool for short-range profit planning purposes. The essential elements that must be considered in such planning include potential changes in selling prices, sales mix, sales volume, variable costs, and fixed costs. Usually such an analysis considers only those costs which are directly traceable to the unit under analysis, but in certain cases common costs are also considered.

Four general approaches to cost-profit-volume analysis include: (1) graphical, (2) equation, (3) contribution margin, and (4) contribution percentage or ratio. All four approaches yield approximately the same results, although in different formats, and all are based on the premise that sufficient sales revenue must be generated to cover both fixed and variable expenses as well as to produce the desired net income.

KEY DEFINITIONS

Common costs—costs which benefit more than one segment of the firm. Any allocation of common costs will be arbitrary.

Contribution margin—the difference between revenues and all variable costs associated with those revenues.

Contribution margin approach—an approach to cost-profit-volume analysis which is similar to the equation approach but which bases its calculations on the contribution margin.

Contribution percentage approach—an approach to cost-profit-volume analysis which uses the contribution margin approach but bases its calculations on the percentage of contribution margin per dollar of sales.

Cost-profit-volume analysis—a technique using the variable costing concept of income determination in anaylzing the impact of potential changes in selling prices, sales mix, sales volume, and variable and fixed costs on short-range profits.

Equation approach—the approach to cost-profit-volume analysis which establishes a basic mathematical relationship between sales, variable costs, fixed costs, and desired net income before taxes, and provides a solution in terms of units.

Full or absorption costing—the traditional type of costing generally used for external reporting purposes where fixed manufacturing overhead costs are included as a part of the cost of goods manufactured according to predetermined rates of application.

Traceable factors—those costs and revenues which may be directly traced on a non-arbitrary basis to a segment of the firm.

Variable or direct costing—a costing approach which includes only the variable portion of manufacturing overhead as a part of the cost of goods manufactured, while treating the fixed portion of manufacturing overhead as a period cost. Variable costing is not generally used for external financial reporting but is an informative management tool.

QUESTIONS

1. From an income determination standpoint, what is the only difference between absorption and variable costing? Explain.

2. Explain the contribution margin approach to decision-making. In your explanation concentrate on the actual format of this type of income statement.

3. When production is more than sales, which method produces the higher income, variable or absorption costing, and why?

4. How is cost-profit-volume analysis used? Give examples.

5. What is the difference between traceable and common costs?

6. Of the following which would you consider common costs?

   a. R & D expenditures
   b. Advertising costs
   c. Variable overhead costs
   d. Depreciation of executive office building
   e. Direct materials costs

7. Explain the equation approach to cost-profit-volume analysis. Does the answer it gives differ from that given under another approach?

8. Name the underlying assumption in cost-profit-volume analysis.

9. Since the variable costing approach is not acceptable for external financial accounting purposes, why do firms bother with it?

EXERCISES

10. You are given the following information about the operations of the Queen Company:

Direct labor costs..................................	$19,000
Direct materials purchases.........................	7,000
Overhead (all variable except fixed rent of $1,000 and depreciation of $2,000)................	14,000
General and administrative expense.................	2,000
Selling expenses...................................	9,000
	$51,000

    There were no beginning inventories. During the year, 10,000 units were produced; 8,000 were sold. There were no inventories of material or work-in-process at year-end—only finished goods.

    Required:

    Prepare statements of cost of goods manufactured under each of the following assumptions:

    1. Full absorption
    2. Variable costing

11.   Given below is cost information for the Sales Company for the month of June:

Sales..	400 units
Variable manufacturing costs......................	$6 per unit
Total fixed manufacturing costs...................	$2,400
Total administrative expense (fixed)...............	$1,200
Finished goods beginning inventory................	0 units
Finished goods ending inventory..................	200 units
Selling price....................................	$25 per unit
Variable selling expense..........................	$1 per unit

Required:

1.   What is the net income under absorption costing?
2.   What is the net income under variable costing?

12.   Given the following break-even chart:

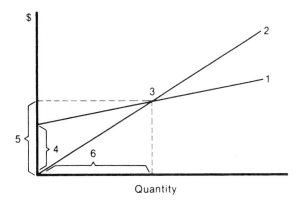

Identify the following items by numbers.

a.   Total revenue line
b.   Total cost line
c.   Total fixed cost
d.   Break-even volume
e.   Break-even sales
f.   Break-even point

13.   The solid lines in the following break-even charts represent the present cost-profit-volume relationships in a firm. The dotted lines represent changes. Explain what financial factors changed the original relationships.

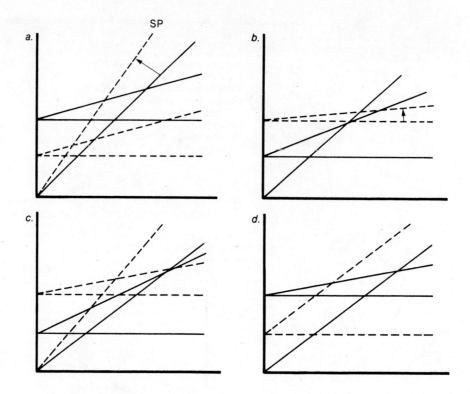

14. Given the following graph:

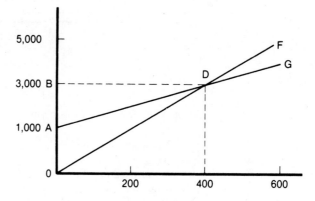

State the equation for total cost and for revenue in numerical terms. (Your answer will consist of 2 equations.)

15. For the last year revenue was $400,000, total variable costs $180,000, total fixed costs $100,000, and net income $120,000. With no change in selling price, costs or level of efficiency, what would the break-even point in sales be?

16.   You are told the following about Jones Company's production costs:

Fixed costs............................... $36,000
Variable costs:
    Materials............................... $2.50 per unit
    Labor................................... $1.70 per unit
    Other processing........................ $ .80 per unit

Required:

1.   What is the *lowest price* at which you can sell the product and not lose money if you intend to produce and sell 60,000 units? (Use the equation method.)
2.   At what price will you sell the product if you desire to have a 15% profit on sales?

17.   The A&M Company has just been formed. In their first year of production, they have a plant capacity of 10,000 units. They feel they will be able to sell all of the 10,000 units that they produce.
     Their costs are:

Direct labor............................... $2.00 per unit
Direct materials........................... $1.00 per unit
Other variable costs....................... $ .50 per unit
Fixed costs................................ $28,000

The company wants to make a profit of $25,000 in the first year. What should their selling price be? (Use the equation method.) What is the contribution margin?

18.   The management of the Richards Company has developed the following estimates of costs and sales, assuming the company is able to operate at full capacity:

Total fixed expenses....................... $ 80,000
Total variable costs....................... 30,000
Total sales revenues....................... 150,000

Fixed expenses are constant at all levels of business activity and variable expenses vary in direct proportion to sales.

Required:

1.   Calculate the break-even point of the Richards Company using the contribution margin ratio approach.
2.   Calculate the break-even point assuming the above *except* that the total expenses at full capacity are composed of $60,000 fixed and $75,000 variable.

PROBLEMS

19. Prepare a cost of goods manufactured statement and an income statement using: (a) variable and (b) absorption costing from the information given below:

Sales:
    Product A............................. 3,500 units @ $27.50
    Product B............................. 4,000 units @ $32.00
Direct labor:
    Cutting: Product A—............. 2 hours @ $2.00
              Product B—............. 2½ hours @ $2.00
    Finishing: Product A—............. 2 hours @ $2.50
              Product B—............. 3 hours @ $2.50
Beginning finished goods inventory........... 0 units
Variable overhead:
    Cutting: Product A & B.......... $ .50 per direct labor hour
    Finishing: Product A & B.......... $1.00 per direct labor hour
Beginning work-in-process................... 0 units
Ending work-in-process..................... 0 units
Direct materials: Product A.............. 2 units @ $1.50
                    Product B.............. 3 units @ $1.50
Fixed overhead........................... $18,000 (applied at a rate of $1.50 per unit of A and $2.40 per unit of B)

Ending finished goods inventory:
    Product A............................. 500 units
    Product B............................. 1,000 units
Beginning raw materials.................... 4,000 units @ $1.50
Ending raw materials...................... 3,000 units @ $1.50
Fixed selling and administrative expense....... $20,000
Purchases of raw materials.................. 22,000 units @ $1.50

20. Crash Products has just perfected a rip-proof "rip-a-way" football jersey which it can sell to the Washington Deadskins LFN football team for $10 per jersey. Crash's economist forecasts that demand for this unique product (fiendishly designed to maim the fingers of enemy tacklers) will be 80 in 19x1 and 110 in 19x2. Product costs are estimated as follows:

	19x1	19x2
Fixed (in total).........................	$100	$100
Variable (per unit)......................	5	6

Because Crash's production facilities can accomodate only a single worker per shift, only 100 jerseys are turned out annually by the organization's skilled craftsman.

Required:

Prepare an income statement using variable costing and one using absorption costing for 19x1 and 19x2. Crash Products uses Fifo to cost their inventories.

21.   Whodunit, Inc. has given you the following information for 19x1 concerning its products. They have hired you to:

a.   Compute the selling price per unit.

b.   Project an income statement for the year using variable costing.

c.   Compute a break-even point expressed in dollars and in units assuming that $20,000 of overhead and the total administrative expenses are fixed but that all other costs are fully variable.

Estimated annual sales...................... <u>25,000</u> units

	Amount	Per Unit
Estimated costs:		
Material	$ 93,750	$3.75
Direct labor.....................	20,000	.80
Overhead	31,250	1.25
Administrative expense.............	<u>50,000</u>	<u>2.00</u>
Total........................	$195,000	$7.80

Selling expenses are expected to be 13% of sales and profit is to amount to $1.77 per unit.

22.   The Buffalo Company has just been formed and plans to produce a product which will sell for $12 per unit. A market survey showed that demand will be less than 15,000 units per year, but did not indicate how much less.

The company has found two machines suitable for its plant. Each of these machines has a capacity of 15,000 units per year. Machine 1 would have fixed costs of $30,000 per year and would yield a profit of $45,000 per year if sales were 15,000 units. Machine 2 has a fixed cost per year of $42,000 and would yield a profit of $48,000 per year at sales of 15,000 units. Variable costs behave linearly for both machines.

Required:

1.   Break-even sales in dollars and units for each machine.

2.   A second survey was taken which indicated that the company's sales will probably average 11,500 units. Which machine should Buffalo buy?

3.   If average sales will be 14,500 units, which machine should Buffalo buy?

(Note: Buffalo Company uses variable costing.)

23.   The Rosen Company makes a single product which has the following costs:

Fixed costs............................... $400 (total)
Variable costs............................ $.10 (per unit)

The income tax rate is 40%. Rosen will make exactly 1,000 units this period.

Required:

1. How much will Rosen have to charge per unit in order to break-even on the sale of the 1,000 units? (Use the equation method.)
2. In order to make a profit of $120 (after taxes) on the sale of 1,000 units, how much will Rosen have to charge per unit?

24. The Sales Company has just been formed to produce Product Z. The first year, the capacity of the plant will be 12,000 units. They will be able to sell all of their production.

    Their costs are:

Direct labor	$2.50 per unit
Raw materials	1.80 per unit
Other variable costs	1.20 per unit
Fixed costs	36,000

    Required:

    1. If the company wishes to make a profit of $30,000 the first year, what should their selling price be? What is the contribution margin?
    2. At the end of the first year, they wish to increase their volume. An increase of $15,000 in annual fixed costs will increase their capacity to 30,000 units. They now want a profit of $70,000 and to achieve this end, they also invest $29,000 in advertising. No other costs change. Under these new conditions, how many units will they have to sell to realize this profit, if their new selling price will be $13 per unit? How many units will they have to sell to break-even?

25. Sam's Pipe Company has a relevant production range of 2,500 to 7,000 units. Total production costs range from $10,500 to $24,900. The pipes sell for $4 per pipe.

    Required:

    1. What is the variable cost per unit?
    2. What is the total fixed cost?
    3. What is the break-even volume? (Use the contribution margin approach.)
    4. If 5,652 pipes are sold, what is the net income under variable costing?
    5. If the break-even point is 4,000 units, what must the contribution margin be?

Chapter 17 continues the introduction of short-range planning and provides a comprehensive example of the budgeting process. Studying this chapter should enable you to:

1. Describe the general budgeting process.

2. Identify and discuss the primary benefits of the budgeting process.

3. Prepare budgets and the associated schedules when given the necessary data.

4. Prepare the pro-forma financial statements that are the final products of the budgeting process.

17

Short-Range Planning

INTRODUCTION

Short-range planning, also referred to as budgeting or profit planning, is a measure of management's financial expectations for the near future, usually the coming year. Often, plans are made on a month-by-month basis. The short-range period is normally considered to be that period in which the firm faces constraining factors. Constraining factors are those factors which cannot be significantly altered in the short-run, such as capacity of equipment, number of employees, or demand for products.

All except perhaps the smallest of firms engage in some type of short-range planning. At a minimum, some analysis of projected cash flows must be considered in order to assure management that the firm will be able to meet its cash requirements during the coming period. If the plans are formalized, then these plans are usually referred to as budgets.

LONG-RANGE VERSUS SHORT-RANGE PLANNING

Long-range planning is also referred to as budgeting. The longer time period involved, however, means that plans developed for the distant future are less reliable and cannot be prepared in as much detail as plans developed for the near future. At the extreme, long-range plans can be considered goals that the firm would like to achieve or attain in the future. Goals are expressed in very general descriptive terms, such as the goal or objective to be the largest firm or the best quality producer in the industry. Intermediate-range plans are considered objectives the firm is striving to achieve in the next three to five years. Examples of intermediate objectives include increasing sales volume, increasing the asset base, and expanding product lines in the next five years.

Most short-range budgets must provide sufficient detail to allow day-to-day functioning at operational levels. Generally, the significant planning decisions are made and the formalized plans are prepared on a segment-by-segment basis for a firm. Examples of segments include divisions, product lines, and sales territories. Management participation is an integral part of the successful budgeting process. The management personnel in each segment should be involved in determining budget inputs, and, in return, these individuals should be held responsible for any variances that occur between actual and budgeted performances.

BENEFITS OF SHORT-RANGE PLANNING

The general benefits of short-range planning in any firm include:

1. Communication and coordination.
2. Before-the-fact control.
3. A basis for after-the-fact control and performance evaluation.
4. Identification of weak areas in the firm.
5. Management motivation.

These are described in the sections which follow.

Communication and Coordination

Profit planning enables a manager to identify the overall short-range plans of the firm and how his or her managerial area fits into this plan. Profit planning also enables a manager to realize before-the-fact what is expected of him and his division.

The efforts of the functional areas of the business are coordinated by planning. For example, a sales forecast is an important consideration in planning product schedules. Advertising campaigns and sales efforts must be coordinated to be fully effective. Raw material purchases must reflect production demand. Short-range financial plans are made in conjunction with projected cash flows.

If the managers of all areas of the business operated independently without a coordinated plan, then each manager would act according to his individual perceptions of the best interests of his department and the firm. The production manager might plan long production runs in order to minimize costs. The purchasing manager would order the largest possible quantities in order to maximize the available discounts. The inventory control manager would minimize inventories in order to reduce the funds committed to inventory and the carrying costs of the inventory. Sales managers would maintain large quantities of finished goods inventories on hand to provide the best possible customer service. To the individual manager, each of these strategies would appear to be in the best interests of the firm. Without studied coordination and assessment of the interaction of the various individual plans and strategies, however, it is possible for any one individual strategy to be counterproductive when considered in light of the firm's overall objectives.

Before-the-Fact Control

The communication and coordination which result from the budgeting process introduce an element of continuous before-the-fact control. Every manager knows what is expected of him in terms of performance in a given budgeting period. The manager then supervises his division and its employees to meet the budgeted goals in the most effective and efficient manner.

In developing budgets, managers must establish and justify a need for resources. This formalization of the segment's needs serves as a control factor in the planning function. Using this method, operating and financial constraints of the firm become obvious to each manager.

A Basis for After-the-Fact Control and Performance Evaluation

Because the budgeting process serves as a basis for measuring a manager's performance, each manager knows that he will be judged by his ability to satisfy the goals of his department budget. Any variations from the budget are analyzed after the performance takes place. If the planning and budgeting process does not take place, control after-the-fact is almost non-existent because of the difficulty in determining what performance should have been attained by a given manager.

**Identification of
Weak Areas
of the Firm**

Through formal planning, weak segments of the firm can be identified. Potential operating and financial factors such as an unsatisfactory contribution margin in a segment, a production bottleneck, a poor sales mix, excessive inventories or accounts receivable, and insufficient cash flows can be readily identified. Any imbalance between segments of the firm becomes apparent in the planning process.

**Motivation for
Management**

When lower-level management is involved in the budgeting process, these managers become directly involved with the goals, objectives, problems, and policies of the firm. The budgeting process assists in identifying the importance of a manager's job in the overall performance of the firm. Coordinated action of all employees toward achieving the firm's goals becomes a major objective of the individual managers. Because the goals of each segment have been established in conjunction with the overall goals and policies of the firm through the coordinating aspects of budgeting, the manager's own self-interests should be served by acting in the best interest of the firm.

**GENERAL
COMPREHENSIVE
BUDGETING
RELATIONSHIPS**

The concept of comprehensive budgeting covers the entire area of planning, control and performance evaluation. Illustration 1 presents the skeletal relationships of the general types of budgets. This illustration should be viewed as the "tip of an iceberg," in that more specific budgets and special budgets are prepared for management at all levels using the general budgets as guidelines. Budgets should be sufficiently detailed and specialized to provide plans for the day-to-day operations at the lowest level of management.

Illustration 1 identifies the major budget categories, their interrelationships and their ultimate articulation into pro-forma or projected financial statements. All budgets except those involving long-range sales forecasts, research and development expenditures, and long-range capital expenditures are covered in this chapter.

The major budgets and pro-forma financial statements developed in this chapter are:

1. Budgeted cost of goods manufactured statement
2. Budgeted cost of goods sold statement
3. Budgeted income statement
4. Cash budget
5. Budgeted stockholders' equity statement
6. Budgeted balance sheet

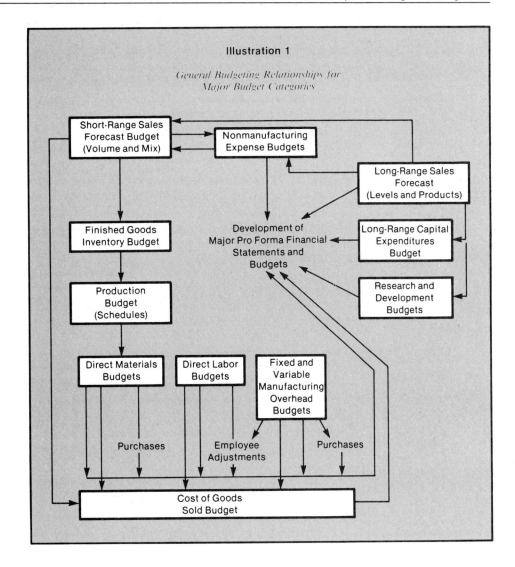

Illustration 1

General Budgeting Relationships for Major Budget Categories

ROLE OF STANDARD COSTS IN BUDGETING

If established attainable standards are available, these standards can serve as the basis for developing the budget. Attainable standards are useful in budget development because standard costs define a series of relationships among various inputs and outputs of production. Once these relationships are established via the standard cost system, sales and/or production forecasts can be expanded into more detailed budgets through the application of the established relationships between the input and output measures. For example, if the standard labor cost for making one unit of a product is two direct labor hours at $4 per hour, then this input measure of two direct labor hours at $4 is equal to the output measure of one unit of product (in terms of a direct labor input measure). If 500 units of the product are forecast for production, direct labor costs of $4,000 (500 units $\times$ 2 hours $\times$ $4) can be budgeted for that product. Since the standard cost for direct labor is $8 per unit of product, the budgeted direct labor cost is $4,000.

BUDGETING: A COMPREHENSIVE EXAMPLE

In July of 19x1, Sax's president requested that the Power Turbine Shaft Division establish a planning, control and performance evaluation system that could be used in the Division's 19x2 operations. The president requested that the variable costing format for measuring income be used for short-range profit planning purposes. The Division's financial staff was given until November 1, 19x1 to establish a planning system and until December 1, 19x1 to submit the Division's month-by-month plans for the first quarter of 19x2.

The finance department analyzed the Power Turbine Shaft Division's operations and established forecasts and management policies for both the operational (or performance) budgets and the financial (or resource) budgets for 19x2. Management considered the standard costs for manufacturing attainable and realistic and recommended that these costs be used wherever possible in the budgeting process. The management policies and forecasts are separated into two categories: (1) those policies and forecasts which primarily affect the operating budgets and (2) those policies and forecasts which primarily affect the financial budgets. As the operating and financial budgets are fundamentally related, this segregation of policies and forecasts is not strict.

Eighteen management policies and forecasts established by Sax Company are listed. The first six policies are related to income statement items and therefore primarily affect the operating budget. The policies and forecasts numbered seven through eighteen are concerned with various balance sheet accounts and, as such, primarily affect the financial budget. The projected balance sheet for December 31, 19x1 for the Power Turbine Shaft Division is presented in Illustration 2. The beginning balances in the permanent accounts are necessary for financial planning for the first quarter of 19x2.

Federal income taxes are not considered in the budgeting process for the Power Turbine Shaft Division, as all income tax budgeting is handled by corporate headquarters.

Illustration 2

Sax Company
Power Turbine Shaft Division
Projected Balance Sheet as of December 31, 19x1

Assets			Liabilities and Stockholders' Equity		
Current Assets:			**Current Liabilities:**		
Cash	$	40,000	Accounts Payable	$	60,000
Accounts Receivable		424,400	Wages Payable		18,000
Direct Materials Inventories:			Total Current		
Steel Billets @ Standard . .		96,000	Liabilities	$	78,000
Ball Bearings @ Standard .		48,000			
Indirect Materials and					
Supplies		30,000			
Work-In-Process @ Standard					
Variable Cost		300,000	**Long-Term Liabilities:**		
Finished Goods @ Standard					
Variable Cost		249,600			
Total Current Assets		$1,188,000	Long-Term Debt		1,200,000
			Total Liabilities		$1,278,000
Long-Term Assets:					
Equipment . . . . $ 600,000					
Less: Accumulated					
Depreciation 60,000					
Net: Equipment	$	540,000	**Stockholders' Equity:**		
Plant $3,000,000					
Less: Accumulated			Stockholders'		
Depreciation . 150,000			Investment		3,300,000
Net: Plant		2,850,000			
Total Long-Term Assets . . .		$3,390,000	Total Liabilities		
Total Assets		$4,578,000	and Stockholders'		
			Equity		$4,578,000

Management Policies and Forecasts Affecting the Operating Budget— 19x2

1. The standard sales price of $50 per power turbine shaft should be maintained during 19x2. New competition has not entered the market, and is unlikely to do so during 19x2. A projected sales forecast, in units, will be developed by the sales manager of the division.

2. The standard variable production cost of $10.40 used previously will be used again for planning purposes. For convenience, the pertinent standards are presented again in Illustration 3.

3. Variable selling costs were $5 per unit sold in 19x1; no change is expected in 19x2.

Illustration 3

Sax Company
Power Turbine Shaft Division

Summary of Standard Variable Manufacturing
Costs Per Unit of Production

Materials @ Standard
1 Steel Billet . . . . $ 4.00
2 Ball Bearings 2.00
Direct Labor @ Standard ½ Hour @ $6.00 per hour 3.00
Variable Manufacturing Overhead @ Standard ° 1.40
$10.40

° Basis of application to product is standard direct labor hours. Application rate is $2.80 per standard direct labor hour.

4. Fixed manufacturing overhead costs are budgeted at $360,000. These costs are incurred uniformly throughout the year at a rate of $30,000 per month. An individual cost breakdown will be presented in a separate budget. Depreciation is a non-cash expense. (See Policy and Forecast items 13 and 14.)

5. Fixed selling and administrative expenses will be budgeted at $2,004,000 in 19x2.

6. Annual interest expense on long-term debt is $132,000, payable in equal monthly payments of $11,000. (See item 17.)

Management Policies and Forecasts Affecting the Financial Budget— 19x2

7. A minimum cash balance of $40,000 is necessary in order to provide sufficient cash to support day-to-day operations. If the Division needs to borrow cash to maintain the $40,000 balance, it can be borrowed from corporate headquarters. Cash must be borrowed and repaid in $5,000 increments.

8. All sales are made by the sales force on a credit basis. Sax Company provides customers with credit terms of net/30. Customers normally pay within 30 days and bad debts are rare.

9. There should always be sufficient direct (raw) materials on hand to meet the production demands for the next two month period.

10. Indirect materials and supplies inventory should be maintained at a level of $30,000. This inventory account will be replenished monthly to maintain a level of $30,000.

11. The work-in-process inventory should be maintained at a balance of approximately $300,000.

12. The finished goods inventory should be maintained at a level sufficient to meet the next two months' demand for power turbine shafts.

13. The original cost of the equipment in the Power Turbine Shaft Division was $600,000. The equipment has an estimated life of 10 years with no salvage value anticipated. Sax Company uses the straight-line method of depreciation. The equipment was purchased on January 1, 19x1. Depreciation expense for equipment will be $5,000 per month in 19x2.

14. The original cost of the plant was $3,000,000. The estimated life of the plant is 20 years. No salvage value is anticipated. As is the case with the equipment, straight-line depreciation will be used in depreciating the plant. The plant was purchased on January 1, 19x1. Depreciation expense will be $12,500 per month in 19x2.

15. Accounts payable represent credit purchases of direct materials on net/30 terms. Accounts payable are paid on time, but never sooner than necessary. Therefore, payments lag behind actual purchases by 30 days.

16. Wages payable are stabilized at approximately $18,000, because Sax's policy is to hold the first two weeks pay earned by each employee. Wages are paid on the fifteenth and on the last business day of each month.

17. A long-term debt of $1,200,000 is outstanding. Interest payments of $11,000 are made monthly. Principal payments of $30,000 per quarter will be made on the loan for 10 years. The initial principal payment will be made on March 31, 19x2.

18. Sax Company has an investment of $3,300,000 that is traceable to the Power Turbine Shaft Division. This represents the stockholders' equity (corporate investment) in the Division.

DEVELOPMENT OF THE MAJOR OPERATING AND PERFORMANCE BUDGETS

Sales Budget (Budget #1)

The sales budget is usually the starting point for short-range profit planning. If the sales projections are inaccurate, all subsequent budgets will be unreliable because these budgets are based, either directly or indirectly, on the sales budgets.

Sales forecasting is an art that relies upon both external and internal information gathered by the marketing or the sales department of the firm. External information sources such as industry periodicals, trade journals, analyses of general economic conditions, and marketing surveys can be used to aid in the development of a sales forecast. Information available internally, such as the firm's past performance and salesperson's estimates, can assist in projecting sales. Sales management assimilates and assesses all available information regarding sales projections, and then uses this information and their professional judgment to establish a reliable sales forecast.

The management of Sax Company requires a monthly sales forecast for the first quarter of 19x2 and for the months of April and May. Forecasts for

April and May are necessary to plan the ending inventories for the first quarter of 19x2 in accordance with management's policies. (See items 9-12 in Management Policies and Forecasts.)

The sales manager reviewed the pertinent estimates of industry demand and the Power Turbine Shaft Division's position in the industry. Each salesperson developed a sales forecast for his or her territory by key (large) customers and in the aggregate for small customers. The sales manager also examined the sales volume for the last three years and checked trends and monthly fluctuations. With the assistance and approval of the other key managers in the Division, the sales manager prepared the following sales budget.

Budget #1
Sales Budget
(January-May, 19x2)

Month	Units	Dollars
January	12,000	$ 600,000
February	12,000	600,000
March	17,000	850,000
Total First Quarter Sales Forecast	41,000	$2,050,000
April	20,000	$1,000,000
May	20,000	1,000,000

Finished Goods Inventory Budget and Production Budget (Budgets #2 and #3)

The production budget is prepared after the sales budget has been finalized. Finished goods inventory serves as the buffer between the level of sales and the level of production. Most firms prefer to maintain a reasonably stable level of production even when faced with fluctuating product demand. Fluctuating production volume causes obvious problems in scheduling and cost control and adversely affects employee morale due to overtime or temporary layoffs.

Most firms maintain some minimum level of finished goods inventory in order to provide satisfactory customer service. There is also a maximum level of inventory that most firms will not exceed because of the cost of carrying inventory, the capital committed to the inventory, and the fear of inventory obsolescence or possible spoilage.

The Power Turbine Shaft Division has a management policy (Item 12 in Management Policies and Forecasts) requiring that the ending finished goods inventory balance be maintained at a level sufficient to meet the next two months' anticipated sales demands. The finished goods inventory balance expected on December 31, 19x1 is 24,000 units. (Illustration 2 shows finished goods inventory at standard cost of $249,600 or 24,000 units.) This quantity of finished goods inventory is sufficient to meet the forecasted January 19x2 sales of 12,000 units and February sales of 12,000 units. At the end of January 19x2, the finished goods inventory should be at a level of 29,000 units, which will meet the forecasted sales for February 19x2 (12,000 units) and March 19x2 (17,000 units). The finished goods inventory budget, Budget #2, for the Power Turbine Shaft Division quantifies management's finished goods inventory policy. The sales budget, Budget #1, is the basis used to establish ending finished goods inventory balances.

Budget #2
Finished Goods Budget
(1st Quarter, 19x2)

Date	Units	Dollars at Standard Variable Cost of $10.40
January 1	24,000	$249,600
January 31	29,000	301,600
February 28	37,000	384,800
March 31	40,000	416,000

The production budget is based upon this fundamental accounting inventory relationship: beginning finished goods inventory plus the cost of goods manufactured less the cost of goods sold is equal to the ending inventory of finished goods. After completing the sales budget and the finished goods budget, production requirements (Budget #3) can be calculated to comply with the specified inventory and sales figures.

Budget #3
Production Budget in Units
(1st Quarter, 19x2)

	January	February	March	Quarter Total
Sales (Budget #1)	12,000	12,000	17,000	41,000
Desired Ending Finished Goods Inventory (Budget #2)	29,000	37,000	40,000	40,000
Total	41,000	49,000	57,000	81,000
Less: Beginning Finished Goods Inventory (Budget #2)	24,000	29,000	37,000	24,000
Production Requirements	17,000	20,000	20,000	57,000

Direct Materials Requirements and Purchases Budgets (Budgets #4, #5 and #6)

Once the production budget is prepared, the raw materials budget and the raw materials purchases budget can be developed. The amount of raw materials necessary depends upon both the ending raw materials inventory requirements established by management and the production requirements established in the production budget. Item 9 of the Management Policies and Forecasts requires that the Power Turbine Shaft Division maintain a level of raw materials inventories at the end of each month that is sufficient to meet the next two months' production demands. Management decided that the standard usage and costs of one steel billet at $4 and two ball bearings at $1 each (from Illustration 3) were realistic and attainable. The December 31, 19x1 direct (raw) materials inventory from Illustration 2 is 24,000 steel billets ($96,000/$4) and 48,000 ball bearings ($48,000/$1). The desired ending raw materials inventories for March 31, 19x2 are large enough to provide for the budgeted April production of 13,000 units and the budgeted May production of 10,000 units as per item 9.

Budget #4
Direct Materials Requirements Budget (in Units)
(1st Quarter, 19x2)

Steel Billets (One per Finished Unit)

	January	February	March	Quarter Total
Production Requirements (Budget #3)	17,000	20,000	20,000	57,000
Desired Ending Direct Materials Inventory	40,000	33,000	23,000	23,000
Total	57,000	53,000	43,000	80,000
Less: Beginning Direct Materials Inventory	24,000	40,000	33,000	24,000
Purchase Requirements	33,000	13,000	10,000	56,000

Ball Bearings (Two per Finished Unit)

	January	February	March	Quarter Total
Production Requirements (Budget #3)	34,000	40,000	40,000	114,000
Desired Ending Direct Materials Inventory	80,000	66,000	46,000	46,000
Total	114,000	106,000	86,000	160,000
Less: Beginning Direct Materials Inventory	48,000	80,000	66,000	48,000
Purchase Requirements	66,000	26,000	20,000	112,000

The preparation of the direct materials purchases budget (Budget #5) requires converting the estimated monthly unit purchases of raw materials into a budget expressed in terms of dollars. The monthly purchase requirements are developed in Budget #4 in units. The direct material purchases budget (Budget #5) is then prepared in terms of dollars. The costs or purchase prices assigned to the purchase requirements in Budget #5 are the standard costs for raw materials found in Illustration 3. Management believes that the standard costs are the best estimate of the purchase prices that the Power Turbine Shaft Division will have to pay for direct materials. The standard cost of steel billets is $4 and the standard cost of ball bearings is $1.

Budget #5
Direct Materials Purchases Budget
(1st Quarter, 19x2)

Steel Billets

	January	February	March	Quarter Total
Purchase Requirements (Budget #4)	33,000	13,000	10,000	56,000
Standard Cost per Unit (Illustration 3)	$ 4.00	$ 4.00	$ 4.00	$ 4.00
Total Billet Purchases	$132,000	$52,000	$40,000	$224,000

Ball Bearings

	January	February	March	Quarter Total
Purchase Requirements (Budget #4)	66,000	26,000	20,000	112,000
Standard Cost per Unit (Illustration 3)	$ 1.00	$ 1.00	$ 1.00	$ 1.00
Total Ball Bearing Purchases	$ 66,000	$26,000	$20,000	$112,000
Total Direct Material Purchases	$198,000	$78,000	$60,000	$336,000

The direct materials usage budget (Budget #6) can be prepared at this point, or it can be included as part of the cost of goods manufactured budget (Budget #12). The direct materials usage budget can be prepared using the relationships inherent in the accounting inventory equation: beginning raw materials inventory plus purchases less the amount transferred to work-in-process equals the ending raw materials inventory. An alternative method is to convert the production requirements from the direct materials requirements budget (Budget #4) into dollars. The direct materials usage budget (Budget #5) converts the unit production requirements from Budget #4 into dollars.

Budget #6
Direct Materials Usage Budget
(1st Quarter, 19x2)

Steel Billets

	January	February	March	Quarter Total
Production Requirements (Budget #4)	17,000	20,000	20,000	57,000
Standard Cost per Unit (Illustration 3)	$ 4.00	$ 4.00	$ 4.00	$ 4.00
Total Usage	$68,000	$80,000	$80,000	$228,000

Ball Bearings

	January	February	March	Quarter Total
Production Requirements (Budget #4)	34,000	40,000	40,000	114,000
Standard Cost per unit (Illustration 3)	$ 1.00	$ 1.00	$ 1.00	$ 1.00
Total Usage	$34,000	$40,000	$40,000	$114,000

Direct Labor Budget (Budget #7)

For the direct labor budget, the Power Turbine Shaft Division uses the standard time of one-half per power turbine shaft and a standard direct labor cost of $6 per hour (Illustration 3). The production schedule, Budget #3, is the basis for developing the direct labor budget (Budget #7).

Budget #7
Direct Labor Budget
(1st Quarter, 19x2)

	January	February	March	Quarter Total
Production Requirements—Units (Budget #3)	17,000	20,000	20,000	57,000
Direct Labor per Unit in Hours	.5	.5	.5	.5
Direct Labor Requirements in Hours	8,500	10,000	10,000	28,500
Direct Labor Cost per Hour	$ 6.00	$ 6.00	$ 6.00	$ 6.00
	$51,000	$60,000	$60,000	$171,000

**Manufacturing
Overhead Budgets
(Budgets #8 and #9)**

Standard costs for manufacturing overhead, which were computed in Illustration 3, are used for planning purposes. The variable manufacturing overhead can be planned on the basis of units of production (Budget #3) or using direct labor hours at standard (Budget #7). The same budgeted cost will result using either basis. Since units of production are used as the basis of activity in the other production related budgets, the activity measure for the variable manufacturing overhead budget (Budget #8) will also be units of production.

The fixed manufacturing overhead costs are budgeted at $360,000 annually (item 4 in Management Policies and Forecasts). Individual items of the fixed overhead costs for the Division were updated to reflect current changes in costs. Management considers the breakdown of fixed manufacturing overhead costs reflected in Budget #9 to be reasonable approximations of 19x2 expenditures for overhead. Because fixed manufacturing overhead costs are linked primarily to the passage of time, management decided that an equal amount should be budgeted for each month of 19x2.

Budget #8
Variable Manufacturing Overhead Costs Budget
(1st Quarter, 19x2)

	January	February	March	Quarter Total
Production Requirements—Units (Budget #3)	17,000	20,000	20,000	57,000
Variable Manufacturing Overhead per Unit Produced:				
Rework Time . . . . $ .10	$ 1,700	$ 2,000	$ 2,000	$ 5,700
Waiting Time 06	1,020	1,200	1,200	3,420
Setup Time 08	1,360	1,600	1,600	4,560
Indirect Materials and Supplies 60	10,200	12,000	12,000	34,200
Indirect Labor 46	7,820	9,200	9,200	26,220
Electricity 10	1,700	2,000	2,000	5,700
Total $1.40	$23,800	$28,000	$28,000	$79,800

Budget #9
Fixed Manufacturing Overhead Costs Budget
(1st Quarter, 19x2)

	January	February	March	Quarter Total
Indirect Materials and Supplies . . .	$ 750	$ 750	$ 750	$ 2,250
Indirect Labor	2,200	2,200	2,200	6,600
Electricity	2,000	2,000	2,000	6,000
Heat	800	800	800	2,400
Equipment Depreciation	5,000	5,000	5,000	15,000
Plant Depreciation	12,500	12,500	12,500	37,500
Factory Property Taxes	6,750	6,750	6,750	20,250
	$30,000	$30,000	$30,000	$90,000

Non-Manufacturing Expense Budgets (Budgets #10 and #11)

The budgeted non-manufacturing expenses include variable selling costs of $5 per unit sold, $2,004,000 annually in fixed selling and administrative expenses, and annual interest expense on long-term debt of $132,000. These expenses were discussed in Management Policies and Forecasts, Items 3, 5, and 6, respectively. The activity basis for establishing the variable selling costs budget is the sales budget (Budget #1), because sales volume determines the amount of variable selling costs.

Over half of the fixed selling and administrative expenses budgeted are for monthly salaries. All other fixed selling and administrative expenses are also prorated into equal monthly installments for budgeting purposes, even though actual expenditures may be considerably more erratic.

Budget #10
Variable Selling Costs Budget
(1st Quarter, 19x2)

	January	February	March	Quarter Total
Forecast Unit Sales (Budget #1)	12,000	12,000	17,000	41,000
Variable Selling Cost per Unit	$ 5.00	$ 5.00	$ 5.00	$ 5.00
Total Variable Selling Cost	$60,000	$60,000	$85,000	$205,000

Budget #11
Fixed Non-Manufacturing Costs Budget
(1st Quarter, 19x2)

	January	February	March	Quarter Total
Selling and Administrative Expenses:				
Salaries	$ 96,000	$ 96,000	$ 96,000	$288,000
Advertising	28,000	28,000	28,000	84,000
Office Supplies	3,000	3,000	3,000	9,000
Travel	8,500	8,500	8,500	25,500
Telephone	5,000	5,000	5,000	15,000
Insurance	1,500	1,500	1,500	4,500
Research and Development	25,000	25,000	25,000	75,000
Total Selling and Administrative Expenses . .	$167,000	$167,000	$167,000	$501,000
Interest Expense	11,000	11,000	11,000	33,000
Total Non-Manufacturing Expenses	$178,000	$178,000	$178,000	$534,000

DEVELOPMENT OF THE MAJOR OPERATING OR PERFORMANCE BUDGETED FINANCIAL STATEMENTS

The major operating or pro-forma budgeted financial statements can be prepared using the Management Policies and Forecasts, and Budgets #1 through #11. The major operating budgeted financial statements are the cost of goods manufactured statement, the cost of goods sold statement, and the income statement.

Budgeted Cost of Goods Manufactured Statement (Budget #12)

The budgeted cost of goods manufactured statement is a projection and analysis of the changes occurring in the work-in-process account during the budgeted period. The work-in-process account at January 1, 19x2 is projected to have a balance of $300,000 (Illustration 2). Management expects to maintain this $300,000 balance in work-in-process throughout the year (item 11 of Management Policies and Forecasts). The variable manufacturing costs which are added to work-in-process each month can be determined from the budgets previously prepared for direct materials, direct labor, and variable manufacturing overhead. The budgeted cost of goods manufactured statement is presented in Budget #12.

```
                              Budget #12
                Budgeted Cost of Goods Manufactured Statement
                     For the Quarter Ending March 31, 19x2
```

	January	February	March	Quarter Total
Beginning Work-In-Process . .	$300,000	$300,000	$300,000	$300,000
Add: Manufacturing Costs				
Direct Materials:				
Steel Billets (Budget #6)	68,000	80,000	80,000	228,000
Ball Bearings (Budget #6)	34,000	40,000	40,000	114,000
Direct Labor (Budget #7)	51,000	60,000	60,000	171,000
Variable Manufacturing				
Overhead (Budget #8)	23,800	28,000	28,000	79,800
Total Available	$476,800	$508,000	$508,000	$892,800
Less: Ending				
Work-In-Process	300,000	300,000	300,000	300,000
Cost of Goods Manufactured	$176,800	$208,000	$208,000	$592,800

Budgeted Cost of Goods Sold Statement (Budget #13)

The budgeted cost of goods sold statement is a projection and an analysis of the changes occurring in the finished goods account during the budget period. The beginning finished goods inventory is budgeted for $249,600 (Budget #2 or Illustration 2). The additional forecast data are taken from the budgeted cost of goods manufactured statement and the finished goods budget. The budgets are prepared on a variable costing basis; therefore, only variable costs are considered in the cost of goods sold.

```
                              Budget #13
                Budgeted Variable Cost of Goods Sold Statement
                            (1st Quarter, 19x2)
```

	January	February	March	Quarter Total
Beginning Finished Goods				
Inventory (Budget #2) . .	$249,600	$301,600	$384,800	$249,600
Add: Budgeted Cost of Goods				
Manufactured				
(Budget #12)	176,800	208,000	208,000	592,800
Total Available	$426,400	$509,600	$592,800	$842,400
Ending Finished Goods				
Inventory (Budget #2) . .	301,600	384,800	416,000	416,000
Cost of Goods Sold	$124,800	$124,800	$176,800	$426,400

**Budgeted Income
Statement
(Budget #14)**

Budget #14, the budgeted income statement, is the forecasted results of operations for the budget period using the variable costing format for income determination. Note that Budget #14 shows two contribution margins—one after variable manufacturing costs are deducted from sales revenues and one after *all* variable costs are deducted from sales revenues. This refinement of the contribution margin approach reveals the source of the various contribution margins. The contribution margin computed by deducting *all* variable costs is the contribution margin available to cover fixed costs and profits. Therefore, it is the more significant of the two contribution margins. The budgeted income statement is presented on an accrual basis, not on a cash flow basis.

Budget #14
Budgeted Income Statement
For the Quarter Ending March 31, 19x2

	January	February	March	Quarter Total
Sales Revenues (Budget #1)	$600,000	$600,000	$850,000	$2,050,000
Less: Variable Cost of Goods Sold (Budget #13) . . .	124,800	124,800	176,800	426,400
Contribution Margin from Manufacturing	$475,200	$475,200	$673,200	$1,623,600
Less: Variable Selling Costs (Budget #10)	60,000	60,000	85,000	205,000
Contribution Margin	$415,200	$415,200	$588,200	$1,418,600
Less:				
Fixed Manufacturing Overhead Costs (Budget #9)	$ 30,000	$ 30,000	$ 30,000	$ 90,000
Fixed Selling and Administrative Costs (Budget #11)	167,000	167,000	167,000	501,000
Interest Expense (Budget #11)	11,000	11,000	11,000	33,000
Total Fixed Expenses	$208,000	$208,000	$208,000	$ 624,000
Budgeted Income Before Taxes	$207,200	$207,200	$380,200	$ 794,600

**DEVELOPMENT OF
THE MAJOR
FINANCIAL OR
RESOURCE
BUDGETS**

Once the operating or performance budgets are prepared, the financial or resource budgets can be prepared. The financial budgets rely mainly on the data included in the beginning balance sheet as presented in Illustration 2, the performance budgets and the Management Policies and Forecasts.

All balance sheet accounts are permanent accounts in which the accounting relationship (beginning balance in the account plus additions to the account less withdrawals from the account equals the ending balance) must be maintained. The ending account balances appear on the budgeted balance sheet. A number of ending balances for the permanent accounts have already been established by the performance budgets or by the Management Policies and Forecasts. Each account on the balance sheet is budgeted individually and then combined with other permanent accounts to develop the budgeted balance sheet. The ending cash balance cannot be ascertained until all other March 31, 19x2 budgeted account balances have been determined because data developed in the other budgeted permanent accounts are necessary in order to develop the cash budget. The accounts are considered in their order on the balance sheet.

Accounts Receivable Budget (Budget #15)

Collections of accounts receivable lag one month behind sales. The ending accounts receivable balance on March 31, 19x2 is equal to sales of $850,000 which are budgeted for March (Budget #1). The beginning accounts receivable for 19x2 is forecasted at $424,400 (Illustration 2).

Budget #15
Accounts Receivable Budget
(1st Quarter, 19x2)

	January	February	March	Quarter Total
Beginning Accounts Receivable (Illustration 2)	$ 424,400	$ 600,000	$ 600,000	$ 424,400
Sales for the Month (Budget #1)	600,000	600,000	850,000	2,050,000
Total	$1,024,400	$1,200,000	$1,450,000	$2,474,400
Ending Accounts Receivable	600,000	600,000	850,000	850,000
Collection of Accounts Receivable	$ 424,400	$ 600,000	$ 600,000	$1,624,400

Inventory Budgets (Budgets #16 and #17)

For the most part, inventory budgets are developed from operating budgets, because the ending inventory balance is dictated by management policy. The direct materials inventory budget is developed using the information provided in the direct materials purchases budget (Budget #5) and the budgeted cost of goods manufactured statement (Budget #12).

The indirect materials and supplies budget is to be maintained at a level of $30,000 (Item 10 in Management Policies and Forecasts). Purchases each month are therefore equal to the amount of indirect materials and supplies used. These data are found in the manufacturing overhead budgets (Budget #8 and #9).

The work-in-process inventory account is to be maintained at a level of $300,000 in order to insure relatively stable production volume requirements (Item 11 in Management Policies and Forecasts).

The finished goods inventory balances are determined by the sales forecast and the requirement that a quantity of finished goods sufficient to meet demand for two months in advance be on hand (Item 12 in the Management Policies and Forecasts). The monthly ending inventory balances required for finished goods are developed in Budget #2. A budget for finished goods inventory levels is also developed by using the budgeted cost of goods manufactured statement (Budget #12) and the budgeted variable cost of goods sold statement (Budget #13).

Budget #16
Direct Materials Budget
(1st Quarter, 19x2)

Steel Billets

	January	February	March	Quarter Total
Beginning Inventory (Illustration 2)	$ 96,000	$160,000	$132,000	$ 96,000
Add: Purchases (Budget #5)	132,000	52,000	40,000	224,000
Total Materials Available	$228,000	$212,000	$172,000	$320,000
Less: Transfers to Work-in-Process (Budget #6)	68,000	80,000	80,000	228,000
Ending Inventory	$160,000	$132,000	$ 92,000	$ 92,000

Ball Bearings

	January	February	March	Quarter Total
Beginning Inventory (Illustration 2)	$ 48,000	$ 80,000	$ 66,000	$ 48,000
Add: Purchases (Budget #5)	66,000	26,000	20,000	112,000
Total Materials Available	$114,000	$106,000	$ 86,000	$160,000
Less: Transfers to Work-in-Process (Budget #6)	34,000	40,000	40,000	114,000
Ending Inventory	$ 80,000	$ 66,000	$ 46,000	$ 46,000

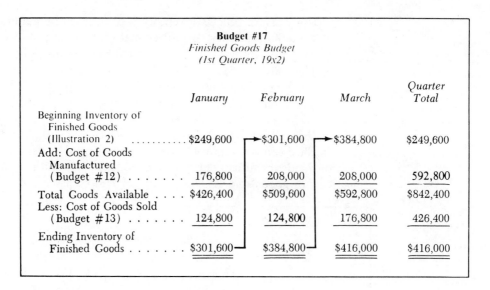

Budget #17
Finished Goods Budget
(1st Quarter, 19x2)

	January	February	March	Quarter Total
Beginning Inventory of Finished Goods (Illustration 2)	$249,600	$301,600	$384,800	$249,600
Add: Cost of Goods Manufactured (Budget #12)	176,800	208,000	208,000	592,800
Total Goods Available	$426,400	$509,600	$592,800	$842,400
Less: Cost of Goods Sold (Budget #13)	124,800	124,800	176,800	426,400
Ending Inventory of Finished Goods	$301,600	$384,800	$416,000	$416,000

Fixed Asset Budget (Budget #18)

The Power Turbine Shaft Division does not anticipate buying, selling, or trading any fixed assets in 19x2. The original cost of the equipment was $600,000. The estimated life of the equipment is 10 years, no salvage value is anticipated and straight-line depreciation is used to depreciate the equipment. Only one year's depreciation (19x1) has been recognized on the equipment prior to the preparation of the 19x2 budget.

The original cost of the plant was $3,000,000. A 20-year life is anticipated with no salvage value and straight-line depreciation is used as the basis for depreciating the plant. Both the equipment and plant depreciation were included in the fixed manufacturing overhead costs budget (Budget #9). The calculation of net book values is presented in Budget #18.

Accounts Payable and Wages Payable Budget (Budget #19)

Accounts payable represent direct material purchases; therefore, the accounts payable budget is based upon the direct material purchases budget (Budget #5). Credit terms in the industry and for the Power Turbine Shaft Division are net/30. The payments of accounts payable lag behind the purchases schedule by 30 days (item 15 of Management Policies and Forecasts). The beginning accounts payable balance of $60,000 (Illustration 2) will be paid in January of 19x2. The January, 19x2, purchases of $198,000 will be paid in February of 19x2.

Wages are paid on the fifteenth and on the last business day of each month. The outstanding wages payable at the end of any month is $18,000; this represents the wages earned by employees for the first two weeks that they are employed (item 16 in Management Policies and Forecasts). The budgeted wages paid are the monthly wages determined in the direct labor budget (Budget #7).

Budget #18
Fixed Asset Budget
(1st Quarter, 19x2)

Equipment

	January	February	March	Quarter Total
Original Cost	$600,000	$600,000	$600,000	$600,000
Less: Beginning Accumulated Depreciation	60,000	65,000	70,000	60,000
Less: Depreciation for the Period (Budget #9)	5,000	5,000	5,000	15,000
Accumulated Depreciation to Date	$ 65,000	$ 70,000	$ 75,000	$ 75,000
Net Book Value	$535,000	$530,000	$525,000	$525,000

Plant

	January	February	March	Quarter Total
Original Cost	$3,000,000	$3,000,000	$3,000,000	$3,000,000
Less: Beginning Accumulated Depreciation	150,000	162,500	175,000	150,000
Less: Depreciation for the Period (Budget #9)	12,500	12,500	12,500	37,500
Accumulated Depreciation to Date	$ 162,500	$ 175,000	$ 187,500	$ 187,500
Net Book Value	$2,837,500	$2,825,000	$2,812,500	$2,812,500

Budget #19
Accounts Payable Budget
(1st Quarter, 19x2)

	January	February	March	Quarter Total
Beginning Accounts Payable (Illustration 2)	$ 60,000	$198,000	$ 78,000	$ 60,000
Add: Purchases of Direct Materials (Budget #5) . .	198,000	78,000	60,000	336,000
Total	$258,000	$276,000	$138,000	$396,000
Less: Payments on Accounts Payable	60,000	198,000	78,000	336,000
Ending Accounts Payable . .	$198,000	$ 78,000	$ 60,000	$ 60,000

Long-Term Debt Budget (Budget #20)

The Power Turbine Shaft Division does not foresee any additional borrowing in 19x2. A current long-term debt of $1,200,000 is outstanding and requires monthly interest payments of $11,000 and principal payments of $30,000 per quarter beginning March 31, 19x2 (item 17 of Management Policies and Forecasts). The current payment schedule is projected in Budget #20.

Budget #20
Long-Term Debt Budget
(1st Quarter, 19x2)

Loan Payments

	January	February	March	Quarter Total
Interest Payments . . .	$ 11,000	$ 11,000	$ 11,000	$ 33,000
Principal Payments . .	–0–	–0–	30,000	30,000
Total	$ 11,000	$ 11,000	$ 41,000	$ 63,000

Balance of Principal

	January	February	March	Quarter Total
Beginning Principal (Illustration 2)	$1,200,000	$1,200,000	$1,200,000	$1,200,000
Less: Principal Payments	–0–	–0–	30,000	30,000
Net Principal	$1,200,000	$1,200,000	$1,170,000	$1,170,000

DEVELOPMENT OF THE MAJOR FINANCIAL OR RESOURCE BUDGETED FINANCIAL STATEMENTS

The next step in the budgeting process is the preparation of three major budgeted resource financial statements:

1. A cash budget
2. A stockholders' equity (corporate investment) statement
3. A budgeted balance sheet

**Cash Budget
Budget #21)**

A cash budget is an analysis of the cash account in terms of cash receipts and disbursements, and as such can facilitate the planning and control of cash flows. One intent of a cash budget is to establish minimum balance requirements so that normal cash needs can be met without borrowing. Determination of a minimum balance also frees surplus cash for investment. Cash budgeting is also necessary in order to anticipate possible cash shortages and thus allow adequate time to arrange borrowing. Cash budgeting is usually planned for very short periods (i.e., weekly or bi-weekly) in order that the budget be as responsive as possible to the cash needs of the company, for there can be drastic financial implications when a firm runs out of cash.

The primary source of cash for the Power Turbine Shaft Division is customer receipts (Budget #15). The cash balance and company borrowing policies (Item 7 of Management Policies and Forecasts) require a minimum cash balance of $40,000 to sustain the operations of the division. Any necessary cash can be borrowed from corporate headquarters, but only in increments of $5,000.

A number of factors affect cash disbursements:

1. The payment schedule for accounts payable for direct material purchases is presented in the accounts payable budget (Budget #19).
2. Wages payable are paid in the month earned and can be determined from the direct labor budget (Budget #7).
3. The long-term debt repayment schedule is found in the long-term debt budget (Budget #20).
4. All variable (Budget #8) and fixed manufacturing overhead costs (Budget #9) are paid in the month incurred except for the semiannual property taxes in Budget #9. The property taxes are paid on June 30 and December 31. (Remember, depreciation is a non-cash expense and therefore is not considered in the cash budget.
5. All non-manufacturing costs (Budgets #10 and #11) are paid in the month incurred.

Budgets for cash receipts and cash disbursements could be prepared separately. A complete cash budget is then prepared which incorporates both receipts and disbursements and reconciles the beginning and ending cash balances. Budget #21, the cash budget, includes all the budgeted factors which affect the cash position.

Budget #21
Cash Budget
(1st Quarter, 19x2)

	January	February	March	Quarter Total
Cash Receipts:				
Collections of Accounts Receivable (Illustration 2, Budget #15) ...	$424,400	$600,000	$600,000	$1,624,400
Cash Disbursements:				
Accounts Payable (Illustration 2, Budget #19) .	$ 60,000	$198,000	$ 78,000	$ 336,000
Payments for Direct Labor (Budget #7)	51,000	60,000	60,000	171,000
Long-Term Debt Principal Repayment (Budget #20)	–0–	–0–	30,000	30,000
Long-Term Debt Interest Payment (Budget #11 or 20)	11,000	11,000	11,000	33,000
Variable Manufacturing Overhead (Budget #8)	23,800	28,000	28,000	79,800
Fixed Manufacturing Overhead (Budget #9)[a]	5,750	5,750	5,750	17,250
Variable Selling Costs (Budget #10)	60,000	60,000	85,000	205,000
Fixed Selling and Administrative Costs (Budget #11)[b]	167,000	167,000	167,000	501,000
Total Disbursements	$378,550	$529,750	$464,750	$1,373,050
Excess (Deficit) of Cash Receipts Over Disbursements	$ 45,850	$ 70,250	$135,250	$ 251,350
Beginning Cash Balance .	40,000	85,850	156,100	40,000
Ending Cash Balance Before Borrowing or Repayment	$ 85,850	$156,100	$291,350	$ 291,350
Borrowing from Corporate Headquarters . . .	–0–	–0–	–0–	–0–
Repayment to Corporate Headquarters . . .	–0–	–0–	–0–	–0–
Ending Cash Balance	$ 85,850	$156,100	$291,350	$ 291,350

[a] Equipment and plant depreciation is not a cash outflow. The monthly cash outflows for fixed manufacturing overhead must be adjusted accordingly. For example, January—[$30,000-$6,750 (property taxes) — $17,500 (depreciation)] = $5,750 net cash outflow.
[b] Interest expense was considered separately in this cash budget. The January through March cash outflows are $178,000 — $11,000 (interest) = $167,000.

Budgeted Stockholders' Equity Statement (Budget #22)

The budgeted stockholders' equity statement, Budget #22, is the projected analysis of the change in Sax Company's investment in the Power Turbine Shaft Division. Corporate headquarters plans no increase or decrease in the investment in the division for the first quarter of 19x2.

Budget #22
Budgeted Stockholders' Equity Statement
(1st Quarter, 19x2)

	January	February	March	Quarter Total
Beginning Corporate Investment (Illustration 2).......	$3,300,000	$3,507,200	$3,714,400	$3,300,000
Add: Income (Budget #14) ...	207,200	207,200	380,200	794,600
Less: Withdrawals by Corporate Headquarters	–0–	–0–	–0–	–0–
Ending Corporate Investment ..	$3,507,200	$3,714,400	$4,094,600	$4,094,600

Budgeted or Pro-Forma Balance Sheet (Budget #23)

The budgeted or pro forma balance sheet in Budget #23 is the result of all budgets developed which involved assets, liabilities, or stockholders' equity. Management Policies and Forecasts have an added impact on the budgeted balance sheet. The function of management is to establish guidelines for obtaining and utilizing resources. If management requires certain balances in given accounts in order to attain the goals and objectives of the firm, then the budget should be prepared in light of these policies. For example, the budgeted balances in indirect materials and supplies, work-in-process, and wages payable were established by Management Policies and Forecasts. All other accounts were affected, either directly or indirectly, by management policies designed to utilize the resources of Sax Company in the most efficient and effective manner.

Budget #23
Budgeted Monthly Balance Sheets
(1st Quarter, 19x2)

	January 31	February 28	March 31
ASSETS			
Current Assets:			
Cash (Budget #21)	$ 85,850	$ 156,100	$ 291,350
Accounts Receivable (Budget #15)	600,000	600,000	850,000
Direct Materials Inventories:			
Steel Billets @ Standard			
(Budget #16)	160,000	132,000	92,000
Ball Bearings @ Standard			
(Budget #16)	80,000	66,000	46,000
Indirect Materials and Supplies . . .	30,000[a]	30,000[a]	30,000[a]
Work-in-Process @ Standard			
Variable Cost	300,000[b]	300,000[b]	300,000[b]
Finished Goods @ Standard			
Variable Cost (Budget #17) . . .	301,600	384,800	416,000
Total Current Assets.	$1,557,450	$1,668,900	$2,025,350
Long-Term Assets:			
Equipment (Budget #18)	$ 600,000	$ 600,000	$ 600,000
Less: Accumulated Depreciation			
(Budget #18)	65,000	70,000	75,000
Net: Equipment (Budget #18) . .	535,000	530,000	525,000
Plant (Budget #18)	3,000,000	3,000,000	3,000,000
Less: Accumulated Depreciation			
(Budget #18)	162,500	175,000	187,500
Net: Plant (Budget #18)	2,837,500	2,825,000	2,812,500
Total Long-Term Assets.	3,372,500	3,355,000	3,337,500
Total Assets.	$4,929,950	$5,023,900	$5,362,850
LIABILITIES AND STOCKHOLDERS' EQUITY			
Current Liabilities:			
Accounts Payable (Budget #19) . .	$ 198,000	$ 78,000	$ 60,000
Wages Payable	18,000[c]	18,000[c]	18,000[c]
Deferred Factory Property Taxes			
(Budget #9)	6,750[d]	13,500[d]	20,250[d]
Total Current Liabilities.	$ 222,750	$ 109,500	$ 98,250
Long-Term Debt (Budget #20) . . .	1,200,000	1,200,000	1,170,000
Total Liabilities	$1,422,750	$1,309,500	$1,268,250
Stockholders' Equity			
Corporate Investment			
(Budget #22)	3,507,200	3,714,400	4,094,600
Total Liabilities and Stockholders'			
Equity.	$4,929,950	$5,023,900	$5,362,850

[a] Item 10, Management Policies and Forecasts
[b] Item 11, Management Policies and Forecasts
[c] Item 16, Management Policies and Forecasts
[d] Deferred factory property taxes are $6,750 per month. The property taxes are paid on June 30 and December 31.

SUMMARY

Most firms employ some form of routine annual budgeting process resulting in segment-by-segment monthly budgets for the coming year. The process normally begins with the development of company objectives and lower management's projection of needs to meet those objectives. The budgeting process culminates in a formal integration of all divisional budgets into a corporate budget. The monthly budgets are updated at given intervals to reflect any new or additional information that may be pertinent.

Short-range planning or budgeting has several general benefits. One primary benefit is that a budget communicates the short-range plans of the firm to each manager and thereby facilitates coordination of the efforts and activities of all segments of the company. The budget process also serves as an element of *before-the-fact* control because each manager must justify his requests for resources. In addition, the budget serves as a basis for *after-the-fact* control by providing a benchmark against which actual performance can be measured. Formal budgeting can identify weak areas of the firm by pinpointing unsatisfactory contribution margins, production bottlenecks, etc. Finally, by involving various personnel in the budgeting process, the budget becomes an effective motivational tool for employees and management.

The basic end-product of the budgeting process is a set of budgeted or pro-forma financial statements. In developing these statements, a firm generally finds it necessary to produce numerous specialized budgets and schedules. The starting point in the budgeting process is generally a projection of sales in units for the budget period. Estimates are then made to determine the level of finished goods inventory and production requirements necessary to meet this anticipated demand for the product. Information from the production budget is then used to forecast direct material requirements and to prepare the purchases budget. The direct labor and manufacturing overhead budgets are also prepared based on the production budget.

The budgets for non-manufacturing expenses are completed and the major budgeted operating statements are then prepared. These statements include the budgeted cost of goods manufactured statement, the budgeted cost of goods sold statement, and the budgeted income statement.

To develop the major financial or resource budgets, the firm must prepare additional budgets and associated schedules for each asset, liability, and owner's equity account. The final result is a budgeted or pro forma balance sheet for the firm.

KEY DEFINITIONS

Budget—formalized plans prepared by management, generally on a segment-by-segment basis, for a specified period in the near future. Budgets may be prepared for a wide range of operating and financial factors such as sales, production and manufacturing expenses. These factors are the basis for the major operating or performance and financial or resource budgeted (pro-forma) financial statements. They may be long or short-term (most firms use both).

Budgeted balance sheet—the projected balance sheet of the firm showing the expected financial position of the firm at a given point in time during or at the conclusion of the budget period.

Budgeted cost of goods manufactured statement—a projection and analysis of the changes occurring in the work-in-process account during the budget period.

Budgeted cost of goods sold statement—a projection and analysis of the changes occurring in the finished goods account during the budget period.

Budgeted income statement—the forecasted results of operations for the budget period.

Budgeted stockholders' equity statement—a projected analysis of investment changes in the firm during the budget period.

Cash budget—an analysis of the cash account in terms of anticipated cash receipts and disbursements in order to establish cash balances over the budget period for the planning and control of cash.

Comprehensive budgeting—a system encompassing and integrating the areas of planning, control and performance evaluation for the entire company.

Intermediate-range planning—planning to achieve objectives for which the firm is striving in the next three to five years.

Long-range planning—planning for the distant future.

Major financial resource budgeted statements—cash budget, stockholders' equity or corporate investment statement, and budgeted balance sheet.

Major operating budgeted financial statements—cost of goods manufactured statement, the cost of goods sold statement, and the income statement.

Short-range planning—also known as budgeting or profit planning, this planning consists of management's financial expectation for the near future, a period in which the firm faces factors which cannot be altered in the short-term.

QUESTIONS

1. What is the definition of constraining factors and how do they relate to short-range planning?

2. Name two specific ways in which long-range planning differs from short-range planning.

3. Two of the benefits of short-range planning are communication and coordination. Why are these two factors important to the firm?

4. How can short-range planning act as a motivator for management?

5. How does short-range planning yield a basis for after-the-fact control?

6. At what stage in the short-range budgeting process is the sales budget formulated? What external sources are used to establish a reliable sales forecast?

7. Why do firms maintain a minimum and a maximum level of inventory?

8. What is a cash budget and what is its purpose?

9. What factors do the normal operating cash receipts of a firm depend on?

10. What is the last budget which is usually made in the short-range profit planning procedure and why is it the last?

EXERCISES

11. The Downhill Ski Company has forecasted sales in February to be 38,500 pairs of skis. The company has three areas for sales: New England, Middle West and Rocky Mountains. The New England area captures about 35% of the sales and the price is $90. The Middle West and Rocky Mountains areas sell 28% and 37%, respectively. The price is $120 in the Middle West and $165 in the Rocky Mountains.

    Required:

    Prepare a sales budget for February showing quantity and dollar sales in each area as well as a total for the company.

12. The Foolery Company has requested the construction of an income budget for sales of $7,200, $6,300, and $7,680. The company accountant has estimated that variable costs are 67% of sales and fixed costs are $2,400 per year.

    Required:

    Prepare the three budgets the Foolery Company has requested.

13. The Nelson Company produces two products: standard and custom. For 19x1, the company plans to produce 4,000 units of each product. These products require the raw materials given below:

	Cost/Unit	Standard	Custom
X	$2.00	2 units	
Y	2.50	1 unit	1 unit
Z	1.25		3 units

Required:

Prepare a material usage budget for 19x1.

14. Given below is the beginning inventory and the desired ending inventory of raw materials for Jones, Inc.

	Beginning		Ending	
Material	No. Units	Cost Per Unit	No. Units	Cost Per Unit
A	400	$.50	300	$.50
B	2,000	.40	2,000	.40
C	600	.90	750	.90

The company plans to produce 40,000 units of Product X and 37,500 units of Product Z. Product X requires 2 units of A, 1 unit of B, and 1 unit of C. Product Z requires 1 unit of B and 3 units of C.

Required:

Prepare a purchases budget in units and dollars for raw materials.

15. You have been asked to prepare a sales budget broken down by month for the first quarter of 19x1.

Required:

Prepare the requested sales budget from the information given below. Your answer should show the sales budget in units and dollars.

Sales price, $10 per unit.
Sales for December, 19x0, 5,000 units.
Sales are expected to increase by 3% each month.

16. Gamma, Inc. plans to produce 25,000 units of Alpha and 29,000 units of Beta. The units go through cutting and finishing processes. Alpha requires 2 hours cutting and ¾ hour in finishing at direct labor rates of $2 and $3.50, respectively. Beta requires 1 hour in cutting and 2 hours in finishing at the same rates.

Required:

Prepare a direct labor budget for Gamma, Inc.

17. Rite, Inc. manufactures pencils. During 19x1, they predict a sales volume of 25,240,000 pencils. At the present time, their finished goods inventory has 1,500,000 pencils. Rite hopes to increase this inventory by 15% at the end of the year. At the present time, there is no work-in-process inventory.

Required:

Prepare a production budget by units.

18. The Task Company is to begin operations in January. They have budgeted January sales of $34,000, February sales of $40,000, March sales of $42,000 and April sales of $38,000.

Required:

Prepare a budget of cash receipts from sales for the first five months of the year if 75% of sales are collected the month following sale, 16% the second month, 6% the third month, and the balance is bad debts.

19. The sales budget of Wackie Toy Co. projects the following level of sales for the second quarter: April 20,000 units, May 22,000 units and June 19,000 units. The finished goods budget shows desired ending inventories as follows: April 30,000 units, May 35,000 units and June 25,000 units. The ending desired inventory for March was 28,000 units.

Required:

Prepare a production budget in units for the second quarter.

20. Vandergelder, Inc. produces hockey sticks with a standard cost of material of $1.75 per stick. The raw materials production requirements for the last quarter of 19x0 are as follows: October = 27,000 units, November = 35,000 units and December = 40,000 units. It requires $\frac{1}{10}$ hours of direct labor per stick at a cost of $3 per hour. Rework costs amount to $.05 per unit. Waiting time is zero and set-up time is $.02 per unit. Indirect materials and supplies total $.40 per unit. Indirect labor is $.15 per unit and electricty is $.08 per unit.

Required:

Prepare the direct materials usage budget, the direct labor budget, and the variable manufacturing overhead budget for the last quarter.

PROBLEMS

21. Lazyman, Inc., a producer of mattresses, has predicted total sales of 190,500 mattresses in 19x1. The company has three outlets for the product: the East Coast, the West Coast, and Southern United States. The mattresses sell for $180, $200 and $215, respectively. The East Coast captures 40% of the market with the other two areas dividing the remainder equally.

In 19x1, it took 40 pounds of stuffing at $2 per pound and 20 yards of material at $1.50 per yard to make one mattress. Lazyman expects the cost of stuffing to go up 15% and the material to go up 8%. It takes 1½ hours of direct labor, which cost $6.50 per hour in 19x1, to make one mattress. Due to a new labor contract, labor costs per hour will rise 20% in 19x2. Because of improved machinery, it will only take 1¼ hours to make one mattress in 19x2. Variable costs will be applied at a rate of $4.50 per direct labor hour. This is the same rate as was used in 19x1. Fixed overhead costs are expected to be $200,000 and administrative costs to be $150,000 in 19x2.

At the end of 19x1, the inventory consisted of 620 finished mattresses, no work-in-process, 800 pounds of stuffing, and 600 yards of material. They plan to increase all of their inventories except work-in-process by 30% at the end of 19x2. Lazyman uses Fifo and variable costing for inventory costing purposes.

Required:

Prepare the following:

1. Production budget in units
2. Direct material requirements budget (in units)
3. Direct material purchase budget (in dollars)
4. Direct material usage budget
5. Direct labor budget
6. Variable manufacturing overhead budget
7. Cost of goods manufactured statement
8. Cost of goods sold statement
9. Income statement

22. During December, 19x1, the Burns Co. sold 40,000 gallons of charcoal lighter. In the first quarter of 19x2, the company expects sales to increase 20% each month. The company normally collects 30% of the sales price in the month of the sale, 50% in the second month, and the remainder in the next month. Sales for November 19x1, totaled 35,000 gallons. A gallon of charcoal lighter sold for $.60 in 19x1, but the company plans to raise the price to $.68 per gallon in 19x2 due to increasing costs.

Required:

You are to prepare a sales budget and an accounts receivable budget for the first quarter of 19x2.

23. During February and March, the Farm Fresh Egg Co. sold 110,000 and 90,000 dozen eggs, respectively. The eggs sell for $.49 per dozen for the small eggs, $.56 for medium eggs, $.60 for large eggs, and $.68 for extra large eggs. The ratio of eggs from small to extra large is 1-3-4-2, respectively. Sales for the second quarter are expected to increase 20% each month. Collections on sales are 50% in the month of the sale, 40% the next month, and 10% the third month.

Required:

Your job is to prepare a sales budget for February through June and an accounts receivable budget for April through June.

24. The condensed income statement of the Howle Manufacturing Corporation for 19x1 is as follows:

Sales (30,000 units)........................		$450,000
Sales returns, allowances and discounts.......		13,500
Net sales.............................		$436,500
Cost of goods sold........................		306,000
Gross profit on sales......................		$130,500
Selling expenses..........................	$60,000	
Administrative expenses....................	30,000	90,000
Net profit before income taxes...............		$ 40,500

The budget committee has estimated the following changes in income and costs for 19x2.

30% increase in the number of units sold.
20% increase in the material unit cost.
15% increase in the direct labor cost per unit.
10% increase in the production overhead cost per unit.
14% increase in the selling expenses.
7% increase in the administrative expenses.

As inventory quantities remain fairly constant, the committee considered that, for budget purposes, any change in inventory valuation can be ignored. The composition of the cost of finished product during 19x1 for materials, direct labor and production overhead, respectively, was in the ratio of 3 to 2 to 1. No changes in production methods or credit policies were contemplated for 19x2.

Required:

Using the above data, you are to prepare the projected 19x2 income statement and compute the unit sales price (rounded to the nearest full cent) at which the Howle Manufacturing Corporation must sell its only product in 19x2 in order to earn a budgeted profit (before income taxes) of exactly $60,000.

(AICPA adapted)

25. The condensed income statement of the Jones Manufacturing Corporation for 19x1 is as follows:

Sales (100,000 units)........................		$3,000,000
Sales returns, allowances, and discounts.......		12,000
Net sales.............................		$2,988,000
Cost of goods sold........................		1,215,000
Gross profit..............................		$1,773,000
Selling expense...........................	$360,000	
Administrative expense....................	840,000	1,200,000
Net profit before income taxes...............		$ 573,000

The budget committee has estimated the following changes in income and costs for 19x2:

> 25% increase in the number of units sold.
> 15% increase in the material cost.
> 20% increase in the direct labor cost per unit.
> 10% increase in the production overhead cost per unit.
> 12% increase in selling expenses.
> 14% increase in administrative expense.

As inventory quantities remain fairly constant, the committee considered that, for budget purposes, any change in inventory valuation can be ignored. The composition of the cost of finished product during 19x1, for materials, direct labor, and production overhead, respectively was in the ratio of 4 to 3 to 2. No changes in production methods or credit policies are contemplated for 19x2.

Required:

Using the above data, you are to prepare the projected 19x2 income statement and compute the unit sales price (rounded to the nearest full cent) at which the Jones Manufacturing Corporation must sell its only product in 19x2 in order to earn a budgeted profit (before income taxes) of $650,000.

(AICPA adapted)

26. Below are given the condensed financial statements of the Flophouse Hotel:

Flophouse Hotel
Balance Sheet
December 31, 19x1

Cash..............................	$ 10,000	
Accounts receivable (net)..............	25,000	
Other current assets...................	5,000	$ 40,000
Fixed assets.........................	$120,000	
Less: Accumulated depreciation........	36,000	84,000
Total Assets......................		$124,000
Accrued payables.....................		$ 20,000
Mortgage payable.....................		40,000
Flophouse, capital....................		64,000
Total Liabilities and Equities..........		$124,000

Flophouse Hotel
Income Statement
Year 19x1

Revenues............................	$250,000
Expenses............................	200,000
Income............................	$ 50,000

Other data:

a. Revenues for 19x2 are expected to increase by 20%.
b. Fixed expenses will remain constant at $100,000; the remaining expenses will continue to vary directly and proportionally with revenue.
c. Accounts receivable at December 31, 19x2 are expected to be 10% of 19x2 revenue.
d. The hotel plans a fixed asset addition on July 1, 19x2, costing $50,000. All fixed assets have a useful life of 10 years and no salvage value.
e. Accounts payable at December 31, 19x2, are expected to aggregate 10% of total expenses.
f. The 19x2 mortgage principal payment is $2,000.
g. The owner plans to withdraw $25,000 during the year.

Required:

Prepare the following for the Flophouse Hotel for 19x2:

1. Operating budget (budgeted income statement).
2. Cash budget.
3. Pro-forma balance sheet as of December 31, 19x2.

Chapter 18 discusses the cost concepts and accounting approaches which are related to the planning of special decisions. Studying this chapter should enable you to:

1. Provide examples of the types of decisions which are commonly referred to as special decisions.

2. Discuss the concept of relevance as it relates to the planning of special decisions.

3. Describe how the accounting records may provide useful information for the special decision-making process.

4. Identify the two characteristics which are common to all costs used for decision-making.

5. Define and give examples of the various classifications of decision-making costs.

6. Discuss and apply the general formats for presenting relevant information for special decision-making.

7. Identify those factors that should be considered in pricing a product.

18

Planning for Special Decisions

INTRODUCTION

Accounting records and the accounting information system serve as the basic means for accumulating information on a historical cost basis for financial accounting purposes. Accounting also plays an important role both in the normal and recurring aspects of budgeting and in the control and performance evaluation functions. For financial accounting purposes, the role of record keeping is basically historical in nature. With regard to managerial accounting, record keeping is a combination of both forward looking projections and, on a selected basis, historical accumulations for purposes of comparison. In both of these instances, the accounting system is designed to capture and communicate recurring information.

The focus of this chapter emphasizes the accounting approaches which may be used for accumulating and presenting the information required for use in making decisions that are neither recurring nor routine. Examples of the type of decisions that fall into the non-recurring or special decision category include:

1. Accept or reject decisions for a special customer order.
2. Make or buy decisions for a specific component of the firm's products.
3. Continuance or discontinuance of an operating segment, such as a sales territory or a product line.
4. Pricing decisions.

RELEVANCE: THE KEY TO DECISION-MAKING

The key to selecting an alternative in any decision-making process is to focus attention on the relevant information. Relevant information for decision-making purposes is that information which differs among the various alternatives under consideration. For example, if you were considering the purchase of a candy bar from a vending machine and all of the candy bars available cost 25 cents, the decision would not be based on the cost of the candy bar since all bars have the identical price. However, if you decided that you wanted a candy bar with peanuts and only two of the candy bars available met this criterion, then this is relevant information. The decision is now narrowed to only two alternatives, but additional relevant information is necessary in order to make the final choice. Thus, if you were allergic to chocolate and one of the two bars with peanuts contained chocolate, then this fact is also relevant to you in making the decision to select the candy bar that contains peanuts but no chocolate. The concept of relevance in the planning of special decisions is identical to the relevance considered in the candy bar example. The relevant factors analyzed in the candy purchasing decision were those factors that differed among the alternatives.

IMPORTANCE OF BOTH QUALITATIVE AND QUANTITATIVE FACTORS

The desire for a candy bar with peanuts but no chocolate is an example of the use of a qualitative factor in a decision-making process. Qualitative factors are not expressed in either numerical or monetary terms, yet for any particular decision, a qualitative factor may be the most important consideration. In fact, for many management decisions, qualitative factors are of primary significance and concern.

Accounting concepts play an important role in developing the quantitative factors which are considered in special decisions. Quantitative factors are those factors that can be expressed in numbers. In some instances, the quantitative factors are estimates or forecasts based on the subjective judgments of knowledgeable people or on specific studies designed to develop the estimates. The only quantitative factor in the candy bar example was the price of 25 cents, which was irrelevant to the decision since all of the available bars cost 25 cents.

DECISION-MAKING COST CONCEPTS

Decision making is, by definition, a process of selecting among various alternatives. The availability of all relevant information for each possible alternative would greatly facilitate this process. However, the cost of gathering all potentially useful information for each alternative is extreme. Therefore, although the accounting information system is not designed in terms of providing special decision-making information, accounting records often serve as a basis for accumulating the data which must be considered in making a special decision. For example, if a company is considering producing (with its existing equipment) a subassembly that it is presently buying, then accounting records could play a major role in developing the data required for the analysis. The cost of using the existing equipment to produce current products can be determined from the accounting records. This cost is then adjusted to reflect the different specifications required for the subassembly. The adjusted data serves as the basis for estimating the costs of manufacturing the subassembly.

Costs applicable to the decision-making process are classified differently than those costs which were defined for income determination purposes and for purposes of planning, control, and performance evaluation. Analysis of costs which are relevant to the decision-making process need not follow particular rules or special formats. These costs may be either product costs or period costs, fixed costs or variable costs, controllable costs or noncontrollable costs, common costs or traceable costs. However, all costs used for decision making do have two common characteristics:

1. They are relevant, i.e., the costs will differ under the various alternatives.
2. They are costs which are anticipated in the future under each of the various alternatives.

The cost definitions and the discussions of these definitions which follow are the basic concepts required in developing the accounting approaches used to analyze special decisions.

Relevant Costs

As previously indicated, relevant costs are those future costs that differ under the various alternatives that the firm is considering. Precision and accuracy are not always primary factors in determining relevance. Many relevant costs must be estimates since the precise cost may be known only after a particular alternative is selected and implemented.

The concepts of relevancy and accuracy are illustrated by the following example. Assume that during the next spring break you intend to visit a resort area. This resort is 1200 miles from your school and you have decided either to drive alone or to fly tourist class. A three hour direct flight is available at a round-trip cost of $400. Driving time is two days each way, thus time spent at the resort will be curtailed if this alternative is chosen. Regardless of whether you fly or drive, 14 nights and 15 days of vacation are available to you. Motel accommodations will cost $20 per day, and you expect to stay at a motel every night, including those nights spent on the road if you choose to drive. Food will cost $9 per day, and your car averages 25 miles per gallon of gasoline at an average cost of $1.50 per gallon. Your best estimate of the other costs such as oil, repairs, etc., total approximately $50. If you do not take your car, you do not anticipate renting a car during your stay at the resort. The resort has a courtesy car available that provides airport transportation at no cost. We will assume that the decision, as far as you are concerned, is strictly one of minimizing your vacation costs.

A summary of the total cost for each alternative follows:

By Car		*By Airplane*	
Oil, repairs, etc.	$ 50	Air fare	$400
Motel—14 nights @ $20	280	Motel—14 nights @ $20	280
Food—15 days @ $9	135	Food—15 days @ $9	135
Gasoline: $\frac{2400 \text{ miles}}{25 \text{ miles per gallon}}$ X $1.50	144		
Total cost by car	$609	Total cost by airplane	$815

As the above analysis indicates, you can save $206 ($815 − $609) by driving instead of flying. Note that in order to make this decision, all the costs do not have to be considered. Only those costs that differ between the alternatives should be considered. Motel and food costs are identical under each alternative; therefore, these costs are irrelevant to the decision. If only relevant costs are considered, the cost data can be presented as follows:

By Car		*By Airplane*	
Oil, repairs, etc.	$ 50	Air fare	$400
Gasoline:			
$\frac{2400 \text{ miles}}{25 \text{ miles per gallon}}$ X $1.50	144		
Relevant cost by car	$194	Relevant cost by airplane	$400

The difference between the two alternatives is still $206—the difference between the relevant costs. Eliminating costs which are common to both alternatives has no bearing on the difference between alternatives.

The degree of accuracy in the accumulation of relevant costs is questionable. Numerous factors, such as accidents or breakdowns of the car, could alter the cost of driving. The price of gasoline could increase or decrease, and the air fare could also change.

This example considered only quantitative decision factors. In addition to these factors, there are numerous qualitative factors to consider: the additional time that might be spent at the resort, the personal inconvenience of driving 2,400 miles, the countryside that can be seen by driving and the safety factors of flying versus driving. None of these factors can be easily quantified and used as direct inputs in the decision-making process. Accounting approaches to decision-making emphasize the quantitative factors and, at most, can only aid in identifying the qualitative factors.

Opportunity Costs

An opportunity cost is a measure of benefits that could have been derived had an alternative choice been made. For example, an opportunity cost could be the income foregone by not choosing the next best alternative which was under consideration. An opportunity cost may not always be measured with a high degree of certainty.

The concept of opportunity cost is related to every activity an individual or a firm undertakes, because an alternative course of action always exists. An opportunity cost is always associated with the commitment of scarce resources. For example, assume that you could work this evening for three hours and earn a total of $10. Instead, you choose to go out on the town and spend $15. You chose an alternative, and the income foregone or the opportunity cost associated with your decision was $10. The fact that you actually spent $15 does not affect what you gave up by choosing to go out rather than to work.

Another example of opportunity cost is illustrated by the decision to scrap defective products instead of reworking these units and selling them in the usual market. If a company had defective products that could be sold for 25 cents per unit as scrap or which could be reworked at an additional cost of 10 cents per unit and sold for 50 cents, then there is an opportunity cost involved for either alternative selected. The opportunity cost of the reworking alternative is the scrap value of 25 cents per unit. The opportunity cost of scrapping is 40 cents (the selling price of 50 cents less the reworking cost of 10 cents per unit). Note that the original production cost is not mentioned in either case as it is irrelevant in measuring opportunity cost. The production cost resulted from the initial decision to produce the units; it had already been incurred under either alternative.

Incremental or Differential Costs

An incremental or differential cost is the difference between the total costs of the various available alternatives. In practice, the term "incremental cost" is often used to describe the difference in costs incurred by producing at two different levels of activity. To illustrate the concept of incremental cost, assume that you decide to rent a car at a fixed charge of $15 a day plus a mileage charge of 20 cents per mile. The rental agency will reimburse you for any gasoline and similar expenses which you might incur. If you drive the car 800 miles in a four-day period, your rental cost is calculated as follows:

Rental Cost for 4 Days and 800 Miles
Fixed Costs—4 days @ $15.00 . . . . $ 60
Variable Costs—800 miles @ $.20 160
Total Rental Costs $220

Assume that you decide to keep the car an additional day in order to make a 150-mile side trip. The incremental costs of keeping the car and making this extra trip are calculated as follows:

Rental Costs—4 Days Versus 5 Days

	4 Days and 800 Miles	5 Days and 950 Miles	Incremental Costs
Fixed Costs—$15.00/Day	$ 60	$ 75	$15
Variable Costs—$.20/Mile	160	190	30
Totals	$220	$265	$45

It should be obvious that incremental or differential costs are always relevant costs when making a selection between or among alternatives.

Escapable or Avoidable Costs

As the term implies, escapable or avoidable costs are those costs which are saved or eliminated by making a particular decision or selecting a certain alternative. The concept of escapable costs is useful for decision-making purposes because, in many instances, certain costs may be avoided when one alternative is selected over another. This cost definition is frequently used in discussing the elimination of a division or a segment of a business.

If elimination of a segment of a firm is an alternative under consideration, escapable costs are limited to those costs that are directly traceable to that segment. Any arbitrarily allocated costs will still be incurred even if the segment is eliminated, and the remaining segments of the firm will be required to absorb these costs. An example of this concept is discussed later in this chapter when the elimination of segments is illustrated.

Out-of-Pocket Costs

Out-of-pocket costs are those costs that require a definite outlay of funds. Relevant out-of-pocket costs are those costs which differ among the various alternatives being considered. Expenses such as depreciation or allocated costs are not considered out-of-pocket costs.

Sunk Costs

Sunk costs are costs which have already been incurred and which cannot be changed regardless of the selected alternative. Sunk costs are irrelevant as far as deciding among alternatives is concerned. An investment in fixed assets is a common example of a sunk cost. Once an asset is acquired, its original cost or net book-value is not considered in making future decisions. A relevant cost is a future cost which differs among the alternatives available. Costs which have already been incurred are neither future expenditures nor do these costs differ under the various alternatives under consideration.

If one alternative calls for the sale of an existing asset, the cash received for that asset and any tax implications of a gain or loss on the sale are relevant to that alternative. The net cash received from the sale of an asset, not the original cost or net book value of the asset, is the relevant information. The cost of retaining an asset is the net selling price of the asset because the cash received could be reinvested. It is impossible to reinvest the original cost or the net book value of a retained asset in another alternative; it is a sunk cost. The original cost is relevant only for purposes of calculating depreciation expense for the income statement, for calculating net book values for the balance sheet, and for determining tax implications regarding a sale.

GENERAL ACCOUNTING FORMATS FOR ARRANGING RELEVANT INFORMATION

Any format used for arranging decision-making information should emphasize those factors that differ among the available alternatives. Two general accounting formats used to arrange relevant information for the use of decision makers include:

1. Incremental cost and/or incremental revenue approach.
2. Contribution margin approach.

Neither of these general formats is applicable to every decision. For example, the contribution margin format requires that both revenues and the related variable costs be known in order for the contribution margin to be computed. In addition, the contribution margin format does not explicitly consider fixed costs; therefore, it is valid only when fixed costs are irrelevant. It should be noted that the contribution margin approach is not a "full" costing approach. Both formats are illustrated in the following special order decision-making process.

SPECIAL ORDERS:
AN EXAMPLE

The Karson Company has idle capacity available in its manufacturing operations. A buyer outside Karson's usual marketing area has made an offer to purchase 50 units of a standard product, Edd, at a price of $1 per unit. Edd is normally sold by the Karson Company for $2. The Karson Company does not currently sell this product in the buyer's geographical area nor does the company plan to sell it in that area in the future. This is essentially a one-time purchase by this potential customer. Any freight expense will be paid by the buyer. If Karson Company sells to this buyer, it will have no impact on its current customers.

The *current* budget for Karson Company is as follows:

Karson Company
Budget for Product
Line-Edd

Relevant Range of Production	400-750 Units
Basis for Fixed Overhead Allocation	500 Units
Budgeted Sales 500 Units @ $2.00	$1,000
Variable Costs 500 Units @ $.75	375
Contribution Margin	$ 625
Fixed Production Costs 500 Units @ $.50	250
Fixed Selling and Administrative Costs	300
Budgeted Income Before Taxes	$ 75

Any approach to the decision to produce the special order for sale at $1 per unit which is based on full or absorption costing would result in a recommendation to reject the order since the proposed selling price is less than the full cost. The current full cost of the product (with the fixed overhead allocated over production of 500 units) is $1.25 per unit [($375 + 250)/500]. Even with fixed overhead of $250 allocated over 550 units of production, the full cost of the product on a per unit basis would be in excess of $1.20 [($412.50 + $250)/550].

However, the additional order of 50 units has come at a time when idle capacity is available and when this additional production will not affect the total fixed overhead costs incurred. A production level of 550 units is well within the relevant range of activity for the firm. Quantitatively, both formats for analyzing this special decision will agree, since fixed costs are not relevant to the decision.

Contribution Margin

	Per Unit	Total for 50 Units
Revenues	$1.00	$50.00
Variable Costs	.75	37.50
Contribution Margin	$ .25	$12.50

The above analysis provides the information necessary to make a decision using the contribution margin approach. The additional sales provide a contribution margin of $12.50 or $.25 per unit, which can be applied to the recovery of the unchanged fixed costs. Thus, given the existence of idle capacity, the decision to sell the additional 50 units of Edd appears to be financially sound.

The following analysis presents the information required to make a decision using the incremental income approach:

Incremental Costs and Revenues

	Budget Without the Order	Budget With the Order	Incremental Costs and Revenues
Budgeted Sales:			
500 units @ $2.00	$1,000.00	$1,000.00	–0–
50 units @ $1.00	–0–	50.00	$50.00
Variable Costs:			
500 units @ $.75	375.00	375.00	–0–
50 units @ $.75	–0–	37.50	37.50
Contribution Margin	$ 625.00	$ 637.50	$12.50
Fixed Production Costs	$ 250.00	$ 250.00	–0–
Fixed Selling and Administrative Costs	300.00	300.00	–0–
Budgeted Income Before Taxes	$ 75.00	$ 87.50	$12.50

If the special order is accepted, the incremental budgeted net income before taxes will be $12.50. Given that all other cost factors remain the same, management should accept the order. Remember, there was idle capacity available. Without this idle capacity, the decision may have been to reject the order.

**MAKE OR BUY:
AN EXAMPLE**

In the short-run, for a firm to consider making component parts for products rather than purchasing those parts from vendors, the firm must have available idle capacity and the ability to make the parts. The question is one of using the idle capacity to produce the parts, using the capacity for other purposes, or allowing the capacity to go unused.

If only quantitative factors are considered in the decision to make or buy a part, the current purchase price must be known. The cost to make the part must also be determined. The only relevant costs for this decision are those costs that would be incurred if the part is made. Any arbitrarily allocated costs that could not be avoided if the part were not made are irrelevant. These costs are incurred by the firm under either alternative.

The accounting department made a study and developed the following cost of manufacturing the part. The normal demand for this part is 25 units per year.

Costs to Manufacture a Component Part

	Per Unit	Total at 25 Units
Direct materials	$ .20	$ 5.00
Direct labor	1.10	27.50
Variable overhead	.30	7.50
Avoidable fixed overhead	.40	10.00
Total	$2.00	$50.00

According to the quantitative data, if the purchase price of the part exceeds $2.00, then the firm should make the part itself.

There are also qualitative factors which should be considered in a make or buy decision. Examples of these qualitative factors include the following:

1. What quality is necessary? Can the firm make a better quality part?
2. Will the idle capacity be available? For how long will it be available?
3. Will current vendors of the part be willing to sell to the firm in the future if the supply of raw materials becomes limited?
4. Will future opportunities be lost because of the lack of idle capacity resulting from a decision to make the part?

The make or buy decision may be used in a number of contexts. For example, should a firm use a service bureau for computer work or establish its own facility? Should in-house salespeople be used or should commissioned factory representatives who sell for a number of firms be used? Should employees be used on special jobs or should consultants be employed?

ELIMINATION OF SEGMENTS: AN EXAMPLE

Elimination of a segment of a business such as a product line, division, or sales territory is based on the incremental (or differential) revenues which are lost and the incremental (or differential) costs which are avoided if the segment is dropped. Recall that conventional financial reports are based on full costs which include the arbitrary allocations of common costs.

Assume that a firm has one plant and three products. The firm prepares financial reports on the basis of full costs by product line. The actual performance for the previous year is presented in the following income statement:

Income Statement by Product Lines

	Product Line #1	*Product Line #2*	*Product Line #3*	*Total*
Net Sales	$200	$400	$400	$1,000
Cost of goods sold:				
Direct labor	64	48	48	160
Direct material	60	90	150	300
Variable overhead	20	40	40	100
Fixed overhead:				
Property taxes	8	6	6	20
Property insurance	4	3	3	10
Depreciation	32	24	24	80
Other	8	6	6	20
Total cost of goods sold	$196	$217	$277	$ 690
Gross margin	$ 4	$183	$123	$ 310
Expenses:				
Selling	12	24	24	60
Advertising	24	48	48	120
Interest	12	12	12	36
General and administrative	15	15	15	45
Total expenses	$ 63	$ 99	$ 99	$ 261
Net income (loss) before taxes	($ 59)	$ 84	$ 24	$ 49

It appears that product Line #1 is somewhat undesirable because it is operating at a loss. It might be erroneously inferred that if this line were dropped, the total net income before taxes for the firm would increase. Before any decisions can be made, however, each cost and expense item must be analyzed to determine which costs and expenses would be eliminated if the product line were dropped. The basis of allocation of each cost must also be identified in order to aid in the determination of that portion, if any, of the cost which would be eliminated by dropping the product line. All revenues from product Line #1 would be lost if the line were discontinued.

Analysis of Incremental Factors

	Product Line #1	Incremental Costs and Revenue of Product Line #1
Net Sales	$200	$200
Cost of goods sold:		
Direct labor	64	64
Direct material	60	60
Variable overhead	20	20
Fixed overhead:		
Property taxes	8	–0–
Property insurance	4	–0–
Depreciation	32	–0–
Other	8	–0–
Total cost of goods sold	$196	$144

	Product Line #1	Incremental Costs and Revenue of Product Line #1
Gross margin	$ 4	$ 56
Expenses:		
Selling	12	3
Advertising	24	–0–
Interest	12	–0–
General and administrative	15	5
Total expenses	$ 63	$ 8
Net income (loss) before taxes	($ 59)	$ 48

If product Line #1 were dropped, product Lines #2 and #3 would then have to absorb $107 (the difference between a $59 loss and $48 before tax income) in common costs which are now allocated to product Line #1. Income before taxes would have been $48 less last year because product Lines #2 and #3 would have had to absorb all of the fixed overhead and all fixed selling and administrative expenses. If a new income statement were prepared for the firm for the prior year, assuming that product Line #1 was dropped, the results would be as follows:

	Total Before Dropping Product Line #1	Incremental Costs and Revenues on Product Line #1	Total Without Product Line #1
Net sales	$1,000	($200)	$800
Cost of goods sold:			
Direct labor	160	(64)	96
Direct materials	300	(60)	240
Variable overhead	100	(20)	80
Fixed overhead:			
Property taxes	20	–0–	20
Property insurance	10	–0–	10
Depreciation	80	–0–	80
Other	20	–0–	20
Total cost of goods sold	$ 690	(144)	$546
Gross margin	$ 310	($ 56)	$254
Expenses:			
Selling	60	(3)	57
Advertising	120	–0–	120
Interest	36	–0–	36
General and administrative . . .	45	(5)	40
Total expenses	$ 261	($ 8)	$253
Net income before taxes	$ 49	($ 48)	$ 1

Without product Line #1, income before taxes is only $1, not $49. If only the incremental revenues and costs are considered, product Line #1 provides a contribution margin of $48 that is available to cover common fixed costs which would not be eliminated if the product line were eliminated.

If a similar analysis were applied to product Lines #2 and #3, it would demonstrate that each of these lines provide substantial funds from operations to cover common costs and contribute toward profits. As long as a segment of the organization provides incremental revenues in excess of incremental costs, the segment is contributing to the recovery of common fixed costs and thus making a contribution toward profit. The firm would reduce its total net income by eliminating such a segment.

PRODUCT PRICING TECHNIQUES

The factors affecting a pricing decision cannot be completely defined as there is neither a consistent theoretical nor practical approach that is appropriate for every situation that a firm might encounter. While the pricing decision is viewed by many firms as a short-run decision, the long-run implications are substantial. In the long-run, the prices charged for the entire line of products sold by a firm must first cover the fixed costs and then provide an acceptable margin of profit. Certain products will never be acceptable on a profit-making basis, but must be carried in order to provide a complete product line. Also, a product in the initial stages of market entry may not generate profits in the short-run.

The factors considered in a pricing decision include the following:

1. The economic considerations of supply and demand at different prices in a given time period.
2. The economic considerations of competition and substitute products.
3. The nature of the product and any competitive advantage which may result from unique capabilities or legal protection such as a patent.
4. Marketing considerations associated with selling and related to factors such as brand name, advertising, promotion, service capabilities, special applications, etc.
5. Legal implications of a given price in a specific market such as those covered under the Robinson-Patman Act which prohibits discriminatory prices that could reduce competition.
6. The investment which is required to produce the volume of product required.
7. The cost of producing the product.

From an accounting standpoint, the emphasis is on the last two items (6 and 7 above). In the short-run, the emphasis in accounting may focus on basic manufacturing costs rather than on the investment required to produce the product. However, it is obvious that the investment required directly affects the cost of producing a product in any given time period. In some instances, it is possible that the investment should never have been made.

The discussion of pricing in this chapter considers two basic short-run cost approaches to pricing: (1) the contribution margin approach and (2) the cost-volume-profit approach.

The Contribution Margin Approach to Product Pricing: An Example

The contribution margin approach is a short-run technique which may be used for product pricing. This method identifies the minimum price that can be charged for a product, assuming fixed costs do not change, without affecting the firm's profit. The minimum cost, and therefore price, is the total of all variable costs incurred in manufacturing and selling the product. Obviously, if the price charged for all products is equal to the variable costs of producing those products, the firm would operate at a loss. The total mix of products must cover all variable and fixed costs, and must provide a profit which allows the firm to obtain a satisfactory return on its investment.

Assume that a firm has developed a product that it wishes to introduce to the greatest potential market. The firm decides that the introductory price should be the lowest possible price that will neither increase nor decrease current profits. Management does not believe that fixed costs have been affected by this product. After reviewing the cost of making the product, the accounting department developed the following cost summary on a contribution margin format for management's use.

Pricing Decision—Using
The Contribution Margin Approach

Direct materials	$ .50
Direct labor	.75
Variable overhead	.30
Distribution costs	.05
Total variable cost	$1.60

If no other costs are involved, the minimum selling price of the product could be set at $1.60. At this price, the current profits from the sale of other products are not eroded. This approach has some merit in bidding situations, where the minimum price based on variable costs can be established and fixed costs do not change. After this absolute minimum is established, management can establish a price that provides a positive contribution margin.

Directly Traceable Costs and the Cost-Profit-Volume Approach to Product Pricing: An Example

When a pricing approach based on costs is made, and fixed costs of any kind are considered, the question of volume must also be considered because the fixed cost per unit decreases as the volume increases. If the firm discussed in the contribution margin approach to pricing example was required to rent a warehouse for one year at a cost of $260 and anticipated an advertising campaign of $500 in addition to the variable costs already considered, the minimum price calculation to allow cost recovery becomes somewhat more complex. The new cost structure for the product would be as follows:

Pricing Decision—Using the Directly
Traceable Costs and the Cost-Profit-Volume Approach

Variable Costs:	
Direct materials	$ .50
Direct labor	.75
Variable overhead	.30
Distribution costs	.05
Variable costs per unit	$1.60
Managed Fixed Costs:	
Warehousing	$260
Advertising	500
Total managed fixed costs	$760

The minimum price the firm must charge is greater than $1.60 per unit if the $760 of managed fixed costs are to be recovered. The problem of volume is now introduced. Management must determine an anticipated volume in order to determine the absolute minimum price possible. The minimum price is

$$\$1.60 \ + \ \frac{\$760}{\text{Anticipated Volume}}$$

If the anticipated volume were 1,000 units, the absolute minimum price would be

$$\$1.60 \ + \ \frac{\$760}{1,000 \ \text{units}} \ = \ \$2.36 \ \text{per unit}$$

At a price of \$2.36, the profits of the firm would neither be increased nor decreased by the sale of this specific product, assuming that other products sold and other costs incurred remain constant.

SUMMARY

The management of a firm is often called upon to make special decisions of a non-recurring nature. Information used for special decisions may include historical data obtained directly from the accounting records as well as future projections based upon this data. In addition, a firm may find it necessary to conduct special studies to generate information which is not generally accumulated in the accounting records but which is required to make a given special decision.

Although both qualitative and quantitative factors are considered in the decision-making process, the accountant is generally concerned with providing only quantitative data; that is, data that can be expressed in numbers. Cost data for special decision making is a primary type of quantitative data provided by accountants.

All costs used for special decision making have two common characteristics. First, they must be relevant costs; that is, the costs must differ among the available alternatives. Second, the costs must be costs that are anticipated or expected in the future if one of the available alternatives is selected.

An opportunity cost measures the benefits that could have been derived had an alternative choice been made. Incremental cost, also referred to as differential cost, is the difference between the total costs of available alternatives. Escapable or avoidable costs are those costs that will be eliminated by selecting a given alternative. Costs that will require a definite outlay of funds, as opposed to depreciation or allocated costs, are often referred to as out-of-pocket costs. Any of the above costs may be relevant costs for special decision-making purposes. Sunk costs, on the other hand, are irrelevant for decision making because they represent past expenditures that cannot be changed regardless of the alternative chosen.

Examples of special decisions include decisions to: (1) accept or reject a special order from a customer, (2) make or buy a component part, (3) continue or eliminate a segment of the business, and (4) determine a price to charge for a product. No single special format exists for presenting information for special decision-making purposes. However, among the formats in general use are the incremental cost and/or revenue approach and the contribution margin approach. Although either format may be used in the analysis of a special decision, the incremental approach is more appropriate in cases where fixed costs are relevant.

KEY DEFINITIONS

Contribution margin approach—a general format for arranging relevant decision-making information showing additional revenues and related variable costs to be incurred under various alternatives in determining a contribution margin.

Escapable or avoidable costs—costs which may be eliminated by making a particular decision or selecting a certain alternative.

Incremental cost and revenue approach—a general format for arranging relevant decision-making information which considers total costs and revenues to be incurred under various alternatives in determining an incremental net income or loss.

Incremental or differential cost—the difference between the total costs of available alternatives.

Opportunity cost—a measurement of benefits that could have been derived had an alternative choice been made.

Out-of-pocket costs—costs requiring a definite outlay of funds.

Relevant costs—future costs which differ under the alternatives under consideration in a decision-making situation.

Sunk costs—those costs which are irrelevant for future decisions because the expenditure has already been made and cannot be changed regardless of the alternative selected.

Appendix A

We have treated direct labor as a proportionately variable cost in most of our analysis because the firm was operating in the relevant range of activity where costs are approximately linear (see Illustration 1). Certain industries, such as the aerospace industry, never reach those volumes of activity that would put them in the relevant range. Therefore, when estimating costs they must deal with the problem that as the same job is repeated labor becomes more efficient. Since there is an observed regularity in the rate of improvement, we can apply the rule that as the cumulative output doubles there is a constant rate of reduction in average labor hours per unit. A commonly used rate is eighty percent. The effects of an eighty percent learning curve is presented in Illustration 2.

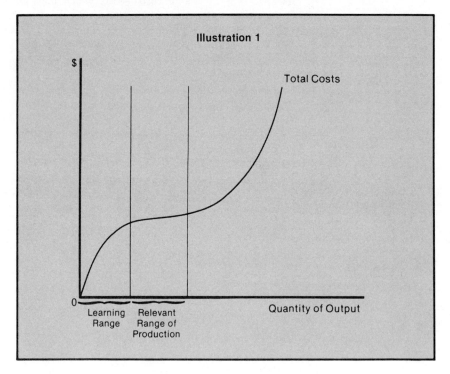

Illustration 1

Because the eighty percent rule gives the average time, it is very useful for many accounting reports or for estimating the cost of total production. But, if the analysis is an attempt to forecast the cost of only certain units in the cumulative production quantity, a certain amount of caution is necessary to derive the incremental time for those units. Refer to Illustration 2, the first

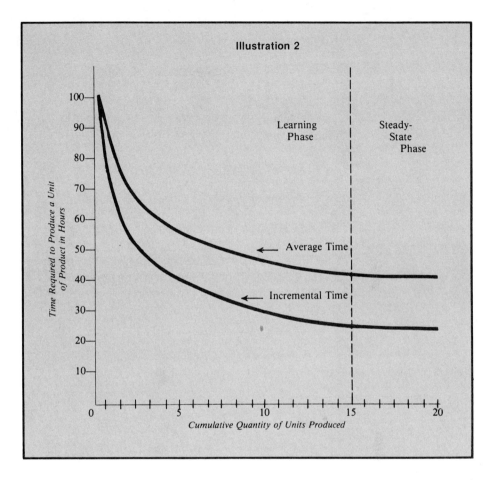

unit produced required 100 hours. If we want to estimate the incremental time to produce the second unit by applying the learning curve rule we need to follow this procedure.

$$
\begin{array}{rl}
\text{Time of First Unit} = & 100 \text{ Hours} \\
\text{Learning Curve Rate} = & \underline{80\%} \\
\text{Cumulative Average Time} = & 80 \text{ Hours}
\end{array}
$$

The cumulative average does not tell us the incremental time to produce the second unit, but is used to determine that the total time for both units is 160 hours:

$$
\begin{array}{rl}
\text{Total Time} = & \text{Average Time} \times \text{Total Number of Units} \\
= & 80 \times 2 = 160 \text{ Hours}
\end{array}
$$

Because we know that the first unit required 100 hours, the incremental time of the second unit is 60 hours.

$$\begin{aligned} \text{Incremental Time} &= \text{Total Time} - \text{Time of Previous Units} \\ &= 160 - 100 = 60 \text{ Hours} \end{aligned}$$

The incremental time for units 3 and 4 (this is another doubling of cumulative production) is 96 hours.

$$\begin{aligned} \text{Average Time of Units 1 and 2} &= 80 \text{ Hours} \\ \text{Learning Curve Rate} &= \underline{80\%} \\ \text{Cumulative Average Time} &= 64 \text{ Hours} \\ \text{Total Time} = 64 \times 4 &= 256 \text{ Hours} \\ \text{Incremental Time} = 256 - 160 &= 96 \text{ Hours} \end{aligned}$$

There are also other rules for estimating the incremental labor hours. One is that, utilizing an 80 percent learning curve, the average incremental time of the added cumulative production is 75 percent of the cumulative average time.

Appendix B

THE ROLE OF QUANTITATIVE TECHNIQUES IN SHORT-RANGE PLANNING AND DECISIONS

In this appendix we examine some quantitative techniques that may be useful in short-range planning and decisions. While the in-depth study of formal decision models and risk or uncertainty is usually considered part of other fields or disciplines, the managerial accountant needs the knowledge and ability to utilize these techniques in the proper circumstances. This includes the ability to recognize when the techniques may be used incorrectly.

Objective vs. Subjective Probabilities

Many formal models require a schedule of probable demand, commonly called a probability distribution. This schedule describes the chance that a possible event will occur out of all possible events. In gaming strategy, where engineered gadgets perform according to natural or physical laws, this is quite simple. We know that from a randomly shuffled deck of cards the probability of drawing a heart is $13 \div 52 = 0.25$. If we draw five cards from the deck, and they are four hearts and one spade, the probability of the next card being a heart is $9 \div 47 = 0.19$ (there are only nine hearts in the remaining forty-seven cards). If several people independently calculated the chance of drawing the card they would all arrive at the same answer, hence, the term objective probability.

In most business situations we are unable to determine the actual probability that an event will occur or even to determine all of the possible events. Because of this, the probability distributions used in the formal models are of necessity only subjective estimates of the underlying probabilities. And as such, we should always be aware that the use of formal models may lead to incorrect decisions if the subjective probabilities do not represent reality.

Determination of Single Point Sales Estimates

When using a single point sales estimate in budgeting, the sales level selected is usually the level having the highest probability of occurrence or the modal event. Because the actual probability distribution is not known, the decision maker assumes a normal distribution which makes the mean and the mode identical and no further calculations are necessary.

When the probability distribution of possible sales levels is skewed the expected value (mean) might be a better estimation than the mode. The mode does not consider the effect of the extreme events while the expected value does. The expected value is the weighted average mean value of all of the possible outcomes. The expected value is computed by multiplying each possible outcome (conditional value) by the probability of its occurrence. Consider the following illustration:

Illustration 3

Weighted Average Expected Value

	Possible Sales Levels	Subjective Probabilities	Expected Value
	$700,000	.20	$140,000
	750,000	.30	225,000
(mode)	800,000	.35	280,000
	850,000	.10	85,000
	900,000	.05	45,000
	Weighted Average Expected Value (mean)		$775,000

Example of Decision Making Under Uncertainty

Each Thursday a storekeeper buys boxes of fresh strawberries. The strawberries cost $1 and sell for $1.75. Because of their perishable nature, any unsold strawberries are worthless. The storekeeper wants to know how many boxes should be purchased each week in order to maximize profits. Based upon past experience, the demand for strawberries is estimated as follows:

Illustration 4

Demand for Strawberries

Demand	Estimated Probability
0	0.00
100 boxes	0.05
150 boxes	0.10
200 boxes	0.20
250 boxes	0.35
300 boxes	0.20
350 boxes	0.10
400 boxes	0.00
	1.00

The strategies to be examined are 100 through 350 boxes. Zero or 400 boxes are not considered because there is no demand at these levels. The solution to the problem is presented in Illustration 5. There is a 75¢ profit on each box sold and a $1 loss on each unsold box.

Illustration 5

Payoff Table Solution

Possible Events Probability of Event Strategies	100 .05	150 .10	200 .20	250 .35	300 .20	350 .10	Expected Value
100	$ 75	$ 75	$ 75	$ 75	$ 75	$ 75	$ 75
150	25	112.50	112.50	112.50	112.50	112.50	108.125
200	− 25	62.50	150	150	150	150	132.50
250	− 75	12.50	100	187.50	187.50	187.50	139.375
300	− 125	− 37.50	50	137.50	225	225	115.625
350	− 175	− 87.50	0	87.50	175	262.50	74.375

The strategy of buying 250 boxes produces the largest expected value. The expected value (EV) for the 250 box strategy is:

$$EV = .05(-75) + .10(12.50) + .20(100) + .35(187.50) + .20(187.50) + .10(187.50) = \$139.375$$

The Value of Perfect Information

In the previous illustration, because the demand was uncertain, the solution was to use the optimum strategy each week; buy 250 boxes. If, however, the demand for strawberries was known with certainty, a different number of boxes would be purchased each week. With perfect information the storekeeper would never lose a sale nor would he ever have to throw away spoiled strawberries. The weighted average weekly profit with perfect information is calculated as follows:

Illustration 6

Average Weekly Profit with Perfect Information

Demand (Boxes)	Conditional Value	×	Probability of Event	=	Expected Value
100	$ 75		.05		$ 3.75
150	112.50		.10		11.25
200	150		.20		30.00
250	187.50		.35		65.625
300	225		.20		45.00
350	262.50		.10		26.25
					$181.875

With perfect information the storekeeper could increase the expected weekly profit by $42.50 ($181.875 − $139.375). The problem, obviously, is that perfect information is not available. If management believes that better information is available, the calculation of the value of perfect information does provide a maximum price that could be paid for such information.

Management of Inventory Costs

The management of inventories involved three types of cost: (1) the fixed costs of setting up for a production run or placing an order, (2) the carrying costs of warehousing, insuring, interest, spoilage, etc., and (3) the stock-out opportunity costs of lost sales and customers.

Illustration of Inventory Management

Peter Ruplinger, Inc. imports diamonds from South Africa and sells them in the San Diego area. Ruplinger is trying to determine the economic order quantity and reorder point for a one carat "D" quality diamond. The following data is available.

Cost of placing an order.................... $ 500
Purchase price of a diamond............... $1,000
Selling price of a diamond.................. $1,100
Cost of borrowed money................... 20%
Annual demand......................... 500
Average time to receive an order........... 3 months

Based on this data, the economic order quantity of 50 diamonds is presented in Illustration 7.

Illustration 7

Economic Order Quantity

Order Quantity	C_s Annual Cost of Placing an Order	C_i Annual Carrying Cost	C Total Annual Cost
	$\left(\dfrac{SD}{Q} = C_s \right)$	$+ \left(\dfrac{IQ}{2} = C_i \right)$	$= \left(C = \dfrac{IQ}{2} + \dfrac{SD}{Q} \right)$
40	$6,250	$4,000	$10,250
50	5,000	5,000	10,000
60	4,167	6,000	10,167

EOQ = Economic order quantity
Q = Size of order in units
D = Annual demand in units
I = Cost of carrying one unit for one year
S = Set up or cost of placing an order

The graphic solution is presented in Illustration 8. A mathematical solution to the economic order quantity can be obtained by setting the first derivative of the total cost function equal to zero.

$$EOQ = \sqrt{\frac{2 \times D \times S}{I}} = \sqrt{\frac{2 \times 500 \times 500}{200}} = 50$$

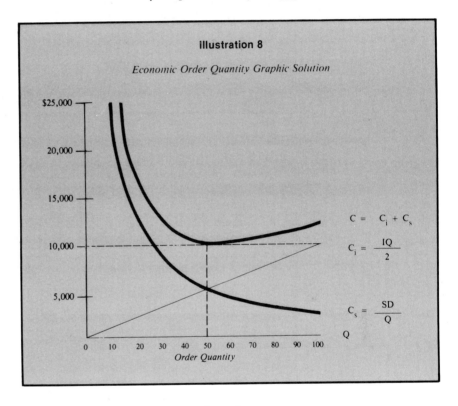

Illustration 8

Economic Order Quantity Graphic Solution

$C = C_i + C_s$

$C_i = \dfrac{IQ}{2}$

$C_s = \dfrac{SD}{Q}$

Order Quantity

The reorder inventory level consists of two parts:

Reorder Point = Lead time stock + Safety stock

The lead time stock is determined by the average demand during the average time that it takes to receive an order:

Lead time stock = 3/12 × 500 = 125

The optimal safety stock will minimize the total cost of carrying safety stock and the opportunity cost of lost sales (stock out costs). In order to analyze the need for safety stock, we need to know what the possible demands might be during the reorder period and the probability of those demands occurring (see Illustration 9).

Illustration 9

Probability of Demand

Demand	Probability	Possible Safety Stock
125	.05	125 − 125 = 0
135	.10	135 − 125 = 10
145	.25	145 − 125 = 20
155	.35	155 − 125 = 30
165	.20	165 − 125 = 40
175	.05	175 − 125 = 50
	1.00	

We can now construct a decision table (Illustration 10). One very important point; there is no cost of running out of stock unless customers are turned away. For example, if Ruplinger reorders when the inventory level is 165 diamonds and 165 customers come in before the new order arrives no sales will be lost. But if 175 customers want diamonds, ten sales will be lost. Because the contribution margin is $100, the loss of ten sales has an opportunity cost of $1,000. With a probability of occurrence of 5%, this strategy has an expected loss of $50 per order or a $500 annual stock out cost. The Company will be ordering ten times a year $\left(\dfrac{D}{Q} = \dfrac{500}{50} = 10 \right)$

Illustration 10

Decision Table for Safety Stock

Safety Stock	Annual Carrying Cost	Annual Stock-out Cost	Total
0	$ 0	$27,000	$27,000
10	2,000	17,500	19,500
20	4,000	9,000 [1]	13,000
30	6,000	3,000 [2]	9,000
40	8,000	500	8,500
50	10,000	0	10,000

[1] $[((30 \times 100).05)10 + ((20 \times 100).20)10 + ((10 \times 100).35)10] = 9,000$
[2] $[((20 \times 100).05)10 + ((10 \times 100).20)10] = 3,000$

With a safety stock of 40 diamonds, the appropriate time to reorder is:

$$\text{Reorder point} = 125 + 40 = 165 \text{ diamonds}$$

LINEAR PROGRAMMING

Linear programming is a mathematical approach to allocating scarce resources in order to maximize profit or reduce cost.

Since its development, linear programming has been applied to a number of production problems. Examples include product mix, raw material mix, capacity allocation problems, make or buy problems, and shipping problems.

Example of Scarce Resource Problem

A small business makes two products, A and B. These products must be machined in department D1 and assembled in department D2. There are 200 hours available in D1 and 300 hours available in D2. While the company can sell all the product B that they produce, the demand for product A is limited to 80 units. Product A requires 2 hours of machining in D1 and 2 hours of assembly in D2. Product B requires 1 hour of machining in D1 and 3 hours of assembly in D2. Product A has a contribution margin of $2.50 per unit. Product B has a contribution margin of $3 per unit.

The objective function in this example is to maximize the contribution margin, where:

$$\text{Total Contribution Margin} = \$2.50A + \$3B \qquad (1)$$

Since the total time required in each department cannot exceed available capacity, we have the following constraints:

Department D1	$2A + 1B \leq 200$	(2)
Department D2	$2A + 3B \leq 300$	(3)

Since the demand for A is limited to 80 units, we have the additional constraint:

For Product A	$A \leq 80$	(4)

These constraints are represented by the three solid lines in Illustration 11.

It should be observed that the optimum solution must always be one of the corners of the area of possible solutions in Illustration 11. These corners are analyzed in Illustration 12. The optimum solution is to produce 75 units of product A and 50 units of product B. This combination provides a total contribution margin of $337.50 which is larger than any of the other possible solutions.

Since our example was very simple and uncomplicated, the graphical approach was easy to apply and understand. Most companies use a mathematical approach, the simplex method, in practice.

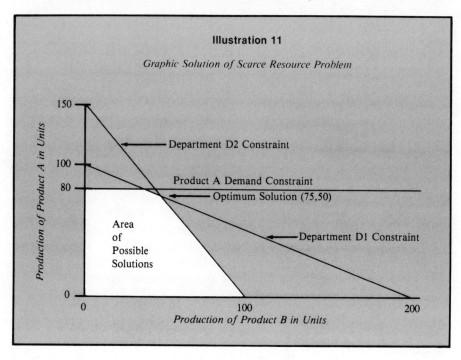

Illustration 11

Graphic Solution of Scarce Resource Problem

Illustration 12

Analysis of Corners Solution

Possible Solutions		Contribution Margin				
A, B		A	+	B	=	Total
0,0		0	+	0	=	0
80,0		200	+	0	=	200
80,40[1]		200	+	120	=	320
75,50[2]		187.50	+	150	=	337.50
0,100		0	+	300	=	300

[1] From equation (2):

$$2(80) + 1B = 200; B = 40$$

[2] From equation (2) and (3):

$$
\begin{array}{rr}
2A + 3B = & 300 \\
- 2A - 1B = & - 200 \\
\hline
0 + 2B = & 100
\end{array}
\quad ; B = 50 \text{ and } A = 75
$$

QUESTIONS

1. What information should be considered relevant in making a non-recurring or special decision?

2. What is the difference between qualitative and quantitative factors used in making a decision? Which factor(s) do accounting records play an important role in developing?

3. Define opportunity costs and explain when they are most likely to be incurred.

4. What is an incremental cost and when is it relevant in making a decision?

5. What classification of cost might be an escapable cost when one considers eliminating a segment of a firm?

6. Why is depreciation not considered an out-of-pocket cost?

7. For what purposes is the original cost of an asset relevant in making a decision?

8. Give two examples stating decision-making situations in which the contribution margin approach would not be appropriate.

9. When a pricing decision is being made, on what factors is the emphasis placed from an accounting standpoint?

10. How is the contribution margin approach used in setting the minimum price for a product?

EXERCISES

11. In 19x1 and 19x2 the Chipper Company overproduced its Product L because of an increasing demand for this product. In 19x3 another company began to produce an improved model of this product which made Chipper Company's Product L obsolete. After inventory was counted in 19x3, they found they had $50,604 of Product L. After considering many alternatives, it was determined that they could sell the product for scrap for $6,850 or recylce it into another product. It will cost $12,500 to rework the product, and it will sell for $20,500. In addition to the additional cost, salesmen will receive 3 percent of the selling price.

Required:

What should be done with Product L?

12. The Squeak-E Tennis Shoe Company sells 20,000 pairs of tennis shoes annually. They have fixed costs of $38,000 and direct costs of $6 per pair. The shoes sell for $9 per pair. Squeak-E has a capacity of 5,000 in excess of the 20,000 pairs of shoes they sell annually. They have just received an offer from a company outside their present sales territory to buy 4,500 pairs of tennis shoes for $6.25 per pair.

Required:

1. Should they accept this order?
2. If Squeak-E did not have the excess capacity, should they accept the order?

13. The Easy Sleep Company is a large manufacturer of waterbeds. Unfortunately, due to the current water shortage, waterbeds have been forbidden by law. Easy Sleep has a $60,000 inventory of waterbeds at the present time. Easy Sleep must make a decision to sell the waterbeds as scrap for a total of $5,000, or modify the beds to be sold as life rafts. The modification will cost a total of $12,000, which includes the purchase of a special machine. (This machine will be sold after the modifications are finished for $3,000.) The total sales expected from the life rafts are $16,000 less 10% sales commissions.

Required:

Should Easy Sleep modify the beds or sell them as scrap?

14. The following income statements were prepared by the accounting department for Russel Company for 19x1. Assume all fixed expenses are allocated on an arbitrary basis to each department.

	Department J	Department K	Department L
Sales............................	$130,000	$200,000	$145,000
Variable cost of goods sold........	90,000	120,000	70,000
Contribution margin from manufacturing	$ 40,000	$ 80,000	$ 75,000
Operating expenses:			
Fixed expenses................	25,000	40,000	35,000
Variable selling expenses........	5,000	8,000	4,000
Fixed selling expenses..........	10,000	16,000	12,000
Net income.....................	0	$ 16,000	$ 24,000

Required:

The president of Russel Company feels Department J should be eliminated. How would you advise her?

15. The following information was made available concerning the four departments of the Roast Company.

	Department A	Department B	Department C	Department D
Sales	$100,000	$20,000	$50,000	$70,000
Variable cost of goods sold...	70,000	10,000	30,000	45,000
Contribution margin from manufacturing..........	$ 30,000	$10,000	$20,000	$25,000
Operating expenses:				
Fixed expenses............	20,000	4,000	10,000	15,000
Variable selling expenses...	10,000	3,000	6,000	12,000
Net income (loss)...........	0	$ 3,000	$ 4,000	($ 2,000)

Chuck Roast, the president of the company, has decided that one department must be dropped. Fixed expenses have been arbitrarily assigned according to the sales of each department. No matter which department is dropped the fixed expenses will be reduced one-fourth.

Required:

Which department should be dropped so as to give the greatest benefit to the company? What will be the company's income?

16. The Z Company makes saws; last year it sold 30,000 saws at a price of $5 and produced them at an average cost of $3. The sales manager thinks 40,000 units could be sold at price of $4.30. The plant manager estimates that 40,000 units could be produced at a cost of $2.80 each.

Required:

What effect will this have on profit?

17. Ralph Company sells three products. Product B has yielded a net loss of $10,000 for the past three years, and there is no reason to expect a change in the future. Company officials also feel that the sales of the three products are not interrelated. Fixed expenses are allocated equally among the products in determining product profitability. Company records show:

	Product A	Product B	Product C
Contribution margin per unit............	$6.50	$4.00	$7.00
Net income (loss).....................	$13,000	($10,000)	$16,000
Total annual fixed expenses are:	$42,000		

Required:

Based on the information given, should Product B be dropped?

18. Allen Tool Company is making plans for the coming year. Management feels that a target profit of $425,000 before income taxes would represent a satisfactory continuation of their growth pattern of earnings, which has been a steady 7% over the last 6 years. Marketing management has studied the market for the coming year and predicted the following sales possibilities.

	Selling Price		Advertising	Unit Sales
Alternative A.......	$5.00	....	No change..........	1,000,000
Alternative B.......	5.00	....	Up $60,000.........	1,120,000
Alternative C.......	5.50	....	No change..........	700,000
Alternative D.......	5.50	....	Up $60,000.........	810,000

Estimated fixed expenses for next year are $825,000 and estimated variable expenses are $3.75 per unit of product. These expense estimates do not include any changes in advertising.

(**Note:**   In your answer show any necessary computations.)

Required:

1. What should the marketing strategy be?
2. Suppose that management decided to change the selling price to $5.25 and raise advertising $45,000. If this will give unit sales of 775,000, will the target profit be achieved?

19. The Davis Company has been producing 20,000 units per month but wants to begin producing 25,000 units per month (capacity is 28,000 units per month) because of an increase in demand for their product. Davis has the following cost structure.

> Selling price = $1.60 per unit
> Variable manufacturing costs = $.35 per unit
> Fixed manufacturing costs = $15,400
> Variable selling expense = 5% of selling price
> Fixed selling expense = $2,000

Required:

1. Determine the incremental revenues and costs.
2. Should Davis produce the additional units?

20. Russel, Inc. has been purchasing a component part from another company since it began operations five years ago. Russel now has a steady demand for its product and feels it has the capacity to produce the component part itself. Russel purchased 120,000 units at a cost of $1.10 per unit last year and feels it will purchase 10% more this year for the same price. If Russel produces this part, its costs will be:

Direct materials............................. $.45 per unit
Direct labor................................. $.30 per unit
Variable overhead........................... $.20 per unit
Avoidable fixed overhead.................... $33,000

Required:

Should Russel Company purchase this part or produce it itself?

PROBLEMS

21. The Silsbee Company has three products. Product #2 has incurred a loss for the past two years; therefore, management would like to drop this line. Given an income statement for 19x1, you are to determine whether the company should drop this product. All "Fixed Overhead" items are allocated to the products as are all items under "Expenses" except selling expenses. Selling expenses are 2% of sales plus an allocated amount.

	Product Line #1	*Product Line #2*	*Product Line #3*	*Total*
Net sales...................	$280,000	$220,000	$300,000	$800,000
Cost of goods sold:				
Direct labor..............	$ 21,000	$ 34,500	$ 20,000	$ 75,500
Direct materials...........	25,000	24,600	24,000	73,600
Variable overhead.........	14,000	19,300	15,200	48,500
Fixed overhead				
Property taxes..........	28,000	22,000	30,000	80,000
Depreciation	56,000	44,000	60,000	160,000
Other..................	24,500	19,250	26,250	70,000
Total cost of goods sold......	$168,500	$163,650	$175,450	$507,600
Gross margin...............	$111,500	$ 56,350	$124,550	$292,400
Expenses:				
Selling expenses...........	$ 26,600	$ 20,900	$ 28,500	$ 76,000
Advertising...............	28,000	22,000	30,000	80,000
General and administrative expenses	42,000	33,000	45,000	120,000
Total expenses..............	$ 96,600	$ 75,900	$103,500	$276,000
Net income before taxes......	$ 14,900	($ 19,550)	$ 21,050	$ 16,400

22. Wilson, Wilson, and Company has three products. Management would like to drop Product X since it has not shown a profit for the past three years. Given below is the company's most recent income statement:

	Product X	Product Y	Product Z	Total
Net sales....................	$450,000	$450,000	$600,000	$1,500,000
Cost of goods sold:				
Direct labor...............	$160,000	$ 70,000	$ 50,000	$ 280,000
Direct materials...........	120,000	45,000	80,000	245,000
Variable overhead..........	56,000	50,000	59,000	165,000
Fixed overhead				
Property taxes...........	30,000	30,000	40,000	100,000
Depreciation	42,000	42,000	56,000	140,000
Other	24,000	24,000	32,000	80,000
Total cost of goods sold.......	$432,000	$261,000	$317,000	$1,010,000
Gross margin...............	$ 18,000	$189,000	$283,000	$ 490,000
Expenses:				
Selling expenses............	$ 25,500	$ 25,500	$ 34,000	$ 85,000
Advertising	36,000	36,000	48,000	120,000
General and administrative				
expenses	48,000	48,000	64,000	160,000
Total expenses..............	$109,500	$109,500	$146,000	$ 365,000
Net income before taxes.......	($ 91,500)	$ 79,500	$137,000	$ 125,000

General and administrative expenses are totally allocated, while selling expenses are 3% of sales plus an allocated amount and advertising expenses are 2% of sales plus an allocated amount.

Required:

You have been asked to determine whether Product X should be dropped.

23. Rick Rock, a well-known criminal, was considering the future revenues he could generate from two possible jobs. Due to risk and capital requirements, Rick can choose only one of the 2 possible alternatives. The breakdown of costs for each job was as follows:

Liquid Liquor Store (Job #1)

1 gun	$ 50
1 get-a-way bicycle	100
1 ski mask	10
1 day's observation	70
1 laundry bag	3
Expected payoff	$ 800

Easy Money Bank (Job #2)

3 guns	$ 240
2 accomplices	2,000
1 get-a-way car	1,000
Floor plans	150
1 ski mask	10
1 week's observation	350
1 attache case	60
Expected payoff	$4,400

Both jobs will be charged $150 for plane tickets to get Rick out of the state.

Required:

1. Which alternative is best for Rick, assuming risk is the same?
2. Which cost(s) is irrelevant in making this decision?
3. What is the opportunity cost of the best alternative?

24. Ira Smart was entering the construction business and was faced with choosing between two possible opportunities; building a $50,000 house or a $70,000 gas station. Ira had already purchased a $10,000 truck that had an expected ten-year life and no salvage value. The breakdown of the costs for each job are as follows:

House

Insurance	$ 600
Workers	15,000
Building permit	1,000
Materials	10,000
Depreciation	1,000
Contract price	50,000

Gas Station

Crane	$ 3,000
Insurance	1,500
Materials	14,000
Building permit	1,000
Workers	20,000
Depreciation	1,000
Contract price	$70,000

Required:

1. Which job is most profitable for Mr. Smart?
2. What is the opportunity cost of the job chosen in "a"?
3. Which costs are irrelevant?
4. Which costs are sunk costs?

25. Harrington, Inc. plans to introduce a new product in 19x1. The company would like to make 10% profit on the sales. They feel that they will be able to sell from 9,000 to 12,000 units in 19x1. Variable costs per unit associated with the new product are:

Direct materials.........................	2 lbs. of x @ $.32 per lb.
	3 lbs. of z @ $.62 per lb.
Direct labor..........................	1¼ hrs. @ $5.20 per hr.
Variable overhead......................	1¼ hrs. @ $2.60 per hr.
Selling and distribution expense...........	$.35 per unit

In order to make this product, fixed production costs will increase by $34,000 per year. An advertising campaign costing $20,000 will also be initiated to promote the product.

Required:

Determine the range of selling prices for sales from 9,000 to 12,000 units.

26. The Kogwell Company is in the business of selling stereo equipment in a college town. Since school has started again, ten college students have applied to buy stereo systems on credit. Since these students only have part-time jobs, they are considered "high-risk" customers. Past experience has shown that 40% of this type of customer will take off with the merchandise and never pay for it. A stereo system sells for $500 and variable costs amount to $325 for the merchandise and $10 for delivery expenses. There are no financing charges.

Required:

Decide if the Kogwell Company should sell the stereo systems to these ten college students. Make your decision based on whether selling the merchandise will result in recovery of the costs necessary to sell the merchandise.

27. The Smith and Jones Company does small remodeling jobs for residential homes and commercial office buildings. Recently they have been offered two major remodeling jobs, both requiring six months to complete. The problem is that both of the jobs must be performed at the same time. The data for each job is:

Job #1

Contract price...............................	**$60,000**

Direct materials............................	$18,900
Direct labor................................	8,560
Indirect materials..........................	4,500
Supervisor's salary (for 6 months)..............	12,500
Warehouse depreciation (for 6 months).........	3,245
Depreciation on tools (for 6 months)...........	2,550

Job #2

Contract price...............................	**$56,000**

Direct materials............................	$17,600
Direct labor................................	7,950
Indirect materials..........................	3,450
Supervisor's salary (for 6 months)..............	12,500
Warehouse depreciation (for 6 months).........	3,245
Depreciation on tools (for 6 months)...........	2,550

The company has one other alternative. They can contract to do two small jobs a month as has been done in the past. The average contract price of one of these jobs is $5,500; direct materials average 30% of contract price, direct labor 20%, and indirect materials 10%.

Required:

1. Which of the three alternatives is the most profitable?
2. Identify which costs are irrelevant to this decision?
3. What are the opportunity costs associated with choosing the best alternative?

28. Costello and Costello Company paves driveways for residential homes. The average driveway costs about $5,000 to pave as determined below:

Direct materials............................	$2,500
Direct labor................................	1,500
Overhead	1,000
	$5,000

The overhead cost includes both fixed and variable costs and it is always allocated to each job by multiplying two-third's times direct labor. Total overhead for the year is $50,000 of which $40,000 is fixed. The remainder is variable and is directly proportional to direct labor.

Mr. Costello has always used a direct markup of 25% on full costs in the past but his wife believes he should change his pricing strategy to the contribution margin approach. He has extra time and capacity to do more jobs than he gets orders for, so he decides to listen to what his wife has to say.

Currently, a customer has offered to pay $4,800 to have his driveway paved. This driveway is what Mr. Costello defines as an "average" driveway and therefore he usually charges $6,250 for the job (25% × $5,000) + $5,000.

Required:

1. Taking his wife's advice, what is the minimum selling price which could be charged if Mr. Costello used the contribution margin approach to pricing?
2. Should Mr. Costello pave this customer's driveway for $4,800?

(CMA adapted)

29. The Bellance Company has designed a new airplane. They have already completed two planes (for demonstration purposes only) at the following costs:

Direct material...............................	$2,000,000
Direct labor..................................	3,000,000
Set-up costs.................................	400,000
Overhead*	900,000
Total.....................................	$6,300,000

> * Overhead is assigned as a percentage of labor cost for purposes of bidding on contracts. While fixed overhead is independent of any particular contract, variable overhead has been observed consistently at ten percent of labor cost.

Required:

1. Prepare an estimate of costs for bidding on a contract for six more airplanes. Assume that the direct labor hourly rate will be unchanged and that the set-up costs can be reused. You should use an 80 percent learning curve as a basis for forecasting pertinent costs.
2. If this were a special order for a foreign customer, would you analyze overhead differently than you did for requirement no. 1?

30. Horace Company employs a standard cost system in the manufacturing of all its products. Based upon past experience, the company considers the effect of an 80 percent learning factor when developing standards for direct labor costs.

   Horace Company is planning for the production of an automatic electrical timing device requiring the assembly of purchased components. Production is planned in lots of five units each. A steady-state production phase with no further increases in labor productivity is expected after the eighth lot. The first production lot of five units required 90 hours of direct labor time at a standard rate of $6 per hour.

Required:

1. Determine the standard amount Horace Company should establish for the total direct labor costs required for the production of the first eight lots of the automatic electrical timing devices.
2. Discuss the factors which should be considered in establishing the direct labor standards for each unit of output produced beyond the first eight lots.

(CMA adapted)

31. The Xyon Company has purchased 80,000 pumps annually from Kobec Inc. The price has increased each year and reached $68 per unit last year. Because the purchase price has increased significantly, Xyon management has asked that an estimate be made of the cost to manufacture it in its own facilities. Xyon's products consist of stamping and castings. The company has little experience with products requiring assembly.

    The engineering, manufacturing, and accounting departments have prepared a report for management which included the estimate shown below for an assembly run of 10,000 units. Additional production employees would be hired to manufacture the sub-assembly. However, no additional equipment, space or supervision would be needed.

    The report states that total costs for 10,000 units are estimated at $957,000 or $95.70 a unit. The current purchase price is $68 a unit so the report recommends a continued purchase of the product.

Components (outside purchases)................	$120,000
Assembly labor*..............................	300,000
Factory overhead**...........................	450,000
General and administrative overhead***..........	87,000
Total Costs................................	$957,000

    * Assembly labor consists of hourly production workers.
    ** Factory overhead is applied to products on a direct labor dollar basis. Variable overhead costs vary closely with direct labor dollars.

Fixed overhead.............	50%	of direct labor dollars
Variable overhead...........	100%	of direct labor dollars
Factory overhead rate........	150%	of direct labor dollars

    *** General and administrative overhead is applied at 10% of the total cost of material (or components), assembly labor and factory overhead.

Required:

1. Was the analysis prepared by the engineering, manufacturing, and accounting departments of Xyon Company and the recommendation to continue purchasing the pumps which followed from the analysis correct? Explain your answer and include any supportive calculations you consider necessary.

2. Assume Xyon Company could experience labor cost improvements on the pump assembly consistent with an 80 percent learning curve. An assembly run of 10,000 units represents the initial lot or batch for measurement purposes. Should Xyon produce the 80,000 pumps in this situation? Explain your answer.

(CMA adapted)

32. The Starr Company manufactures several products. One of its main products requires an electric motor. The management of Starr Company uses the economic order quantity formula (EOQ) to determine the optimum number of motors to order. Management now wants to determine how much safety stock to order.

Starr Company uses 30,000 electric motors annually (300 working days). Using the EOQ formula, the company orders 3,000 motors at a time. The lead time for an order is five days. The annual cost of carrying one motor in safety stock is $10. Management has also estimated that the cost of being out of stock is $20 for each motor they are short.

Starr Company has analyzed the usage during past reorder periods by examining the inventory records. The records indicate the following usage patterns during the past reorder periods:

Usage During Lead Time	Number of Times Quantity Was Used
440	6
460	12
480	16
500	130
520	20
540	10
560	6
	200

Required:

1. Using an expected value approach, determine the level of safety stock for electric motors that Starr Company should maintain in order to minimize costs.
2. What would be Starr Company's new reorder point?
3. What factors should Starr Company have considered to estimate the out-of-stock costs?

(CMA adapted)

33. Vendo, Inc. has been operating the concession stands at the University football stadium. The University has had successful football teams for many years; as a result, the stadium is always full. The University is located in an area which suffers no rain during the football season. From time to time, Vendo has found itself very short of hot dogs and at other times it has had many left. A review of the records of sales of the past five seasons revealed the following frequency of hot dogs sold.

	Total Games
10,000 hot dogs	5 times
20,000 hot dogs	10 times
30,000 hot dogs	20 times
40,000 hot dogs	15 times
	50 total games

Hot dogs sell for 50 cents each and cost Vendo 30 cents each. Unsold hot dogs are given to a local orphanage without charge.

Required:

1. Assuming that only the four quantities listed were ever sold and that the occurrences were random events, prepare a payoff table (ignore income taxes) to represent the four possible strategies of ordering 10,000, 20,000, 30,000, or 40,000 hot dogs.
2. Using the expected value decision rule, determine the best strategy.
3. What is the dollar value of perfect information in this problem?

(CMA adapted)

34. *Part A*

The Witchell Corporation manufactures and sells three grades: A, B, and C of a single wood product. Each grade must be processed through three phases—cutting, fitting, and finishing—before it is sold.
  The following unit information is provided:

	A	B	C
Selling price	$10.00	$15.00	$20.00
Direct labor	5.00	6.00	9.00
Direct materials	.70	.70	1.00
Variable overhead	1.00	1.20	1.80
Fixed overhead	.60	.72	1.08
Materials requirements in board feet	7	7	10
Labor requirements in hours:			
Cutting	3/6	3/6	4/6
Fitting	1/6	1/6	2/6
Finishing	1/6	2/6	3/6

Only 5,000 board feet per week can be obtained.
  The cutting department has 180 hours of labor available each week. The fitting and finishing department each have 120 hours of labor available each week. No overtime is allowed.
  Contract commitments require the company to make 50 units of A per week. In addition, company policy is to produce at least 50 additional units of A, 50 units of B, and 50 units of C each week to actively remain in each of the three markets. Because of competition only 130 units of C can be sold each week.

Required:

Formulate and label the linear objective function and the constraint functions necessary to maximize the contribution margin.

Part B

The graph provided presents the constraint functions for a chair manufacturing company whose production problem can be solved by linear programming. The company earns $8 for each kitchen chair sold and $5 for each office chair sold.

Required:

1. What is the profit maximizing production schedule?
2. How did you select this production schedule?

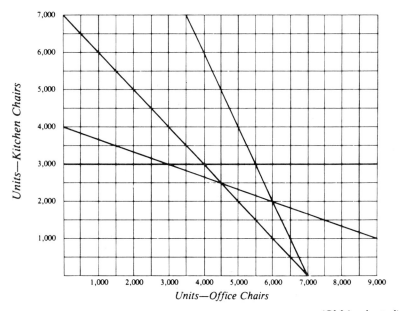

(CMA adapted)

35. The Robney Company is a restaurant supplier that sells a number of products to various restaurants in the area. One of their products is a special meat cutter with a disposable blade.

The blades are sold in packages of twelve for $20 per package. After a number of years, it has been determined that the demand for the replacement blades has a constant rate of 2,000 packages per month. The packages cost the Robney Company $10 each from the manufacturer and require a three-day lead time from date of order to date of delivery. The ordering cost is $1.20 per order and the carrying cost is 10% per annum.

Robney is going to use the economic order quantity formula:

$$EOQ = \sqrt{\frac{2(\text{Annual requirements}) (\text{Cost per order})}{(\text{Price per unit}) (\text{Carrying cost})}}$$

Required:

1.   Calculate:

    a.   The economic order quantity.
    b.   The number of orders needed per year.
    c.   The total cost of buying and carrying blades for the year.

2.   Assuming there is no reserve (e.g., safety stock) and that the present inventory level is 200 packages, when should the next order be placed? (Use 360 days equal one year.)
3.   Discuss the problems that most firms would have in attempting to apply this formula to their inventory problems.

(CMA adapted)

36.   Jackston Inc. manufactures and distributes a line of Christmas toys. The company had neglected to keep its doll house line current. As a result, sales have decreased to approximately 10,000 units per year from a previous high of 50,000 units. The doll house has been redesigned recently and is considered by company officials to be comparable to its competitors' models. The company plans to redesign the doll house each year in order to compete effectively. Joan Blocke, the sales manager, is not sure how many units can be sold next year, but she is willing to place probabilities on her estimates. Block's estimates of the number of units which can be sold during the next year and the related probabilities are as follows:

Estimated Sales in Units	Probability
20,000	.10
30,000	.40
40,000	.30
50,000	.20

The units would be sold for $20 each.

The inability to estimate the sales more precisely is a problem for Jackston. The number of units of this product is small enough to schedule the entire year's sales in one production run. If the demand is greater than the number of units manufactured, then sales will be lost. If demand is below supply, the extra units cannot be carried over to the next season and would be given away to various charitable organizations. The production and distribution cost estimates are listed below.

	Units Manufactured			
	20,000	30,000	40,000	50,000
Variable costs............	$180,000	$270,000	$360,000	$450,000
Fixed costs..............	140,000	140,000	160,000	160,000
Total Costs............	$320,000	$410,000	$520,000	$610,000

The company intends to analyze the data to facilitate making a decision as to the proper size of the production run.

Required:

Prepare a payoff table for the different sizes of production runs required to meet the four sales estimates prepared by Joan Blocke for Jackston, Inc. If Jackston, Inc. relied solely on the expected monetary value approach to make decisions, what size of production run would be selected?

(CMA adapted)

37. Excelsion Corporation manufactures and sells two kinds of containers—paperboard and plastic. The company produced and sold 100,000 paperboard containers and 75,000 plastic containers during the month of April. A total of 4,000 and 6,000 direct labor hours were used in producing the paperboard and plastic containers, respectively.

The company has not been able to maintain an inventory of either product, due to the high demand; this situation is expected to continue in the future. Workers can be shifted from the production of paperboard to plastic containers and vice versa, but additional labor is not available in the community. In addition, there will be a shortage of plastic material used in the manufacture of the plastic container in the coming months due to a labor strike at the facilities of a key supplier. Management has estimated there will be only enough raw material to produce 60,000 plastic containers during June.

The income statement for Excelsion Corporation for the month of April is shown below. The costs presented in the statement are representative of prior periods and are expected to continue at the same rates or levels in the future.

Excelsion Corporation
Income Statement
For the Month Ended April 30, 19x1

	Paperboard Containers	Plastic Containers
Sales	$220,800	$222,900
Less: Returns and allowances	$ 6,360	$ 7,200
Discounts	2,440	3,450
	$ 8,800	$ 10,650
Net sales	$212,000	$212,250
Cost of sales:		
Raw material cost	$123,000	$120,750
Direct labor	26,000	28,500
Indirect labor (variable with direct labor hours)	4,000	4,500
Depreciation—machinery	14,000	12,250
Depreciation—building	10,000	10,000
Cost of Sales	$177,000	$176,000
Gross profit	$ 35,000	$ 36,250
Selling and general expenses:		
General expenses—variable	$ 8,00	$ 7,500
General expenses—fixed	1,000	1,000
Commissions	11,000	15,750
Total Operating Expenses	$ 20,000	$ 24,250
Income before tax	$ 15,000	$ 12,000
Income taxes (40%)	6,000	4,800
Net income	$ 9,000	$ 7,200

Required:

The management of Excelsion Corporation plans to use linear programming to determine the optimal mix of paperboard and plastic containers for the month of June to achieve maximum profits. Using data presented in the April income statement, formulate and label the

1. Objective function.
2. Constraint functions.

(CMA adapted)

38. The Unimat Company manufactures a unique thermostat which yields dramatic cost savings from effective climatic control of large buildings. The efficiency of the thermostat is dependent upon the quality of a specialized thermocoupler. These thermocouplers are purchased from Cosmic Company for $15 each.

Since early 19x1, an average of 10 percent of the thermocouplers purchased from Cosmic have not met Unimat's quality requirements. The number of unusable thermocouplers has ranged from 5 to 25 percent of the total number purchased and has resulted in failures to meet production schedules. In addition, Unimat has incurred additional costs to replace the defective units because the rejection rate of the units is within the range agreed upon in the contract.

Unimat is considering a proposal to manufacture the thermocouplers. The company has the facilities and equipment to produce the components. The engineering department has designed a manufacturing system which will produce the thermocouplers with a defective rate of 4 percent of the number of units produced. The schedule presents the engineers' estimates of the probabilities that different levels of variable manufacturing cost per thermocoupler will be incurred under this system. The variable manufacturing cost per unit includes a cost adjustment for the defective units at the 4 percent rate. Additional annual fixed costs incurred by Unimat if it manufactures the thermocoupler will amount to $32,500.

Estimated Variable Manufacturing Cost Per Good Thermocoupler Unit	Probability of Occurrence
$10	10%
12	30
14	40
16	20
	100%

Unimat company will need 18,000 thermocouplers to meet its annual demand requirements.

Required:

Prepare an expected value analysis to determine whether Unimat Company should manufacture the thermocouplers.

(CMA adapted)

39. Hermit Company manufactures a line of walnut office products. Hermit executives estimate the demand for the double walnut letter tray, one of the company's products, at 6,000 units. The letter tray sells for $80 per unit. The costs relating to the letter tray are estimated to be as follows for 19x1:

    a.   Standard manufacturing cost per letter tray unit—$50.
    b.   Costs to initiate a production run—$300.
    c.   Annual cost of carrying the letter tray in inventory—20 percent of standard manufacturing cost.

In prior years, Hermit Company has scheduled the production for the letter tray in two equal production runs. The company is aware that the economic order quantity (EOQ) model can be employed to determine optimum size for production runs. The EOQ formula as it applies to inventories for determining the optimum order quantity is shown below.

$$EOQ = \frac{2 \text{ (annual demand) (cost per order)}}{\text{(cost per unit) (carrying cost)}}$$

Required:

Calculate the expected annual cost savings Hermit Company could experience if it employed the economic order quantity method to determine the number of production runs which should be initiated during the year for the manufacture of the double walnut letter trays.

(CMA adapted)

40. The Jon Co. has just agreed to supply Arom Chemical Inc. with a substance critical to one of Arom's manufacturing processes. Due to the critical nature of ths substance, Jon Co. has agreed to pay Arom Chemical Inc. $1,000 for any shipment that is not received by Arom on the day it is required.

Arom Chemical Inc. establishes a production schedule which enables it to notify Jon Co. of the necessary quantity 15 days in advance of the required date. Jon Co. can produce the substance in 5 days. However, capacity is not always readily available which means that Jon Co. may not be able to produce the substance for several days. Therefore, there may be occasions when there are only one or two days available to deliver the substance. When the substance is completed by Jon Co.'s manufacturing department and released to its shipping department, the number of days remaining before Arom Chemical Inc. needs the substance will be known.

Jon Co. has undertaken a review of delivery reliability and costs of alternative shipping methods. The results are presented in the following table.

Shipping Method	Costs Per Shipment	Probability that the shipment will take _____ days					
		1	2	3	4	5	6
Motor freight	$100	—	—	.10	.20	.40	.30
Air freight	200	—	.30	.60	.10	—	—
Air express	400	.80	.20	—	—	—	—

Required:

Prepare a decision table which can be used by Jon Co.'s shipping clerk to decide which delivery alternative to select. Use the expected monetary value decision criteria as the basis for constructing the table.

(CMA adapted)

Chapter 19 discusses the basic steps of the capital budgeting process, with special emphasis on evaluating and choosing among alternative long-term investments. Studying this chapter should enable you to:

1. Identify constraints affecting a firm's use of capital.
2. Discuss the principal types of data used to make capital budgeting decisions.
3. Explain how income tax considerations may affect the capital budgeting decision.
4. Describe the basic steps in developing a capital budget on a project-by-project basis.
5. Apply the various techniques of evaluating and/or ranking alternative investment possibilities.
6. Discuss sensitivity analysis and the cost of prediction errors.

19

Long-Range Planning: Capital Budgeting

INTRODUCTION

In the previous chapter, the emphasis was on making a choice from among two or more alternatives when only revenues, cost savings, and costs are relevant to the decision. In that context the commitment of resources was not a relevant financial factor. In this chapter, however, the long-term investment of the firm's resources is a major consideration in the decision-making process.

Long-range investments imply a use of capital by the firm. Suppliers of capital demand an acceptable return on this resource. Management must balance the firm's demand for capital necessitated by new investments with the available supply of capital. The process of managing the supply and demand of capital and making decisions with regard to the use of available capital is referred to as capital budgeting. The capital budget is a list and analysis of all the long-range investments in which the firm is considering investing its available supply of capital. Acceptable capital investments must be consistent with the goals and objectives of the firm.

A capital budget may be regarded as both short and long-term. The capital budgeting decision considers both the firm's financial ability to provide acceptable returns on current and future capital and the degree to which the investment meshes with the firm's other short and long-range goals.

Once management has committed the firm's capital to specific long-term investments, the firm may have limited its potential investment alternatives for some time into the future. Once a capital investment is made, it is normally difficult to modify at a later date without incurring considerable losses. Usually, the original outlay for any investment can only be recovered through the use of the asset involved.

TYPES OF ACCOUNTING INFORMATION NECESSARY FOR CAPITAL BUDGETING DECISIONS

Accounting information which may prove useful in capital budgeting decisions includes both accrual and cash flow data. Accrual accounting information is based on generally accepted accounting principles which normally have a tendency to average the various financial factors involved in determining revenues, costs, and investments. Therefore, analysis based on accrual accounting information will reflect this averaging approach.

Generally accepted accounting principles are not considered in estimating cash inflows and outflows. Thus, the cash flows from an investment proposal will not necessarily coincide with either the income or the accrual accounting cost savings from an investment. For example, an investment in an asset usually requires an immediate cash outlay for the acquisition cost of the asset. From an accrual accounting standpoint, this cost is allocated to the appropriate time periods over the asset's projected life through the process of depreciation.

INCOME TAX IMPLICATIONS FOR CAPITAL BUDGETING DECISIONS

Income tax implications with regard to any revenues, cost savings, or expenses associated with a capital investment must be considered. Assuming a 40 percent income tax rate, revenues or cost savings represent an after tax inflow of 60 percent of their gross amount (100 percent—40 percent). In other words, revenues (or cost savings in excess of expenses) associated with the proposed capital investment are taxed at 40 percent; 60 percent of the gross amount accrues to the firm. Likewise, expenses requiring a cash outlay have an after tax cost of only 60 percent of their stated amount.

Another income tax factor that should be considered in capital budgeting decisions is the effect of the depreciation taken on long-term investments upon taxable income and cash flows. Although it is a non-cash expense, depreciation is an allowable deduction for income tax purposes and as such causes a lower taxable net income and, consequently, lower taxes. The depreciation allowance indirectly reduces cash outflows by lowering the income tax liability. For example, assume a firm purchases an asset at a cost of $10,000 and depreciates this asset electing the straight-line method, using a useful life of five years with no salvage value. The firm will recognize depreciation expense of $2,000 a year ($10,000 ÷ 5 years). If the firm's effective tax rate is 40 percent, that firm will realize an $800 tax savings ($2,000 × .40) in each of the five years the asset is depreciated.

THE CAPITAL BUDGET

Proposals for capital expenditures may be initiated by any group within the organization. Employees may propose an idea via suggestions to management; the research and development department may develop new products or alter current products so as to require capital outlays; technological change may introduce new methods; product demand may necessitate additional plant, equipment, warehouses, offices or other assets; or assets may simply wear out and necessitate replacement.

The process of developing the capital budget on a project-by-project basis may be divided into five steps: [1]

1. Initiating the idea and specifications.
2. Reviewing the request.
3. Making a decision regarding the request.
4. Controlling the project's progress and funds.
5. Conducting a post-audit of the results of the decision.

The five steps are presented here in order to structure the coverage and discussion of long-range capital investments. In practice, the distinction among these steps may not be as apparent or clear-cut as the above listing would lead one to believe.

---

[1] Six steps might be more appropriate if the firm wishes to consider the available alternative financing techniques.

**INITIATION
OF THE
IDEA AND
SPECIFICATIONS**

In firms where numerous capital expenditure requests must be considered, the format of the request and the channels through which the request must be routed or directed are normally identified in the firm's policy manual. The sponsor of the request usually develops the basic idea with the aid of the appropriate supporting personnel from accounting, management, industrial engineering, the legal department, etc. If a specific department has the responsibility for developing the specifications and the capital expenditure request form for projects, the input of the original sponsor may be limited to developing the idea and basic estimates of the benefits and costs. An example of a request for a capital expenditure is presented in Illustration 1.

**Sax Company
Capital Expenditure Request**

Project Title _____ Date _____

Project No. _____

Proposal Overview (Attach Detail)
Direct Capital Required _____ Depreciation Technique _____
Working Capital Required _____
Project Life _____
Average Revenues or Cost Savings _____
Average Period Expenses _____
Net Added Profits Before Taxes _____
Net Added Profits After Taxes _____

Average Annual Cash Flow _____

Justification:
Cash Payback _____ Present Value Index _____
Accounting Rate of Return _____ Internal Rate of Return _____
Net Present Value _____
Comments:

(Division)	Approval Date	(Corporate)	Approval Date
Project Sponsor _____		_____	
General Manager _____		_____	
Division Controller _____		_____	

**REVIEW OF
THE REQUEST**

If a firm is large and has numerous capital budgeting proposals, the request is normally reviewed by the sponsor's supervisor. The decision to accept or reject the proposal may be made at a lower level of management provided that the request is within the manager's capital budget limit. For example, department heads may have the authority to approve projects with a cost of up to $4,000 on an individual basis, with a maximum total of $15,000 in expenditures established for a given year. A division manager may be able to approve expenditures of up to $30,000 with an aggregate limit of $150,000 in any given year. The president may be authorized to approve expenditures of up to $500,000 with an annual aggregate of $5,000,000. Normal procedures indicate that major capital expenditures should be approved by the board of directors.

The basis for establishing the various limits on expenditures at different levels within the organization is developed at the annual budget review session with top management. At this session, current proposals and related estimates are reviewed, combined and coordinated with ongoing projects from prior years and with projects in other segments or divisions of the organization. As might be expected, the forms and procedures for capital budgeting decisions in smaller firms are usually not as clearly developed or as formal as they are in larger firms.

**MAKING A
DECISION
REGARDING
THE REQUEST**

There are numerous tools or techniques available to aid management in making capital budgeting decisions. Each of these techniques has strengths and weaknesses. Management normally employs several of these techniques. The most difficult part of the capital budgeting decision may well be obtaining quantifiable input data, i.e., the information and forecasts surrounding the project. After the initial proposal is prepared, making additional calculations to develop an unbiased perspective regarding a decision does not usually require significant effort or cost. If the firm has a computer facility or access to a computer service bureau, a program is usually available which will handle the basic techniques discussed in this chapter.

The techniques used to analyze proposed capital budgeting decisions may be classified into two general categories: (1) those techniques that ignore the time value of money and (2) those techniques that consider the time value of money.

**Techniques
That Ignore
Time Value**

There are several project evaluation techniques which do not consider the time value of money. While none of these methods should be used exclusively, they do have the advantages of being simple and easy to compute. They provide management with a quick method to facilitate a review of project feasibility. However, if the project involves large cash flow streams, the unadjusted evaluation techniques should generally be used as additional information to supplement a time value adjusted technique. Four project evaluation techniques which ignore the time value of money are discussed in the following section of this chapter.

No Choice or Urgency— Making the Decision

The distinguishing characteristic of the no choice or urgency technique is the real or implied need to make a decision immediately because of the particular circumstances at hand. This approach is the least desirable of the various capital budgeting techniques because, due to the urgency of the situation, profitability considerations are not analyzed, but rather are left to chance.

Urgency implies quick remedial action rather than deliberative action undertaken after a careful analysis of the available alternatives. If the potential resources involved are not great, the urgency criterion is probably justified. An effective planning scheme and a limitation on the amount of investment involved reduces the probability of large expenditures being made using the no choice or urgency plea as the basis for the decision.

Qualitative Reasons— Making the Decision

A second capital budgeting technique which does not consider the time value of money is based on qualitative rather than quantitative reasoning. In every capital budgeting decision, there are certain qualitative aspects that must be considered in addition to the available quantitative information. However, a capital budgeting decision based solely on qualitative criteria should be made only when the qualitative statements can be made with some degree of accuracy and when there is no quantifiable information available.

Qualitative reasoning is considered in many decisions made in areas such as organizational behavior or social commitment of resources. For example, if a firm chooses to install a lunchroom for its employees, this decision cannot be evaluated solely on its monetary returns. The lunchroom may have positive social value for the company which in and of itself justifies the investment. Although an investment in an employee lunchroom may produce quantifiable benefits for the firm in the form of increased revenues, decreased costs, increased productivity, lower employee turnover, or more satisfied employees, these benefits can only be measured indirectly in relation to the capital investment.

Qualitative reasons involved in capital budgeting decisions range from such factors as employee incentive plans to community relations activities for profit-oriented companies. In these decisions, it is frequently difficult to specify and quantify the benefits attributable to the investment except by comparing some aspect of the firm or its activities before and after the decision to see if a change appears to have taken place.

Payback Period— Making the Decision

The payback period is the amount of time required to produce net cash flows sufficient to recover the initial investment outlay. The payback technique does not consider the timing of the receipt of money, but is based totally on an analysis of cash flows. Moreover, the payback method does not measure the profitability of a project. This method is a simple calculation which determines the amount of time required to recover, in cash flows, the initial net investment in an asset.

The payback technique is widely used for a rough analysis of small investments that do not justify or warrant in-depth study or analysis. Despite its simplicity, the approach does have merit in the following situations:

1. If a company-wide policy requires payback within a stated time period for all capital investments below a selected dollar limit, the payback technique can effectively and efficiently screen small investment proposals before a formal request for expenditure is prepared.
2. If there is an element of uncertainty with regard to the estimates of future cash inflows or cost savings, the payback calculation provides a measure of how soon the firm can expect to recover its initial investment.
3. If cash flow is a major problem for a firm, timing of the cash returns from an investment may be considered crucial; thus the payback technique may provide relevant information.

The payback approach may be applied in several ways. The general formula is as follows:

$$\text{Payback period} = \frac{\text{Net original investment}}{\text{Annual cash inflows or cost savings}}$$

As long as the annual cash inflows are equal in amount, this general formula is applicable. If unequal cash inflows are expected, average cash inflows may be used or the projected unequal cash inflows for each year may be reviewed in order to determine the payback period.

To illustrate the use of the payback technique, assume that Sax Company is considering a labor-saving device that costs $1,000 and provides the following cash flow savings:

Year	Cash Flow Savings	Cumulative Cash Flow	Cumulative Cash Flow Net of Investment
1	$ 400	$ 400	($600)
2	300	700	(300)
3	300	1,000	0
4	300	1,300	300
5	200	1,500	500
Total	$1,500		

The average cash savings is $300 ($1500/5 years). Using this average cash savings, the payback period is calculated as follows:

$$\text{Payback} = \frac{\$1,000}{\$300} = 3\frac{1}{3} \text{ years}$$

If the cash savings are reviewed by specific years, the payback period is three years because $1,000 is recovered in the first three years.

The major weakness of the payback method is the disregard for the timing of the receipts and therefore the time value of money. A managerial decision which demonstrates the problem caused by a disregard for the time value of money is shown below:

	Investment A	Investment B
Cash Outflow	$1,000	$1,000
Cash Inflows		
Year 1	$ 200	$ 700
Year 2	300	200
Year 3	500	100
Payback Period	3 Years	3 Years

Alternative Investments A and B have the same investment outlays, same payback periods and are equally important to the firm. However, because capital available for investment is limited, only one investment can be selected. Since the payback period is the same for both Investment A and Investment B either alternative is equally desirable if the payback method is used as the sole criterion in choosing between these investments. An analysis of the timing of the cash flows expected under Investment B, however, points out that this investment provides a greater cash flow in the first year than does Investment A. Because there is a time value associated with future cash receipts (that is, a dollar today is of greater value to the firm than a dollar to be received next year), investment B is the better choice. The payback technique ignores the time value of money and thus is not an effective gauge of an investment's worth. The payback calculation is useful as a ranking technique in that it provides an index of the cash recovery period for an investment being contemplated. Payback should not be considered a comprehensive criterion in a capital budgeting analysis.

Accountant's Rate of Return—Making the Decision

The accountant's rate of return (ARR, also referred to as the unadjusted rate of return or accounting rate of return) also fails to consider the time value of money. Accrual accounting income is used as the basis for benefit measurement. Since income is considered in the formula, the technique does give some recognition to profitability.

The formula used for the accountant's rate of return is:

$$\frac{\text{Average incremental increase in annual net income}}{\text{Net original investment outlay}}$$

The accountant's rate of return may also be computed using the average investment outlay as the denominator. The formula then becomes:

$$\frac{\text{Average incremental increase in annual net income}}{\left(\dfrac{\text{Original investment } + \text{ Salvage value}}{2} \right)}$$

The payback example can be used to illustrate the use of the accountant's rate of return, if certain additional assumptions are made. The labor-saving device considered in the payback example will be depreciated using the straight-line method over an expected life of five years. The salvage value of the asset at the end of five years is estimated to be $100. Sax Company wishes to make the analysis on a before-tax basis using both the original investment and the average investment.

$$\text{ARR using original investment} = \frac{(\$1,500/5 \text{ years}) - \$180 \text{ Depreciation}}{\$1,000}$$

$$= \frac{\$300 - \$180}{\$1,000} = 12\%$$

$$\text{ARR using average investment} = \frac{(\$1,500/5 \text{ years}) - \$180 \text{ Depreciation}}{\left(\dfrac{\$1,000 + \$100 \text{ Salvage}}{2} \right)}$$

$$= \frac{\$300 - \$180}{\$550} = 21.8\%$$

The accounting rate of return, like the payback technique, is a ranking technique. Alternative investments may be ranked in the order of their profitability to provide another measure to be used in making the capital budgeting decision.

TIME VALUE OF MONEY TECHNIQUES

Capital budgeting techniques which consider the time value of money are referred to as discounted cash-flow methods. A dollar today has a greater value than does a dollar one year from now; moreover, a dollar to be received one year from now has a greater value to a firm today than a dollar to be received five years from now. Money has value over time because it can be invested and a return on the investment can be realized.

The emphasis of capital budgeting techniques that consider the time value of money is on the timing and magnitude of cash flows. Two general discounted cash flow techniques available to assist in making capital budgeting decisions are the net present value method and the internal rate of return method. These two techniques and a variation of the net present value technique, the present value index, are considered in this chapter.

The concept of present value is discussed in the Appendix to this chapter. One must understand the Appendix and must be able to use Tables 1 and 2 at the end of this chapter prior to considering the net present value and the internal rate of return techniques. If you are unfamiliar with this concept, you should read the Appendix on Present Value before continuing with the chapter material.

The techniques that employ the concept of the time value of money usually consider the impact of income taxes on cash flows utilized in the analysis. If income tax implications are not considered, the analysis of cash flows is incomplete and inaccurate. Two similar pre-tax investment alternatives may produce entirely different results on an after-tax basis. For this reason, after-tax cash flows should be used in an analysis in which income taxes are a relevant factor.

Net Present Value—Making the Decision

The net present value technique requires that the management of a firm specify the minimum desired rate of return on an after-tax basis which must be earned on capital investments in order to make them acceptable to the firm. This minimum acceptable rate is usually referred to as the cost of capital. In essence, the net present value technique discounts all projected outflows and inflows of cash back to the present period using the cost of capital as the discount rate. If the present value of anticipated cash inflows exceeds the present value of anticipated cash outflows, the project is acceptable because the investment is earning an after-tax return which is greater than the cost of capital. If the present value of projected cash inflows is equal to the present value of projected cash outflows, then the net present value of the project is zero, and the project is earning exactly the cost of capital. If the net present value is negative, the project is earning less than the cost of capital because the present value of anticipated cash outflows is greater than the present value of anticipated cash inflows.

More than one of the alternatives under consideration may be capable of earning a return greater than the minimum return acceptable to management. When more than one alternative is acceptable using the net present value criterion, management will further compare the acceptable alternatives and then make its decision. The following example illustrates the use of the net present value technique and the alternative means of approaching an investment decision.

Northern Printing Company is considering the purchase of a new offset printing press at a cost of $15,000. This press has an estimated useful life of five years and will result in a savings in operating costs of $5,000 per year over its useful life. The straight-line method of depreciation will be used and no salvage value is anticipated at the end of its useful life. The printing press will require an overhaul costing $2,500 (considered a maintenance expense) at the end of the third year. Northern has alternative investment possibilities for the $15,000 that will yield a return of 16 percent after taxes. Because this alternative exists, the management of Northern has decided to use a rate of 16 percent as the cost of capital in evaluating the possible purchase of the printing press. In the past, Northern has averaged a 40 percent tax rate on its earned income. Management anticipates that a similar tax rate will be incurred in the future. If the offset printing press does not earn a projected return of 16 percent after taxes, Northern Printing Company does not wish to invest its resources in this project.

Part A of Illustration 2 identifies the cash flow impacts of the printing press on an annual basis. The discounting factors used are taken from Table 1 at the end of this chapter, Present Value of $1. Part B of Illustration 2 uses the annuity table, Table 2, at the end of this chapter, Present Value of Annuity of $1 Per Period. For purposes of illustration, assume that all inflows or outflows of cash, with the exception of the initial investment, take place at the end of the year.

In Part A of Illustration 2, the present value of the initial outlay of $15,000 is $15,000, because the money is paid out immediately. The cost savings realized each year are discounted to reflect their current dollar value if the rate of return on the funds is 16 percent. The cost savings are also multiplied by 60 percent (100% − the income tax rate of 40%) to reflect the related income tax implications. If the printing press is purchased, the reductions in costs cause income to rise by $5,000 per year. At a 40 percent income tax rate, an additional $2,000 in income taxes is incurred annually. Therefore, the $5,000 reduction in costs is worth only $3,000 to Northern Printing Company after taxes.

The depreciation on the asset represents a tax shelter amounting to $3,000 per year. No cash is paid or received for depreciation, but it is a tax deductible expense used in arriving at taxable income for the period. Net income before taxes is reduced by the annual depreciation charge of $3,000, and income taxes are reduced by 40 percent of $3,000. The tax savings resulting from depreciation expense reduces the outflow of cash required to pay income taxes. Therefore, it is considered a cash inflow just as a cost savings is considered an inflow.

Net Present Value Technique

Part A: Year by Year Discounting

Inflows Year	Description	Before Tax	After Tax	Present Value Factor- 16%	Present Value
1	Operating Savings.....	$ 5,000	$ 3,000[a]	.862	$ 2,586.00
1	Depreciation	3,000	1,200[b]	.862	1,034.40
2	Operating Savings.....	5,000	3,000	.743	2,229.00
2	Depreciation	3,000	1,200	.743	891.60
3	Operating Savings.....	5,000	3,000	.641	1,923.00
3	Depreciation	3,000	1,200	.641	769.20
4	Operating Savings.....	5,000	3,000	.552	1,656.00
4	Depreciation	3,000	1,200	.552	662.40
5	Operating Savings.....	5,000	3,000	.476	1,428.00
5	Depreciation	3,000	1,200	.476	571.20
			Total Inflows		$13,750.80

Outflows					
0	Printing Press Investment	$15,000	$15,000	1.000	$15,000.00
3	Overhaul Expense.....	2,500	1,500[a]	.641	961.50
			Total Outflows		$15,961.50
			Net Present Value		($2,210.70)

Part B: Using the Annuity Table for the Same Inflows and Outflows Occurring in Multiple Years

Inflows	Description	Before Tax	After Tax	Factor	Present Value
1–5	Operating Savings.....	5,000	3,000	3.274	$ 9,822.00
1–5	Depreciation	3,000	1,200	3.274	3,928.80
			Total Inflows		$13,750.80

Outflows					
0	Printing Press........	$15,000	$15,000	1.000	$15,000.00
3	Overhaul Expense.....	2,500	1,500	.641	961.50
			Total Outflows		$15,961.50
			Net Present Value		($2,210.70)

[a] Savings or Operating expenses are multiplied by 1 — the tax rate (in this example: 1 − .40 = .60).
[b] Depreciation expenses are multiplied by the tax rate.

The overhaul expense at the end of the third year will not increase the life of the asset. This expense represents a cash outlay that will be incurred and which will be deductible at the end of year three for income tax purposes. With a 40 percent tax rate, the effective cost of the overhaul is 60 percent of the cash outlay of $2,500, or $1,500. Without this overhaul, the net income before taxes for the period would be $2,500 higher and additional taxes of $1,000 (.40 × $2,500) would have to be paid. Thus, the net cost of the overhaul is $1,500.

Note the difference between the treatment of depreciation, a tax deductible item, and the overhaul which is also a deductible item for tax purposes. If no cash is paid for a tax deductible item, the amount of the effective cost savings is the tax rate multiplied by the amount of the tax deduction. If cash is paid for a tax deductible item, the effective cost (not the cost savings) of the item is 100 percent minus the tax rate. As shown in Illustration 2, the depreciation tax savings is considered an inflow and the overhaul cost is considered an outflow in the analysis.

The same principles underlying the calculations in Part A of Illustration 2 are also applicable to Part B. By using the annuity table to calculate the present values of the inflows and outflows for the two annuities (cost savings and depreciation tax savings), the time required to perform the calculations on a year-by-year basis has been reduced.

The net present value of the offset printing press is a negative $2,210.70. The present value of the outflows exceeds the present value of the inflows by that amount. Therefore, this potential investment is not expected to earn the required 16 percent after-tax return. Rather, the investment will earn something less than 16 percent. Had the net present value of the inflows exceeded the net present value of the outflows, then this investment could be expected to earn a rate of return in excess of 16 percent and would, therefore, have been an acceptable project for the company.

The net present value technique is the theoretically correct capital budgeting decision guide. It is not a ranking technique nor does it provide an answer that specifies the magnitude of the projected effective return on an investment.

Present Value Index—Making the Decision

The present value or profitability index converts the present value of the inflows and outflows as determined by the net present value method into an index. To derive this index, the present value of the inflows is divided by the present value of the outflows. The higher the ratio, the higher the rate of return per dollar invested in the proposed project. A ratio of less than one indicates that a proposed project is expected to earn a return less than the desired rate of return. A proposed project with a present value index of one will earn exactly the desired rate of return, while a present value index greater than one indicates a return in excess of the desired rate of return.

The previously discussed net present value technique provides an answer stated in terms of current dollars. If only net present values are considered in selecting alternative projects, large dollar projects will normally have a net present value greater than that for small projects, even though the large projects may not be earning a rate of return as great as that earned by the small projects. The usefulness of the present value index is that different projects or investments can be ranked in terms of their relative profitability. The absolute dollar values for all projects can be converted to a relative measure of the profitability through the present value index. The present value index of the offset printing press in Illustration 2 is:

$$\text{Present value index} = \frac{\text{Present value of inflows}}{\text{Present value of outflows}}$$

$$= \frac{\$13,750.80}{\$15,961.50} = .861$$

An index of .861 indicates that the project will not earn the 16 percent rate of return or stated cost of capital.

Internal Rate of Return With Equal Cash Flows—Making the Decision

In the net present value technique discussed above, the required rate of return (cost of capital) is specified and the results indicate if the project will earn that rate, a greater rate or a smaller rate but the actual rate the project will earn is not determined. The internal rate of return or the time adjusted rate of return method determines the effective rate of return that a proposed project *will* earn over its expected life. The internal rate of return for the proposed project is then compared to the required rate of return to determine whether to accept or reject the project. The internal rate of return is that interest rate that equates the present value of the inflows with the present value of the outflows for the investment. The following example will illustrate the calculation of an approximation of the internal rate of return when the expected cash flows from a project are equal each period and therefore approximate an annuity.

Harry's Garage is considering purchasing a wheel alignment machine costing $10,000 to be placed into service in 19x1. Harry estimates that this machine will generate $10,000 annually in additional revenues and will cost $6,000 to operate on an annual basis. The machine has an estimated life of ten years with no salvage value anticipated. The straight-line method is used to depreciate the machine. Harry is currently taxed in the 50 percent tax bracket. He would like to know the effective annual rate of return on this machine on an after-tax basis.

To find the internal rate of return for Harry, the initial step is to determine the net annual after-tax cash flows generated by the wheel alignment machine.

Sales revenue (cash)		$10,000
Less: Expenses:		
Operating costs (cash)	$6,000	
Depreciation (non-cash)	1,000	7,000
Net income before taxes		$ 3,000
Income taxes (cash)		1,500
Net income after taxes		$ 1,500
Add back: Depreciation (non-cash)		1,000
Net annual cash flow		$ 2,500

If the potential investment has a minimal salvage value and if the payback on the investment is less than one-half the life of the asset, the payback method can be used in conjunction with the Present Value of an Annuity of $1 Per Period shown in Table 2 at the end of this chapter to approximate the internal rate of return.

$$\text{Payback period} = \frac{\$10,000}{\$2,500} = 4 \text{ years.}$$

The payback period on the wheel alignment machine is four years, less than one-half the estimated life of the machine. Next, go to Table 2 at the end of this chapter and scan horizontally the ten time period row (the life of the machine) to find the table value that approximates the payback period of four years. A table factor of exactly four does not exist, but if it did, it would fall somewhere between 4.192 and 3.923, the amounts for the 20 and 22 percent columns. The actual rate of return on the wheel alignment machine is between 20 and 22 percent. Precision may be increased by interpolation between the two rates, but given the measure of uncertainty in the initial estimates, the range of the two rates is probably adequate.

A proof of the solution for the internal rate of return for the wheel alignment machine is as follows:

Discounted at 22 percent	_Inflow_	_Outflow_
Initial costs......................................		$10,000.00
Sales revenues ($10,000 × 3.923 × .5)..........	$19,615.00	
Operating costs ($6,000 × 3.923 × .5)..........		11,769.00
Depreciation tax savings		
($1,000 × 3.923 × .5)	1,961.50	
Present values....................................	$21,576.50	$21,769.00
Net present value...........................	($192.50)	

Discounted at 20 percent	*Inflow*	*Outflow*
Initial costs...............................		$10,000.00
Sales revenue ($10,000 × 4.192 × .5)...........	$20,960.00	
Operating costs ($6,000 × 4.192 × .5)..........		12,576.00
Depreciation tax savings		
($1,000 × 4.192 × .5)	2,096.00	
Present values.............................	$23,056.00	$22,576.00
Net present value..........................	$480.00	

If the cash inflows and outflows are discounted at a rate of 22 percent, then it can be seen that the investment has a net present value of a negative $192.50 and therefore earns an internal rate of return of less than 22 percent. If the investment is discounted at 20 percent, the net present value is a positive $480.00. The discount factor which would make the present values of the inflows and outflows equal lies at some point between those two rates.

Internal Rate of Return With Unequal Cash Flows—Making the Decision

Significantly unequal annual cash flows preclude the use of the payback period and the present value of an annuity table to approximate the internal rate of return, except as an initial starting point. To illustrate the calculation of the internal rate of return with unequal cash flows, the Northern Printing Company example from Illustration 2 is used. For convenience, the basic data are reproduced in the following example:

> Initial cost—$15,000
> 5 year life
> Straight-line depreciation—$3,000 per year
> Overhaul at the end of 3 years—$2,500
> Annual operating cost savings—$5,000
> Tax rate = 40%

The initial step is to approximate the area of the Present Value of Annuity of $1 Per Period table (Table 2) that will be utilized.[2] Once again, an estimate of the payback period can be used to isolate the appropriate present value of an annuity factor.

---

[2] An alternative approach, which will not be covered, would entail solving the formula for the discount (interest) rate that would produce a zero net present value. That specific discount rate would be the internal rate of return.

Year	Calculations of After-Tax Cash Flow		Cumulative Cash Flow
0	Initial cost.............................	($15,000)	($15,000)
1	($5,000 × .6) + ($3,000 × .4)...............	4,200	(10,800)
2	($5,000 × .6) + ($3,000 × .4)...............	4,200	(6,600)
3	($2,500 × .6) + ($3,000 × .4)...............	2,700	(3,900)
4	($5,000 × .6) + ($3,000 × .4)...............	4,200	300
5	($5,000 × .6) + ($3,000 × .4)...............	4,200	4,500

Payback period = approximately 4 years.

In the five time period row, the table factor of four years falls between 4.1002 and 3.9927, the amounts for the 7 and 8 percent columns of the Present Value of an Annuity Table—shown in Table 2 at the end of this chapter. Discounting of the cash outflows and inflows at 7 and 8 percent for this investment is shown as follows:

Discounted at 7 Percent

	Year	Description	Before Tax	After Tax	PV Factor	Present Value
Inflows						
	1-5	Operating savings	$ 5,000	$ 3,000	4.1002	$12,300.60
	1-5	Depreciation	3,000	1,200	4.1002	4,920.24
		Total inflows:				$17,220.84
Outflows	0	Printing press	$15,000	$15,000	1.0000	$15,000.00
	3	Overhaul expense	2,500	1,500	.8163	1,224.45
		Total outflows:				$16,224.45
		Net present value:				$ 996.39

Discounted at 8 Percent

	Year	Description	Before Tax	After Tax	PV Factor	Present Value
Inflows	1-5	Operating savings	$ 5,000	$ 3,000	3.9927	$11,978.10
	1-5	Depreciation	3,000	1,200	3.9927	4,791.24
		Total inflows:				$16,769.34
Outflows	0	Printing press	$15,000	$15,000	1.0000	$15,000.00
	3	Overhaul expense	2,500	1,500	.7938	1,190.70
		Total outflows:				$16,190.70
		Net present value:				$ 578.64

At 7 percent the net present value of the investment is a positive $996.39, while using the 8 percent discount rate produces a net present value of $578.64. Since the use of an 8 percent discount rate produces a positive net present value, the actual internal rate of return for the printing press is somewhat greater than 8 percent. If a 10 percent discount rate is used, the net present value will be negative. Therefore, the internal rate of return must be between 8 and 10 percent. Unequal cash flows require calculating with different trial discount rates until the two adjacent rates are found that identify the crossover point of the net present value. That is, one rate produces a positive net present value and the adjacent rate produces a negative net present value. The "true" internal rate of return could be found by interpolation after finding the crossover point.

Time Value of Money and Accelerated Depreciation

The straight-line method of depreciation has been used in each of the examples in this chapter in order to allow the reader to focus upon the concepts illustrated. In practice, many companies use accelerated depreciation methods for income tax purposes in order to achieve greater tax savings in the early years of an asset's life. Accelerated methods increase depreciation expense in the early years of an asset's life, thereby reducing income and increasing after-tax cash flows. While depreciation expense in the later years is reduced causing increased income and decreased after-tax cash flows, the advantage of the use of accelerated depreciation is nonetheless real, because of the timing of the cash flows and the time value of money.

Since 1981, the only accelerated method which may be used for Federal tax purposes is the Accelerated Cost Recovery System (ACRS) which was introduced by the 1981 Economic Recovery Tax Act. The Tax Reform Act of 1986 modified the ACRS procedures. For tangible personal property (such as equipment), ACRS generally provides for the use of a statutory method approximating the 200 percent declining balance method with a switch to straight-line after the mid-point life. In addition, there are half-year, mid-quarter and mid-month conventions which must be used when assets qualifying for ACRS treatment are placed in service or sold during the year. Therefore, a full discussion of ACRS is beyond the scope of this text. The straight-line method of depreciation is used for all illustrations and problems to emphasize the concepts of capital budgeting without the complications of different depreciation techniques.

CONTROLLING THE PROJECT'S PROGRESS AND FUNDS

Once a capital investment decision has been made by management, the next step in the capital budgeting process becomes important. Control must be established over the resources committed to the project and over the progress of the project. A budget and cost record is established for each project of the firm. The budget and actual costs must agree if a budget overrun is to be avoided. The original capital expenditure proposal is based on the best information available at the time the proposal is initiated. Therefore, variances are to be expected, but the variances should be explainable. As a rule of thumb, large capital expenditures should have smaller variances on a percentage basis, because they justify more in-depth planning.

The progress of the project must also be closely monitored. Many capital expenditure projects are closely related to the activities of other segments of the organization. When this interrelationship exists, a delay in the completion of one project could cause problems in other segments of the organization. Project delays usually mean increased costs. Illustration 3 is an example of a format which may be used for a capital expenditure budget for a firm.

When a project is significantly off budget in terms of either dollars or time, an investigation should be undertaken. It may be necessary to revise the appropriation or the date of completion in order to coordinate expenditures for the entire firm.

Capital Expenditure Budget

Sax Company Capital Expenditure Budget for 19x1							
Project Origination	Total Budgeted	Budgeted For This Year	Actual For This Year	Under (Over) For This Year	Under (Over) to Date	Estimated Under (Over) For Total Project	Comments

Corporate:
  Project No. 9457
  Project No. 9459							

Power Turbine Shaft:
  Project No. 9425
  Project No. 9426							

Filters:
  Project No. 8567
  Project No. 8973
  Project No. 9367							

Tanks:
  Project No. 9410
  Project No. 9411							

Total ($)							

POST-AUDIT OF THE RESULTS OF THE DECISION

A post-audit of all major capital expenditures and a sample of the smaller expenditures should be made after completion of the projects in order to determine if the benefits expected from the projects did in fact accrue to the firm. There are certain problems associated with post-audits. Many expenditures are not independent of other operations, and the benefits derived from such expenditures are often neither easily nor objectively measurable. In addition, it may be necessary to convert the accounting records from an accrual basis to a cash flow basis if the original decision to make the expenditure was based on cash flows.

Post-audits can assist in identifying past mistakes made in planning capital expenditures, and can, hopefully, improve future inputs into this type of decision. In addition, the individuals responsible for preparing the estimates will probably be more cautious in their treatment of the capital expenditure decision when they are aware that their estimates will be reviewed upon the completion of the project and the subsequent start of operations.

SENSITIVITY ANALYSIS AND COST OF PREDICTION ERRORS

The cash flows that we have used in our capital budgeting models are only expected values. There is always the possibility that the actual cash flow will deviate from the expected cash flow. This possibility is called risk or uncertainty.

Sensitivity analysis attempts to analyze how susceptible a decision is to the uncertainty of the expected cash flows. Conceptually this means that expected cash flows should be examined in accordance with their probability distributions. However, in business decisions we are usually confronted with subjective probabilities as opposed to the objective probabilities we are used to in many gaming decisions. Therefore, the underlying probabilities and probability distributions are not capable of direct measurement but can only be estimated by expert opinion.

Alternative ways to allow for risk apart from estimating probability distributions include using (1) pessimistic predictions of cash flows, (2) shorter expected lives, (3) higher costs of capital, and (4) sensitivity analysis and cost of prediction errors.

As a start, assume that our estimates of the cash flows will not be completely accurate (because they are just that—estimates). It also follows that if we had known the actual cash flows when we were making the decision and with this true information the same decision would have been made, then our prediction errors did not cost the company anything. But if knowledge of the true parameters would have caused us to make some other decision, the cost of the prediction errors is measured by the incremental profit that would have been earned by making the alternative decision.

For example, assume that John decided to bet on a horse because he predicted that it would win by 10 lengths. Actual results are that the horse wins by 2 lengths. John's prediction error cost him nothing because if he had known the true parameter he would have made the same decision to bet the horse to win. However, in another example, John is trying to decide how many shoes to order for his store. Assume that he buys them for $15 and sells them for $25. Based upon his estimate that there is a demand for 100 of these shoes, John places his order accordingly. Actual demand is 110 customers. In this example there is a cost to John because of his prediction error. This is the opportunity cost of the lost sales. John could have made another $100 if he had known the true demand [10 shoes $\times$ ($25 $-$ $15) = $100].

In summary, a decision is labeled as being very sensitive if very small errors in the estimated cash flows would lead to regret that the decision was made. A decision is considered very insensitive if there could be large errors in the predictions and the same decision would still be made. Finally, we recognize that prediction errors need not have a cost to the company if the less than perfect information still leads to the correct decision.

SUMMARY

The process of managing the demand for capital and planning the use of available capital is referred to as capital budgeting. Capital budgeting includes analyzing and selecting alternative long-range investments which insure that the firm will meet both current and future profitability demands. Information required in the capital budgeting process is based on both accrual accounting and cash flow data. In addition, a firm must consider the income tax implications of any investment under consideration.

The process of developing a capital budget on a project-by-project basis is divided into five basic steps: (1) initiating the idea and specifications; (2) reviewing the request; (3) making a decision regarding the request; (4) controlling the project progress and funds; and (5) conducting a post-audit of the results of the decision.

In making the decision regarding a particular capital investment request, a firm may choose to use various financial analysis techniques. The payback technique is a simple calculation which determines the amount of time required to recover, in cash, the initial net investment in an asset. The accountant's rate of return or unadjusted rate of return method is a measure of profitability, but does not consider the time value of money. Both the payback method and accountant's rate of return are tools that can be used to rank the relative desirability of alternative investments and are useful tools when employed along with other methods of analysis.

Capital budgeting techniques which consider the time value of money are referred to as discounted cash flow approaches. Among these techniques are the net present value technique, present value index and the internal rate of return technique. These approaches place emphasis on the timing and magnitude of cash flows. Since the predicted cash flows are only expected values, there is the risk or uncertainty that the actual cash flows will be different. Sensitivity and cost of prediction error analysis attempts to assess the seriousness of this risk or uncertainty.

Appendix

When resources, usually cash, are invested there is an opportunity cost involved. An opportunity cost is defined as the income foregone by not choosing the next best alternative investment. When projects which require the use of resources are short-term, the opportunity cost is usually not substantial because the investment is only committed for a short period of time and will soon be converted back to cash and made available for possible reinvestment. When such projects have a long life, however, the cash inflows and outflows will occur over a long time period. The value of the cash flows over a long time period are not equal in terms of the value of a cash flow today (the present value).

The present value of $1 received today is $1 because it can be invested in assets with a value of $1 or deposited in a savings account to accumulate interest. The present value of $1 to be received one year from now is less than $1 because the opportunity to invest it and earn a return is lost for one year. The rational economic person would not give up $1 today to receive $1 a year from now because he could invest or save the $1 today and receive more than a $1 a year from now.

Calculating the Present Value of a Future Single Sum

The amount that would have to be invested today in order to receive $1 a year from now can be determined by using the following formula:

$$\text{Present value} = \frac{\text{Future value}}{(1 + \text{Interest rate})^N}$$

(Where N = the number of time periods to receipt or payment.)

If an interest rate of 10 percent and an annual interest compounding period[3] are assumed, the numerical formula for the present value of $1 to be received one year from now is:

$$\text{Present value} = \frac{\$1}{(1 + .10)^1}$$
$$= \frac{\$1}{1.10}$$
$$= \$.90909$$

---

[3] An interest compounding period is that period over which interest will be calculated. If the compounding period is one year on bank savings accounts and interest is stated at 4%, the interest on $1 for a year would be $1 × .04 = $.04. If interest is to be compounded semi-annually, the interest on one dollar for a year would be $1 × .02 = $.02 plus $1.02 × .02 = $.0204. The total interest would be $.0404 under semi-annual compounding. The additional $.0004 in interest with semi-annual compounding is the interest on the $.02 interest from the first-half of the year.

The present value of $1 one year from now with annual compounding is $.90909. If a 10 percent return on investment could be earned, the rational economic person would consider receiving $.90909 today the same as receiving $1 one year from today, given all other factors are equal. The sum of $.90909 will equal $1 one year from now at a 10 percent annual compounding as can be seen from the following calculation.

$$
\begin{aligned}
\text{Future value} &= \text{Present value} \times (1 + \text{Interest rate})^N \\
&= \$.90909 \, (1 + .10)^1 \\
&= \$.90909 \times 1.10 \\
&= \$1.00 \text{ (rounded)}
\end{aligned}
$$

To illustrate the calculation of the present value of a lump sum payment occurring more than one interest period in the future, assume that an investor could earn 10 percent compounded annually on his investment. The investor needs to plan his investment so that at the end of 3 years, he will have accumulated enough funds to pay a debt of $1 due the third year. To determine what sum must be invested today in order to meet the debt of $1 three years from now, the present value formula can be solved as follows:

$$
\begin{aligned}
\text{Present value} &= \frac{\$1}{(1 + .10)^3} \\[2mm]
&= \frac{\$1}{1.331} \\[2mm]
&= \$.7513
\end{aligned}
$$

The sum of $.7513 must be deposited at 10 percent interest compounded annually in order to produce one dollar at the end of three years. The calculation of interest per year and the total interest to date is presented in the following table.

Year	(1) Beginning of Year Principal and Accumulated Interest	×	(2) Interest Rate	=	(3) Interest For This Year	(1) + (3) End of Year Principle and Accumulated Interest	Interest to Date
1	$.75130	×	.10	=	$.07513	$ .82643	$.07513
2	.82643	×	.10	=	.08264	.90907	.15777
3	.90907	×	.10	=	.09097	1.00000	.24874

Fortunately, the calculations of present values do not have to be computed manually for each individual receipt or disbursement. Tables have been developed from the formulas that provide a present value factor for $1 for any time period and at any interest rate. Table 1, Present Value of $1 is presented at the end of this chapter. This table provides the present value factors for computing the present value of a lump sum amount to be received in some future number of periods discounted at a given interest rate.

To illustrate the use of Table 1, assume that the present value of $1 is to be calculated at a 10 percent discount rate compounded annually for a three-year period. Go to Table 1 in the 10 percent column and look down the row to the present value factor for three periods. The present value factor is 0.7513; therefore, the present value of $1 to be received three interest periods from today discounted at a rate of 10 percent is $1 × .7513 = $.7513.

Calculating the Present Value of an Annuity

An annuity is a series of equal payments or receipts of cash to be paid or received over a number of equal time periods. An ordinary annuity will have equal payments or receipts at the end of each equal time period. The present value of any stream of payments or receipts can be calculated using the present value formula for a single sum or Table 1 and computing the present value for each amount for each time period. Alternatively, the present value of an annuity table (Table 2) may be used to find the present value of the cash stream.

Assume that $1 is to be received at the end of each year for the next three years and interest is to be calculated at 10 percent compounded annually. There are several ways that the present value of this cash flow can be computed. Two ways to compute the present value were discussed in the prior section of this Appendix when the present value of a single sum was calculated.

Alternative One: The present value of the total stream can be calculated by using the present value formula:

$$
\begin{aligned}
\text{Present value} &= \frac{\$1}{(1 + .10)^1} + \frac{\$1}{(1 + .10)^2} + \frac{\$1}{(1 + .10)^3} \\[2mm]
&= \frac{\$1}{1.10} + \frac{\$1}{1.21} + \frac{\$1}{1.331} \\[2mm]
&= \$.9091 + \$.8264 + \$.7513 \\[2mm]
&= \$2.4868
\end{aligned}
$$

Alternative Two: The present value can be calculated using Table 1.

Inflows	×	Present Value Factors	=	Present Value
$1	×	.9091	=	$ .9091
$1	×	.8264	=	.8264
$1	×	.7513	=	.7513
$1	×	2.4868	=	$2.4868

The third alternative is to use Table 2, Present Value of Annuity of $1 Per Period, at the end of this chapter. Table 2 is a summation of Table 1. To understand this, look at the present value factors for 10 percent for one time period on both tables. They are both .9091. Now look at the present value factors for two time periods at 10 percent. In Table 1, the present value factor is 0.8264. In Table 2, the present value factor is 1.7355; the sum of the first time period factor of 0.9091 plus the second time period factor of 0.8264 from Table 1.

If the present value of a $1 annuity at the end of each year for three years is to be calculated using Table 2, look at the 10 percent column and the row for the three periods to find the present value factor of 2.4869. *One* annuity payment or receipt is multiplied by the present value factor to compute the present value of the annuity, in this case $1 × 2.4869 = $2.4869. There is a slight rounding difference (at the fourth decimal point) between alternatives one and two as compared to alternative three.

KEY DEFINITIONS

Accountant's rate of return—a measure of the profitability of various capital expenditures which expresses the related incremental increases in income as a percentage of the net original or average investment outlay.

Capital budgeting—a process of planning and managing the investment of the firm's capital on a long-term basis. A capital budget includes a listing and analysis of all investment alternatives in which the firm is considering investing its supply of capital.

Cost of capital—the minimum acceptable rate of return (usually on an after-tax basis) required by the management of a firm to be earned by a capital expenditure.

Cost of prediction error—is measured by the incremental profit that would have been earned by making the alternative decision.

Internal rate of return—that interest rate which, when used to discount the cash flows, will make the present value of the inflows exactly equal to the present value of the outflows of the investment.

Net present value method—technique that discounts all projected cash outflows and inflows related to a capital project back to the present period using the cost of capital as the discount rate.

Payback method—a technique used to consider alternative capital expenditures which does not measure profitability but merely calculates the amount of time required to recover the initial net investment in an asset.

Post-audit—a review of major capital expenditures made after the completion of a project in order to determine if benefits actually accrued to the firm as planned.

Present value index—a relative measure of profitability for ranking capital investment projects which is computed by dividing the present value of inflows by the present value of outflows.

Sensitivity analysis—attempts to assess the possible effects of risk or uncertainty on predicted cash flows.

Present Value Tables

Table 1

Present Value of $1

Periods (n)	1%	1½%	2%	2½%	3%	3½%	4%	4½%	5%	6%	7%	8%	10%
1	0.9901	0.9852	0.9804	0.9756	0.9709	0.9662	0.9615	0.9569	0.9524	0.9434	0.9346	0.9259	0.9091
2	0.9803	0.9707	0.9612	0.9518	0.9426	0.9335	0.9246	0.9157	0.9070	0.8900	0.8734	0.8573	0.8264
3	0.9706	0.9563	0.9423	0.9286	0.9151	0.9019	0.8890	0.8763	0.8638	0.8396	0.8163	0.7938	0.7513
4	0.9610	0.9422	0.9238	0.9060	0.8885	0.8714	0.8548	0.8386	0.8227	0.7921	0.7629	0.7350	0.6830
5	0.9515	0.9283	0.9057	0.8839	0.8626	0.8420	0.8219	0.8025	0.7835	0.7473	0.7130	0.6806	0.6209
6	0.9420	0.9145	0.8880	0.8623	0.8375	0.8135	0.7903	0.7679	0.7462	0.7050	0.6663	0.6302	0.5645
7	0.9327	0.9010	0.8706	0.8413	0.8131	0.7860	0.7599	0.7348	0.7107	0.6651	0.6227	0.5835	0.5132
8	0.9235	0.8877	0.8535	0.8207	0.7894	0.7594	0.7307	0.7032	0.6768	0.6274	0.5820	0.5403	0.4665
9	0.9143	0.8746	0.8368	0.8007	0.7664	0.7337	0.7026	0.6729	0.6446	0.5919	0.5439	0.5002	0.4241
10	0.9053	0.8617	0.8203	0.7812	0.7441	0.7089	0.6756	0.6439	0.6139	0.5584	0.5083	0.4632	0.3855
11	0.8963	0.8489	0.8043	0.7621	0.7224	0.6849	0.6496	0.6162	0.5847	0.5268	0.4751	0.4289	0.3505
12	0.8874	0.8364	0.7885	0.7436	0.7014	0.6618	0.6246	0.5897	0.5568	0.4970	0.4440	0.3971	0.3186
13	0.8787	0.8240	0.7730	0.7254	0.6810	0.6394	0.6006	0.5643	0.5303	0.4688	0.4150	0.3677	0.2897
14	0.8700	0.8118	0.7579	0.7077	0.6611	0.6178	0.5775	0.5400	0.5051	0.4423	0.3878	0.3405	0.2633
15	0.8613	0.7999	0.7430	0.6905	0.6419	0.5969	0.5553	0.5167	0.4810	0.4173	0.3624	0.3153	0.2394
16	0.8528	0.7880	0.7284	0.6736	0.6232	0.5767	0.5339	0.4945	0.4581	0.3936	0.3387	0.2919	0.2176
17	0.8444	0.7764	0.7142	0.6572	0.6050	0.5572	0.5134	0.4732	0.4363	0.3714	0.3166	0.2703	0.1978
18	0.8360	0.7649	0.7002	0.6412	0.5874	0.5384	0.4936	0.4528	0.4155	0.3503	0.2959	0.2502	0.1799
19	0.8277	0.7536	0.6864	0.6255	0.5703	0.5202	0.4746	0.4333	0.3957	0.3305	0.2765	0.2317	0.1635
20	0.8195	0.7425	0.6730	0.6103	0.5537	0.5026	0.4564	0.4146	0.3769	0.3118	0.2584	0.2145	0.1486
21	0.8114	0.7315	0.6598	0.5954	0.5375	0.4856	0.4388	0.3968	0.3589	0.2942	0.2415	0.1987	0.1351
22	0.8034	0.7207	0.6468	0.5809	0.5219	0.4692	0.4220	0.3797	0.3418	0.2775	0.2257	0.1839	0.1228
23	0.7954	0.7100	0.6342	0.5667	0.5067	0.4533	0.4057	0.3634	0.3256	0.2618	0.2109	0.1703	0.1117
24	0.7876	0.6995	0.6217	0.5529	0.4919	0.4380	0.3901	0.3477	0.3101	0.2470	0.1971	0.1577	0.1015
25	0.7798	0.6892	0.6095	0.5394	0.4776	0.4231	0.3751	0.3327	0.2953	0.2330	0.1842	0.1460	0.0923
26	0.7720	0.6790	0.5976	0.5262	0.4637	0.4088	0.3607	0.3184	0.2812	0.2198	0.1722	0.1352	0.0839
27	0.7644	0.6690	0.5859	0.5134	0.4502	0.3950	0.3468	0.3047	0.2678	0.2074	0.1609	0.1252	0.0763
28	0.7568	0.6591	0.5744	0.5009	0.4371	0.3817	0.3335	0.2916	0.2551	0.1956	0.1504	0.1159	0.0693
29	0.7493	0.6494	0.5631	0.4887	0.4243	0.3687	0.3207	0.2790	0.2429	0.1846	0.1406	0.1073	0.0630
30	0.7419	0.6398	0.5521	0.4767	0.4120	0.3563	0.3083	0.2670	0.2314	0.1741	0.1314	0.0994	0.0573
40	0.6717	0.5513	0.4529	0.3724	0.3066	0.2526	0.2083	0.1719	0.1420	0.0972	0.0668	0.0460	0.0221
50	0.6080	0.4750	0.3715	0.2909	0.2281	0.1791	0.1407	0.1107	0.0872	0.0543	0.0339	0.0213	0.0085

Table 1 Continued

Present Value of $1

12%	14%	15%	16%	18%	20%	22%	24%	25%	26%	28%	30%	40%	50%
0.893	0.877	0.870	0.862	0.847	0.833	0.820	0.806	0.800	0.794	0.781	0.769	0.714	0.667
0.797	0.769	0.756	0.743	0.718	0.694	0.672	0.650	0.640	0.630	0.610	0.592	0.510	0.444
0.712	0.675	0.658	0.641	0.609	0.579	0.551	0.524	0.512	0.500	0.477	0.455	0.364	0.296
0.636	0.592	0.572	0.552	0.516	0.482	0.451	0.423	0.410	0.397	0.373	0.350	0.260	0.198
0.567	0.519	0.497	0.476	0.437	0.402	0.370	0.341	0.328	0.315	0.291	0.269	0.186	0.132
0.507	0.456	0.432	0.410	0.370	0.335	0.303	0.275	0.262	0.250	0.227	0.207	0.133	0.088
0.452	0.400	0.376	0.354	0.314	0.279	0.249	0.222	0.210	0.198	0.178	0.159	0.095	0.059
0.404	0.351	0.327	0.305	0.266	0.233	0.204	0.179	0.168	0.157	0.139	0.123	0.068	0.039
0.361	0.308	0.284	0.263	0.225	0.194	0.167	0.144	0.134	0.125	0.108	0.094	0.048	0.026
0.322	0.270	0.247	0.227	0.191	0.162	0.137	0.116	0.107	0.099	0.085	0.073	0.035	0.017
0.287	0.237	0.215	0.195	0.162	0.135	0.112	0.094	0.086	0.079	0.066	0.056	0.025	0.012
0.257	0.208	0.187	0.168	0.137	0.112	0.092	0.076	0.069	0.062	0.052	0.043	0.018	0.008
0.229	0.182	0.163	0.145	0.116	0.093	0.075	0.061	0.055	0.050	0.040	0.033	0.013	0.005
0.205	0.160	0.141	0.125	0.099	0.078	0.062	0.049	0.044	0.039	0.032	0.025	0.009	0.003
0.183	0.140	0.123	0.108	0.084	0.065	0.051	0.040	0.035	0.031	0.025	0.020	0.006	0.002
0.163	0.123	0.107	0.093	0.071	0.054	0.042	0.032	0.028	0.025	0.019	0.015	0.005	0.002
0.146	0.108	0.093	0.080	0.060	0.045	0.034	0.026	0.023	0.020	0.015	0.012	0.003	0.001
0.130	0.095	0.081	0.069	0.051	0.038	0.028	0.021	0.018	0.016	0.012	0.009	0.002	0.001
0.116	0.083	0.070	0.060	0.043	0.031	0.023	0.017	0.014	0.012	0.009	0.007	0.002	
0.104	0.073	0.061	0.051	0.037	0.026	0.019	0.014	0.012	0.010	0.007	0.005	0.001	
0.093	0.064	0.053	0.044	0.031	0.022	0.015	0.011	0.009	0.008	0.006	0.004	0.001	
0.083	0.056	0.046	0.038	0.026	0.018	0.013	0.009	0.007	0.006	0.004	0.003	0.001	
0.074	0.049	0.040	0.033	0.022	0.015	0.010	0.007	0.006	0.005	0.003	0.002		
0.066	0.043	0.035	0.028	0.019	0.013	0.008	0.006	0.005	0.004	0.003	0.002		
0.059	0.038	0.030	0.024	0.016	0.010	0.007	0.005	0.004	0.003	0.002	0.001		
0.053	0.033	0.026	0.021	0.014	0.009	0.006	0.004	0.003	0.002	0.002	0.001		
0.047	0.029	0.023	0.018	0.011	0.007	0.005	0.003	0.002	0.002	0.001	0.001		
0.042	0.026	0.020	0.016	0.010	0.006	0.004	0.002	0.002	0.002	0.001	0.001		
0.037	0.022	0.017	0.014	0.008	0.005	0.003	0.002	0.002	0.001	0.001	0.001		
0.033	0.020	0.015	0.012	0.007	0.004	0.003	0.002	0.001	0.001	0.001			
0.011	0.005	0.004	0.003	0.001	0.001								
0.003	0.001	0.001	0.001										

Table 2

Present Value of Annuity of $1 Per Period

Periods (n)	1%	1½%	2%	2½%	3%	3½%	4%	4½%	5%	6%	7%
1....	0.9901	0.9852	0.9804	0.9756	0.9709	0.9662	0.9615	0.9569	0.9524	0.9434	0.9346
2....	1.9704	1.9559	1.9416	1.9274	1.9135	1.8997	1.8861	1.8727	1.8594	1.8334	1.8080
3....	2.9410	2.9122	2.8839	2.8560	2.8286	2.8016	2.7751	2.7490	2.7232	2.6730	2.6243
4....	3.9020	3.8544	3.8077	3.7620	3.7171	3.6731	3.6299	3.5875	3.5460	3.4651	3.3872
5....	4.8534	4.7826	4.7135	4.6458	4.5797	4.5151	4.4518	4.3900	4.3295	4.2124	4.1002
6....	5.7955	5.6972	5.6014	5.5081	5.4172	5.3286	5.2421	5.1579	5.0757	4.9173	4.7665
7....	6.7282	6.5982	6.4720	6.3494	6.2303	6.1145	6.0021	5.8927	5.7864	5.5824	5.3893
8....	7.6517	7.4859	7.3255	7.1701	7.0197	6.8740	6.7327	6.5959	6.4632	6.2098	5.9713
9....	8.5660	8.3605	8.1622	7.9709	7.7861	7.6077	7.4353	7.2688	7.1078	6.8017	6.5152
10....	9.4713	9.2222	8.9826	8.7521	8.5302	8.3166	8.1109	7.9127	7.7217	7.3601	7.0236
11....	10.3676	10.0711	9.7868	9.5142	9.2526	9.0016	8.7605	8.5289	8.3064	7.8869	7.4987
12....	11.2551	10.9075	10.5753	10.2578	9.9540	9.6633	9.3851	9.1186	8.8633	8.3838	7.9427
13....	12.1337	11.7315	11.3484	10.9832	10.6350	10.3027	9.9856	9.6829	9.3936	8.8527	8.3577
14....	13.0037	12.5434	12.1062	11.6909	11.2961	10.9205	10.5631	10.2228	9.8986	9.2950	8.7455
15....	13.8651	13.3432	12.8493	12.3814	11.9379	11.5174	11.1184	10.7395	10.3797	9.7122	9.1079
16....	14.7179	14.1313	13.5777	13.0550	12.5611	12.0941	11.6523	11.2340	10.8378	10.1059	9.4466
17....	15.5623	14.9076	14.2919	13.7122	13.1661	12.6513	12.1657	11.7072	11.2741	10.4773	9.7632
18....	16.3983	15.6726	14.9920	14.3534	13.7535	13.1897	12.6593	12.1600	11.6896	10.8276	10.0591
19....	17.2260	16.4262	15.6785	14.9789	14.3238	13.7098	13.1339	12.5933	12.0853	11.1581	10.3356
20....	18.0456	17.1686	16.3514	15.5892	14.8775	14.2124	13.5903	13.0079	12.4622	11.4699	10.5940
21....	18.8570	17.9001	17.0112	16.1845	15.4150	14.6980	14.0292	13.4047	12.8212	11.7640	10.8355
22....	19.6604	18.6208	17.6580	16.7654	15.9369	15.1671	14.4511	13.7844	13.1630	12.0416	11.0612
23....	20.4558	19.3309	18.2922	17.3321	16.4436	15.6204	14.8568	14.1478	13.4886	12.3034	11.2722
24....	21.2434	20.0304	18.9139	17.8850	16.9355	16.0584	15.2470	14.4955	13.7986	12.5504	11.4693
25....	22.0232	20.7196	19.5235	18.4244	17.4131	16.4815	15.6221	14.8282	14.0939	12.7834	11.6536
26....	22.7952	21.3986	20.1210	18.9506	17.8768	16.8904	15.9828	15.1466	14.3752	13.0032	11.8258
27....	23.5596	22.0676	20.7069	19.4640	18.3270	17.2854	16.3296	15.4513	14.6430	13.2105	11.9867
28....	24.3164	22.7267	21.2813	19.9649	18.7641	17.6670	16.6631	15.7429	14.8981	13.4062	12.1371
29....	25.0658	23.3761	21.8444	20.4535	19.1885	18.0358	16.9837	16.0219	15.1411	13.5907	12.2777
30....	25.8077	24.0158	22.3965	20.9303	19.6004	18.3920	17.2920	16.2889	15.3725	13.7648	12.4090
40....	32.8347	29.9158	27.3555	25.1028	23.1148	21.3551	19.7928	18.4016	17.1591	15.0463	13.3317
50....	39.1961	34.9997	31.4236	28.3623	25.7298	23.4556	21.4822	19.7620	18.2559	15.7619	13.8007

Table 2 Continued

Present Value of Annuity of $1 Per Period

8%	10%	12%	14%	15%	16%	18%	20%	22%	24%	25%	26%	28%	30%	40%	50%
0.9259	0.9091	0.893	0.877	0.870	0.862	0.847	0.833	0.820	0.806	0.800	0.794	0.781	0.769	0.714	0.667
1.7833	1.7355	1.690	1.647	1.626	1.605	1.566	1.528	1.492	1.457	1.440	1.424	1.392	1.361	1.224	1.111
2.5771	2.4869	2.402	2.322	2.283	2.246	2.174	2.106	2.042	1.981	1.952	1.923	1.868	1.816	1.589	1.407
3.3121	3.1699	3.037	2.914	2.855	2.798	2.690	2.589	2.494	2.404	2.362	2.320	2.241	2.166	1.849	1.605
3.9927	3.7908	3.605	3.433	3.352	3.274	3.127	2.991	2.864	2.745	2.689	2.635	2.532	2.436	2.035	1.737
4.6229	4.3553	4.111	3.889	3.784	3.685	3.498	3.326	3.167	3.020	2.951	2.885	2.759	2.643	2.168	1.824
5.2064	4.8684	4.564	4.288	4.160	4.039	3.812	3.605	3.416	3.242	3.161	3.083	2.937	2.802	2.263	1.883
5.7466	5.3349	4.968	4.639	4.487	4.344	4.078	3.837	3.619	3.421	3.329	3.241	3.076	2.925	2.331	1.922
6.2469	5.7590	5.328	4.946	4.772	4.607	4.303	4.031	3.786	3.566	3.463	3.366	3.184	3.019	2.379	1.948
6.7101	6.1446	5.650	5.216	5.019	4.833	4.494	4.192	3.923	3.682	3.571	3.465	3.269	3.092	2.414	1.965
7.1390	6.4951	5.988	5.453	5.234	5.029	4.656	4.327	4.035	3.776	3.656	3.544	3.335	3.147	2.438	1.977
7.5361	6.8137	6.194	5.660	5.421	5.197	4.793	4.439	4.127	3.851	3.725	3.606	3.387	3.190	2.456	1.985
7.9038	7.1034	6.424	5.842	5.583	5.342	4.910	4.533	4.203	3.912	3.780	3.656	3.427	3.223	2.468	1.990
8.2442	7.3667	6.628	6.002	5.724	5.468	5.008	4.611	4.265	3.962	3.824	3.695	3.459	3.249	2.477	1.993
8.5595	7.6061	6.811	6.142	5.847	5.575	5.092	4.675	4.315	4.001	3.859	3.726	3.483	3.268	2.484	1.995
8.8514	7.8237	6.974	6.265	5.954	5.669	5.162	4.730	4.357	4.033	3.887	3.751	3.503	3.283	2.489	1.997
9.1216	8.0216	7.120	6.373	6.047	5.749	5.222	4.775	4.391	4.059	3.910	3.771	3.518	3.295	2.492	1.998
9.3719	8.2014	7.250	6.467	6.128	5.818	5.273	4.812	4.419	4.080	3.928	3.786	3.529	3.304	2.494	1.999
9.6036	8.3649	7.366	6.550	6.198	5.877	5.316	4.844	4.442	4.097	3.942	3.799	3.539	3.311	2.496	1.999
9.8181	8.5136	7.469	6.623	6.259	5.929	5.353	4.870	4.460	4.110	3.954	3.808	3.546	3.316	2.497	1.999
10.0168	8.6487	7.562	6.687	6.312	5.973	5.384	4.891	4.476	4.121	3.963	3.816	3.551	3.320	2.498	2.000
10.2007	8.7715	7.645	6.743	6.359	6.011	5.410	4.909	4.488	4.130	3.970	3.822	3.556	3.323	2.498	2.000
10.3711	8.8832	7.718	6.792	6.399	6.044	5.432	4.925	4.499	4.137	3.976	3.827	3.559	3.325	2.499	2.000
10.5288	8.9847	7.784	6.835	6.434	6.073	5.451	4.937	4.507	4.143	3.981	3.831	3.562	3.327	2.499	2.000
10.6748	9.0770	7.843	6.873	6.464	6.097	5.467	4.948	4.514	4.147	3.985	3.834	3.564	3.329	2.499	2.000
10.8100	9.1609	7.896	6.906	6.491	6.118	5.480	4.956	4.520	4.151	3.988	3.837	3.566	3.330	2.500	2.000
10.9352	9.2372	7.943	6.935	6.514	6.136	5.492	4.964	4.524	4.154	3.990	3.839	3.567	3.331	2.500	2.000
11.0511	9.3066	7.984	6.961	6.534	6.152	5.502	4.970	4.528	4.157	3.992	3.840	3.568	3.331	2.500	2.000
11.1584	9.3696	8.022	6.983	6.551	6.166	5.510	4.975	4.531	4.159	3.994	3.841	3.569	3.332	2.500	2.000
11.2578	9.4269	8.055	7.003	6.566	6.177	5.517	4.979	4.534	4.160	3.995	3.842	3.569	3.332	2.500	2.000
11.9246	9.7791	8.244	7.105	6.642	6.234	5.548	4.997	4.544	4.166	3.999	3.846	3.571	3.333	2.500	2.000
12.2335	9.9148	8.304	7.133	6.661	6.246	5.554	4.999	4.545	4.167	4.000	3.846	3.571	3.333	2.500	2.000

NOTE: To convert this table to values of an annuity in advance, take one less period and add 1.0000.

1. Define capital budgeting. Is it used for short or long-term planning? Explain.

2. What kind of accounting information is necessary for capital budgeting decisions?

3. Name three ways in which the initiation of a capital expenditure may come about. Who or what governs the format and channels of a capital budget request in a large firm?

4. Who normally makes the ultimate decision on a major capital expenditure? If the expenditure is not a major one, who may make the ultimate decision instead?

5. When is the "no choice" or urgency technique for making a decision justified? Why is this technique considered the least favorable of the capital budgeting techniques?

6. What is the primary purpose of using the payback technique in making a capital budgeting decision?

7. What are two similarities between the payback technique and the accountant's rate of return when used to make a decision?

8. Using the net present value technique, how does one decide whether the project is acceptable or not?

9. What are some of the ways management allows for risk or uncertainty in capital budgeting decisions?

10. What is meant by sensitivity analysis?

11. Why is the cost of prediction errors often considered an opportunity cost?

EXERCISES

12. Compute the net present value of these three individual cases at a rate of 10%.

	Outlay	Future Period Inflows			
	0	1	2	3	4
A	($2,000)	$1,150		$1,150	
B	($2,000)	$1,150			$1,150
C	($2,000)		$1,150	$1,150	

Required:

a. Which of these three investments is the most desirable?
b. Which is more desirable using 6% interest?

13. Compute the internal rate of return for each of the following independent investments.

	Outlay	Future Period Inflows		
	0	1	2	3
A	($3,000)	$1,575		$1,735
B	($3,000)	$1,500	$1,780	
C	($3,000)		$1,700	$1,690

Required:

If the investments are mutually exclusive, which one would you choose?

14.   Compute the payback period for each of these independent cases.

	Cost of Investment	Cash Proceeds per Year
A	$20,000	$5,000
B	$15,000	$3,000
C	$24,000	$8,000

Required:

Based on this information, which of these investments is the best?

15.   The James Company purchased a machine several years ago for $20,000. Its book value is $8,000. The company is considering purchasing a new machine for $22,500. The salvage value of the old machine at this time is $3,275. Ignoring taxes, what is the net cash outlay for the new asset?

16.   Weido, Inc. is considering the purchase of a new machine for $2,200. The machine has a life of 5 years and a salvage value of $200. It will be depreciated on a straight-line basis. Cash inflows will be:

Year	Inflows
1	$ 600
2	800
3	500
4	750
5	650
Total	$3,300

Required:

Determine the accountant's rate of return using:

a.   the original investment
b.   the average investment

17.   A nonprofit organization is considering the purchase of a certain depreciable capital asset. The asset costs $10,000.

It is expected that the asset will bring an incremental increase in annual net income of $3,500 for each year of its five-year life. The desired discount rate is 10%. Since it is a nonprofit organization, income taxes and depreciation are ignored.

Required:

a. What is the payback period?
b. What is the accountant's rate of return on original investment?
c. What is the net present value of the investment?
d. What is the present value index?

18. You are considering an outlay of X dollars which will produce an annual benefit of Y dollars per year for Z years. Your cost of capital is 10%.

Use the following alternative choices to answer *a* to *c* below:

1. 0%
2. exactly 10%
3. equal to or greater than 10%
4. equal to or less than 10%
5. greater than 10%
6. less than 10%
7. none of the above
8. cannot determine from the data given

a. If the present value of the Y dollars per year for Z years is X dollars, the return from the investment is _____.
b. If the present value of the Y dollars per year for Z years is X + 1 dollars, the return from the investment is _____.
c. If the present value of the Y dollars per year for Z years is X—1 dollars, the return from the investment is _____.

19. Jess, Inc. is considering purchasing a new machine for $18,000. It will have a useful life of 10 years, a salvage value of $3,000, and be depreciated on a straight-line basis.

The old machine, which cost $15,000, has been depreciated for 5 of its 15 year useful life. It is not expected to have any salvage value at the end of 15 years. It is being depreciated using straight-line. At the present time, the machine can be sold for $9,000. Any gain or loss on the sale can be considered ordinary income.

The company's cost of capital is 12 percent. The tax rate is 40 percent. The new machine will save the company $2,500 per year.

Required:

Using the net present value method, decide whether the company should purchase the new machine.

20. A firm is considering the purchase of a new piece of equipment. Below are the basic data relevant to this purchase.

Initial cost—$24,000
8-year life
Salvage value—$2,000

Straight-line depreciation
Overhaul at the end of year four—$6,000
Operating cost savings—$7,000 per year
Tax Rate—50%

Required:

Determine this equipment's internal rate of return. Round to the nearest dollar.

21. A company is considering purchasing a new machine for $12,000. The new machine will have a useful life of 10 years and a salvage value of $2,000. It will be depreciated on a straight-line basis.

   The old machine, which cost $10,000, also has a useful life of 10 more years but has been fully depreciated for tax purposes. It can be sold for $500 at the present time.

   The company's cost of capital is 6%, and the tax rate is 50 percent. The new machine will save the company $2,000 per year.

Required:

Using the net present value method, decide whether the company should purchase the new machine.

22. The Fattening Donuts Company was deciding what size fryer to purchase. Machine A is capable of producing 120 donuts per minute while machine B can produce 180 donuts per minute. It has been calculated that Machine A will produce a cash flow savings of $400 each year for 5 years, while machine B will produce a cash flow savings of $100 the first year and that amount will double each year through the fifth year. Machine A can be purchased for $1,400 while the cost of machine B is $1,800.

Required:

a. Calculate the payback period of both machines using the average cash inflows.
b. Given the results of "*a*" above, which machine should be purchased?

23. Bob, the barber, was considering purchasing a new machine that would be used to stimulate the scalp and speed hair growth. Faster hair growth would mean more hair cuts and increased revenues. The machine costs $1,700 and has a useful life of 4 years with a salvage value of $100. The expected cash inflows that will be generated are:

Year	Inflows
1	$ 600
2	$ 700
3	$ 600
4	$ 500
	$2,400

Required:

Determine the accountant's rate of return using:

a. the original investment
b. the average investment.

24. Determine the present value of $1,000 due in five years at each of the following interest rates:

a. 6 percent
b. 8 percent
c. 10 percent

25. An investor wishes to have $5,000 available at the end of five years. State the amount of money that must be invested at the present time if the interest rate is:

a. 6 percent
b. 8 percent
c. 12 percent

26. Determine the present value of an annuity for a period of five years with annual payments of $2,000, assuming that the interest rate is:

a. 7 percent
b. 10 percent
c. 12 percent

27. What is the maximum amount you would be willing to pay at the present time in order to receive 10 annual payments of $1,000 beginning one year from now? The current interest rate is 10 percent.

PROBLEMS

28. The Acme Company is currently using a machine which was purchased on January 1, 19x1 at a cost of $8,600. It was assigned a useful life of 8 years and a salvage value of $600. The straight-line method of depreciation is used. The company is considering replacing this machine on January 1, 19x4 with a new machine which would cost $9,000. The new machine would have a useful life of 5 years and a salvage value of $1,000. The straight-line method of depreciation would be used.

With the new machine, expected direct labor savings would be $1,250 per year for the five years. The old machine can be sold immediately for $3,500. Assume that the tax impact from the sale of the old machine occurs immediately when the sale is made.

The tax rate is 40 percent. The cost of capital (or rate of discount) is 16 percent.

Required:

Determine the following as they relate to the purchase of the new machine.

a. Net cash flow per year
b. Present value of the net outlay
c. Payback period
d. Advantage (or disadvantage) of the new machine (in present value)

29. Rental, Inc. is considering the purchase of six garden tillers to add to its rental fleet. The following estimates have been made:

Cost of six tillers	$15,000
Rental Receipts (annual)	12,000
Expenses:	
Maintenance	3,000
Advertising	800
Depreciation (5 year life)	3,000
Salvage value at end of 5 years	–0–

Assume that advertising is not a deductible expense for tax purposes and that a 40% tax rate applies to all other revenue and expense items.

Required:

a. Determine the after-tax cash flow per year.
b. Find the net present value of the investment (assume a 14% cost of capital).
c. Find the internal rate of return of the investment.

30. The Dizzy Company is considering a new mixing machine. They have narrowed the decision down to two choices but are unsure how to arrive at a final decision. It is your job to analyze the two machines so that the management of Dizzy can make their final decision. Assume a 40% tax rate, sum-of-the-years digit depreciation, and a 10% cost of capital.

	Machine A	Machine B
Cost	$47,000	$60,000
Useful life	5 years	5 years
Salvage value	$ 2,000	–0–
Annual before-tax cost savings	$14,500	$18,000

31. The Concerned Company is considering purchasing a replacement machine on January 1, 19x2. The present machine was acquired on January 1, 19x1 at a cost of $12,000 and was assigned a useful life of 6 years, no salvage value and depreciated on a straight-line basis. If it is replaced, it can be sold immediately for $9,000. You may assume that any gain or loss on the sale is treated as ordinary income or expense for tax purposes and the tax impact from the sale of the present machine occurs immediately when the sale is made.

The list price of the replacement machine is $16,000. Shipping charges are $300 and installation is $200. Double-declining balance depreciation will be used on the new machine. The new equipment will have a useful life of 5 years and a salvage value of $1,500.

Estimated cash savings before taxes and depreciation will be $2,500. The income tax rate is 40 percent and all savings are assumed to take place at the end of each year.

The firm's cost of capital is 12 percent.

All calculations should be in dollars only (round cents).

Required:

Decide whether the company should replace the present equipment using both the payback method and the net present value method.

32. The Aggie Corporation of Snook, Texas is considering construction of a new motel containing 180 rooms.

   The motel will cost $3,250,600 which will be paid to the contractor on the day the motel opens for business.

   Additional information:

   1. Assume a 360 day operating year.
   2. Half of the rooms are single rooms and half are double rooms (i.e., one and two person rooms only).
   3. The daily rate is $13.00 for a single room and $24.00 for a double room.
   4. The motel will operate at full capacity for all 360 days.
   5. Cash operating expenses are expected to be $675,000 per year, assumed payable at the *end* of each year.
   6. Assume all room rentals will be collected at end of each year.
   7. Assume no income taxes, i.e., ignore taxes.
   8. Assume a cost of capital of 10%.
   9. Owner plans to keep the motel for 7 years and then sell it for $500,000.

   Required:

   You are to decide whether this is a good investment using the net present value method and the present value index.

33. Taylor, Inc. has hired you for all of their capital budgeting decisions. Mr. Taylor, president of Taylor, Inc. feels that payback is the best method to use. You, however, feel that net present value analysis will yield more information and allow you to make a wiser decision. The company wants to purchase some new machinery. Given the information below, you are to use both methods of analysis and make a decision on investing. Taylor, Inc. requires a ten year maximum payback. Discuss your decision.

	Old Machine	New Machine
Cost	$10,000	$20,000
Useful life remaining	15 years	15 years
Depreciation method	Straight-line	Straight-line
Accumulated depreciation. . . .	$10,000	$ –0–
Scrap value at present	$ 400	N/A
Scrap value in 15 years	$ –0–	$ 500
Direct labor saving/year		$ 3,000
Additional electricity costs per year		$ 500

Tax rate—40%
Time value of money—8%

34. Fritz Company is considering an investment in a new machine to improve the production of one of their products. The old machine requires a great deal of maintenance because of its age, so the company feels it will save about $10,000 per year in maintenance costs if it purchases the new machine. The power bill will increase by $.06 per unit but the company will also be saving $.48 per unit in labor costs. The machine will cost $375,000 and has a useful life of 10 years with no salvage value at that time. It will be depreciated on the straight-line basis. Production will equal sales in all years. In years 1 through 5 production will be 90,000 units but it will increase by 20,000 units in each of the remaining years. The old machine is fully depreciated and will be abandoned in a field behind the factory.

Required:

If the company's minimum rate of return is 12% and a tax rate of 40%, should the investment be undertaken? Find the internal rate of return for the investment. (Round to the nearest cent.)

35. Franco, Inc. has been using the payback method as the sole criterion for capital budgeting decisions. You are the newest member of the Franco staff, having just graduated from college. You realize from courses you have taken that payback is not the best criterion. You feel that the net present value method is better, but so far have been unable to convince management of this.

Management is preparing to purchase a new machine for their new product. The machine appears very good using payback but, again, you are not certain they are making the right decision. There are three machines to choose from; Machine 1 is the one management wants to purchase. From the information given below, prepare an analysis using both the payback method and the net present value method. Use specific cash flows for payback, not the average cash flows. Make your recommendations to management. (Round cents to dollars.)

	Machine 1	Machine 2	Machine 3
Cost................	$25,000	$30,000	$28,000
Useful life..........	6 years	6 years	6 years
Depreciation method.....	Straight-line	Straight-line	Straight-line
Scrap value in 6 years.....	$ 400	$ 600	$ 1,000
Before-tax cash flow per year:			
Year 1............	$10,000	$ 6,000	$11,000
Year 2............	9,000	7,000	10,000
Year 3............	8,000	7,500	8,800
Year 4............	4,000	8,000	7,500
Year 5............	3,000	6,000	7,000
Year 6............	2,000	4,000	6,000

Tax rate = 40%
Cost of capital = 10%
Maximum payback period 4 years

36. Beta Corporation recently learned of a patent on the production of a semi-automatic paper collator that can be obtained at a cost of $60,000 cash. The semi-automatic model is vastly superior to the manual model that the corporation now produces. At a cost of $40,000, present equipment could be modified to accommodate the production of the new semi-automatic model. Such modifications would not affect the remaining useful life of 4 years or the salvage value of $10,000 that the equipment now has. Variable costs, however, would increase by one dollar per unit. Fixed costs, other than relevant amortization charges, would not be affected. If the equipment is modified, the manual model cannot be produced.

The current income statement relative to the manual collator appears as follows:

Sales (100,000 units @ $4)............		$400,000
Variable costs..........	$180,000	
Fixed Costs °..........	120,000	
Total Costs..................		$300,000
Net Income before income taxes.......		$100,000
Income taxes (40%)................		40,000
Net Income after income taxes........		$ 60,000

° All fixed costs are directly allocable to the production of the manual collator and include depreciation on equipment of $20,000, calculated on the straight-line basis with a useful life of 10 years.

Market research has disclosed three important findings relative to the new semi-automatic model. First, a particular competitor will certainly purchase the patent if Beta Corporation does not. If this were to happen, Beta Corporation's sales of the manual collator would fall to 70,000 units per year. Second, if no increase in the selling price is made, Beta Corporation could sell approximately 190,000 units per year of the semi-automatic model. Third, because of the advances being made in this area, the patent will be completely worthless at the end of 4 years.

Required:

Prepare a schedule which shows the after-tax cash flows for the two alternatives. Assume that the corporation will use the sum-of-the-years' digits method for depreciating the costs of modifying the equipment.

Also, by using the net present value method, decide whether Beta Corporation should manufacture the semi-automatic collator. Assume the cost of capital is 18% and all operating revenues and expenses occur at the end of the year.

(CMA, adapted)

37. James Company is trying to decide whether to handle a new automotive product which has an expected life of eight years. Using the data below, determine whether this venture will be profitable. (Round cents to the nearest dollar.) Use the net present value method.

1. The new product will require new factory equipment costing $1,200,000. The useful life of the equipment is eight years, with no salvage value at the end of that time. The depreciation schedule is:

Year	Depreciation
1	$ 266,667
2	233,333
3	200,000
4	166,667
5	133,333
6	100,000
7	66,667
8	33,333
	$1,200,000

2. The new product will be produced in an old plant the company already owns which is not in use. The old plant has a book value of $50,000 and is being depreciated on a straight-line basis at $5,000 annually. The estimated sales value of the building is $40,000; this price should remain stable over the next eight years. The plant is likely to be depreciated for at least ten more years and would have no salvage value.

3. The company's tax rate is 40%. Its cost of capital is 12%.

4. Net cash inflows from operations before depreciation and income taxes will be $450,000 in years 1, 2, and 3, $670,000 in years 4, 5, and 6, and $160,000 in years 7 and 8.

5. An initial sales promotion in year 1 will amount to a cost of $400,000. $25,000 will be spent on promotion in all other years. The entire amount is deductible for income tax purposes in the year of the expenditure.

38. A.J. Voit was considering replacing his coal truck with a new model that would lower his expenses, therefore providing increased savings. Voit's old truck had a book value of $27,500, a remaining life of 10 years and a market value of $5,000. Should the old truck be retained, its salvage value at the end of ten years would be $5,000. The new truck had a list price of $55,000 and a useful life of 10 years with a $5,000 scrap value. The cost savings generated by the new truck will be $3,000 yearly for repair costs. The new model will also run more efficiently and create a savings of $.20 per mile. Assume that the tax impact from the sale of the old truck occurs immediately when the sale is made. The truck is driven 10,000 miles annually.

The tax rate is 40 percent. The cost of capital is 10 percent. Assume straight-line depreciation is used for the trucks.

Required:

Determine whether Voit should invest in the new truck. Use the net present value method.

39. The Grahm Company is considering three mutually exclusive proposals, all of which would require an initial cash outlay of $90,000. The company has estimated that the net cash proceeds from each proposal would be:

	Proposal A	Proposal B	Proposal C
End of Year 1	$50,000	$30,000	$30,000
2	40,000	30,000	30,000
3	30,000	30,000	60,000
4	20,000	30,000	20,000
5	20,000	30,000	20,000
6	20,000	30,000	20,000

Since only one of the three proposals can be accepted, the president of the company has argued that the decision should be made on the basis of a present value analysis. However, the treasurer of the company believes that the decision should be made on the basis of a payback analysis.

Required:

Rank the three proposals as to their desirability by: (a) the present value method (cost of capital is 12%), and (b) payback method. (Note: Do not consider taxes.)

40. The Edwards Corporation is considering adding a new stapler to one of its product lines. More equipment will be required to produce the new stapler. There are three alternative ways to acquire the needed equipment: (1) purchase general-purpose equipment, (2) lease general-purpose equipment, (3) build special-purpose equipment. A fourth alternative, purchase of the special-purpose equipment, has been ruled out because it would be prohibitively expensive.

The general-purpose equipment can be purchased for $125,000. The equipment has an estimated salvage of $15,000 at the end of its useful life of ten years. At the end of five years the equipment can be used elsewhere in the plant or be sold for $40,000.

Alternatively, the general-purpose equipment can be acquired by a five-year lease for $40,000 annual rent. The lessor will assume all responsibility for taxes, insurance, and maintenance.

Special-purpose equipment can be constructed by the Contract Equipment Department of the Edwards Corporation. While the department is operating at a level which is normal for the time of year, it is below full capacity. The department could produce the equipment without interfering with its regular revenue-producing activities.

The estimated departmental costs for the construction of the special-purpose equipment are:

Materials and parts	$ 75,000
Direct Labor (DL)	60,000
Variable overhead (50% of DL$)	30,000
	$165,000

Engineering and management studies provide the following revenue and cost estimates (excluding lease payments and depreciation) for producing the new stapler depending upon the equipment used:

	General-Purpose Equip. Leased	General-Purpose Equip. Purchased	Self-Constructed Equipment
Unit selling price	$5.00	$5.00	$5.00
Unit production costs:			
Materials	$1.80	$1.80	$1.70
Conversion costs	1.65	1.65	1.40
Total unit production costs	$3.45	$3.45	$3.10
Unit contribution margin	$1.55	$1.55	$1.90
Estimated unit volume	40,000	40,000	40,000
Estimated total contribution margin	$62,000	$62,000	$76,000
Other costs:			
Supervision	$16,000	$16,000	$18,000
Taxes and insurance	–0–	3,000	5,000
Maintenance	–0–	3,000	2,000
Total	$16,000	$22,000	$25,000

The company will depreciate the general-purpose machine over ten years. At the end of five years the accumulated depreciation will total $80,000. The present value of the depreciation for the first five years is $62,100. The special-purpose machine will be depreciated over five years. The present value of the depreciation will be $48,400. Its salvage value at the end of that time is estimated to be $30,000.

The company uses an after-tax cost of capital of 10 percent. Its marginal tax rate is 40 percent.

Required:

Calculate which of the three options would be the best using the net present value method. Hint: The present value of the depreciation over the next five years has been given and you *do not* have to calculate it.

(CMA, adapted)

41. Davis, Inc. is considering purchasing a new machine which has an expected life of 10 years. Using the data below, determine whether this venture will be profitable. (Round cents to the nearest dollar.)
1. The new machine, which will cost $40,000, will have a useful life of 6 years. At the end of that time, it is expected to have a salvage value of $1,000. The depreciation schedule is:

Year	Depreciation
1	$11,143
2	9,286
3	7,429
4	5,571
5	3,714
6	1,857
	$39,000

2. The new machine will not be replacing an old machine. It will be used to handle an increase in demand for the company's product.
3. Net cash inflows from operations before depreciation and taxes will be $9,500 in years 1 through 3, $12,000 in years 4 and 5, and $8,000 in year 6.
4. The company's tax rate is 40% with a cost of capital of 10%.

42. Based upon estimated demand, Lucy Stores purchased one thousand crates of oranges at $10 per crate. Management had originally estimated that all one thousand crates would be sold at $15 per crate. Actually only eight hundred crates were sold at $13.50 per crate and the other two hundred crates were sold to a frozen juice company for $5.00 per crate.
Required:
Analyze the cost of Lucy's prediction errors.

43. Based upon estimated demand for the Christmas season. Ruplinger, Inc. acquired 200 diamond pendants. With a cost of $500 each Ruplinger expected a good profit with an estimated selling price of $800. After purchasing the pendants, but before any sales, the retail price rose to $1,000 each. Also, after the 200 pendants were sold, 50 customers had to be turned away because of the lack of inventory.

Required:

Analyze the cost of these prediction errors for Ruplinger, Inc.

Chapter 20 introduces the concept of responsibility accounting and the role it plays in management accounting systems. Studying this chapter should enable you to:

1. Distinguish between controllable costs and direct costs and explain why this distinction is important to responsibility accounting.

2. Discuss the general types of responsibility centers.

3. Explain how a typical responsibility accounting system functions.

4. Describe a performance report and explain how it is used in a responsibility accounting system.

5. List and evaluate the guidelines which have been developed for assigning controllability.

6. Recognize the problems created by the existence of service department costs.

7. Identify the usual types of transfer prices and discuss the advantages and disadvantages of each.

8. Describe the types of variances typically used in the performance evaluation of a profit center.

9. Know and apply the basic return on investment formula.

10. Discuss the problems involved in defining the concept of assets utilized.

11. Discuss how the use of a responsibility accounting system might result in suboptimization of organizational goals.

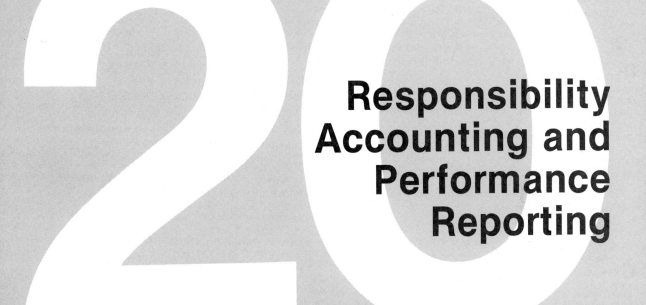

20

Responsibility Accounting and Performance Reporting

INTRODUCTION

Responsibility accounting is an accounting system which emphasizes the human element of the firm and its effect on operations. Responsibility accounting stresses the control or influence that a manager can exert within the segment of the organization which operates under his direction. Ideally, the manager's participation in establishing the budget for his segment and his responsibility for its operations is based on those economic factors that he can control or at least influence. The manager is held responsible for attaining the performance level which was budgeted for his segment.

Responsibility accounting aids in the delegation of authority by permitting the various levels of management within the firm to make decisions regarding those economic factors which they can control. Accounting information is collected and classified on the basis of the responsibility structure of the organization. This information, in part, is the same information which is collected for planning and financial accounting purposes, but is reclassified to meet responsibility accounting needs.

CONTROLLABLE ECONOMIC FACTORS

The controllable economic factors which are found in any firm include revenues, costs, assets, liabilities, and stockholders' equity. Somewhere in the management hierarchy, decisions regarding all of these factors are made. Responsibility accounting identifies the individuals who are making these decisions and aids in holding these individuals accountable for their decisions and actions.

Two classifications or definitions of costs are appropriate for responsibility accounting purposes: controllable costs and noncontrollable costs. These concepts of controllable and noncontrollable may also be applied to revenues, assets, liabilities, and owners' equity as will be explained later in this chapter.

CONTROLLABLE VERSUS NONCONTROLLABLE COSTS

Responsibility accounting requires that costs be classified in terms of the ability of individuals to influence costs in a given time period. The following definition of controllable costs, while more stringent than need be for responsibility accounting, is nonetheless applicable: A controllable cost is a cost which can be traced to a specific responsibility center on a nonarbitrary basis and which can be directly influenced by the manager of that center in a given time period. A noncontrollable cost cannot be directly influenced by the responsibility center manager. Thus it is the managers who influence specific costs who should participate in planning those costs and who should be held accountable for those costs during the operating period. If the entire firm is considered to be a responsibility center, all costs are considered controllable by someone at some level in the organization. Therefore, in assigning costs to a responsibility center, the controllability of costs by someone in that center is a primary consideration.

There are certain common misconceptions regarding controllable costs, fixed costs, variable costs, direct or traceable costs, and indirect or common costs. It is important to note that the dichotomy of fixed and variable costs has no relationship to controllable and noncontrollable costs. All costs within a given responsibility center can be classified either as direct or indirect costs. Direct costs are those costs that can be traced to a given segment of the organization (in this case, a responsibility center) on a non-arbitrary basis. Theoretically, if a responsibility center was eliminated, the direct cost would also be eliminated. All controllable costs are direct costs, because controllable costs can be traced to a specific cost center. However, all direct costs in a responsibility center may not be controllable by the manager of that center. For example, depreciation on equipment might be traceable to a production foreman's responsibility center, even though the foreman cannot control that particular cost.

Indirect or common costs are those costs which are common to more than one segment of the organization (in this case, the responsibility center). Any cost assignment is based on some arbitrary method of allocation. Therefore, all indirect costs are noncontrollable costs for any specific responsibility center.

At each level within the organization, a manager is held directly responsible for the controllable costs of his operation. In addition, he is also responsible for the controllable costs of those segments which are headed by his subordinates. This structure of responsibility provides for the delegation of authority at the lowest possible level of management and recognition of the chain of command and span of control principles.

FORMS OF RESPONSIBILITY CENTERS

Responsibility centers can be classified based on the financial factors which the manager in charge of the responsibility center can influence. A common method of classification is to consider a responsibility center as either a cost center, a profit center or an investment center. Each of these forms of responsibility centers is discussed below.

Cost Centers

The difference between a cost center and an expense center is related to the concept of period versus product costs. The costs of an expense center are usually period costs, while the costs of a cost center normally relate to product costs which are inventoried until the goods are sold. The terms cost and expense center are often considered to be interchangeable in practice.

In a production department where output can be measured objectively in dollars and a specific output is associated with a given cost level, the term cost center is usually used in describing the segment. The segment manager is then held accountable for a specific dollar output at a given cost level.

Cost centers or expense centers are established when conditions are such that the responsible manager can influence only costs. For a cost to be incurred in a given cost center, that cost center should be required to produce a specified amount of output. Since, in certain cases, output cannot feasibly be measured in terms of dollars, the term expense center may be appropriate. Examples of such cases are the accounting department's and purchasing department's contributions to the firm.

Profit Centers

Profit centers are established in those situations where the responsibility center manager can influence both the expenses and revenues of the center. In practice, all or part of the revenues reported by many profit centers are actually the result of sales to other segments of the firm. The price attached to these "intersegment" sales is called a transfer price. For managerial accounting purposes, a profit center must have measurable outputs if a transfer price is to be used to measure intersegment sales. Of course, for financial accounting purposes, only sales to third parties are considered in determining income. The profit center concept is useful, however, in that it allows the manager to make decisions concerning costs and revenues in attaining the expected profit for his segment.

Investment Centers

The investment center concept places the responsible manager in a situation that is analogous to running his own business. The investment center manager is held responsible for producing a future planned income by utilizing a certain amount of invested capital. In other words, the investment center manager can influence revenues, expenses, and the capital invested in his segment. This manager must utilize all resources available to him in order to acquire the best overall results possible. Most divisions of large corporations are actually investment centers, but the term is not widely used in practice. Instead, investment centers are usually referred to as profit centers.

ORGANIZATION STRUCTURE AND RESPONSIBILITY ACCOUNTING

To be effective, responsibility accounting systems are developed along the decison-making lines of authority. If the organizational structure is developed on the basis of authority and decision-making responsibilities, then planning, control and performance reporting can be developed using the same organizational structure.

The job descriptions for the managers in the various responsibility centers should identify the functions, responsibilities, and authority of the manager with respect to his position. Each manager should be concerned with the controllable economic factors that fall within his sphere of responsibilities. In addition, the integration provided by the planning function should assure that the responsibility centers will all act in the best interests of the entire firm. In other words, the ideal situation is for a manager to act in the best interests of his segment while also simultaneously acting in the best interests of the firm as a whole.

ILLUSTRATION OF RESPONSIBILITY ACCOUNTING COST CENTERS

As was previously stated, the responsibility accounting system should be related to the general lines of accountability and authority found in the company's organization chart, if at all possible. A partial organization chart of Sax Company is presented in Illustration 1. Only the segment which is related to the Power Turbine Shaft Division is included in detail.

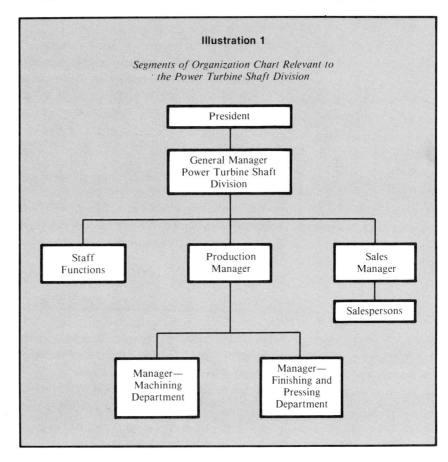

Illustration 1

Segments of Organization Chart Relevant to the Power Turbine Shaft Division

The budgets found in the chapter on Short-Range Planning are developed for the entire division on an accrual accounting basis. For responsibility accounting purposes, these budgets have limited usefulness because the format and detail does not permit the assignment of specific managerial responsibility. To be useful for responsibility accounting purposes, the forecast budgets would have to be recast according to the responsibility format, starting at the lowest level of management where controllable factors can be identified and where the decision-making process takes place. Illustration 2 is an example of a responsibility forecast budget for the manager of the machining department for the month of February 19x1.

The forecast budget, and ultimately, the entire performance report for the machining department is based on those factors subject to the control of the machining department manager. Illustration 2 is only one potential format for such a responsibility budget. A firm generally uses that format which best meets the needs of its management.

The forecast budget (column 1) for the machining department is prepared using established standards for the controllable costs at a level of 20,000 units of production. Last month's (January) production of 17,000 units represents the year-to-date production costs at the beginning of February. The actual controllable costs incurred in producing the 17,000 units are given in column four of Illustration 2. The flexible (control) budget for the year-to-date is developed by considering the year-to-date variances (column 6), and the actual controllable costs (column 4). For example, the direct labor cost at standard that should have been used to date is the actual cost of $33,500 plus the favorable variance of $500, for a total cost of $34,000.

During February, the machining department completed 21,000 units of the product. This department had the same dollar amount of work-in-process inventory at the end of the month as it had at the beginning of the month. The forecast budget was developed on the basis of 20,000 units of production, but 21,000 units were actually produced. To prepare a performance report when there are variable controllable costs involved, a flexible budget or a control budget must be prepared after-the-fact, but before any variances can be calculated. The control budget considers the actual activity that took place at the standard cost of producing that activity. Actual costs accumulated in the records are then compared with the standard costs at the same level of activity (21,000 units for February). Illustration 3 shows the completed responsibility report for the machining department.

The performance report presented in Illustration 3 for the machining department manager includes more detail than is necessary for a variance analysis of the controllable costs. All six columns of Illustration 3 should be reviewed in order to understand the use of responsibility accounting for planning, control, and performance evaluation purposes.

Illustration 2

Responsibility Budget
Machining Department

Manager—Machining Department
Month *February*

Forecast Production 20,000
Actual Production

	Per Unit	(1) *Forecast Budget at Standard* [a]	(2) *Flexible (Control) Budget at Standard*	(3) *Actual This Month*	(4) *Actual Year To Date* [b]	(5) *Variances (Unfavorable) This Month*	(6) *Variances (Unfavorable) Year To Date* [c]
Controllable Costs:							
Direct Labor	$2.00	$ 40,000			$ 33,500		$500
Direct Materials	4.00	80,000			68,000		–0–
Rework Time	.05	1,000			500		350
Setup Time	.04	800			1,020		(340)
Indirect Materials & Supplies	.30	6,000			4,900		200
Total Controllable Costs	$6.39	$127,800			$107,920		$710

[a] Column (1) refers to the budget for one month only. In this case, it represents the forecast for the month of February.
[b] This column pertains to January performance only. None of the performance in February is yet included in the actual to date.
[c] This column is explained in the text.

Illustration 3

Responsibility Report
Machining Department

Manager—Machining Department
Month *February*

Forecast Production 20,000
Actual Production 21,000

	Per Unit	(1) *Forecast Budget at Standard* a	(2) *Flexible (Control) Budget at Standard* b	(3) *Actual This Month* c	(4) *Actual Year To Date* d	*Variances (Unfavorable)* (5) *This Month* e	(6) *Year To Date* f
Controllable Costs:							
Direct Labor	$2.00	$ 40,000	$ 42,000	$ 43,000	$ 76,500	($1,000)	($ 500)
Direct Materials	4.00	80,000	84,000	84,400	152,400	(400)	(400)
Rework Time	.05	1,000	1,050	800	1,300	250	600
Setup Time	.04	800	840	700	1,720	140	(200)
Indirect Materials & Supplies	.30	6,000	6,300	5,500	10,400	800	1,000
Total Controllable Costs .	$6.39	$127,800	$134,190	$134,400	$242,320	($ 210)	$ 500

a Column one is the original forecast budget for 20,000 units of production at the standard cost.
b Column two is the flexible or control budget prepared at the end of the reporting period. The basis for this budget is actual activity, 21,000 units, at the standard cost.
c Column three is the actual controllable costs incurred at the actual production level of 21,000 units.
d Column four is actual production costs for the year-to-date (for January and February). When column four is added to column three, the sum of the two equals the actual year-to-date, column four.
e The variances from the budgeted amounts for the month of February represents the difference between columns two and three—the control budget and the actual costs at 21,000 units. These variances are presented in column five.
f Column six shows the variances between the control budget and actual costs for the year-to-date. To develop column six, the year-to-date variances on February 1 (from Illustration 2) and the variances for February from column five must be summed.

The forecast budget (column 1) included in the responsibility report presented in Illustration 3 is not needed for variance analysis purposes. The basis of performance reporting for a cost center is the comparison of budgeted costs and actual costs for the output produced. Measures other than cost factors, such as percentage of volume attained, efficiency ratios, and cost ratios are also usually developed. In certain situations, these measures may be more important than cost variances.

The actual collection of costs and related information for responsibility accounting takes place on a regular basis. Actual performance reporting for financial control takes place as frequently as management deems necessary to evaluate a given cost center. The performance report should be viewed as an additional cost control tool for the use of the responsible manager as well as a performance evaluation tool for the use of his superiors.

THE RESPONSIBILITY ACCOUNTING SYSTEM

Performance reports are integrated by responsibility levels. If a subordinate is responsible for a given financial factor, the subordinate's superior is also responsible for that same factor. The organization chart presented in Illustration 1 outlines the levels of responsibility in the Power Turbine Shaft Division. Performance reporting, both within the Division and to the President of Sax Company, follows the lines of authority and responsibility established by the organization chart.

The reporting relationships established for responsibility accounting are identified in Illustration 4. Each of the reports is condensed at the next level of management by reporting only the "bottom line" of subordinates' performance reports.

The total controllable costs which were included on the performance report of the manager of the machining department become a single line on the report of the production manager. The production manager's performance report also includes the bottom line from the finishing and pressing department manager's report. The production manager is also held responsible for the other costs of production which neither the manager of the machining department nor the manager of the finishing and pressing department can influence. As the production manager can influence only costs, his sphere of responsibility is a cost center.

The bottom line on the production manager's performance report becomes one line of the general manager's performance report. The controllable cost totals of the sales manager and division staff are also a part of the general manager's performance report. All Power Turbine Shaft Division costs which are controllable by the general manager appear on the general manager's performance report. In addition, the general manager has controllable revenues from the sales manager's performance report. Therefore, at a minimum, the general manager's sphere of responsibility may be considered a profit center. If the general manager can also

Illustration 4

Sax Company

Responsibility Accounting Performance Reports
President—Month February

	Budget		Variances (Unfavorable)	
	This Month	Year To Date	This Month	Year To Date
Controllable Income:				
→Power Turbine Shaft Division	$119,100	$ 300,700	($6,200)	($2,480)
Other Divisions °	256,000	552,000	2,000	4,500
Total Controllable Income	$375,100	$ 852,700	($4,200)	$2,020
Controllable Costs:				
Other Corporate Costs °	150,000	300,000	(5,000)	(6,000)
Controllable Income	$225,100	$ 552,700	($9,200)	($3,980)

Power Turbine Shaft Division
General Manager—Month February

	Budget		Variances (Unfavorable)	
	This Month	Year To Date	This Month	Year To Date
Controllable Revenues:				
Sales Manager	$575,000	$1,175,000	($5,000)	($3,000)
Controllable Costs:				
Sales Manager	134,000	270,500	500	2,000
→Production Manager	219,250	396,800	(250)	720
Division Staff	73,500	147,000	(1,500)	(1,600)
Other Division Costs °	29,150	60,000	50	(600)
Controllable Income	$119,100	$ 300,700	($6,200)	($2,480)

Production Manager
Month February

	Budget		Variances (Unfavorable)	
	This Month	Year To Date	This Month	Year To Date
Controllable Costs:				
→Machining Department	$134,190	$ 242,320	($ 210)	$ 500
Finishing and Pressing Department	71,190	128,820	190	900
Other Costs °	13,870	25,660	(230)	(680)
	$219,250	$ 396,800	($ 250)	$ 720

Machining Department
Manager—Month February

Forecast Production This Month	20,000
Actual Production This Month	21,000
Actual Production Year to Date	38,000

	Budget		Variances (Unfavorable)	
	This Month	Year To Date	This Month	Year To Date
Controllable Costs:				
Direct Labor	$ 42,000	$ 76,500	($1,000)	($ 500)
Direct Materials	84,000	152,400	(400)	(400)
Rework Time	1,050	1,300	250	600
Setup Time	840	1,720	140	(200)
Indirect Materials and Supplies	6,300	10,400	800	1,000
Total Controllable Costs	$134,190	$ 242,320	($ 210)	$ 500

° These numbers are condensed. In an actual report, detail would be presented.

influence capital investment, then his sphere of responsibility is an investment center.

The controllable income for the Power Turbine Shaft Division can be traced to a single line item included on the company president's performance report. The company president is held responsible for all of the subordinates within the firm. His sphere of responsibility is obviously an investment center because the president can control revenues, costs, and capital investments.

MANAGEMENT BY EXCEPTION

After the forecast budgets are developed with the participation of management, it is up to the managers to meet or achieve the plans as stated in their budgets. When actual results are recorded and the performance reports are prepared, management need only consider the significant variances from the budget. The performance report should place major emphasis on variances, because variances should be the focus of management's attention. The reports in Illustration 4 contain the minimum information necessary for the month or year-to-date variances. The emphasis on variances assists management in concentrating its attention on the exceptions from the budget. This is called management by exception. In order to increase the emphasis on variances, many firms express variances both in dollars and as percentages of the budget. The budgeted amounts found in the performance reports are dependent on the emphasis of management and on the type of responsibility center producing the report (i.e., cost center, profit center, or investment center).

THE REPORTING CYCLE

The timing of reporting is crucial because reports must meet the needs of management. If the nature of a responsibility center's operations are such that a daily report is necessary for control purposes, then that center should receive the performance report on a daily basis. Remember, responsibility reporting is considered a tool for management use, not a threat. Variances are early warnings to management that something needs attention. The more important the item is to management, the more critical the time factor becomes.

Each manager should receive only those reports he needs. Again, a sensitive area may warrant daily reporting. However, a manager whose operations do not require daily or weekly reports should not be included on the same reporting cycle as a manager of a more sensitive area. Typically, the longest internal reporting cycle is about one month.

Non-current information is of little value in identifying problem areas. Managers need up-to-date information in order to correct current problems. A performance report delivered today which presents an analysis of the operations which is three months old has limited usefulness in correcting current problems or measuring current performance.

IDENTIFYING
RESPONSIBILITY

Controllability is not always easy to identify due to the fact that very few cost items fall under the decision-making sphere of a single individual. Responsibility accounting requires that the individual with the most influence over costs be responsible and be held accountable for those costs. An American Accounting Association Committee identified guidelines that could be used, along with good judgment, in making the controllability decision.[1]

1. If a person has authority over both the acquisition and the use of the service, he should be charged with the cost of such service.
2. If the person can significantly influence the amount of cost through his own action, he may be charged with such cost.
3. Even if the person cannot significantly influence the amount of cost through his own direct action, he may be charged with those elements with which management desires him to be concerned, so that he will help to influence those who are responsible.

The first two guidelines are workable, but implementing the third can cause difficulties. The interrelationships of decisions also pose certain difficult, but solvable, problems in assigning cost responsibility.

For example, production planning may plan the number of units to be produced and the quantity and quality of the raw materials to be purchased. The purchasing department then acquires the raw materials. A number of events can occur that could affect variances from the point of purchase to the warehousing of the finished goods:

1. There may be a variance from the standard price. If this is the case, the purchasing manager will be held responsible for this variance.
2. It is possible that the material price variance would be favorable, but the materials could be of substandard quality. A production foreman requisitions the materials, rejects them due to their low quality, and, as a result, has an idle work force on his hands. If the foreman accepts the materials, with or without knowledge of their low quality, a host of other variances can arise. Because of the low quality of the materials, an unfavorable materials usage variance is probable. The labor usage variance could well be unfavorable due to the difficulty involved in working with low quality materials. Scrap and rework variances will be unfavorable. The obvious solution for the foreman is to reject the materials. However, if the favorable materials price variance were greater than all of the production related unfavorable

---

[1] "Report of Committee on Cost Concepts and Standards," *The Accounting Review*, April 1956, p. 189.

variances, and if the final product were of the quality desired by the firm, the materials should be used. This would be to the over-all advantage of the firm.

3. Suppose that the materials price variance was unfavorable because a higher quality material was purchased. The purchasing manager will show the unfavorable variance on his performance report. The production foreman's performance report will not be affected by the price of the raw materials used, but the high quality raw materials may have a favorable impact on a number of the production variances. The overall favorable or unfavorable impact can only be measured by considering all of the variances produced by using the higher priced, higher quality materials.

Responsibility for Service Department Costs

Service departments also present problems in responsibility accounting. If a maintenance department is responsible for the upkeep of production equipment, maintenance costs are still affected by the degree of care exercised by production personnel. Although maintenance is held responsible for the costs of maintaining equipment, production personnel can certainly influence the total maintenance costs incurred.

An approach to solving this problem of "dual responsibility" is to charge each department a standard price per hour for every hour of maintenance the department uses. This charge appears as an expense on the performance report of the department using the service. If maintenance costs exceed the department's maintenance budget, then the user department's manager will incur an unfavorable cost variance.

The maintenance department is responsible for staffing its work force in order to meet both scheduled maintenance and any emergencies which may arise. Maintenance users are then billed at a standard rate for maintenance services with a separate billing for any costs for materials or parts. Theoretically, the maintenance department could make a "profit" in the sense that its billings could exceed its costs. The attempt of this internal pricing scheme is to reduce excessive requests for services. The services will no longer be viewed as *free* by the user departments. Cost responsibility is placed with managers who can influence the costs.

PERFORMANCE REPORTING FOR PROFIT CENTERS AND INVESTMENT CENTERS

Responsibility accounting permits the decentralization of decision making in that the manager of each responsibility center is charged with making decisions with regard to that operation. The efforts of the individual managers are coordinated by top management, company policy, planning and any other methods for coordination that may be established by the firm.

In effect, decentralization places each profit or investment center manager in a position similar to an independent entrepreneur operating under a minimum set of constraints or policies. This procedure provides incentives for managers because performance, and therefore bonuses, are measured as if an individual manager were a sole proprietor with that segment of the firm as his own business.

The definition of the financial components of income and invested assets for both profit centers and investment centers poses certain problems from an accounting standpoint. Among these problems are: (1) determining the appropriate measure of revenues when intracompany sales are made between segments or divisions of the firm, and (2) defining assets invested in a center for purposes of calculating the return on investment for investment centers.

TRANSFER PRICING FOR INTRACOMPANY SALES

A transfer price is the price that one segment of an organization pays to another segment within the same organization for the output or service of the supplying segment. In determining the performance of each unit, a transfer price is the basis for: (1) interunit sales from the viewpoint of the selling unit, and (2) variable costs to the buying unit. For financial reporting purposes, the firm recognizes a sale only when goods or services are sold to buyers external to the firm and not when one segment or division of a company sells to another. However, for purposes of performance measurement by segments, an internal sale is considered in calculating segment income; otherwise, the responsible manager would be encouraged to make only external sales in order to maximize income. Of course, top management wishes to establish transfer prices which will maximize the objectives of the firm as a whole.

Generally, the manager of a responsibility center attempts to operate his unit in such a manner as to maximize the profits of the center. Establishing a fair transfer price permits segment managers to make decisions that are in the best interest of the segment as well as in the best interests of the entire firm. These transfer prices are usually market-based, cost-based and/or negotiated. In most cases a transfer price is a combination of these bases.

Market-Based Transfer Prices

If a competitive market price is available for a product also sold internally, then the equitable transfer price, from both a theoretical and practical viewpoint, is the external competitive market price adjusted for any savings in cost, such as selling expenses. If savings are realized as a result of the ability of a unit to sell its product within the firm, then those savings should be fairly distributed or allocated between the buying and selling units. Examples of factors resulting from intersegment sales which may cause cost savings include improved planning, more efficient production runs or the elimination or reduction of selling and distribution expenses. A market-based transfer price for intersegment sales is the closest approximation to an "arm's length" transaction.

Any shortcomings of a market-based transfer price are usually related to the operations or uncertainties concerning the market place. Few markets are truly competitive in an economic sense and any price may be affected by the presence of a few large buyers or sellers. Market prices are also influenced by such factors as supply and demand, quantity discounts and product quality. All of these factors must be considered when an internal transfer price based on market price is established for internal company use.

Cost-Based Transfer Prices— Full Cost

Transfer prices for intersegment sales based on full cost or full cost-plus are common for the following reasons:

1. Certain products have limited or nonexistent outside markets.
2. The full cost transfer price concept is understandable to both the buyer and the seller.
3. Cost accumulations are made for inventory costing purposes so a "cost figure" is readily available.

If the transfer price is based on the actual costs incurred, then the supplying segment may have little incentive to control its costs because the full cost will be recovered by the transfer price. On the other hand, if a normal or standard cost transfer price is used, then this measure of costs which *should* have been incurred by the supplying segment provides an incentive to control costs. The use of a normal or standard cost is also consistent with the basic concepts of responsibility accounting because any efficiencies or inefficiencies are identified with the responsibility center where the cost is incurred.

Cost-Based Transfer Prices— Variable Cost

A variable cost or variable cost-plus transfer price may be justified on a theoretical basis since this transfer price is consistent with the traditional "short-run" economic decision model of a firm. A "short-run" economic decision model assumes that the manager of the supplying segment cannot influence the fixed costs of the segment in the short-run. Therefore the manager is accountable for only the variable costs of the segment and the interunit sales price should be determined using only variable costs as a base.

Negotiated Transfer Prices

Most transfer pricing approaches are negotiated in practice because an equitable price for both the selling and buying segments must be established if the price is to be meaningful. When transfer prices are based on negotiation, both the supplying and the buying segment managers arrive at a fair transfer price considering any information concerning costs and market conditions available to them. A truly negotiated transfer price assumes that neither manager involved in the negotiations has an unfair bargaining position.

In any negotiated transfer price, some arbitration procedure may be necessary in order to neutralize friction or unreasonable positions assumed by one or both of the managers. For all practical purposes, if the buying segment *must* purchase the goods or services internally or the selling segment *must* sell to the buying segment, an unfair bargaining situation may develop. In these cases, company policy or company transfer price formulas may be used to establish the price.

RETURN ON INVESTMENT AS A MEASURE OF PERFORMANCE

When a manager is able to influence revenues, costs and capital investments in a segment, that manager is said to be responsible for an investment center. Performance measures for an investment center should consider the profit element in relation to the size of the asset base used to earn that profit. A performance measure that attempts to relate income (from the income statement) to the assets utilized (from the balance sheet) is the concept of return on investment. The general formula for return on investment (ROI) is as follows:

$$\text{ROI} = \frac{\text{Income}}{\text{Assets utilized}}$$

The exact definitions for both income and assets utilized may vary from firm to firm. The two elements in the equation, income and assets utilized to earn that income, may be analyzed in terms of their respective components:

$$\text{ROI} = \text{Profit margin on sales} \times \text{Sales turnover of assets}$$

$$= \frac{\text{Income}}{\text{Sales}} \times \frac{\text{Sales}}{\text{Assets utilized}}$$

The profit margin on sales is a measure of the profitability of a firm while the turnover of assets is an indication of the assets used in relationship to the sales level achieved during the same accounting period.

These ratios identify two of the factors that a manager in an investment center should be able to control or influence. The return on investment for a center may be improved by increasing sales, reducing expenses, reducing the level of the assets utilized or by some combination of these three factors. The relationship of the profit margin on sales and the turnover of assets describes the relationship between profit planning and asset (or capital) management. A firm that experiences a two percent profit margin and an asset turnover of ten times in a given accounting period provides the same return on investment as a firm with a ten percent profit margin and an asset turnover of two times per period. In both of these cases, the return on investment is 20 percent.

Firm A	*Firm B*
ROI $= 2\% \times 10 = 20\%$	ROI $= 10\% \times 2 = 20\%$

PROBLEMS IN DEFINING ASSETS UTILIZED

In order to effectively use the ROI measure to evaluate the performance of an investment center manager, a consistent definition of assets utilized must be established. Responsibility accounting for investment centers requires that the investment center manager be able to influence the "package" of assets for which he is held responsible. Most managers of an investment center have inherited the majority of the fixed assets of their center from the prior manager. The age and condition of the assets, the depreciation policy in use and the original cost of the assets all play a significant role in the measurement of the appropriate asset base to be used. These factors must be considered in developing a planned or target return on investment. A commonly accepted measure of assets used is total net assets (total original cost of assets less any accumulated depreciation on those assets).

Joint assets pose an additional problem. Many large corporations have established centralized cash, accounts receivable, and long-term debt management; therefore, investment centers in these firms do not have control over cash, accounts receivable or long-term debt. These financial factors are managed by corporate headquarters. In these instances, the centrally-managed financial factors are allocated to the various investment centers involved. An attempt is made to impute the values (including interest expense and interest payable for long-term debt) that would be reported in the financial statements of the investment center if the segment could control these financial factors. This procedure forces the investment center manager to consider and control the factors used as the basis for the allocation of the joint assets if he is to maintain control of ROI for his investment center.

**PERFORMANCE
EVALUATION OF
PROFIT CENTERS**

The analysis of variances of a profit center should explain why actual income differed from the forecast budgeted income for the accounting period under consideration. The general types of variances that can be used to analyze and explain the reasons for the difference between the forecasted income and the actual income are: [2]

1. Sales volume variance
2. Sales mix variance
3. Price variance
4. Expense variance

Illustration 5 presents the variance worksheet that will be used in preparing the performance report that Mr. Gess, the manager of the Industrial Filter Division of Sax Company. The division produces and sells over 100 different filters all with different contribution margins.

The controllable revenues and costs of this division are used to illustrate performance evaluation and reporting for a profit center even though Sax Company considers the Industrial Filter Division to be an investment center. In a later section of this chapter, Mr. Gess's controllable assets and income statement information will be considered in an illustration of the performance evaluation of an investment center.

Illustration 5 includes only controllable revenues and costs in order to be consistent with the concept of responsibility accounting. Each of the columns included in the variance worksheet should be reviewed prior to the preparation of the profit center performance report.

The forecast budget is based on the anticipated sales volume and mix of filters for the Industrial Filters Division. The selling prices and costs included in the budget are the standard prices and costs for the Division. This budget was prepared prior to the start of the accounting period.

The control budget is prepared after the end of the accounting period. At that point, the actual quantities of filters sold are known. The control budget is a flexible budget prepared after-the-fact using the actual quantity and mix sold at the standard selling prices and costs. Any differences between the individual price or cost factors found on the forecast and control budgets are caused by changes in the volume or mix of products sold since both budgets use standard prices and costs in their preparation. Therefore this variance can be broken down into two component parts: the sales volume variance and the sales mix variance.

The column on the variance worksheet headed "actual" is taken directly from the accounting records of the Division. Actual costs and prices at actual volume and mix are shown in these accounts. If the actual data are compared with the data in the control budget, variances can

---

[2] There are other methods of calculating sales volume and mix variances in addition to the approaches used in this text. A contribution margin approach is used here to analyze these two variances.

Illustration 5

Sax Company
Industrial Filter Division
Variance Worksheet

	Forecast Budget (Forecast volume and mix at standard prices and costs) (1)		Control Budget (or Flexible Budget) (Actual volume and mix at standard prices and costs) (2)		Actual (Actual volume and mix at actual prices and costs) (3)		Variances* Volume/Mix (2-1)	Variances* Price/Expense (Cost) (3-2)
	Budget	Budget	Budget	Budget	Actual	Actual		
Sales Revenue...........	$1,500	100%	$1,400	100.0%	$1,500	100%	($100)	$100
Less: Variable Costs								
Cost of Goods Sold.........	810	54	700	50.0	840	56.0	110	(140)
Sales Commissions.........	150	10	140	10.0	150	10.0	10	(10)
Contribution Margin.........	540	36	$ 560	40.0	$ 510	34.0	$ 20	($ 50)
Less: Fixed Costs								
Manufacturing Overhead.....	$ 270	18	$ 270	19.3	$ 283	18.9	0	($ 13)
Selling & Administrative.....	195	13	195	13.9	122	8.1	0	73
Total Fixed Costs...........	$ 465	31%	$ 465	33.2%	$ 405	27.0%	0	$ 60
Income Before Taxes........	$ 75	5%	$ 95	6.8%	$ 105	7.0%	$ 20	$ 10

*Stated as favorable or (unfavorable) as to the impact on income.

be identified as either selling price or expense (cost) variances because the actual volume and mix of products sold are used in preparing the control budget.

The performance report should identify the impact of the variances on income since a profit center manager is held responsible for achieving an established budgeted income figure. Variances are calculated in order to isolate specific impacts on profits when all other factors are held constant. For example, the sales volume variance should provide an explanation of the impact of sales volume on profits. The impact of product mix, sales prices and costs are separated from the sales volume variance.

**Sales
Volume Variance**

If the actual volume of products sold at standard prices differs from the forecasted volume of products sold at standard prices, then the result is a sales volume variance. The formula for calculating the sales volume variance is as follows:

$$\begin{matrix} \text{Sales} \\ \text{Volume} \\ \text{Variance} \end{matrix} = \left[\begin{matrix} \text{Forecasted} \\ \text{Volume} \\ \text{of Sales at} \\ \text{Standard Prices} \end{matrix} - \begin{matrix} \text{Actual Volume} \\ \text{of Sales at} \\ \text{Standard Prices} \end{matrix} \right] \times \begin{matrix} \text{Forecasted} \\ \text{Contribution} \\ \text{Margin} \\ \text{Percentage} \end{matrix}$$

The forecasted sales volume at the standard price is $1,500. The actual sales volume at the standard price is $1,400. Sales volume at standard prices decreased; therefore, the variance is unfavorable. The forecast contribution margin is 36 percent. If the results for the Industrial Filter Division are substituted in the formula, the sales volume variance is:

$$\begin{aligned} \text{Sales Volume Variance} &= (\$1,500 - \$1,400) \times .36 \\ &= \$36 \text{ Unfavorable Variance} \end{aligned}$$

If all financial factors except sales volume had occurred as forecasted, actual income would have been $36 less than budgeted income as a result of the decline in sales volume.

**Sales Mix
Variance**

If the contribution margin percentage for the forecasted mix and standard prices and costs (forecast budget) differs from the contribution margin percentage for the actual mix and standard prices and costs (control budget), then a sales mix variance results. The forecast budget contribution margin percentage from Illustration 5 is 36 percent ($540/$1,500). The contribution margin percentage from the control budget is $560/$1,400 or 40 percent. The formula for calculating the sales mix variance is:

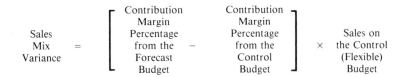

If the contribution margin percentage used in the control budget is greater than the contribution margin percentage in the forecast budget, the resulting sales mix variance is favorable. This is because the actual mix of products sold at the standard prices and costs represents a more profitable mix than was originally forecasted or anticipated. Sales volume does not affect the contribution margin percentage. Even if the forecast budget sales volume had doubled, the control contribution margin percentage would be the same as the forecasted contribution margin so long as the sales mix remained constant.

If the results from the Industrial Filter Division are used in the formula, the sales mix variance is calculated as follows:

$$\text{Sales Mix Variance} = (.36 - .40) \times \$1,400$$
$$= \$56 \text{ Favorable Variance}$$

The impact on actual income as compared to forecasted income is a favorable $56 because the actual mix of products sold was a more profitable mix than was originally anticipated and budgeted.

Sales Price Variance

The sales price variance is taken directly from the variance worksheet. This variance is the difference between standard prices at actual volume and mix (control budget) and actual prices at actual volume mix (actual). In the case of the Industrial Filter Division, sales revenue at actual volume and mix and standard price totaled $1,400. Actual sales revenues are $1,500 (from Illustration 5). Actual revenues exceeded control budget revenues by $100; therefore, the sales price variance is a favorable $100.

Sales commissions increased by $10 due to an increase in actual prices charged customers over the standard prices. It could be argued that the actual sales price variance was $90 ($100 increase in revenues less $10 increase in commissions) because of the impact of sales commissions.

Expense Variances

The expense variances or cost variances are taken directly from the variance worksheet presented in Illustration 5. Variable cost variances represent the traditional approach to variance analysis. Standard costs at actual volume and mix (control budget) are compared with actual costs at actual volume and mix (actual amounts). If actual amounts are less than standard, the variance is favorable. The variable cost expense variances include an unfavorable cost of goods sold variance of $140 and, as indicated above, an unfavorable sales commissions expense of $10. The variance in sales commissions was caused by the favorable sales price variance and, as previously stated, may be considered a reduction in the sales price variance on a performance report.

Fixed cost variances may also be taken directly from the variance worksheet presented in Illustration 5. There are no volume or mix variances for fixed costs because the budgeted fixed costs are not affected by volume or mix changes within the relevant range.[3] The fixed cost variances are caused by spending. Manufacturing overhead has exceeded the budgeted amount by $13. The selling and administrative expense variance is a favorable variance of $73. The impact of these expense variances on actual before-tax income is on a one-to-one basis, that is, for every dollar of favorable expense variance, actual income increases by a dollar over budgeted before-tax income.

PERFORMANCE REPORTS FOR PROFIT CENTERS

The performance report for the Industrial Filter Division of Sax Company presented in Illustration 6 is based on the worksheet presented in Illustration 5. A performance report, such as the one shown in Illustration 6, explains the major reasons for achieving $105 in profit instead of the forecasted profit of $75. The format of the performance report for the Industrial Filter Division begins with the forecasted budgeted income and then analyzes the volume and mix variances in order to arrive at the control budgeted income. The impact of the sales price variances and the expense variances on the control budget income is then computed in order to arrive at the actual income before taxes.

The net effect of the operations of the current period results in an income amount in the Industrial Filter Division that is $30 more than the amount originally budgeted. Illustration 6 summarizes the combination of factors that caused the net $30 favorable variance from budgeted income before taxes.

PERFORMANCE EVALUATION OF INVESTMENT CENTERS

The management of Sax Company views the Industrial Filter Division as an investment center. The balance sheet used to determine the assets or capital employed in this Division is based on the traceable assets, liabilities and corporate investment. In other words, only those balance sheet factors which are directly traceable to the Industrial Filter Division are used to determine the capital utilized in the Division.

---

[3] Remember that Sax Company uses the variable costing approach for internal planning, control and performance evaluation. Fixed manufacturing costs are treated as period costs.

Illustration 6

Sax Company
Industrial Filter Division
Performance Report
Manager: Mr. Gess
( ) = Unfavorable

Forecast Budgeted Income Before Taxes....................................	$ 75
Sales Volume Variance ($1,500 — $1,400) X .36 =......................	(36)

Sales Mix Variance:

Forecast Budget Contribution Margin $\dfrac{\$\ 540}{\$1,500} = .36$

Control Budget Contribution Margin $\dfrac{\$\ 560}{\$1,400} = .40$

Change in Contribution margin caused
   by Change in Mix...................... = .04

Sales Mix Variance $1,400 X .04 =.....................................	56
Control Budgeted Income Before Taxes..................................	$95
Sales Price Variances:	
Increased Prices to Customers $1,500 — $1,400 =......................	100
Less: Increase in Salesmen's Commissions $100 X .10 =.................	(10)
Cost of Goods Sold Cost Variances......................................	(140)
Fixed Cost Spending Variances:	
Manufacturing Overhead...	(13)
Selling and Administrative..	73
Actual Income Before Taxes..	$105

Management recognizes that a measure of return-on-investment (ROI) is only one indication of overall performance. Since no single correct means of calculating return on investment exists, all divisions of the firm that are considered investment centers may be held responsible for two different budgeted rates of return: a rate-of-return on total traceable assets and a rate-of-return on traceable corporate investment. In these measures, the budgeted assets or the budgeted corporate investment at the end of the year is used as the basis for the ROI calculation. The use of the budgeted assets utilized provides the division managers with a target asset package or corporate investment.

The rate of return on total traceable assets is important because it provides a measure of how well the responsible manager utilized the resources that were available to him. Return on corporate investment traceable to the division is used to provide a measure of the financial performance of the firm's capital investment in that division. Each division may borrow money externally and, through the use of leverage, increase its return on corporate investment. Cash could also be borrowed internally from corporate headquarters. When cash is borrowed from corporate headquarters, corporate investment in that division is increased. When cash is sent to corporate headquarters, corporate investment is reduced.

Sax Company has established and maintains a monthly reporting system. Rates of return are calculated on a monthly basis to assure the adherence of a division to its budgets and to encourage the responsible manager to attempt to attain the budgeted returns on investment. Illustration 7 presents the budgeted and actual balance sheets for the past year for the Industrial Filter Division.

The worksheet analyzing the income statement variance was presented in Illustration 5.

BUDGETED ROI VERSUS ACTUAL ROI

The budgeted returns for the year using budgeted end-of-year total assets and corporate investment from Illustration 7 and the forecast budgeted income from Illustration 5 are as follows:[4]

$$\text{ROI on Total Assets} = \text{Profit Margin} \times \text{Asset Turnover}$$

$$= \frac{\text{Profit}}{\text{Sales}} \times \frac{\text{Sales}}{\text{Assets Utilized}}$$

$$= \frac{\$75}{\$1,500} \times \frac{\$1,500}{\$600}$$

$$= .05 \times 2.5$$

$$= .125 \text{ or } 12\frac{1}{2}\%$$

$$\text{ROI on Corporate Investment} = \frac{\text{Profit}}{\text{Sales}} \times \frac{\text{Sales}}{\text{Corporate Investment}}$$

$$= \frac{\$75}{\$1,500} \times \frac{\$1,500}{\$300}$$

$$= .05 \times 5$$

$$= .25 \text{ or } 25\%$$

The results for the year using actual end-of-year total assets and corporate investment from Illustration 7 and the actual income from Illustration 5 are as follows:

---

[4] It is common to use average total assets and average corporate investment for the accounting period instead of end-of-year totals. End-of-year totals could be influenced by last minute decisions and could present a distorted perspective when compared to averages.

Illustration 7

Sax Company
Industrial Filter Division
Budgeted and Actual Balance Sheets
Manager: Mr. Gess

	Budget	Actual	Variances
ASSETS			
Current Assets:			
Cash..........................	$ 20	$ 20	$ 0
Accounts Receivable...................	100	60	(40)
Direct Materials Inventories.............	50	20	(30)
Indirect Materials and Supplies...........	10	5	(5)
Work-in-Process Inventories.............	30	30	0
Finished Goods on a Variable			
Costing Basis.......................	90	65	(25)
Long-Term Assets:			
Equipment (Net of Accumulated			
Depreciation)	100	100	0
Plant (Net of Accumulated			
Depreciation)	200	200	0
Total Assets............................	$600	$500	($100)
LIABILITIES AND STOCKHOLDERS' EQUITY			
Current Liabilities:			
Accounts Payable......................	$ 75	$ 80	$ 5
Wages Payable........................	50	40	(10)
Long-Term Liabilities:			
Long-Term Debt.....................	175	180	5
Stockholders' Equity:			
Corporate Investment..................	300	200	(100)
Total Liabilities and Stockholders'			
Equity............................	$600	$500	($100)
Return on Total Assets (Income from			
(Illustration 5)	12½ %	21 %	
Return on Corporate Investment			
(Income from Illustration 5)	25 %	52½ %	

$$\text{ROI on Total Assets} = \frac{\$105}{\$1,500} \times \frac{\$1,500}{\$500}$$

$$= .07 \times 3$$

$$= .21 \text{ or } 21\%$$

$$\text{ROI on Corporate Investment} = \frac{\$105}{\$1,500} \times \frac{\$1,500}{\$200}$$

$$= .07 \times 7.5$$

$$= .525 \text{ or } 52½\%$$

Mr. Gess, the manager of the investment center, was able to exceed the budgeted return on total assets by increasing both the actual profit margin and asset turnover compared to budget. The budgeted profit margin was 5 percent and the budgeted asset turnover was 2.5 times. The actual profit margin and budgeted asset turnover was 7 percent and 3 times, respectively.

An analysis of the increased profit margin can be made form Illustration 6. The sales volume, sales commissions, cost of goods sold and manufacturing overhead variances were all unfavorable, but were less in total than the favorable variances for sales mix, sales prices, and selling and administrative expenses. Thus a net favorable variance resulted in a 2% increase in the profit margin.

Budgeted and actual total revenues were the same. To increase asset turnover, Mr. Gess reduced assets by $100. This reduction may, in fact, represent only a short-run improvement in the utilization of resources if the budgeted amounts in Illustration 7 are assumed to be the amounts necessary to fund the operations of the Division over a long-run period.

The actual return on corporate investment exceeded the budgeted return by 27.5 percent. Mr. Gess accomplished the increased return by increasing the profit margin by 2 percent and decreasing corporate investment by $100. The decrease in corporate investment was sufficient to increase the turnover of corporate investment from a budgeted 5 times to an actual turnover of 7.5 times.

In addition to the cash transfers made to corporate headquarters (which reduced corporate investment in the Division by $100), Mr. Gess reduced accounts receivable by $40, direct materials inventories by $30, indirect materials and supplies by $5 and finished goods inventory by $25. He increased accounts payable by $5 and long-term debt by $5. Wages payable was reduced by $10. The variances from budget for these balance sheet accounts must be considered in view of the Division's needs before any statements or conclusions may be made regarding Mr. Gess's management approach.

If the performance report presented in Illustration 6 and the budgeted and actual balance sheets and other analyses included in Illustration 7 are all considered, the following statements can be made concerning Mr. Gess's management of the Industrial Filter Division.

1. The sales volume variance was an unfavorable $36 because budgeted sales were not attained.
2. The sales mix variance was a favorable $56. The actual mix included a greater proportion of the more profitable filters than was originally budgeted.

3. The sales prices charged to some or all customers were higher than standard. This enabled the division to make an additional $100 in gross sales revenues or $90 net after the increased sales commisions.

4. The production cost variances charged to the cost of goods sold for the year were unfavorable and thus decreased the division's income by $140.

5. The fixed cost spending variances totaled $60 favorable. This increased the income of the division by $60.

6. The division's actual income before taxes was $105. This was $30 above the forecast budget income.

A selected measure of income is used as the numerator in all return-on-investment equations. The denominator will always be based on a selected measure of resources utilized. By controlling or influencing either the numerator or the denominator (or both) the manager can influence ROI. The denominators as defined by the Sax Company are total traceable assets for the first measure and traceable corporate investment for the second measure.

Mr. Gess increased the numerator, income before taxes, without increasing revenues. The denominator was reduced by decreasing the assets utilized and decreasing corporate investment by the same amount. Total liabilities did not change from budgeted, although individual balances in the accounts were changed.

Responsibility Accounting and Human Behavior

Decisions are made by managers at all levels of an organization. Top management develops the goals and objectives of the firm and all management should work together to attain these goals and objectives. Individual managers also have their own personal goals which they are striving to attain. Professional goals are generally only one aspect of personal goals. Any aspect of control should result in decisions which are both in the best interest of the firm's goals and objectives and in the best personal interest of the manager.

If responsibility accounting is to be a useful tool in planning, control, and performance evaluation, then the entire system must be designed to eliminate or reduce the potential of a manager making decisions that appear to be in his own best interest, but are not in the best interest of the firm. The responsibility accounting system must be useful and provide performance measures based on controllable factors. Some reward structure must be developed, even if it is only verbal, to provide incentives for management and employees to act in the best interests of the firm.

SUMMARY

Under a responsibility accounting system, a manager participates in establishing the budget for the economic factors over which he has control or influence. He is then held responsible for reaching that budget. The responsibility system is generally integrated into the regular accounting system and includes information regarding controllable economic factors.

Responsibility centers are normally classified according to the economic factors that the manager of the center can influence. In the most common type of responsibility center, the cost or expense center, only costs are considered controllable by the manager of the center. The manager is generally held responsible for a specified amount of output given the costs incurred. Only those costs which are under the control of the manager are considered in evaluating his performance. A cost center typically refers to the control of the manager over product costs whereas an expense center refers to a manager's control over non-manufacturing costs. A profit center exists in those circumstances where the manager can influence both revenues and expenses associated with his segment. In the most comprehensive form of responsibility centers, the investment center, the manager is similar to a sole proprietor in that he has control over capital investments as well as revenues and expenses.

The responsibility accounting system is generally developed along lines of organizational authority. Managers at each level are responsible for their own individual financial factors as well as those of their subordinates. The system typically uses a performance report that emphasizes variances from the budget. These reports are prepared at intervals which permit the timely and effective correction of deviations from the budget.

Since control is often difficult to identify with any given individual, controllability must at times be delegated for responsibility accounting purposes. Guidelines have been established in order to assist in the controllability decision. In addition, service department costs may create problems and require the use of an allocation process, for example the charge of an internal "expense" for each hour of service consumed by a department.

Responsibility accounting for profit centers and investment centers is similar to that for cost centers. Additional financial factors, however, must be taken into account. While the cost center is concerned only with controllable costs, the profit center is responsible for controllable revenues and costs. The investment center is responsible for controllable capital investments as well as controllable revenues and costs. Although responsibility accounting for these additional financial factors permits considerable decentralization, it also creates new problems.

One of the problems associated with responsibility accounting for profit centers relates to the measurement of revenues when sales are made between company segments. The primary types of transfer prices used to measure such revenues are: (1) market-based price, (2) cost-based price, and (3) negotiated price. Each of these transfer prices has its advantages and disadvantages and the actual transfer price used by a firm will probably be a combination of these methods.

The procedure for evaluating the performance of profit centers includes a detailed analysis of the variances from budgeted net income. The variances generally included in such an analysis are: (1) sales volume variance, (2) sales mix variance, (3) sales price variance, and (4) cost or expense variance. The first three variances are related to revenues realized by the center and the cost or expense variance is related to costs incurred by the center.

Responsibility accounting for investment centers also requires a method for evaluating performance. One common performance evaluation technique is to relate income to the assets utilized to earn that income. This relationship is determined by calculating the return on investment (ROI). However, the return on investment calculation requires that the amount of assets utilized be known.

The performance evaluation of an investment center may include more than one ROI calculation since "assets utilized" may be defined several ways. For instance, the actual rate of return on total traceable assets may be calculated in addition to the usual calculation of the rate of return on corporate investment. Budgeted ROI and actual ROI are compared and an analysis of any differences between the two is made. In addition, a firm may wish to analyze the various components of the ROI figure to determine if the desired ROI is being met in an acceptable manner.

KEY DEFINITIONS

Control budget—a flexible budget prepared at the end of an accounting period using the actual quantity and mix sold at the standard selling prices and costs.

Controllable cost—a cost that can be traced to a specific responsibility center on a non-arbitrary basis and is influenced by the manager of that center in a given time period.

Cost-based transfer price—a transfer price which may be based on the actual, standard or variable costs of the supplying segment.

Cost center—a type of responsibility center where the manager influences only costs and is held accountable for a specific output at a given cost level.

Direct costs—costs which can be traced to a given segment or responsibility segment of the organization on a non-arbitrary basis. All direct costs may not necessarily be controllable costs of a specific responsibility center.

Expense variances—the differences between the standard and actual costs or expenses at the actual volume and mix.

Indirect costs—costs which are common to more than one segment or responsibility center of the organization. All indirect costs are non-controllable costs for any particular responsibility center.

Investment center—a type of responsibility center where the manager can influence revenues, expenses, and capital invested in his center to attain the best performance possible.

Management by exception—when variances from the budgets are emphasized in reporting procedures so that management concentrates its attention on these variances or exceptions from the budget.

Market-based transfer price—a transfer price based on the external market price less any savings in cost; it is the closest approximation to an arm's length transaction that segments can achieve.

Negotiated transfer price—a transfer price which is established by agreement of both the selling and buying segments of the firm.

Non-controllable cost—a cost which cannot be directly influenced by the manager of the responsibility center.

Profit center—a type of responsibility center where the manager can influence both revenues and expenses for his center.

Responsibility accounting—an accounting system in which the accountability for costs is assigned to a segment manager of the firm based on the amount of control or influence he possesses over those costs.

Responsibility performance reports—reports concerning the performance of various responsibility centers of the firm with respect to controllable costs. They report variances that result from a comparison of budgeted and actual controllable costs.

Return on investment—measures the ability of a firm, or segment within a firm, to utilize available resources effectively by expressing profit or income as a percentage of invested assets.

Sales mix variance—occurs when the contribution margin percentage at the forecasted mix and standard prices and costs (forecast budget) differs from the contribution margin percentage at actual mix and standard prices (control budget).

Sales price variance—the difference between standard prices at actual volume and mix (control budget) and actual prices at actual volume and mix.

Sales volume variance—occurs when the actual sales volume of products sold at the standard prices (control budget) differs from the forecasted sales volume of products sold at the standard prices (forecast budget).

Transfer price—the price that one segment of a firm pays to another segment of the same firm for the output or service of the supplying segment.

QUESTIONS

1. What is responsibility accounting? What additional accounting costs are added by responsibility accounting?

2. What is a controllable cost? How are controllable costs related to direct costs?

3. What is a profit center and what does it accomplish?

4. In what two ways is the timing of responsibility reporting crucial?

5. In what manner may the problem of dual responsibility among service departments possibly be solved?

6. What is a transfer price and why does it pose certain problems in performance measurement by segments?

7. What are the shortcomings of a market-based transfer price? A cost-based transfer price?

8. The return on investment formula is made up of two components: margin on sales and turnover of capital. Explain what each of these respective components signify.

9. What is the reason for a sales mix variance? Does volume affect this variance?

10. What is the difference between a sales price and expense variance?

11. What causes a fixed cost variance when the variance costing approach is used? What impact does this variance have on actual income?

EXERCISES

12. Determine whether each of the following costs is controllable or noncontrollable by a manufacturing department manager.

    a. Depreciation on building and equipment
    b. Supplies and indirect materials
    c. Rent on building
    d. Heat, light and power
    e. Maintenance and repair costs
    f. Salary of salespersons
    g. Direct labor
    h. Rework time

13. You have been hired by the Par Golf Company to look into its cost system to determine the cause of the increased costs in making golf clubs. In touring the factory you have learned that to make a wood club, certain materials are required. Jack Palmer, the president of Par Golf, had required that some system for standards be established and you have found them to be:

1 head @ $4
1 shaft @ $1
1 grip @ $2

During the past year, you have discovered that 10,000 woods were produced at a total cost of $71,800. Mr. Palmer said that this was an unfavorable variance of $1,800 and he wants to know where to lay the blame. Your investigation shows that Joe Duffer was the purchasing agent for shafts. Since Joe considered all shafts to be equal, he got the cheapest shaft possible at $.90. Unfortunately, this required the assembly department to use 12 shafts to successfully complete 10 clubs. Other information showed actual costs of:

10,100 heads at a total cost of $40,000
10,200 grips at a total cost of $21,000

Required:

1. Calculate the total material quantity and price variances.
2. Who should be given the shaft variance?

14. Given below are the controllable costs for the assembly division of the Hays Manufacturing Company for October.

Budgeted production was 4,000 units.
Actual production was 5,000 units.

Standard costs:

Direct labor..................................	$5 per unit
Direct material..............................	3 per unit
Supplies	$ .75 per unit
Other.......................................	.10 per unit

Actual costs for the month were as follows:

Direct labor..................................	$25,850
Direct material..............................	14,600
Supplies	3,500
Other.......................................	500

Required:

Prepare a responsibility accounting performance report showing variances for the assembly division for October.

15. The Love Tennis Company has been experiencing dissension between its purchasing and manufacturing divisions. The division that has the largest favorable variance has been promised a free tennis lesson with the company pro, Rod Connors. Your job is to determine the material and labor variances and assign them to the competing divisions.

The standard racket is comprised of:

String, 80 ft.@$.05 per foot	=	$ 4
Frame @ $6	=	6
Grip @ $1	=	1
Total standard material cost per racket =		$11

The standard time required to construct a racket is 1 hour at $5 per hour. The standard string using is a high quality catgut. In an attempt to win the contest for the purchasing division, Billy Riggs, a real hustler, purchased a cheaper nylon string at 4¢ a foot. Unfortunately, 100 feet of string per racket was required and this also increased the direct labor time per racket to 1.1 hours.

During the past month, 5,000 rackets were completed. The following data were available:

5,100	frames used	– total cost	=	$30,400
5,200	grips used	– total cost	=	$ 5,400
5,500	direct labor	– total cost	=	$25,000

Required:

1. Calculate material quantity and price variances. Calculate direct labor efficiency and rate variances.
2. Assign the variances previously calculated to the division responsible.

16. Bob Smart is general manager of the Production Division of the Texas Auto Company. One of his responsibilities is the acquisition of raw materials from the purchasing department which orders them from an outside supplier.

Assume that the standard price per unit of raw material is $2.50. 1,000 units of raw material are ordered by the purchasing department at a price of $1.50 per unit, but the materials ordered are of sub-standard quality. If the production division works with the inferior raw material, the following variances are anticipated: a $500 unfavorable material usage variance and a $700 unfavorable labor usage variance.

Required:

Should the production manager accept or reject the shipment of sub-standard raw material? Support your answer.

17. Sleeper, Inc. forecasted sales of 500,000 mattresses at $150 per mattress. At the end of the year, the company determined that it had sold 498,000 mattresses at an average price of $158 per mattress. The forecasted contribution margin percentage was 42%.

Required:

Determine the sales volume variance and the sales price variance.

18. The Thomson Company has two divisions. Division 1 normally sells 75% of its output to Division 2 for $10, the same price as it sells to other customers.
   Given below are the results for the year:

	Division 1	Division 2
Sales to outsiders..............	$15,000	$200,000
Sales to Division 2..............	45,000	0
Total......................	$60,000	$200,000
Transfer costs.................	0	45,000
Other variable costs............	15,600	35,000
Contribution margin..........	$44,400	$120,000
Fixed costs...................	25,000	80,000
Net income before taxes.......	$19,400	$ 40,000

Required:

1. Prepare a report consolidating the two divisions.
2. If Division 2 could purchase the product from an outside source for $9 by purchasing their total needs from that source, should Division 1 meet this price? Assume that Division 1 can sell no more than 75% of their production to outsiders. (Consider this from the viewpoint of the overall company.)

19. Division C of the Glaser Company has the following budget for 19x1:

	Forecast Budget
Sales @ $10/unit*.........................	$40,000
Variable costs @ $5/unit*..................	20,000
Contribution margin......................	$20,000
Fixed costs..............................	10,000
Net income before taxes....................	$10,000

* Weighted average based on forecast sales mix.

The weighted average contribution margin on the control budget is $15,000, which is a 48 percent contribution margin. Actual sales in 19x1 were $35,000, variable costs were $16,000 and fixed costs were $11,000. Total assets for Division C were budgeted at $30,000 but were actually $35,000.

Required:

Prepare a variance worksheet in good form for 19x1 assuming that Division C is a profit center.

20. You have been hired by East Money Inc. to work in their cost accounting department. Your first job is to calculate the ROI. Unfortunately, the sales figures for the past year have been lost. Eager to show your technical skill you state that you can still calculate ROI with only the income of $60,000 and the investment of $720,000 being known.

Required:

Calculate the ROI and show how the volume of sales has no effect.

PROBLEMS

21. Department A of the Stonewall Company has been purchasing the rods it uses in concrete slabs from Department B of the same company for $50 per ton. Department A purchases about 90% of the production of B. In the current year, B expects to have sales of about 1,600 tons. The remaining 10% of B's sales are to outside customers for $51 with terms of 2/10, n/30. Approximately 60% of the outside sales were paid within ten days, and about 3% of the outside sales are never paid.

A has been negotiating with several other suppliers for these rods and finds it can purchase from an outside supplier for $48 per ton. Unless Department B lowers its price, A will use the outside supplier.

After doing some market research, B feels that it can sell 90% of its present capacity to outside customers for $51 @ 2/10, n/30, or 95% for $50 @ 2/10, n/30. Under these two arrangements, Department A will buy all purchases from outsiders.

Variable costs for the rods are $20 per ton and fixed costs are $21,000 per year. Selling expenses are $1.50 per ton if sold to outside customers.

Required:

If Department B does not consider the rest of the firm, what should it do?

22. Alcorn, Inc. has 2 divisions, R and S. R sells approximately 80% of its output to S for $15, but charges outside customers $15.50 because Alcorn must pay its salesman 3% of the selling price on sales to outside customers.

Given below are the results for 19x1:

	Division R	Division S
Sales to outsiders.	$ 9,300	$72,000
Sales to Division S.	36,000	0
Total.	$45,300	$72,000
Transfer costs.	0	36,000
Variable costs.	9,000	9,600
Sales commission.	279	2,160
Contribution margin.	$36,021	$24,240
Fixed costs.	23,000	10,000
Net income before taxes.	$13,021	$14,240

Required:

1. Prepare a report consolidating the two divisions.
2. If Division S could purchase the product for $14.25 from an outside source, should R meet this price? Assume R could sell 90% of their production to outsiders for $15. If R sells to S, it can still sell 20% of its production to outside customers for $15.50. (Consider this from the viewpoint of the overall company.)

23. Robin Smith is the regional sales manager for International Fragrances, Inc. As such, she is responsible for the management of sales personnel in her area, including the determination of sales salaries. Company policy, however, requires that a mimimum salary of $12,000 per year be paid to each sales person.

As a sales manager, Ms. Smith is also responsible for budgeting and arranging for all local and regional advertising and other selling expenses in her area. National advertising is handled by the corporate offices of International Fragrances with total annual costs allocated to each regional area.

Cost information for Ms. Smith's region follows below:

Total sales salaries: (13 sales personnel). .	$215,000
Local advertising and promotion.	78,000
Regional advertising and promotion.	155,000
National advertising.	200,000
Display, set-up costs.	12,000
Miscellaneous expenses.	7,500

Required:

Given the above information, prepare a schedule of controllable and noncontrollable costs for Ms. Smith.

24. The Marshall Door Corporation is organized on a functional basis and uses a responsibility accounting system. The production division, one of the five main divisions, is supervised by a general manager. The production division consists of three producing departments and three service departments.

During July, 10,000 units were produced by the production division. Given below are the controllable costs incurred by the six departments and the manager. Also, shown in the first column are the budgeted totals.

	Budget Totals	Direct Material	Direct Labor	Manufacturing Overhead	Total
Producing Departments					
1	$187,000	$25,000	$65,000	$100,000	$190,000
2	122,000	15,000	40,000	65,000	120,000
3	66,500	8,000	22,000	37,000	67,000
Service Departments					
A	10,000	0	0	7,500	7,500
B	8,000	0	0	10,000	10,000
C	4,500	0	0	5,000	5,000
Production Manager	13,000	0	0	13,000	13,000

Required:

Prepare a cost responsibility accounting report showing all controllable costs for the production manager of the production division for July. Show all variances.

25. John Able is the manager of the Finishing and Processing Division at the Houston Plant of the Morgan Company. His responsibility report for March is as follows:

	Flexible Budget	Actual	Variances (unfavorable)
Controllable Costs:			
Direct materials	$10,000	$12,500	($2,500)
Direct labor	5,000	6,900	(1,900)
Supplies	850	600	250
Repairs and maintenance	1,000	1,200	(200)
Total controllable costs	$16,850	$21,200	($4,350)

Additional data:

1. 5,000 pounds of raw material at a price of $2 per pound were budgeted for March ($10,000). During March the purchasing department could not obtain the materials at $2 per pound. The price increased to $2.50 per pound. Therefore, 5,000 pounds of raw material were obtained at a price of $2.50 per pound ($12,500).

2. When the budget was prepared in January, the labor rate was $5 per hour. However, the labor rate was increased to $6 per hour when a union contract was signed in February. Also, 100 hours of overtime were authorized during March even though no amount of overtime had been approved by the budget. Overtime was paid at a rate of 1½ times the regular rate ($9 per hour). This overtime was incurred during an emergency in which Mr. Able's department aided another department. The budget allowed 1,000 hours; the actual hours worked conformed to the budgeted hours plus the 100 authorized overtime hours.

Required:

1. Is the given responsibility report for Mr. Able's department a fair one? Mr. Able argues that he should not be charged with the unfavorable variances resulting from direct materials and direct labor. Do you agree with Mr. Able's argument?
2. Prepare a revised responsibility report showing only those costs controllable by Mr. Able and variances chargeable to him.

26. Baker and Carr Enterprises consists of four divisions which are supervised by the manufacturing Vice President; the four divisions are the assembly division, the finishing and processing division, the machining division and the packing division. Each division is supervised by a manager and each division consists of several departments. Each department is supervised by a department head. Responsibility accounting performance reports are prepared monthly for each department head, the division manager and the Vice President.

The finishing and processing division consists of two departments. The following data for the finishing and processing division for December show the controllable costs of the manager:

	Department X		Department Y	
	Budgeted	Actual	Budgeted	Actual
Controllable costs:				
Direct materials...............	$12,000	$12,500	$ 9,500	$ 9,400
Direct labor..................	25,000	27,500	18,000	16,500
Supplies.....................	2,000	1,600	1,200	1,350
Repairs and maintenance.......	1,000	950	700	850
Total controllable costs.........	$40,000	$42,550	$29,400	$28,100

Additional data:

Total controllable costs for the other three divisions for December were as follows:

	Budgeted	Actual
Assembly division.................	$135,000	$132,600
Machining division...............	117,500	120,200
Packing division.................	175,600	172,050

Required:

1. Prepare a performance report for the division manager of finishing and processing assuming that "Other Costs" for this division are:

Budgeted............................	$100,000
Actual...............................	99,000

2. Prepare a performance report for the manufacturing Vice President assuming that "Other Costs" for his segment are:

Budgeted............................	$ 55,000
Actual...............................	57,100

27. The Cooke Company is composed of three divisions: marketing, production, and administrative services. The approved (flexible) budgets for each division for March are as follows:

	Marketing Manager	Production Manager	Administrative Services Manager
Controllable costs:			
Direct materials..................	0	$18,000	0
Direct labor.....................	0	32,500	0
Salaries	$55,000	40,000	$75,000
Supplies........................	3,800	750	9,500
Maintenance....................	1,200	1,200	1,200
Total	$60,000	$92,450	$85,700

The actual costs incurred by each division are as follows:

	Marketing	Production	Administrative Service
Controllable costs:			
Direct materials..................	0	$21,800	0
Direct labor.....................	0	30,050	0
Salaries	$55,600	40,000	$73,000
Supplies........................	3,650	800	9,250
Maintenance....................	1,200	1,200	1,200
Totals.......................	$60,450	$93,850	$83,450

Required:

1. Prepare a responsibility accounting performance report for the production division.
2. Prepare a performance report for the Vice President in charge of all three divisions. In preparing the report it is permissible to use only "Total Controllable Costs" for each division. Assume that "Other Costs" for the Vice President are:

Budgeted............................	$25,000
Actual...............................	25,600

Appendix A: Present Value Tables

Table 1

Present Value of $1

Periods (n)	1%	1½%	2%	2½%	3%	3½%	4%	4½%	5%	6%	7%	8%	10%
1......	0.9901	0.9852	0.9804	0.9756	0.9709	0.9662	0.9615	0.9569	0.9524	0.9434	0.9346	0.9259	0.9091
2......	0.9803	0.9707	0.9612	0.9518	0.9426	0.9335	0.9246	0.9157	0.9070	0.8900	0.8734	0.8573	0.8264
3......	0.9706	0.9563	0.9423	0.9286	0.9151	0.9019	0.8890	0.8763	0.8638	0.8396	0.8163	0.7938	0.7513
4......	0.9610	0.9422	0.9238	0.9060	0.8885	0.8714	0.8548	0.8386	0.8227	0.7921	0.7629	0.7350	0.6830
5......	0.9515	0.9283	0.9057	0.8839	0.8626	0.8420	0.8219	0.8025	0.7835	0.7473	0.7130	0.6806	0.6209
6......	0.9420	0.9145	0.8880	0.8623	0.8375	0.8135	0.7903	0.7679	0.7462	0.7050	0.6663	0.6302	0.5645
7......	0.9327	0.9010	0.8706	0.8413	0.8131	0.7860	0.7599	0.7348	0.7107	0.6651	0.6227	0.5835	0.5132
8......	0.9235	0.8877	0.8535	0.8207	0.7894	0.7594	0.7307	0.7032	0.6768	0.6274	0.5820	0.5403	0.4665
9......	0.9143	0.8746	0.8368	0.8007	0.7664	0.7337	0.7026	0.6729	0.6446	0.5919	0.5439	0.5002	0.4241
10......	0.9053	0.8617	0.8203	0.7812	0.7441	0.7089	0.6756	0.6439	0.6139	0.5584	0.5083	0.4632	0.3855
11......	0.8963	0.8489	0.8043	0.7621	0.7224	0.6849	0.6496	0.6162	0.5847	0.5268	0.4751	0.4289	0.3505
12......	0.8874	0.8364	0.7885	0.7436	0.7014	0.6618	0.6246	0.5897	0.5568	0.4970	0.4440	0.3971	0.3186
13......	0.8787	0.8240	0.7730	0.7254	0.6810	0.6394	0.6006	0.5643	0.5303	0.4688	0.4150	0.3677	0.2897
14......	0.8700	0.8118	0.7579	0.7077	0.6611	0.6178	0.5775	0.5400	0.5051	0.4423	0.3878	0.3405	0.2633
15......	0.8613	0.7999	0.7430	0.6905	0.6419	0.5969	0.5553	0.5167	0.4810	0.4173	0.3624	0.3153	0.2394
16......	0.8528	0.7880	0.7284	0.6736	0.6232	0.5767	0.5339	0.4945	0.4581	0.3936	0.3387	0.2919	0.2176
17......	0.8444	0.7764	0.7142	0.6572	0.6050	0.5572	0.5134	0.4732	0.4363	0.3714	0.3166	0.2703	0.1978
18......	0.8360	0.7649	0.7002	0.6412	0.5874	0.5384	0.4936	0.4528	0.4155	0.3503	0.2959	0.2502	0.1799
19......	0.8277	0.7536	0.6864	0.6255	0.5703	0.5202	0.4746	0.4333	0.3957	0.3305	0.2765	0.2317	0.1635
20......	0.8195	0.7425	0.6730	0.6103	0.5537	0.5026	0.4564	0.4146	0.3769	0.3118	0.2584	0.2145	0.1486
21......	0.8114	0.7315	0.6598	0.5954	0.5375	0.4856	0.4388	0.3968	0.3589	0.2942	0.2415	0.1987	0.1351
22......	0.8034	0.7207	0.6468	0.5809	0.5219	0.4692	0.4220	0.3797	0.3418	0.2775	0.2257	0.1839	0.1228
23......	0.7954	0.7100	0.6342	0.5667	0.5067	0.4533	0.4057	0.3634	0.3256	0.2618	0.2109	0.1703	0.1117
24......	0.7876	0.6995	0.6217	0.5529	0.4919	0.4380	0.3901	0.3477	0.3101	0.2470	0.1971	0.1577	0.1015
25......	0.7798	0.6892	0.6095	0.5394	0.4776	0.4231	0.3751	0.3327	0.2953	0.2330	0.1842	0.1460	0.0923
26......	0.7720	0.6790	0.5976	0.5262	0.4637	0.4088	0.3607	0.3184	0.2812	0.2198	0.1722	0.1352	0.0839
27......	0.7644	0.6690	0.5859	0.5134	0.4502	0.3950	0.3468	0.3047	0.2678	0.2074	0.1609	0.1252	0.0763
28......	0.7568	0.6591	0.5744	0.5009	0.4371	0.3817	0.3335	0.2916	0.2551	0.1956	0.1504	0.1159	0.0693
29......	0.7493	0.6494	0.5631	0.4887	0.4243	0.3687	0.3207	0.2790	0.2429	0.1846	0.1406	0.1073	0.0630
30......	0.7419	0.6398	0.5521	0.4767	0.4120	0.3563	0.3083	0.2670	0.2314	0.1741	0.1314	0.0994	0.0573
40......	0.6717	0.5513	0.4529	0.3724	0.3066	0.2526	0.2083	0.1719	0.1420	0.0972	0.0668	0.0460	0.0221
50......	0.6080	0.4750	0.3715	0.2909	0.2281	0.1791	0.1407	0.1107	0.0872	0.0543	0.0339	0.0213	0.0085

Table 1 Continued

Present Value of $1

12%	14%	15%	16%	18%	20%	22%	24%	25%	26%	28%	30%	40%	50%
0.893	0.877	0.870	0.862	0.847	0.833	0.820	0.806	0.800	0.794	0.781	0.769	0.714	0.667
0.797	0.769	0.756	0.743	0.718	0.694	0.672	0.650	0.640	0.630	0.610	0.592	0.510	0.444
0.712	0.675	0.658	0.641	0.609	0.579	0.551	0.524	0.512	0.500	0.477	0.455	0.364	0.296
0.636	0.592	0.572	0.552	0.516	0.482	0.451	0.423	0.410	0.397	0.373	0.350	0.260	0.198
0.567	0.519	0.497	0.476	0.437	0.402	0.370	0.341	0.328	0.315	0.291	0.269	0.186	0.132
0.507	0.456	0.432	0.410	0.370	0.335	0.303	0.275	0.262	0.250	0.227	0.207	0.133	0.088
0.452	0.400	0.376	0.354	0.314	0.279	0.249	0.222	0.210	0.198	0.178	0.159	0.095	0.059
0.404	0.351	0.327	0.305	0.266	0.233	0.204	0.179	0.168	0.157	0.139	0.123	0.068	0.039
0.361	0.308	0.284	0.263	0.225	0.194	0.167	0.144	0.134	0.125	0.108	0.094	0.048	0.026
0.322	0.270	0.247	0.227	0.191	0.162	0.137	0.116	0.107	0.099	0.085	0.073	0.035	0.017
0.287	0.237	0.215	0.195	0.162	0.135	0.112	0.094	0.086	0.079	0.066	0.056	0.025	0.012
0.257	0.208	0.187	0.168	0.137	0.112	0.092	0.076	0.069	0.062	0.052	0.043	0.018	0.008
0.229	0.182	0.163	0.145	0.116	0.093	0.075	0.061	0.055	0.050	0.040	0.033	0.013	0.005
0.205	0.160	0.141	0.125	0.099	0.078	0.062	0.049	0.044	0.039	0.032	0.025	0.009	0.003
0.183	0.140	0.123	0.108	0.084	0.065	0.051	0.040	0.035	0.031	0.025	0.020	0.006	0.002
0.163	0.123	0.107	0.093	0.071	0.054	0.042	0.032	0.028	0.025	0.019	0.015	0.005	0.002
0.146	0.108	0.093	0.080	0.060	0.045	0.034	0.026	0.023	0.020	0.015	0.012	0.003	0.001
0.130	0.095	0.081	0.069	0.051	0.038	0.028	0.021	0.018	0.016	0.012	0.009	0.002	0.001
0.116	0.083	0.070	0.060	0.043	0.031	0.023	0.017	0.014	0.012	0.009	0.007	0.002	
0.104	0.073	0.061	0.051	0.037	0.026	0.019	0.014	0.012	0.010	0.007	0.005	0.001	
0.093	0.064	0.053	0.044	0.031	0.022	0.015	0.011	0.009	0.008	0.006	0.004	0.001	
0.083	0.056	0.046	0.038	0.026	0.018	0.013	0.009	0.007	0.006	0.004	0.003	0.001	
0.074	0.049	0.040	0.033	0.022	0.015	0.010	0.007	0.006	0.005	0.003	0.002		
0.066	0.043	0.035	0.028	0.019	0.013	0.008	0.006	0.005	0.004	0.003	0.002		
0.059	0.038	0.030	0.024	0.016	0.010	0.007	0.005	0.004	0.003	0.002	0.001		
0.053	0.033	0.026	0.021	0.014	0.009	0.006	0.004	0.003	0.002	0.002	0.001		
0.047	0.029	0.023	0.018	0.011	0.007	0.005	0.003	0.002	0.002	0.001	0.001		
0.042	0.026	0.020	0.016	0.010	0.006	0.004	0.002	0.002	0.002	0.001	0.001		
0.037	0.022	0.017	0.014	0.008	0.005	0.003	0.002	0.002	0.001	0.001	0.001		
0.033	0.020	0.015	0.012	0.007	0.004	0.003	0.002	0.001	0.001	0.001			
0.011	0.005	0.004	0.003	0.001	0.001								
0.003	0.001	0.001	0.001										

Table 2

Present Value of Annuity of $1 Per Period

Periods (n)	1%	1½%	2%	2½%	3%	3½%	4%	4½%	5%	6%	7%
1....	0.9901	0.9852	0.9804	0.9756	0.9709	0.9662	0.9615	0.9569	0.9524	0.9434	0.9346
2....	1.9704	1.9559	1.9416	1.9274	1.9135	1.8997	1.8861	1.8727	1.8594	1.8334	1.8080
3....	2.9410	2.9122	2.8839	2.8560	2.8286	2.8016	2.7751	2.7490	2.7232	2.6730	2.6243
4....	3.9020	3.8544	3.8077	3.7620	3.7171	3.6731	3.6299	3.5875	3.5460	3.4651	3.3872
5....	4.8534	4.7826	4.7135	4.6458	4.5797	4.5151	4.4518	4.3900	4.3295	4.2124	4.1002
6....	5.7955	5.6972	5.6014	5.5081	5.4172	5.3286	5.2421	5.1579	5.0757	4.9173	4.7665
7....	6.7282	6.5982	6.4720	6.3494	6.2303	6.1145	6.0021	5.8927	5.7864	5.5824	5.3893
8....	7.6517	7.4859	7.3255	7.1701	7.0197	6.8740	6.7327	6.5959	6.4632	6.2098	5.9713
9....	8.5660	8.3605	8.1622	7.9709	7.7861	7.6077	7.4353	7.2688	7.1078	6.8017	6.5152
10....	9.4713	9.2222	8.9826	8.7521	8.5302	8.3166	8.1109	7.9127	7.7217	7.3601	7.0236
11....	10.3676	10.0711	9.7868	9.5142	9.2526	9.0016	8.7605	8.5289	8.3064	7.8869	7.4987
12....	11.2551	10.9075	10.5753	10.2578	9.9540	9.6633	9.3851	9.1186	8.8633	8.3838	7.9427
13....	12.1337	11.7315	11.3484	10.9832	10.6350	10.3027	9.9856	9.6829	9.3936	8.8527	8.3577
14....	13.0037	12.5434	12.1062	11.6909	11.2961	10.9205	10.5631	10.2228	9.8986	9.2950	8.7455
15....	13.8651	13.3432	12.8493	12.3814	11.9379	11.5174	11.1184	10.7395	10.3797	9.7122	9.1079
16....	14.7179	14.1313	13.5777	13.0550	12.5611	12.0941	11.6523	11.2340	10.8378	10.1059	9.4466
17....	15.5623	14.9076	14.2919	13.7122	13.1661	12.6513	12.1657	11.7072	11.2741	10.4773	9.7632
18....	16.3983	15.6726	14.9920	14.3534	13.7535	13.1897	12.6593	12.1600	11.6896	10.8276	10.0591
19....	17.2260	16.4262	15.6785	14.9789	14.3238	13.7098	13.1339	12.5933	12.0853	11.1581	10.3356
20....	18.0456	17.1686	16.3514	15.5892	14.8775	14.2124	13.5903	13.0079	12.4622	11.4699	10.5940
21....	18.8570	17.9001	17.0112	16.1845	15.4150	14.6980	14.0292	13.4047	12.8212	11.7640	10.8355
22....	19.6604	18.6208	17.6580	16.7654	15.9369	15.1671	14.4511	13.7844	13.1630	12.0416	11.0612
23....	20.4558	19.3309	18.2922	17.3321	16.4436	15.6204	14.8568	14.1478	13.4886	12.3034	11.2722
24....	21.2434	20.0304	18.9139	17.8850	16.9355	16.0584	15.2470	14.4955	13.7986	12.5504	11.4693
25....	22.0232	20.7196	19.5235	18.4244	17.4131	16.4815	15.6221	14.8282	14.0939	12.7834	11.6536
26....	22.7952	21.3986	20.1210	18.9506	17.8768	16.8904	15.9828	15.1466	14.3752	13.0032	11.8258
27....	23.5596	22.0676	20.7069	19.4640	18.3270	17.2854	16.3296	15.4513	14.6430	13.2105	11.9867
28....	24.3164	22.7267	21.2813	19.9649	18.7641	17.6670	15.6631	15.7429	14.8981	13.4062	12.1371
29....	25.0658	23.3761	21.8444	20.4535	19.1885	18.0358	1o.9837	16.0219	15.1411	13.5907	12.2777
30....	25.8077	24.0158	22.3965	20.9303	19.6004	18.3920	17.2920	16.2889	15.3725	13.7648	12.4090
40....	32.8347	29.9158	27.3555	25.1028	23.1148	21.3551	19.7928	18.4016	17.1591	15.0463	13.3317
50....	39.1961	34.9997	31.4236	28.3623	25.7298	23.4556	21.4822	19.7620	18.2559	15.7619	13.8007

Table 2 Continued

Present Value of Annuity of $1 Per Period

8%	10%	12%	14%	15%	16%	18%	20%	22%	24%	25%	26%	28%	30%	40%	50%
0.9259	0.9091	0.893	0.877	0.870	0.862	0.847	0.833	0.820	0.806	0.800	0.794	0.781	0.769	0.714	0.667
1.7833	1.7355	1.690	1.647	1.626	1.605	1.566	1.528	1.492	1.457	1.440	1.424	1.392	1.361	1.224	1.111
2.5771	2.4869	2.402	2.322	2.283	2.246	2.174	2.106	2.042	1.981	1.952	1.923	1.868	1.816	1.589	1.407
3.3121	3.1699	3.037	2.914	2.855	2.798	2.690	2.589	2.494	2.404	2.362	2.320	2.241	2.166	1.849	1.605
3.9927	3.7908	3.605	3.433	3.352	3.274	3.127	2.991	2.864	2.745	2.689	2.635	2.532	2.436	2.035	1.737
4.6229	4.3553	4.111	3.889	3.784	3.685	3.498	3.326	3.167	3.020	2.951	2.885	2.759	2.643	2.168	1.824
5.2064	4.8684	4.564	4.288	4 160	4.039	3.812	3.605	3.416	3.242	3.161	3.083	2.937	2.802	2.263	1.883
5.7466	5.3349	4.968	4.639	4.487	4.344	4.078	3.837	3.619	3.421	3.329	3.241	3.076	2.925	2.331	1.922
6.2469	5.7590	5.328	4.946	4.772	4.607	4.303	4.031	3.786	3.566	3.463	3.366	3.184	3.019	2.379	1.948
6.7101	6.1446	5.650	5.216	5.019	4.833	4.494	4.192	3.923	3.682	3.571	3.465	3.269	3.092	2.414	1.965
7.1390	6.4951	5.988	5.453	5.234	5.029	4.656	4.327	4.035	3.776	3.656	3.544	3.335	3.147	2.438	1.977
7.5361	6.8137	6.194	5.660	5.421	5.197	4.793	4.439	4.127	3.851	3.725	3.606	3.387	3.190	2.456	1.985
7.9038	7.1034	6.424	5.842	5.583	5.342	4.910	4.533	4.203	3.912	3.780	3.656	3.427	3.223	2.468	1.990
8.2442	7.3667	6.628	6.002	5.724	5.468	5.008	4.611	4.265	3.962	3.824	3.695	3.459	3.249	2.477	1.993
8.5595	7.6061	6.811	6.142	5.847	5.575	5.092	4.675	4.315	4.001	3.859	3.726	3.483	3.268	2.484	1.995
8.8514	7.8237	6.974	6.265	5.954	5.669	5.162	4.730	4.357	4.033	3.887	3.751	3.503	3.283	2.489	1.997
9.1216	8.0216	7.120	6.373	6.047	5.749	5.222	4.775	4.391	4.059	3.910	3.771	3.518	3.295	2.492	1.998
9.3719	8.2014	7.250	6.467	6.128	5.818	5.273	4.812	4.419	4.080	3.928	3.786	3.529	3.304	2.494	1.999
9.6036	8.3649	7.366	6.550	6.198	5.877	5.316	4.844	4.442	4.097	3.942	3.799	3.539	3.311	2.496	1.999
9.8181	8.5136	7.469	6.623	6.259	5.929	5.353	4.870	4.460	4.110	3.954	3.808	3.546	3.316	2.497	1.999
10.0168	8.6487	7.562	6.687	6.312	5.973	5.384	4.891	4.476	4.121	3.963	3.816	3.551	3.320	2.498	2.000
10.2007	8.7715	7.645	6.743	6.359	6.011	5.410	4.909	4.488	4.130	3.970	3.822	3.556	3.323	2.498	2.000
10.3711	8.8832	7.718	6.792	6.399	6.044	5.432	4.925	4.499	4.137	3.976	3.827	3.559	3.325	2.499	2.000
10.5288	8.9847	7.784	6.835	6.434	6.073	5.451	4.937	4.507	4.143	3.981	3.831	3.562	3.327	2.499	2.000
10.6748	9.0770	7.843	6.873	6.464	6.097	5.467	4.948	4.514	4.147	3.985	3.834	3.564	3.329	2.499	2.000
10.8100	9.1609	7.896	6.906	6.491	6.118	5.480	4.956	4.520	4.151	3.988	3.837	3.566	3.330	2.500	2.000
10.9352	9.2372	7.943	6.935	6.514	6.136	5.492	4.964	4.524	4.154	3.990	3.839	3.567	3.331	2.500	2.000
11.0511	9.3066	7.984	6.961	6.534	6.152	5.502	4.970	4.528	4.157	3.992	3.840	3.568	3.331	2.500	2.000
11.1584	9.3696	8.022	6.983	6.551	6.166	5.510	4.975	4.531	4.159	3.994	3.841	3.569	3.332	2.500	2.000
11.2578	9.4269	8.055	7.003	6.566	6.177	5.517	4.979	4.534	4.160	3.995	3.842	3.569	3.332	2.500	2.000
11.9246	9.7791	8.244	7.105	6.642	6.234	5.548	4.997	4.544	4.166	3.999	3.846	3.571	3.333	2.500	2.000
12.2335	9.9148	8.304	7.133	6.661	6.246	5.554	4.999	4.545	4.167	4.000	3.846	3.571	3.333	2.500	2.000

NOTE: To convert this table to values of an annuity in advance, take one less period and add 1.0000.

Appendix B: General Motors Corporation and Consolidated Subsidiaries

CONSOLIDATED FINANCIAL STATEMENTS

General Motors Corporation and Consolidated Subsidiaries

RESPONSIBILITIES FOR FINANCIAL STATEMENTS

The following financial statements of General Motors Corporation and consolidated subsidiaries were prepared by the management which is responsible for their integrity and objectivity. The statements have been prepared in conformity with generally accepted accounting principles and, as such, include amounts based on judgments of management. Financial information elsewhere in this Annual Report is consistent with that in the financial statements.

Management is further responsible for maintaining a system of internal accounting controls, designed to provide reasonable assurance that the books and records reflect the transactions of the companies and that its established policies and procedures are carefully followed. From a stockholder's point of view, perhaps the most important feature in the system of control is that it is continually reviewed for its effectiveness and is augmented by written policies and guidelines, the careful selection and training of qualified personnel, and a strong program of internal audit.

Deloitte Haskins & Sells, independent certified public accountants, are engaged to examine the consolidated financial statements of General Motors Corporation and its subsidiaries and issue reports thereon. Their examination is conducted in accordance with generally accepted auditing standards which comprehend a review of internal accounting controls and a test of transactions. The Accountants'

Report appears on page 41.

The Board of Directors, through the Audit Committee and its Common Stock Classification Oversight Subcommittee (both composed entirely of non-employe Directors), is responsible for assuring that management fulfills its responsibilities in the preparation of the financial statements. The Committee selects the independent public accountants annually in advance of the Annual Meeting of Stockholders and submits the selection for ratification at the Meeting. In addition, the Committee reviews the scope of the audits and the accounting principles being applied in financial reporting. The independent public accountants, representatives of management, and the internal auditors meet regularly (separately and jointly) with the Committee to review the activities of each and to ensure that each is properly discharging its responsibilities. To ensure complete independence, Deloitte Haskins & Sells have full and free access to meet with the Committee, without management representatives present, to discuss the results of their examination, the adequacy of internal accounting controls, and the quality of the financial reporting.

Chairman

Chief Financial Officer

STATEMENT OF CONSOLIDATED INCOME

For the Years Ended December 31, 1986, 1985 and 1984 (Dollars in Millions Except Per Share Amounts)	1986	1985	1984
Net Sales and Revenues (Notes 1 and 2)			
Manufactured products	$101,506.9	$95,268.4	$83,699.7
Computer systems services	1,306.8	1,103.3	190.2
Total Net Sales and Revenues	102,813.7	96,371.7	83,889.9
Cost and Expenses			
Cost of sales and other operating charges, exclusive of items listed below	88,298.0	81,654.6	70,217.9
Selling, general and administrative expenses	5,203.5	4,294.2	4,003.0
Depreciation of real estate, plants and equipment	3,499.6	2,777.9	2,663.2
Amortization of special tools	2,596.1	3,083.3	2,236.7
Amortization of intangible assets (Note 1)	498.0	347.3	69.1
Special provision for scheduled plant closings and other restructurings (Note 6)	1,287.6	–	–
Total Costs and Expenses	101,382.8	92,157.3	79,189.9
Operating Income	1,430.9	4,214.4	4,700.0
Other income less income deductions—net (Note 7)	983.1	1,299.2	1,713.5
Interest expense (Note 1)	(953.7)	(892.3)	(909.2)
Income before Income Taxes	1,460.3	4,621.3	5,504.3
United States, foreign and other income taxes (credit) (Note 9)	(300.3)	1,630.3	1,805.1
Income after Income Taxes	1,760.6	2,991.0	3,699.2
Equity in earnings of nonconsolidated subsidiaries and associates (dividends received amounted to $1.7 in 1986, $100.5 in 1985 and $706.1 in 1984)	1,184.1	1,008.0	817.3
Net Income	2,944.7	3,999.0	4,516.5
Dividends on preferred stocks	10.8	11.6	12.5
Earnings on Common Stocks	$ 2,933.9	$ 3,987.4	$ 4,504.0
Earnings attributable to:			
$1-2/3 par value common stock	$ 2,607.7	$ 3,883.6	$ 4,498.3
Class E common stock (issued in 1984)	$ 136.2	$ 103.8	$ 5.7
Class H common stock (issued in December 1985)	$ 190.0	–	–
Average number of shares of common stocks outstanding (in millions):			
$1-2/3 par value common	317.6	316.3	315.3
Class E common (issued in 1984)	63.8	66.5	36.3*
Class H common (issued in December 1985)	63.9	–	–
Earnings Per Share Attributable to (Note 10):			
$1-2/3 par value common stock	$8.21	$12.28	$14.27
Class E common stock (issued in 1984)	$2.13	$1.57	$0.16*
Class H common stock (issued in December 1985)	$2.97	–	–

Reference should be made to notes on pages 30 through 41. Certain amounts for 1984 have been reclassified to conform with 1985 classifications.

Earnings and earnings per share attributable to common stocks in 1985 and 1984 have been restated to reflect the Class E common stock amendment approved by the stockholders in December 1985.

*Adjusted to reflect the two-for-one stock split in the form of a 100% stock dividend distributed on June 10, 1985.

CONSOLIDATED BALANCE SHEET

December 31, 1986 and 1985 (Dollars in Millions Except Per Share Amounts)

ASSETS	1986	1985
Current Assets		
Cash	$ 150.7	$ 179.1
United States Government and other marketable securities and time deposits—at cost, which approximates market of $3,881.0 and $4,933.1	3,868.1	4,935.3
Total cash and marketable securities	4,018.8	5,114.4
Accounts and notes receivable (Note 11):		
Nonconsolidated subsidiaries and associates (including GMAC and its subsidiaries—$1,387.1 and $4,038.7)	1,607.0	4,126.9
Other (less allowances)	9,697.3	3,155.1
Inventories (less allowances) (Note 1)	7,235.1	8,269.7
Contracts in process (less advances and progress payments of $2,345.7 and $2,525.3) (Note 1)	1,590.6	1,453.8
Prepaid expenses	2,619.6	2,136.1
Total Current Assets	26,768.4	24,256.0
Equity in Net Assets of Nonconsolidated Subsidiaries and Associates (principally GMAC and its subsidiaries—Note 11)	7,232.3	5,718.5
Other Investments and Miscellaneous Assets—at cost (less allowances)	2,308.4	3,069.8
Common Stocks Held for the GM Incentive Program (Note 3)	190.3	190.2
Property		
Real estate, plants and equipment—at cost (Note 12)	55,240.7	47,267.1
Less accumulated depreciation (Note 12)	27,658.0	24,325.0
Net real estate, plants and equipment	27,582.7	22,942.1
Special tools—at cost (less amortization)	2,793.7	1,710.9
Total Property	30,376.4	24,653.0
Intangible Assets—at cost (less amortization) (Note 1)	5,717.2	5,945.3
Total Assets	$72,593.0	$63,832.8

LIABILITIES AND STOCKHOLDERS' EQUITY	1986	1985
Current Liabilities		
Accounts payable (principally trade)	$ 6,368.0	$ 7,322.2
Loans payable (Note 14)	2,730.1	2,655.2
United States, foreign and other income taxes payable	333.1	243.1
Accrued liabilities and deferred income taxes (Note 13)	13,416.9	12,078.0
Total Current Liabilities	22,848.1	22,298.5
Long-Term Debt (Note 14)	4,007.3	2,500.2
Payable to GMAC (Note 11)	5,500.0	300.0
Capitalized Leases (including GMAC and its subsidiaries—$35.8 and $76.1)	318.0	367.0
Other Liabilities	6,991.7	6,879.8
Deferred Credits (including investment tax credits—$1,505.3 and $1,328.8)	2,249.9	1,962.6
Stockholders' Equity (Notes 3, 4, 5 and 15)		
Preferred stocks ($5.00 series, $153.0 and $169.3; $3.75 series, $81.4)	234.4	250.7
Common stocks:		
$1-2/3 par value common (issued, 319,383,830 and 318,853,315 shares)	532.3	531.4
Class E common (issued, 53,507,119 and 66,227,137 shares)	5.4	6.6
Class H common (issued, 66,585,332 and 65,495,316 shares)	6.6	6.6
Capital surplus (principally additional paid-in capital)	6,332.6	6,667.8
Net income retained for use in the business	23,888.7	22,606.6
Subtotal	31,000.0	30,069.7
Accumulated foreign currency translation and other adjustments (Note 1)	(322.0)	(545.0)
Total Stockholders' Equity	30,678.0	29,524.7
Total Liabilities and Stockholders' Equity	$72,593.0	$63,832.8

Reference should be made to notes on pages 30 through 41. Certain amounts for 1985 have been reclassified to conform with 1986 classifications.

STATEMENT OF CHANGES IN CONSOLIDATED FINANCIAL POSITION

For the Years Ended December 31, 1986, 1985 and 1984 (Dollars in Millions)	1986	1985	1984
Source of Funds			
Net income	$ 2,944.7	$ 3,999.0	$ 4,516.5
Depreciation of real estate, plants and equipment	3,499.6	2,777.9	2,663.2
Amortization of special tools	2,596.1	3,083.3	2,236.7
Amortization of intangible assets (Note 1)	498.0	347.3	69.1
Deferred income taxes, undistributed earnings of nonconsolidated subsidiaries and associates, etc.—net	(562.9)	(471.7)	(1,316.1)
Total funds provided by current operations	8,975.5	9,735.8	8,169.4
Increase in long-term debt	2,885.3	965.9	1,074.1
Increase in payable to GMAC	5,200.0	—	—
Issuances of common stocks	327.6	2,883.3	614.0
Other—net	393.8	331.4	2,010.6
Total	17,782.2	13,916.4	11,868.1
Use of Funds			
Cash dividends paid to stockholders (Note 15)	1,663.1	1,616.9	1,523.7
Expenditures for real estate, plants and equipment:			
Operations	8,086.3	6,099.2	3,595.1
Hughes acquisition	—	1,948.7	—
Expenditures for special tools	3,625.3	3,075.0	2,452.1
Intangible assets arising from acquisitions (Note 1)	270.0	4,354.0	2,006.3
Increase (Decrease) in other working capital items	3,058.4	(866.2)	(1,964.6)
Decrease in long-term debt	1,378.2	883.1	1,793.9
Repurchases of common and preferred stocks, less shares reissued	679.4	127.8	11.8
Investments in nonconsolidated subsidiaries and associates	117.1	130.9	99.3
Total	18,877.8	17,369.4	9,517.6
Increase (Decrease) in cash and marketable securities	(1,095.6)	(3,453.0)	2,350.5
Cash and marketable securities at beginning of the year	5,114.4	8,567.4	6,216.9
Cash and marketable securities at end of the year	$ 4,018.8	$ 5,114.4	$ 8,567.4
Increase (Decrease) in Other Working Capital Items by Element			
Accounts and notes receivable:			
Nonconsolidated subsidiaries and associates	($ 2,519.9)	$ 159.9	$ 307.0
Other	6,542.2	(235.8)	86.7
Inventories	(1,034.6)	910.0	738.2
Contracts in process	136.8	1,453.8	—
Prepaid expenses	483.5	1,707.8	(568.9)
Accounts payable	954.2	(2,578.7)	(101.2)
Loans payable	(74.9)	430.8	(1,830.8)
United States, foreign and other income taxes payable	(90.0)	375.8	(416.6)
Accrued liabilities and deferred income taxes	(1,338.9)	(3,089.8)	(179.0)
Increase (Decrease) in other working capital items	$ 3,058.4	($ 866.2)	($ 1,964.6)

Reference should be made to notes on pages 30 through 41. Certain amounts for 1985 and 1984 have been reclassified to conform with 1986 classifications.

NOTES TO FINANCIAL STATEMENTS

NOTE 1. Significant Accounting Policies

Principles of Consolidation

The consolidated financial statements include the accounts of the Corporation and all domestic and foreign subsidiaries which are more than 50% owned and engaged principally in manufacturing or wholesale marketing of General Motors products as well as defense, electronics and computer services. General Motors' share of earnings or losses of nonconsolidated subsidiaries and of associates in which at least 20% of the voting securities is owned is included in consolidated income under the equity method of accounting.

Revenue Recognition

Sales are generally recorded by the Corporation when products are shipped to independent dealers. Provisions for normal dealer sales incentives and returns and allowances are made at the time of sale. Costs related to special sales incentive programs are recognized as sales deductions when these incentive programs are announced.

Certain sales under long-term contracts, primarily in the defense business, are recorded using the percentage-of-completion method of accounting. Under this method, sales are recorded equivalent to costs incurred plus a portion of the profit expected to be realized on the contract, determined based on the ratio of costs incurred to estimated total costs at completion. Profits expected to be realized on contracts are based on the Corporation's estimates of total sales value and cost at completion. These estimates are reviewed and revised periodically throughout the lives of the contracts, and adjustments to profits resulting from such revisions are recorded in the accounting period in which the revisions are made. Estimated losses on contracts are recorded in the period in which they are first identified.

Inventories

Inventories are stated generally at cost, which is not in excess of market. The cost of substantially all domestic inventories other than the inventories of GM Hughes Electronics Corporation (GMHE) is determined by the last-in, first-out (LIFO) method. If the first-in, first-out (FIFO) method of inventory valuation had been used for inventories valued at LIFO cost, such inventories would have been about $2,203.8 million higher at December 31, 1986 and $2,196.3 million higher at December 31, 1985. As a result of decreases in LIFO eligible U.S. inventories, certain LIFO inventory quantities carried at lower costs prevailing in prior years, as compared with the costs of current purchases, were liquidated in 1986 and 1985. These inventory adjustments favorably affected income before income taxes by approximately $38.2 million in 1986 and $20.9 million in 1985. The cost of inventories outside the United States and of the inventories of GMHE is determined generally by FIFO or average cost methods.

Major Classes of Inventories

(Dollars in Millions)	1986	1985
Productive material, work in process and supplies	$4,042.5	$5,591.5
Finished product, service parts, etc.	3,192.6	2,678.2
Total	$7,235.1	$8,269.7

Contracts in Process

Contracts in process are stated at costs incurred plus estimated profit less amounts billed to customers and advances and progress payments received. Engineering, tooling, manufacturing and applicable overhead costs, including administrative, research and development and selling expenses, are charged to cost of sales when they are incurred. Contracts in process include amounts relating to contracts with long production cycles. Although shown as a current asset, approximately $230.0 million of the 1986 amounts are not expected to be collected within one year. Under certain contracts with the United States Government, progress payments are received based on costs incurred on the respective contracts. Title to the inventories relating to such contracts (included in contracts in process) vests with the United States Government.

Depreciation and Amortization

Depreciation is provided on groups of property using, primarily, an accelerated method which accumulates depreciation of approximately two-thirds of the depreciable cost during the first half of the estimated lives of the property.

Expenditures for special tools are amortized over short periods of time because the utility value of the tools is radically affected by frequent changes in the design of the functional components and appearance of the product. Amortization is applied directly to the asset account. Replacement of special tools for reasons other than changes in products is charged directly to cost of sales.

Income Taxes

Investment tax credits are generally deferred and amortized over the lives of the related assets (the "deferral method"). In 1985, Electronic Data Systems Corporation (EDS) changed its method of accounting for investment tax credits from the flow-through method to the deferral method used by the Corporation. The effect of the change was to reduce 1985 earnings attributable to Class E common stock by $0.41 per share and defer the recognition of investment tax credits to earnings attributable to Class E common stock in future years. GMHE recognizes investment tax credits as a reduction of income tax expense in the year that the assets which give rise to the credits are placed in service (the "flow-through method").

The tax effects of timing differences between pretax accounting income and taxable income (principally related to depreciation, sales and product allowances, vehicle instalment sales, benefit plans expense and profits on long-term contracts) are deferred. Provisions are made for estimated United States and foreign taxes, less available tax credits and deductions, which may be incurred on remittance of the Corporation's share of subsidiaries' undistributed earnings less those deemed to be permanently reinvested.

Pension Program

As described in Note 8, the Corporation adopted Statement of Financial Accounting Standards (SFAS) No. 87, Employers' Accounting for Pensions, effective January 1, 1986 for its U.S. and Canadian pension plans and will adopt the new accounting standard for other foreign pension plans by 1989. Adoption of SFAS No. 87 had the effect of reducing 1986 pension expense by $640.9 million and increasing consolidated net income by $330.5 million or $0.96 per share of $1-2/3 par value common stock, $0.04 per share of Class E common stock and $0.34 per share of Class H common stock. In addition, a change in pension plan actuarial assumptions made in June 1986, as recommended by GM's independent actuary to reflect the increased yield on investments, had the effect of decreasing 1986 pension expense by $381.6 million and increasing 1986 consolidated net income by $195.6 million or $0.61 per share of $1-2/3 par value common stock.

Product Related Expenses

Expenditures for advertising and sales promotion and for other product related expenses are charged to costs and expenses as incurred; provisions for estimated costs related to product warranty are made at the time the products are sold. Expenditures for research and development are charged to expenses as incurred and amounted to $4,157.7 million in 1986, $3,625.2 million in 1985 and $3,075.8 million in 1984.

Interest Cost

Total interest cost incurred in 1986, 1985 and 1984 amounted to $1,137.0 million, $944.9 million and $932.5 million, respectively, of which $183.3 million, $52.6 million and $23.3 million, related to certain real estate, plants and equipment acquired in those years, was capitalized.

Foreign Currency Translation

Assets and liabilities of operations outside the United States, except for operations in highly inflationary economies (principally in Latin America) or those that are highly integrated with the U.S. operations of the Corporation (principally in Canada), are translated into U.S. dollars using current exchange rates, and the effects *(continued)*

NOTES TO FINANCIAL STATEMENTS (continued)

NOTE 1. (concluded)

of foreign currency translation adjustments are deferred and included as a component of stockholders' equity. For operations in highly inflationary economies or that are highly integrated with U.S. operations, foreign currency translation adjustments are generally included in income. Exchange and translation gains (losses) included in net income in 1986, 1985 and 1984 amounted to $102.2 million, $54.1 million and ($114.8) million, respectively.

Acquisitions and Intangible Assets
Effective December 31, 1985, the Corporation acquired Hughes Aircraft Company (Hughes) and its subsidiaries for $2.7 billion in cash and cash equivalents and 50 million shares of General Motors Class H common stock having an estimated total value of $2,561.9 million. In addition, the Corporation has contingently agreed to pay the Howard Hughes Medical Institute (Institute) on December 31, 1989, for each share of Class H common stock issued in connection with the acquisition and held by the Institute on that date, the amount, if any, by which the market value per share of Class H common stock is below $60; provided that such payment shall not be greater than $40 per share. Any payment required under this contingency provision will be charged to capital surplus.

The acquisition was accounted for as a purchase. In view of the current policy of the Department of Defense and a previous decision of the Armed Services Board of Contract Appeals, there is substantial uncertainty as to the recoverability through contracts with the U.S. Government of any increase in the book values of the net assets of a defense contractor as a result of a business combination accounted for as a purchase. Accordingly, the amounts assigned to the tangible net assets of Hughes at the date of acquisition did not differ materially from the historical net book values. The purchase price exceeded the net book value of Hughes by $4,244.7 million, which was assigned as follows: $500.0 million to patents and related technology, $125.0 million to the future economic benefits to the Corporation of the Hughes Long-Term Incentive Plan (LTIP), and $3,619.7 million to other intangible assets. The amounts assigned to the various intangible asset categories are being amortized on a straight-line basis: patents and related technology over 15 years, the future economic benefits of the Hughes LTIP over 5 years and other intangible assets over 40 years. Amortization is applied directly to the asset accounts.

Because the acquisition was made effective December 31, 1985, the Statement of Consolidated Income includes the operations of Hughes beginning January 1, 1986. Pro forma results of operations of General Motors as though the acquisition of Hughes had been effective at the beginning of 1985 and 1984 are as follows:

(Dollars in Millions)	Pro Forma	
	1985	**1984**
Net Sales and Revenues	$102,537.1	$89,706.2
Net Income	$ 4,023.5	$ 4,476.4
Earnings Per Share Attributable to:		
$1-2/3 par value common stock	$11.89	$13.61
Class E common stock	$ 1.57	$ 0.16
Class H common stock	$ 2.44	$ 2.59

For the purpose of determining earnings per share and amounts available for dividends on common stocks, the amortization of intangible assets arising from the acquisition of Hughes is charged against earnings attributable to $1-2/3 par value common stock. The effect on the 1986 earnings attributable to $1-2/3 par value common stock was a net charge of $95.0 million, consisting of the amortization of the intangible assets arising from the acquisition, the profit on intercompany transactions and the earnings of GMHE attributable to $1-2/3 par value common stock.

On October 18, 1984, the Corporation acquired EDS and its subsidiaries for $2,501.9 million. The acquisition was consummated through an offer to exchange EDS common stock for either (a) $44 in cash or (b) $35.20 in cash plus two-tenths of a share of Class E common stock plus a nontransferable contingent promissory

note issued by GM. This note is payable seven years after closing in an amount equal to .2 times the excess of $62.50 (post-split) over the market price of the Class E common stock at the maturity date of the note. Holders may tender their notes for prepayment at discounted amounts beginning five years after closing.

In December 1986, the Corporation reacquired 11,791,790 shares of Class E common stock and related contingent notes issued in the acquisition from certain employes and former stockholders of EDS for $751.5 million (see Note 15), including $343.2 million attributable to contingent notes. The cost of the contingent notes, less certain income tax benefits, was assigned principally to intangible assets, including goodwill.

If the market price of Class E common stock at the maturity date of the notes were to equal the market price at December 31, 1986, $24.88 a share, the aggregate additional consideration for contingent notes outstanding at December 31, 1986 would be $394.0 million. Any additional consideration will be charged to goodwill and amortized over the remaining life of that asset.

The acquisition of EDS was accounted for as a purchase. The purchase price in excess of the net book value of EDS, $2,179.5 million, was assigned principally to existing customer contracts, $1,069.9 million, computer software programs developed by EDS, $646.2 million, and other intangible assets, including goodwill, $290.2 million. The cost assigned to these assets is being amortized on a straight-line basis over five years for computer software programs, about seven years for customer contracts, ten years for goodwill and varying periods for the remainder. Amortization is applied directly to the asset accounts.

The Statement of Consolidated Income includes the operations of EDS since October 18, 1984. For the purpose of determining earnings per share and amounts available for dividends on common stocks, the amortization of these assets is charged against earnings attributable to $1-2/3 par value common stock. The effect on the 1986, 1985 and 1984 earnings attributable to $1-2/3 par value common stock was a net charge of $260.2 million, $241.0 million and $31.7 million, respectively, consisting of the amortization of the intangible and other assets arising from the acquisition less related income tax effects, the profit on intercompany transactions and the earnings of EDS attributable to $1-2/3 par value common stock.

Earnings per share of $1-2/3 par value common stock would have been reduced by $0.66 in 1984 if the acquisition of EDS had been consummated at the beginning of that year.

NOTE 2. Net Sales and Revenues

Net sales and revenues includes sales to:

(Dollars in Millions)	**1986**	**1985**	**1984**
Nonconsolidated subsidiaries and associates	$ 845.3	$ 289.1	$ 121.6
Dealerships operating under dealership assistance plans	$2,435.3	$2,090.1	$1,917.4

Unrealized intercompany profits on sales to nonconsolidated subsidiaries and to associates are deferred.

NOTE 3. General Motors Incentive Program

The General Motors Incentive Program consists of the General Motors Bonus Plan, the General Motors Performance Achievement Plan and the General Motors Stock Option Plans. The Program was approved by the stockholders in 1982 and will be submitted for their approval at the 1987 Annual Meeting. The Program is administered by the Incentive and Compensation Committee of the Board of Directors (the Committee).

Bonus Plan
Under the provisions of the Bonus Plan, the maximum amount that may be credited to the reserve for awards for any year is

(continued)

NOTES TO FINANCIAL STATEMENTS (continued)

NOTE 3. (concluded)

equal to 8% of the amount by which net earnings exceed $1 billion; provided, however, that the amount credited may not exceed the amount paid out as dividends on common stock during the year. The Committee may, at its discretion, direct that for any year an amount less than the maximum amount be credited to the reserve.

The Committee determined that the credit to the reserve for 1986 would be $169.1 million, and on February 2, 1987, the Committee granted awards of $169.1 million. In 1985, a credit of $260.7 million was made to the reserve. Actual awards for 1985 were $218.6 million. In 1984, a credit of $269.2 million was made to the reserve, an amount $35.0 million less than the maximum which could have been credited under the formula. Actual 1984 awards totaled $224.1 million.

Performance Achievement Plan
Under the provisions of the Performance Achievement Plan, the Committee established target awards for the initial three-year phase-in period ended in 1984, for the first five-year period ended in 1986, and for five-year periods ending in 1988 and 1990. Awards are established based on targeted relationships between Corporation earnings and worldwide industry sales during the award periods; the percentages of the target awards ultimately distributed to the participants are determined by the Committee based on actual results in relation to the established goals and individual performance. Accruals for awards under this plan were $8.9 million, $21.5 million and $33.2 million, respectively, for the three years ended December 31, 1986, 1985 and 1984.

Stock Option Plans
Incentive and nonqualified stock options granted under the Stock Option Plans generally are exercisable one-half after one year and one-half after two years from the dates of grant; the option prices are 100% of fair market value on the dates of grant. Options generally expire ten years from the dates of grant and are subject to earlier termination under certain conditions.

Stock Appreciation Rights (SARs) relating to outstanding stock options have been granted to certain officers of the Corporation. These SARs provide holders with the right to receive cash equal in value to the appreciation in the Corporation's common stock over the option price of the shares under option. These SARs are not exercisable during the first six months of their terms and can only be exercised during a quarterly "window period" following release of GM's quarterly or annual press release of earnings, and may be exercised only upon surrender of the related options and only to the extent that the related options are exercisable. SARs expire with the related options.

The utilization of SARs requires an accrual each year for the appreciation on the rights expected to be exercised. The amount of such accrual is dependent on the amount, if any, by which the fair market value of the common stock exceeds the related option price and on changes in fair market value during the period. Accruals for SARs were minimal in 1986, ($2.7) million in 1985 and $13.9 million in 1984.

Changes in the status of outstanding options were as follows:

$1-2/3 par value common stock	Option Prices	Shares Under Option
Outstanding at January 1, 1984	$38.25-$72.88	3,100,294
Granted	77.19	615,355
Exercised: Options	38.25-72.88	(794,828)
SARs	38.25-72.88	(231,539)
Terminated	38.25-72.88	(48,039)
Outstanding at December 31, 1984	38.25-77.19	2,641,243
Granted	67.94	1,132,605
Exercised: Options	38.25-72.88	(365,798)
SARs	38.25-72.88	(35,970)
Terminated	38.25-72.88	(30,692)
Outstanding at December 31, 1985	38.25-77.19	3,341,388
Granted	68.32	1,244,325
Exercised: Options	38.25-77.19	(385,984)
SARs	38.25-77.19	(51,859)
Terminated	38.25-77.19	(96,066)
Outstanding at December 31, 1986	$38.25-$77.19	4,051,804

The Corporation intends to deliver newly issued $1-2/3 par value common stock upon the exercise of the stock options. Options for 2,288,809 shares were exercisable at December 31, 1986; the maximum number of shares for which additional options may be granted under the Plans was 3,301,449 at December 31, 1986.

Common Stocks Held for the GM Incentive Program
Common stocks held for the GM Incentive Program are stated substantially at cost and are used exclusively for payment of Incentive Program liabilities.

(Dollars in Millions)	1986		1985	
	Shares	Amount	Shares	Amount
Balance at January 1	2,669,664	$190.2	2,072,694	$144.2
Acquired: $1-2/3	993,860	74.8	1,629,809	118.7
Class E	334,148	12.9	29,427	1.0
Class H	377,676	15.7	—	—
Delivered: $1-2/3	(1,406,299)	(100.8)	(1,023,688)	(73.0)
Class E	(29,721)	(1.0)	(38,578)	(.7)
Class H	(39,256)	(1.5)	—	—
Bal. at Dec. 31: $1-2/3	2,228,108	163.2	2,640,547	189.2
Class E	333,544	12.9	29,117	1.0
Class H	338,420	14.2	—	—
Total	2,900,072	$190.3	2,669,664	$190.2

NOTE 4. EDS Incentive Plans

The GM Board of Directors has approved and adopted the 1984 Electronic Data Systems Corporation Stock Incentive Plan in accordance with stockholder approval obtained in connection with GM's acquisition of EDS. Under this Plan, shares, rights or options to acquire up to 40 million shares of Class E common stock may be granted or sold during the ten-year life of the Plan.

The EDS incentive and compensation committee has granted to key employes rights to purchase a total of 6,710,040 shares of Class E common stock at prices of $0.05 and $0.10 per share. Class E shares sold under this Plan are subject to restrictions and vest over a ten-year period from the date the stock purchase rights are granted. An expense of $17.1 million and $13.2 million was recorded for these awards in 1986 and 1985, respectively.

In 1985, the committee also granted incentive stock options at a price of $35.82 per share under the provisions of the 1984 Plan.

(continued)

NOTES TO FINANCIAL STATEMENTS (continued)

NOTE 4. (concluded)

The option price is equal to 100% of the fair market value of Class E common stock on the date the options were granted. These incentive stock options expire six years from dates of grant and are subject to earlier termination under certain conditions. Changes in the status of outstanding options were as follows:

Class E common stock	Shares Under Option
Granted in 1985	4,082,500
Terminated	(38,300)
Outstanding at December 31, 1985	4,044,200
Exercised	(1,000)
Terminated	(255,450)
Outstanding at December 31, 1986	3,787,750

At December 31, 1986, options for 939,100 Class E common shares were exercisable, and the maximum number of shares for which additional shares, rights or options may be granted or sold under the Plan was 29,501,210 shares.

As a part of the agreement for the acquisition of EDS by GM, the 2,270,160 unvested shares of EDS common stock sold under the EDS 1977 Stock Incentive Plan were converted at the date of the acquisition into an equal number of unvested shares of Class E common stock (4,540,320 shares on a post-split basis). In addition, EDS employes holding unvested shares under the 1977 Plan may receive deferred compensation payments under certain conditions. These payments are intended to compensate employes for the income tax consequences of realizing certain income taxed at ordinary income rates rather than at long-term capital gain rates.

EDS also has a bonus plan under which awards are granted to key executives and employes. The amounts accrued for this plan were $23.2 million in 1986 and $16.9 million in 1985.

NOTE 5. GMHE Incentive Plans

In 1985, stockholder approval was obtained in connection with GM's acquisition of Hughes for a GMHE Incentive Plan. Under this Plan, shares, rights or options to acquire up to 10 million shares of Class H common stock may be granted or sold during the ten-year life of the Plan.

In 1986, contingent upon approval of the Board of Directors, the GM Incentive and Compensation Committee granted nonqualified stock options at a price of $39.50 per share to acquire 39,455 shares under the provisions of the GMHE Plan. The option price is equal to 100% of the fair market value of Class H common stock on the date the options were granted. These nonqualified options generally expire ten years from the dates of grant and are subject to earlier termination under certain conditions.

At December 31, 1986, no options for Class H common shares were exercisable, and the maximum number of shares for which additional shares, rights or options may be granted or sold under the Plan was 9,960,545 shares.

Prior to the acquisition of Hughes, the Hughes board of directors adopted the Hughes Long-Term Incentive Plan (LTIP). The LTIP was developed to provide incentives to employes to remain with Hughes, a factor considered significant in preserving the value of Hughes for a buyer. The LTIP provided approximately 1,000 key scientists, engineers and managers of Hughes with restricted cash units, which entitle participants to receive payments from a trust established and funded pursuant to the terms of the LTIP. Concurrent with the acquisition of Hughes, $250 million was contributed to the trust by Hughes, and Hughes incurred a non-recurring preacquisition charge of about $125 million (net of the related income tax effects). In 1986, the LTIP was amended to allow participants on a one-time basis to convert restricted cash units to Class H common stock. A total of 113,517 restricted cash units were converted to 3.7 million shares of Class H common stock at a price of $40.06 per share.

Hughes also maintains supplemental compensation plans under which awards are currently granted to officers and other key employes. Amounts available for awards under the plans totaled $26.2 million in 1986.

Key employes of GMHE and Delco Electronics Corporation also participate in the General Motors Incentive Program.

NOTE 6. Special Provision for Scheduled Plant Closings and Other Restructurings

In 1986, the Corporation announced plans to close certain manufacturing and assembly plants over the next three years and to restructure certain other operations. The 1986 results of operations include a special provision of $1,287.6 million for costs associated with these scheduled plant closings and other restructurings that can be reasonably estimated at the present time. This provision includes $802.9 million for scheduled plant closings in the U.S. and $484.7 million for various other restructurings of foreign operations. As a result of plant closings and other restructurings, consolidated net income was reduced by $291.3 million or $0.92 per share of $1-2/3 par value common stock.

NOTE 7. Other Income Less Income Deductions

(Dollars in Millions)	1986	1985	1984
Other income: Interest	$813.6	$1,328.3	$1,466.8
Other	223.3	143.6	302.4
Income deductions	(53.8)	(172.7)	(55.7)
Net	$983.1	$1,299.2	$1,713.5

NOTE 8. Pension Program and Postemployment Benefits

The Corporation and its subsidiaries have a number of defined benefit pension plans covering substantially all employes. Plans covering U.S. and Canadian represented employes generally provide benefits of negotiated stated amounts for each year of service as well as significant supplemental benefits for employes who retire with 30 years of service before normal retirement age. The benefits provided by the plans covering U.S. and Canadian salaried employes are generally based on years of service and the employe's salary history. The Corporation and its consolidated subsidiaries also have certain nonqualified pension plans covering executives which are based on targeted wage replacement percentages and are generally unfunded currently.

Plan assets are primarily invested in United States government obligations, equity and fixed income securities, commingled pension trust funds and insurance contracts. The Corporation's funding policy with respect to its qualified plans is to contribute annually not less than the minimum required by applicable law and regulation nor more than the maximum amount which can be deducted for Federal income tax purposes.

During the fourth quarter of 1986, the Corporation adopted SFAS No. 87, Employers' Accounting for Pensions, with respect to all its U.S. and Canadian defined benefit pension plans, effective January 1, 1986. Application of SFAS No. 87 had the effect of increasing 1986 net income by $330.5 million or $0.96 per share of $1-2/3 par value common stock, $0.04 per share of Class E common stock and $0.34 per share of Class H common stock. In addition, the change in pension plan actuarial assumptions made in June 1986, as recommended by GM's independent actuary to reflect the increased yield on investments, had the effect of increasing 1986 net income by $195.6 million or $0.61 per share of $1-2/3 par value common stock.

Total pension expense of the Corporation and its consolidated subsidiaries amounted to $821.0 million in 1986, $1,674.8 million in 1985, and $1,618.4 million in 1984. The 1985 and 1984 pension expense does not include amounts for the Corporation's recently acquired Hughes subsidiary. Net periodic pension cost (credit) for 1986 of U.S. plans and plans of subsidiaries outside the United States for which SFAS No. 87 has been adopted included the components shown on the next page.

(continued)

NOTES TO FINANCIAL STATEMENTS (continued)

NOTE 8. (concluded)

(Dollars in Millions)	U.S. Plans	Non-U.S. Plans
Benefits earned during the year	$ 622.3	$ 17.8
Interest accrued on benefits earned in prior years	2,517.7	81.7
Return on assets		
—Actual	($6,711.2)	($153.9)
—Less deferred gain	4,365.8 (2,345.4)	37.3 (116.6)
Net amortization	(59.7)	(24.0)
Net periodic pension cost (credit)	$ 734.9	($ 41.1)

The following table reconciles the funded status of the Corporation's U.S. and non-U.S. plans for which SFAS No. 87 has been adopted with amounts recognized in the Corporation's Consolidated Balance Sheet at December 31, 1986 and January 1, 1986.

Measurement dates used for the Corporation's principal U.S. plans are October 1 and December 31. For non-U.S. plans, the measurement date used was November 30.

(Dollars in Millions)	U.S. Plans				Non-U.S. Plans	
	December 31, 1986		January 1, 1986		December 31, 1986	January 1, 1986
	Assets Exceed Accum. Benefits	Accum. Benefits Exceed Assets	Assets Exceed Accum. Benefits	Accum. Benefits Exceed Assets	Assets Exceed Accum. Benefits	Assets Exceed Accum. Benefits
Actuarial present value of benefits based on service to date and present pay levels						
Vested	$12,092.9	$14,728.0	$ 8,578.4	$11,514.4	$ 766.6	$ 658.6
Nonvested	963.8	2,951.9	192.4	1,785.7	58.7	47.2
Accumulated benefit obligation	13,056.7	17,679.9	8,770.8	13,300.1	825.3	705.8
Additional amounts related to projected pay increases	2,126.4	53.7	2,127.4	61.4	56.5	46.3
Total projected benefit obligation based on service to date	15,183.1	17,733.6	10,898.2	13,361.5	881.8	752.1
Plan assets at fair value	16,797.5	15,287.3	13,708.0	12,102.0	1,411.1	1,259.0
Projected benefit obligation (in excess of) or less than plan assets	1,614.4	(2,446.3)	2,809.8	(1,259.5)	529.3	506.9
Unamortized net amount resulting from changes in plan experience and actuarial assumptions	1,684.7	1,509.0	—	—	34.1	—
Unamortized net obligation or (asset) at date of adoption	(2,529.3)	1,884.6	(2,723.7)	2,019.2	(338.0)	(357.7)
Prepaid pension cost recognized in the Consolidated Balance Sheet	$ 769.8	$ 947.3	$ 86.1	$ 759.7	$ 225.4	$ 149.2

The weighted average discount rate used in determining the actuarial present values of the projected benefit obligation shown in the above table for U.S. plans was 8.5% at December 31, 1986 and 10.9% at January 1, 1986 and for non-U.S. plans was 10.25% at December 31, 1986 and 11.0% at January 1, 1986. The rate of increase in future compensation levels of U.S. salaried employes was 5.6% at December 31, 1986 and 5.8% at January 1, 1986 and of non-U.S. salaried employes was 5.0% at both dates. Benefits under the hourly plans are generally not based on wages and therefore no benefit escalation beyond existing negotiated increases was included. The expected long-term rate of return on assets for both U.S. and non-U.S. plans was 10.0%. The assumptions for non-U.S. plans were developed on a basis consistent with that for U.S. plans, adjusted to reflect prevailing economic conditions and interest rate environments.

The actuarial present value of accumulated benefits for the pension plans of subsidiaries outside the United States for which SFAS No. 87 has not yet been adopted has not been determined in the manner calculated and shown above. The total of these plans' pension funds and balance sheet accruals, less pension prepayments and deferred charges, exceeded the actuarially computed value of vested benefits by approximately $580.9 million at December 31, 1986 and $485.1 million at December 31, 1985.

In addition to providing pension benefits, the Corporation and certain of its subsidiaries provide certain health care and life insurance benefits for retired employes. Substantially all of the Corporation's employes, including employes in some foreign countries, may become eligible for those benefits if they reach normal retirement age while working for the Corporation. The Corporation recognizes the cost of providing those benefits primarily by expensing the cost as incurred. The cost of such benefits amounted to $864.5 million in 1986, $836.5 million in 1985 and $806.1 million in 1984.

A program for early retirement or special separation is being offered to certain salaried employes. Expenses accrued in 1986 for the program were $88.2 million.

NOTES TO FINANCIAL STATEMENTS (continued)

NOTE 9. United States, Foreign and Other Income Taxes (Credit)

(Dollars in Millions)	1986	1985	1984
Taxes estimated to be payable currently:			
United States Federal	($2,176.2)	$1,465.4	$1,151.7
Foreign	524.2	287.3	662.5
State and local	(200.5)	147.9	140.1
Total	(1,852.5)	1,900.6	1,954.3
Taxes deferred—net:			
United States Federal	1,413.8	(386.7)	8.3
Foreign	(202.4)	54.9	(170.6)
State and local	148.0	(4.6)	32.1
Total	1,359.4	(336.4)	(130.2)
Investment tax credits deferred—net:			
United States Federal	168.2	49.0	(15.1)
Foreign	24.6	17.1	(3.9)
Total	192.8	66.1	(19.0)
Total taxes (credit)	($ 300.3)	$1,630.3	$1,805.1

Investment tax credits entering into the determination of taxes estimated to be payable currently amounted to $568.6 million in 1986, $427.6 million in 1985 and $311.6 million in 1984.

The deferred taxes (credit) for timing differences consisted principally of the following: 1986—$173.3 million for depreciation, $954.1 million for sales and product allowances, $420.9 million for vehicle instalment sales, $247.8 million for benefit plans expense and ($184.5) million for profits on long-term contracts; 1985—$269.0 million for depreciation, ($608.1) million for sales and product allowances and $125.1 million for pollution control bonds; and 1984—$762.6 million for benefit plans expense, ($305.5) million for sales and product allowances, $387.6 million for vehicle instalment sales, ($240.3) million for interest, ($125.1) million for pollution control bonds and ($435.7) million for the domestic international sales corporation (DISC).

Income before income taxes included the following components:

(Dollars in Millions)	1986	1985	1984
Domestic income	$ 87.4	$3,690.5	$4,513.6
Foreign income	1,372.9	930.8	990.7
Total	$1,460.3	$4,621.3	$5,504.3

The consolidated income tax (credit) was different than the amount computed at the United States statutory income tax rate for the reasons set forth in the table below.

(Dollars in Millions)	1986	1985	1984
Expected tax at U.S. statutory income tax rate	$671.7	$2,125.8	$2,532.0
Investment tax credits amortized	(375.8)	(361.5)	(330.6)
Foreign tax rate differential	19.9	(7.2)	135.9
State and local income taxes	29.6	77.4	93.0
Deferred income tax reversal on the DISC	—	—	(421.3)
Taxes on undistributed earnings of subsidiaries	—	—	(112.2)
Research and development credit	(86.7)	(147.0)	(73.5)
Tax benefit from restructuring of foreign operations	(404.0)	—	—
ESOP credit and related adjustments	(76.4)	(75.2)	(42.2)
Tax effect of foreign dividends	(96.2)	(19.3)	(7.5)
Other adjustments	17.6	37.3	31.5
Consolidated income tax (credit)	($300.3)	$1,630.3	$1,805.1

NOTE 10. Earnings Per Share Attributable to and Dividends on Common Stocks

Earnings per share attributable to common stocks have been determined based on the relative rights of $1-2/3 par value common, Class E common and Class H common stocks to participate in dividends. The effect on earnings per share of $1-2/3 par value common stock resulting from the assumed exercise of outstanding options and delivery of bonus awards is not material. The operations of the EDS and GMHE Incentive Plans do not have a material dilutive effect on earnings per share of Class E common or Class H common stocks, respectively, at this time.

Dividends on the $1-2/3 par value common stock are declared out of the earnings of GM and its subsidiaries, excluding the Available Separate Consolidated Net Income of EDS and GMHE.

In connection with the authorization of the Class H common stock issued in December 1985 in the acquisition of Hughes, the stockholders of the Corporation approved certain amendments to the General Motors Certificate of Incorporation to redefine the earnings available for payment of dividends on Class E common stock. As a result of the amendment, earnings attributable to Class E common stock are determined and reported on a basis consistent with the earnings that the GM Board of Directors had previously treated as available for payment of dividends on that class. Because the amendment was retroactive to the date that the Class E common shares were first issued, previously reported earnings and earnings per share attributable to common stocks were restated. The amendment had the effect of increasing earnings per share attributable to $1-2/3 par value common stock by $0.27 per share in 1985 and $0.05 per share in 1984.

Dividends on the Class E common stock are declared out of the Available Separate Consolidated Net Income of EDS earned since the acquisition of EDS by GM. The Available Separate Consolidated Net Income of EDS is determined quarterly and is equal to the separate consolidated net income of EDS, excluding the effects of purchase accounting adjustments arising from the acquisition of EDS, multiplied by a fraction, the numerator of which is the weighted average number of shares of Class E common stock outstanding during the period and the denominator of which is currently 121.9 million shares.

Dividends on the Class H common stock are declared out of the Available Separate Consolidated Net Income of GMHE earned after December 31, 1985, the date the Hughes acquisition was made effective. The Available Separate Consolidated Net Income of GMHE is determined quarterly and is equal to the separate consolidated net income of GMHE, excluding the effects of purchase accounting adjustments arising from the acquisition of Hughes, multiplied by a fraction, the numerator of which is the weighted average number of shares of Class H common stock outstanding during the period and the denominator of which is currently 200 million shares.

The denominators used in determining the Available Separate Consolidated Net Income of EDS and GMHE will be adjusted as deemed appropriate by the Board of Directors to reflect subdivisions or combinations of the Class E common and Class H common stocks and to reflect certain transfers of capital to or from EDS and GMHE.

Dividends may be paid on common stocks only when, as and if declared by the Board of Directors in its sole discretion. The Board's policy with respect to $1-2/3 par value common stock is to distribute dividends based on the outlook and the indicated capital needs of the business. The current policy of the Board of Directors with respect to the Class E common and Class H common stocks is to pay cash dividends approximately equal to 25% of the Available Separate Consolidated Net Income of EDS and GMHE, respectively, for the prior year.

NOTES TO FINANCIAL STATEMENTS (continued)

NOTE 11. General Motors Acceptance Corporation and Subsidiaries

Condensed Consolidated Balance Sheet (Dollars in Millions)

	1986	1985
Cash and investments in securities	$ 3,295.5	$ 2,787.7
Finance receivables—net	73,516.7	65,725.7
Notes receivable from General Motors Corporation	5,500.0	300.0
Other assets	8,468.7	6,634.8
Total Assets	$90,780.9	$75,448.2
Short-term debt	$50,968.4	$42,642.9
Accounts payable and other liabilities (including GM and affiliates—$1,387.1 and $4,038.7)	7,800.7	8,548.0
Long-term debt	25,629.7	19,110.5
Stockholder's equity	6,382.1	5,146.8
Total Liabilities and Stockholder's Equity	$90,780.9	$75,448.2

Condensed Statement of Consolidated Income (Dollars in Millions)

	1986	1985	1984
Gross Revenue	$13,069.9	$ 9,755.8	$ 8,098.6
Interest and discount	6,188.5	5,121.8	4,772.4
Other expenses	5,696.3	3,613.0	2,541.4
Total Expenses	11,884.8	8,734.8	7,313.8
Net Income	$ 1,185.1	$ 1,021.0	$ 784.8

Interest is paid to General Motors on settlements of wholesale financing of product sales which are made beyond transit time.

Under the special rate programs sponsored by General Motors, an interest rate differential is paid to GMAC. These payments are included in unearned income by GMAC and are recognized over the life of the related contracts. Amounts recognized constituted less than 11% of GMAC gross revenues in 1986, compared with 3% in 1985 and 4% in 1984.

For marketing and financial reasons, GM assumed part of the dealer inventory financing previously provided by GMAC. Accordingly, on September 30, 1986, General Motors entered into a five-year financing agreement with GMAC which provides that GMAC will extend loans to GM up to a maximum of $12 billion which will bear interest at floating market rates. This financing agreement ensures that GMAC's ongoing funding activities continue and returns to GMAC the approximate amount of interest it would have earned had it retained the dealer inventory financing business. At December 31, 1986, $5,200 million was outstanding under this agreement at a rate of 7.4%.

NOTE 12. Real Estate, Plants and Equipment and Accumulated Depreciation

(Dollars in Millions)	1986	1985
Real estate, plants and equipment (Note 14):		
Land	$ 610.9	$ 599.2
Land improvements	1,438.2	1,297.8
Leasehold improvements—less amortization	68.0	79.4
Buildings	10,930.0	9,545.6
Machinery and equipment	35,326.5	29,580.9
Furniture and office equipment	1,959.8	1,407.8
Satellites and related facilities	284.1	270.0
Capitalized leases	938.2	968.0
Construction in progress	3,685.0	3,518.4
Total	$55,240.7	$47,267.1
Accumulated depreciation:		
Land improvements	$ 853.0	$ 759.9
Buildings	4,929.9	4,453.6
Machinery and equipment	20,548.8	18,149.5
Furniture and office equipment	803.7	479.4
Satellites and related facilities	46.3	—
Capitalized leases	476.3	482.6
Total	$27,658.0	$24,325.0

Gross property increased in 1986 by $1,467.9 million as a result of foreign currency translation adjustments. Net book value increased $617.0 million because of such adjustments.

NOTE 13. Accrued Liabilities and Deferred Income Taxes

(Dollars in Millions)	1986	1985
Taxes, other than income taxes	$ 1,228.8	$ 1,158.3
Payrolls	2,174.9	2,353.5
Employe benefits	372.5	571.1
Dealer and customer allowances, claims, discounts, etc.	3,938.6	4,659.7
Other, including deferred income taxes	5,702.1	3,335.4
Total	$13,416.9	$12,078.0

NOTE 14. Long-Term Debt

(Dollars in Millions)	Interest Rate	Maturity	1986	1985
GM:				
U.S. dollars:				
Notes	12.20 %	1988	$ 75.0	$ 150.0
Notes	14.70	1991	250.0	250.0
Notes	8.125	1991	300.0	—
Notes	7.50	1993	400.0	—
Debentures	8.625	2005	102.4	102.4
Debentures	8.125	2016	500.0	—
Other	6.59	1988-2001	151.4	57.8
Other currencies:				
British pounds	10.92	Indefinite	181.0	21.7
Japanese yen	7.91	1991	139.2	—
Swiss francs	7.00	1996	161.9	—
German marks	5.75	1996	104.1	—
Other			—	.2
Consolidated subsidiaries:				
U.S. dollars	8.82	1988-2011	839.2	987.1
Spanish pesetas	11.73	1988-92	526.3	629.1
German marks	5.04	1988-96	89.7	70.9
Austrian schillings	6.40	1988	10.0	84.1
Other currencies	Various	1988-95	265.6	241.3
Total			4,095.8	2,594.6
Less unamortized discount (principally on 14.7% notes due 1991)			88.5	94.4
Total			$4,007.3	$2,500.2

(continued)

NOTES TO FINANCIAL STATEMENTS (continued)

NOTE 14. (concluded)

At year-end 1986, the Corporation and its consolidated subsidiaries had unused short-term credit lines of approximately $3.0 billion and unused long-term credit agreements of approximately $1.8 billion. Long-term debt at December 31, 1986 and 1985 included approximately $597 million and $702 million, respectively, of short-term obligations which are intended to be renewed or refinanced under long-term credit agreements. Long-term debt (including current portion) bore interest at a weighted average rate of approximately 10.8% at December 31, 1986 and 12.5% at December 31, 1985.

In 1981, the Corporation and a subsidiary arranged a private financing of $500 million in 14.7% notes due 1991. An option to acquire certain real estate in 1991 was also granted. The option holder may deliver the notes in payment for the real estate.

Under the sinking fund provisions of the trust indenture for the Corporation's 8⅝% Debentures due 2005, the Corporation is to make annual sinking fund payments of $3.0 million in 2002 and $11.8 million in each of the years 2003 and 2004.

Maturities of long-term debt in the years 1987 through 1991 are (in millions) $401.4 (included in loans payable at December 31, 1986), $397.0, $156.8, $177.0 and $1,379.4.

Loans payable at December 31, 1985 included the current portion of long-term debt in the amount of $446.9 million.

NOTE 15. Stockholders' Equity

The preferred stock is subject to redemption at the option of the Board of Directors on any dividend date on not less than thirty days' notice at the redemption prices stated in the following table plus accrued dividends.

Holders of $1-2/3 par value common stock, Class E common stock and Class H common stock are entitled to one, one-quarter and one-half vote per share, respectively, on all matters submitted to the stockholders for a vote. The liquidation rights of common stockholders are based on per share liquidation units of the various classes and are subject to certain adjustments if outstanding common stock is subdivided, by stock split or otherwise, or if shares of one class of common stock are issued as a dividend to holders of another class of common stock. At December 31, 1986, each share of $1-2/3 par value common, Class E common and Class H common stock was entitled to a liquidation unit of approximately one, one-quarter and one-half, respectively.

In December 1986, the Corporation reacquired 11,791,790 shares of Class E common stock and related contingent notes issued in the EDS acquisition from certain employes and former stockholders of EDS for $751.5 million, including $389.1 million, or $33 per share, attributable to Class E common stock (see Note 1).

After December 31, 1994 or December 31, 1995, the Board of Directors may exchange $1-2/3 par value common stock for Class E common stock or for Class H common stock, respectively, if the Board has declared and paid certain minimum cash dividends during each of the five years preceding the exchange. If GM should sell, liquidate, or otherwise dispose of EDS or Hughes (or substantially all of the other business of GMHE), the Corporation will be required to exchange $1-2/3 par value common stock for Class E common or Class H common stock, respectively. In the event of any exchange, the Class E common or Class H common stockholders will receive $1-2/3 par value common stock having a market value at the time of the exchange equal to 120% of the market value of the Class E common or Class H common stock exchanged.

The Certificate of Incorporation provides that no cash dividends may be paid on the $1-2/3 par value common stock, Class E common stock, Class H common stock or any series of preference stock so long as current assets (excluding prepaid expenses) in excess of current liabilities of the Corporation are less than $75 per share of outstanding preferred stock. Such current assets (with inventories calculated on the FIFO basis) in excess of current liabilities were greater than $75 in respect of each share of outstanding preferred stock at December 31, 1986 and 1985.

The equity of the Corporation and its consolidated subsidiaries in the accumulated net income or loss, since acquisition, of associates has been included in net income retained for use in the business.

At December 31, 1986, consolidated net income retained for use in the business attributable to $1-2/3 par value common, Class E common and Class H common stocks was $23,530.9 million, $206.2 million and $151.6 million, respectively.

(Dollars in Millions Except Per Share Amounts)	1986	1985	1984
Capital Stock:			
Preferred Stock, without par value, cumulative dividends (authorized, 6,000,000 shares):			
$5.00 series, stated value $100 per share, redeemable at Corporation option at $120 per share:			
Outstanding at beginning of the year (1,693,294 shares in 1986, 1,698,294 in 1985 and 1,835,644 in 1984)	$169.3	$169.8	$183.6
Reacquired on the open market (163,100 shares in 1986, 5,000 in 1985 and 137,350 in 1984)	(16.3)	(.5)	(13.8)
Outstanding at end of the year (1,530,194 shares in 1986, 1,693,294 in 1985 and 1,698,294 in 1984)	153.0	169.3	169.8
$3.75 series, stated value $100 per share, redeemable at Corporation option at $100 per share:			
Outstanding at beginning of the year (814,100 shares in 1986, 858,000 in 1985 and 1,000,000 in 1984)	81.4	85.8	100.0
Reacquired on the open market (43,900 shares in 1985 and 142,000 in 1984)	–	(4.4)	(14.2)
Outstanding at end of the year (814,100 shares in 1986 and 1985 and 858,000 in 1984)	81.4	81.4	85.8
Preference Stock, $0.10 par value (authorized, 100,000,000 shares in 1984), no shares issued	–	–	–
Common Stock, $1-2/3 par value (authorized, 1,000,000,000 shares):			
Issued at beginning of the year (318,853,315 shares in 1986, 317,504,133 in 1985 and 315,711,299 in 1984)	531.4	529.2	526.2
Reacquired on the open market and cancelled (761,390 shares)	(1.3)	–	–
Newly issued shares used for bonus deliveries and sold under provisions of the Stock Option Plans and the Dividend Reinvestment Plan (1,291,905 shares in 1986, 1,349,182 in 1985 and 1,792,834 in 1984)	2.2	2.2	3.0
Issued at end of the year (319,383,830 shares in 1986, 318,853,315 in 1985 and 317,504,133 in 1984)	$532.3	$531.4	$529.2

(continued)

NOTES TO FINANCIAL STATEMENTS (continued)

NOTE 15. (continued)

(Dollars in Millions Except Per Share Amounts)	1986	1985	1984
Class E Common Stock, $0.10 par value (authorized, 190,000,000 shares in 1984):			
Issued at beginning of the year (66,227,137 shares in 1986 and 29,082,382 in 1985)	$ 6.6	$ 2.9	$ —
Reacquired from certain employes and former stockholders of EDS (11,791,790 shares)	(1.2)	—	—
Issued as a public offering (3,125,000 shares)	—	.3	—
Two-for-one stock split in the form of a 100% stock dividend (31,742,670 shares)	—	3.2	—
Reacquired on the open market (2,417,206 shares in 1986 and 651,804 in 1985)	(.2)	(.1)	—
Issued in the acquisition of EDS in 1984 (11,371,268 shares)	—	—	1.1
Issued in conjunction with EDS Incentive Plans and other employe stock plans (1,488,978 shares in 1986, 2,928,889 in 1985 and 2,270,160 in 1984) (Note 4)	.2	.3	.2
Issued to $1-2/3 par value common stockholders as a dividend (15,440,954 shares)	—	—	1.6
Issued at end of the year (53,507,119 shares in 1986, 66,227,137 in 1985 and 29,082,382 in 1984)	5.4	6.6	2.9
Class H Common Stock, $0.10 par value (authorized, 600,000,000 shares in 1985):			
Issued at beginning of the year (65,495,316 shares)	6.6	—	—
Issued in conjunction with GMHE Incentive Plans and other employe stock plans (4,156,598 shares)	.3	—	—
Reacquired on the open market (3,066,582 shares)	(.3)	—	—
Issued in the acquisition of Hughes in 1985 (50,000,000 shares)	—	5.0	—
Issued to $1-2/3 par value common stockholders as a dividend (15,495,316 shares)	—	1.6	—
Issued at end of the year (66,585,332 shares in 1986 and 65,495,316 in 1985)	6.6	6.6	—
Total capital stock at end of the year	778.7	795.3	787.7
Capital Surplus (principally additional paid-in capital):			
Balance at beginning of the year	6,667.8	3,347.8	2,136.8
Preferred stock:			
Stated value in excess of repurchase price of shares reacquired on the open market	6.2	2.9	16.2
$1-2/3 par value common stock:			
Repurchase price in excess of par value of shares reacquired on the open market and cancelled	(52.1)	—	—
Proceeds in excess of par value of newly issued shares used for the GM Incentive Program and the Dividend Reinvestment Plan	89.5	90.7	109.7
Class E common stock:			
Repurchase price in excess of par value:			
Shares reacquired from certain employes and former stockholders of EDS	(387.9)	—	—
Shares reacquired on the open market	(92.0)	(125.8)	—
Amounts in excess of par value:			
Issued as a public offering	—	193.3	—
Issued in the acquisition of EDS	—	—	499.2
Issued in conjunction with EDS Incentive Plans and other employe stock plans	68.6	34.7	.8
Issued as a dividend	—	—	585.1
Amount transferred to Class E common stock in conjunction with two-for-one stock split in the form of a 100% stock dividend	—	(3.2)	—
Class H common stock:			
Repurchase price in excess of par value of shares reacquired on the open market	(134.3)	—	—
Amounts in excess of par value:			
Issued in conjunction with GMHE Incentive Plans and other employe stock plans	166.8	—	—
Issued in the acquisition of Hughes	—	2,556.9	—
Issued as a dividend	—	570.5	—
Balance at end of the year	6,332.6	6,667.8	3,347.8
Net Income Retained for Use in the Business:			
Balance at beginning of the year	22,606.6	20,796.6	18,390.5
Net income	2,944.7	3,999.0	4,516.5
Total	25,551.3	24,795.6	22,907.0
Dividend of one Class E common share for each 20 shares of $1-2/3 par value common outstanding	—	—	586.7
Dividend of one Class H common share for each 20 shares of $1-2/3 par value common outstanding	(.5)	572.1	—
Cash dividends:			
Preferred stock, $5.00 series, $5.00 per share	7.8	8.4	8.9
Preferred stock, $3.75 series, $3.75 per share	3.0	3.2	3.6
$1-2/3 par value common stock, $5.00 per share in 1986 and 1985 and $4.75 in 1984	1,588.0	1,581.2	1,497.5
Class E common stock, $0.40 per share in 1986, $0.195 in 1985 and $0.045 in 1984 (post-split)	25.9	12.4	1.2
Class H common stock, $0.60 per share	38.4	—	—
Cash payments in lieu of fractional shares of common stock issued as a dividend:			
Class E common	—	—	12.5
Class H common	—	11.7	—
Total cash dividends	1,663.1	1,616.9	1,523.7
Balance at end of the year	$23,888.7	$22,606.6	$20,796.6

(continued)

NOTES TO FINANCIAL STATEMENTS (continued)

NOTE 15. (concluded)

(Dollars in Millions)	1986	1985	1984
Accumulated Foreign Currency Translation and Other Adjustments:			
Balance at beginning of the year:			
Accumulated foreign currency translation adjustments	($ 675.0)	($ 789.5)	($ 661.8)
Net unrealized gains on marketable equity securities	130.0	71.7	91.3
Changes during the year:			
Accumulated foreign currency translation adjustments	192.2	114.5	(127.7)
Net unrealized gains (losses) on marketable equity securities	30.8	58.3	(19.6)
Balance at end of the year	(322.0)	(545.0)	(717.8)
Total Stockholders' Equity	$30,678.0	$29,524.7	$24,214.3

NOTE 16. Segment Reporting

Industry Segments

Prior to 1986, General Motors operated predominantly in the automotive products industry and, accordingly, did not present industry segment data. While the major portion of the Corporation's operations in 1986 was derived from the automotive products industry segment, it also produces products and services in the defense and other nonautomotive products industry segments. The automotive products segment consists of the manufacture, assembly and sale of automobiles, trucks and related parts and accessories. The defense products segment includes military vehicles, radar and weapon control systems, guided missile systems, as well as defense satellites. The other nonautomotive products segment consists of the design, installation and operation of business information and telecommunication systems; the design, development and manufacture of locomotives; engines for drilling, marine and stationary applications; commercial satellites and specialized automated production and test equipment. Because of the high degree of integration, substantial interdivisional and intersegment transfers of materials and services are made. Intersegment sales and revenues are made at negotiated selling prices.

Substantially all of General Motors' automotive and nonautomotive products are marketed through retail dealers and through distributors and jobbers in the United States and Canada and through distributors and dealers overseas. To assist in the merchandising of General Motors' products, GMAC and its subsidiaries offer financial services and certain types of automobile insurance to dealers and customers. In addition, subsidiaries of GMAC are engaged in mortgage banking operations.

Information concerning operations by industry segment is displayed below.

1986	Automotive Products	Defense Products	Other Non-automotive Products	Total
	(Dollars in Millions)			
Net Sales and Revenues:				
Outside	$90,740.2	$ 7,760.8	$ 4,312.7	$102,813.7
Intersegment	123.4	—	3,179.9	—
Total net sales and revenues	$90,863.6	$ 7,760.8	$ 7,492.6	$102,813.7*
Operating Profit	$ 2,014.3**	$ 285.8	$ 145.8	$ 2,445.9
Identifiable Assets at Year-End	$42,400.9	$ 8,733.6	$10,774.1	$ 61,908.6
Depreciation and Amortization	$ 5,188.9	$ 443.5	$ 961.3	$ 6,593.7
Capital Expenditures	$10,257.3	$ 500.2	$ 954.1	$ 11,711.6
Operating Profit				$ 2,445.9
Corporate Expenses				(1,015.0)
Operating Income				$ 1,430.9
Identifiable Assets				$ 61,908.6
Equity in Net Assets of Nonconsolidated Subsidiaries and Associates				7,232.3
Corporate Assets				13,312.9
Eliminations				(9,860.8)
Total Assets				$ 72,593.0

*After elimination of intersegment transactions.
**Includes a special provision for scheduled plant closings and other restructurings of $1,287.6 million.

Geographic Segments

Net sales and revenues, net income (loss), total and net assets and average number of employes in the U.S. and in locations outside the U.S. for 1986, 1985 and 1984 are summarized on the next page. Net income (loss) is after provisions for deferred income taxes applicable to that portion of the undistributed earnings not deemed to be permanently invested, less available tax credits and deductions, and appropriate consolidating adjustments. Interarea sales and revenues are made at negotiated selling prices.

(continued)

NOTES TO FINANCIAL STATEMENTS (continued)

NOTE 16. (concluded)

1986	United States	Canada	Europe	Latin America	All Other	Total*
			(Dollars in Millions)			
Net Sales and Revenues:						
Outside	$82,977.0	$ 5,600.1	$10,675.8	$1,798.7	$1,762.1	$102,813.7
Interarea	8,366.1	7,817.4	462.2	899.2	59.7	—
Total net sales and revenues	$91,343.1	$13,417.5	$11,138.0	$2,697.9	$1,821.8	$102,813.7
Net Income (Loss)	$ 3,058.0	$ 381.9	($ 343.3)**	$ 32.6	($ 257.5)	$ 2,944.7
Total Assets	$57,668.8	$ 3,643.8	$ 7,590.3	$3,022.9	$1,862.5	$ 72,593.0
Net Assets	$27,525.0	$ 2,131.6	($ 593.2)	$1,299.1	$ 459.1	$ 30,678.0
Average Number of Employes (in thousands)	632	43	123	59	19	876

1985						
Net Sales and Revenues:						
Outside	$80,204.7	$ 5,283.7	$ 7,671.6	$1,841.9	$1,369.8	$ 96,371.7
Interarea	8,893.8	8,494.6	322.8	995.5	483.7	—
Total net sales and revenues	$89,098.5	$13,778.3	$ 7,994.4	$2,837.4	$1,853.5	$ 96,371.7
Net Income (Loss)	$ 3,624.3	$ 473.7	($ 372.1)	$ 308.3	$ 9.1	$ 3,999.0
Total Assets	$50,796.0	$ 2,920.1	$ 5,960.6	$3,054.2	$1,634.6	$ 63,832.8
Net Assets	$26,710.0	$ 1,906.4	($ 765.7)	$1,327.8	$ 572.2	$ 29,524.7
Average Number of Employes (in thousands)	561	44	125	59	22	811

1984						
Net Sales and Revenues:						
Outside	$69,355.6	$ 4,411.6	$ 6,735.7	$1,642.0	$1,745.0	$ 83,889.9
Interarea	7,276.5	8,170.0	242.2	823.6	401.7	—
Total net sales and revenues	$76,632.1	$12,581.6	$ 6,977.9	$2,465.6	$2,146.7	$ 83,889.9
Net Income (Loss)	$ 3,872.0	$ 762.2	($ 291.1)	$ 94.4	$ 61.5	$ 4,516.5
Total Assets	$41,692.7	$ 2,833.5	$ 4,425.7	$2,874.0	$ 932.0	$ 52,144.9
Net Assets	$22,149.7	$ 1,628.9	($ 439.2)	$1,016.7	$ 41.7	$ 24,214.3
Average Number of Employes (in thousands)	511	41	122	49	25	748

*After elimination of interarea transactions.
**Includes the effect of the termination of the heavy-duty truck portion of GM's European commercial vehicle operations.

NOTE 17. Profit Sharing Plans

Profit Sharing Plans were established, effective January 1, 1983, under which eligible United States hourly and salaried employes share in the success of the Corporation's U.S. operations. Under the Plans' provisions, 10% of profits, as defined, are shared when the Corporation's U.S. income before income taxes plus equity in U.S. earnings of nonconsolidated subsidiaries (principally GMAC) exceeds 10% of the net worth of U.S. operations plus 5% of the difference between total assets of U.S. operations and net worth of U.S. operations. Amounts applicable to subsidiaries incorporated in the U.S. that are operating outside of the U.S., as well as amounts

applicable to associates, are excluded from the calculation. Ten percent of the profits in excess of the minimum annual return, less a diversion for the Guaranteed Income Stream Benefit Program and Income Protection Plan and that portion of profit sharing allocable to nonparticipating employes, are distributed to eligible U.S. employes by March 31 following the year earned.

GM's earnings in 1986 were not sufficient to generate a payout under the profit sharing formula. The accrual for profit sharing was $180.3 million in 1985 and $281.9 million in 1984. The profit sharing calculation for 1986 is shown below.

(Dollars in Millions)				1986
Minimum Annual Return	January 1, 1986	December 31, 1986	Average	
Total Assets in the U.S.	$50,796.0	$57,668.8		
Deduct assets of excluded subsidiaries and associates	706.5	1,015.1		
Total Assets of U.S. operations as defined in the Plans	$50,089.5	$56,653.7	$53,371.6	
Net Assets in the U.S.	$26,710.0	$27,525.0		
Deduct net assets of excluded subsidiaries and associates	701.9	685.6		
Net Worth of U.S. operations as defined in the Plans	$26,008.1	$26,839.4	26,423.7 X 10% =	$2,642.4
Other assets of U.S. operations			$26,947.9 X 5% =	1,347.4
Minimum Annual Return as defined in the Plans				$3,989.8

(continued)

NOTES TO FINANCIAL STATEMENTS (concluded)

NOTE 17. (concluded)

(Dollars in Millions)	1986
Profits as Defined in the Plans	
Net Income in the U.S.	$3,058.0
Add (Deduct): Net income of excluded subsidiaries and associates	(111.2)
Income taxes of U.S. operations	(610.0)
Provision for the General Motors Incentive Program applicable to U.S. operations	135.5
Profit sharing accrual	—
Profits as defined in the Plans	$2,472.3

Profit Sharing Accrual	
Profits as defined in the Plans	$2,472.3
Deduct Minimum Annual Return as defined in the Plans	3,989.8
Profits (less than) Minimum Annual Return	($1,517.5)

NOTE 18. Commitments and Contingent Liabilities

Minimum future commitments under operating leases having non-cancellable lease terms in excess of one year, primarily for real property, aggregating $2,759.8 million, are payable $538.9 million in 1987, $358.0 million in 1988, $258.7 million in 1989, $189.7 million in 1990, $140.1 million in 1991 and $1,274.4 million thereafter. Certain of the leases contain escalation clauses and renewal or purchase options. Rental expenses under operating leases were $882.4 million in 1986, $690.0 million in 1985 and $223.0 million in 1984.

There are serious potential liabilities under government regulations pertaining primarily to environmental, fuel economy and safety matters. There are also various claims and pending actions against the Corporation and its subsidiaries with respect to commercial matters, including warranties and product liability, civil rights, antitrust, patent matters, taxes and other matters arising out of the conduct of the business. Certain of these actions purport to be class actions, seeking damages in very large amounts. The ultimate liability under these government regulations and the amounts of liability on these claims and actions at December 31, 1986 were not determinable but, in the opinion of the management, the ultimate liability resulting should not have a material adverse effect on the Corporation's consolidated financial position.

ACCOUNTANTS' REPORT

**Deloitte
Haskins + Sells**

1114 Avenue of the Americas
New York, New York 10036

General Motors Corporation, its Directors and Stockholders: February 5, 1987

We have examined the Consolidated Balance Sheet of General Motors Corporation and consolidated subsidiaries as of December 31, 1986 and 1985 and the related Statements of Consolidated Income and Changes in Consolidated Financial Position for each of the three years in the period ended December 31, 1986. Our examinations were made in accordance with generally accepted auditing standards and, accordingly, included such tests of the accounting records and such other auditing procedures as we considered necessary in the circumstances.

In our opinion, these financial statements present fairly the financial position of the companies at December 31, 1986 and 1985 and the results of their operations and the changes in their financial position for each of the three years in the period ended December 31, 1986, in conformity with generally accepted accounting principles consistently applied during the period except for the change in 1986, with which we concur, in the method of accounting for pensions as described in Notes 1 and 8 to the Financial Statements.

Deloitte Haskins + Sells

SUPPLEMENTARY INFORMATION

Selected Quarterly Data
(Dollars in Millions Except Per Share Amounts)

	1986 Quarters				1985 Quarters			
	1st	2nd	3rd	4th	1st	2nd	3rd	4th
Net sales and revenues	$26,820.1	$27,625.3	$22,841.0	$25,527.3	$24,182.5	$25,056.9	$22,491.7	$24,640.6
Operating income (Loss)	1,365.4	1,085.8	(251.5)	(768.8) *	1,511.8	1,485.3	(20.9)	1,238.2
Income (Loss) before income taxes	1,391.2	1,087.4	(207.5)	(810.8)	1,632.2	1,664.4	74.8	1,249.9
United States, foreign and other income taxes (credit)	475.2	377.9	(236.2)	(917.2)	781.8	716.5	(172.4)	304.4
Income after income taxes	916.0	709.5	28.7	106.4	850.4	947.9	247.2	945.5
Equity in earnings of nonconsolidated subsidiaries and associates	282.9	308.9	316.4	275.9	221.3	211.4	269.3	306.0
Net income	1,198.9	1,018.4	345.1	382.3	1,071.7	1,159.3	516.5	1,251.5
Dividends on preferred stocks	2.8	2.7	2.6	2.7	2.9	2.9	3.0	2.8
Earnings on common stocks	$ 1,196.1	$ 1,015.7	$ 342.5	$ 379.6	$ 1,068.8	$ 1,156.4	$ 513.5	$ 1,248.7
Earnings attributable to:								
$1-2/3 par value common stock	$ 1,116.1	$ 928.1	$ 253.3	$ 310.2	$ 1,048.6	$ 1,132.8	$ 485.1	$ 1,217.1
Class E common stock	$ 29.9	$ 33.2	$ 37.5	$ 35.6	$ 20.2	$ 23.6	$ 28.4	$ 31.6
Class H common stock (issued in December 1985)	$ 50.1	$ 54.4	$ 51.7	$ 33.8	—	—	—	—
Average number of shares of common stocks outstanding (in millions):								
$1-2/3 par value common	317.3	317.8	317.8	317.7	316.2	316.4	316.4	316.3
Class E common	65.6	64.6	64.2	60.8	64.7**	67.8	66.7	67.0
Class H common (issued in December 1985)	65.3	63.9	63.3	63.2	—	—	—	65.5
Earnings per share attributable to:								
$1-2/3 par value common stock***	$3.52	$2.92	$0.80	$0.97	$3.32	$3.58	$1.53	$3.85
Class E common stock	$0.46	$0.51	$0.58	$0.58	$0.32**	$0.35	$0.43	$0.47
Class H common stock (issued in December 1985)	$0.77	$0.85	$0.82	$0.53	—	—	—	—
Cash dividends per share of common stocks:								
$1-2/3 par value common	$1.25	$1.25	$1.25	$1.25	$1.25	$1.25	$1.25	$1.25
Class E common	$0.10	$0.10	$0.10	$0.10	$0.045**	$0.05	$0.05	$0.05
Class H common (issued in December 1985)	$0.15	$0.15	$0.15	$0.15	—	—	—	—

Operating data as well as earnings and earnings per share attributable to $1-2/3 par value common and Class H common stocks for the first three 1986 quarters have been restated to reflect the adoption in the fourth quarter of Statement of Financial Accounting Standards (SFAS) No. 87, Employers' Accounting for Pensions, effective January 1, 1986. Previously reported earnings and earnings per share, respectively, attributable to such common stocks were as follows (in millions and in dollars): $1-2/3 par value common stock—$986.3 [$3.11], $892.7 [$2.81] and $176.7 [$0.56]; Class H common stock—$44.8 [$0.69], $49.1 [$0.76] and $46.9 [$0.74]. The effective income tax rates and credits for the 1986 quarters reflect the earnings, the continuing amortization of U.S. investment tax credits and, in the fourth quarter, recognition of tax benefits from restructuring foreign operations.

The effective income tax rates and credit for the 1985 quarters reflect the favorable impact of U.S. investment tax credits. Earnings and earnings per share attributable to common stocks in 1985 have been restated to reflect the Class E common stock amendment approved by the stockholders in December 1985. Previously reported earnings and earnings per share, respectively, attributable to common stocks for the first three quarters of 1985 were as follows (in millions and in dollars): $1-2/3 par value common stock—$1,030.8 [$3.26], $1,113.9 [$3.52] and $461.6 [$1.46]; Class E common stock—$38.0 [$0.63], $42.5 [$0.67] and $51.9 [$0.78].

*Includes a special provision for scheduled plant closings and other restructurings of $1,216.6 million.

**Adjusted to reflect the two-for-one stock split in the form of a 100% stock dividend distributed on June 10, 1985.

***Includes favorable (unfavorable) effects on earnings per share of: adoption of SFAS No. 87 in 1986: first quarter—$0.41, second quarter—$0.11, third quarter—$0.24, fourth quarter—$0.20; revisions to pension plan actuarial assumptions in 1986: second quarter—$0.32, third quarter—$0.10, fourth quarter—$0.19; and foreign exchange/translation activity [1986: first quarter—$0.26, second quarter—($0.14), third quarter—($0.02), fourth quarter—($0.14); 1985: first quarter—($0.18), second quarter—($0.23), third quarter—$0.38, fourth quarter $0.28].

(continued)

SUPPLEMENTARY INFORMATION (concluded)

Selected Quarterly Data (concluded)

(Dollars in Per Share Amounts)		1986 Quarters				1985 Quarters			
		1st	2nd	3rd	4th	1st	2nd	3rd	4th
Stock price range:									
$1-2/3 par value									
common*:	High	$88.63	$86.38	$78.75	$75.00	$85.00	$75.13	$73.88	$77.25
	Low	$68.38	$74.63	$66.88	$65.88	$72.50	$66.00	$65.75	$64.25
Class E common**:	High	$47.25	$49.63	$48.75	$37.25	$36.00	$42.00	$46.50	$43.63
	Low	$36.13	$42.63	$32.50	$24.75	$20.63	$29.75	$35.00	$32.88
Class H common									
(issued Dec. 1985)***:	High	$49.25	$47.75	$43.25	$44.00	–	–	–	$50.00
	Low	$32.63	$41.13	$39.00	$36.63	–	–	–	$38.00

*The principal market is the New York Stock Exchange and prices are based on the Composite Tape. $1-2/3 par value common stock is also listed on the Midwest, Pacific and Philadelphia stock exchanges. As of December 31, 1986, there were 857,333 holders of record of $1-2/3 par value common stock.

**The principal market is the New York Stock Exchange and prices are based on the Composite Tape. As of December 31, 1986, there were 456,471 holders of record of Class E common stock. 1985 first and second quarter data have been adjusted to reflect the two-for-one stock split on June 10, 1985.

***The principal market is the New York Stock Exchange and prices are based on the Composite Tape. As of December 31, 1986, there were 540,297 holders of record of Class H common stock. Market prices were on a "when issued" basis prior to December 31, 1985.

Selected Financial Data

(Dollars in Millions Except Per Share Amounts)	1986	1985	1984	1983	1982
Net sales and revenues	$102,813.7	$96,371.7	$83,889.9	$74,581.6	$60,025.6
Earnings attributable to $1-2/3 par value common stock	$ 2,607.7	$ 3,883.6	$ 4,498.3	$ 3,717.3	$ 949.8
Cash dividends on $1-2/3 par value common stock	1,588.0	1,592.9	1,510.0	879.3	737.3
Dividend of Class E common shares	–	–	586.7	–	–
Dividend of Class H common shares	(.5)	572.1	–	–	–
Net income retained in the year	$ 1,020.2	$ 1,718.6	$ 2,401.6	$ 2,838.0	$ 212.5
Earnings per share attributable to $1-2/3 par value common stock	$8.21	$12.28	$14.27	$11.84	$3.09
Cash dividends per share of $1-2/3 par value common stock	5.00	5.00	4.75	2.80	2.40
Per share dividend of Class E common shares	–	–	1.90	–	–
Per share dividend of Class H common shares	–	1.94	–	–	–
Net income per share retained in the year	$3.21	$ 5.34	$ 7.62	$ 9.04	$0.69
Earnings attributable to Class E common stock (issued in 1984)	$ 136.2	$ 103.8	$ 5.7	–	–
Cash dividends on Class E common stock (issued in 1984)	25.9	12.4	1.2	–	–
Net income retained in the year	$ 110.3	$ 91.4	$ 4.5	–	–
Earnings per share attributable to Class E common stock	$2.13	$1.57	$0.16*	–	–
Cash dividends per share of Class E common stock	0.40	0.195	0.045*	–	–
Net income per share retained in the year	$1.73	$1.375	$0.115*	–	–
Earnings attributable to Class H common stock (issued Dec. 1985)	$ 190.0	–	–	–	–
Cash dividends on Class H common stock (issued Dec. 1985)	38.4	–	–	–	–
Net income retained in the year	$ 151.6	–	–	–	–
Earnings per share attributable to Class H common stock	$2.97	–	–	–	–
Cash dividends per share of Class H common stock	0.60	–	–	–	–
Net income per share retained in the year	$2.37	–	–	–	–
Average number of shares of common stocks outstanding (in millions):					
$1-2/3 par value common	317.6	316.3	315.3	313.9	307.4
Class E common (issued in 1984)	63.8	66.5	36.3*	–	–
Class H common (issued in December 1985)	63.9	–	–	–	–
Cash dividends on capital stocks as a percent of net income	56.5%	40.4%	33.7%	23.9%	77.9%
Expenditures for real estate, plants and equipment	$ 8,086.3	$ 8,047.9**	$ 3,595.1	$ 1,923.0	$ 3,611.1
Expenditures for special tools	$ 3,625.3	$ 3,075.0	$ 2,452.1	$ 2,083.7	$ 2,601.0
Cash and marketable securities	$ 4,018.8	$ 5,114.4	$ 8,567.4	$ 6,216.9	$ 3,126.2
Working capital	$ 3,920.3	$ 1,957.5	$ 6,276.7	$ 5,890.8	$ 1,658.1
Total assets	$ 72,593.0	$63,832.8	$52,144.9	$45,694.5	$41,397.8
Long-term debt and capitalized leases	$ 4,325.3	$ 2,867.2	$ 2,772.9	$ 3,521.8	$ 4,745.1

Financial data for years prior to 1986 have not been restated for the adoption effective January 1, 1986 of Statement of Financial Accounting Standards No. 87, Employers' Accounting for Pensions. The effect of adopting SFAS No. 87 was to increase net income for 1986 by $330.5 million or $0.96 per share of $1-2/3 par value common stock, $0.04 per share of Class E common stock and $0.34 per share of Class H common stock. Earnings and earnings per share attributable to common stocks in 1985 and 1984 have been restated to reflect the Class E common stock amendment approved by the stockholders in December 1985. Financial data for years prior to 1983 have not been restated for the adoption of Statement of Financial Accounting Standards No. 52, Foreign Currency Translation. The effect of adopting SFAS No. 52 was to reduce net income for 1983 by about $422.5 million or $1.35 per share of $1-2/3 par value common stock.

*Adjusted to reflect the two-for-one stock split in the form of a 100% stock dividend distributed on June 10, 1985.

**Includes $1,948.7 million of net property acquired in Hughes acquisition.

Index